GOOD NEWS
FOR MODERNS

Nero James Pruitt

GOOD NEWS FOR MODERNS

The Cover Design is Paul in Athens. Raphael 1483-1520.

iUniverse books may be ordered through booksellers or by contacting:

iUniverse
1663 Liberty Drive
Bloomington, IN 47403
www.iuniverse.com
1-800-Authors (1-800-288-4677)

Scriptures taken from the NEW AMERICAN STANDARD BIBLE,
Copyright © 1960,1962,1963,1968,1971,1972,1973,1975,1977,1995
by The Lockman Foundation. Used by permission.*

ISBN: 978-1-4917-6327-8 (sc)
ISBN: 978-1-4917-6328-5 (e)

Library of Congress Control Number: 2015904082

Print information available on the last page.

iUniverse rev. date: 04/28/2016

CONTENTS

FOREWORD

This book could belong in the self-help section of a book store if people who do not need to make drastic changes in their lives often shop there. It is an attempt to look at the *New Testament* and the lessons of history as resources to live our lives in the twenty-first century. I approach the former skeptically, believing that is a human work. I view history with this commonplace observation: there are many who came before us whose bodies are now dust as one day ours will be but from their lives we can gain insights.

Here are two notes of style. I have italicized all the books of the *Bible* and all *Bible* verses and parts of verses that I quote in the text of this book.[1] I have put the birth and death years for many of the historical figures that I cite. In some instances, I have just used the years that they were in a high office, for example the papacy. My purpose in the smaller sense is to provide context and in the larger sense to allude to the shortness of human life. This brevity of our existence is a piece of wisdom handed to us in both the *Old* and *New Testaments* and by William Shakespeare (1564 – 1616):

Old Testament: *"As for the days of our life, they contain seventy years,*
Or if due to strength, eighty years,
Yet their pride is but labor and sorrow;
For soon it is gone and we fly away." (Psalm 90:10)

New Testament: *"Come now, you who say, "Today or tomorrow we will go to such and such a city, and spend a year there and engage in business and make a profit. Yet you do not know what your life will be like tomorrow. You are just a vapor that appears for a little while and then vanishes away." (James 4:13-14)*

Shakespeare: "All the world's a stage, and all the men and women merely players: they have their exits and their entrances; and one man in his time plays many parts, his acts being seven ages." (*As You Like It*)

This insight from Shakespeare was the opening line spoken by my father Nero Pruitt (1916 – 2003) at his valedictorian speech graduating from Waco High School in Waco, Texas in 1934. I dedicate this book to him.

PROLOGUE

In 1987 the light from an exploding star in a nearby galaxy reached earth and was observed, photographed and placed on magazine covers. That star had exploded about 168,000 years previously. When that light was over half-way on its journey to earth, a group of about a thousand hunter-gatherers left a land mass that tens of millenniums later Europeans named Africa. Those hunter-gatherers were the probable ancestors of all humans now alive.[2] The time spans involved here are but a fractional glimpse of the immense age and consequent size of our universe which is billions of years old and billions of light years in size. Much of this we have learned only in the last century. During this past hundred years we have also been to the Moon and landed robots with cameras on Mars and found water there. (We have found water on the Moon too.) We have sent space craft over 900 million miles to the planet Saturn - it took about seven years - and discovered a moon about one-third of a mile in diameter. We have microscopes through which we can see atoms. We have telephones that we conveniently carry on our persons that allow us to speak anywhere in the world. Millions of people fly through the air every hour. We can project images anywhere on earth to homes and cell phones. In this century also, tens of millions have died at the hands of other humans and even now food production and the purification of water can be taken for granted only in developed countries. One can make both optimistic and pessimistic predictions of the next several decades.[3]

In this ancient and huge universe, what is the significance of the Christian religion which began two thousand years ago in the Near East?

It is the aim of this book to show the relevance of Christianity and to recommend a form of Christianity that will fit in any future scenario. Chapters 1-8 attempt to show Christianity's relevance by exploring the diversity embedded within it. I look at the claim that the *Bible* is error-free, at the prestige it holds within our society, at Jesus, Paul and the struggles within the *New Testament* to accommodate various views. Chapters 9-11 recommend one variety of Christianity for our time. I call it monotheistic Christianity and I attempt to ground it in the *New Testament* and American history.

John Locke (1632 -1704) published *The Reasonableness of Christianity* in 1695. He did not see any need to prove the existence of God. He thought Newtonian physics showed that a creator was inevitable. He saw that the only essential belief for salvation was that Jesus is the Messiah and the Son of God. To Locke, this simplicity showed that Christianity is a religion of reason and common sense.[4] We don't have to agree with any of Locke's particulars to appreciate his effort to simplify. This book - sort of an update to *The Reasonableness of Christianity* - is to identify the essence of Christianity so that the religion can prosper and help society and individuals prosper in the decades ahead.

This book examines the *New Testament* of the Christian *Bible*. It finds within the *New Testament* different answers to the question, "What is a Christian?" It relies on the *New Testament* text and lessons from American history and Christian history to describe a Christian religion for the future that is broad and inclusive. It hopes for a religion that is portable and that has the strengths of unity and diversity. Christians, by this approach, may believe in the atoning death of Jesus Christ on a cross near Jerusalem about two thousand years ago for our individual sins - or they may not. This book finds support for this diversity not in diversity seminars but in the pages of the *New Testament*. It is not a diversity that is talked about or well-known but it is so close to the surface that we can perceive it just below the currents.

Let me state my point of view at the outset. I believe in God but it is a shaky belief bolstered by intuition, habit, and an instinct that something or someone must have started the universe. This idea of a first cause leads me to belief although I know that it does not for many. But the reality that any God that might exist allows the innocent – and animals[5] – to suffer pulls me toward disbelief. I think - and this is another shaky belief - that our deaths do not end our existence but that somehow we unite with God. I could be wrong but what would it matter? In short, I often doubt like the Apostle Paul[6] whom I write about extensively in this book.

People live briefly on the earth but to paraphrase Abraham Lincoln (1809-1865) we are connected by mystic chords of memory to all who lived before us. The message that touched so many of them can be adapted for our era. It is that God is probably present and can possibly be somewhat understood and that the *New Testament* can be a guide for many people.

I write for people who do not need to make major changes in their lives in order to be or stay successful. They do not, for example, need to go to church. But they can still be encouraged by the Christian religion, a religion which, even in the pages of the *New Testament*, took diverse forms. My intended audiences are people who, as Samuel Johnson said, often need to be reminded rather than informed.[7] I would add that the reminding needs to be respectful, coming from a peer with all the limitations of a single human being.

In 1803 President of the United States Thomas Jefferson (1743-1826) wrote to the famous physician Benjamin Rush (1745 -1813) that "I am a Christian in the only sense that (Jesus) wished any one to be; sincerely attached to his doctrines, in preference to all others; ascribing to himself every *human* excellence; and believing he never claimed any other." (Italics are in the original.)[8] As students of his life know, Christianity in the sense of conduct versus proper beliefs defined Jefferson's religion.[9] It may not be generally appreciated, however, that Jefferson's approach had some basis in the *New Testament*. Any careful reading of the *New Testament* shows a tension between those who believed in a deified Jesus Christ and those, still considering themselves his followers, who saw him as only a great man. This book examines this tension and draws from it meaning for contemporary life. In modern terms, it explores the diversity embedded in the *New Testament*. This book makes occasional references to history for three primary purposes:

- To show the prestige that the *Bible* has had in our culture.
- To use the quotes of American statesmen and others to show that religion based on conduct, rather than doctrinal assent, is a common expression of Christianity.
- To set the foundation for a more inclusive, God-centered Christianity.

I hope to persuade others that Christianity may hold more appeal than they may have thought. The way I will try to do that is to show that in its founding documents it was an inclusive religion. My favored variation is what I would call God-centered ethical living. It has roots in the *New Testament* and in American history.

This book is not one of original research. I have no training in languages or theology. I do not attend any church but I did until I was about thirty-five and have reflected upon these topics in middle age, like Thomas Jefferson and many others. My reflections have led me to read about 150 books and to consider the views of many eminent authors who writings have influenced my own thinking. Where I think it has been helpful, I have included lengthy quotes from some of these authors and have tried hard to maintain the context of the quote and to offer an accurate interpretation of it. I regret any instances in which I may have misunderstood the intent of one of these sources. I have tried to synthesize the themes coming from these books and apply them as I see fit in order to help others.

A non-exhaustive list of these scholars and writers includes:

Sydney Ahlstrom, Donald Harman Akenson, Charlotte Allen, John L. Allen Jr., Pope Benedict XVI, Randall Balmer, Richard Bauckham, Walter Bauer, Alex Beam, Marcus J. Borg, Paul Boyer, Fawn Brodie, Raymond E. Brown, WRF Browning, Lars Brownworth, Matthew Bunson, Eugene E. Campbell, Joel Carmichael, James Carroll, Paolo Cesaretti, Father Michael Collins, Harvey Cox, John Dillenberger, Ross Douthat, James DG Dunn, Susan Dunn, Lena Einhorn, Bruce Feiler, Harry Emerson Fosdick, David Gelernter, Dieter Georgi, Nancy Gibbs, Justo L. Gonzales, Ondina E. Gonzales, Edgar J. Goodspeed, Michael Grant, Andrew Greeley, Robin Griffith-Jones, Paul C. Gutjahr, Victor Davis Hanson, Martin Hengel, James Hitchcock, Michael Hout, Hubert Jedin, Philip Jenkins, Paul Johnson, JND Kelly, Karen L. King, David Klinghoffer, Jon Krakauer, Herbert Krosney, Michael J. Kruger, Amy-Jill Levine, Bernard Lewis, CS Lewis, Gerd Ludemann, Rich Lowry, Hyam Maccoby, Diarmaid MacCulloch, Burton L Mack, Martin Marty, Scotty McLennan, Jon Meacham, John P. Meier, Jean Milet, Joshua Muravchik, WOE Oesterley, Richard N. Ostling and Joan K. Ostling, Elaine Pagels, Jaroslav Pelikan, F. N. and M. A. Peloubet, J Phillips, Robert Pinsky, Charles Francis Potter, Matthew A. Price, Stephen Prothero, Jonathan L. Reed, Yves Renouard, Don Richardson, Theodore H. Robinson, Joan Roughgarden, Culbert Gerow Rutenber, EP Sanders, Annette Sandoval, Wolfgang Schrage, Anna Maria Schwemer, William Smith, John Shelby Spong, Donald Spoto, Rodney Stark, Lee Strobel, Jon M. Sweeney, James D. Tabor, Burton H. Throckmorton, Jr., Greg Tobin, Tevi Troy, Robert E. Van Vorst, Steven Waldman, Williston Walker, George Weigel, Claude Welch, L. Michael White, Robert Louis Wilken, Garry Wills, AN Wilson, Ben Witherington III, David Wolpe, Thomas E. Woods, Jr., NT Wright.

These are writers of diverse points of view and scholarly profile. From all of them I have learned a lot and I hope I have provided succinct overview and application for busy readers.

CHAPTER 1

Introduction

Christianity is a religion which from its origin and throughout its history has been understood in diverse ways.

Within about fifty years of the crucifixion of Jesus Christ a man known to history as Luke wrote an account of a movement started in Jesus's name. That account was in two volumes. We know these two volumes as the *Gospel of Luke* and the *Book of Acts* in the *New Testament*. [10] Within the latter we learn of the Apostle Paul[11] who may not have ever seen Jesus but came to be devoted to him. But Paul came into contention with Jesus's family and those who were closest to him in life. We learn in the *Book of Acts* that some members of the early Jesus movement tried to kill Paul. How this came to be is an interesting story and it is relevant two thousand years later because it shows that diversity of beliefs was at the very beginnings of Christianity.

A large amount of diversity can be found in modern Christianity from Pentecostalism, to high church Anglicanism, to the Vatican, to Salt Lake City, to the Watchtower Society, to the *Christian Science Monitor*, between black and white Americans, between Protestants, Catholics, Eastern Orthodox, within these large bodies and with other Christian groups around the world. What is less well understood is that the pages of the *New Testament*, reveal a significant amount of diversity in the origin of Christianity. That *New Testament* diversity properly understood broadens the understanding of what it means to be a Christian. So does the Christian experience in the United States of America.

Many people may want to be considered as Christians but reject what they understand it may require them to believe. But these people can, if they want, find a place in Christianity - whether or not they decide to go to church in the future. This group may be ready. In one study of American adults who identified themselves as belonging to "no religion," 9 of 10 also told researchers that they pray.[12] According to a May 2007 Gallup Poll 78% of Americans believe in God and 70% believe in the Devil.[13] Another study

1

showed that "(w)ell over 80 percent" of Americans pray quite regularly.[14] These are numbers that run ahead of the number of people who attend church once a week or almost every week which was reported by Gallup in 2010 to be forty-three percent.[15]

This book is written with great respect for the belief that Jesus of Nazareth was divine and that he died a substitutionary death on behalf of every individual, providing those who accept him eternal life. This respect is a foundation for this book[16] even as I argue for a broader understanding of Christianity.

Although the *New Testament* is quoted in this work extensively, there is no premise that it or the *Bible* as a whole are somehow without any mistakes or in terms of the modern debate among American Christians, inerrant. This is an important point. The humanity of the *Bible* as a whole and the *New Testament* in particular as opposed to the deification[17] of this book allows for an understanding that is crucial for the survival of Christianity: that there is more than one way to be a Christian. Much then turns on the issue of inerrancy for the future of Christianity.

The next chapter opposes the view that the *Bible* is somehow an error-free book. That is necessary because the fundamentalist view about this book has prevented many people from learning what it actually has to say. But my comments here should not obscure the great prestige of the *Bible* and the role it could have in life.

CHAPTER 2

Inerrancy

There are twenty-seven "books" in the New Testament. The earliest was not written until at least twenty years after the crucifixion of Jesus. The most recent was completed about one hundred years after Jesus's death. We have none of the original manuscripts and the copies we do have contain variances. The final formation of the twenty-seven books into our New Testament collection did not occur until the late fourth century. There are obvious contradictions in the texts.

In about 1815, John Adams (1735 – 1826), who had been the second president of the United States, tried to debate the infallibility of the *Bible* by letter to his son, John Quincy Adams (1767 – 1848) the US Ambassador in London, and eventually the sixth president of the United States. John Quincy protested that he had not thoroughly studied scripture and replied that he preferred to rely on faith: "I am not called upon to be its judge."[18] The younger Adams's view may have changed over time but stated here it is a close approximation of what many Americans believe today.

In the United States today, millions of Christians attest to a belief that the *New Testament* is without error and inspired in each particular word by God. A 2011 study done by the Gallup organization reported that the statement "the *Bible* is the actual word of God and is to be taken literally, word for word" was agreed-to by 30% of respondents. Gallup reported that this percentage had held fairly consistent over the previous twenty years.[19]

Evangelical institutions agree. Dallas Theological Seminary's doctrinal statement asserts in part: "We believe that 'all Scripture is given by inspiration of God', by which we understand the whole *Bible* is inspired in the sense that holy men of God 'were moved by the Holy Spirit' to write the very words of Scripture."[20] Western Seminary asserts that "God's inerrant Word is central to our teaching, …"[21] Intervarsity Christian Fellowship, which was founded in 1941 and has a presence in over 500 college and university campuses in the US, makes this statement: "(We believe) the unique divine inspiration, entire trustworthiness and authority of the *Bible*."[22]

3

What these evangelicals seem to mean as they assent to these sorts of statements is that the *Bible* is inerrant – without error: "The Holy Spirit of God superintended the human writers in the production of Scripture so that what they wrote was precisely what God wanted written."[23] This echoes a papal view issued over one hundred years ago. In 1903 Pope Leo XIII wrote in *Providentissimus Deus* that the whole *Bible* was "a letter written to us by our heavenly father." (Therefore), "it would be impious to confine the truth of inspiration to certain parts of the holy writings and to grant that the inspired writer ever erred....For all books accepted in the sacred canon are, throughout and in every part, written at the dictation of the Holy Spirit." [24],[25]

Most of these evangelicals, however, temporize. For example, Campus Crusade for Christ, a sixty year-old evangelical association[26], posts on its web site that "The sole basis of our beliefs is the *Bible*, God's infallible written Word, the 66 books of the *Old* and *New Testaments*. We believe that it was uniquely, verbally and fully inspired by the Holy Spirit, and that it was written without error (inerrant) in the **original manuscripts**." [27] (Emphasis added). The "Campus Crusade Compromise" can be disregarded because it expresses faith in a book that does not exist – the original manuscript. We don't have it. All we have are copies of copies of copies many times removed and these are not consistent at the level that inerrancy would require.

Fuller Theological Seminary in Pasadena, California has wrestled with the issue of inerrancy and attracted critics from other evangelicals. It describes its belief this way: "Where inerrancy refers to what the Holy Spirit is saying to the churches through the Biblical writers, we support its use. Where the focus switches to an undue emphasis on matters like chronological details, precise sequence of events, and numerical allusions, we would consider the term misleading and inappropriate."[28]

But what does the "Fuller Compromise" mean except that readers of the *New Testament* are allowed to decide as individuals what is accurate and what is not and whatever they decide will be OK with Fuller? That will of course lead to different conclusions. Most will probably consider it unimportant that the *Book of Acts* claims that Paul's traveling companion Timothy did not accompany him to Athens on a trip [29] but that Paul said he did in *I Thessalonians* 3: 1-3. But, it may be very important whether the Apostle Paul acted publicly and boldly in Jerusalem during his first visit there as a Christian as described in *Acts* 9: 26-30 and reprised in *Acts* 22:17-21 or just met with the Apostle Peter and James the brother of Jesus and that even after that was unknown to the churches of the area as described in *Galatians* 1:18-24.[30] The importance in either understanding or reconciling this difference

4

goes to how Paul learned and initially formulated the Christian gospel. Does the Fuller Compromise allow us to pick which version we prefer? In fact, the Fuller Compromise is probably mid-point on a route between inerrancy and regarding the *Bible* like all other books.

The Campus Crusade and Fuller Compromises are a nod to modern sensibilities and probably an attempt to avoid the ridicule heaped on fundamentalists in this country since at least the 1920s. But other than that, they are dodges. All evangelical groups want us to take the *Bible* as infallible in some way. The clearest want us to accept the current English language *Bible* as error-free. This compels two inter-related observations. First, the object of faith is a book - a book printed by recognizable publishing houses and distributed conventionally. Second, the act of faith in this book is a further step, after expressing faith in Jesus Christ.

The most famous Protestant of our time exemplifies this second step of faith. The great evangelist Billy Graham (1918 -) was confronted with doubts about the literalism of the *Bible* in his early ministry. Could a whale really have swallowed Jonah?[31] Here is how he resolved them: On a night-time hike in the 1940s, he wandered off the trail, opened his *Bible* and prayed:

"Father, I am going to accept this as thy Word—by faith! I'm going to allow faith to go beyond my intellectual questions and doubts, and I will believe this to be your inspired Word."[32]

"Thy Word" still comes down to a book. For many, faith in a book is an unexamined concept. On the one hand, the *Bible* is a book like no other. It has been translated into more languages and distributed in more copies than any other book. Many American families have a decades-old edition, given at some family milestone and annotated in now barely readable penmanship.[33] Yet, it is a book that can be read and critiqued – even by non-specialists.

There are two obvious reasons to doubt that the *Bible*[34] is error-free:

- The *New Testament* took nearly three hundred years from the events it reported to reach final form.
- There are important inconsistencies in the *New Testament*.

Formation

Let me briefly review the essential history.

The 27 books of the *New Testament* were written between about 50 AD and 130 AD.[35]

Paul's letters were written in the 50s and appear to have preceded the four Gospels because Paul does not mention the Gospels. Also, the Gospel writers appear to have known about the destruction of Jerusalem which occurred in 70 AD.[36] Scholarly consensus holds these approximate dates for the Gospels:

- *Mark*: About 70 AD.
- *Matthew* and *Luke*: Since they apparently used *Mark* as a source and it needed time to circulate, about 80-85 AD.
- *John*: Since it has the most sophisticated and complex theology which took time to develop, about 90-95 AD.[37]

The Apostle Paul used scribes to write the letters that became *New Testament* books. *Romans* 16:22 records that one named Tertius put himself into the *New Testament* with a verse that is seldom committed to memory in the world's Sunday Schools: *"I Tertius, who write this letter, greet you in the Lord."* *Galatians* 6:11 (*"See with what large letters I am writing to you with my own hand."*) and *I Corinthians* 16:21: (*"The greeting is in my own hand-Paul."*) suggest Paul signing letters that he had dictated to Tertius or some other scribe. The original writings were probably on papyrus and deteriorated over time. Hence, they were copied over and over by scribes. These scribes were initially nonprofessionals and in later centuries, professionals.[38] But their role was crucial.

The work of these scribes exists today in a very uneven fashion. In some cases, the handwritten copies or manuscripts are of the entire *New Testament*. In others, just a fragment is preserved. The earliest manuscript of any part of the *New Testament* is of this section from the eighteenth chapter of the *Book of John*, verses 31–33 and 37-8, found in Egypt about a century ago.

> *"So Pilate said to them, 'Take Him yourselves, and judge Him according to your law.' The Jews said to him, 'We are not permitted to put anyone to death,' to fulfill the word of Jesus which He spoke, signifying by what kind of death He was about to die. Therefore Pilate entered again into the Praetorium, and summoned Jesus and said to Him, 'Are You the King of the Jews?' Therefore Pilate said to Him, 'So You are a king?' Jesus answered, 'You say correctly that I am a king For this I have been born, and for this I have come into the world, to testify to the truth Everyone who is of the truth hears My voice.' Pilate said to Him, 'What is truth?' And when he had said this, he went out again to the Jews and said to them, 'I find no guilt in Him.'"*

This fragment is about the size of a credit card[39] and it apparently came into existence about one hundred years after the life of Christ.

The earliest manuscripts of Paul's letters date from about 200 AD. The earliest manuscripts we have of the Gospels are from about the same time. Our first complete copy of *Mark* is from about 350 AD. We have about 5700 Greek manuscripts of part or all of the *New Testament*. The vast majority were made after the 700s.[40] There are hundreds of thousands of variations within the manuscripts. None are exactly alike (except the smallest ones).[41] That is unsurprising. When copied, the early Greek texts including the *New Testament* had no punctuation, no differentiation between lower case and uppercase letters and no space between words.[42] In the early years of Christianity, they were copied by people who were possibly illiterate themselves.[43] This, of course, negates Campus Crusade's escape clause.[44]

In an era without printing presses or academic standards, tampering with written letters – either intentionally or unintentionally - was a problem. A threat issued at the very end of the last book of the *New Testament* underscores this issue: *"If anyone adds anything to (the words of this book), God will add to him the plagues described in this book. And if anyone takes words away from this book of prophecy, God will take away from him his share in the tree of life and in the holy city, which are described in this book."* [45] *II Thessalonians* 2:2 warns people of that time not to be alarmed by a false letter purporting to come from Paul. We read in *II Peter* 3:16 of people distorting Paul's letters. Scholars estimate that *II Thessalonians* was written late in the first century[46] and *II Peter* was written in the 120s – 130s.[47]

In the third century the church father Origen (abt. 185- abt. 254) wrote "the differences among the manuscripts have become great, either through the negligence of some copyists or through the perverse audacity of others."[48]

We know that many people in the small churches addressed in Paul's letters were illiterate since Paul notes in *I Thessalonians* 5:27 that his letter was to be read aloud. Furthermore, *Colossians* 4:16 notes that that letter was to be read aloud and *I Timothy* 4:13 calls for the public reading of scriptures. *Revelation* 1:3 blesses both those who read and those who hear the words of that book. In *Acts* 4:13 the Apostles Peter and John are called uneducated. About a century later, the anti-Christian Roman Celsus wrote that Christians were lower class people.[49],[50]

We also know that some writings were lost. In *I Corinthians* 5:9 (*"When I wrote to you before…"*) and possibly *II Corinthians* 2:4 (*"Oh, how I hated to write that* letter…") Paul refers to a letter or letters from him missing to history unless they are somehow embedded in *II Corinthians*.[51] In *I Corinthians* 7:1 (*"Now, about those questions you asked in your last letter…"*) Paul refers to a missing letter from the Corinthians to him. *II Corinthians* 3:1 (*"Are we beginning to be like those false teachers of yours who …bring long letters of recommendation with them?…."*) mentions letters from Paul's opponents that we do not have and *Colossians* 4:16 (*"After you have read this letter, pass it on to the church at Laodicea so they can read it, too. And you should read the letter I wrote to them."*) mentions a missing letter to the Laodiceans.[52] Paul was remembered to have kept parchments on which he may have written notes[53] so possibly he wrote rough drafts of some letters before he dictated.

Luke explicitly relied on other sources. The *Gospel of Luke* opens with these words:

> *"Inasmuch as many have undertaken to compile an account of the things accomplished among us, just as they were handed down to us by those who from the beginning were eyewitnesses and servants of the word, it seemed fitting for me as well, having investigated everything carefully from the beginning, to write it out for you in consecutive order, most excellent Theophilus; so that you may know the exact truth about the things you have been taught."*[54]

From this it is clear that Luke had oral and written sources and that he did additional work so he could *"write it out for you in consecutive order."* Luke did not regard the original accounts as inerrant but went about to do the work to bring up the standard. Who wrote those accounts? Modern scholarship has concluded that Luke had as sources the *Gospel of Mark*, possibly a book of sayings known to moderns at "Q" about which we will have more to say later and other material. This other material included certain parables and narratives of lasting fame – the Good Samaritan[55], the Prodigal Son[56], the story of the ten lepers who were healed by Jesus but only one of them returned to thank him[57], the calling of Zacchaeus (from a sycamore tree)[58], the disagreement between Martha and Mary.[59] Matthew had the same two sources - *Mark* and "Q" - and also added unique material.[60]

There is at least one other example of a *New Testament* writer working from the text of an earlier *New Testament* book. The tiny *Book of Jude*, found near the end of the *New Testament* was written possibly toward the end of the first century[61] to rail against false teachers. It appears to have been used as a source for *II Peter* which incorporates much of it. [62]

The *Book of Acts* is mostly written in the standard third person, as a reporter might cover a story. There are portions, however, which go abruptly into the first person plural, the so-called "we" sections. These appear to be cut-and-pasted into Luke's narrative, although possibly from another document that Luke himself wrote.[63] They include:

- *Acts* 16: 10-7 – Paul going to Macedonia and making the first European convert, Lydia.
- *Acts* 20: 5-15 – Paul returning to Troas and Paul apparently raising a young man from the dead.
- *Acts* 21:1-18 – Paul traveling on to Jerusalem and a warning from the Holy Spirit that "the Jews" meant trouble for him there and then a meeting with James.
- *Acts* 27:1-28:16 – Paul traveling as a captive to Rome through Malta.

The concept that the "we" sections represent another document is bolstered by the observation that none has any major conflicts with Paul's letters as we will note occurs in other sections of *Acts*. [64] Moreover, in *Acts*, unlike the *Gospel of Luke*, Luke may not have relied on any other sources than his own notes captured in the "we" sections. [65]

John also may have relied on at least one other source and possibly more. At the conclusion of the Gospel the author of John writes a few comments about a mysterious *"disciple whom Jesus loved"* - sometimes referred to as the *"Beloved Disciple"* - and then writes: *"This is the disciple who is testifying to these things and has written them, and we know that his testimony is true."*[66] Another source might be inferred from *John* 20: 30-31. It reads: *"Many other signs therefore Jesus also performed in the presence of his disciples which are not written in this book; but these have been written that you may believe that Jesus is the Christ, the Son of God; and that believing you may have life in His name."*[67] This sounds like an ending in and of itself, concluding an account of several miracles that are cited to prove that Jesus was the Messiah who gives life.

Both of these endings hint at editing from oral or written traditions. Was there a text of Jesus's miracles going around the area that the author of *John* incorporated along with information from the *"disciple whom Jesus loved"*[68] If so, it would seem that like Luke, the author of *John* worked over the material, editing it to make his Gospel. We know that he left information out of his account so as not to go on too long. As noted, *John* 20:30 shows that Jesus performed other miracles than the ones listed in *John*.[69] *John* 21:25 alludes to unmentioned activities of Jesus, stating *"I suppose that if all the other events in Jesus's life were written, the whole world could hardly contain the books."*[70]

If other documents and oral histories were edited, with information left out and with two possible endings, one would expect certain disjointedness. There are indeed some examples of apparent disjointedness. *John* 5:1 announces a visit by Jesus to Jerusalem which is in the southern part of the country. Events transpire there as described throughout chapter 5. *John* 6:1 then records, *"After this Jesus went to the other side of the Sea of Galilee..."* Galilee was about a hundred miles north, in the opposite end of the country. *John* chapters 13 through 17 is primarily an account of Jesus talking to his disciples in the hours before his arrest. These chapters are packed with sublime concepts including admonitions to love one another and a prayer for unity. But there is a weird piece of dialog. The disciples are aware that Jesus is to leave them but they don't understand what this means. In chapter 13 verse 36 Peter asks him, *"Lord, where are you going?"* In chapter 14 verse 5 Thomas persists. *"We have no idea where you are going,..."* However, in chapter 16 verse 5 Jesus says, *"not one of you is asking where I am going."* These accounts in *John* can be tortuously reconciled but the simplest explanation is that the author relied on at least two and probably multiple sources and in parts of his narrative effected a clumsy integration.

Over the first three centuries after Christ, the emerging orthodox church was but one of several claimants to true Christianity and the historical context was one of scribal inconsistency, illiteracy, lost documents and other sources that were primary for the *New Testament* "books." Some of the rivals to the emerging orthodox began to collect writings, those of Paul and others.[71] In response, the orthodox gradually worked toward a consensus about what to include in the canon. The evidence of this work toward agreement has been found in recent centuries.

For example, consider the Muratorian Canon, a fragment named after the Italian Scholar LA Muratori who discovered it in the eighteenth century. The physical document was anonymously written and dated from the eighth century. It is thought by most scholars to be a copy of another document dating from the late second century although at least one dates it in the fourth century. It lists *Luke* as "the third book of the Gospel" and *John* as the "fourth" so we assume *Matthew* and *Mark*. In addition it lists eighteen of the current 27 *New Testament* books as sacred scriptures. It does not include these five: *Hebrews, James, I* and *II Peter* and *III John*. It specifically rejects many others. [72] The Muratorian Canon, then, reflects a debate of an earlier era over what *New Testament* books were to be considered scripture. In the fourth century, Eusebius[73] wrote of questions regarding status of these books that eventually reached the *New Testament* canon: *James, II Peter, II John, III John, Jude* and *Revelation.*[74]

What do we know about how and when that debate was resolved?

There seems to have been some criteria. The Gospels root Jesus in specific history and were supposedly written by apostles or close followers of Jesus – Matthew, Mark, Luke and John. The letters tie to apostles who were in turn allegedly tied to Jesus. These five apostles were Paul, Peter, John, James and Jude. [75] However, even these books took time to gain acceptance. *Hebrews* (thought to be from Paul) had adherents in Alexandria but not as many elsewhere. The letters ascribed to James, Peter, John, and Jude faced some skeptics; the first to be universally accepted was *I John*. The controversy around *Revelation* (thought to be written by the Apostle John) had to do with a view that it was apocalyptic and too anti-Roman.[76]

Some books were close calls but were excluded. One was the *Shepherd of Hermas* written in the middle second century. This work was often cited respectfully and was even included in the canon by some of the early church leaders.[77] Moreover, there were problems with the written-by-an-apostle test. "Of the 27 books of the *New Testament*, only eight were almost certainly written by the authors to whom they are traditionally ascribed: the seven undisputed letters of Paul[78] and the *Revelation of John*."[79] But these types of doubts did not emerge until the scholarship of the nineteenth century.[80]

The 27 books of the *New Testament* were first described exclusively by a Bishop named Athanasius (abt. 293 – 373) of Alexandria in the year 367. This list was recognized as the *New Testament* canon by a council at Rome in AD 382 by Pope Damasus with the advice of Jerome (347-420)[81] and at Carthage in AD 397.[82]

What this shows us, of course, is that the authority of scriptures that we now know of as the *New Testament* relies on people over a long period of time working often in competition with others who also claimed to follow Jesus. This underscores the Catholic position questioning the Protestant Reformers's claim of *sola scriptura*. The Catholic view goes something like this: 1. Christ had promised to always be with his Church. 2. Certain doctrines and practices not explicitly in the *Bible* had developed over time. 3. In this instance (the authority of scripture) the Church itself had determined the canon. 4. Therefore, it was impossible to give the *Bible* authority over the Church.[83]

Contradictions

Contradictions in the *New Testament* are easily found. They come in several categories

First, there are **Inconsistent but Reconcilable** sections. These are accounts of events that are dissimilar, but both could be true. These are events described by one or more writers with at least one version containing details not in at least one of the others - but in no way refuted by any of the other accounts.

According to *Matthew, Mark* and *Luke,* Jesus spoke to a man about the path to eternal life. The writers all agreed he was rich, but only *Matthew* added that he was young and only *Luke* added that he was a ruler. That story has come down to us as the story about the Rich Young Ruler.[84] We know that Jesus was a carpenter according to *Mark* 6:3. But no other Gospels report that fact although *Matthew* reports that he was the son of a carpenter. [85] *Luke*[86] and *John*[87] simply report that he was Joseph's son. There is inconsistency but it can be reconciled: Jesus was a carpenter. His father was one too. His father was named Joseph.

Much more familiar to us are the accounts of the birth of Jesus in *Matthew* and *Luke.* Both accounts have Jesus born in Bethlehem[88] of Judea which was in the southern part of Israel about one hundred miles from Nazareth. But after that, the accounts vary significantly. *Matthew* has the wise men[89] and *Luke* has the shepherds visiting the baby Jesus, but neither has both. But both accounts could be true, though incomplete, and two thousand years later we celebrate the Christmas[90] story with both shepherds and wise men. Beyond this, the reconciling remains possible but becomes more difficult. We learn from the *Matthew* story that Jesus's family had a house in Bethlehem where it appears that Jesus was born[91] but we don't learn about any manger. That's only in *Luke.*[92] Also, since as *Matthew* reports that Herod the Great, the Roman client king of Israel, killed the male infants two years old or younger, Mary and Joseph may have stayed in Bethlehem at least that long. In fact, if we just read *Matthew,* it appears that Bethlehem was their home and they relocated to Nazareth because as *Matthew* recounts, Mary and Joseph thought it would be safer and it was a fulfillment of prophecy,[93] nothing about it being a homecoming. Only Matthew has the holy family temporarily fleeing to Egypt.[94],[95]

The arrest of Jesus is described differently in the Gospels. For example, note the differences between *Mark* and *John. Mark* 14:36 has Jesus saying, "*remove this cup from me yet not what I want but what you want.*" But *John* 18:11 quotes

Jesus differently: *"Am I not to drink the cup the Father has given me?"* In *Mark* 14:50-52, his followers fled – one left all his clothing in his haste. But in *John* 18:8-9 Jesus told the soldiers: *"Let these men go."* He could have said both things about the cup and he could have commanded the soldiers to let his men go right before they fled. It makes a strange account but that is how we have to reconcile matters if we stick with inerrancy.[96]

We know of Joseph of Arimathea, the man who prepared Jesus's body for burial, according to all four Gospels.[97] Who was he? According to *Mark*[98] he was *"a prominent member of the Council, who was himself waiting for the kingdom of God."* According to *Matthew*[99] he was *"a rich man from Arimathea who had himself become a disciple of Jesus."* *Luke*[100] asserts that he was a member of the Council, a good and upright man, who had not consented to their decision and action. He came from the Judean town of Arimathea and he was waiting for the kingdom of God. *John*[101] calls him a disciple of Jesus, but secretly because he feared the Jews.[102] We will discuss later how the evolution in our knowledge of Joseph of Arimathea sheds light on the resurrection of Jesus.

There was a Roman centurion at the cross who is treated very respectfully in all three Synoptics.[103] What he actually said differs in one account, however. *Mark* records this quote, *"Surely this man was the Son of God!"*[104] *Matthew* notes that there was an earthquake and that the centurion and those with him who were guarding Jesus were terrified, and exclaimed, *"Surely he was the Son of God!"*[105] According to *Luke*, the centurion (again speaking alone) said *"Surely this was a righteous man."*[106]

When I was a boy in Sunday School in the 1960s, I quoted Jesus that anyone who is not against us is for us. I thought it reflected a healthy tolerance. I was quickly "corrected" by a teacher who said that I had gotten it backwards. It wasn't until years later that I realized that we were both correct, that Jesus had said both quotes.[107]

There are interesting questions when we juxtapose the *Book of Acts* and the letters of Paul. Paul wrote to the church in Thessalonica that he worked with them day and night and that he converted them from paganism. As he puts it in the ninth verse of the first chapter, his converts had *"turned to God from idols."* Yet in *Acts* 17, it seems as though he was there for only three weeks and mainly tried to convert Jews. Paul wrote a very personal letter to the Philippians, mentioning several people, but he does not mention either a jailer or a businesswoman named Lydia who were very prominent in his first visit to Philippi as described in *Acts* 16.[108] In *Acts*, it is recorded that Paul visited the cities of Derbe, Lystra, Iconium and Psidian Antioch (chapters 13 and 14). He typically started preaching in the synagogues and was opposed by the Jews. These cities were in the region of Galatia.[109] In *Galatians*, Paul does not mention these cities. In *Galatians* 4: 13-17 he recalls that he preached the gospel to them the first time as they were nursing him back to health from an illness. This seemingly important event goes unmentioned in *Acts*. In his letter to the Romans, Paul talks of travel plans that include a trip to Rome and he greets many people living there. In *Acts*, he was arrested and taken to Rome for trial. The writer of *Acts* seems unaware of any previous written contact between Paul and the Romans and has him spending time with Jewish leaders trying to convert them. In the *Book of Acts* we learn that Paul was a tentmaker (*Acts* 18:3), a Roman citizen (*Acts* 16: 37-39 – invoked to secure an official apology for imprisonment - and *Acts* 22:25-28 – invoked to dissuade a flogging[110]) and that he was taught in Jerusalem by the sage Gamaliel (*Acts* 22:3). He does not make mention of any of these assertions in his letters.[111]

One of the most interesting disjunctions between the *Book of Acts* and one of the letters comes as we consider Paul's escape from the city of Damascus in modern Syria. According to Paul's own writing he was evading government agents. *II Corinthians* 11:32-3 reads *"When I was in Damascus, the governor under King Aretas kept guards at the city gates to catch me. I had to be lowered in a basket through a window in the city wall to escape from him."* In verse 31 Paul assures the reader that he is *"not lying."* According to *Acts* 9:23-24, he was evading *"the Jews."* In theory, both the Jews and the governmental officials could have been looking for him.

(There is a possible story here. As we have noted, Paul wrote to the Galatians that he did not go to Jerusalem for three years after his conversion. *"Instead, I went away into Arabia, and later I returned to the city of Damascus."* [112] It has been assumed by many that he went off by himself to work out his view of Christianity. However, another possibility has been suggested. The keys are the mention of "Arabia" in *Galatians* and "Aretas" in *II Corinthians*. Marcus J. Borg and John Dominic Crossan[113] have pointed out that at that very time, Herod Antipater, the son of Herod the Great[114] had insulted the Arab King Aretas by divorcing his daughter to marry Herodias. A war resulted just as Paul was trying to spread a Jewish/Christian gospel in "Arabia", making him an enemy of Aretas and occasioning his escape. All this is plausible and, if so, Paul's first mission ended ignominiously. However, even if it did end with disappointment - and we cannot be sure that it did – yet another point to consider is what Paul may have learned in Arabia. Martin Hengel and Anna Maria Schwemer have speculated that Paul may have gained insights about the patriarch Abraham who was revered in those territories. In his letters he referred to Abraham a total of nineteen times in *Romans, II Corinthians* and *Galatians*. He also drew from what he undoubtedly saw in Arabia to make an important point in *Galatians* 4:25-31 about the freedom of the Christian. Verses 25 and 26 read: *"Now this Hagar is Mount Sinai in Arabia and corresponds to the present Jerusalem, for she is in slavery with her children. But the Jerusalem above is free; she is our mother…"* Hengel and Schwemer also point out that we know from the Jewish historian Josephus (37– abt.100) that some of the people regarded Herod Antipater's defeat at the hand of Aretas as punishment for the execution of John the Baptist.[115])

These examples do not erode the doctrine of inerrancy. The rich man seeking eternal life was remembered differently but not inconsistently by different writers. Luke did not say that he was old in refutation of Matthew saying he was young. Joseph of Arimathea could have had the various experiences and qualities that the Gospel writers ascribe to him. The centurion and the others could have said both that Jesus was the Son of God and that he was innocent. If Jesus's comments about his support appear inconsistent, they are reconcilable in different circumstances. The *Matthew* quote came in the context of hostile questions linking Jesus to Satan; the *Mark* quote came in the context of someone unaffiliated with Jesus doing good. If Paul chose not to mention Lydia, the first convert in Europe, in his letter to the Philippians it does not mean that the account in *Acts* is mythical - just that the purpose of the letter did not require reference to her (or he forgot about her). *Luke* does not record that no wise men came to see the baby Jesus, just that shepherds did. The writer of *Acts* may not have known about the letter to the Romans and Paul, under police custody, may have decided not to meet with Christians. Both government agents and Jewish representatives could have been surveiling Paul in Damascus.

There are, however, other inconsistencies that are not possible to reconcile. These are either insignificant to the doctrines of Christianity except insofar as inerrancy is one of those doctrines, or very significant. We will look at these separately, making the second category that of the **Inconsistent, Irreconcilable and Insignificant.**

These can be understood in questions:

Question: After Jesus's baptism, what did God say?

Answer: After the baptism of Jesus *Mark* has God saying, *"You are my son."* (*Mark* 1:11). *Matthew* has God saying, *"This is my son."* (*Matthew* 3: 17).[116]

Question: How did Jesus enter Jerusalem?

Answer: Compare the triumphal entry into Jerusalem as told in *Mark* 11:1-10 and *Matthew* 21:1-9. *Mark* has Jesus's disciples getting a colt and then Jesus sitting on it. *Matthew* has Jesus's disciples getting a colt and a donkey and then Jesus sitting on both of them. (That seems odd. John P. Meier traces it this way: *Matthew* puts a quote from *Zechariah* 9:9 introduced by *Isaiah* 62:11. *Matthew* doesn't recognize the poetic parallelism in *Zechariah* and has Jesus literally on two animals.[117])

Question: What time of day was Jesus crucified?

Answer: According to *Mark* 15:25 it was third hour or 9:00 AM but according to *John* 19:14-16, it was about the sixth hour or 12 noon.[118] Moreover in *Mark* - followed by *Matthew* and *Luke* - Jesus has a Passover meal the night before his death. In *John* the meal is not a Passover but he dies on Passover. *John* seems to want Jesus to be the Passover lamb.[119]

Question: When Jesus was on the cross, which of the other two crucified men mocked him and why were they crucified?

Answers: According to *Matthew* 27: 44 and *Mark* 15: 27 and 32 both mocked him. They were "robbers." According to *Luke* 23: 32, 39-43, one mocked him and one did not. They were "criminals." To the one that did not, Jesus gave one of his most famous sayings: *"Truly I tell you, today you will be with me in Paradise." John* 19:18 and 32 mention two others but does not call them criminals or say that they mocked Jesus.

Questions: How did the traitor[120] Judas die, who bought the field associated with his death and how did it get its name?

Answers: According to *Matthew* 27: 2-10, Judas hanged himself, the priests used the money he had received as a bribe to buy a field which was called the "Field of Blood" either because it was bought with blood money or because it was a place to bury strangers. However, according to *Acts* 1: 18-19 Judas fell headlong and burst in the middle and his intestines gushed out and he bought the field which was called the "Field of Blood" because he (Judas) bled on it. [121]

Question: Who met the women at the now-empty tomb?

Answers: According to *Matthew*, an angel with very white clothes did.[122] According to *Mark* a young man dressed in a white robe met them.[123] According to *John* it was two angels in white.[124] *Luke* is close to this version but writes that it was two men in clothes that gleamed like lightning.[125]

16

Question: When Paul (known at the time as Saul) was on the road to Damascus, and he was knocked off his horse [126]and encountered the Lord, what happened to his traveling companions?

Answers: According *Acts* 9:7 Paul's companions heard the voice that Paul did, but saw no one and were left standing, but according to Paul's account before King Agrippa, the great grandson of Herod the Great, recorded in *Acts 26*, they all fell to the ground with no mention of seeing the light or hearing a voice. Paul's account to a mob in Jerusalem as recorded in *Acts 22:9*, can be reconciled with his companions falling or not falling because the subject is not addressed.

Do any of these inconsistencies undermine the Christian faith? No, unless, to repeat, the Christian faith requires every word and every account of the *New Testament* to be accurate. These discrepancies are only important two thousand years later as a standing refutation to those who would insist that the words of the *Bible* are perfect.

An additional example in this category is a very close call. There is an irreconcilable inconsistency, but it may or may not be insignificant.

There is an apparent conflict in the *New Testament* between how Paul reported that he learned the basics of the Christian gospel and how it is reported it in *Acts*. I alluded to it earlier in the chapter. Here now is more detail.

The *Acts* account looks like a cover-up, or at least the minimizing of the cleavage between Paul and the Jewish-Christians.[127] The author Luke recounts that Paul went to Jerusalem after his conversion to confer with the people *("the apostles")* who had lived with Jesus. The details include their quite understandable response that Paul could not be trusted, the vouching for Paul by a Christian named Barnabas, Paul's boldness in speaking for Jesus *"in and out among them in Jerusalem"* and his escape to Tarsus aided by the Jerusalem-Christians.[128] Luke also records a second trip to Jerusalem with Barnabas to bring money[129] before the climactic Council of Jerusalem covered in *Acts* 15 and *Galatians* which I will describe later.

In *Galatians* 1-2 Paul stakes his entire ministry on his independence from the Jewish-Christians. To the Galatians Paul claimed that he did not go to Jerusalem for three years after his conversion. He states that on this trip he only saw Peter and James, explicitly not any other apostles.[130] He then, according to his account in *Galatians*, did not go again for fourteen years and only then in response to a *"revelation."* He further claimed that the Christians in Jerusalem did not know what he looked like. The account in

Acts is difficult to reconcile with this. It becomes even more difficult to do so with more accounts from *Acts*:

- According to *Acts* 7:58-8:3 Paul was active in the persecutions and this might have caused him to be known there.
- According to *Acts* 22:3 although he had been born in Tarsus he was *"brought up"* in Jerusalem.

But he wrote the Galatians as earlier he had written the Corinthians that, he was *"not lying."*[131] (This was a man who lived in controversy with other Christians.)

Since Paul's understanding of Christianity came to be dominant in the churches, this difference to some is one of the most significant in the *New Testament*. Did he get his understanding from the followers of Jesus who lived in Jerusalem or did he go off and work it out by himself?

In the interest of balance, I have read two analyses of these portions of scripture which could reconcile this discrepancy. Justo L. Gonzales[132] suggests a long period of time - perhaps the three years mentioned in *Galatians* 1 - between *Acts* 9:19 and *Acts* 9:23:

- Verse 19 concludes Paul's initial meeting with Ananias in Damascus and reads: *"and he took food and was strengthened."*
- Verse 23 concludes Paul's contentious dealings with Jews in Damascus and reads: *"When **many days** had elapsed, the Jews plotted together to do away with him,"* (Emphasis added).

If the "many days" covered a three year period, this could make Paul's trip to Jerusalem in *Acts* 9:26-30 the same as the two-week trip in *Galatians* 1. The logic would continue that after that visit, Paul spent time in Tarsus and the environs (*Acts* 9:30) or the regions of Syria and Cilicia (*Galatians* 1:21) which are about the same. However, there are some points still to consider that make this scenario only possible:

- *Acts* does not mention any trip to "Arabia." *Galatians* 1:17 does.
- *Acts* does not say how long the visit to Jerusalem was. *Galatians* 1:18 says it was two weeks.
- *Acts* 9:27 says that Barnabas introduced Paul to the apostles. *Galatians* does not say anything about an introduction and that Paul conferred only with Peter and James.

Martin Hengel's and Anna Maria Schwemer's views cohere in part with those of Gonzales as they conclude that during the "many days" time frame in *Acts* 9:23 Paul left Damascus to evangelize in "Arabia" and then returned to Damascus as Paul noted in *Galatians* 1:17. However, they conclude about *Acts* 9: 26-30 that the scene of Paul being in Jerusalem and appearing before the apostles is "unhistorical." They further conclude that this may have been an attempt at polishing Paul's image against detractors who later said he was furtive and cowardly. *Acts* 9:29-30 has him acting quite boldly in Jerusalem: *"And he was talking and arguing with the Hellenistic Jews[133]; but they were attempting to put him to death. But when the brethren learned of it, they brought him down to Caesarea and sent him away to Tarsus."* A legendary aspect to this account is also suggested in that *Acts* 22:17-21 reports this scene quite differently: Here it is not the Jewish-Christians who got Paul out of Jerusalem; it is Jesus Christ who did, with the specific charge that he preach to the Gentiles.

Finally, Hengel and Schwemer deal with the trip by Paul from Antioch to Jerusalem when he went with Barnabas to bring money as described in *Acts* 11:27-30 and 12:25. They conclude that in *Galatians* Paul may have just neglected to mention this trip or that he left Antioch with Barnabas but stayed outside of the city of Jerusalem. This does not seem consistent with the text which says in *Acts* 12:25: *"And Barnabas and Saul returned from Jerusalem..."*[134]

My view is this: the exposure Paul had in Jerusalem according to *Acts* is not reconcilable to Paul's own write-up in *Galatians*. Yet, the *Galatians* account of Paul visiting with Peter is not defeated in the *Acts* account. It was probably a two-way information exchange in an intense two-week period in Jerusalem. Ultimately - and, again, this is a close call – the discrepancies here are not significant for understanding the Christian gospel. We will discuss this further in Chapter 10.

There is a third category which does call into question key aspects of the Christian faith - that of the **Inconsistent, Irreconcilable and Significant.** These are accounts in which the questions that are caused by the inconsistencies raise important issues that have ambiguous answers in the *New Testament*.

How did sin come into the world and how can we be saved? According to Paul in *Romans* 5:12 and following, *"Sin came into the world through one man"* (Adam) and in *Romans* 10:9 Paul writes without qualification that if you *"confess with your mouth that Jesus is Lord and believe in your heart that God raised him from the dead, you will be saved."* However, according to *I Timothy*

2: 14-15 *"it was not Adam who was deceived by Satan. The woman was deceived, and sin was the result"* and women will *"be saved through childbearing"* if they live in faith, hope, love and modesty.

What is the status of non-Christian/non-Jew? A sermon in Athens is ascribed by the author of *Acts* to Paul. It appears in chapter 17. This sermon is about God. In it, Paul refers to a nearby altar *"to the unknown god"* and says in verse 23 that what they have worshipped in ignorance is the true God. Fortunately, God has overlooked this ignorance and is now telling everyone that they should repent (verses 30-31). His letter to the Romans is far less emollient. It is clear in chapter 1 that the non-Christian/non-Jew *"knew God (but) did not honor him as God and God has given them over to degrading passions…worthy of death."* So, for those who have worried about people who never heard about God - at least in the years before Christ and maybe afterwards – there are two answers. In Athens, Paul says that they did not know God but that God overlooks it; in the letter to the Romans Paul's judgment is harsh.

In *I Thessalonians*, Paul addresses the end times. We learn that the end will come a time when we don't expect it – like a thief in the night according to chapter 5 verse 2. In *II Thessalonians,* the writer is apparently concerned that the readers may have had their convictions disturbed by rumors that the end had already come. The writer assures them that it has not and, moreover, that it will not come until, specifically, the *"man of lawlessness"* is revealed and he takes his place in the Temple of God, displaying himself as God. The writer asks in chapter 2 verse 5, *"Do you remember that while I was still with you I was telling you these things?"*

In summary, on key questions such as the authenticity of the Apostle Paul's message, on the nature of God's relationship to mankind, and on the end times, the *New Testament* offers a debate more than a guide. Within this debate, one can discern a more diverse original Christianity than is commonly understood.

The discussion on inerrancy within the United States has been polarizing for nearly one hundred years. This is not an edifying argument. In fact, if we avoid it the Christian movement will have a good chance of thriving. Those millions of Americans who believe that the *Bible* is error-free do not need to give up or even reexamine that belief. All that is necessary to reconcile with those who do not believe the *Bible* is error-free is to append the following to the types of creedal statements that appeared at the beginning of this chapter:

"We do not, however, exclude from Christian fellowship those who do not believe in inerrancy of the *Bible*." That would resolve a major Christian split.

This is a safe place for evangelicals to land. In fact, evangelicals may be starting to question inerrancy. Christian writers have acknowledged for more than a generation that errors had crept into the copying of the *New Testament*. Most of them probably would assert as did one that "(t)he fact is that in about 90 per cent of the *New Testament* the manuscripts all agree; the differences occur in a small percentage of passages, and do not affect fundamental Christian doctrine."[135]

Let's look further. Journalist Lee Strobel has interviewed various scholars on the topic of inerrancy.[136]

As to the variations in the text, Strobel's sources assert that these are for the most part insignificant. These include, for example, a scribe substituting "Lord" for "Jesus", misspellings, two spellings for John. He notes that in *Romans* 5:1 - one letter is the difference between *"we have peace"* and *"let us have peace."* He notes that about 2200 of the approximately 5700 Greek manuscripts are lectionaries - sections of scripture for daily readings. Sometimes the word "Jesus" might be used instead of "he." One scholar is quoted, "No cardinal or essential doctrine is altered by any textual variant that has plausibility of going back to the original." Examples of this include:

- *Mark* 9:29 - In that verse Jesus answers his disciples's question about why they could not cast out a demon by saying: *"This kind can be cast out only by prayer."* Some manuscripts add *"or fasting."*
- *I Corinthians* 14:34-5 - These verses read: *"Women should be silent during the church meetings. It is not proper for them to speak. They should be submissive, just as the law says. If they have any questions, they should ask their husbands at home, for it is improper for women to speak in church meetings."* But many scholars believe that these may have been inserted by later scribes.[137]
- *I Corinthians* 9:20 – This verse reads: *"When I was with the Jews, I lived like a Jew to bring the Jews to Christ. When I was with those who follow the Jewish law, I too lived under that law. **Even though I am not subject to the law**, I did this so I could bring to Christ those who are under the law."* Some scholars believe that the highlighted phrase would not have been in the original.

Strobel also concludes that these passages are not considered authentic to scripture though they are in the Bible:

- *John* 7:53-8:11 – The story of the woman caught in adultery which contains this famous quote: "*If any one of you is without sin, let him be the first to throw a stone at her.*"
- *Mark* 16:9-20 – A post-resurrection appearance of Jesus.[138]
- *I John* 5: 7-8 – The clearest statement in the *New Testament* of the doctrine of the Trinity which reads in its entirety as follows: "*For there are three that testify: the Spirit, the water and the blood; and the three are in agreement.*"[139]

Daniel B. Wallace referred to a study on the discrepancy between *Mark* 2:26 and *I Samuel* 21:1-6. In the Gospel account Jesus described an event that happened "*when Abiathar was high priest.*" But the *Old Testament* account indicates that this happened when Abiathar's father, Ahimelech was high priest. Wallace considered several ways to reconcile this apparent discrepancy. "In the end, I didn't have a conclusion, but I said whatever you do with this, don't throw out Christ if you're going to question inerrancy. And I think that's fair. Personally, I believe in inerrancy, but I am not going to die for inerrancy. I will die for Christ. That's where my heart is, because that's where salvation is...The *Bible* wasn't hanged on a cross; Jesus was."[140]

In conclusion, the evangelical position gives up a lot of ground. Strobel quotes one scholar as criticizing the statement: "Find me one error and I'll throw out the whole *Bible*." This scholar goes on that this turns "the *Bible* into the Fourth person of the Trinity, as if it should be worshipped."[141] Further, evangelical writers acknowledge scribal errors and there appear to be out and out errors that they accept as such. There are sections that don't belong. All of this is a cautious stepping away from inerrancy. The problem is that Strobel and the scholars are not challenging the harmful statements of the evangelical institutions who are therefore allowed to create a caricature of Christianity based on a magic book.

The *New Testament* may be the most-studied work ever written.[142] Evangelicals often assert that the quality of the *New Testament* manuscripts is "unequalled in the ancient Greco-Roman world."[143] That is most likely true and we can agree with Donald Harman Akenson that the *New Testament* is a "surpassing wonder." [144] However, evangelicals need to consider carefully the doctrine of inerrancy and their statements on it found, for example, at the beginning of this chapter. It is far past time. John Henry Newman of the Oxford Movement in nineteenth century England saw that the study of history was a threat to the inerrancy that characterized the Protestantism of his day. He wrote, "To be deep in history is to cease to be a Protestant."[145] Newman led a Catholic revival and his goals were good but one can certainly shuck inerrancy and remain Protestant. In 1920 Harry Emerson Fosdick characterized the Fundamentalists's position on inerrancy as follows: "They insist that we must all believe in the historicity of certain special miracles, preeminently the virgin birth of our Lord; that we must believe in a special theory of inspiration—that the original documents of the Scripture, which of course we no longer possess, were inerrantly dictated to men a good deal as a man might dictate to a stenographer." [146] To what degree could evangelicals deny Fosdick's characterization today? It seems very consistent with the doctrinal statements of Campus Crusade, *Et al.* quoted earlier.

In conclusion to this discussion on inerrancy, I offer a simple comment and a restatement of the major point of this chapter.

Simple Comment:

We can hold that the heart of life is a personal experience with the risen Christ. Inerrancy is not a requirement for some of the varieties of Christianity.

Restatement:

To look at the *Bible* as a human book opens up avenues to see the different types of believers that the authors and ultimate editors had in scope. Some background is important here. Early Christians dealt with the issue of four different Gospels. Tatian an Assyrian Christian in the mid-second century attempted to solve the problem by writing a harmonization which was used in Syria for several centuries as the authoritative Gospel. It was called the *Diatessaron*, meaning "through four." Marcion (abt. 85 – abt. 160), at about the same time, resolved the problem another way. He rejected all but *Luke* and revised it somewhat. Irenaeus (abt. 130- abt. 200) embraced the diversity of the four Gospels and accepted them all with this famous statement late in the second century: "It is not possible that the Gospels can be either more or fewer in number than they are. For, since there are four zones of he world in which we live, and four principal winds, while the church is scattered throughout the world, and the pillar and the ground of the Church is the Gospel...it is fitting that we should have four pillars."[147],[148]

The early Christians bought this argument and even embellished it. *Revelation 4: 6-7 reads: "In front of the throne was a shiny sea of glass, sparkling like crystal. In the center and around the throne were four living beings, each covered with eyes, front and back. The first of these living beings was like a lion; the second was like an ox; the third had a human face; and the fourth was like an eagle in flight."* These *"four living beings"* were matched in art and legend with the four Gospels. *Matthew* was symbolized by a man, *Mark* by a lion, *Luke* by an ox, and *John* by an eagle. More prosaically, "because there were four Gospels rather than one, a certain variety of interpretation of Jesus was built into the *New Testament* from the start." [149]

The study of these variations in the Gospels has been one of the major projects of modern Christian research.[150] To see how the same story is treated a little differently by the writers of the Gospels brings with it recognition of diversity. These variations are called redactions and we will discuss them further in Chapter 4. For now, here is an example.

Mark 10:46-52 recounts the healing of blind Bartimaeus who calls Jesus the *"Son of David"* and asks for mercy as Jesus and the disciples were leaving Jericho. The triumphal entry to Jerusalem in *Mark* 11:1-10 follows. Some years later *Matthew* 20:29-34 recounts the healing of two blind men who call Jesus the *"Son of David"* and ask for mercy as Jesus and the disciples were leaving Jericho. The triumphal entry to Jerusalem in *Matthew* 21:1-9 follows. At about the same time, *Luke* 18:35-43 recounts the healing of a blind man who calls Jesus the *"Son of David"* and asks for mercy as Jesus and the disciples were approaching Jericho. The triumphal entry to Jerusalem in *Luke* 19:28-38 follows but after the story of Zacchaeus and a parable. These stories are so alike that they must have come from a common source but they are not identical. To further complicate things, *Matthew* has a very similar story earlier in his narrative. *Matthew* 9:27-31 recounts Jesus's healing of two blind men. They call him *"Son of David."* It is certainly possible to reconcile all this. (Perhaps Jesus healed Bartimaeus, then two unnamed blind men, then another unnamed blind man and then stopped to tell a parable which two of the three Gospel writers ignored and then went into Jerusalem.) But it is not necessary to make these stretches. It is simpler and more logical to conclude that the whole incident comes from *Mark* 10:48 by way of *Matthew* 20:31 of which *Matthew* 9:27 is a "weak reduplication"[151] and that somewhere along the way Bartimaeus was changed into two unnamed men.

What is the point of this? It is just this: within the *New Testament* there are important variations. If we study these types of variations as we will later in this book they teach us different lessons. If we read the *New Testament* in this way, rather than as a book that cannot tolerate error, we can see that the authors were addressing different Christian groups. The existence of these groups shows that there was more than one way to be a Christian. This book will describe some of the ways. Further, if we walk away from inerrancy, we can still revere the *Bible* and recognize that the *Bible*, and for the purposes of this book, the *New Testament*, holds a lot of prestige. As Marcus Borg has said: "Christianity is centered in the *Bible*...the foundation upon which Christianity is built, without which the structure will fall into ruins." [152] Minimally, it should be possible to respect the *New Testament* as an important document that has come down to us through many centuries in a form similar to the original manuscripts as a wonderful treasure of our civilization, referred to frequently in history and culture. In the next chapter we will look at some of the ways.

CHAPTER 3

The Role of the *New Testament* in our Culture

The United States is saturated with place names and geographical designations related to the Bible. American rhetoric has been heavily conditioned by allusions to scripture.

The American Religious Identification Survey (ARIS) has recently demonstrated that the percentage of Americans who say that they have no religion has gone from 8.2% in 1990 to 15% 2009. Some context is important, however. America in the seventeenth and eighteenth centuries was not very religious. In Salem, Massachusetts, "the setting for *The Crucible*, 83% of taxpayers by 1683 confessed to no religious identification." It was the First Amendment to the Constitution which guaranteed freedom of religion that caused church growth and today, about 75% of the population considers itself Christian. As with much of modern life, American Christianity is more diverse than in generations past but our geography and our history reflect this Christian orientation.[153]

On Christmas Day of 1741 the Moravians in America named their Pennsylvania settlement after one of the most famous towns in history, Bethlehem. [154] The Moravians also founded Nazareth a few miles away, a town that now has about six thousand inhabitants. The influence of the *New Testament* and of Christian history on naming is felt throughout the US in both Spanish and English. In California alone, one can find cities named after Jesus's father, John the Baptist and the four Gospels: San Jose, San Juan Bautista, San Mateo, San Marcos, San Lucas and North San Juan. Jesus's mother is the source for the name of one of the best-known cities in the world - *El Pueblo de Nuestra Señora la Reina de los Ángeles del Río de Porciúncula* (The Town of Our Lady the Queen of the Angels on the *Porciúncula* River) which we know as Los Angeles. Los Angeles also commemorates St. Francis of Assisi (1181/2-1226). *Porciúncula* is a place near Assisi where he died.[155]The angel that announced the births of both John the Baptist [156]and Jesus [157] and who explained the visions of the *Old Testament* figure of *Daniel* [158] is honored nearby by the town of San Gabriel. [159] In the vicinity is a port town named for Peter, San Pedro.[160] Florida honors Peter in another language with its St. Petersburg. Minnesota has St. Paul while California honors the Apostle in Spanish with its San Pablo. San Diego honors the Apostle James. (Its professional baseball team is the "Padres," Spanish for Priests.)

The city of Philadelphia draws from *Revelation* 3:7. That verse, quoting someone *"like the Son of Man" (Revelation* 1:13) reads: *"Write this letter to the angel of the church in Philadelphia. This is the message from the one who is holy and true, the one who has the key of David. What he opens, no one can close; and what he closes, no one can open."* [161]Then it goes on in that vein. More prosaically, Pennsylvania draws its name from William Penn (1644 - 1718), a rich Quaker who was granted Pennsylvania by King Charles II in settlement of a family debt. He founded the colony as a haven for persecuted Quakers and named its principal city, Philadelphia - "brotherly love." Penn said, "liberty of conscience is everyman's natural right." [162]

The name of Bethesda, Maryland comes from a pool mentioned in *John* 5:1-17 where Jesus performed a healing. Salem, viewed by many commentators as short for Jerusalem and found in the *Old* and *New Testament* (*Genesis* 14:18, *Psalm* 76:2 and *Hebrews* 7:1-2), is the name of towns in Massachusetts, Oregon, Virginia, West Virginia, New Hampshire, Connecticut, New York and Illinois. The state of Utah has a Jerusalem about one hundred miles from Salt Lake City. *Acts* 17:10-13 - mentions Berea, a city in modern Macedonia. The writer of *Acts* commends the citizens of Berea because they received Paul's message *"very eagerly and examined the scriptures every day to see whether these things were so."* Berea is the name of a town in Kentucky. Canaan or a word related to Canaan is mentioned 158 times in the *Old Testament*, referred to by Stephen the Martyr [163] and Paul [164] in sermons in *Acts* and in *Matthew*, a Canaanite woman comes to Jesus to ask him to heal her demon-possessed daughter. A strange conversation takes place. She was not Jewish and Jesus says: *"It is not right to take the children's bread and throw it to the dogs."* She responds: *"Yes, Lord, yet even the dogs eat the crumbs that fall from their master's table."* He commends her faith and heals her daughter.[165] Canaan, New York was founded by settlers from Canaan, Connecticut in 1759. (There is also a New Canaan, Connecticut.)

The *New Testament* records that Antioch was a base of operations for Paul and a hub of Christian activity.[166] In that era it was an important city but by the year 500AD it had declined.[167] However, it lives on in the US. There are at least nineteen cities or counties in the US named Antioch[168] and in 2008

Money Magazine put Antioch California on its list of America's best small cities. As noted, Paul (then Saul) escaped from Damascus. Today in the US there is a Damascus in at least five states. Fourteen thousand people live in Corinth Mississippi. Smyrna was one of the seven churches of *Revelation*.[169] Polycarp (70-156), an early Christian martyr, was its Bishop.[170] Smyrna, Georgia was settled as a religious encampment in the 1820s and burned to the ground by the Union army during the Civil War. Today it has a population of about forty thousand. Three thousand people live in Philippi, West Virginia – also the site of a Civil War battle - named in honor of the town to which Paul addressed a letter. Abilene, Kansas was named in a reference to *Luke* 3:1. In the 1800s it was famous for its stockyards and the Chisholm Trail terminated there. About seven thousand people live there now. There are Abilenes in Georgia, Texas and Virginia.

This just scratches the surface. Locations in the US named after Christian historical figures include such California cities and jurisdictions as San Francisco, Santa Clara, San Anselmo,[171] San Bernardino,[172] Serra Mesa[173] (a community within San Diego), San Juan Capistrano[174] and Santa Rosa.[175] Calvin[176] (Michigan), Brigham City [177](Utah), St. Augustine (Florida)[178] and Clovis (New Mexico)[179] also honor Christian heroes. One of the oldest place names in the US honoring a Christian hero is the Saint Lawrence River which forms part of the boundary between Canada and the United States. It was named by Jacques Cartier a French explorer in 1535.[180]

In 1691 a group of Spanish soldiers came across an Indian settlement in what is now Texas and named it San Antonio in honor of a Catholic born in Portugal in 1195 and venerated as Saint Anthony of Lisbon and Saint Anthony of Padua.[181] The battle of the Alamo was fought there in 1836. In recent years the city's National Basketball Association team, the "Spurs," has consistently been an outstanding performer. Erasmus High School is a public high school in New York City. [182]Its founders included Alexander Hamilton (1755 or 1757 – 1804) and Aaron Burr (1756 – 1836).[183]In frontier Alaska, the Russians once established a fort called New Archangel, now a part of the city of Sitka. The Archangel is identified by Paul as an announcer of the Rapture – discussed in Chapter 9 - in *I Thessalonians* 4:16 and *Jude* 1:9 names him as Michael. He is mentioned as a combatant in a cosmic battle in *Revelation* 12:7 and possibly *Daniel* 10:13, 20, 21 and 12:1.[184] Gabriel and Michael are the only two angels named in the *New Testament*.[185] Alaska also has a Resurrection River, Resurrection Bay and Resurrection Peninsula near Seward.

Santa Fe, New Mexico directly translates to Holy Faith.[186] Santa Cruz, California means Holy Cross. Corpus Christi, Texas translates to "Body of Christ." Sacramento, California means sacrament. The southernmost subrange of the Rocky Mountains located in northern New Mexico and southern Colorado occasionally evinces a red color at sunrises and sunsets, especially when the mountains are covered with snow. They are called the Sangre de Cristo Mountains which is Spanish for "Blood of Christ." California has Mount Diablo (Spanish for Devil Mountain). Christian doctrine lives in certain place names. The Catholic teaching of the Assumption is that at the end of her life on earth Mary was bodily assumed into heaven. The state of Louisiana has parishes which are political subdivisions like counties. Twenty-two parishes are in Cajun areas, an ethnic group with French ancestors. One of the counties is named Assumption. Plains, Georgia, population less than 700, is the birthplace of the thirty-ninth President of the United States, Jimmy Carter (1924 -). It derives its name from *Daniel* 3:1 in which the "plain of Dura" in ancient Babylon was the site of an idol before which the faithfulness of the Hebrew minority was tested.[187]

In the late 600s, the city of Constantinople was successfully defended by the Byzantine Empire relying on fortified walls and "Greek Fire" delaying the Islamic invasion of Europe through the Balkans by eight centuries.[188] In 732 French soldiers armed only with swords, shields, axes, javelins, and daggers and under the command of Charles "The Hammer" Martel put themselves in the path of an invading Muslim cavalry near the Loire River. After a ferocious battle – we know it as the Battle of Tours or Poitier – the Muslims retreated back across the Pyrenees. What would all these places in America be named today if these battles had gone the other way?[189] History does not disclose its alternatives.[190],[191]

(From an historical standpoint, Christian triumphalism here is wide of the mark. By 800, Muslim Spain was at least four centuries ahead of the rest of Western Europe. It was more tolerant. It was more economically evolved. It had far more books and learning. Certainly in the 800s, its architecture was more splendid. By contrast, "...the peoples of the West were obliged to accept the governance, protection, exploitation, and militant creed of a warrior caste and its clerical enforcers, an overlordship sustained by a powerful military machine and an omnipresent ecclesiastical apparatus. The European shape of things to come was set for dismal centuries following one upon the other until the Commercial Revolution and the Enlightenment molded new contours." A Muslim ambassador from Baghdad encountered a group of Vikings or Norsemen - the ancestors of modern Norwegians - in the tenth century. His report: "They are the filthiest race that God ever created."[192])

American statesmen and others have frequently used Biblical language.

In the early settlement of what became the United States, Captain John Smith (abt. 1580 - 1631), faced with a food crisis, gave an order quoting the *New Testament*: *"He who does not work, neither shall he eat."*[193]

In the early 1600s a pestilence - an infectious disease, possibly a viral hepatitis to which the Indians had no natural defenses - struck Indian villages in costal New England. It came from French sailors who were immune and it decimated the Indian population. A European, arriving by ship, saw the skeletal remains and pronounced the area a "new-found Golgotha."[194]

In another century-and-a-half, pastors provided religious justification for the American Revolution. Some linked the Stamp Act of 1765 which required legal documents to be affixed with a tax stamp to the Mark of the Beast.[195] Thomas Paine (1737 – 1809) wrote in *Common Sense*: "Monarchy is ranked in scripture as one of the sins of the Jews."[196]

John Adams, negotiating in France for an end to the American Revolutionary War, said he would need the "patience of Job" [197] to deal with Benjamin Franklin (1706 – 1790), his fellow commissioner.[198] When told that because of the resultant peace treaty with England of 1782 he would be "called blessed" by every American, Franklin demurred, "The blessing promised to peacemakers, I fancy, relates to the next world. In this they seem to have a greater chance of being cursed."[199] After the American victory at Yorktown, when the ability of the Congress to pay army officers was a major issue, some of them complained that George Washington (1732 – 1799) was indifferent. Washington subsequently referred to them as "the old leven (leaven)."[200] At least one of these officers referred to the incompetent Continental Congress as "the Grand Sanhedrin of the Nation."[201] On June 28, 1787, Benjamin Franklin called for daily prayer during the Constitutional Convention asking if they had forgot their powerful friend. He alluded to the *New* and *Old Testaments*. He said of God that not a sparrow fell to the ground without his notice.[202] He quoted that *"except the Lord build the House they labor in vain that build it."*[203] He said without God's help they would be like the Builders of Babel.[204] (Franklin was famously secular and this may have been an attempt to play to the crowd or to find a formula that would encourage consensus – but even so, it is significant that he chose Biblical imagery.[205])

Early America's blend of religion and secularism can also be seen in Benjamin Rush's attestation that he "as much believed the hand of God was employed in this work (the writing of the Constitution) as that God divided the Red Sea[206] to give a passage to the children of Israel, or had fulminated the ten commandments from Mount Sinai." [207](Signer Gouverneur Morris of

Pennsylvania [1752 – 1816] took a more worldly approach and wrote that "while some may have boasted of it as a work from Heaven, others have given it a less righteous origin. I have many reasons to believe that it is the work of plain honest men, and such, I think it will appear."[208]) One comment opposing ratification of the Constitution came from a delegate to the Massachusetts nominating convention who worried that the federal government would swallow up "us little folks...just as the whale swallowed Jonah."[209] Another delegate in answering him said "There is a time to sow and a time to reap[210]; we sowed our seed when we sent men to the federal convention, now it is the harvest...."[211] At the Virginia ratifying convention Edmund Randolph (1753 – 1813) who had come to support the Constitution was criticized severely by Patrick Henry (1736 – 1799) and responded that if their friendship should fall "let if fall, like Lucifer, never to rise again."[212]

Thomas Jefferson in 1793 in response to the violence of the French Revolution made this audacious statement: "Rather than (that the French Revolution) should have failed, I would have seen half the earth desolated. Were there but an Adam and an Eve left in every country, and left free, it would be better than as it now is."[213]

When George Washington died, Thomas Jefferson quoted *II Samuel* 3:38, "I felt on his death, with my countrymen that verily a great man hath fallen in Israel."[214] Jefferson was familiar with the *Bible*. In the 1790s, he described some of his former political allies whom he felt had gone a different way from him, as people who had been "Samsons in the field and Solomons in the council but who have had their heads shorn by the Harlot England."[215] Abigail Adams (1744 – 1818), facing the difficulties of raising a family, managing a farm and living near the ongoing battles in the American Revolution, all while separated from her husband, who was performing diplomatic duty in Europe, noted, that "a cheerful countenance and a merry heart...does good like a medicine."[216] During her husband's single term as president, she referred to his political enemies as "false brethren," [217] a term the Apostle Paul used – along with other atmospherics - to describe other Christians who opposed him. [218]In 1795 Alexander Hamilton, observing what he viewed as insincere efforts of comity between the camps of John Adams and Thomas Jefferson wrote sarcastically to a friend that "the Lion & the Lamb" were going to lie down together. He was observing the earliest developments of America's two-party system.[219]

After Washington's death, John Adams, concerned that he was not getting due credit for the establishment of the United States, wrote to Benjamin Rush that people seemed to think that the country was started when "Dr.

Franklin's electrical rod smote the earth and out sprung General Washington. That Franklin electrified him with his rod and thence forward these two conducted all policy, negotiation, legislation and war."[220] As Secretary of State, John Quincy Adams accepted the presidency of the American Bible Society. He opposed what he saw as intolerance among evangelicals. Adams preferred the moral beauty of Christ's teachings, downplaying doctrine: "It is enough for us to know that God hath made foolish the wisdom of this world."[221] In considering a run for the presidency in 1824, John Quincy Adams wrote, "would that this cup might pass from me."[222]

Here is Andrew Jackson (1767 – 1845)[223] after he lost the 1824 election for the presidency and as he blamed Henry Clay (1777-1852) for the loss: "So you see the Judas of the West has closed the contract and will receive the thirty pieces of silver. His end will be the same."[224], [225] In Andrew Jackson's presidency, his major domestic crisis was with the Bank of the United States, a chartered but privately owned institution. When, to weaken the bank, Jackson ordered the withdrawal of federal deposits, an admiring newspaper likened this action to Jesus driving the money changers from the Temple.[226]

In the 1820s Martin Van Buren (1782 – 1862) who was later President of the US was in the Senate and John Quincy Adams was President. Adams picked former Federalist Party members for posts along with members of the Jeffersonian Republican Party. Van Buren, a Republican, objected and complained that Adams didn't care if his support came from "Jew or Gentile."[227]

As a member of the Tennessee legislature in the 1830s, future president Andrew Johnson (1808 – 1875) opposed convict labor in the interests of free labor holding that "...Adam, the father of the race was a tailor by trade, sewing fig leaves together for aprons;...Joseph, the husband of Mary, was a carpenter, and our savior probably followed the same trade; the Apostle Paul was a tentmaker..." [228] In 1831, a Virginia slave, Nat Turner (1800 – 1831), who led a slave uprising believed that the time was near that *"the first shall be last and the last shall be first."* [229] His rebellion lasted two days with massacres on both sides. [230] In 1836 Angelina Grimke (1805 – 1879), an abolitionist, published *Appeal to the Christian Women of the South*. She pointed to the *Old Testament* figure of Esther[231] and the women around Jesus[232] as examples to follow for reform. [233] In the election of 1836, John Quincy Adams thought that candidates Martin Van Buren and William Henry Harrison were "the golden calves [234] of the people, and their dull sayings are repeated for wit, and their grave inanity is passed off for wisdom." In 1841 an aged John Quincy Adams argued before the US Supreme Court in the *Amistad* case over a group of Africans taken into US custody after they took over a ship. He told the justices that he hoped that someday they would enter heaven hearing, *"Well done, thou good and faithful servant."* [235] Here is Andrew Jackson, after the presidency and after the 1844 election which secured a goal of his, the annexation of Texas: "I am now like Simeon of old; having seen my country safe, I am prepared to depart in peace....I await with resignation the call of my God." [236] In Congressional debates that eventually led to the Compromise of 1850 southern Members of Congress worried about territories encompassing present day New Mexico, California, Utah, Oregon and others coming into the United States as non-slave states and the political impact that would have on the slave-holding South. One thought the South would be as powerless as a shorn Samson. [237] In those same debates, William Seward, opposing the extension of slavery, asserted that "There is a higher law than the Constitution...." He said that he and his peers were "stewards" of the "Creator of the Universe." He was mocked as one who "may have imagined himself to be Lazarus...sent on furlough to the world..." [238]

In 1858 Abraham Lincoln accepted the nomination for the US Senate from the Illinois Republican convention with a speech that history has called the "House Divided" speech. This title derives from a single sentence in the speech - "A house divided against itself cannot stand" - which paraphrases a statement of Jesus recorded one time in the *New Testament.* [239] Lincoln went to the *Old Testament* to describe the Declaration of Independence calling it the "apple of gold" within the Constitution's "picture of silver."[240]

In 1859, the abolitionist John Brown (1800 – 1859) led an attack on an armory at Harpers Ferry, Virginia. He was captured and hanged. Ralph Waldo Emerson (1803 – 1882) wrote that he made "the gallows as glorious as the cross."[241] During the 1860 campaign Abraham Lincoln following the norms for presidential candidates in that era made almost no political speeches. His stated position on slavery was moderate: to tolerate it where it existed but to oppose its expansion. Shortly before the election he was asked to repeat his position to offer some assurances to the South and to those who worried about his election breaking up the Union. He refused, wanting to withhold comment until he assumed office. He awkwardly quoted scripture: *"If they hear not Moses and the prophets, neither will they be persuaded though one rose from the dead."*[242]

"The Battle Hymn of the Republic" sung by the Union soldiers of the Civil War has several *New Testament* references.[243] Lincoln referred to God as "my Maker" in 1862 when he told his cabinet that he had made a bargain with God that if the rebel army was driven out of Maryland -the battle of

Antietam had been won shortly before - that he would issue the Emancipation Proclamation.[244]

In 1863, Congressman Thaddeus Stevens (1792 – 1868) declined an invitation to attend the ceremonies with Abraham Lincoln dedicating a cemetery known as Gettysburg with the statement, "Let the dead bury the dead."[245] In occupied Richmond in 1865 as the Civil War was drawing to a close, Abraham Lincoln was told that the Confederate President Jefferson Davis (1808 – 1889) should be hanged, to which he closely paraphrased *Matthew* 7:1 "Let us judge not that we not be judged."[246] Young James Garfield (1831-1881) who became the United States's twentieth President grew up in the Western Reserve and in a small school house is said to have won a *New Testament* in a reading contest. He must have read it [247] because it affected his language. As an Ohio state senator, Garfield said in 1861 of the coming Civil War: "I am inclined to believe that the sin of slavery is one of which it may be said that without the shedding of blood there is no remission." [248] After the war, American poet and diplomat James Russell Lowell (1819-1891), speaking for the victorious North and urging a Reconstruction, said, "The South called for war and we have given it to her. We will fix the terms of peace ourselves and we will teach the South that Christ is disguised in a dusky race." [249]

In the 1884 presidential election reformers who bolted the Republican Party to support the Democratic candidate Grover Cleveland (1837 – 1908) were sometimes called Mugwumps. Republican regulars also called them "brawling Pharisees."[250] In that same campaign a famous slur had *New Testament* roots. One of the earliest Christian congregations in history was the church at Rome[251] to which the Apostle Paul addressed his most famous letter. In the centuries following, Rome became the seat of the Catholic hierarchy and in even later centuries, references to the city became a type of Protestant invective. The Republican candidate James G. Blaine (1830 – 1893) was defeated in 1884 and a major contributing factor was the cry of one of his supporters, a Protestant minister, that Blaine's opponents, the Democrats, were the party of "Rum, Romanism and Rebellion." It was a reference to alcohol, Catholicism and the recent Civil War and it did not go over well with Irish-American voters.[252]

In one of the most famous political speeches in American history, William Jennings Bryan (1860-1925), a 36 year-old Democrat from Nebraska, electrified the 1896 convention and went on to be nominated for President three times. (He lost to William McKinley [1843 – 1901] in 1896 and 1900 and William Howard Taft [1857–1930] in 1908, each time by a greater margin.) In defense of abandoning the gold standard in federal monetary policy he intoned, "You shall not press down upon the brow of labor this crown of thorns, you shall not crucify mankind upon a cross of gold."[253]

Sixteen years later Theodore Roosevelt (1858–1919) made an obscure *New Testament* reference when he said during the 1912 campaign that his opponent Woodrow Wilson (1856 – 1924) should belong to the Ananias Club.[254] Roosevelt knew other parts of the *Bible*. As a New York state Assemblyman in 1883, he had said of political opponents, "No good thing will come out of Nazareth."[255] In yet another *New Testament* reference that far more people at that time than now would understand, Roosevelt said, at the end of his 1912 losing campaign that he could not keep the Progressive Party – which had split off from the Republican Party that year – together adding "there are no loaves and fishes."[256] Roosevelt's other opponent that year, President Taft, said of Roosevelt that by manipulation and deceit, "he is seeking to make his followers 'Holy Rollers.'"[257] In 1918 the journalist Heywood Broun (1888–1939) heard a courtroom speech by the Socialist leader Eugene V. Debs (1855-1926). Debs was a great orator of that era. Broun said that the speech was "one of the most beautiful and moving passages in the English language. He was for that one afternoon touched with inspiration. If anyone told me that tongues of fire danced upon his shoulders as he spoke, I would believe it."[258] Commenting that his conversion to Socialism was gradual, Norman Thomas (1884-1968) wrote that there was no vision or "Road to Damascus."[259]

In 1921 President Warren Harding (1865–1923) called for reduction of arms: "It was my fortune recently to see a demonstration of modern warfare. It is no longer a conflict in chivalry, no more a test of militant manhood. It is only cruel, deliberate, scientific destruction." He asked the crowd to join him in the Lord's Prayer.[260] Americans often comment on a perceived lack of difference between the two major political parties. In 1928, commenting on the presidential election and similarities between Democrat Al Smith (1873–1944) and Republican Herbert Hoover (1874 – 1964), humorist Will Rogers (1879–1935) said: "If a man could tell the difference between the two parties, he could make a Sucker out of Solomon."[261] In 1940 the Republicans did a spoof on the Twenty-Third Psalm that began, "Roosevelt is my shepherd. I live in want...."[262] Hoover, by that time a former president, got into the act by paraphrasing a Beatitude:[263] "Blessed are the young, for they shall inherit the national debt."[264] FDR, working against entrenched economic interests in the 1930s, talked of cleansing the temple of "money changers."[265]

James 1:12 – "*Blessed is a man who perseveres under trial; for once he has been approved, he will receive the crown of life which the Lord has promised to those who love Him"* - is sometimes invoked by Alcoholics Anonymous.[266], [267] Joseph Smith (1805 – 1844), the founder of Mormonism, "arguably the most influential native-born figure in American religious history and certainly the most fascinating" and who may have had up to thirty wives[268], claimed that he prayed to God for wisdom as called for in *James* 1:5.[269] [270] In looking back on the criticism he said he faced after telling others of his first vision at age 14-15, Smith alluded to *Acts* 26: "I have thought since, that I felt much like Paul when he made his defense before King Agrippa, and related the account of the vision he had when he 'saw a light and heard a voice'; but still there were but few who believed him. Some said he was dishonest, others said he was mad, and he was ridiculed and reviled; but all this did not destroy the reality of his vision." [271] In the 1876 election, Mark Twain (1835 – 1910) [272]said that the Republican Rutherford B. Hayes (1822 – 1893) would defeat Samuel Tilden (1814 – 1886): Hayes "is as bound to go to the White House as Tilden is to go to the devil when the last trumpet blows."[273] He had just written *The Adventures of Tom Sawyer.* [274] Mark Twain later wrote an essay called "To the Person Sitting in Darkness." [275] It was in response to imperialism and questioned the blessings of Western Civilization from the point of view of the subjugated. In 1949 Secretary of State Dean Acheson (1893–1971) referred to "the 25th Chapter of the *Gospel of St. Matthew* beginning with verse 24" in describing why he would not turn his back on accused traitor and convicted perjurer Alger Hiss (1904 – 1996). A portion of verse 36 reads: *"I was in prison, and you visited me.* "[276]

President Truman wrote in his diary in 1945 that the atom bomb might be "the most terrible bomb in the history of the world" and wondered if it could be "the fire of destruction" cited in the *Bible.* [277] Addressing the American public in 1946 about worldwide food shortages, former president Herbert Hoover said: "Of the Four Horsemen of the Apocalypse, the one named War has gone - at least for a while. But Famine, Pestilence and Death are still charging over the world." [278] Decrying the arms race in 1953, President Dwight Eisenhower (1890 – 1969) said, "this is no way of life at all...Under the cloud of threatening war, it is humanity hanging from a cross of iron."[279] In 1964 Lyndon Johnson (1908-1973) running for re-election to the presidency, liked to quote from the *Book of Isaiah* - *"Come, let us reason together"* - as a way of trying to show his differences with his opponent, Barry Goldwater (1909 – 1998). [280]

Both President John F Kennedy (1917–1963) and President Reagan (1911–2004) invoked *Matthew* 5:4, telling audiences that America was like a "city upon a hill."[281] At a Mass at President Kennedy's death Richard Cardinal

Cushing offered a requiem from a sixth-century Latin prayer with this beginning:[282]

"Dies irae! dies illa
Solvet saeclum in favilla
Teste David cum Sibylla^"

("Day of wrath and terror looming!
Heaven and earth to ash consuming,
David's word and Sibyl's truth foredoomimg!")

This reference derives from several *Bible* verses including *II Peter* 3:7[283] which reads: "*And by the same word, the present heavens and earth have been stored up for fire. They are being kept for the day of judgment, when ungodly people will be destroyed...*"

President Lyndon Johnson, complaining about bad press coverage of his presidency often joked that if he ever was able to walk on water, reporters would say he couldn't swim.[284] In 1976 candidate for president Jimmy Carter alluded to Jesus's statement in the Sermon on the Mount to the effect that anyone who lusts for a woman has in effect committed adultery and said: "I've looked upon a lot of women with lust. I've committed adultery in my heart many times. This is something that God recognizes I will do - and I have done it - and God forgives me for it. But that doesn't mean that I condemn someone who not only looks on a woman with lust but who leaves his wife and shacks up with somebody out of wedlock." Carter went on to urge tolerance and to persuade others not to be proud of being relatively less sinful - a theologically sound point. [285] In later years, Carter has pointed to *Hebrews* 11:1 - "*Now faith is the substance of things hoped for, the evidence of things not seen*"[286] - to describe his religion.

When Ronald Reagan was in the hospital in 1981 after an assassination attempt, Democrat Speaker of the House Tip O'Neill (1912–1994) visited and was shocked at Reagan's gauntness. Reagan and O'Neil were rivals but O'Neill kissed Reagan's face and the two Irish-American politicians recited the Twenty-Third Psalm. [287] George HW Bush (1924 -), the president who succeeded Reagan was asked if he were a born again Christian[288] and responded that, "I'm clear-cut affirmative to that." [289] In 1992 at the Democratic national convention, the Reverend Jesse Jackson (1941 -) said that the Herod the Great [290] was "the (then Vice President Dan) Quayle of his day." [291]

In his first inaugural in 1993, President Bill Clinton (1946 -) quoted Paul's letter to the *Galatians*, "*And let us not be weary in well-doing, for in due season, we shall reap, if we faint not.*"[292] On August 18, 1998, the day after Clinton's testimony before a grand jury acknowledging "inappropriate physical contact" with an intern, escalating an already-major scandal, the Clinton family left on a vacation. Hillary Clinton's (1947 -) press secretary released this statement: "Clearly, this is not the best day in Mrs. Clinton's life. This is a time when she relies on her strong religious faith." [293]

Former Senator Dale Bumpers (1925 -) defending President Clinton in the Senate in 1999 said in a statement that would deeply move Hillary Clinton: "Where were the elements of forgiveness and redemption, the very foundation of Christianity?"[294] In 2000 Vice President Al Gore (1948 -) attempted to quote *Matthew* 6:21 to stress his views on environmentalism. [295] In 2004, Senator John Kerry (1943 -), trying to cut into President Bush's margin among church-attending Americans repeatedly invoked the *Epistle of James* to the effect that "*faith without works is dead.*"[296] Howard Dean (1948 -), a Democratic candidate for president at the same time and, later chair of the Democratic Party wrote, "When you think of the *New Testament*, [Republicans] get about two of the values, and we get about 27." [297] In 2004 Howard Dean located the *Book of Job* in the *New Testament*.[298]

In the 2008 election, after Barack Obama's (1961 -) concluding speech at the Democratic National Convention, MSNBC's Chris Matthews (1945 -) worked in two *New Testament* references, probably only one intentionally, when he enthused, "you know, I've been criticized for saying he inspires me, and to Hell [299] with my critics! ... In the *Bible*, they talk about Jesus serving the good wine last. [300] I think the Democrats did the same." [301] At his inaugural, President Barack Obama, said, "in the words of Scripture, the time has come to set aside childish things." [302]

Social movements in the US have historically quoted the *New Testament*. Samuel Sewall (1652-1730), one of judges in the Salem witch trials and the only judge who publicly confessed that it was a mistake, later wrote an anti-slavery book: *The Selling of Joseph* (1700).[303] He dealt with many Biblical arguments for slavery and rebutted them, in part, by quoting *Matthew* 7:12 – the Golden Rule (*"Do unto others as you would have them do to you."*) [304]Nearly one hundred years later, Anthony Benezet (1713-1784), a Philadelphia Quaker and abolitionist also used *Matthew* 7:12 in his attack on slavery. In the 1850s southern leaders such as Jefferson Davis argued that the *Bible* supported slavery and that blacks came to Christianity "through the portal of slavery alone." Daniel Webster (1782-1852) answered the first, acknowledging that "the teachings of Jesus Christ" contained no prohibition of slavery but said that it was not "kindly affectioned." He added that slavery did not let "the oppressed go free."[305]

Thomas Jefferson argued in the Virginia legislature in 1776 to disestablish the Anglican Church. He thought that without state support religion would thrive. Dealing with objections to the contrary, he quoted *Matthew* 16:18 that the gates of hell would not prevail against it. [306] In the Central Intelligence Agency headquarters auditorium in Langley Virginia, along one wall is the verse: *"And Ye shall know the Truth and Truth shall Make You Free"* - a favorite verse of spy Allen Dulles. [307]

In addition to the *New Testament's* place in the vocabulary of the American people, its concepts clearly underpin American values. Christianity helped create a sense of individualism. Sin and salvation are personal.[308]

Paul wrote that people were important but not infallible when he informed the Romans that *"... the good that I want, I do not do, but I practice the very evil that I do not want."* [309]James Madison made a similar point when he acknowledged in Federalist 51 that people were not "angels" adding, "if angels were to govern men, neither external nor internal controls on government would be necessary. In framing a government which is to be administered by men over men, the great difficulty lies in this: you must first enable the government to control the governed; and in the next place oblige it to control itself."[310] Here is how Alexander Hamilton put it in Federalist 85: "I never expect to see a perfect work from imperfect man." Hamilton also wrote, "A fondness for power is implanted, in most men, and it is natural to abuse it, when acquired." [311]

It was this insight of the value [312] but the limitations of humans that helped lead to the Constitutional system of checks and balances[313] and divided government is now a hallmark of our democracy. As Louis Brandeis (1856 – 1941) said in the early twentieth century, the doctrine of separation of powers was adopted "not to promote efficiency but to preclude the exercise of arbitrary power." [314]

Another *New Testament* insight that aided the development of modern political values was Jesus's recognition of different spheres for God and "Caesar."[315] Jesus thereby set the basis for limited government and the individual conscience. Conversely, when he said *"My kingdom is not of this world"*[316] he put limits on the church. The First Amendment of the Constitution recognized these distinct areas of life and set the new country on a different path than Europe. [317] Late in life, James Madison articulated how the United States protected religion: "Among the features peculiar to the political system of the United States, is the perfect equality of rights which it secures to every religious sect."[318]

This calls for more emphasis. Secularism in the modern political meaning - the idea that religious and political authority are different, and can or should be separated – is in a profound sense Christian. This secularism - or separation - is rooted in Jesus's teachings and in the long struggle against the Roman Empire. "In the course of the centuries, Christian jurists and theologians devised or adapted pairs of terms to denote this dichotomy of jurisdiction: sacred and profane, spiritual and temporal, religious and secular, ecclesiastical and lay."[319] Although there was not separation of church and state as moderns understand the term, there did develop a distinction. Pope Gelasius I (492-496) articulated the classical theory of the Two Swords which held that God granted two swords of rule, one (temporal) to the state, the other (spiritual) to the Church. These swords were to be used separately but in coordination. Several centuries later, John of Salisbury (abt. 1120 - 1180) taught that both swords belonged to the Church, which then granted temporal power to the civil government. He also justified rebellion.[320] This is one of the most remarkable developments in world history. It impacts us greatly even today. "… (T)he values of America and Europe - even secular values - are decisively shaped by Christianity. (The outspoken atheist) Richard Dawkins (1941 -) has even identified himself as a 'cultural Christian.'"[321]

Adam Smith (1723 – 1790) saw religious pluralism as contributing to social tranquility. In *The Wealth of Nations* he called for a thousand small sects. "The teachers of each little sect, finding themselves almost alone, would be obliged to respect those of almost every other sect, and the concessions which they would mutually find it both convenient and agreeable to make to one another....(would result in) publick tranquility." [322]

Jesus also taught that servanthood was the ideal metaphor for leadership[323] laying the basis to see people as citizens rather than subjects. Jesus's and Paul's teachings support the notion that human lives have worth and all lives count equally. Jesus died for people[324], even when they were apart from God[325]and in his circles human differences are muted.[326]

To summarize the last two chapters:

- The *New Testament* is a wonderful book, highly relevant to our society. It is not surprising that in the 1830s Alexis de Tocqueville wrote: "There is no country in the world where the Christian religion remains a greater influence over the souls of men than in America." [327]
- The *New Testament* is not an error-free book.

- The way it was formed and some of its internal inconsistencies support the concept that there are different understandings of what it could mean to be a Christian
- It has given us secularism, individual rights, citizenship.

We now turn to the *New Testament*, investigating its internal diversity. By properly understanding it, we will be able to identify different types of Christians.

CHAPTER 4

Jesus

Paul is the earliest and by far the best-known of the New Testament writers. His view of Jesus came to be dominant. But Pauline writings are emphatically not our only source for information about Jesus. We can also learn about Jesus by considering the Gospels and some of his close associates.

Scholars believe that *I Thessalonians*, a message that fits on four single-space typewritten pages in modern English, is the first of Paul's letters and the oldest book of the *New Testament*. In this letter, Paul recollected his visit to a town in what is modern-day Turkey. The people he addressed were Gentiles. He encouraged them to continue to believe in Jesus. Jesus was a Jew who had been executed for treason about two decades previously[328] by the Romans who controlled that part of the world but whom Paul said was alive. Paul also assured them that they and their cohorts who had died would some day see Jesus.

Besides *I Thessalonians*, most scholars accept that Paul authored these other *New Testament* books (in chronological order in the 50s): *I* and *II Corinthians, Philippians, Philemon, Galatians* and *Romans*.[329] These letters stress that Jesus is alive and that through him people could be forgiven for their sins. Paul told people that even though they would see Jesus one day, they needed to live normal lives in the meantime. He advised people to pay taxes and respect the government[330] and he had some concern for an orderly worship service.[331] He wanted to make sure that people did not take their belief in Jesus as a license to live immorally.[332] His letters taught that this risen Jesus had superseded Jewish law but that the Jews and the Christians were still somehow integrally related. His constant theme was that Jesus was alive and through faith people could have forgiveness of sins and live a good life. The points to stress for purposes of this book are:

- That Paul had a point of view about Jesus.
- That this point of view can be compared with those of his contemporaries who are also represented in the pages of the *New Testament*.

- That where differences are apparent, there is no particular reason to accept Paul's version as the only authentic Christianity.

But who was Jesus and in what sense did people like Paul come to regard him as still alive?

At the time that Paul wrote the first letter to the Thessalonians there was, of course, no *New Testament* canon. So what did these first early bands of Christians know about Jesus?

They probably had heard that:

- He was born shortly prior to the death of Herod the Great in 4 BCE.
- In his mid or late twenties he went into the wilderness and associated with John the Baptist who became his mentor and, after some time we assume, was baptized by John.
- After John was taken into custody by the ruler of Galilee who was a son of Herod the Great, Jesus began his own ministry.
- He taught about the Kingdom of God.
- He spoke mainly to peasants and avoided cities except Jerusalem.
- He was a great teacher, using figures of speech, one-liners and stories.
- He was a healer and an exorcist.
- He transgressed social norms, associating with outcasts and women.
- His followers saw him as filled with the Holy Spirit.
- He went to Jerusalem on a Passover when he was about 30. There was conflict and he was crucified.
- Some of his followers saw him again after his death, not as a ghost but as the living Lord.[333]

As described in the *New Testament*, the picture rounds out further.

History knows him as Jesus of Nazareth. But here there is a point to resolve. According to *Matthew* 9:1, Capernaum may have been Jesus's "own city"[334] and according to *Mark* 2:1-2 he may have had a home in Capernaum. According to *Matthew* 2:15-17 he hosted parties there and *Matthew* 3:20-35 indicates that he may have preached to crowds in and around his house. He paid his taxes there.[335] Why isn't he called Jesus of Capernaum instead of Jesus of Nazareth? Well, the precedent is set in the *New Testament* itself as he is referred to as a Nazarene or of Nazareth by the writer of *Matthew*[336], a demon-possessed man [337], the crowd around Blind Bartimaeus [338], an unnamed girl provoking Peter's denial while Jesus was in custody [339], the mob arresting Jesus in response to Jesus's question, *"For whom are you looking?"*[340], Pilate [341], a young man in a white robe greeting Mary Magdalene and two other women at the Empty

Tomb [342], the travelers on the Road to Emmaus [343], Peter at Pentecost [344], Peter performing a miracle in Jerusalem [345], Peter on trial [346], Stephen's accusers [347], Jesus in a vision to Paul [348], and Paul to Agrippa and his court.[349] His identification with Nazareth, rather than Capernaum, then, is attested to in all four Gospels and the *Book of Acts* and seems secure.

The reality of where Jesus lived is pretty prosaic. His hometown was Nazareth but he moved about 20 miles away to Capernaum later.[350] According to *Matthew* 4:12-13, he was in the area of the Jordan River about one hundred miles from Nazareth at the time of his baptism and subsequent temptations and then returned to Galilee after the arrest of John the Baptist by Herod Antipater, not to his home town of Nazareth but to Capernaum. In fact, it is likely that John the Baptist's ministry was terminated at the very time that Jesus was going through his temptations and that Jesus upon discovering this left the wilderness area and returned north.[351] However, the move may have happened for a different reason. According to *Luke* 4:16-31, Jesus left Nazareth because his neighbors objected to him applying an *Isaiah* prophecy to himself in the synagogue and drove him out. They even tried to kill him. Thereafter, he went to Capernaum. This discord with his neighbors may have been compounded by a rift with his family[352] although in *John* 2:12 after the wedding at Cana he went to Capernaum for a few days and his mother and brothers went with him. In any case, the move seems to have jump-started his popularity. From *Luke* 4:31-37 we learn that he preached in the synagogue at Capernaum[353] every Sabbath day and that *"the news about Jesus spread through every village in the entire region."* (verse 37). The move, however it was occasioned, was to a bigger locale. Recent archaeological work suggests that in Jesus's time Nazareth was "an out-of-the-way hamlet of around 50 houses on a patch of about four acres"[354] with no great wealth,[355] with workshops and craftsmen.[356],[357]

The *New Testament* Gospels – *Matthew, Mark, Luke* and *John*[358] - which are accounts of Jesus's life - make up about forty-five percent of the *New Testament*. Tradition holds that *Matthew* was written by Matthew a disciple who was a tax collector, *Mark* by Mark a secretary of Peter[359], *Luke* by Luke a traveling companion of Paul and *John* by John of the Twelve. All these traditions go back to about a century after these books were written and I will use these traditional names in designating these authors. However, if *Matthew* was written by Matthew the tax collector, it is odd that it is in the third person. The calling of Matthew to discipleship in *Matthew* 9:9 gives no indication that he is the author. He is mentioned in *Matthew* 9:9 and 10:3 where he is described as either hanging around the tax office or as a tax collector and in *Mark* 3:18 and *Luke* 6:15. He was in the "Upper Room" according to *Acts* 1:13. [360],[361] There is speculation that the author of *Mark* was John Mark who traveled with Paul in *Acts* and whose mother was the Mary who owned property in Jerusalem according to *Acts* 12:12. There is further speculation that he was the young man described as escaping from Gethsemane in *Mark* 14:51-52. One early historian wrote that Mark was a friend of Peter and got information from him.[362] The *Bible* makes no claim that anyone named Luke wrote *Luke*; the co-authorship of the Third Gospel and the *Book of Acts* will be discussed in Chapter 7. As we have noted, to some *John* 21:24 is evidence that someone other than John of the Twelve at least contributed to the Fourth Gospel.

Here are some basic facts to remember about these Gospels:

- All were written after Paul's letters and even after his death. They were written between about 70 AD and 95 AD.[363]
- *Mark* – though the second in the order of our *New Testament* – was the first written of these Gospels.[364] It may have been based on some written sources.[365]
- As we have seen, the author of *Luke* acknowledged other written sources.[366] *John* also probably had multiple sources.
- *John* explicitly left out some information.[367]

The Gospels were written in such a way so as to attempt to root them in history. *Luke 2:2* records that Jesus was born during the reign of Augustus Caesar *"when Quirinius was governor of Syria."* The Third Gospel also sets the context *"in the days of Herod (the Great), king of Judaea"* in *Luke* 1:5. *Matthew* 2:1 mentions Herod (the Great) and the first Gospel starts with a genealogy. Mark gives less detail but still reports in *Mark* 1:9 that Jesus began his ministry *"in those days"* – meaning the days of John the Baptist. John talks about the Word which was *"in the beginning with God"* in *John* 1:2 and affirms that the Word was made flesh in human history in *John* 1:14.[368]

The Gospels contain mundane details like the comment that other boats were in the sea at the time that Jesus and his disciples embarked on a trip that led to him ordering the waves to be calm [369] or the observation that a little girl recovering from a coma or fever was hungry.[370], [371] But they also have an artistry [372] that shows up in different ways. The Gospels developed through at least two stages. First, oral tradition about Jesus was eventually written down. Second, these writings were reshaped by the evangelists for their own particular audiences.[373] This shaping is of great interest to the question of the diverse ways to be a Christian.

As noted, there is a scholarly consensus that the authors of *Matthew* and *Luke* had the *Gospel of Mark* before them as they separately wrote their Gospels. They often added or changed material. I alluded to the changes that Matthew and Luke applied to the story of Blind Bartimaeus in Chapter 2. These types of changes are called redactions and they show what an author chose to highlight or ignore. If Matthew or Luke redacted a story from *Mark* it was because they wanted to say it differently and possibly address different types of Christians.

Here is an example of how Luke changed *Mark* some fifteen years later. In *Mark* 15 at his trial before Pilate, Jesus answered Pilate's question about whether he was king of the Jews with this: *"Yes, it is as you say."* [374] After that he had no more to say until his final words. Pilate was *"amazed"* at his silence. [375] He was sentenced, flogged and crucified. He was mocked by the soldiers, the people passing by the cross, the religious leaders and even the robbers crucified with him. But he was silent until at the end on the cross he said, *"My God, my God, why have you forsaken me?"*[376] This portrays a man in shock and then despair.

In *Luke* 23 Jesus gives a similar answer to Pilate.[377] But he continues to speak after that. To the people he passed on his way to the crucifixion he expressed concern for them[378] and on the cross he forgave his executioners with the famous words, *"Father forgive them for they know not what they do."*[379] To the thief on the cross he says that both of them would be in Paradise *"today."* [380] Finally, in a loud voice Jesus says, *"Father, into your hands I commit my spirit."* [381] This is not shock; it is at least equipoise and it is a remarkable reorientation of Mark's account, particularly when Luke also asserts that in the lead-up to his arrest Jesus was in "agony."[382]

Here is an example from a familiar story about Jesus that Luke and John also redact. *Mark*, written about forty years after Jesus's death, tells of a time when Jesus came to a house in Bethany owned by a man named Simon who was formerly a leper.[383] A woman goes into the house and anoints Jesus with perfume. Some people in the house are indignant over the waste. Writing a decade or so later, Matthew tells a very similar story.[384] Luke recalls that Simon was a Pharisee, says nothing about him being a leper and has him indignant and oblivious to the beauty of the woman's act.[385] Writing still later, John also locates this scene in Bethany at the home of Jesus's friends Mary and Martha.[386] Judas the traitor is the one who is identified as the indignant, oblivious one. So, it is possible to conclude that these are two or three separate accounts. But it is more plausible that something like this happened as recounted in *Mark* and then was changed later to make a point. Luke's point was to bash Pharisees, John's to expose Judas.[387]

It is illuminating to see what the other Gospel writers changed from *Mark* and to consider the reasons. Here are three more examples, all of which concern the Apostle Peter.

1. One of the key events of Christianity cited down through the ages is the identification of Jesus as the Messiah by his closest follower, Peter. Mark recounts Peter's identification of Jesus this way. At Caesarea Philippi[388]Jesus asked his disciples who they thought he was. Peter answered that he was the Christ. Jesus told them to tell no one. Matthew tells the story this way: Jesus asked his disciples, in effect, who he, the Son of Man[389] was. Peter answered that he was the Christ, the son of the living God. Jesus then announced that he would build his church on Peter's faith. Matthew turned this whole occasion into an elevated role of Jesus and a future role for Peter in the building of the church.[390] The difference in how Mark and Matthew treated Peter is sharpened in the immediate sequel to this story. The *Gospel of Mark* has Jesus proceeding to tell the disciples about his coming death and resurrection. Peter then reprimands Jesus. Jesus in turn reprimands Peter and utters these words to Peter, "*Get away from me, Satan!*" *Matthew* contains the same story, including the labeling of Peter as Satan, but he softens all of it with an explanatory note that is not contained in the original story as told in *Mark*. Peter's reprimand of Jesus contains this explanation: "*'Heaven forbid, Lord,' he said. 'This will never happen to you'*"! This shows a loyal side of Peter, not acknowledged in *Mark*.[391]

2. Peter's role may be bolstered in another of Matthew's redactions, the story of the Temple Tax. This story is only in *Matthew*. It is, in and of itself, therefore a redaction. The story has two levels. First, it is light-hearted. Peter told Jesus that people were inquiring about whether Jesus paid Temple taxes. Jesus told him to "*go to the lake and throw out your line. Take the first fish you catch; open its mouth and you will find a four-drachma coin. Take it and give it to them for my tax and yours.*"[392] It seems pretty simple and straightforward. But Matthew's selection of this account and his placement of it in his narrative reveals more and that is the second level of this story.

This story is inserted between a section in which Jesus tells his apostles of his death and resurrection (*Matthew* 17:22-33) and a teaching about becoming like a child in order to be great in the kingdom of heaven (*Matthew* 18:1-5). *Mark* and *Luke* have similar (but not identical) passages but do not have the story of the Temple Tax.[393] Matthew's account throughout this section puts the disciples in a better light than does Mark's account. For example, Mark says, but Matthew does not, that upon hearing the death and resurrection account the disciples did not understand. Mark strongly implies that the disciples were arguing who among them was the greatest. Matthew has them merely coming to Jesus and asking, *"Who is greatest in the kingdom of heaven?"* The account of the Temple Tax fits *Matthew's* agenda. It builds up Peter. Peter acts as Jesus's spokesman. The tax is paid *"for me and for you."* [394] As seen in *Matthew* 18:1ff this caused jealousy on the part of the disciples and led to more teaching from Jesus. [395]

3. Finally, we see Matthew adding nuance to Peter's greatest embarrassment. He does it by the most negative of examples. We have noted earlier the difference between Matthew's account of Judas's suicide and the account found in *Acts*. A question to ponder here is why did Matthew add the suicide story to Mark's account? Let's consider the context. Matthew positions the story almost immediately after the Apostle Peter's bitter weeping on the occasion of his famous denials that he knew Jesus, even as Jesus was on trial for his life. Mark covers the weeping but does not segue to Judas. Matthew's apparent intent was to contrast repentance (of Peter) and despair (of Judas). Luke, like Mark, does not cover Judas's death in his gospel although he does in *Acts* in a context that does not include Peter. [396]

These redactions all serve to build up Peter and those allied with him and thus were part of a deliberate program by the writer of *Matthew* and his colleagues. As we will note in Chapter 8, the promotion of Peter served the interests of an emerging church as opposed to the interests of other Christians.

In addition to redactions, the artistry of the Gospels can be seen as they interpret the same material differently. Jesus told stories about feasts that served to make a point. Luke and Matthew interpret the same stories of the wedding feasts and banquets differently. Matthew sees the story of the feast as a comment of the requirements put on anyone who would become a follower of Jesus: a man was kicked out of the wedding feast because he didn't have the proper clothing. This is the place of an oft-quoted scripture: *"many are called but few are chosen."* [397] The fourteenth chapter of *Luke*, however records two parables about feasts and neither of them have the meaning ascribed to Jesus in *Matthew*:

- One has a message of humbleness: *"For everyone who exalts himself will be humbled, and he who humbles himself will be exalted."* [398]
- One has a message of talking the gospel to the world: *"Go out to the highways and hedges and compel people to come in, that my house may be filled."* [399]

(The first part of this last verse is another oft-quoted scripture. The second part – *"compel people to come in"* – has its own history. In the fourth century both Augustine and Ambrose of Milan drew attention to this parable to justify the use of coercion in bring about conversions.[400] In the fifteenth century, Christopher Columbus also used it as a rationale for using force to convert the indigenous peoples he encountered in America.[401])

If the redactions and the varying interpretations of the same material help us to understand Jesus, the stark division between the Synoptics and the *Gospel of John* emphatically add dimension to the picture and *John* is a far different book than *Matthew, Mark* or *Luke*.[402] Let's scratch the surface. The Synoptics but not *John* report the Transfiguration of Jesus.[403] This may be because John did not need the story of Transfiguration because he covered the concept in a different way.[404] The glory of Jesus and of God through Jesus are shown often.[405] More subtly, *John* may cover a significantly longer time period than the Synoptics. There is a clue that this is the case but it is hidden.

There is talk in *Mark* 2 about Jesus's disciples picking and eating grain on the Sabbath.[406] This underlies a controversy portrayed in the *New Testament* as working on the Sabbath which in some form could be a violation of Jewish religious law. Jesus, according to this account, dealt with questions about his disciples "working" by proclaiming a principle: *"The Sabbath was made to meet the needs of people, and not people to meet the requirements of the Sabbath."* That is one lesson from this story. There is another. Jesus in *Mark* 2 refers to an *Old Testament* scripture to make his point. He said to his interrogators *"haven't you ever read in the Scriptures what David did when he and his companions were hungry? He went into the house of God (during the days when Abiathar was high priest) and broke the law by eating the sacred loaves of bread that only the priests are allowed to eat. He also gave some to his companions."* The problem is that, according to the *Old Testament*, this event happened when Ahimelech - not Abiathar - was high priest.[407] Did Jesus make an error in his citation? Was he misquoted? Did the copyists get it wrong? (After all, Ahimelech was Abiathar's father.) The episode has been a standing lesson against inerrancy. (We noted it in Chapter 2.)[408]

There may be another important point in this story. David as the *Old Testament* records was a man after God's own heart[409] and was anointed king.[410] But he did not assume the throne of the king for several years and in fact was a wanted man.[411] Jesus's allusion to David as a wanted man implicitly made a comparison to himself. Like David, Jesus was already king but had not yet taken the full role.[412]

There may be yet another important point in this story however other than the intended lesson of the true meaning of the Sabbath or the derived lesson about inerrancy or the present and coming lordship of Christ. In context, this story may be saying something important about the length of Jesus's ministry on earth.

Since the grain was ripe, this scene evidently took place in the autumn of a year. Now, Mark uses the word "immediately" repeatedly[413] and by *Mark* 11 it is the last week of Jesus's life at which point the Passover - which is in the spring - is first mentioned.[414] But *John* mentions three Passovers.[415] It leads to the logical conclusion that *Mark* covers less than a year and *John* covers two to three years. James Tabor believes at least one year that is missing in the Synoptics can be accounted for in *John*. *Mark* 1:12-13 records that after Jesus was baptized he withdrew for 40 days and was tempted by Satan. *Matthew* and *Luke* add details. The next verse *Mark* 1:14 reads: *"Now after John was arrested, Jesus came to Galilee proclaiming the good news of the kingdom of God."* Thus, John the Baptist is removed in *Mark* quickly after the baptism of Jesus. These are the events which, according to the *Gospel of John*, happened between Jesus's baptism referred to in *John* 1:32-34 and John the Baptist's imprisonment referred to in *John* 3:24:

- The calling of Andrew, Peter, Philip and Nathanial (*John* 1:35-51).
- The wedding at Cana (*John* 2: 1-12).
- The cleansing of the Temple (*John* 2:13-25)
- The encounter of Nicodemus (*John* 3: 1-21).
- Baptisms performed by both Jesus and John the Baptist (*John* 3:22-23).
- John the Baptist's deferring to Jesus's greater role (*John* 3:24-36).[416]

Eusebius came to a very similar conclusion writing in the 300s "...it is evident that the three evangelists recorded only the deeds done by the Saviour for one year after the imprisonment of John the Baptist, and indicated this in the beginning of their account." Eusebius cites language from

- *Matthew* 4:12 – *"Now when Jesus heard that John had been taken into custody, He withdrew into Galilee;"*
- *Mark* 1:14 - *"Now after John had been taken into custody, Jesus came into Galilee, preaching the gospel of God,"*
- *Luke* 3:20 – *"Herod (Antipater) also added this to them all: he locked John up in prison."*

Eusebius went on: "They say, therefore, that the apostle John, being asked to do it for this reason, gave in his Gospel an account of the period which had been omitted by the earlier evangelists, and of the deeds done by the Saviour during that period; that is, of those which were done before the imprisonment of the Baptist."[417]

Most of *John's* stories are not in the Synoptics and vice versa. Chapters 1-12 of *John* cover the two to three years. *John* 13-19 covers twenty-four hours. Jesus never tells a parable in *John*, he does not proclaim the kingdom of God, or institute the Lord's Supper.[418] Here are just two of the many key differences in how Jesus is portrayed. In *Matthew* 11:38, Jesus refuses to perform a sign to prove his identity and in his temptations by the Devil in *Matthew* 4:1-11 and *Luke* 4:1-13 he refuses to jump from the Temple. But in *John* signs are a way of showing his identity.[419] Another specific example is that in *Mark* Jesus discretely raises Jairus's daughter from the dead [420] but in *John*, his resurrection of Lazarus is very public. [421] In *Mark* he heals the girl in private, with only her parents and three of his disciples; in *John*, crowds are looking on.

The *Book of John* develops the highest view of Jesus within the four Gospels.[422] This Gospel identifies Jesus with God. Jesus claims in the tenth chapter, verse 30 that *"the Father and I are one."* Part of this insight may have derived from communal struggles these Christians had with their Jewish friends at the end of the first century. Between the lines of the *Gospel of John* one senses that the early Christians were part of the local synagogues and then drifted away into their own fellowships. These could have been the stages:

- The Jewish stage of the Johannine community is shown in the calling of certain Jewish followers and also the signs source referred to in Chapter 2 of this book. Note that *John* 20:30-31 indicates that the miracles were to convince people (Jews) that Jesus was the Messiah, to show that he was empowered by God as his representative.[423]
- Eventually there were expulsions from the synagogue. See the story of the healing of the man born blind in chapter 9[424], especially *John* 9:22 in which the formerly blind man's parents were said to be *"afraid of the Jewish leaders, who had announced that anyone saying Jesus was the Messiah would be expelled from the synagogue."*
- After the expulsion, an "us versus them" mentality emerged. Often in *John* the adversaries are called "the Jews." A high Christology emerged. Jesus came to be seen as the embodiment of the message: *John* 8:58 - *"Before Abraham was, I am."*; *John* 1:14. – *"And we have seen his glory, the glory of the Father's one and only Son."* [425]

We will examine this deeper reading of *John* further in Chapter 8.

Jesus is the key figure of world history. We date our calendar by him. We pray to him, use him as a swear word and celebrate his birth, death and resurrection. What more do the Gospels say about him?

He was in his early thirties[426] and was estranged from his own family. It may have started even before birth. Mary was confused when an angel told her she was pregnant[427] even though she tried hard to understand.[428] At the baby Jesus's presentation in the Temple, Mary was "astounded" at the comments of Simeon.[429] When Jesus was twelve, he separated from his parents in Jerusalem. When they found him he said, *"Why is it that you were looking for Me? Did you not know that I had to be in My Father's house?"*[430] His parents did not understand what he was saying.[431] We know nothing more about his life through childhood, his teenage years and his twenties except that he grew and matured.[432] We have one clue that he was religious: when he began his ministry, the scriptures note that he went to the synagogue in Nazareth *"as was his custom."*[433] He may not have been physically strong.[434] When he began his ministry, his brothers did not accept him.[435] His family tried to take him into custody because they considered him mentally ill. [436] His townspeople tried to throw him off a cliff. [437] Jesus rejected Mary at some point.[438]

He put out a challenge to the authorities unlike *New Testament* contemporaries or near-contemporaries like Theudas[439] or Judas the Galilean.[440] Nor was he like the *"Egyptian who started a revolt and led four thousand terrorists out into the desert some time ago"* …"[441] These revolts and others were during his era[442], [443] and at times Jesus may have been linked with them.[444] He compelled his followers not to tell anyone that he was the Messiah [445] perhaps in order to dissociate himself from those he regarded as counterfeits. But he did not mount a direct military challenge. He taught pacifism. He urged love of enemies. He tended to stay within the Jewish faith but was willing to set aside some of its restrictions in the name of humanity, famously forgiving an adulterer.[446] He did so even in the face of the zero-tolerance command from *Leviticus*, that *"If a man commits adultery with another man's wife—with the wife of his neighbor—both the adulterer and the adulteress must be put to death."*[447]

To quote one scholar, "…Jesus was stigmatized by his critics as a bon vivant[448], a glutton and drunkard, a friend of toll collectors and sinners (*Matthew* 11:19), a demoniac or mad man (*Mark* 3:20-30 and *John* 8:48). A traveling entourage of husbandless female supporters, some of whom were former demoniacs who were now giving Jesus money or food, would only have heightened the suspicion and scandal Jesus already faced in a traditional peasant society."[449],[450] Yet, like a mystic he fasted and had long times of prayer.

Jesus must have given people a sense of extraordinary closeness to God. He forgave sins. That is important even for those who do not believe that our sins were forgiven by the atonement on the cross. To quote another scholar: those who cling to "the gruesome idea that human sin could only be forgiven by the death of Jesus on the cross must miss the point of such Gospel stories. This was the essence of Jesus's teaching and this was what caused scandal to those, like the Pharisees or the Essenes[451], who believed that forgiveness could only be offered to the pure." [452]

Jesus may have been a commanding presence. He taught in Capernaum with great authority every Sabbath.[453] He also may have had some affluence. It appears that he dressed well. All four Gospels report that at his crucifixion, the Roman soldiers divided up his clothes.[454] When he was a boy his family could afford an annual trip to Jerusalem.[455] He was frequently addressed as teacher[456] or rabbi[457] which indicated some professional training. We do know that unlike the vast majority he could read.[458] His associates may also have had some affluence. His followers included James and John who were in the fishing business and had employees.[459] Peter was apparently in partnership with them.[460] Peter may also have owned two homes - his home town was Bethsaida[461] but he had a house in Capernaum.[462] Jesus had wealthy followers such as Joseph of Arimathea[463], Joanna, the wife of one of Herod Antipater's key associates[464], Jairus[465] and Zacchaeus.[466] He once told a parable using money as the metaphor indicating that he knew the basics of loaning at interest even though such practices were outlawed in his society. This is captured in *Luke* 19: 11-27 with this in verse 23: *"'Then why did you not put my money in the bank, and having come, I would have collected it with interest?'"*[467]

There is one more clue to consider from the writings of Paul. In *II Corinthians* chapter 8 Paul was urging the church in Corinth to donate money. Verse 9 reads: *"For you know the grace of our Lord Jesus Christ, that though He was rich, yet for your sake He became poor, so that you through His poverty might become rich."* Although this verse is usually interpreted to mean that Jesus Christ temporarily gave up a heavenly station to assume life on earth, at least one commentator suggests that this passage could indicate that Jesus was once a rich man.[468]

So was Jesus once affluent? Those who would answer in the negative might point to his teachings. Some examples:

- In *Matthew* 25: 42-43 he seems to condition salvation upon helping the poor by saying: *"For I was hungry, and you didn't feed me. I was thirsty, and you didn't give me a drink."*

- In *Luke* 4: 18 he announced that, *"The Spirit of the LORD is upon me, for he has anointed me to bring Good News to the poor."*
- In *Luke* 14:21 in one of Jesus's parables the head of a household is throwing a large party but is angered that people are not coming. He says, as the point of the metaphor: *"Go quickly into the streets and alleys of the town and invite the poor..."*

Arguably, these teachings (and many similar ones) do not lead to a conclusion that Jesus was either poor or born poor. Other once-rich and even still-rich people have urged themselves and others to help the poor. But another story might lead to that conclusion. According to Jewish law at the time of Jesus's birth, the dedication of a newborn baby was accompanied by an animal sacrifice. It was normally to be of a young lamb but *Leviticus* 12:8 provided that, *"But if she cannot afford a lamb, then she shall take two turtledoves or two young pigeons."* At the baby Jesus's presentation at the Temple his parents took the cheaper route. As *Luke* 2:24 reads: *"So they offered the sacrifice required in the law of the Lord—'either a pair of turtledoves or two young pigeons.'"*[469]

My summary: Was Jesus wealthy or poor or somewhere between? We don't know.

One way to better understand Jesus is to consider who his close associates were. Here we will look at several, leaving Peter and Jesus's family including John the Baptist for Chapter 7.

The Twelve Apostles

The twelve disciples of Jesus are listed four times in the scriptures: *Matthew* 10:2-4, *Mark* 3:16-19, *Luke* 6:14-16 and *Acts* 1:13. The order and names vary only slightly. However, references to the Twelve may be misleading. Jesus also had supporters who helped him with food, lodging and expenses. These included Zacchaeus (*Luke* 19: 1-10), Lazarus (*John* 12: 1-2), a man with a pitcher who led disciples to the Last Supper (*Mark* 14:13; *Luke* 22:10), an anonymous person who prepared the Last Supper (*Matthew* 26:18; *Mark* 14: 14-15 and *Luke* 22:11-12), women including Mary Magdalene who traveled with Jesus from Galilee all the way to the crucifixion, a journey of about one hundred miles (*Mark* 15:40-41; *Luke* 8:1-3) and possibly Simon the Leper (*Mark* 14:3). *Luke* records in chapter 9 that Jesus commissioned the Twelve to heal diseases and sent them out to proclaim the kingdom (*Luke* 9:1-2). Then in chapter 10 he expands the program: *"Now after this the Lord appointed **seventy** others, and sent them in pairs ahead of Him to every city and place where He Himself was going to come."*[470] Later *"the **seventy** returned with joy, saying, 'Lord, even the demons are subject to us in your name.'"* (Emphasis added).

The Twelve were apparently important associates of Jesus and the number was highly symbolic. He was, in effect, reassembling Israel around himself. This delved deep into the history of his culture as Israel had not had twelve tribes since the 700s BC when the Assyrians invaded and carried off ten of the tribes leaving only the tribes of Benjamin and Judah (the "Jews") in the south and some Levites.[471]

The Twelve are mentioned nearly thirty times in the in the *New Testament*. They follow Jesus from Galilee to Jerusalem. They were at the Last Supper.[472] Minus Judas, they saw appearances of the resurrected Jesus in Galilee where they received the Great Commission[473] to make disciples of Jesus throughout the world.[474] Minus Judas, they were given a report of the resurrection from the women who first saw the risen Jesus and later along with others told the Emmaus travelers that, *"the Lord has really risen and has appeared to Simon (Peter)."* Following that, the eleven saw Jesus himself, talked with him and then witnessed his ascension into Heaven.[475] The eleven were in the Upper Room[476] and quickly picked a replacement for Judas.[477] As the Jerusalem Church grew, they learned to delegate authority.[478] We will see that the Twelve moved from center stage in the *New Testament*. However, there is one more mention and it at least shows their place in the mindset of some early followers of Jesus. The writer of *Revelation*, in describing his vision of heaven, wrote: *"And the wall of the city had twelve foundation stones, and on them were the twelve names of the twelve apostles of the Lamb."*[479]

Within the Twelve, however, there was a select group. It included Peter and the brothers James and John.

James and John of the Twelve

We will focus on John since as we will see, he lived longer than James.[480] The brothers were often referred to in the Gospels as the "sons of Zebedee"[481] They either directly or through their mother had schemed for positions in the kingdom of Heaven.[482] John and James were two of Jesus's earliest followers. As noted, they were business partners in the fishing industry with Peter and also their father.[483] Along with Peter, the two brothers were part of Jesus's inner circle. Here are some examples: the brothers were with Peter and Jesus at the healing Peter's mother,[484] at the healing of the Jairus's daughter,[485] at a scene where Jesus made a great catch of fish and told them: *"Do not fear, from now on you will be catching men,"*[486] at the Transfiguration,[487] on the Mount of Olives in private conversation with Jesus,[488] praying with him at Gethsemane a little ways off from the rest of the disciples,[489] and in Galilee at a resurrection appearance by Jesus.[490]

As the Jerusalem church started, John was a central figure. Paul later wrote of him as one of the "pillars."[491] He was with Peter near the Temple where Peter performed a healing miracle which resulted in a crowd scene and their arrest. At the ensuing trial the High Priest and his associates made notice of Peter's and John's confidence and merely told them not to *"speak or teach at all in the name of Jesus. But Peter and John answered and said to them, 'Whether it is right in the sight of God to give heed to you rather than to God, you be the judge; for we cannot stop speaking about what we have seen and heard.'"*[492] Paul wrote that John was at the Council of Jerusalem[493], a crucial conference that we will discuss in Chapter 7.

What can we reasonably infer from all this about John? Along with his brother, he may have had a volatile temperament. Jesus nicknamed them *"Sons of Thunder."*[494] But John changed over time. At one point a Samaritan village rejected Jesus. John along with his brother asked Jesus if they *"should we call down fire from heaven to burn them up?"*[495] But as a leader in the Jerusalem Church John accompanied Peter on a missionary trip to Samaria.[496] In summary, he was a businessman,[497] with a strong personality who became a church leader and he evolved over time. Such was one type of person drawn to Jesus.

The *"Disciple Whom Jesus Loved"*

There is a person mentioned several times in the *Gospel of John* and we turn to him as another of Jesus's associates. But first, there is a point of controversy. This person may or may not be the Apostle John, the individual whom we have just discussed. I will take the view that they are two different people. Let me explain.

I introduced the *"disciple whom Jesus loved"* in Chapter 2 in discussing possible sources for the *Gospel of John*. Who was he? Traditionally, this disciple has been assumed to be the Apostle John the son of Zebedee and thus one of the Twelve[498] and the author according to *John* 21:24[499] of *John*.

However, there are other views. All this is of great importance in understanding Jesus because we are trying to learn about one of the closest people to him, possibly his best friend during his earthly ministry and in whose care he placed his own mother.[500]

Here is some background.

Unlike the Synoptics, there is no list of the Twelve in *John* although the Twelve are referred to in four instances. The first three are closely connected in an account in which many of his followers were deserting Jesus. Jesus then *"said to the **Twelve**, 'You do not want to go away also, do you?' Simon Peter answered*

Him, 'Lord, to whom shall we go? You have words of eternal life. We have believed and have come to know that you are the Holy One of God.' Jesus answered them, 'Did I Myself not choose you, the Twelve, and yet one of you is a devil?' Now He meant Judas the son of Simon Iscariot, for he, one of the Twelve, was going to betray Him."[501] From these verses we can corroborate with the Synoptics that Peter and Judas were in the Twelve. The fourth instance explicitly put Thomas in the Twelve. *John* 20:24 follows a resurrection appearance by Jesus and reads: *"But Thomas, one of the Twelve, called Didymus, was not with them when Jesus came."* (Emphases added). *John* goes on to give us the story of Doubting Thomas. From these we can corroborate with the Synoptics that Thomas also was in the Twelve.

Who – according to *John* - were some of the other disciples? They are introduced as follows:

- Andrew and an anonymous disciple are introduced in *John* 1:35-40. The Synoptics's lists include Andrew in the Twelve.
- Philip is introduced in *John* 1:43. The Synoptics's lists include Philip in the Twelve.
- Nathanial is introduced in *John* 1:45. The Synoptics's lists do not include Nathanial in the Twelve but he is often conflated with Bartholomew who is listed.
- James and John are introduced in *John* 21:2, although they are not named – only called the *"sons of Zebedee."* The Synoptics's lists include James and John in the Twelve.
- Also in *John* 21:1-2 two anonymous disciples are mentioned and it appears from the context of *John* 21:7, that one of them is the *"disciple whom Jesus loved."*

In contrast to the Synoptics, Andrew is given roles apart from Peter:

- He joins the Jesus movement, leaving John the Baptist, before Peter. In fact, Andrew introduces Peter to Jesus in *John* 1:35-43.
- At the feeding of the five thousand, he is the one to mention to Jesus that a boy has some food in *John* 6:8.
- Along with Philip he tells Jesus toward the end of his ministry that some Gentiles were hoping to see him in *John* 12:20-22.

Also, *John* introduces new disciples:

- Nicodemus is introduced in *John* 3:1-21.
- Lazarus is introduced in *John* 11:1.
- Mary the wife of Clopas is introduced in *John* 19:25.

Finally, at least two disciples are given more prominence than they were in the Synoptics. Mary and Martha from Bethany are mentioned in *Luke* 10:38-42. It is the account in which Martha is concerned that her sister is not helping with the meal arrangements and Jesus responds in verses 41-42: *"Martha, Martha, you are worried and bothered about so many things; but only one thing is necessary, for Mary has chosen the good part, which shall not be taken away from her."* The *Gospel of John* gives a whole chapter to the sisters and Lazarus.

Nicodemus, Lazarus, Mary and Martha were from in or around Jerusalem - where the *"disciple whom Jesus loved"* may have lived.

Aside from the distinction noted above in *John* 21 between John the son of Zebedee and the *"disciple whom Jesus loved"* there are additional strong arguments that they were two different people. The Synoptics list three major events that took place during Jesus's ministry: the Transfiguration[502], his reviving of the daughter of Jairus[503] and his prayers in the Garden of Gethsemane.[504] As noted, John was present at each of these. Others who were there were his brother and Peter. Yet, in the *Gospel of John* these events are not mentioned which, if this John were the author, seems strange. In fact, the Apostle John is mentioned about twenty times in the Synoptics and none of those instances are reported in *John*. An event in the *Book of Acts* when juxtaposed with one in the *Gospel of John* also suggests that John of the Twelve and the *"disciple whom Jesus loved"* were two different people. In *Acts* 4:1-23 the High Priest Annas and his colleague Caiaphas become acquainted with Peter and John after their arrest in Jerusalem. However, according to *John* 18:15 a disciple who is by inference the *"disciple whom Jesus loved"* was known to the high priest who at the time was Caiaphas according to *John* 18:13.

What, then, do we know about the *"disciple whom Jesus loved"*?

This disciple may have been younger than the others. Consider:

- He could outrun Peter (*John* 20: 3-4).
- His eyesight was better than others (*John* 21:7).
- Jesus established him as a witness possibly because of his expected longevity (*John* 21:22-24).[505]

As a relatively young man, he may have joined the group late and been left out of lists of the Twelve.[506] One scholar suggests that this disciple became one of Jesus's successors like James or Peter or Paul.[507] Lazarus whom Jesus loved[508] appears in *John* 11 and 12 and then not again and in *John* 13 we see the first explicit reference to the *"disciple whom Jesus loved."* *Mark* tells of only one young man who stayed behind when Jesus was arrested[509] and *John* shows that the *"disciple whom Jesus loved"* was at the cross. Could these references be to Lazarus?[510]

Possibly.

But Richard Bauckham believes that the *"disciple whom Jesus loved"* was a man named John but was not John of the Twelve. He further believes that the *"disciple whom Jesus loved"*:

- Wrote the *Gospel of John*.
- Wrote the three Johannine letters.
- Lived a long life.
- Lived out his life in Ephesus.[511]

Bauckham relies on his reading of the Fourth Gospel plus his research into the writings of patristic sources to reach these conclusions.[512]

He notes or infers that the *"disciple whom Jesus loved"* appears in:

- *John* 1:35 – As one of the first two disciples, even before Peter. This is by inference.
- *John* 13:23-26 - At the Last Supper in a place of honor.
- *John* 18:15-16 – In the high priest's courtyard after Jesus's arrest. This is by inference.
- *John*19:25-27 - At the cross.
- *John* 19:35 - As an eyewitness to the soldiers stabbing the body of Jesus on the cross. This is by inference.
- *John* 20:2-10 – At the Empty Tomb.
- *John* 21:2, 7, 20-24 – At the Sea of Galilee.

It is this last verse that may be decisive: *John* 21:24 which, to quote again, reads*: "This is the disciple who is testifying to these things and wrote these things, and we know that his testimony is true."*

Bauckham believes that *"John* 21:24 means that the Beloved Disciple composed the Gospel, whether or not he wielded the pen. He could have received assistance of various kinds in the process of composition or his work could have been edited by someone else, but the statement requires that he was substantially responsible both for the content and for the words of the book."

Jesus's associations with the Twelve, with John of the Twelve and with the *"disciple whom Jesus loved"* (if indeed he was a different person that John of the Twelve) show his appeal to a diverse group of people. We will see in Chapter 7 how his associations with Peter and with his own family emphasize this point.

For now, we will look at some of the other aspects of his personality that we glean from the Gospels.

Jesus's empathy for the unfortunate may have derived from ambiguous circumstances in his own family. In one of the earliest accounts we have of Jesus, his townspeople identified him as the *"Mary's son"*[513], omitting any mention of his father in a patriarchal culture. A later account added Joseph, although not by name.[514] There are other hints that Jesus may have been taunted with illegitimacy. In a portion of what we call the *Magnificat* in which Mary thanks God for choosing her to give birth to Jesus, she refers to her "low estate." [515] *John* 8:41 records a statement by Jesus's enemies that may imply that they thought that he was born out of wedlock. They said, with some apparent incongruity, *"We are not illegitimate children."* Across the centuries, one can unconsciously put an emphasis on the *"We"* in that sentence. There is at least one hint in history. "We have independent testimony from Celsus around 180 that Jews were telling stories about Mary's conception of Jesus by a Roman soldier named Panthera."[516] In this context, it is worth noting that Roman soldiers were treated respectfully in the Gospels: In *Luke* 3:14 some soldiers asked John the Baptist, *"And what should we do?"* He simply told them to do their jobs: *"Don't extort money and don't accuse people falsely—be content with your pay."* In *Luke* 7: 9 Jesus said about a centurion, *"I tell you, I have not found such great faith even in Israel."* Then, at the crucifixion, *"when the centurion, who stood there in front of Jesus, heard his cry and saw how he died, he said, 'Surely this man was the Son of God!'"* (*Mark* 15:39).

Jesus's teaching stands for the ages. Although he once told his followers not to go into any village of the non-Jewish Samaritans,[517] he also told a story about what modern people would call cross-cultural communications between Jews and a good Samaritan.[518] The world now has hundreds of hospitals named after that story and, as a further example of its place in our heritage, it has been invoked more than five hundred times in US House and Senate debates in the last couple of decades.[519] His story of forgiveness of the Prodigal Son[520] is a staple. His one-liners – the blind leading the blind[521], blessed are the peacemakers[522], faith the size of a mustard seed is sufficient for great things[523], do not put your lamp under a basket[524], seek and you will find[525], a prophet not being honored in his own country[526] and more – are also staples. He urged people not to obsess over material gains since God, who took care of the *"lilies of the field"* would care for them.[527] He urged people to go the extra mile in dealing with others[528] and even to love one's enemies.[529] He mocked self-righteousness, telling people they worried too much about other's minor faults (a speck in the eye) but excused their own faults even when these shortcomings were, by comparison to the other person's, like having a log in the eye.[530] (And he said it much better than that.) He accused the religious leaders of *"strain(ing) out a gnat but swallow(ing) a camel."*[531] Even Jesus's enemies regarded him as a gifted teacher.[532] Like most great teachers his style was to press his listeners to think for themselves and at times his followers did not understand his metaphors.[533] About sixty-five parables are ascribed to Jesus.[534] In fact, Matthew, quoting some unknown source, writes that at one point, *"he did not say anything to them without using a parable..."*[535] The Gospel writers remember at least two purposes for his style of parables but these purposes are contradictory depending on the context. *Mark 4:12* reports that Jesus used parables *"in order that the crowd might not understand."* This is part of *Mark's* "messianic secret" [536]approach to Israel's rejection of Jesus. *Matthew 13* is a chapter of parables with this difference: Jesus resorts to parables *because* the crowds have not understood and have rejected him especially in Galilee [537] or at best they waver. *Matthew 13:13* makes this clear: *"Therefore I speak to them in parables; because while seeing they do not see, and while hearing they do not hear, nor do they understand"* In *Matthew 13:36*, Jesus takes his followers into a house to privately explain a parable. [538] Even in the *Book of John* which contains no parables as such, Jesus talks figuratively. In *John 10:1-16*, he identifies himself as *"the good shepherd"* and the *"the door of the sheep"*[539] and in *John 15:1-6* he tells his followers, *"I am the vine, you are the branches. He who abides in me, and I in him, he it is that bears much fruit, for apart from me you can do nothing."*

He urged people to strive for timeless values or, in the language we have in the Sermon on the Mount[540], *"treasure in heaven."* He said memorable things like the last shall be first[541] and he talked of counter-wisdom, a different way of looking at things that was not obvious.[542] He talked about his way as the "narrow" gate or door.[543]

The Gospels record that he performed miracles. The first three Gospels list thirty-two miracles with an emphasis on calming storms, healings and exorcisms. John described seven more [544]and referred to *"many other miraculous signs"* which he implied were literally too numerous to list.[545] One early account has Jesus recognizing after a miracle that power had proceeded out of him.[546]

Were these miracles supernatural interventions? Here is Rodney Stark: "To make miracles plausible, all that is needed is to postulate the existence of a God who created the universe, nothing more. Surely a God who created the natural laws could suspend them at will. Moreover, *unless* physical laws are violated, there is no miracle. So was Lazarus raised from the dead? Perhaps and perhaps not. But if God exists he *could* have been. Was Mary a virgin (when she gave birth to Jesus)? She *could* have been.[547] Did the resurrection occur? It *could* have. Some believe these things happened, some believe they didn't ..." [548]

There is a *New Testament* suggestion that at least some of these miracles were in the eyes of the beholders, subject to individual outlooks. They seemed according to *Mark* to depend on faith. Mark reports that Jesus once went to his home town, taught in the local synagogue, was rejected by the townspeople, then made the statement that has become famous, *"Prophets are not without honor, except in their home town." Mark* then adds that Jesus *"**could** do no deed of power there"* except for some healing and that he was astonished at their unbelief.[549] (Emphasis added).

So, do miracles depend on people having faith? It may depend on which Gospel writer we consult. Writing some ten to fifteen years later, Matthew tells a similar story but with the twist that Jesus apparently *chose* not to do any miracles there because of their unbelief.[550]

One can also see these miracles as the way people explained how they saw Jesus some 40-70 years after his death. How did they see him? In *II Corinthians* 5:19 Paul thought God was in Jesus. *Mark* 1:1-11 and *Matthew* 1:23 make similar points. Luke saw Jesus coming from and returning to God - *Luke* 1:26-35, 24:50-53, and *Acts* 1:1-11. John had Jesus asserting his oneness with God in *John* 1:14, 5:17, 5:20, 10:30 and 17:1ff. In explaining that God was somehow in Jesus, the writers of the *New Testament* turned to the *Old Testament* God who was reported to have worked wonders. They attributed those same types of wonders to Jesus to explain his relationship to God. This is how I view the accounts of the miracles of Jesus.[551]

This point needs emphasis even if it alienates some readers. I view Jesus of Nazareth as the most important human that ever lived whose life points the way to a better life for other humans and who shows symbolically the possibility of a life beyond death. I do not view him as a supernatural miracle worker but can appreciate intellectually why some do. Like Isaac Newton (1643–1727) I believe that Jesus was subordinate to God although like Benjamin Franklin I think there is "no harm" in believing in Jesus as God.[552] I, however, see these reports of miracles as parabolic – the blind see and we gain insight, the paralytic is healed and we too can be given new direction, Jesus returns from the dead and so might we.

There are several reasons for my belief that Jesus was a human: scriptures which show him as subordinate to God, scriptures that show that his sonship to God, special though it was, came sometime after his birth, and scriptures that show him as mortal.

Subordinate to God

Psalm 110:1 was key verse to the early Christians: *"The LORD says to my Lord: 'Sit at My right hand until I make Your enemies a footstool for Your feet.'"*

Here are the ways in which this verse was considered by the writers of the *New Testament*

- *Matthew 22: 41-45 – "Now while the Pharisees were gathered together, Jesus asked them a question: 'What do you think about the Christ, whose son is He?' They *said to Him, 'The son of David.' He *said to them, 'Then how does David in the Spirit call Him "Lord," saying, "THE LORD SAID TO MY LORD, 'SIT AT MY RIGHT HAND, UNTIL I PUT YOUR ENEMIES BENEATH YOUR FEET'"? If David then calls Him "Lord," how is He his son?' No one was able to answer Him a word, nor did anyone dare from that day on to ask Him another question."*
- *Mark 12:35-36 – "And Jesus began to say, as He taught in the temple, 'How is it that the scribes say that the Christ is the son of David? David himself said in the Holy Spirit, "THE LORD SAID TO MY LORD, 'SIT AT MY RIGHT HAND, UNTIL I PUT YOUR ENEMIES BENEATH YOUR FEET.'"'"*
- *Luke 20: 41-43 – "Then He said to them, 'How is it that they say the Christ is David's son? For David himself says in the book of Psalms, "THE LORD SAID TO MY LORD, 'SIT AT MY RIGHT HAND, UNTIL I MAKE YOUR ENEMIES A FOOTSTOOL FOR YOUR FEET.'"'"*
- *Acts 2:34-35 – "For it was not David who ascended into heaven, but he himself says: 'THE LORD SAID TO MY LORD, "SIT AT MY RIGHT HAND. UNTIL I MAKE YOUR ENEMIES A FOOTSTOOL FOR YOUR FEET.'"'"*
- *Romans 8:34 – "Who is the one who condemns? Christ Jesus is He who died, yes, rather who was raised, who is at the right hand of God, who also intercedes for us."*
- *Ephesians 1:19-20 – "These are in accordance with the working of the strength of His might which He brought about in Christ, when He raised Him from the dead and seated Him at His right hand in the heavenly places,…"*
- *Colossians 3:1 – "Therefore if you have been raised up with Christ, keep seeking the things above, where Christ is, seated at the right hand of God."*
- *Hebrews 1:3 – "…When He had made purification of sins, He sat down at the right hand of the Majesty on high,"*

- *Hebrews* 1:13 – *"But to which of the angels has He ever said, 'SIT AT MY RIGHT HAND, UNTIL I MAKE YOUR ENEMIES A FOOTSTOOL FOR YOUR FEET'"*?
- *Hebrews* 8:1 – *"Now the main point in what has been said is this: we have such a high priest, who has taken His seat at the right hand of the throne of the Majesty in the heavens"*
- *Hebrews* 10:11-13 – *"Every priest stands daily ministering and offering time after time the same sacrifices, which can never take away sins; but He, having offered one sacrifice for sins for all time, sat down at the right hand of God, waiting from that time onward 'UNTIL HIS ENEMIES BE MADE A FOOTSTOOL FOR HIS FEET.'"*
- *Hebrews* 12:1-2 – *"...let us run with endurance the race that is set before us, fixing our eyes on Jesus, the author and perfecter of faith, who for the joy set before Him endured the cross, despising the shame, and has sat down at the right hand of the throne of God."*
- *I Peter* 3:22 – *"Corresponding to that, baptism now saves you— not the removal of dirt from the flesh, but an appeal to God for a good conscience—through the resurrection of Jesus Christ, who is at the right hand of God, having gone into heaven..."*

James DG Dunn writes of *I Corinthians* 15:24-28 that: "In effect it is the nearest we have in the *New Testament* to an exposition of the crucial text, *Psalm* 110:1, that so influenced the first Christians." Here is this section of scripture quoted at length:

"... then comes the end, when He hands over the kingdom to the God and Father, when He has abolished all rule and all authority and power. For He must reign until He has put all His enemies under His feet. The last enemy that will be abolished is death. For HE HAS PUT ALL THINGS IN SUBJECTION UNDER HIS FEET. But when He says, 'All things are put in subjection,' it is evident that He is excepted who put all things in subjection to Him. When all things are subjected to Him, then the Son Himself also will be subjected to the One who subjected all things to Him, so that God may be all in all."

To me and to others, the concept of *Psalm* 110 as explained by the earliest Christian writers[553] is strong evidence that God is greater than Christ and that at the end, God will be all in all. Since I am a monotheist, I cannot see Jesus as a lesser God. Hence, I conclude that he was a human.[554]

<u>Jesus' Sonship Came After His Birth</u>

Certain scriptures make it appear as though Jesus became the Son of God some years after his birth. *Romans* 1:3-4 is one example: *"concerning His Son,* *who was born of a descendant of David according to the flesh, who was declared the Son of God with power **by the resurrection from the dead**..." (Emphasis added).* Paul, in fact, may be citing an ancient creed.

Also, some of the speeches in *Acts* apparently allude to early traditions about Jesus that seem to indicate that his sonship to God occurred some period of time after his birth:

- *Acts* 2:36 - Luke has Peter expressing a view that *"God has made him both Lord and Christ."*
- *Acts* 13:32-33 - Luke has Paul linking Jesus's sonship to the resurrection: *"And we preach to you the good news of the promise made to the fathers, that God has fulfilled this promise to our children in that He raised up Jesus, as it is also written in the second Psalm, 'YOU ARE MY SON; TODAY I HAVE BEGOTTEN YOU.'"*

These scriptures are evidence of a tradition older than the Gospels, an adoptionist Christology,[555] which holds that Jesus became God's son at either his baptism or the resurrection. In adoptionist Christianity we are pretty close to recognizing Jesus of Nazareth as a person anointed or set aside at some point in his life rather than God himself.[556]

Jesus's humanity.

There are two categories to consider.

Theological category:

Paul depicts Christ as a type of second Adam. This is summarized in *I Corinthians* 15:45 which reads: *"So also it is written, 'The first MAN, Adam, BECAME A LIVING SOUL.' The last Adam became a life-giving spirit."* It is driven home in two other sections:

- *Romans* 5:12-19. In his passage, Paul writes of sin and grace, Verse 15 is key: *"But the free gift is not like the transgression. For if by the transgression of the one the many died, much more did the grace of God and the gift by the grace of the one Man, Jesus Christ, abound to the many."*
- *I Corinthians* 15:21-22. In this passage, Paul writes of death and resurrection: *"For since by a man came death, by a man also came the resurrection of the dead. For as in Adam all die, so also in Christ all will be made alive."*[557]

<u>Everyday category:</u>

These speeches in *Acts* show Jesus as mortal:

- Peter at Pentecost: *"Men of Israel, listen to these words: Jesus the Nazarene, a man attested to you by God with miracles and wonders and signs which God performed through Him in your midst, just as you yourselves know— this Man, delivered over by the predetermined plan and foreknowledge of God, you nailed to a cross by the hands of godless men and put Him to death." (Acts 2:22-24)*
- Peter near the Temple in Jerusalem: *"The God of Abraham, Isaac and Jacob, the God of our fathers, has glorified His servant Jesus, the one whom you delivered and disowned in the presence of Pilate, when he had decided to release Him." (Acts 3:13)*

Accounts in the Synoptics show his townspeople in Nazareth marveling at how he could suddenly seem so wise. One reads: *"He came to His hometown and began teaching them in their synagogue, so that they were astonished, and said, 'Where did this man get this wisdom and these miraculous powers? Is not this the carpenter's son? Is not His mother called Mary?,...'" (Matthew 13:54-55.* A similar account is in *Mark* 6:2-3 and a more detailed one in *Luke* 4: 14-30) The reaction of his peers in Nazareth is not surprising since scripture records that while growing up in that small town he was *"increasing in wisdom and stature." (Luke 2:52.)* [558]

Finally, in conclusion, I agree with NT Wright who said, "With Jesus, it is easy to be complicated and hard to be simple."[559] I have tried hard to be simple. For me he was a great human, but I respect the view that he was God.

But with all this, Jesus did not succeed in his own time the way Mohammad later did or even in the way that Moses once did. He was crucified.

Then – according to the *New Testament* - came the resurrection.

We will focus on the resurrection and its significance in Chapter 11. Here we note that the Gospels "were written with the conviction that Jesus had risen from the dead, and left behind an empty tomb in Jerusalem to prove it; and that he had appeared in various mysterious ways to some of his followers." [560] In the earliest account in the Gospels, a woman known to history and culture as Mary Magdalene went to the tomb.[561] Mary Magdalene is only mentioned twelve times in the *New Testament* and only once aside from the crucifixion and resurrection[562] but for centuries she has been an object of fascination. Some early churchmen, including Augustine, called Mary Magdalene the

"Apostle to the Apostles. [563] In 591, however, she was identified as a sinner, which led to her reputation as a prostitute by Pope Gregory I.[564] There is a ninth century legend that she was buried in France in Aix-en-Provence. [565] She is considered by the Roman Catholic, Eastern Orthodox, and Anglican churches to be a saint, with a feast day of July 22.[566]

According to *Mark*, Mary Magdalene accompanied by two other women, one of them possibly Jesus's own mother,[567] went to the tomb which was more like a cave where he had been placed. Here is what happened: *"...they saw a young man dressed in a white robe sitting on the right side, and they were alarmed. 'Don't be alarmed,' he said. 'You are looking for Jesus the Nazarene, who was crucified. He has risen! He is not here. See the place where they laid him. But go, tell his disciples and Peter, "He is going ahead of you into Galilee. There you will see him, just as he told you."' Trembling and bewildered, the women went out and fled from the tomb. They said nothing to anyone, because they were afraid."*[568]

The story in *Mark* ends there.[569] Other Gospels and other accounts in the *New Testament* have stories about mistaken identities[570], eating[571], disappearing[572], commissioning[573], confronting "Doubting Thomas[574]," appearances up north in Galilee[575], appearances in Judea[576], appearing over a period of forty days[577], appearing to more than five hundred people at the same time[578], ascending into the sky [579] and more. But in the account of the earliest Gospel no one saw him.[580]

In summary, Jesus was a unique figure who predicted a new societal arrangement based on the Jewish God. He had an empathy with the unfortunate and died disillusioned. His resurrection was understood in different ways by different followers and his followers –all devout Jews – referred to themselves as the Way, united around a belief that Jesus was still alive. That is an important message to us and we will cover that message in Chapter 11.

The designation the Way may indeed hearken back to John the Baptist's mission as recorded in all four Gospels –to prepare the "way" for the Lord.[581] Jesus's own teaching was that he himself was the way - in an answer to Thomas's specific question: *"Lord, we do not know where you are going; how know we the way?"*[582] Several passages in *Acts* referred to the growing movement as the Way.[583] Paul himself used the term (according to Luke).[584] Luke changes the metaphor only slightly when he describes the return of Paul and Barnabas to the Antioch congregation after their first missionary journey noting that they *"related all that God had done with them, and how he had opened a door of faith for the Gentiles."* [585]

We now turn to the Apostle Paul.

CHAPTER 5

Paul

Paul did not write very much about Jesus's earthly life. When he did, he even showed a willingness to change some of Jesus's teachings. His enemies were typically other Christians.

Early Christians may have called themselves the Way but the Way soon included many travelers in different lanes. Indeed, the problem of Christians over the next few centuries was to pick a lane and stop swerving. James the brother of Jesus, who spoke for the Jewish followers of Jesus, presided over a coalition in Jerusalem.[586] There were disputes within that group based first on cultural diversity[587] and within a generation on the Christian mission to non-Jews. Christian groups developed in Antioch, Alexandria, Athens, Rome and other Mediterranean cities and except for Antioch, the *New Testament* tells us very little about what they taught or believed. In Damascus, the figure of Saul emerged and became the Apostle Paul of world history.

Of the *New Testament* figures, Paul is the only one whom we know by his own writing.[588] Jesus himself, John the Baptist, James, Mary Magdalene, the Blessed Virgin Mary, and Peter left no writings. We know that Paul was born in Tarsus, in modern-day Turkey. Paul Johnson estimates that he was born about 9AD making him about 12 years younger than Jesus.[589] Tarsus was a cosmopolitan city. Stabo, an ancient writer, saw it as culturally alongside Athens.[590] At some point in the early part of his life, Paul became very conservative. Much later he wrote to the Galatians about this period that he had been *"advancing in Judaism beyond many of my contemporaries among my countrymen, being more extremely zealous for my ancestral traditions."*[591] To the Philippians he said that he was *"circumcised the eighth day, of the nation of Israel, of the tribe of Benjamin, a Hebrew of Hebrews; as to the Law, a Pharisee; as to zeal, a persecutor of the church; as to the righteousness which is in the Law, found blameless."*[592] To the Corinthians he defended himself against Jewish-Christians by claiming that his roots were as conservative as theirs: *"Are they Hebrews? So am I. Are they Israelites? So am I. Are they descendants of Abraham? So am I."*[593] Paul was energetic, working hard that he *"might save some."*[594] He had a sense of self-importance. He saw himself as superior in such matters as observing the law[595], hard work[596] and even speaking in tongues.[597] One of the most relevant personal stories in Western civilization is that this individual went from a tolerant, worldly culture in Tarsus first to fundamentalist Jewish beliefs then to a different knowledge of Jesus Christ. [598]

Paul, the *"Apostle to the Gentiles"*, set himself apart from Jesus's brother James and his closest follower Peter whom he described as the *"Apostle to the Jews."*[599] He traveled for ten or more years in big cities throughout the Aegean basin spreading a different brand of Christianity than that of the original followers. As he traveled he frequently received messages from groups of Jesus followers that he had helped set up in a previous city. Often the news was not good and he responded in typical Pauline fashion: he wrote letters – some of which survive – to address problems.

From these letters, we can infer an often overlooked reality and it is of large significance for understanding that a diversity of beliefs in the twenty-first century can properly be labeled as "Christian." *Paul had enemies within the Jesus movement.* In Jerusalem alone, the *New Testament* teaches that thousands of followers of Jesus were opposed to Paul.[600] Some of them said his presence was contemptible,[601] some tried to kill him[602] and others took pleasure in his troubles with the authorities.[603] Paul returned full measure. He condemned those who preached "another Jesus" or a "different gospel."[604] He called those who would find the meaning of Jesus closer to Judaism, "dogs."[605] He talked of an opposition that caused his followers to keep on "biting and devouring" each other.[606] He said these types of people "bewitched"[607] his converts and caused them to "(fall) from grace." [608]

He labeled his enemies in Corinth as false apostles[609] and sarcastically as super apostles.[610] His comments were not merely indecorous. His "epistles…suggest doctrinal bitterness and unresolved controversy"[611], and what his language lacked in poetry it certainly made up in vividness. It was not sport, it was spite - at one point the same person who could write the paean to love that we find in *I Corinthians* 13, could lash out at Christians who urged circumcision saying, in effect, that he hoped they would mutilate themselves.[612], [613]Some moderns think that these enemies of Paul were the Jews or others opposed to Christianity. But they were Jewish followers of Jesus. *II Corinthians* 11:26 records Paul saying he was in danger *"from his own people."*

Paul's attacks on other Christians indicate unhealthy amounts of anxiety and self-doubt. At the time of his death he was known for a few letters written to isolated groups, an historical footnote at best, rejected by his fellow Christians.

Certain passages in *Revelation* seemed to be aimed at Paul.[614] Certainly Paul or a close follower is the most likely object of this scorn: *"... I have a few things against you: you have some there who hold the teaching of Balaam, who taught Balak to put a stumbling block before the sons of Israel, so that they might eat food sacrificed to idols..."*[615] Paul, or someone like him, is certainly targeted by such invective as people who *"say they are apostles but are not"* or who *"say they are Jews, but they are not."*[616] Justin Martyr who lived approximately 100-165 and was an early Christian apologist and Catholic saint recognized by Pope Leo XIII (1878-1903) did not quote Paul in any of his existing writings.[617]

Paul died, in all likelihood, a bereft figure and a martyr in 64AD. A reference from *I Clement* [618] that Paul died in Rome of "rivalry and grudge" among Christians suggests that the Christians who wanted to kill him in Jerusalem had counterparts in Rome.[619] The *New Testament Book of II Timothy*, written, as noted earlier, after Paul's death but attributed to him has "Paul" saying, *"As you know, everyone from the province of Asia has deserted me."*[620] Luke got near to the end but did not record Paul's death, possibly out of deference to the Romans.[621]

Scholars have been aware of the cleavage between Paul and other Christians for two hundred years. Johann Salomo Semler (1725-1791) "made a distinction between Petrine, Judaizing parties, in the early church, and Pauline, anti-Judaic (groups) that was to play a great role in later discussions."[622] In our time, NT Wright has said that "...despite those who have tried to keep them apart, very early Christianity should itself properly be seen as a sub-branch of first-century Judaism."[623]

These, then become key questions: in Christianity, what is the role of Paul, his Christian enemies and other competitors and how is it relevant today? We will cover these questions in this chapter and then in Chapter 6-8 look at other types of *New Testament* Christians.

So, at its essentials, what is Pauline doctrine?

Paul established churches in the eastern Mediterranean, usually in urban centers, by convincing people that the Jewish God was the only one to worship, that Jesus was his son, that Jesus had died both for the sins of the world and to ensure that people would also survive death and that Jesus was returning soon to judge the earth. Paul linked Jesus's death and resurrection with an interpretation of the Jewish scriptures.[624]

Paul seems to have been saying that Jesus's death-and-resurrection allowed people to be freed from the burden of their individual shortcomings and mistakes, their sin. I think he taught that these guilty feelings should not burden them and that Christ, still alive, could unite with each individual and allow him or her to live a better life. This life would be characterized by love of other humans. There would be a final reward after death.

Pauline Christians believe in justification by faith. What does this mean? *Romans* the tenth chapter the ninth verse has provided this soothing message for two thousand years –"*... if you confess with your mouth, 'Jesus is Lord,' and believe in your heart that God raised him from the dead, you will be saved.*"[625] Pauline Christians are less concerned with the actual teachings *of* Jesus and more interested in Paul's teachings *about* Jesus. [626] For them, as for Paul, it is a matter of "*first importance*" [627] that Jesus died for them and rose from the dead. They do not care that about all that Paul had to say about Jesus was that he was a Jew[628], that he had brothers[629], that one of his brothers was named James[630], that he ministered among the Jews,[631] that he was betrayed (possibly),[632] that he was crucified[633] and that he had twelve disciples to whom he appeared after his resurrection. [634],[635]

At its worst, justification by faith leads to the behavior that stunned Paul in the Corinthian church. This included at the least greed, idol worship, swindling, drunkenness and incest.[636] At its best, it allows humans to accept their imperfections and, by God's grace, try to do better. Its historical champions are St. Augustine (354 – 430), Martin Luther (1483 – 1546) [637]and recently Billy Graham and the person that Graham called the greatest Christian witness of the twentieth century, Pope John Paul II (1920 – 2005).[638]

Paul's core message - to emphasize - was about Jesus and his "revelation" was that Jesus had been crucified for our sins, risen from the dead, and that by faith in him we could be forgiven of our state of sin and live a good life forever. To put it still another way, he wanted to replace a legal and religious code with the God-given redemptive power of Jesus Christ. He did not expect people to accept that grace and then live immorally and his list of what this included was quite extensive. Even beyond the problems he found at Corinth, he listed: "*sexual immorality, impurity and debauchery; idolatry and witchcraft, hatred, discord, jealousy, fits of rage, selfish ambition, dissensions, factions and envy; drunkenness, orgies, and the like.*"[639]

He understood that people would only come to that belief in Christ instinctively and that to many it would just seem foolish. He wrote to the Corinthians that "*...we preach Christ crucified, to Jews a stumbling block and to Gentiles foolishness, but to those who are the called, both Jews and Greeks, Christ the power of God and the wisdom of God. Because the foolishness of God is wiser than men,*" *and the weakness of God is stronger than men.*"[640] Paul's Christianity was not based in hard, verifiable facts. It was based on his experiences. Paul had heard the good news often, but he was brought to grasp and accept it only by a special vision. That vision was important enough to be told three times by the writer of *Acts*, although with contradictory details.[641] About his core message, he claimed that he *"received it by revelation from Jesus Christ"*[642] and then went out of his way to add that after getting that revelation, he did not consult with anyone.[643] Even years later when he did go to consult with others he said it was a *"in response to a revelation."*[644] He did not regard Jesus from an historical perspective.[645] He talked about visions and going to the *"third Heaven"* and to *"paradise."*[646] He expanded Christianity into Europe based on a "vision."[647] The *Book of Acts* records that Paul saw Jesus while in a trance.[648] He talked about Jesus being "in him."[649] He described *"God's secret wisdom"* as something that *"No eye has seen, no ear has heard, no mind has conceived…"*[650] His institution of the Lord's Supper was what he had *"received from the Lord."*[651] He described the end times in what he said was *"by the word of the Lord."*[652]

At least that is primarily how Paul derived his message and his doctrine. He also apparently applied considerable intellectual effort. In a subsequent chapter we will talk of an important council where Paul's views were tested by the leaders of the Christian movement in Jerusalem. By the time of that council Paul had been a follower of Christ for about seventeen years. All of his surviving letters are in the period after the council and thus, we can conclude that he gave the matter a lot of thought.[653] He also heard the basic message from others and learned from his and their reading of the Jewish scriptures. He wrote to the Corinthians for example about what he had "received" and listed the key points (the ones he called of "first importance.") These key points were *"that Christ died for our sins according to the Scriptures, and that He was buried, and that He was raised on the third day according to the Scriptures, and that He appeared to Cephas, then to the twelve. After that He appeared to more than five hundred brethren at one time, most of whom remain until now, but some have fallen asleep; then He appeared to James, then to all the apostles; and last of all, as to one untimely born, He appeared to me also."*[654]

We can derive at least three insights here:

- Paul's theology may have been a combination of revelation, the teachings of others and study.
- These "others" may have included Jewish-Christians like James and Peter whom Paul eventually challenged.
- Above all, Paul's relationship with Jesus was a very intense experience for him.

Since Paul has had such an outsized impact on Christianity, the actual relationship between him and Jesus should be examined. It is a relationship that can be looked at from several vantage points.

Jesus's and Paul's lives had certain similarities. Both had received some of their training in Jerusalem – Jesus as a twelve year-old[655] and Paul, in his own words before a Jerusalem mob, *"I am a Jew, born in Tarsus of Cilicia, but brought up in this city, educated under Gamaliel, strictly according to the law of our fathers, being zealous for God just as you all are today."*[656] For both, the middle portion of their life is unknown. Both were, at a time of crisis, of some concern to the wife of a Roman official. Jesus: Matthew wrote that while Pilate was *"sitting on the judgment seat, his wife sent him a message, saying, 'Have nothing to do with that righteous Man; for last night I suffered greatly in a dream because of Him.'"*[657] Paul: Luke records that after Paul's trial in Caesarea before King Agrippa, *"...The king stood up and the governor and Bernice, and those who were sitting with them, and when they had gone aside, they began talking to one another, saying, 'This man is not doing anything worthy of death or imprisonment.'"*[658]

The extreme of this point of view is that of Lena Einhorn who makes an argument that Jesus, the radical Egyptian who is mentioned in *Acts* 21:38 and by the Jewish historian Josephus and Paul were in fact the same person. Einhorn notes that like the Egyptian, Jesus had thousands of followers in the wilderness and she reasons from *John* 18:3,12 that up to a thousand Roman troops may have been needed to arrest Jesus. She holds that Jesus's death was too quick as he was strong enough just before the moment of death, to talk and shout. From this she posits that Jesus did not die on the cross. Einhorn notes that according to *John* 19:38-40 Joseph of Arimathea and Nicodemus used 75 pounds of myrrh and aloes. Myrrh and aloe were used for healing and disinfecting wounds in ancient times and aloe was an ancient pain-killer.[659] She notes that after the crucifixion and the subsequent conversion of Paul, *Galatians* 1 and 2 and *Acts* 9 show Paul mostly staying away from Jerusalem for 17 years and the church in Judea and Galilee and Samaria prospering. She claims that Irenaeus, living about 200 AD, seems to have conveyed that Jesus lived long after the crucifixion and that the church father Jerome said that Paul and his parents were born in Galilee.[660] Einhorn's view – while intriguing - represents a radical fringe.[661] I know of no other supporters of it.

More significantly, the *New Testament* teachings by Paul and Jesus had some similarities. Both held that observing legal precepts for societal acclaim or justification from God was harmful. Jesus told a parable called the Laborers in the Vineyard in which all workers including those who were hired late for the job received the same pay and he gave the specific morale of this story as *"So the last shall be first, and the first last."*⁶⁶² In the Sermon on the Mount Jesus taught against ostentatiousness in giving to the needy and in prayer and fasting. He led into this whole topic by this warning: *"Beware of practicing your righteousness before men to be noticed by them; otherwise you have no reward with your Father who is in heaven"* ⁶⁶³ Paul took the idea of the motive of doing good farther claiming *"...no flesh will be justified in His sight; for through the Law comes the knowledge of sin."*⁶⁶⁴ He had, a few years earlier, explained this with more context in the second chapter of *Galatians*, verse 16, writing that *"a man is not justified by the works of the Law but through faith in Christ Jesus, even we have believed in Christ Jesus, so that we may be justified by faith in Christ and not by the works of the Law; since by the works of the Law no flesh will be justified."* There are those who see this – let's call it doing good for goodness's sake and not seeking credit from anyone or even God – as an evolving principle: "No doubt this development had begun to take place long previously, but we do not get such pointed evidence both of the development and its effects as is given in the *New Testament*." ⁶⁶⁵

Another similarity between the teachings of Jesus and Paul is around the idea of ritual. Paul writes to the Romans that *"all food is clean, but it is wrong for a man to eat anything that causes someone else to stumble."*⁶⁶⁶ Jesus is quoted in *Mark* that *"nothing outside a man can make him 'unclean' by going into him."* ⁶⁶⁷ Each looked at substance over form.

There are some clues that Paul was aware of an oral tradition about what Jesus taught. In *I Corinthians* 13 he speculated about faith moving mountains, a possible echo of Jesus's famous comments⁶⁶⁸ on the topic. In his letter to the Thessalonians, Paul talked about the return of the Lord coming at an unexpected time, like a thief in the night;⁶⁶⁹ Jesus told a story with a similar point, closing with the same metaphor, *"But be sure of this, that if the head of the house had known at what hour the thief was coming, he would not have allowed his house to be broken into."*⁶⁷⁰ Also in that letter to the Thessalonians, Paul counseled alertness, saying *"let us not be like others, who are asleep."*⁶⁷¹ This may derive from Jesus's parable about the people who went to sleep and did not have enough oil for their lamps as told in *Matthew* 25.⁶⁷² Paul and Jesus talked about *"old leaven"* – Jesus applying it to Pharisees and Herod Antipater and Paul applying it to backsliding church members.⁶⁷³ Paul wrote to the Corinthians about expelling church members in a way that echoed Jesus's teaching on the subject. ⁶⁷⁴ Paul's teaching in *Romans* contains injunctions such as *"Bless those who persecute you,*[675] *never pay back evil with more evil*[676]*,... never take revenge."*[677] These echo the Sermon on the Mount in which Jesus says, *"I say, love your enemies! Pray for those who persecute you!"*[678] Paul's teaching in *Romans* 13 about government – "If you owe taxes, pay taxes" - calls to mind one of Jesus's most quoted sayings to *"Render to Caesar the things that are Caesar's, and to God the things that are God's."*[679] When Paul told the Galatians that *"The entire law is summed up in a single command: 'Love your neighbor as yourself,'"* [680] it sounds a lot like Jesus's greatest commandment.[681]

These similarities of teaching are not surprising. What *is* surprising is that they are relatively rare. After all, when Paul was writing, the stories of Jesus were fresh and talked-about. Furthermore, there are many areas when Paul seems to take the focus away from Jesus. This – like the reality that Paul had enemies within the Jesus movement - is of large significance for understanding that a diversity of beliefs in the twenty-first century can properly be labeled as "Christian." Aside from the few examples mentioned, Paul does not say much about Jesus's life and teachings on earth.[682]

As noted, the Gospels attest to Jesus's miracles but Paul didn't mention any. Paul never wrote of Jesus's family except for two references to his brother James, one of them negative.[683] He mentioned other brothers of Jesus, though not by name and only once.[684] He only once alluded to the Twelve disciples.[685] He only mentioned Peter three times and one of these is disparaging.[686] He mentioned one of Jesus's key disciples John once. [687]

In his surviving letters Paul missed simple opportunities to link his teaching with Jesus's life and teaching. When he does cite events from Jesus's life, he does so because it stresses to his readers that they should follow what Jesus said or did. Why, then, doesn't he do this more often? He warns his readers about temptation[688] and lets them know that it is common to humanity[689] and a threat to faith[690] but he does not refer to Jesus's temptations. This is all the more significant because the writer of *Hebrews did* cite Jesus's overcoming of temptations as encouragement for believers.[691] When Paul talks about his opponents among non-Christian Jews, why doesn't he speak of Jesus's opposition from the Jewish leaders? In pleading for unity between Gentiles and Jews in *Galatians*, Paul might have mentioned Jesus's story of the Good Samaritan. Also, it has not gone unnoticed, that although he often described Jesus as divine or near divine, he did not cite the virgin birth even once.[692], [693] [694]

So we know Paul knew Peter and that he knew James, Jesus's brother. So, why don't his existing letters talk much of Jesus? Theories include:[695]

- There is the strong assumption that Paul did not know Jesus personally. That may well be the case and would go a long way to explaining why he rarely cited Jesus's teachings. However, it is not certain that he did not know him. They were contemporaries and may have been in Jerusalem at about the same time. Could Paul have known Jesus? To the Corinthians, Paul wrote, *"Therefore from now on we recognize no one according to the flesh; even though we have known Christ according to the flesh, yet now we know Him in this way no longer."*[696] Certainly this admits to a more philosophical or historical interpretation, rather than the simple statement that Paul knew Jesus as he knew James and Peter. But it leaves open other possibilities such as that the two had at least a passing acquaintance.
- In an overlapping reason to the above, possibly Paul didn't know the stories about Jesus. (However, this is doubtful since he had apparently spent two weeks as Peter's house guest a mere six or so years after the crucifixion.[697])
- Possibly he knew the stories about Jesus but had no occasion to write about them. His letters addressed other topics.[698]
- Possibly he knew the stories but saw them as irrelevant. Paul's message was mostly about the death and resurrection of Jesus. All else was off-message. He told the Corinthians that he determined to know nothing except *"Christ crucified."* [699]

Only on the rarest occasions did he cite directly any of Jesus's teachings. Paul records his words at the Last Supper[700] and possibly two other sayings – that Christians should pay their preachers[701] and that they should not get divorced. [702] In these two topics, Paul felt free to change Jesus's teachings.

<u>Paying Preachers:</u> An analysis of the ninth chapter of *I Corinthians* suggests that Paul changed the commandment of Jesus to pay preachers into a right which could be claimed or turned down: although he alludes to Jesus in verse 14 as commanding that those who preach the gospel should receive their living from the gospel he asserts in a question in verse 6 that *"... is it only I and Barnabas who must work for a living?"* It is hard to reconcile that sort of tampering with Christ's words with inerrancy but it does underscore Paul's independence of thought.[703]

<u>Divorce:</u> Paul's independence of thought is more obvious on the topic of divorce. Jesus prohibited men from leaving their wives[704]; Paul prohibited

husbands *and* wives from dissolving marriage[705], which he says is *"from the Lord"* and is a reasonable enough expansion of Jesus's core teaching.[706] However, he also appears to have softened Jesus's anti-divorce position. In *Mark* 10:2-12, *Matthew* 5:31-32, *Matthew* 19:3-12, and *Luke* 16:18 Jesus's teachings on divorce are stricter than those of Moses. This goes against Jesus's typical trend – for example on the keeping of the Sabbath[707] or other rituals. Paul, however, adds an exception that although Christians should stay married to an unbelieving spouse who consents to live with them that, if the unbelieving spouse leaves, the believer is *"not under bondage."* He is bold enough to preface this exception with this amazing statement: *"To the rest I say this (**I, not the Lord**)."*[708](Emphasis added). This is an important concept far beyond the issues of marriage and divorce: Paul is willing to explicitly modify one of Jesus's teachings.[709],[710]

A final example jumps out. One of Jesus's most famous, controversial and difficult- to-follow teachings is to love one's enemies. Paul agreed but the reason that Jesus gave for doing this was far more aesthetic than Paul's reason. Jesus taught in the Sermon on the Mount: *"love your enemies! Pray for those who persecute you! In that way, you will be acting as true children of your Father in heaven."*[711] Paul changed the reason, teaching the Romans: *"if your enemy is hungry, feed him; if he is thirsty, give him something to drink; for by so doing you will heap burning coals on his head."*[712] The pairing of these two teachings in Holy Scripture recognizes the complexity of human motives and shows Paul's originality.[713]

In conclusion, in key areas Paul changes what Jesus said. This is a significant sign that Pauline Christianity is a variety of the religion of Jesus. Although Paul may not have taken an *a la carte* approach to Jesus's teaching, his originality was breathtaking. He tampered with Jesus's teachings and ignored much of it. He set his visions up against the experience of Jesus's closest followers and possibly Jesus's mother whom he never even mentions although she was part of the Jesus movement in Jerusalem.[714] It may be discouraging to some to see this division among the early followers of Jesus. Another way to look at it is that from the earliest beginning, Christianity showed a diverse face.

But this diversity did not come easily. It required an historical process. After Paul's probable execution, "(m)ost of the churches he had established in the Near East reverted to the ideas of his Jewish-Christian opponents. By the time of his death, his fame was at a very low ebb."[715] His invective against fellow Christians had been futile. After a possible defeat at Antioch and the rude reception in Jerusalem, Paul had an undistinguished record. After his death at least two of the churches with which he had been associated showed that they had deep-rooted problems. Ephesus had "left (its) first love" and needed to "repent" according to *Revelation* 2:4-5. Laodicea as noted earlier had become lukewarm according to *Revelation* 3:16. To a fair-minded contemporary, Paul's motives would have justified both praise and criticism but in the end he was probably seen as inconsequential, flotsam in the Jesus movement of his time. But as Walter Laqueur has observed, "History does not consist of races in which only the winners qualify for the next round, as in the Olympic Games."[716] Paul, as we will see in Chapter 10, resurfaced within a generation. His innovative approach to the life and message of Jesus Christ and the ferment he caused with the original followers of Jesus produced Christianity as history came to regard it.

CHAPTER 6

The Other Christians of the
New Testament: Part 1

*From the New Testament and from reasonable inferences, we can now conclude that
there were people of the New Testament era who considered themselves followers of
Jesus Christ but who did not agree with Paul. Some of these disagreements were
major and some were minor. The most important group was the Jewish-Christians
and they were led for at least three generations by members of Jesus Christ's family.*

The Jewish-Christians were led by the Pillars: Peter, Jesus's brother James[717]
and John, so named by Paul.[718]

Paul visited the Pillars at least twice. [719] Their role in the *New Testament* is
somewhat ambiguous, particularly in the case of Peter. Mark includes the
famous story of Jesus calming the waters, a story that has been rendered in
art and legend for centuries. He reports that the disciples were in a boat, in a
storm that was reaching crisis levels and saw Jesus walking toward them on
the water. Mark reports that they were terrified but that Jesus got into the boat
and made the storm cease. Mark concludes with the note that the disciples
lacked understanding and their hearts were hardened. We now understand
that Matthew wrote some ten to fifteen years later and that he probably had
Mark's account before him. Matthew redacts the story. Matthew reports the
storm, the terror, and the calming of the water but he changes the ending.
He has Peter temporarily trusting Jesus to the point of walking on the water
and writes that the disciples worshipped Jesus saying that he was the Son of
God.[720] Mark, then, initially sees them as a clueless group. Matthew later gives
them more credit, as befitting future Pillars.

The Pillars saw value in Jerusalem and the keeping of Jewish purity codes.
Although they revered Jesus Christ, they were concerned with the types of
innovation led by Paul. They saw themselves as keepers of a strict doctrine
while others backslid. They, especially James, may have made some connection
between the kingdom of God and the Temple-based kingdom in Jerusalem.
That position persisted into the very end of Jesus's life on earth as we read

that at his ascension [721] the disciples asked him *"Lord, is this the time when you will restore the kingdom to Israel?"*[722] In short, their role is unclear but their position was supported by Matthew who took opportunities to promote Peter. [723] One of the underreported facts of the early church is this: *The early Jewish-Christians were heavily influenced by members of Jesus's family and in the case of James were actually led by Jesus's brother.* The Pillars and the family overlapped. They represent a variant of Christianity that has *New Testament* support. So let's look at what the *Bible* and history have to say about Jesus Christ's parents, brothers, sisters and extended family.

There is little mention in scripture of Joseph the father of Jesus (*"as was thought"*[724]) although *Matthew* mentions that he was a "righteous man."[725] In the *New Testament*, outside of the birth narratives in *Matthew* and *Luke*, Jesus is linked with his mother and brothers.[726] The silence in the *New Testament* about Joseph suggests the possibility that he died relatively early and Jesus took on the responsibility of raising younger siblings until he was about 30. More important, the *New Testament* (again outside of the birth narratives) makes little mention of Mary the mother of Jesus and Paul ignores her.

That's pretty significant: Paul ignored the person who became the second most referred to and revered figure in Christian history, regarded by at least one church council as the "Mother of God."[727] What do we know about her? Tradition holds that Mary lived out her life in Ephesus. Ephesus was an ancient city, even in Jesus's time. It was a Roman provincial capital with a stadium that held twenty-five to thirty thousand spectators. At the end of their lives, the Roman general Mark Antony (83BC – 30BC) and his Egyptian lover Cleopatra (69BC-30BC) lived there together.[728] According to the *Book of Acts*, Jews, including some who were followers of John the Baptist, lived the area.[729] It is located in modern Turkey and it is desolate today.[730] It was one of the seven churches of Asia[731], addressed in the *Book of Revelation*.[732] The *Gospel of John* might have been written there[733] and according to the *New Testament*, *I Corinthians* was written there.[734] *Acts* chapter 19 recounts Paul's stay in Ephesus as characterized by miracles, demonstrations of the Holy Spirit's power over other spirits and voluntary book burnings by "sorcerers" who had become convinced of Paul's message. The value of these books was estimated at fifty thousand drachmas.[735] (Recall: according to *Matthew* 17:27, two drachmas was enough to pay the annual Temple Tax for an individual.) Ultimately however, vested commercial interests harassed Paul in the name of the "Temple of Artemis." These interests incited a mob to chant *"Great is Artemis of the Ephesians!"* [736]In *I Corinthians* 15:32, Paul implies that he fought "wild beasts" in

Ephesus.[737] Paul stayed there two-to-three years according to *Acts* 19:8, 10 and 20:31. While living in Ephesus, he also may have written *Galatians* and *II Corinthians*.[738] In what scholars call a pastoral letter[739], Timothy is imagined as left by Paul in charge of Ephesus.[740]

So Ephesus plays large in Paul's life and also possibly in Mary's.[741]

Did Paul, while residing in Ephesus, ever meet Mary, the mother of Jesus? What would they have discussed? What was Mary's point of view? We don't know because Paul and the early church wrote her out of the narrative. But we do know that in history she made a remarkable comeback which we will discuss in Chapter 8.[742]

Joseph is revered in history, although not nearly as much as Mary. He was declared the "protector of the Universal church" in 1870 by Pius IX and he is the patron saint of Belgium. His feast days are March 19 and May 1. He is also the patron saint of Canada, carpenters, the church, the dying, fathers, Korea, Peru, social justice, and working men.[743] The Catholic Church designated May 1 as St Joseph the Worker Day in part to provide a non-Marxist alternative for labor activism.[744]

Matthew 13:55-6 and *Mark* 6:3 mention that Jesus had sisters although none are named. We know that at one time his sisters may have joined other family members in looking for him. (*Mark* 3:32 states that his mother and brothers – and some manuscripts add, sisters [745]– came to find him.) One of these sisters may have been named Salome but very little, if anything, is known about her. Here is speculation. *Mark* 15:40 reads that near the cross was *"Mary the mother of James the younger and of Joses, and Salome."* Various commentators – Rodney Stark and James Tabor, for example - think that this Mary was Mary the mother of Jesus. If so, Jesus had a sister or half-sister named Salome.[746] Since Jesus's sisters were remembered in Christian tradition but not in the Gospels they must not have been as prominent as his female disciples – Mary Magdalene, Mary and Martha, - who were mentioned.[747] (Incidentally, Paul also had at least one sister according to *Acts* 23:16. That sister is unnamed but her son, also unnamed, tipped off Paul to an ambush and thereby probably saved his life.)

Matthew 13:55-6 and *Mark* 6:3 also indicate that Jesus had four brothers - James, Joses, Judas and Simon. Jesus's brothers may have traveled with him because according to Paul in *I Corinthians* 9:5 at least two of them were on the mission field with their wives. It is safe to assume they were Paul's competitors because he never mentions them directly in his lists of supporters and because of his theological difficulties with the oldest one, James, revealed as we shall see in Paul's letter to the Galatians.

Jesus's extended family may also have been involved in his ministry and in the early Jesus movement after his death. Here is the logic. Hegesippus was an early Christian writer living in the 110-180 time period. None of his writing survives, except as quoted in other writings. Hegesippus wrote that Jesus's father Joseph had a brother named Clopas.[748] The name is extremely rare, only two other certain occurrences of it are known.[749] One of these is in *John 19:25*: *"Standing near the cross were Jesus's mother, and his mother's sister, Mary (the wife of Clopas), and Mary Magdalene."* We can therefore be somewhat sure that the man to whom this verse of the Fourth Gospel refers is the same Clopas, Joseph's brother.[750] Clopas also may have been nearby because Luke names a "Cleopas" as one of the two disciples in his account of the Road to Emmaus.[751] The close spellings and these other circumstances force a question: Could the two disciples on the Road to Emmaus have been a family team - Uncle Clopas and Aunt Mary?[752]

The writer of the letter of *Jude* identifies himself as *"Jude...a brother of James."*[753] Jude is listed in *Mark* 6:3 and *Matthew* 13: 55-57 as a brother of Jesus. He may be the Jude mentioned by Luke twice in the lists of the twelve apostles (*Luke* 6:16 and *Acts* 1:13)[754] but that is far from certain.[755] It may be that he was the son or the brother of James which could make him the brother or the nephew of Jesus. Details aside, all one can be sure of is that tradition holds that Jude was part of Jesus's family and some evidence in scripture supports this notion. The *Book of Jude* was probably written at the end of the first century.[756] Even if Jude is a pseudonym it would have only made sense if at that late date there was respect for Jesus's family.

James and Jude as well as other family members are attested to in history. Eusebius quoted Hegesippus that James was the "brother of the Lord" and Clement of Alexandria (abt.150 - 215) that, "Peter, James and John, after the Ascension of the Savior did not claim pre-eminence...but chose James the Righteous as Bishop of Jerusalem." Eusebius also reported that the grandsons of Jude "who was said to be Jesus's brother humanly speaking" were hauled before Roman authorities who let them go when they asserted that the kingdom promised by Christianity was not of the world.[757] Eusebius further wrote that the first fifteen Bishops of Jerusalem were "of the circumcision" [758] and it has been suggested by Richard Bauckham that these were not fifteen successive Bishops but a mixture of bishops and elders serving roughly simultaneously, with a strong influence from Jesus's family. In Bauckham's take on Eusebius, James the brother of Jesus was the first Bishop. Jesus's cousin Simon, the son of Clopas was the second bishop. The grandsons of Jude, Zoker and James, served together along with elders. Bauckham rightly notes that elders were part of the Jerusalem scene in the *Book of Acts* - as early as *Acts* 11:30 and *Acts* 15.[759] The pre-Paul Jesus movement was probably the business of an entire family that may have extended across three generations.[760],[761]

How is it that Jesus's family and the Jewish-Christians they led were lost to history? Here are some possible reasons: the influence of Paul lowered their profile and the doctrine of Mary's perpetual virginity marginalized all the siblings to cousins and eventually oblivion.

I am no expert on the development of the Roman Catholic point of view on this matter but the view that Mary had other children was condemned by the Church at least as long ago as the fourth century.[762] There are three schools of thought about Jesus's familial relationship to James, Joses, Judas and Simon. The traditional Catholic view is that they were cousins. Another view is that they were children of Joseph by a previous marriage. (Although if they were children of Joseph from a previous marriage it would seem that they were unrelated to Jesus due to the doctrine of the Virgin Birth.) Another is that they were children of Joseph and Mary. In any event, it seems clear that they were raised in the same household as Jesus and as adults were part of his movement:

- *Matthew* 12: 46-47 – *"As Jesus was speaking to the crowd, his mother and brothers stood outside, asking to speak to him. Someone told Jesus, 'Your mother and your brothers are outside, and they want to speak to you.'"*
- *Matthew* 13:55 - *"He's just the carpenter's son, and we know Mary, his mother, and his brothers..."*
- *Luke* 8: 19-2 - *"Someone told Jesus, 'Your mother and your brothers are outside, and they want to see you.'"*
- *John* 2:12 - *"After the wedding [at Cana] he went to Capernaum for a few days with his mother, his brothers, and his disciples."*
- *Acts* 1:14 - *"They all met together and were constantly united in prayer, along with Mary the mother of Jesus, several other women, and the brothers of Jesus."*

For whatever reasons, the *New Testament* has little to say about them, including Mary and James.[763] One way that Mary herself was marginalized was perverse: there is a proliferation of Marys in the *New Testament* and it has become difficult to keep them straight.[764] That James was pushed to the side becomes obvious in that even though Paul asserted that Jesus had appeared to James after the Resurrection[765], there is no such cite in any of the four Gospels.

It is not only Mary and the rest of Jesus's extended family that end up on the cutting room floor. The Twelve for the most part disappear from Acts[766] and the loyal retainer Peter is also marginalized.

Peter is still a key figure in the early part of the *Book of Acts*. But then he dwindles. Following an escape from prison Peter went to a safe house and asked the people there to pass the word to James that he was out of prison. Then, he *"went to another place."*[767] After that, except for a supporting role to James at the Council of Jerusalem in *Acts* 15, a negative role to Paul at Antioch in *Galatians* 2, and some apparent influence in Corinth[768], Peter, who up to then had been mentioned over 150 times in the *New Testament*, disappeared.[769] Peter had early-on correctly identified Jesus's role and consequently received the *"keys of the kingdom of heaven."*[770] He had walked on water. He had cut off an assailant's ear prompting Jesus's famous quote, *"Put your sword back into its place; for all those who take up the sword shall perish by the sword. Or do you think that I cannot appeal to My Father, and He will at once put at My disposal more than twelve legions of angels?"*[771] He received possibly the first appearance from the risen Christ.[772] He had been given a direct order from Jesus to *"Tend My sheep."*[773]

He kept the early followers of Jesus from drifting away before more forceful leaders like James the brother of Jesus and Paul arrived, and for that reason alone he is one of the most important people in history. He preached the sermon at the first Pentecost, which resulted in speaking in tongues and three thousand conversions.[774]

Peter also helped symbolize the breakout to the Gentiles. This story is told in great detail and it is important to see that it had a prequel.

First he slipped out of strict orthodoxy by visiting the Samaritans in *Acts* 8. Traditionally, the Samaritans accepted Jewish Law but not the Temple. Their heterodoxy is enshrined for all time in the story of the Good Samaritan. Peter's colleague Philip had been to Samaria first. Then Peter and John arrived to check out the situation. The Samaritan Christians received the Holy Spirit and Peter and John returned to Jerusalem by way of Samaritan villages where they preached.[775] The story of the Gentiles is picked up in *Acts* 10 by a focus on Cornelius, a Roman soldier. Nearly two chapters detail the type of person Cornelius was, the miraculous message to Peter, Peter's reaction, his trip to Cornelius's home with some other Christians, the conversion, and the reaction of the Jewish-Christians upon hearing the news.[776]

But then after all this, Peter simply goes to another place and basically vanishes from the *New Testament*. The hand-off is to James who did none of those things and even opposed Jesus before the resurrection (according to *John* 7:5) and, to a far greater extent, Paul. History has winners and also-rans and it also has comeback stories. As we will see in Chapter 8, history promoted Peter to iconic status and the Catholic Church recognizes Peter as the first Pope (albeit a non-celibate one[777]).

The Catholic Church claims many of these Pillars and family members as saints. Protestants like me have found this irrelevant. Perhaps we should take another look. We can respect at least a core reality represented by these lives and legends. That is that they are standing examples to the diversity of Christianity at its point of origin. If these people were important in that early era, their views loom large as we understand the multi-sidedness of Christianity. What were those beliefs? There are some answers in passages of the *New Testament* and other ancient literature. In some instances the passages we will look at are straightforward and in other instances they are esoteric but this part should not be lost: some of their beliefs have a modern tone to them.

Whoever wrote the *Epistle of James* found near the end of the *New Testament* represented the family of Jesus. This writer spoke less of grace and forgiveness and more of good works, less of beliefs and more of ethics and actions.[778] A verse in *James* summarizing an entire argument holds that "*just as the body without the spirit is dead, so also faith without works is dead.*"[779] Jesus Christ is mentioned sparingly in *James*: once in the introduction, [780] and once as an exhortation to treat people fairly.[781] His atoning-for-sins death, his resurrection and the miracles are not mentioned. There are, however, parallels to Jesus's *teachings* in such matters as the swearing of oaths,[782] the concept that loving one's neighbor fulfills the law,[783] that the rich should fear judgment,[784] and the idea of the rich fool. [785]

James stresses a very day-to-day definition of religion – caring for the needy and keeping "pure." It teaches that self-deception ruins religion. "*If anyone thinks himself to be religious, and yet does not bridle his tongue but deceives his own heart, this man's religion is worthless.*"[786] Since *James* refers to the readers's meeting place as a synagogue, [787] there is strong reason to assume that he is addressing Jewish-Christians in this letter. Additionally, *James's* examples of good behavior come from the *Old Testament*: Abraham,[788] Rahab,[789] Job [790] and Elijah.[791]

Even the style of *James* evokes an important piece of Jewish literature. With its sayings pertaining to good works, *James* has been called the "the *Proverbs* of the *New Testament*."[792] That approach of wisdom sayings can be found in another "document" embedded in the *New Testament* to be discussed below.

This Jewish orientation of this epistle is not surprising. The Jewish-Christians were wedded to the Temple. John the Baptist's father was a priest there.[793] The aged Simeon and Anna greeted the baby Jesus there.[794] Peter and John performed at least one miracle in Temple precincts [795] and also preached there.[796] Paul went to the Temple in his last visit to Jerusalem at James's urging.[797] The Jewish-Christians would acknowledge that Jesus once called the Temple a "den of robbers" and famously cleansed it[798] but would probably liken that to a modern American saying that he/she respected the office of the presidency but disdained the incumbent.[799] The Jewish-Christians would claim that Jesus directed his mission toward Jews.[800] As noted, he once called Gentiles "dogs."[801] He frequently condemned Samaritans[802]and the Samaritans in turn often asked him to leave their territories.[803] James's role in Christianity will be discussed further in Chapter 7.

The Jewish-Christians of the *New Testament* did not have a Eucharist. They saw themselves as another Jewish group attending the Temple[804] and with their own synagogues.[805] (In that era there were specialized synagogues.[806]) They were seen by the authorities as a *"sect of the Nazarenes"*[807] which may be a working description of Christianity as a messianic sect within first century Judaism.[808] They also apparently had their unique religious calendar, different from what Paul emphasized, prompting him to assail some of his own converts that the Jewish-Christians had compromised them with the complaint, *"how can you turn back again to the weak and worthless elementary principles of the world, whose slaves you want to be once more? You observe days and months and seasons and years!*[809] Guidance in the *Book of Colossians* may also be directed toward shunning an alternate religious calendar: *"...don't let anyone condemn you for what you eat or drink, or for not celebrating certain holy days or new moon ceremonies or Sabbaths."* [810]

One can easily guess at the Pillars's view toward Paul. They would complain that he made little or no mention of Jesus's teachings, that he disparaged Jewish Law and that he elevated faith over good conduct. They would probably note that they knew Jesus personally and Paul did not. They would remember that Peter and James protected Paul when he first went to Jerusalem as a new follower of Jesus and, doubtless, instructed him about Jesus.[811] Most crucially, though, they would see that they represented and were part of Jesus's family and that Paul was a late-comer and a corrupter of the message of Jesus.

The Jewish-Christians would be astonished and dismayed at the success of Pauline Christianity. They saw him as an upstart, an arriviste. In their time they saw Paul as someone who made headlines but not history. The hard-liners among them held that Gentile Christians had to be circumscribed and hold to the Law of Moses.[812]

There is a possible off-shoot of the Jewish-Christians which is found in the pages of the *New Testament*. We can attempt to identify it by making inferences from the Apostle Paul's criticisms and by consideration of certain passages in *Acts*. I speak of the "super apostles" noted earlier. In this I draw on the work of Dieter Georgi.[813]

Paul criticized the super apostles in *II Corinthians*. He referred to his opponents in that sarcastic manner because they saw themselves - in Paul's view inappropriately - quite positively. But this was also recognition that the Corinthian people had given them great prestige. Paul wrote twice - and it sounds defensive, especially in repetition - that he was just as prestigious:

- *II Corinthians* 11:5: *"For I consider myself not in the least inferior to the most eminent apostles."*
- *I Corinthians* 12:11: *"...for in no respect was I inferior to the most eminent apostles,..."*

Who were the super apostles? We know that they were Jewish-Christians from chapter 11 verses 22 and 23 of *II Corinthians*. Paul wrote these well-known lines: *"Are they Hebrews? So am I. Are they Israelites? So am I. Are they descendants of Abraham? So am I. Are they servants of Christ?—I speak as if insane—I more so ..."*

As Jewish-Christian missionaries they were on ground that had been ploughed in the previous centuries by Jewish missionaries who had contributed to a significant growth in Judaism. Josephus noted that the Jews in Antioch "were constantly attracting to their religious ceremonies multitudes of Greeks and these they had in some measure incorporated with themselves into their community." Often the missionaries were wandering magicians or "spirit filled." There was a *New Testament* tradition of Jewish wonder-working missionaries:

- *Acts* 6:8-10- Stephen the Martyr. Verse 8 reports that *"Stephen, full of grace and power, was performing great wonders and signs among the people."*
- *Acts* 8:9-13 - Simon the magician of Samaria with Philip the deacon. Verse 11 reports that people were *"were giving (Simon) attention because he had for a long time astonished them with his magic arts."*
- *Acts* 13:6-12 - Bar-Jesus or Elymas of Paphos with Paul. Verse 6 reports that this person was *"a magician."*

- *Acts* 14:8-18 Paul and Barnabas were seen as gods. Verse 11 reports that the people said of them that "*The gods have become like men and have come down to us.*"
- *Acts* 19:11-20 - Some Jews were traveling around casting out evil spirits in the name of Jesus including the seven sons of a Jewish High Priest named Sceva near Ephesus. Verse 13 reports that they were "*Jewish exorcists.*"

Let's look further at the four designations of *II Corinthians* 11:

- "Hebrews." To quote Georgi: "When adversaries of Paul praised themselves before their audiences as 'Hebrews,' they could count on attention, they could build on their listeners's expectation of something special which was grounded in their Hebrew origin, in Hebrew history and culture." Paul's opponents were probably using a technique that the non-Christian Jewish missionaries before them had used.
- "Israelites." This referred primarily to the past as the foundation for the religious strength of the Jews. To quote Georgi: "The special characteristics of that which was Israelite pointed beyond the limits of the people, according to Hellenistic – Jewish understanding." This is similar to the third designation, "descendants of Abraham."
- "Descendants of Abraham." Abraham was an exalted figure in the ancient/pagan world. He was seen as the first colonizer and the real starter of civilization. There was a tradition based on *Genesis* 14:15 and 25:2 that he had been king of Damascus. Josephus wrote of Abraham that "He was a man of ready intelligence on all matters, persuasive with his hearers." *Genesis* 12:10 records that Abraham went to Egypt to escape a famine. Josephus said he went to Egypt to compete with the religious leaders there.
- "Servants of Christ." To quote Georgi: "One may conclude that, like Paul and other early Christian proclaimers, the opponents of Paul thought of themselves as envoys of Christ, as Christ's personal representatives. Accordingly, the adversaries of Paul functioned principally as Jesus-missionaries. They apparently differed from Paul in demonstratively emphasizing the importance of their role, or - to use the words of Paul (*II Corinthians* 11:16-23) - they boasted and bragged about it." Verse 18 reports of the super apostles: "*Since many boast according to the flesh, I will boast also.*" The super apostles, then, were popular and making inroads in Corinth and they were a threat to Paul. James Tabor holds that they were not only Jewish-Christian missionaries, but that they were actually the Jerusalem apostles.[814]

Peter was the man in the middle. His sermon in *Acts* 2 provides a helpful perspective on the early beliefs of the Jewish-Christians. He regarded Jesus as a prophet in the long line of Jewish heroes and he advised his listeners to *"Repent and be baptized."*[815] Much more than a Pauline message, that was Jewish renewal, from the program of the *New Testament* figure, John the Baptist. This "Baptism of John," it seemed, was sufficiently important to the life of the earliest of Jesus's followers that it remained in the *New Testament* and in history for centuries.

What do we know about John the Baptist and the "Baptism of John?" First, we know that Jesus himself alluded to it to keep his interrogators off-balance. According to the Synoptics, when he was asked a hostile question about the source of his authority he offered to answer if the "chief priests" and others would answer a question for him on whether the Baptism of John came from Heaven, or was of human origin. The Synoptic accounts all agree that the chief priests felt trapped - they could not answer that it was from God and if they said it was of human origin, they feared the reaction of the people.[816]

The "Baptism of John" was a piece of Jewish-Christianity and the *New Testament* has more to say about it. In an effort to better understand the core beliefs of these Jewish-Christians we turn to the Baptism of John in the next section.

Apollos and John the Baptist

A shadowy figure known as Apollos appears in the *Books of Acts, I Corinthians* and *Titus.* Apollos was an Egyptian Jew from Alexandria.

Alexandria was the Hellenic, Roman and Christian capital of Egypt. It ranked second to Rome in wealth and second to Athens in literature and science. It had a diverse population and Alexander the Great who founded the city in 332 BC welcomed Jews.[817] Alexandria was the "cultural successor to war-devastated Athens." By the third century BC it became the City of the Mind. It had the largest Jewish community in the ancient world. Also in the third century BC, a group of Jewish scholars translated the Hebrew scriptures into Greek, the *Septuagint*, which, somewhat expanded and revised, came to be called the *Old Testament*. The *Septuagint* became popular in the Greek-speaking world with Jews but also among Gentiles who were looking for a monotheistic religion. These for the most part did not convert to Judaism but became known as "God-fearers."[818] They were many of the first Gentile Christian converts to Christianity. Alexandria was the city of Ptolemy (death - 283BC), Cleopatra (death - 30BC), Euclid (death - early third century BC), Philo (death - 45AD), Clement (death - 215AD), Origen (death - 254AD), Arius (death - 336 AD), Athanasius (death - 373AD).[819] Alexandria is mentioned in the *New Testament* several times. Some of the opponents of Stephen were Alexandrians (*Acts* 6:9), Apollos was an Alexandrian (*Acts* 18:24), a ship that Paul while in custody took toward Rome was an Alexandrian vessel and a replacement ship was also Alexandrian (*Acts* 28:11).[820] In *New Testament* times, Alexandria was one of the most cultured cities in the Roman Empire but also one of the most volatile due to clashes between Jews and Gentiles.[821]

Church historian Eusebius wrote that Mark brought Christianity to Alexandria and the bishopric of Alexandria traces to this day to Mark.[822] We know very little from the *New Testament* about Alexandrian Christianity[823] but Apollos is its representative.

Apollos was learned and knew the scriptures. He spoke passionately and taught accurately. He was excellent in public debate. He preached about Jesus but was said to only have partial knowledge.[824] He encouraged a splinter group in Corinth[825] and may have had a different slant on things than Paul. Not only the faction in Corinth, but also at least one in Ephesus[826] may have been more in Apollos's camp than Paul's but Paul saw himself and the Egyptian on the same team.[827] In the account in *Acts* we learn that Apollos was initially "only" acquainted with the "Baptism of John." A little later, Paul discovers the same teaching – "John's baptism" - in Ephesus.[828]

Was Paul jealous of Apollos? He may have been. He wrote the Corinthians *"When I came to you, brothers, I did not come with eloquence or superior wisdom …"*[829] This may be an oblique criticism of Apollos with Paul showing (false?) modesty about his own verbal gifts in comparison to Apollos. This is substrata within the *New Testament*, out of sync with the overall Pauline message, and for that reason very probably authentic. The authors and compilers of the *New Testament* whose overall motive was to magnify Paul's message would not have had any reason other than accuracy [830] to add these accounts about Apollos and the "Baptism of John" because they are inconsistent with that message.[831] They show that Apollos, whoever he was, was not simply a downloader of the Pauline message. It appears, rather, that Apollos preached a version of Christianity more consistent with the ministry of John the Baptist than the message of Paul. It is hard to sort out the factions but Apollos appears to have been from the Jewish-Christian cohort.[832]

John the Baptist is mentioned dozens of times in all four Gospels and in *Acts*. We hear that he was Jesus's relative and whether or not this is literally true, it is further evidence that Jesus's work started as a family operation.[833] At the least, like Jude's claim to be James's brother, it shows respect for the tradition of the family. However, within the *New Testament* there is a constant downplay of him. In approximate order of appearance:

- *Mark* 1:7 - John baptized Jesus.
- *Matthew* 3:13 - John tried to stop Jesus from being baptized by him.
- *Luke* 3:19-21 – There is an implication that Jesus was baptized after John's incarceration.
- *Matthew* 11:2-3 and *Luke* 7:18-19 - From prison, he communicated with Jesus through intermediaries asking a very basic question – *"Are you the Messiah we've been expecting, or should we keep looking for someone else?"* - which seems to contradict earlier claims that he recognized Jesus even before birth (*Luke* 1:76). To say the least, this sows doubt about whether John the Baptist truly recognized the validity of Jesus's program, much like Paul's work throws doubt on Peter and James.
- *Acts* 13:25 – Paul preached to Jews in the Diaspora[834] that John the Baptist said of Jesus, *"I am not worthy to untie the thong of the sandals on his feet."*[835]
- It is clear in both *John* and *Acts* that Jesus's baptism which is "of the spirit" is better than John's water baptism.[836]
- *John* 1:29 and 3:30 - No mention of baptizing.

As noted, the *Gospel of John* may well have been written in a stronghold of those who favored John the Baptist, Ephesus. Yet, it seems particularly concerned with relegating John the Baptist to his place as a forerunner of Jesus. Note:

- *John* 1:6ff; 20ff: *"God sent a man, John the Baptist, to tell about the light so that everyone might believe because of his testimony"* and *"He (John the Baptist) came right out and said, 'I am not the Messiah.'"*
- *John* 1:29 – *"The next day John saw Jesus coming toward him and said, 'Look! The Lamb of God who takes away the sin of the world!'"*
- *John* 3:28-30 – *"You yourselves know how plainly I told you, 'I am not the Messiah. I am only here to prepare the way for him.' He who has the bride is the bridegroom; but the friend of the bridegroom, who stands and hears him, rejoices greatly because of the bridegroom's voice. So this joy of mine has been made full. He must increase, but I must decrease."*[837],[838]

91

However, the Gospels and the *Book of Acts* also show that:

- In some sense, the Twelve recognized that the Baptism of John was the beginning of their movement. When it came time to replace Judas, one qualification for candidates was that the individual needed to have been with them since the time of the Baptism of John.[839]
- John the Baptist's appeal was populist[840] and he had a following that contrasted with that of Jesus. *Mark* records that *"now John's disciples and the Pharisees were fasting. Some people came and asked Jesus, 'How is it that John's disciples and the disciples of the Pharisees are fasting, but yours are not?'"*[841]
- There were people who thought John the Baptist had returned from the dead.[842]

Thus, John the Baptist may have been a very important personage. As noted earlier, one scholar has concluded that the prayer that we know as the Lord's Prayer was actually composed by John the Baptist.[843] Historical records indicate John the Baptist's following continued long after his death.[844] Josephus had more to say about John the Baptist that he did about Jesus (although very little about either).[845],[846]

If John the Baptist was a potential rival to Jesus – even a friendly rival – what were his core teachings beyond repentance and baptism? We don't know exactly[847] but as reported in the *New Testament*, they are entirely ethical. He counseled ordinary people to share their possessions[848], government officials to be honest[849] and Roman soldiers not to exploit civilians.[850] He spoke of a coming kingdom.[851] He confronted the most powerful man in the district and was imprisoned.[852] Later he was executed and Jesus took the occasion to withdraw from the immediate area.[853]

John the Baptist practiced baptism for the remission of sins and he baptized Jesus.[854] He was not a miracle worker.[855] Although he allied with Jesus, he taught a message devoid of Jesus as a sacrifice for sins and he focused on behavioral imperatives. Isn't it very possible that Apollos took that message into the Mediterranean word?[856]

As Donald Harman Akenson has summarized:

- John the Baptist came first and Jesus was his disciple.
- Jesus became his own master and after his death James and Paul became his disciples.
- At least some of John the Baptist's followers stayed with his version of faith in God.

- From the late 20s to the 60s there were, therefore, at least three versions of Christianity: John the Baptist's, James's and Paul's.[857]

If indeed, the religion of Apollos was the "Baptism of John" we can envision alternative histories. AN Wilson wrote: "Had Paul been a weaker personality than Apollos, or had he never written his epistles[858] it could easily have been the case that 'the Baptism of John' would have been the religion which captured the imagination of the ancient world, rather than the Baptism of Christ. Instead of the Sermon on the Mount, devotees would know all about the Sermon on the River-bank. Instead of stories about the heroic last days of Jesus, they would have preserved stories of John the Baptist in prison, John the Baptist having his head chopped off, and, no doubt, John the Baptist appearing after his death to his chosen followers." [859]

From an historical standpoint, one can assume that this alternative came close to taking off.[860] As noted, the resurrection of John the Baptist was already a rumor in *New Testament* times. Some of Jesus's contemporaries thought that Jesus was John the Baptist returned to life.[861] The disciples confirmed that this rumor was out there.[862] Other contemporaries thought that John the Baptist was Elijah[863], the *Old Testament* prophet who had never died.[864]Jesus himself suggested that John the Baptist was Elijah, "*if you are willing to accept it.*" [865] The modifier is important. *Luke* 1:17 suggests that the Elijah-John the Baptist connection was more metaphorical because it has the angel Gabriel saying that the latter will come "*in the spirit and power of Elijah.*" John the Baptist characteristically spoke more plainly. When asked if he was Elijah, he answered, "No."[866]

John the Baptist was slated to be remembered for his teachings rather than a return from the dead. While he did not create a new religion, he greatly influenced at least one branch of what came to be known as the Christian religion and not merely as a herald of Jesus Christ. His ethical teachings were at the core of the Jewish-Christians and the family of Jesus. There is evidence of these beliefs in a two additional documents. The first is admittedly theoretical but has received lots of scholarly attention in the last century. The second was assumed to exist for centuries but has only been discovered in our time.

Q and The *Gospel of Thomas*

For more than a century, scholars have speculated that a book of sayings of Jesus may have circulated in the Jewish homeland prior to the writing of the Gospels. This "book" may have been a common source for *Matthew* and *Luke*. The clue pointing in this direction is that although these two Gospels relied heavily on *Mark*[867] they share about 250 verses which are *not* found in *Mark*. Labeled "*Q*" for the German word *Quelle*, translated into English as "source", this bit of literary analysis may be a hint of another group of Christians.

Q includes only one miracle – the healing of a Roman centurion's servant.[868] *Q* also makes no explicit statement about Jesus's birth, atonement or resurrection.[869] These 250 verses are mostly ethical statements by Jesus and with a lot of materiel about John the Baptist. *Q* connects us with the first followers of Jesus. The *Q* people may not have been worshipping a risen Christ as in Pauline congregations. They were pondering his sayings as a way of thinking about the kingdom of God. At some point the *Q* people turned away from both apocalypticism and Jewish-Christian customs.[870]

Was there a tradition of such sayings? There is evidence that this was the case. Paul learned of Jesus both in the Diaspora and in Jerusalem and as we have seen may have used some of the sayings of Jesus in his writings. When he cited the Second Coming of Christ he called it *"according to the Lord's own word"* [871] even though we have no such record. In introducing both the Lord's Supper and the resurrection he talked about what he had "received."[872] In Paul's letter to the Philippians, in the second chapter he appears to be quoting from a song about Jesus in verses six through eleven:

"who, although He existed in the form of God, did not regard equality with God a thing to be grasped, but emptied Himself, taking the form of a bond-servant, and being made in the likeness of men. Being found in appearance as a man, He humbled Himself by becoming obedient to the point of death, even death on a cross. For this reason also, God highly exalted Him, and bestowed on Him the name which is above every name, so that at the name of Jesus EVERY KNEE WILL BOW, of those who are in heaven and on earth and under the earth, and that every tongue will confess that Jesus Christ is Lord, to the glory of God the Father."

Luke and John, as we have seen, relied on other writers[873] and all the Gospels themselves are evidence that there must have been stories that circulated for decades about how Jesus was betrayed by one of his own disciples and then specifically denied by one of his closest ones and that the others fled. The stories must have recounted that he was crucified by order of the Roman governor Pontius Pilate with some claim that he was the king of the Jews.

There are scholars committed to the one-time existence of *Q*. Here is John Dominic Crossan on *Q*: "I prefer to call *Q* the *Q Gospel*." Here is Burton Mack: "You still hear that: *only a hypothesis*....There will be a text! It's going to have a Library of Congress number!"[874] But there are opposing points of view.

EP Sanders has written: "I believe that Luke and Matthew copied *Mark* and that Luke also copied *Matthew.*" Eta Linnemann has noted: "(O)nly about 42% of the words in Matthew's and Luke's putative *Q* passages are in fact identical."[875] Michael Goulder believes that Luke used *Mark* and *Matthew* rendering the existence of *Q* unnecessary. He identifies what he calls "Minor Agreements" between *Matthew* and *Luke* against *Mark*. Here is one of his examples. Both *Matthew* 26:68 and *Luke* 22:64, but not *Mark* 14:65, add the question *"Who hit you?"* when Jesus, in custody, is attacked by soldiers. His point runs something like this:

- *Q* is devoid of any direct comment of the last week of Jesus's life, the crucifixion week.
- This is an example of *Luke* and *Matthew* agreeing on a comment that did not come from *Mark* and could not have come from *Q* since, again, *Q* does not cover this crucial week.
- The author of *Luke* probably got this verse from *Matthew* as he did other material attributed to *Q*.
- Hence, *Q* is unnecessary.[876]

These waters are too deep for a nonspecialist like me. But it seems that a written or oral understanding of Jesus's sayings was probably available in Palestine in the early decades after the crucifixion. There is evidence of this in one of the best-known *New Testament* verses. The Apostle Paul in *Acts* 20:35 quotes Jesus as saying that *"It is more blessed to give than to receive."* That quote is found nowhere else in the *New Testament* and strongly suggests that Luke, writing in the 80s or later, may have had access to a compendium of Jesus's teachings from as much as fifty years earlier.[877]

There is a far less known example of a *New Testament* writer quoting an extra-Biblical source. In the midst of railing against false teachers, the writer of *Jude* in verses 14 and 15 quotes a book known as *I Enoch*: *"Behold, the Lord came with many thousands of His holy ones, to execute judgment upon all, and to convict all the ungodly of all their ungodly deeds which they have done in an ungodly way, and of all the harsh things which ungodly sinners have spoken against Him."*[878]

Jude may also quote from yet another non-*New Testament* source, known as the *Testament of Moses*, a work no longer extant but cited in other works. This is complicated but illuminating to our major point that a diversity of Christianity co-exists in the pages of the *New Testament*. Here is the analysis.

Jude 9 talks of a dispute between the Devil and the angel Michael over Moses's body and burial. In the context of the *Testament of Moses*, the Devil has slandered Moses by saying that he had once murdered an Egyptian.[879] Michael – even though he is *"one of the mightiest of the angels"* and even though Moses was a righteous man and the charge was slander - did not take it upon himself to dismiss the charge recognizing that only God was the judge. *Jude* 9 reads: *"But Michael the archangel, when he disputed with the devil and argued about the body of Moses, did not dare pronounce against him a railing judgment, but said, 'The Lord rebuke you!'"* The writer of *Jude* used this (rather obscure) example to preach against false teachers who were essentially antinomian, claiming to be their own judges. That is the whole point. He was as a skillful exegete, utilizing a Jewish text[880] and addressing Jewish-Christian audience.

Decades later, an anonymous author wrote *II Peter* and incorporated most of *Jude*. When the writer came to *Jude* 9 he probably was confused and simply wrote that good angels did not presume to disrespect bad people as a lesson in humility for his Gentile audience. But it is a different nuance. Whereas *Jude* stood for the process, that only God is the ultimate judge, *II Peter* seems to be saying that we should show the ungodly and the demons respect. *II Peter* 2:11 reads in part: *"…angels who are greater in might and power do not bring a reviling judgment against them before the Lord.."* These are strange twists and turns within the supposed inerrant word of God. A fundamentalist would try to find that both outlooks are true – that God is the only true judge and that somehow, some way, even demons are worthy of respect. For others, the most sensible view is that *Jude* and *II Peter* show two diverse groups of Christians getting a different message. [881] But the main point is this: we can see that this is one more example of reliance on an extra-biblical text[882] much like some speculate that Luke and Matthew relied on a document that we call *Q*.[883]

The surviving teachings of John the Baptist, the *Epistle of James* and *Q* have certain commonalities. They reflect, in American terms, a more Jeffersonian view of Christianity, one that stresses behavior over belief. [884] So might this text which was discovered in the twentieth century.

In 1945 in Nag Hammadi, Egypt a farmer found a sealed jug buried near a cliff. Within the jug were several bound papyrus documents. It took decades but scholars determined that a portion of these documents constituted a group of 114 "sayings"; we might call them verses. Apparently, a group of Christians circulated this text in Syria in the second century. These sayings are reportedly Jesus's own words to individuals and groups. This is the *Gospel of Thomas*, written in the Coptic language of ancient Egypt.[885]

This gospel, of course, is not in the *New Testament* but some possible traces of it have been identified by at least one scholar. Elaine Pagels theorizes that the community behind the *Gospel of Thomas* and the community behind the *Gospel of John* may have been rivals due to the starkly contrasting view of Jesus represented by each. Further, the writer of *John* may have taken a swipe at the *Thomas* community by three negative references about the Apostle Thomas that do not appear in other Gospels of the *New Testament*:

- First, when the disciples hear that Jesus is about to take a personal risk by going toward Judea to raise Lazarus, Thomas says *"Let us go also that we may die with him."* (*John* 11:16).

- Second, as Jesus forecasts his death and departure Thomas misunderstands and says, *"We do not know where you are going. How can we know the way?"* (*John* 14:5).

- Third, even after Jesus's return, when he confers the power of the Holy Spirit on the disciples, John specifies that Thomas is not present: *"Thomas...was not with them."* (*John* 20:24). Compare this to *Matthew* 28:16 which reports that the eleven disciples – remember Judas was dead – met with the resurrected Jesus in Galilee and *Luke* 24:33-6 which reports that the eleven disciples met with the resurrected Jesus in Jerusalem.[886]

We know him in history as "Doubting Thomas."[887]

Pagels would add the *Gospel of Thomas* to the *New Testament* canon and when asked to name a Christian text that she "couldn't do without," she answered, that there would be two: the *Gospels of Mark* and *Thomas*.[888]

Other scholars downplay the significance of the *Gospel of Thomas* in comparison with *Matthew, Mark, Luke* and *John* believing that it is from the late second century and that anything in it that goes back to Jesus reflects the tradition already preserved in the canonical Gospels.[889] John P. Meir asserts: "Claims that later apocryphal gospels and the Nag Hammadi material supply independent and reliable historical information about Jesus are largely fantasy." [890] It has also been noted that Origen read and rejected the inspiration of the *Gospel of Thomas*.[891]

Like Q, the *Gospel of Thomas* is a book of sayings. The sayings, like Q, point at ethics. Saying 6, for example, reads in part, "His disciples asked him (and) said to him: 'Do you want us to fast? And how shall we pray (and) give alms? What diet should we observe?' Jesus said: 'Do not lie, and what you abhor, do not do...'" Some of the sayings in *Thomas* are more enigmatic than Q. Saying 80 reads, "Jesus said: 'He who has known the world has found the body; and he who has found the body, the world is not worthy of him.'"

Some of the sayings hint at social upheaval. Saying 64, for example, reads, "Traders and merchants [shall] not [enter] the places of my Father." The affinity of the *Gospel of Thomas* to the Jewish-Christian world view is shown in Saying 12 which contains a reference to their first post-Jesus leader, his brother James: "The disciples said to Jesus, 'We know that you are going to leave us. Who will be our leader?' Jesus said to them, 'No matter where you are you are to go to James the Just, for whose sake heaven and earth came into being.'"

The *Gospel of Thomas* like Q consists primarily of teachings attributed to Jesus. A comparison between Q and *Thomas* shows that:

- Each is about the same length.
- Both are sayings.
- About one-third of the sayings of *Thomas* have parallels in Q.
- Many more of *Thomas's* sayings are enigmatic. [892]

Thomas like Q may appeal to those who have trouble accepting Jesus's death as an atonement or who don't believe in a literal resurrection but still consider themselves Christians because they try to follow the teachings of Jesus.[893] The *Gospel of Thomas* does not teach that salvation comes from belief in the death and resurrection of Jesus but by knowing his secret teachings. As Saying 1 states: "Whoever finds the interpretation of these sayings will not taste death."

For these people, a new look at Christianity may now be available. As Elaine Pagels has noted, "Over the last 150 years or so, we have gained access to over forty gospels, letters, and other early Christian works. We can now see more clearly that the early history of Christianity was tumultuous - a time of intense reflection, experimentation, and struggle involving every fundamental issue."[894] Yet most of this scholarship has not been available to the general public until the last thirty or so years.[895] Of these gospels, *Thomas* is preeminent.

Thomas, like Q,[896] *James* and John the Baptist present a Jesus with almost no miracles whereas the Gospels list - as noted earlier - at least 32 and assert many more. These texts also do not make claims that Jesus is God or that he is a sacrifice for sins of humanity.[897] Although Paul testified to preaching nothing but *"Christ Crucified,"*[898] these texts emphasize the ethical teachings of Jesus.[899] They may have much more in common with Paul's Jewish-Christian enemies, the family of Jesus and with the main body of Judaism itself. They also might have much more in common with many modern people.

The early Christians managed the diversity between the Jewish-Christians and the Pauline Christians by complicated negotiations. We will review those negotiations and the resulting agreement in the next chapter. After that, we will review more *New Testament* examples of diversity within the ranks of Pauline Christianity.

CHAPTER 7

Acts and the Council

In Acts (written in the 80s) and in Paul's letter to the Galatians (written in the 50s) we learn of one of the most important negotiated agreements in world history, the agreement reached at the Council of Jerusalem in about 49AD. This agreement allowed Christianity to spread through a message of freedom.

The *Book of Acts* was written in about 80 AD.[900] Mainstream scholars assume that "Luke" or at least some individual wrote both the third canonical Gospel and *Acts*.[901] They point to similar beginnings. *Luke* starts: *"Inasmuch as many have undertaken to compile an account of the things accomplished among us, just as they were handed down to us by those who from the beginning were eyewitnesses and servants of the word, it seemed fitting for me as well, having investigated everything carefully from the beginning, to write it out for you in consecutive order, most excellent Theophilus; so that you may know the exact truth about the things you have been taught."* [902] *Acts* starts: *The first account I composed, Theophilus*[903], *about all that Jesus began to do and teach, until the day when He was taken up to heaven, after He had by the Holy Spirit given orders to the apostles whom He had chosen. To these He also presented Himself alive after His suffering, by many convincing proofs, appearing to them over a period of forty days and speaking of the things concerning the kingdom of God."*[904]

There are other literary similarities. In *Luke* God was behind Jesus's ministry. In *Acts* God was behind the church. In *Luke* Jesus was baptized and received the Holy Spirit. In *Acts* the church was baptized and received the Holy Spirit. In *Luke* the Spirit enabled Jesus to do miracles and preach. In *Acts* the Spirit enabled Christians to do miracles and preach. In *Luke* Jesus healed sick, cast out demons, raised the dead. In *Acts* the Christians did. In *Luke* the Jewish authorities confronted Jesus in Jerusalem. In *Acts* the same authorities confronted the apostles. In *Luke* Jesus is imprisoned, condemned and executed. In *Acts* some of his followers are imprisoned, condemned and executed.[905]

Who was Luke? Was this a real individual who traveled with Paul and wrote the Third Gospel and the *Book of Acts*? The *Bible* does not make that claim.[906]

Someone(s) named Luke appear(s) in the *New Testament* in *Acts* 13:1 (*"Lucius of Cyrene"*), *II Timothy* 4:11 (*"Only Luke is with me."*) and *Colossians* 4:14 (*"Luke, the beloved physician"*). Luke (we will assume a singular person) may have been Libyan as Cyrene was an ancient Greek colony in present day Libya.[907]

The Libyans were an important element in the earliest Christianity:

- Simon, the bystander near Golgotha who was, according to all the Synoptics, pressed into service to carry Jesus's cross was Cyrene.[908] Mark adds this line: *"Simon was the father of Alexander and Rufus."* Rufus and Alexander may also have been known to the readers of *Mark*. As Richard Bauckham writes, "I regard it as a good general rule - not without exceptions - that where the early Gospel tradition preserves the names of characters in the Gospel story (other than those of public figures such as Pilate and Caiaphas), these named people were Christians well known in the early church."[909] Paul wrote *"Greet Rufus, a choice man in the Lord, also his mother and mine."*[910]
- Visitors to Jerusalem from *"parts of Libya belonging to Cyrene"* were at Peter's Pentecost sermon.[911]
- Cyrenians from the Synagogue of the Freedmen argued with Stephen.[912]
- After the persecution following Stephen's death Cyrenians brought Christianity to Antioch.[913]

The Libyans's implantation of Christianity in Antioch became one of the decisive events in all of world history because it set in motion a chain of events that led to the take-off of the career of the Apostle Paul. First, the followers of Jesus in that city made a significant impression and they came to the attention of the Christian authorities remaining in Jerusalem. Those leaders sent a trusted man named Barnabas to investigate and Barnabas retrieved Paul to assist him.[914] Possibly Luke and Paul met there. From the references to Lucius (Luke?), Simon, Rufus and Alexander, and the migration to Antioch we might conclude that the Cyrenian Christians were yet another branch in the first century – and a very important one. If so, Luke was their champion.

According to the Catholic Church, Luke is the patron saint of artists. His feast day is October 18. He is also the patron saint of butchers, glassworkers, notaries, painters, physicians, and surgeons. He allegedly lived to age 84 and died in Greece.[915]

About one-fourth of the *Book of Acts* consists of sermons by Peter, Stephen and Paul. *Acts* affirms the Pauline version of Christianity while acknowledging other variants. It talks of rapid, exciting church growth. [916] It talks of executions within the movement of dishonest believers[917] and prison guards,[918] and of satisfyingly gruesome deaths of Judas[919] and Herod Agrippa the grandson of Herod the Great.[920] It talks of miracles caused even by Peter's shadow,[921] or by contact with handkerchiefs and aprons touched by Paul.[922] It mentions persecutions,[923] Paul being stoned nearly to death, then getting up and returning to the same city.[924] Both Peter[925] and Paul[926] could raise the dead and Paul could nonchalantly shake off a venomous snake that had bitten him.[927] *Acts* reports on a sorcerer named Simon[928] and another one named Bar-Jesus who worked for a Roman official,[929] of angels,[930] of prison escapes,[931] of Paul striking someone blind as he himself had been blinded,[932] of people who thought Paul and his associate Barnabas were Greek gods,[933] of a Roman officer worshipping Peter,[934] of a slave fortune teller who is possessed by a spirit,[935] of a prophet named Agabus with links to the Jerusalem Christians who accurately predicted both a worldwide famine and later that Paul would face danger in Jerusalem[936]and a cohort of Jewish exorcists representing themselves as sons of the priest.[937] *Acts* tells of Paul's conversion and asserts that before that he was trying to execute Christians.[938] *Acts* has surprising twists. Matthias is picked by the apostles in *Acts* 1 and never mentioned again and Paul is picked by Jesus in *Acts* 9 and shapes Christianity. *Acts* 6:4 asserts that the Twelve picked the seven men to oversee resource distribution but that preaching would remain the responsibility of the Twelve: ("...*we will devote ourselves to prayer and to the ministry of the word.*") But in *Acts* 7 and *Acts* 8 two of these seven men - Stephen and Philip – preach memorably.

Acts does all this and yet it also repeatedly asserts that it is offering only a summary of events.[939]

It is striking that Paul's letters and those later attributed to him (and those attributed to Peter) make no mention of miraculous deeds.[940] One would think he would have cited them. The closest he came were references to what Christ had done through him by *"the power of signs and wonders,"* [941] that his message was not just words but *"power"*,[942] that his message was actually unimpressive by human standards but was *"a demonstration of the Spirit and of power,"*[943] and that – and this in the context of telling the Corinthians that he had gone up into the *"third heaven"* – *"the signs of a true apostle were performed among you with utmost patience, signs and wonders and mighty works."*[944] When Paul bragged, it was usually about his weaknesses because they showed his dependence on God.[945]

The unbelievable[946] accounts in *Acts* are told alongside commonplace details such as that when Peter escaped from prison he first went to a private home owned by an apparent follower of Jesus named Mary[947] who it turned out was the mother of Mark. We learn that the person answering the door was named Rhoda who was so excited to see him that she forgot to invite him in.[948] A couple of apparently different Alexanders are mentioned in *Acts*.[949] It is duly recounted that Paul thought the denizens of Mars Hill in Athens were very religious,[950] that in Corinth, Paul, fed up by disputants in the local synagogue, went next door to the house of Gentile named Justus Titus,[951] that Paul rented a hall in Ephesus from someone named Tyrannus,[952] that Paul had traveling companions that included men named Tychicus[953] and Trophimus[954], [955] that Paul had a nephew in Jerusalem,[956] that he had prepared the police for his arrival[957] and that he had a fair amount of money on his person[958] and possibly used it to bribe or corrupt at least one of his captors.[959] (In Paul's defense, he was dealing with Felix who was a shark. Felix had been appointed the Roman procurator by emperor Claudius in 53 AD. He was a cruel administrator and a profligate one. He was a former slave and Tacitus said he "practiced all sorts of cruelty and lasciviousness." His time in office was characterized by troubles and sedition. When Festus succeeded him he was recalled to Rome where Jews from Caesarea complained about him. He would have been executed but Nero spared him. Drusilla, his third wife, was the daughter of Herod Agrippa mentioned in *Acts* 12:1 and therefore was a sister to the brother-sister team of Agrippa and Bernice who appeared in *Acts* 25. According to *Acts* 24:24, Drusilla visited Paul when he was in prison for two years under Felix.[960] Drusilla died when the volcano Vesuvius blew up in 79.[961] Felix may have been a very dangerous enemy as Luke records that he *"was quite familiar with the Way."*[962] However, even if Paul did bribe Felix, he still had enough cash on hand to rent quarters in Rome sufficient for him to welcome *"all who came to see him. Boldly and without hindrance he preached the kingdom of God and taught about the Lord Jesus Christ"* for two years.[963])

In *Acts* there are lists of the seven Hellenists appointed as deacons in Jerusalem[964] and of five prophets and teachers at Antioch.[965] Most of these men were nobodies but there were some who were not. Five had significant mention in the *New Testament* – Stephen, Philip, Barnabas and Paul and possibly Lucius of Antioch as Luke. Another, Manaen of Antioch, was politically connected. He *"had been brought up with Herod the tetrarch* (Antipater)."[966]

Philip may be a unique case. It is important to distinguish this Philip because two other important people in the *New Testament* have the same name. Philip the brother of Herod Antipater was a political ruler. The desertion of his wife Herodias for his brother according to *Matthew* and *Mark* led indirectly to the execution of John the Baptist.[967] Philip was also the name of one of the

Twelve.[968] By the number of mentions in the *New Testament*, he may have been one of the more important ones after Peter, James, John, and Andrew (and, of course, Judas). Like Andrew, this Philip may have initially been one of John the Baptist's disciples. When he came over to Jesus he recruited Nathanial to the Twelve.[969] Philip may have also helped a group of Gentiles reach Jesus: toward the end of Jesus's ministry *"(s)ome Greeks who had come to Jerusalem for the Passover celebration"* wanted to see Jesus and they approached Philip who worked through Andrew.[970]

The third Philip, like Stephen, was a Hellenistic Jew who opposed Temple worship[971] and as such would have been at some odds with James and the Jewish-Christians. As noted, after Stephen's martyrdom he went to Samaria – between Jerusalem and Galilee – to tell the Samaritans about Jesus. Peter and John followed him. This took the message of Jesus into precincts where he himself had been rejected. Later Philip converted an Ethiopian official[972] and still later he resided in Caesarea with four of his daughters.[973] He is thought to have lived out his life in Hierapolis in modern Turkey.[974] Samarian Christianity persisted for several centuries.[975] The Ethiopian is only mentioned here in the *New Testament*, but the church that traces itself to this event endures until the present time. Both of these groups of Jesus's followers add to the diversity of the *New Testament*.

Alongside with the miracles, and the commonplace names, it is of note that some of the claims in *Acts* have been verified. For example, according to *Acts* 18:12-17 when Paul was at Corinth he was hauled before Gallio[976] who was proconsul of Achaia. In 1905 an inscription discovered at Delphi a town in modern Greece showed that Gallio a brother of Seneca the philosopher was indeed in the region of Corinth during that time.[977] *Acts* 18:2 talks of Paul meeting Aquila and Priscilla in Corinth and reports that this couple had left Rome because the Emperor Claudius had ordered all the Jews to leave. The Roman historian Suetonius (abt. 69/75 – after 130) said of Claudius who ruled from 41-54: "Because the Jews of Rome caused continuous disturbances at the instigation of Chrestus, he expelled them from the city." [978] Additionally, *Romans* 16:23 identifies an Erastus as the Corinth city treasurer and he may be referred to again in *Acts* 19:22 and *II Timothy* 4:20.[979] In 1929 archaeologists working in Corinth found an inscription supporting this.[980]

The broad story of *Acts* is of the expansion of Christianity, through Paul and, to a lesser degree, Peter to the wider world. This movement began at Pentecost with Peter placing the life of Jesus in Jewish history and calling on people to repent. We read more about the opening to the Gentiles occasioned by the scattering of Hellenist believers after the murder of

Stephen. *"They preached the word of God, but only to Jews. However, some of the believers who went to Antioch from Cyprus and Cyrene began preaching to the Gentiles about the Lord Jesus."*[981] In *Acts* 9 Paul converts and subsequently begins a program for Gentiles. One of the most important verses in the whole *Bible* may be *Acts* 16:9: *"During the night Paul had a vision of a man of Macedonia standing and begging him, 'Come over to Macedonia and help us.'"* The actions that followed took Christianity into Europe. Some two thousand years later, Hilaire Belloc (1870 – 1953) wrote, "The faith is Europe and Europe is the faith." [982],[983]

Acts, in the words of a modern commentator, Ernst Haenchen "tells about the age of the apostles in order to edify the Christians and woo the Gentiles." Luke writes from a distance, conscious of his role. He was also conscious of what centuries later American political thinkers would call "posterity." [984] (Paul, on the other hand, handled immediate problems in the churches he founded in most of his letters.) Luke analyzes the first generation of Christians not to tell every detail of each sub-group (we would call them denominations) but for these interrelated purposes:

- To bring unity to the movement.
- To help people see the problem of the role of the Gentiles and how it was solved.[985]
- To show the government that the Christians could be accepted. Thus he has every Roman or Roman-related authority that Paul went before declaring him innocent:
  - A. *Acts* 18:12-16 – Gallio at Corinth when Paul was accused of leading people to worship God in unlawful ways: *"'....I refuse to judge such matters.' And he threw them out of the courtroom."*
  - B. *Acts* 19: 37 - The town clerk at Ephesus said that Paul's friends were *"neither temple robbers nor blasphemers of our goddess."*
  - C. *Acts* 23:29 - Claudius Lysias of Jerusalem wrote to Governor Felix that Paul *"was accused concerning questions of their, (the Jewish) law but was charged with nothing deserving dearth or imprisonment."*
  - D. *Acts* 26: 30-31 – Agrippa, Festus, Bernice: *"Then the king, the governor, Bernice, and all the others stood and left. As they went out, they talked it over and agreed, 'This man hasn't done anything to deserve death or imprisonment.'"*[986])

Jerusalem and Antioch

The diversity of early Christianity can be seen in the two main cities of the *Book of Acts*: Jerusalem and Antioch. In a way, the latter was like a spin-off but by the 40s it had become the most dynamic of the Christian communities. But Jerusalem was still the headquarters of the movement and those who remained tried to lead that movement in a more conservative direction.

The Jerusalem church suffered attacks. Emperor Claudius appointed Herod Agrippa, a Jew, as King of Judea and Samaria.[987] He took charge of Jerusalem. He executed the Apostle James, the brother of the Apostle John. In so doing he killed one of the Sons of Thunder who had been close to the Zealots.[988] Herod Agrippa then arrested Peter - who was known to have raised a sword against the soldiers at Jesus's arrest.[989] He may have done this to please the upperclass Jews (*Acts* 12:3). James of the Twelve, then, disappears from history – as do all of the other original Twelve apostles except Peter and the Apostle John who is mentioned very sparingly. But then, like Peter, this James resurfaces in history and legend. He is sidelined in scripture but becomes the St. James of the Catholic tradition. His "life-after-death" becomes a strong example - the Virgin Mary is a stronger example by many times – of the power of the Christian story in history.

We find that:

- James is supposedly buried at Santiago de Compostela in Galicia in Spain.
- His body was either miraculously transported there in a rudderless boat or by the apostles.
- Santiago de Compostela is the third most holy city in Catholicism – after Jerusalem and Rome.
- The pilgrimage to his grave – "The Way of St. James" - has been the most popular pilgrimage for Western European Catholics since the Middle Ages, making James one of the patron saints of pilgrimage.
- Catholics celebrate his feast day on July 25.
- The authenticity of his bones was certified by Pope Leo XIII in 1884.
- According to the Catholic Church, James is the patron saint of arthritis, of Chile, furriers, Guatemala, Nicaragua, pharmacists, pilgrims, and Spain. [990]

Why is there this link to Spain? That is the stuff of legend.

In 844 in Castile, the Christians perceived the help of James the brother of John in their battles against Islam. The historian Edward Gibbon (1737 – 1794) wrote: "a stupendous metamorphosis was performed in the ninth century when from a peaceful fisherman of the Lake of Gennasareth, the Apostle James was transformed into a valorous knight, who charged at the head of Spanish chivalry in battles against the Moors." *Santiago Matamoros* became a stalwart of the *Reconquista*. He was at Valencia in 1094 and Alarcos in 1195. As Cervantes said in *Don Quixote*, "St James the Moorslayer, one of the most valiant saints and knights the world ever had ... has been given by God to Spain for its patron and protection."[991] He is known as Matamoros, the Moorslayer. There are four cities in Mexico named Matamoros.[992] With a slightly different spelling -Matamoras – there are towns in Indiana (an unincorporated town), Ohio (about 1000 people) and Pennsylvania (about 2300 people). So, the young fisherman who followed Jesus and who must have heard his teachings on nonviolence often and who became the first of the Twelve to be martyred is known for warfare, although one doubts if many of the citizens of the three townships in the US are concerned with this paradox.[993] This James also has a role in the history of the Mormon church. He is alleged to have appeared to Joseph Smith in the setting up of his church as did his brother John, John the Baptist and Peter in 1829.[994]

However, to return to the situation in first century Jerusalem, the judicial murder of James of the Twelve had an important and immediate side effect. Very possibly, it created an opportunity for the other James, the brother of Jesus, to rise higher in the Jerusalem church. By *Acts* 12:17, as we have noted, when Peter escaped from prison he prioritized the brother James in getting out the message that he was free. (*"Go tell James and the brothers."*) By *Acts* 15 James the brother of Jesus is a leading figure. From a careful reading of *Acts* 11:27–12:25, it appears that Paul was in or near Jerusalem at this time and, if so, would have witnessed the rise of James, the brother of Jesus.[995] This promotion is all the more noteworthy since as noted James may not have been a follower of Jesus during Jesus's earthly ministry.[996]

There is also evidence in Paul's own writing of this career growth of James the brother of Jesus. In a fourteen-year period in the 30s and the late 40s, framed by *Galatians* 1:18-19 and *Galatians* 2: 1,9-10, James surpassed Peter in significance as the order of mention changes:

- In the first reference Paul talks of visiting Peter and James in Jerusalem three years after his conversion: *"Then three years later I went to Jerusalem to get to know Peter, and I stayed with him for fifteen days. The only other apostle I met at that time was James, the Lord's brother."*
- In the second reference he talks of a return visit fourteen years later where he saw *"James and Cephas (Peter) and John."*

In summary, this is how the Jerusalem Jesus movement came to be led by James the brother of Jesus. It took the death of Jesus, the death one of his close associates and the indictment of Peter, turning him into a fugitive. Initially, the Jerusalem Jesus movement was united[997] and grew to include priests.[998] There were later difficulties and James himself was executed over the protests of the Pharisees in about 62 AD.[999] However, these Jewish-Christians hung on through the Roman wars[1000] and were continuously led as we have noted by a member of Jesus's family.[1001] This tells us even more about the Jewish-Christians. It shows us that they fit comfortably into the Jewish culture and that although they may have hoped for Rome's expulsion from their land, they were not revolutionaries. If Jesus had been a revolutionary it is unlikely that his brother James could have remained in Jerusalem.[1002]

The city of Antioch was in the Syrian province of the Roman Empire, about 350 miles north of Jerusalem.[1003] Stephen's martyrdom broke up a group that had been waiting for the Second Coming and the End-of-the-World. According to *Acts* 11:19 the believers in Jesus traveled to Phoenicia, Cyprus and Antioch. They probably also went to Damascus as the *New Testament* reports several times that Saul (Paul) was on the road there to arrest them.[1004] In essence, they went to set up farm teams to be under the control of the Jerusalem church although the eventual effect was to create diversity.

Of these four places it was in Antioch where we learn of the views of the now-dispersed Greek-speaking Jews. Members of the church in Jerusalem were concerned when they heard that Antiochan Jews were accepting Gentiles into the Christian community.[1005] They learned that this had been instigated by immigrants from Cyprus[1006] and as noted they sent Barnabas (who was from Cyprus[1007]) to investigate. In a crucial accreditation, Barnabas approved of what he saw and Antioch became one of the great Christian cities over the next few centuries. "No city, after Jerusalem, is so intimately connected with the history of the apostolic church."[1008]

When Barnabas went to get Paul to join him,[1009] the church's mission to non-Jews began in earnest.[1010] In Antioch, Paul developed his views of Jesus Christ – that he was God's sacrifice for our sins and was elevated to the level of a deity - and took these beliefs to the mission field.[1011]

It was in Antioch where the followers of Jesus were first called Christians[1012] and where Paul, their champion, was confronted by representatives of Jesus's brother and Peter for supposed errors.[1013],[1014] The term "Christian" is only used two other times in the *New Testament* and both times with a strong Pauline connection. In *Acts* a political leader said at Paul's trial that he himself could possibly be persuaded to become a Christian.[1015] In *I Peter* which promotes Paul in various ways,[1016] the term "Christian" is used for the only other time.

[1017] It is safe to conclude, therefore, that the term "Christian" applied to one branch of the diverse followers of Jesus, some group that we might call a denomination. First-century Christians then line up as a variation of the Way with such designations as the Pillars, the Q people, the Thomas people[1018], the Saints, the Christians, Apollos, and others.[1019] All had an understanding of Jesus that at key points differed.

The *Book of Acts* downplays all of these differences in the interest of the unity that Luke is promoting.

As Burton Mack put is: "Luke was a daring genius for his time. He saw the significance of major centers of Christian instruction; imagined that the church could be an institution united under a single authority in Rome; sensed the danger of the difference between Jewish-Christianity, with its roots in the Jesus traditions, and gentile Christianity, with its roots in the Christ cult; and wrote his two-volume history to suggest that the two traditions had merged into one. He chose Peter and Paul as two representatives of the two types of Christianity and so constructed their sermons and their missions to illustrate the agreements. In doing so, Luke purposefully left out of the account the many different varieties of Christian experimentation that were still accumulating during this time...." [1020] In Luke's version, the role of the Twelve is preserved in *Acts* even as it is moving off the stage.[1021] After the ascension of Jesus, for example, the first action of the apostles was to select a replacement for Judas. They chose Matthias who then disappeared from the *New Testament*. He seems important only as a figure of continuity[1022] and then the continuity of the Twelve became a non-issue within a generation even - as we will note in Chapter 8 – within the *Book of Acts*.[1023]

We don't know how all the differences were managed. We only know of one particular case – that of the differences between Paul and the leaders of the Jerusalem church, the Pillars.

The Council of Jerusalem

Leaders of the Jesus movement met in Jerusalem in about 49AD[1024] to consider an unforeseen development: the spread of their movement into non-Jewish settings. The precipitating issue was a disagreement between James's representatives and Paul on whether non-Jewish-Christians needed to be circumcised to be saved. The larger question, however, was how to manage differences among Christians. This conclave was crucially important, one of the turning points in world history easily matching the significance of the American Constitutional Convention of 1787.

This Council is described in both the *Book of Acts*[1025] and Paul's letter to the Galatians.[1026] *Acts* was written about thirty years after the event and *Galatians* was written within three-four years after the event. *Acts* records that the Council included the *"apostles and elders"* and describes it once as a *"whole assembly."* Peter, James, Barnabas and Paul are mentioned. Paul's account to the Galatians adds John and Titus and notes that the latter was a Gentile and was not required to be circumcised.[1027] The men in that room had endured hardship. James and John had lost their brothers.[1028] As noted the situation for Christians in Jerusalem since Paul's visit some fourteen or so years previously had grown more dangerous with the persecution by Herod Agrippa covered in *Acts* 12. Peter, Barnabas and Paul had been on the road for years. The Council was meeting at a tumultuous time with the expulsion of Jews from Rome in the near background.

The Council was called to judge the teachings of Paul. The accounts differ. Paul's account, whereas more contemporaneous, had a strong personal agenda. Paul reports this event as one in which he attended on his own volition, because of a revelation, that a two-way dialog occurred and that his views were completely endorsed. He inserts gratuitously that he was not at all impressed with the Jerusalem leaders (*"what they were makes no difference to me"*).[1029] The account in *Acts* is much more like a summons to a tribunal.[1030] The Council reached an agreement to send a message to the non-Jewish-Christians. It was recorded as a decree in the fifteenth chapter of *Acts* verses 23 through 29 as follows:

"The apostles and elders, your brothers, To the Gentile believers in Antioch, Syria and Cilicia: Greetings. We have heard that some went out from us without our authorization and disturbed you, troubling your minds by what they said. So we all agreed to choose some men and send them to you with our dear friends Barnabas[1031] *and Paul— men who have risked their lives for the name of our Lord Jesus Christ. Therefore we are sending Judas and Silas*[1032] *to confirm by word of mouth what we are writing. It seemed good to the Holy Spirit and to us not to burden you with anything beyond the following requirements: You are to abstain from food sacrificed to idols, from blood, from the meat of strangled animals and from sexual immorality. You will do well to avoid these things. Farewell."*

This is a message of freedom. The letter to the Galatians, Paul's description of this historic event, has been called the *Magna Carta* of Christian liberty.[1033] The Council imposed an easy burden of ideology, calling to mind Jesus's statement that *"my burden is light."*[1034] It stripped Christianity of ethnicity[1035] and made it a universal religion. The four prohibitions - eating animals sacrificed to idols, eating meat with its blood, eating animals killed by strangulation and *porneia* - are prohibited to Israelites and resident aliens in exactly the same order in *Leviticus* 17-18 as in *Acts* 15:29.[1036]

The Council managed differences but certainly did not create perfect harmony.

In fact, differences of interpretation (Paul characteristically asserted that those who disagreed with him were acting in bad faith.) busted up some of the major figures of the *New Testament*.

We read in *Acts* that after the Council of Jerusalem Paul and Barnabas had a conflict about whether to include John Mark[1037] on their next trip and parted company. It may have been more complicated. We know from the *Galatians* account that they had a major disagreement in Antioch over the application of the Council's decision.[1038] It's important to recall that we don't have Barnabas's side of the story and he may not have been acting hypocritically. After all, he was an honorable figure in *Acts* and Paul notes in *I Corinthians* 9:6 that he stayed on the mission field and even supported himself. We also read in *Galatians* that Peter and Paul came to differences.[1039]

The Synagogue of the Freedmen - who had opposed Stephen[1040] - may have been the site of great opposition and Paul's Jewish-Christian enemies persisted within the Christian movement for many years. A group called the Ebionites were "the descendants of Paul's Judaizing opponents (who) maintained that the Mosaic law was universally obligatory. Their gospel was written around the middle of the second century. They believed that Jesus so fulfilled Jewish law that God chose him as Messiah."[1041] Eusebius said of the Ebionites: "...they considered him a plain and common man, who was justified only because of his superior virtue, and who was the fruit of the intercourse of a man with Mary. In their opinion the observance of the ceremonial law was altogether necessary, on the ground that they could not be saved by faith in Christ alone and by a corresponding life."[1042]

Scholars believe the letters of *I* and *II Timothy* and *Titus* were written from about 120AD–130AD to rebut this point of view and to consolidate Pauline teaching. These letters are concerned with false teaching and with guarding the "*deposit*" of faith.[1043] The last letter is quite blunt, teaching that "*...there are many rebellious men, empty talkers and deceivers, especially those of the circumcision, who must be silenced because they are upsetting whole families, teaching things they should not teach for the sake of sordid gain. ...*"[1044] This is a direct put-down of the Jewish-Christians and a rejection of their hardline position at the Council enunciated in their opening statement: "*...some of the* *sect of the Pharisees who had believed stood up, saying, 'It is necessary to circumcise them and to direct them to observe the Law of Moses.'"*[1045]

Both comments shun the complexity of arguments and simply spout the party line. But on this issue at the Council, Paul was skating on thin ice. The Council evaded pronouncing on circumcision in the same way that the Founders of the United States Constitutional system in 1787 avoided mentioning slavery although it was the largest issue before them.[1046] Like James Madison of Virginia, James of Jerusalem bought time. Some attempt was made to smooth over differences but the key-one, circumcision, was left unmentioned.[1047]

Paul portrayed three elements at the Council and characteristically he used both invective and condescension in his descriptions:

- *"False brothers (who) had infiltrated our ranks to spy on the freedom we have in Christ Jesus and to make us slaves."* These were often called Judaizers.[1048]
- *"Those who seemed to be important"* or *"Pillars"* – or at least reputed Pillars. As noted, the key figures were Peter, Jesus's brother James and John.[1049]
- Himself and Barnabas.

Paul was able to win over the Pillars – but by what tactics? There are intriguing hints that it involved money. In his account of the Council Paul claimed that all the Jerusalem leaders wanted of him was to *"remember the poor"* as he was already inclined to do.[1050] As to remembering the poor, the *Acts* account is silent [1051]and the money may have been for the Jerusalem community rather than poor people *per se*. (Why would the poor in Jerusalem have special status over other poor?[1052]) We know that Paul was capable of amassing money. In one instance early in Paul's ministry – actually, when he was still called Saul and apprenticed to Barnabas – he was entrusted with money in Antioch to transport to Jerusalem.[1053] His letters show his determination to continue this fundraising.[1054]

These contributions may have been a *quid pro quo* for keeping silent about circumcision, demonstrating that the Jewish-Christians were the strongest element within the early movement. They, in turn, may have explained to "false brothers" and other Jews that Paul's payment was the Gentile equivalent of the Temple Tax required by Jewish males.[1055] They may have redefined the settlement from one of freedom to merely managing the terms that Gentile Christians could join with Jews without violating the consciences of the Jews.[1056] Like most bargainers they may also have stressed what they had in common with Paul, that with all their diversities he and they still agreed on a simple formula (which itself is subject to many interpretations): "The human Jesus is the exalted Lord."[1057] In short, James and his colleagues had a tricky problem with Paul. They probably did not want their cash cow to either stray too far or to get slaughtered. They wanted him at the circumference of the movement but not at the center. Until the end of their lives they probably saw him as a franchisee of their centralized operation.

Did Paul buy a seat at the table for his brand of Christianity? Perhaps, and if the scenario we have described is not how the financial arrangement worked, there is an alternative. Perhaps the money Paul collected was for an ascetic community in Jerusalem under the leadership of James. As shown in *Acts* 2:44-45 and *Acts* 4:32 - 5:11, there was at least one such community within the Jerusalem Church. They may have been known as the "Poor Ones" although as noted earlier, private ownership also seemed to exist. In any event, the money situation was a touchy one. In *Romans* 15:31, Paul expressed a fear that the Jewish-Christians might not accept his collection and according to *Acts* 21:17-24 this may have been a problem.[1058]

In addition to the strategic use of money to win his points, Paul also distorted the findings of the Council. Paul took the message of freedom and extended it further. He set the dietary regulations aside in the context of the *New Testament* itself writing *"eat anything sold in the meat market without raising questions of conscience, for, 'The earth is the Lord's, and everything in it.'"*[1059] So, Paul not only modified Jesus's teachings (paying preachers, divorce), he also abrogated three-fourths of the written decision of the Council of Jerusalem.[1060] This made him lasting enemies.

Moreover, the Pillars themselves may have seen the four prohibitions of the Council as less than scriptural commands. The formula is essentially reiterated some years later in *Acts*.[1061] The context is Paul's last visit to Jerusalem and the formula is uttered by James and the other elders at a meeting in which they encourage Paul to visibly respect the Jewish rituals to ease concerns of Jewish-Christians. James and the elders label the Council formula as "**our judgment**" rendering it – one thinks – as less than a command of the Lord and more as a good faith attempt to bridge differences. This is a downgrade from the description of the origin of the requirements in *Acts* 15 which was: *"For it seemed good to **the Holy Spirit** and to us..."* (Emphases added).[1062],[1063]

Yet, with all of the difficulties in its implementation, the Council of Jerusalem incubated Christianity as we know it. Paul took the decision of the Council and ran with it. In *Acts* 16:4 we read: *"Now while they were passing through the cities, they were delivering the decrees which had been decided upon by the apostles and elders who were in Jerusalem, for them to observe."* The Council, then, kept the nascent movement from immediately hardening into opposing factions.[1064] By placing minimal requirements on the Gentile believers, Jesus's own brother James allowed the Christian movement to flourish and in the centuries ahead come to dominate Europe. The Council's written decision quoted in its entirety above, is one of the most important documents in Western Civilization.[1065] The Council's significance for modern times is that it shows discussion and the building of consensus among different types of Christians.[1066] Within this concoction, a line-up similar to the one identified by Paul could be more neutrally seen as: James who offered the compromise and Peter who later may have waffled as centrists, the Jewish-Christians about whom James later warned Paul[1067] as hard-liners and Paul and the late Stephen[1068] as radicals.[1069]

To summarize:

The mix of Christians was more complicated than Antioch versus Jerusalem. What was Peter's side of the Antioch controversy described in *Galatians*? What was James's perception of the risen Christ which, according to Paul, James experienced alone?[1070] Who started Apollos's "church" in Alexandria or the church in Damascus? What exactly did they believe? What exactly did Apollos believe? We know that there were churches in Galilee and Samaria but we don't know if they were dependent on Jerusalem which was several travel days away.[1071] Even if they were technically dependent, given how loose and disorganized the chain of command was as evidenced in the controversy at Antioch, there could have been other interesting variations in these locales.

Luke moved past all of this in the interest of unity. His combined work *Luke-Acts* is longer than all thirteen letters attributed to Paul. The sermons in *Acts* of Peter and Paul represent in some part the thoughts of Luke. He created a view that the only important evangelizing was associated with Paul and spread west to Rome. He was a Greek writing for Greeks, ignoring the Aramaic-speaking peoples and was lukewarm toward Jewish-Christians. He idealized the apostolic age[1072] which later fed the need for tradition and sound doctrine.[1073] *Acts* is a fantastic story with much that we don't have to accept as hard history.[1074] But here is the key: its author interpreted the Council of Jerusalem and the life of Paul in a way that made it clear that two types of Christianity were acceptable: the religion of Jesus's family and the religion of Paul which was the variety that he favored. Within Pauline Christianity, as we shall see in the next chapter, there were additional diversities.

CHAPTER 8

The Other Christians of the *New Testament*: Part 2

After Paul and his first generation colleagues and adversaries had passed from the scene, and as the Jesus movement survived, there were other, newer varieties of followers of Jesus. Most of these fell somewhere in the Pauline tradition. Some of these have modern analogs. The most important, from the vantage of history, were the Institutionalists.

Beyond the acknowledged writings of Paul, there are other letters and writings in the *New Testament* that can be examined to determine what kind of beliefs animated people claiming to be followers of Jesus. The important point to keep in mind is that when there is criticism of some group in the *New Testament* (and there is a lot of very harsh criticism) we typically only have one the side of the story. Drawing from these attacks, I will list several types of Christians. I will spend the most time on the group which was not criticized and which historically outran the others. I call them the Institutionalists and to many they are Christianity. There is overlap in these categories and it is not my intent to describe hard and fast differences but rather to show the variations in the *New Testament* within what came to be known as Christianity.

The Pietistic Church.

Although *I Corinthians* 15 and *Romans* 6, talk of a future resurrection of people, the writers of *Ephesians* and *Colossians* seem to have taken the position that it had already happened. In this way and in related ways, these books sound like Paul, but ever-so-slightly have a different focus. Salvation is represented as a radical change from a dissolute life to being relocated immediately to present-day union with Christ. The author of *Ephesians* (claiming to be Paul) talks of a past that included living *"in the passions of our flesh, following the desires of flesh and senses..."* [1075] By contrast the real Paul talks of a past that was essentially *"blameless."*[1076] *Ephesians* teaches that Christians are *"seated us with him (Christ) in the heavenly realms."* [1077] The real Paul sees our life in heaven to come in the future. As he wrote the Romans: *"Or don't you know that all of us who were baptized into Christ Jesus were baptized into his death? We were therefore buried with him through baptism into death in order that, just as Christ was raised from the dead through the glory of the Father, we too may live a new life. If we have been united with him like this in his death, we will certainly also be united with him in his resurrection."*[1078] There are similar passages in *I Thessalonians* and *I Corinthians.*[1079]

This type of Christian may be described in the letter of *Colossians* which is also a letter ascribed to Paul, but considered by many to be authored by someone else.[1080] The people addressed in this letter may have been learning and following a type of Jewish mysticism. They were criticized for adhering to certain dietary protocols and observing certain holidays.[1081] This suggests some form of Jewish Christianity. But they also followed certain ascetic customs that "Paul" characterizes as *"self-abasement and the worship of angels."*[1082] To counter this, *Colossians* elevates Christ and stresses concepts common to Paul's accepted letters such as forgiveness through Christ.[1083] However, the writer goes beyond this to stress that believers have been raised with Christ and their lives are *"hidden with Christ in God."*[1084] This is the *Ephesians*-like difference from the more future orientation in *Romans* which Paul taught. In short, there may have been, in addition to the Jewish mystical form of Christianity, a variety, closer to Paul, which held that Christians had already experienced the raising with Christ. It is a type of Christianity that is other-worldly.

The Christians addressed in these letters, that I am labeling as the Pietists, may have had a broad influence. Colossae was destroyed in an earthquake in 61 AD and by the time of the letter bearing its name was nonexistent. Thus the letter may well have been a circular.[1085] The letter that we know as *Ephesians* may also have been a type of circular letter with the words *"in Ephesus"* added into the preface by a later scribe who lived in Ephesus.[1086] Consequently, both letters may have been copied and read throughout the region influencing multiple Christian groups and eventually winning a place in the canon.

The Pietistic Christians were otherworldly but also tended to live by practical rules of daily life. *Colossians* 3:18-4:1 and *Ephesians* 5:21-6:9 explain reciprocal requirements between husbands and wives, parents and children and masters and slaves. [1087] These epistles contradict the Pauline stance that in Christ such distinctions are a nullity.[1088] They are evidence of a more rules-oriented Christianity and for the type of Institutionalism that we will cover below. Diversity, in other words, began to take hold even in the Pauline churches.

One senses a second-generation problem. The other-worldliness and the household rules were attempts to give up apocalypticism, achieve cohesiveness and put down rumors. In many ways, this aptly describes a Christian variant some twenty centuries downstream. It is easy to identify Christian groups whose doctrines are otherworldly and who in many instances believe in the inerrancy of scripture but whose business practices and home life are well regulated. There is seemingly no inconsistency in living a well-organized life and yet still professing a belief that the devil once argued with an angel about the disposition of Moses's body (*Jude* 9), that Christians will ascend into the air to meet Jesus (*I Thessalonians* 4: 17-19), that Jesus spent roughly Friday and Saturday of Holy Week in Hell trying to save the damned (*I Peter* 3:19-20) or that God once threw angels into Hell. (*II Peter* 2:4).

The Mormons might be an example. The *Book of Mormon*, published in 1830, holds that North American Indians had horses and wheel-carts and steel, claims that are supported by no archaeologist. It teaches that Indians were descendants of ancient Hebrews which is refuted by DNA evidence.[1089] The Mormons of the 1840s believed they were gathering in Zion in Utah Territory and they praised God for miraculously sending seagulls to eat crop-destroying crickets. (The seagull is the state bird of Utah.) But the Mormons eventually brought hundreds of thousands of immigrants to the US [1090] and in addition to the return of Christ, these Mormons were also concerned with acquiring such practical goods as saws, paint, turpentine, screws, boots, shoe leather and many other supplies for the building of what became Salt Lake City and many other towns in the West.[1091]

Esoteric religious beliefs matter very little to most of those either inside or outside such faith groups. On the inside, most of the devout are concerned with establishing good ties and raising strong families. On the outside most, at least in the modern United States, are tolerant of the beliefs of others. Where it does matter is when these sorts of beliefs are understood to be necessary for membership into Christianity itself rather than as characteristic of one particular Christian group.

The New Deal Christians.

Another group of Christians can be inferred from the *New Testament Book of Hebrews*. *Hebrews* came to be included in the canon because Christians of the 200s and 300s believed Paul wrote it. But the authorship is far from certain. Scholars have suggested as other possible authors Barnabas, Apollos and Priscilla. Origen of Alexandria said: "As for who has written it, only God knows."[1092]

Here is possible context to the *Book of Hebrews*: Partly to defend themselves in the first century and early second century era, Christians claimed an allegiance to Judaism. As the two religions separated, however, Christians came to lose the status and protection that Judaism provided. Hence, some were considering converting or re-converting to historical Jewish congregations. The writer of *Hebrews* was concerned about this possibility. He or she wrote warnings like these:

- *"So we must listen very carefully to the truth we have heard, or we may drift away from it."*[1093]
- *"That is why the Holy Spirit says, 'Today when you hear his voice, don't harden your hearts as Israel did when they rebelled, when they tested me in the wilderness.'"*[1094]
- *"For it is impossible to bring back to repentance those who were once enlightened—those who have experienced the good things of heaven and shared in the Holy Spirit, who have tasted the goodness of the word of God and the power of the age to come— and who then turn away from God. It is impossible to bring such people back to repentance; by rejecting the Son of God, they themselves are nailing him to the cross once again and holding him up to public shame."*[1095]

The writer tried to create an antidote to anyone forsaking Christianity. That antidote was called a New Covenant. These Christians were told that Christianity is better than Judaism, fulfilling it. In *Hebrews* 8: 10-12, here is God describing the New Covenant that applies to the Christians:

"I WILL PUT MY LAWS INTO THEIR MINDS,
AND I WILL WRITE THEM ON THEIR HEARTS.
AND I WILL BE THEIR GOD,
AND THEY SHALL BE MY PEOPLE.
AND THEY SHALL NOT TEACH EVERYONE HIS FELLOW CITIZEN,
AND EVERYONE HIS BROTHER, SAYING, 'KNOW THE LORD,'
FOR ALL WILL KNOW ME,
FROM THE LEAST TO THE GREATEST OF THEM.
FOR I WILL BE MERCIFUL TO THEIR INIQUITIES,
AND I WILL REMEMBER THEIR SINS NO MORE"[1096]

Here is the writer of *Hebrews* describing the power of this New Covenant: *"When He said, 'A new covenant,' He has made the first obsolete. But whatever is becoming obsolete and growing old is ready to disappear."*[1097]

If the people for whom *Hebrews* was written were primarily Jewish-Christians or at least Gentiles with a sympathy toward Judaism, they may have been another variant within the Pauline movement. The variation may be understood at the very basic level of the meaning of Christian faith. *Hebrews* 10:38 quotes *Habakkuk 2:4* - "But **my righteous one shall live by faith.**" (Emphasis added) and here an interesting *New Testament* contrast emerges as we note that Paul quotes the same verse but gives it a different meaning. In *Romans* 1: 16-17 he wrote: *"For I am not ashamed of the gospel, for it is the power of God for salvation to everyone who believes, to the Jew first and also to the Greek. For in it the righteousness of God is revealed from faith to faith; as it is written, 'But **the righteous man shall live by faith.**'"* (Emphasis added). In *Galatians* 3:11 he wrote, *"Now that no one is justified by the Law before God is evident; for, '**the righteous man shall live by faith.**'"* (Emphasis added). For Paul, *Habakkuk's*[1098] claim was foundational to his thinking and faith meant trust in Jesus's death and resurrection as the means by which people are reconciled to God. The writer of *Hebrews* had a different take on faith. A few verses after the quote from *Habakkuk*, comes this famous statement in *Hebrews* 11:1: *"Now faith is the assurance of things hoped for, the conviction of things not seen."* For the writer of *Hebrews*, then, faith is confidence that God would fulfill his promises and that is foundational to *his*[1099] thinking. We will see the phenomenon of Paul and another *New Testament* writer deriving different meanings from the same *Old Testament* verse again in Chapter 11.[1100]

I will call the Christians addressed in *Hebrews* New Deal Christians in recognition of the New Covenant presented to them. I do not perceive a direct descendant of the New Deal Christians as a stand-alone group of Christian believers in the twenty-first century. Rather, I view them as a transitional group with their core beliefs embedded in most if not all denominations. They are, however, one more example of *New Testament* diversity.

The "Red-Letter Christians."

Throughout history, there have been those that took the words of Jesus, particularly the Sermon on the Mount, as a guide for all of life. I call them – and the term is not original with me – the "Red-Letter Christians." The term derives from modern editions of the *Bible* which have printed words attributed to Jesus in the color red.[1101] Red-Letter Christians tend to associate with such values as promoting peace talks, eliminating poverty through government action and fighting racism and in the United States, they tend to be associated with liberal Democrat prescriptions to these problems. These Christians have a clear preference for the statements of Jesus over other statements in the *New Testament*. For example, Senator Barack Obama as a presidential candidate in 2008 defending his position on civil unions for gays said: "If people find that controversial then I would just refer them to the Sermon on the Mount, which I think is, in my mind, for my faith, more central than an obscure passage in *Romans*."[1102]

The Red-Letter Christians are an early twenty-first century cohort with many antecedents. In history this type of Christian has embraced *Luke's* version of the Beatitudes in *Luke* 6 which casts *Matthew's* beatitudes in a more socially progressive light. The first Gospel's *"blessed are the poor in spirit"*[1103]is rendered in *Luke* as *"blessed are the poor."* [1104] The first Gospel's *"blessed are those who hunger and thirst for righteousness"* [1105]becomes *Luke's "blessed are the hungry."*[1106]

Luke also includes reverse beatitudes which have been hurled at society's elite ever since:

"Woe to you who are rich,
  for you have your only happiness now.
Woe to you who are fat and prosperous now,
  for a time of awful hunger awaits you.
Woe to you who laugh now,
  for your laughing will turn to mourning and sorrow.
Woe you who are praised by the crowds,
  for their ancestors also praised false prophets."[1107]

Luke's version of the beatitudes has been a foundational text for those who see their faith as an ongoing challenge to society's structures.

So is the account taken from *Matthew, Mark* and *Luke* of the Rich Young Ruler.[1108] This is the story about a man who came to Jesus seeking the path to eternal life. Jesus told him that he needed first to sell his possessions and give the money to the poor. This story has had a stupendous impact throughout history. It led Anthony of Egypt born in about 250 to establish monasticism.[1109] Anthony lived to age 100. Constantine, the first Roman emperor who publicly embraced Christianity, was said to have visited him for counsel.[1110] All subsequent monastic movements stem from Anthony.[1111],[1112] About a thousand years later, the story of the Rich Young Ruler inspired the founder of the mendicant Waldenses. In 1176, a man known variously as Valdez or Waldo was a merchant in Lyon. He provided for his family and gave away the rest of his money. He gathered a group and his group was denied the right to preach and was eventually excommunicated. The Waldenses attempted to literally follow the *New Testament*.

They endured over centuries and many became Protestants. Some migrated as far as Latin America. By some reckoning the Waldensians could be considered the oldest Protestants but the original problem that Rome had with them was less over doctrine and more over their lay preaching. There is a close parallelism between the Waldensians of the twelfth century and the original followers of St. Francis of Assisi in the thirteenth except that the Franciscans stayed within the church.[1113]

St. Francis also was inspired by a passage from *Matthew*.

Francis had a somewhat raucous youth. According to one source, he was raised "indulgently and carelessly ... (and was) taught shameful and detestable things full of excess and lewdness... He boiled in the sins of youthful heat." He was involved in "every kind of debauchery." His conversion in his early 20s around 1206 followed war, imprisonment, a long recuperation and a vision to build rebuild a dilapidated church building at Sam Damiano. He was led by a vision of Jesus speaking from *Matthew* 10:7, 9 - "*Go, preach as you go, saying, 'the kingdom of heaven is at hand. Take no gold, nor silver, nor copper in your belt'.*"" This led to a public confrontation with his wealthy father before a bishop at which he repaid his father money his father demanded and even all his clothing, appearing before the local crowd naked.

Francis, unlike many of his contemporaries, preached love for the material world and did not condemn marriage and sex. He composed a hymn mentioning "brother son" and "sister moon" showing ecological sensitivities centuries ahead of his time. Unlike other itinerant preachers he stayed away from the theme of damnation.

Francis founded an order and later visited the Middle East with the Fifth Crusade during which he visited the sultan al-Malik al-Kamil and tried unsuccessfully to convert him and bring about peace. After the fall of the crusaders his order alone was allowed by the Moslems to remain. In 1228 Pope Gregory IX canonized Francis.

A modern historian has written that "in Francis of Assisi medieval piety had its highest and most inspiring representative."[1114] Pope Pius XI (1857 – 1939) officially designated Francis "the second Christ" or *alter Christus*. Francis is, after Jesus and the Virgin Mary, possibly the most admired Christian in history. Catholic tradition holds that Francis was the first person in history to show the *stigmata* - Christ's wound on his hands and feet. He also introduced the nativity scene to devotion. According to the Catholic Church, the patron saint of animals is St. Francis. His feast day is October 4. He is also the patron saint of ecologists, Italy, merchants and zoos. [1115]

Leo Tolstoy (1828-1910) was a nineteenth century precursor of the Red-Letter Christians. Like Francis, in mid-life Tolstoy resolved a spiritual crisis by his study of the Gospels, particularly the Sermon on the Mount. The message of his novel *Resurrection* (1899) was that the teachings of Jesus were to be read literally.[1116] His new understanding led him to a radical pacifism. He came to see his opponents as falling into two camps: "conservative Christian patriots" and "atheistic revolutionists." He rejected most of the institutional church of his day writing: "So-called believers believe that Christ-God, the second person of the Trinity, descended upon earth to teach men by His example how to live; they go through the most elaborate ceremonies for the consumption of the sacraments, the building of churches, the sending out of missionaries, the establishment of priesthoods, for parochial administration, for the performance of rituals; but they forget one little detail, - to do what He said."

He went on, saying: "According to the interpretations of the church, He (Jesus) taught that He was the second person of the Trinity, the Son of God the Father and that He came into the world to atone by His death for Adam's sin. But every one who has read the Gospels knows that Christ taught nothing of the sort, or at least but spoke very vaguely on these topics. .... In what, then, does the rest of Christ's teaching consist? It is impossible to deny, and all Christians have always recognized the fact, that the chief aim of Christ's teaching is to regulate men's lives, - how they ought to live with regard to one another." He rejected war, the justice system and any type of coercion.[1117]

Would Tolstoy or someone like St. Francis have been an effective leader of the church? It is possible but it seems improbable for this type of Christianity to be suited for political leadership in any era. One who failed was an Italian hermit named Peter of Morrone who in 1294 was elected Pope after the College of Cardinals had deadlocked for over two years and Peter had rebuked them in writing. He took the name Celestine V. Celestine was a humble man, refusing to be inaugurated in Rome and riding to his coronation on August 29, 1294 on a donkey. He was over eighty and his elevation was testimony to Franciscan ideas of a reformed church. He offered plenary indulgence to all who attended his coronation and went to confession. This was a popular "people-first" move because it meant that the sins of everyday people would be forgiven without any need for further expiation in Purgatory[1118] which required financial sacrifices on the part of surviving relatives.

As Pope he issued two decrees. One had to do with the selection of future popes by confirming the decision of an earlier Pope that the College of Cardinals was to meet in a conclave. The second decree announced the right of any Pope to abdicate. After five months he exercised that right. His resignation letter stated "the desire for humility, for a purer life, for a stainless conscience, the deficiencies of his own physical strength, his ignorance, the perverseness of the people, his longing for the tranquility of his former life." For a pope to resign was unprecedented[1119], and his resignation demonstrated the burden of the papacy, the need for more than idealism and honesty as job qualifications and the power of the College of Cardinals. No pope since then has taken the name Celestine. He is the patron saint of bookbinders.

Celestine V has been called "the most inept pope in history." The next Pope was twenty years younger and temperamentally quite different. Pope Boniface VIII canceled Celestine's leniencies and served ten tumultuous years during which he issued the bull *Unam Sanctam*, declaring that the Pope was the rightful ruler of the world. Its key language: "Now, therefore, we declare, say, determine and pronounce that for every human creature it is necessary for salvation to be subject to the authority of the Roman pontiff"[1120]

After that, the papacy fell into more than a hundred years of controversy. First came the Avignon papacy (1305-78) when the popes quit Rome and then came the Great Schism (1378-1415) characterized by competing popes.[1121]

Yet, we have seen practical effects of the Tolstoyan take on Christianity. In 1910, shortly before his death Tolstoy wrote a young lawyer whom the world would know as Mohandas Gandhi (1869–1948) about the contradiction between the teachings of the church and the teachings of Christ. In the decades that followed, Gandhi used passive resistance to force the British to quit India. In turn, Gandhi's influence was studied by a seminary student - the son, grandson and great-grandson of Baptist ministers named Martin Luther King (1929-1968).[1122] King later wrote about the Montgomery bus boycott: "When the protest began, my mind, consciously or unconsciously, was driven back to the Sermon on the Mount, with its sublime teaching on life, and to the Gandhian method of nonviolent resistance." When asked why he had not become a Marxist, Martin Luther King responded: "Because of the overpowering force of the figure of Jesus." [1123]

The relevance of the Red-Letter Christians and their pacifism in a nuclear age should not be discounted.[1124] Yet, the Red-Letter Christians are not the only authentic voice of Christianity. President Barack Obama made this clear in receiving the Nobel Peace Prize in 2009:

"We must begin by acknowledging the hard truth that we will not eradicate violent conflict in our lifetimes. There will be times when nations -- acting individually or in concert -- will find the use of force not only necessary but morally justified. I make this statement mindful of what Martin Luther King said in this same ceremony years ago – 'Violence never brings permanent peace. It solves no social problem: it merely creates new and more complicated ones.' As someone who stands here as a direct consequence of Dr. King's life's work, I am living testimony to the moral force of nonviolence. I know there is nothing weak -- nothing passive -- nothing naive -- in the creed and lives of Gandhi and King. **But as a head of state sworn to protect and defend my nation, I cannot be guided by their examples alone.** I face the world as it is, and cannot stand idle in the face of threats to the American people. For make no mistake: Evil does exist in the world. A nonviolent movement could not have halted Hitler's armies. Negotiations cannot convince al Qaeda's leaders to lay down their arms. To say that force is sometimes necessary is not a call to cynicism -- it is a recognition of history; the imperfections of man and the limits of reason."[1125] (Emphasis added).

There are others in history whose actions might not flow from the Sermon on the Mount but nevertheless stood up to governments in the name of Christ. As such they might be considered Red-Letter Christians also. Some examples include:

- Francisco de Vitoria (1483–1546) and Bishop Bartolome de Las Casas (1484-1566). In the 1500s news of Spanish mistreatment of the Indians prompted reflection and sympathy in the Church leading to thoughts of international law. The foundation was that as humans were created in the image of God and given a rational nature they had a unique position in creation and were entitled to treatment from other people that no other creature could claim. De Vitoria and De Las Casas were key voices.[1126] De Las Casas refused Mass to some slaveholders. [1127]

- The Cristero rebels in the 1920s Mexico. The Cristeros were armed peasants who fought the government's attack on the Catholic religion for three years to preserve their religious freedoms. Priests went on strike. Women joined the men in the fighting. More than thirty thousand Cristeros and about twice that many government troops were killed. In 2000 Pope John Paul II beatified twenty-five Cristero martyrs.[1128]

- Archbishop Oscar Romero of El Salvador (1917-1980). Romero stood for justice and the rights of the poor in a violence-torn El Salvador. He died a martyr's death, gunned down in a church. The Church of England has placed a statue of him in Westminster Abbey.[1129]

The Institutionalists

Developing the *New Testament* canon, a formal structure and negotiated answers to the question of whether Jesus was God and/or human was the work of church councils and leaders in the early centuries. Consensus proved difficult and there were ongoing conflicts.

Accepted scripture emerged slowly. The first prompt may have been the Jewish orientation of the early church: as Judaism was a religion with a holy book so it was natural that the Christian off-shoot would develop scriptures. We see that starting in the *Gospel of Matthew*. The writer puts Jesus's words on par with the teachings of Moses by this formula: *"You have heard that it was said,... but I say to you..."*[1130] From *I Timothy*, we hear one of Jesus homespun sayings labeled scripture.[1131] *II Peter* labels Paul's letters as scripture and alleges that people were twisting them[1132] and even discourages private interpretation of scripture.[1133]

It took challenges from other Christians for those Christians that became the Orthodox – I call them the Institutionalists - to develop a canon of accepted scripture. During the second century, Marcion of Sinope[1134] taught an extreme form of Pauline Christianity. Marcion rejected what he perceived as the *Old Testament* God of wrath.[1135] He developed a "canon" of ten Pauline letters which included all of ours minus *I* and *II Timothy* and *Titus*[1136] and a version of *Luke*. Marcion believed that *Luke* was the only genuine Gospel because of its supposed connection with Paul's letters.[1137] He taught that the God of Jesus had nothing in common with the *Old Testament* God.[1138] Marcion even edited Paul's letters to remove Jewish influences.[1139] In essence, "the small collection of Pauline letters which were cherished at the beginning of the second century in the 'churches' of Rome - doubtless just as in similarly oriented Corinth, in Antioch and Smyrna - were then surpassed and replaced by Marcion's more complete collection." Marcion was determined to give his churches as solid a Pauline basis as he could. Marcion may have saved *Galatians* for us since he came from a region which was close to Galatia and after him there are far more mentions of it. (In any case, it was from this letter that Marcion supported his break with the *Old Testament*.) Also, we may owe the private[1140] letter of *Philemon* to Marcion. Finally, he may have brought *Colossians* to Rome's attention since, again, we hear of it after him far more than before him.[1141]

Marcion who died about 160 was eventually excommunicated[1142] but the Marcionite churches flourished for another three hundred years.[1143] In the end, however, the Marcionites could not address the need of the Romans for a religion with ancient roots which Pauline Christianity could furnish through its connection with Judaism.[1144]

The Montanist sect of the 150-250AD era also challenged orthodoxy and also contributed indirectly to the development of the canon. Montanus was a religious leader who joined the Christian movement and was baptized about 155 AD. However, he came into conflict with the emerging orthodoxy by his emphasis on new revelation and by counter-organizing. Montanus and his followers took to speaking in tongues and issuing prophecy. They were apocalyptic and eventually suppressed. The Montanists may have encouraged a reaction against at least two of their favorite texts which survive in the *New Testament*: *Hebrews* and *Revelation*.[1145] Still another force challenging the orthodox was Gnosticism, with the *Gospel of Thomas*, its twenty-first century artifact.[1146]

Of course there were responses to these challenges. One compromise to Marcion's anti-Jewish views was offered in the *Letter of Barnabas* written about 130, probably in Alexandria. It "offered Christians a compromise solution to the problem of the proper significance for them of the Hebrew law. This compromise held that the Jewish scriptures were true, not literally as the Jews believed, but allegorically." This letter was accepted as scripture by some church fathers, including Clement and Origen.[1147] The lasting response to Marcion, the Montanists and the Gnostics, however, was the church leaders's commencement of serious work on the canon. They reaffirmed their reliance on the *Old Testament* and began the multi-generational process of determining the content of the *New Testament* canon which was finally completed in the late 300s.[1148]

The formation of a coherent message and a leadership structure also filled up the early centuries of the Church. The first need was - as we would put it today - to stay on message. From *Jude* we hear that it was *"necessary to write and appeal to you to contend for the faith that was once for all entrusted to the saints."*[1149] Thus, as with the letter to *Hebrews,* we see the concept of faith come to mean something different than Paul's trusting relationship in Jesus. It now took on a meaning closer to this: the content of the teaching of Christianity.[1150] From *II Thessalonians* we read of the importance of *"tradition"* in order, probably among other things, to obtain glory and to avoid idleness.[1151] In *I John* most *"visions"* are labeled out-of-bounds.[1152] *II Peter*[1153] makes overt claims to tradition by claiming to be written by the Apostle Peter[1154] and even citing his experience at the Mount of Transfiguration with Jesus.[1155]

Several of the *New Testament* books - including *I* and *II Timothy, I* and *II Peter, Titus, II Thessalonians* and *Jude*[1156]- stress the development of a formal leadership structure. This organizational orientation is reflected, for example, as Timothy and Titus are imagined as left by Paul in charge of Ephesus [1157]and Crete.[1158] As noted in Chapter 7, scholars believe that *I* and *II Timothy* and *Titus* were written with an agenda of promoting institutionalization of the churches.[1159] Scholars also believe that all three letters were written by the same person.[1160] *I Peter* promotes institutionalism by telling the young to respect the elders[1161] and by giving specific advice to elders that includes in *I Peter* 5: 2-3 this general guidance: *"Care for the flock that God has entrusted to you. Watch over it willingly, not grudgingly— not for what you will get out of it, but because you are eager to serve God. Don't lord it over the people assigned to your care, but lead them by your own good example."*

Church leadership took a much more formal tone. Consider, for example, leadership qualities in the days of *Acts* 6. Leaders were to be *"men of good repute, full of the Spirit and wisdom."*[1162]The exigencies of a later time required bishops who could *"hold firm to the sure word as taught, so that he may be able to give instruction in sound doctrine and also to confute those who contradict it."*[1163] The harum-scarum church in Corinth had so many problems and yet Paul did not appeal to a leadership group because there wasn't a leadership group. Decades later, bishops and overseers were in charge. The leadership that these later *New Testament* letters promoted was exclusively male. Whereas Paul had many females in leadership roles, the writer of *I Timothy* has this put-down of women: *"...Adam was not deceived, but the woman was deceived and became a transgressor. Yet she will be saved through childbearing..."* [1164]

As accepted scripture, a message and a structure all emerged, so did a solid front against enemies. In the later *New Testament* letters there is invective and scurrility not against Jewish-Christians like in Paul's day, but against unnamed false teachers. They are called *"lovers of themselves, lovers of money, boasters, arrogant, abusive, disobedient to their parents, ungrateful, unholy, inhuman, implacable, slanderers, profligates, brutes, haters of good, treacherous, reckless, swollen with conceit, lovers of pleasure rather than lovers of God."*[1165] The nature of their teaching is unclear but *I Timothy* and *Titus* may well be attacking Gnostics with their disparaging of endless genealogies and mythologies.[1166] But who knows the other side of the story? They may have been free-flowing spirit-led Christians like those in Corinth a generation or two earlier. Similarly, as noted above, the writer of *II Peter* worried that Paul's message was twisted and misinterpreted. But it may well have been the case that he was just describing a different type of Christian, one who took Paul's message on grace and forgiveness to a more tolerant life style.

The lines are impossible to draw, but Paul himself seems to have anticipated at least a variant of this problem. He wrote the Romans that *"…why not say (as some people slander us by saying that we say), 'Let us do evil so that good may come?'"*[1167] In sum these second century churches had to stanch the flow of defectors and so the *New Testament* letters warned against what *Hebrews* called *"diverse teachings".*[1168]

It is in *I Peter* that the need for institutionalism becomes most apparent. Here is some background. In about 111, Pliny the Younger (abt. 61–abt. 112) was sent by the emperor Trajan (52–117) to Bithynia, a Roman province in modern-day Turkey to serve as governor. Before this time, we have no surviving written comments about Christians from any non-Christian, non-Jewish source. Christianity just wasn't on the Roman radar screen. Pliny's job as governor was primarily to collect taxes and maintain public order. Pliny wrote Trajan in about 112 AD seeking advice on how to handle Christians because he was getting complaints about them. The complaints were unclear but Pliny showed some knowledge of Christ and Christians:

- That Christians lived moral lives.
- That Christians worshipped Christ in songs as a god.[1169]
- That no Christian could revile or curse Christ.[1170]

But he showed no knowledge of Christian writings and he viewed Christianity as a superstition.[1171] In this way Christians were probably coming to the attention of other governors. This too is reflected in the *New Testament.*[1172] It is important to remember that a hundred years after the life of Christ the number of Christians was still tiny.[1173] Christians may not have broken imperial laws but were sometimes participants in civil disturbances[1174] often because they did not worship the state gods and thus were blamed for community misfortune. Local bullies may have also turned on them because Christians were exclusivists.[1175] They exchanged ritual kisses.[1176] The Lord's Supper was equated with cannibalism.

The majority of judicial proceedings against Christians during the second century seems to have been under the power of authorities to suppress disturbances rather than specific criminal charges. Christians were typically charged with atheism and anarchy.[1177] In some instances, as Pliny's and Trajan's correspondence suggests, identification as a Christian was a criminal charge but by performing sacrifices the accused could get acquittals. As a consequence, it is not surprising that in the time of Pliny many people moved in and out of Christianity. [1178], [1179]

It is highly relevant to all this that *I Peter* is addressed to people in Bithynia[1180] who were being *"slandered."*[1181] *I Peter* was a type of circular letter and must have been copied and read throughout Bithynia. The word for suffering appears more than any *New Testament* book. *I Peter* 4:4 indicates that much of the persecution arose from other citizens. They were causing a *"fiery ordeal"* according to *I Peter* 4:12. *I Peter* takes the tack of advising Christians to keep their heads down, unify and await a better day. There is counsel to live good lives among the pagans.[1182] There is counsel to obey the government.[1183]There is, however, recognition that they may suffer for doing good. [1184]

There are two possible early artifacts of the Institutional church in the *New Testament* itself. One is a passage in the *Book of Acts*. Even by the time of the Council of Jerusalem, a leadership class separate from the twelve apostles had emerged in Jerusalem. *Acts* 11:30 first mentions elders. It is significant that when the Apostle James, the brother of the Apostle John, was martyred, he was not replaced as Judas had been.[1185] There was no need. They had a permanent leadership group which could naturally evolve. When the Council of Jerusalem met, the leadership consisted of "apostles and elders."[1186] There was no mention of the Twelve.

Another possible early artifact of the new institutionalism was the *Gospel of Matthew* which blends Pauline universalism with respect for Jewish tradition. It is assumed by many scholars that Matthew wrote in Antioch between 80 and 90. For at least twenty years the Jewish- Christians had held sway in Antioch, stemming from their victory over Paul described in *Galatians*. But in the post-war world, Gentile Christians were becoming more numerous and influential and Matthew's Gospel may well be an attempt to honor the Jewish traditions but describe that faith as applicable to all. To add to the complications, Matthew was writing in a time when Jewish-Christians were struggling with other Jews and facing ostracism.[1187]

The Jewish traditions are acknowledged early in *Matthew* through literary parallels. In *Exodus* 1 and 2 Moses is born in the midst of a general slaughter of Hebrew baby boys on the order the king. In *Matthew* 2 Jesus is born in the midst of a slaughter of Jewish baby boys by the order of Herod the Great. Both are taken to safety – Moses within Egypt and Jesus to Egypt. Joseph the father of Jesus is modeled after Joseph the *Old Testament* patriarch. Both got messages in dreams.

- Joseph the father of Jesus: In *Matthew* 1:20-25 an angel tells him that Jesus was conceived of the Holy Spirit. In *Matthew* 2:13 an angel tells him to take his family and flee to Egypt. In *Matthew* 2:19 an angel tells him to take his family back into Israel. In *Matthew* 2: 22-23 God tells him to avoid Judaea and he ends up in Nazareth.

- Joseph the Patriarch: In *Genesis* 37:5-11 he dreamed about imagery showing his superiority over his brothers. In *Genesis* 40 Joseph interprets dreams of other prisoners in Egypt. In *Genesis* 41 Joseph interprets dreams of the pharaoh.

Beyond the literary devices, there is some unsubtle pro-Jewish commentary. In the pre-Easter era, Jesus instructs his followers not to go into non-Jewish areas to preach[1188] and he tells a worried non-Jewish mother that, *"I was sent only to the lost sheep of the house of Israel"* and as noted even likens her to a dog.[1189] Moreover, traditional Jewish-Christians were assured by *Matthew* in the words of Jesus in the Sermon on the Mount that he *"did not come to abolish the law of Moses or the writings of the prophets"*[1190] If this is not a direct refutation of Paul's teaching that *"we know that a person is made right with God by faith in Jesus Christ, not by obeying the law"* and that *"no one will ever be made right with God by obeying the law"*[1191] then it at least speaks to the diversity of *New Testament* Christianity. Moreover, it is difficult to square Jesus's statement about the law first codified in *Matthew* that *"until heaven and earth disappear, not even the smallest detail of God's law will disappear ..."*[1192] with Paul's claim that when he was around people *"who follow the Jewish law, I too lived under that law. Even though I am not subject to the law"* and that when he was with non-Jews *"who do not follow the Jewish law, I too live apart from that law."*[1193]

Yet, *Matthew* moves toward more universalism. After his resurrection *Matthew's* Jesus proclaims universalism based on baptism, his teachings and his continued presence, telling his followers: *"I have been given all authority in heaven and on earth. Therefore, go and make disciples of all the nations, baptizing them in the name of the Father and the Son and the Holy Spirit. Teach these new disciples to obey all the commands I have given you. And be sure of this: I am with you always, even to the end of the age."*[1194] *Matthew* hinges this great change on the crucifixion/resurrection. The author uses the apocalyptic sign of an earthquake, both at the cross[1195] and then a few days later at the Empty Tomb[1196] and he is the only Gospel writer to do so although earthquakes feature large in the *New Testament.*[1197] In short, *Matthew* may have been somewhat of a corrective to the excesses of Pauline theology – shown in its stress of Judaism – but also accepting a universal message.[1198]

Let's examine how the institutionalized church took root. Although it is difficult for moderns to understand this, for at least a century Christianity attracted very little official notice within the Roman Empire. Pliny the Younger's uncle (Pliny the Elder [23 – 79]) had written a book, *Natural*

History, about generation after the death of Jesus. The section on Palestine did not mention Jesus or the beginnings of Christianity even though by that time many of the books of the *New Testament* had already been written. The Roman historian Tacitus (abt. 56- abt. 120) summarized the state of Palestine between 14 and 37 as: "under Tiberius all was quiet." [1199] Indeed, there are only three mentions of Jesus or Christianity in Roman literature in the first ninety years after Jesus's death[1200] and these could have been written on a few pages.[1201] They include, besides the Pliny/Trajan correspondence, the comments of two ancient historians.

Suetonius as we have noted wrote around 120 AD about Claudius who was emperor from 41-54. Claudius expelled Jews from Rome because of the instigator "Chrestus." He probably - but not certainly - meant "Christus" but this still shows how vague and incorrect the understanding of Christianity was. The *New Testament* tie-in is *Acts* 18:1-2. which introduces Aquilla and Priscilla and allows that they "*had left Italy when Claudius Caesar deported all Jews from Rome.*" Suetonius was unimpressed with Christians. He viewed them as "a class of men given to a new and malevolent superstition."[1202]

Tacitus wrote in about 116 about the events of the 64 fire in Rome during Nero's reign. He wrote, "The founder of this name, Christ, had been executed in the reign of Tiberius by the procurator Pontius Pilate."[1203] He said Christians were hated for their "shameful acts." He said that Christianity was a "deadly superstition." He said that many Christians were convicted not so much for arson but for "hatred of the human race." He also said that they had "a guilt which deserved the most exemplary punishment." Although Tacitus was negative about Christians he was neutral toward Christ. He cited his death as a Roman matter - no mention of Judaism. He did not explain the Christian movement by Jesus's resurrection. He listed none of Jesus's teachings. For him it came down to the Christians following a man executed by Rome and therefore deserving of death themselves and Nero's error was in causing sympathy for such a group.[1204]

Yet from a tiny group, the Christians loyal to Paul's understanding of the faith grew to dominate the Roman Empire within a few centuries. Rodney Stark has argued that this expansion did not depend on mass conversions like in *Acts* 2:41 ("*Those who believed what Peter said were baptized and added to the church that day—about 3,000 in all.*") but could be accomplished by incremental growth. Stark uses the model of the Mormon church growth from 1830 to the present to make his case.[1205] During the start-up period of Christianity travel – due to Roman administrative control - was easier than it had ever been or would be for the next eighteen hundred years. While the church in Jerusalem spent the first generation in patient waiting, Paul traveled.[1206] He traveled as much or more by sea as by land.[1207] Paul's network, and the networks of others, launched this steady growth. It spread throughout the Mediterranean region as seen in that both *James* and *I Peter* are addressed to Jews in the Diaspora.[1208]

From that base, slow and consistent growth continued. The Christians had an optimistic view, ahead of their time. They survived the destruction of Jerusalem and an off-and-on three-century struggle with the Roman Empire. If there were a thousand Christians in 40, an annual growth rate of 3.4% would have made for a Christian majority in the Roman Empire by the year 350.[1209] This growth was largely an urban phenomenon. Although Jesus preached in villages or hillsides, there is no record of Paul doing so. By the 100s there were outstanding Christian centers – Carthage, Alexandria, Ephesus, Antioch and Rome.[1210]

Institutionalism, as noted, was a reaction to enemies. For hundreds of years Roman pagan intellectuals attacked Christianity as an apostasy from Judaism.[1211] Beginning in the second century they took aim at the Christian faith, often in modern tones. The work of most of these intellectuals was destroyed by Christian authorities in the fourth and fifth centuries and what we have are lengthy excerpts appearing in refutations of their work.[1212] From these sources we glean information about Celsus who lived in the second century and wrote that Jesus was a magician who learned magic in Egypt. He added that Christians formed "associations contrary to our laws." Celsus also took the tack that Christians had severed religion from the idea of the nation and that the deification of Jesus threatened monotheism.[1213] Celsus also accused Christians of causing moral decline by easy forgiveness.[1214] Celsus believed that:

- Jesus was illegitimate. His father was a Roman soldier named Pantera.
- Jesus was not divine.
- Jesus was not born in Bethlehem.
- The story of the wise men and the killing of the children were made-up.
- Jesus did not do any miracles.
- Jesus did not predict his own death.
- The teaching that God allowed Jesus to die for the sins of the world is perverse.
- The resurrection of Jesus was wishful thinking on the part of his followers.[1215]

132

Porphyry[1216] (abt. 234-abt. 305) was born in Tyre a costal city in modern Lebanon[1217] about fifty miles from Beirut. His parents were Syrian. As a young man he traveled to Rome where his reputation as a philosopher was established. His antichristian writings were countered by Christians for centuries; St. Augustine called him "the most learned of philosophers."

Among Porphyry's contentions are many that are familiar:

- The genealogical lists in *Matthew* and *Luke* were inconsistent.
- The birth stories of Jesus were inconsistent.
- The *New Testament* disagrees on the time of day that Jesus died.
- There were variations in the account of Jesus's baptism.
- Jesus cites a passage in *Matthew* 27: 3-10 as coming from Jeremiah but it actually comes from Zechariah.

Porphyry appears to have wanted to incorporate Christianity into the framework of the Roman world. He wrote: "There is one God whom all men worship, and Jesus, like other pious men worshipped this God and taught others to venerate him. By his teaching Jesus directed men's attention to the one God, but his disciples fell into error and taught men to worship Jesus." This next of his comments could be embraced today by many who consider themselves Christians: "Does the Christian faith rest on the preachings of Jesus or on the ideas forged by his disciples in the generations after his death?" One of Porphyry's most famous quotes sounds like it could have been uttered by Thomas Jefferson: "The Gods have proclaimed Christ to have been most pious, but the Christians are a confused and vicious sect."[1218]

Julian the Apostate, a nephew of Constantine and emperor from 361-363, wanted to return Rome to its pre-Christian religions. Julian held that his Christian Constantian relatives and predecessors were criminal and failed to practice the religion they preached.[1219] (He had a point: Constantine had executed one of his wives in a succession struggle.) Julian saw Judaism as an ally against the radical religion of Christianity. He even wrote an anti-Christian treatise, *Against the Galileans.*[1220] While preparing for war against Persia he offered to rebuild the Temple in Jerusalem. Both the military campaign and the Temple project were part of his anti-Christian strategy. The campaign was to give paganism great prestige much as his uncle Constantine had achieved for Christianity fifty years earlier. The rebuilding of the Temple was to expose Jesus as a false prophet because he had said that it would not be rebuilt until the end of time. But Julian's death in battle and an earthquake intervened and his projects never got off the ground.[1221]

In short, the intellectual attacks and persecutions slowed the growth of the Christian movement but did not stop it. In the end it came to dominate and then survive the Roman Empire. In the forty generations between the fall of Rome[1222]and the Age of Discovery, the church kept western civilization alive and helped it develop.[1223]

Debates over the nature of Christ

With Institutionalism, debates regarding the nature of Christ grew large and became a crisis in the fourth and fifth centuries.

Here is some background. First there, were interminable debates about the relationship of Christ to God.

Monarchians believed that God, Jesus, and the Holy Spirit were one and the same person. Trinitarians believed in one God but with three separate persons. Modalists who were sometimes called Sabellians after one of their leaders tried to affect a compromise and said that the Trinity represented three aspects of the same God and not three separate persons. Subordinationists believed that Jesus as "son" was inferior to God the father. Adoptionists believed Jesus was a human being whom God had later filled with the divine Logos.

Paul of Samosata[1224] was a third-century Adoptionist and bishop of Antioch. Antiochenes were committed to the humanity of Jesus and focused on the majesty of God. Paul of Samosata referred to Jesus simply as "the Nazarene," a human being like everyone else who came into his divine role. He noted *Luke* 2: 52 which held that as a boy, Jesus had *"kept increasing in wisdom and stature, and in favor with God and men."*

Arius of Alexandria (abt. 250 – 336) tried to balance Adoptionism and Modalism. He promoted the concept that Jesus was in some way created by God against the Trinitarian position of Athanasius, also of Alexandria and a younger contemporary of Arius. Arius, seeing Jesus as less than God, also pointed to scripture affirming Jesus's humanity, particularly *Luke* 2:52. Athanasius stood for what became the Nicene Creed of 325, that all three persons of the Trinity were fully equal.[1225] Athanasius considered monotheism a bedrock of Christianity (within a Trinitarian framework) stating: "The rule of more than one is the rule of none." He saw the balance in nature as an implication of one God and he thought that Arianism destroyed Christian monotheism by creating another god.[1226] Athanasius fought bitterly.[1227] This dispute rivaled the Protestant Reformation of a millennium later in its intensity and in its impact on the church.

Athanasius was banished from Alexandria five times. In exile he lived in Trier, Rome and with monks in the Egyptian desert.[1228] He had the nickname of "Athanasius against the world."[1229]

For the next half-century after the Council of Nicaea, Christians worked on improving the wording of the creed and began to talk about God in a Trinitarian manner. It was the work of intellectuals but followed avidly by the people. Gregory of Nyssa, made the famous quote which speaks of the theological fervor of that era in light-hearted tones saying that "the populace argued furiously about impenetrable issues, and even the baker, when you asked him for the price of bread, replied that in the Trinity the Father is greater than the Son." [1230]

The Council of Constantinople (381) affirmed the Nicene Creed and added a key section recognizing that the Holy Spirit "proceeds from the Father" (God). This is drawn from *John* 15:26 which quotes Jesus to his followers: *"When the Helper comes, whom I will send to you from the Father, that is the Spirit of truth who proceeds from the Father, He will testify about Me."* The important distinction within the creed was that Christ was "begotten of the Father." The arguments then shifted from the relationship of Christ to the Father to a second phase, the way in which Christ combined both human and divine nature.[1231] It was a grinding and sometimes violent conflict.

Here is how James Hitchcock puts it: "… the slow vanquishing of Arianism only settled one side of the christological controversy - whether Jesus was fully divine. In part, precisely because of her strong affirmation of His divinity, the Church then found herself wracked with conflict over the question of His humanity. Antioch and Alexandria continued to represent alternative Christologies, now centering on the nature of Jesus, with the former positing both human and divine natures, united but distinct, the latter a total union of the two in which the human nature was absorbed by the divine." [1232]

Here is some background on the "nature-of-Christ" debates:

In about 428 a cleric named Nestorius who had been born in present-day Turkey became patriarch of Constantinople. He tactlessly opposed the title "Bearer of God" as applied to Mary. He saw that nomenclature as a confusion of the divine and the human in Jesus Christ. Nestorius held that one may call Mary Bearer of Christ but not Bearer of God. There was a quick reaction. His opponents saw Nestorius as denying the principle, prevalent in Alexandria, of the unity of Jesus Christ. There was also political overtones as all the

Christian centers - Rome, Alexandria, Antioch, and Constantinople - were positioning themselves to gain advantage.[1233]

Various church councils ensued:

- Council of Ephesus - 431: The title for Mary as *Theotokos* or the Mother of God was affirmed and Nestorius excommunicated.[1234] But the Council also held that Christ had two natures.
- Second Council of Ephesus - 449: The Council held that Jesus was not fully human. There were riots. The views of Pope Leo I the Great were rejected leading the Pope to call it the "robber council."
- Council of Chalcedon - 451: Pope Leo I sent his "Tome" teaching that Jesus was one divine person with two natures.[1235]

The Council of Chalcedon asserted that Christ was fully God and fully human and it is a landmark council in church history. The Chalcedon formula on Christ was: "the same perfect in divinity and perfect in humanity, the same truly God and truly man, of a rational soul and a body; consubstantial with the Father as regards his divinity, and the same consubstantial with us as regards his humanity..." This view came to dominate the Catholic, Protestant and Eastern Orthodox churches ever since.[1236]

This triumph, however, effectively divided the followers of Jesus and created outcasts. Who were the non-Chalcedon Christians, the ones who were cut off from what became orthodoxy?

- Most Egyptian Christians refused to consent the decisions of Chalcedon and became the separate Coptic (Egyptian) church. They held that Christ had one nature which was divine; they were called Monophysites. It was the Monophysites with their base in Alexandria that most worried the emperors in Constantinople. The attempts to negotiate an acceptable Christological formula were complicated by the perspective of Rome. The Monophysite cause reached east and south and converted Ethiopia.[1237] These Copts thrived for centuries. Indeed because of them "it would be quite feasible to write an Egyptian-centered history of the first five or six hundred years of Christianity."[1238] The Ethiopian Copts persist until the present day.[1239]
- The Nestorians were strong in territories that we now know as Iran and Iraq. They came to be called the Church of the East.[1240] They held, along with the Nicene Creed, that Christ had two natures but also held that these two natures were not absolutely united in the

sense that the Chalcedon Christians believed. Hence, Mary was not the Mother of God. By the sixth century the Church of the East was well established and was a great missionary force, extending into China where centuries later it was observed by Marco Polo. Settlers and missionaries from the Church of the East also reached India and may have linked with a small group of Christians already there. They became known as "Thomas Christians" after the Apostle. These believers lived peacefully with neighbors for centuries. The Church of the East developed its own traditions. For example, it remembered the Biblical *Book of Jonah* in which the lead character tried to avoid going to the Assyrian city Nineveh.[1241] The Church had a bishop there completing his work. Recognizing Christ's two natures gave the Church of the East more of an optimistic outlook than the emphasis on sin preached in the West by Augustine. (If Jesus had a whole human nature, then human nature was by definition good.)[1242] However, from the Middle Ages forward, persecution from the Mongols and later from a predominantly Islamic society decimated the Church of the East. Its near-extermination was an incalculable loss to the world.[1243] In modern times remnants of it have been targeted in Iraq.[1244] In 1994 Pope John Paul II met with a patriarch of the Church of the East for the purpose of establishing ecumenical relations and bridging differences in how the two communions saw the person of Jesus Christ.[1245]

In many ways the Monophysites and the Nestorians were orthodox. Around 800 the great Nestorian patriarch Timothy who lived in the Mesopotamian city of Seleucia listed doctrines that were shared by the Nestorians, the Monophysites and the heirs of Chalcedon. These included: the Trinity, the Incarnation, baptism, adoration of the cross, the Eucharist, the two *Testaments*, the resurrection of the dead, eternal life, the return of Christ and the last judgment. However, the schisms continued. "Most of the discord arose out of debates surrounding linguistic misunderstandings in a doctrine that is highly complex and often difficult to follow."[1246]

The endless debates trying to solve the problems of the Trinity and the nature of Christ helped lead to the success of Islam whose message was straightforward. The Koran taught that "Unbelievers are those who say, 'God is one of three.' There is but one God."[1247] Christianity's doctrinal ambivalence was easily overcome by the new, monotheistic religion.[1248] Of the five great patriarchates of the Christian church - Alexandria, Jerusalem[1249], Antioch, Constantinople and Rome - the first three were taken by Islam in an eight year period in the 630s. Islam also took Damascus during that period. In 674 it took Tarsus. A couple of centuries later, the Christians burned Tarsus to the ground in retaliation for the Muslims sacking another *New Testament* city, Thessalonica. In the 900s, Constantinople re-took Antioch and Damascus.[1250] All of these wars were fought in the lands of the *New Testament*. From the time of Mohammed, much of the discord and the vulnerability to Islam was because of political differences within the empire. As Alexander Schmemann (1921-1983) asked, "Is it not tragic that one of the main reasons for the rejection of Orthodoxy by almost the whole non-Greek East was its hatred for the empire? .... This was the price the Church paid for the inner dichotomy (of the union of church and state) under Constantine."[1251]

In a triumph of process over substance, the issues associated with the Trinity even split the eastern and western sections of the Roman Empire.

Here is background to that split:

As noted, the Nicene creed was augmented at Constantinople in 381 to note that the Holy Spirit "proceeds from the Father." In the late 500s "*filioque,*" which means "and the son", was added by the Spanish church to bolster the Trinitarian position against the ruling Arian Visigoths. This custom spread throughout the West. "During Charlemagne's reign, when relations between the Franks and the Byzantines were tense, the *filioque* issue was the source - and also the excuse - of long controversies."[1252]

In 1054 Michael Cerularius the Patriarch of Constantinople wrote the Pope Leo IX addressing him as "brother." He objected to the Pope adding the word *filioque* to the Nicene Creed. The Eastern Church agreed with the concept but objected to the Pope's unilateral decision to change the Creed. It thought only a full council could make this decision. The papacy had taken hundreds of years to concur with the Spanish church but Cerularius still compared the Pope to Judas for this move. The crisis was exacerbated by a personality issue. An irascible, anti-eastern cardinal named Humbert acting as an ambassador to discuss a military alliance on behalf of Pope Leo IX was poorly treated in Constantinople. In response he placed a note excommunicating the patriarch of Constantinople on the altar of Hagia Sophia, the Church of Holy Wisdom. The patriarch excommunicated him in return. These excommunications of course widened the breach.

As the centuries rolled by after that, Constantinople's leaders continued to feel the pressure of Islam but they had trouble deciding who their enemies were – the Moslems or the Christian West. The issue of *filioque* remained sore point. Other sore points were the question of the primacy of Rome and the sacking of Constantinople in 1204 by the West.[1253] Intense negotiations occurred at various times. The two sides achieved unity at the Council of Lyon in 1274 and the Council of Ferrara-Florence in 1439. However, in both cases the agreements were debated at length later with the local authorities and not truly implemented. Constantinople fell to the Turks in 1453 and is now Istanbul.

After the fall of Constantinople the spiritual leadership of the Eastern Orthodox shifted to Moscow. At a synod in 1620 the Russian Orthodox declared that the Romans had undermined the Trinity by inserting the *filioque* in the Creed.

More centuries rolled by. In 1965 Pope Paul VI reached agreement with the leadership of the Eastern Orthodox church to cancel the excommunications of 1054. Subsequently, Pope John Paul II hosted the Eastern Orthodox patriarch and during an ecumenical Mass left out the word *filioque*. It attracted little controversy.[1254],[1255]

During these seemingly-interminable controversies, the Institutional church managed to produce two figures, one truly world-wide and it also produced the most lasting institution in world history.

The Apostle Peter

The Institutionalists helped promote the historical reputation of Peter to the point that by 391 when Emperor Flavius Theodosius mandated Christianity throughout the Roman Empire he asserted: "it is our will that all the peoples we rule shall practice that religion that Peter the Apostle transmitted to the Romans."[1256]

This was not inevitable. Peter is unique in the Gospels, both as a symbol and as a realistically-described individual.[1257] The *New Testament* is very hard on him. He is a hypocrite,[1258] a *"so-called pillar"*,[1259] perhaps a *"big-shot apostle"*,[1260] Satan,[1261] ineffectual at cutting off the servant's ear,[1262] a blocker of Jesus's mission,[1263] a mis-interpreter of the Transfiguration,[1264] a factional leader,[1265] and as traveling with his wife even though Jesus counseled leaving one's family.[1266]

Among the Twelve only Peter "stands out as often engaged in missionary journeys"[1267] but even here, the Pauline *New Testament* compares him poorly to Paul. In *Acts* he only gets as far as Samaria.[1268] According to Paul he gets to Antioch[1269] and possibly Corinth.[1270] Paul may have made an oblique dig at Peter in *I Corinthians* 10:4 ("*that Rock was Christ*") by redirecting Peter's nickname. (Peter's name in Greek meant Rock with Cephas the equivalent in Aramaic.)[1271] Moreover, it is strange to call Peter the Rock. That is a *New Testament* description of Jesus as in *Acts* 4:11 by Peter himself and in *I Peter* 4:5-8 Christians are called rocks. Pauline writing refers to Christ as a rock three times.[1272]

However, the emerging Pauline church in the centuries after Peter and Paul began to emphasize apostolic succession and government by bishops and this redounded to Peter's historical reputation. Two books of the *New Testament* are ascribed to him. Moreover, in an effort to exonerate him from the heresy suggested in *Galatians*, some Christians came to see him as an equivocator rather then a tool of James's emissaries and that view gets some support in Paul's description of the event. As noted, according to Paul, there were three parties at Antioch: Paul, the Judaizers and Peter. The Judaizers were heretics and Peter was "weak." The proper response to weakness is seen in the idea of tolerance toward a "*weaker brother*" found in *Romans* 14:1 - which had to deal with vegetarianism and keeping of the Sabbath. The Judaizers's insistence on circumcision, on the other hand, was more serious and amounted to heresy.[1273] This fits with a view of Peter as error-prone but directionally correct and he is saved in history.

The Blessed Virgin Mary

One of the unintended consequences of the lengthy Christological debate was the promotion of Mary. The logic of a more god-like Christ resulted in the elevation of Mary as the "Mother of God." In the second century Irenaeus thought of her as the second Eve and she came to be seen as a type of mediator. In the late twentieth century Pope John Paul II authorized a commission to study whether Mary is a co-redeemer of the human race.[1274]

To say that she is iconic is the greatest of understatements. She has fit into many cultures. The veneration of Mary is one of the many traditions that has roots in the churches based in Syria and Mesopotamia. Eastern churches had a reverence of Mary.[1275] In about 622 the Persians besieged Constantinople. During the siege the patriarch walked the walls holding an icon of the Virgin Mary. This was a relic believed to have been painted by Luke which had been brought to Constantinople in the 400s. It allegedly terrorized the barbarians assisting the Persians and the siege failed.[1276] By the 1600s it was believed that Mary had appeared in Mexico in the previous century. She was revealed in a vision left by rose petals to be an olive-skinned Mary known to history as the Virgin of Guadalupe. In the early 1900s, revolutionary armies fought under her banner. Octavio Paz wrote in 1974 that "the Mexican people, after more than two centuries of experiments, have faith only in the Virgin of Guadalupe and the National Lottery." Carlos Fuentes said, "...one may no longer consider himself a Christian, but you cannot truly be considered a Mexican unless you believe in the Virgin of Guadalupe." [1277] "Our Lady" is a term of affection and respect for Mary. According to the Catholic Church the patron saint of North America and Mexico is Our Lady of Guadalupe.[1278]

Our Lady of Lourdes is the patron saint of bodily injury. Traditional Catholics hold that in 1858 Mary appeared to a young girl. Mary was dressed in white and referred to herself as the "Immaculate Conception." On the Lourdes site spring waters causing cures emerged. Lourdes is now a popular pilgrimage site attracting four million people a year. In the 1800s, a statue commemorating the Virgin Mary was crafted by a Bolivian fisherman. Our Lady of Copacabana is the patron saint of that country. Our Lady of Charity is the patron saint of Cuba, "the Virgin of Caridad."

Our Lady of Grace is the patron saint of the Dominican Republic. The title is a reference to Gabriel's address to Mary in *Luke* 1:28 in which the angel tells Mary that she is "*highly favored*." Our Lady of Peace is the patron saint of El Salvador. (Mary was anointed "Queen of Peace" in El Salvador in 1966.)

In 1291 Mary's home in Nazareth was suddenly found in Loretto Italy. Our Lady of Loretto is the patron saint of homebuilders. In 1854, Pope Pius IX declared that the Blessed Virgin Mary was born without original sin, or was immaculately conceived, and lived a sin-free life.[1279] In 1950 Pope Pius XII surmised that since the Blessed Virgin Mary was born without original sin she was elevated (body and soul) to heaven upon her death. Our Lady of the Assumption is the patron saint of France.

Our Lady Help of Christians is the patron saint of New Zealand. In 1964, Pope Paul VI honored Mary as the protector of both Australia and New Zealand. Immaculate Conception is the patron saint of Portugal. She is also the patron saint of Brazil, Corsica, Tanzania and the United States. Our Lady of Europe is the patron saint of Gibraltar bestowed on Mary in 1979.

Our Lady of Sorrows is the patron saint of Slovakia. Mary's seven sorrows are as follows: 1) The arrest of Christ, 2) Christ being taken to Pontius Pilate for conviction, 3) Christ found guilty before Pilate and the Jewish people, 4) The crucifixion of Christ, 5) The death of Christ on the cross, 6) Christ being brought down from the cross, and 7) The burial of Christ.

Our Lady of Lujan is the patron saint of Uruguay, Paraguay and Argentina.[1280] Pope Pius V (1566-72), a reform Pope, attributed the victory in the Battle of Lepanto in 1571 over the Turks which ended Turkish dominance in the Mediterranean to the Blessed Virgin Mary. Pope Clement XI (1700-1721) made the feast of the Immaculate Conception in honor of the Blessed Virgin Mary obligatory throughout Christendom in 1708[1281] The Virgin Mary is said to have appeared in a village in Hebei Province to rescue Chinese Catholics during the Boxer Rebellion in 1900. There are annual festivities there honoring her which is a concern to the Chinese government.[1282]

Mary is also is also the patron saint of India, Malta[1283], and South Africa.

For Henry Adams (1838-1918), the grandson and great-grandson of American presidents and America's most important historian, the Virgin Mary was the force behind the Norman cathedrals of Europe to which he was drawn near the end of his life. He said, "Symbol or energy, the Virgin had acted as the greatest force the Western world ever felt, and had drawn man's activities to herself more strongly than any other power, natural or supernatural, had ever done...."[1284], [1285]

I have a final thought on the role of Mary and it is laden with speculation. How did she rise so far? Could her own effort have been a factor? Consider the *Gospel of Luke*. As noted, Luke wrote his Gospel from oral and written sources. He wrote in Greek but the quality of the Greek in most of the Gospel and his companion *Book of Acts* is not present in the first chapters of *Luke*. Those chapters include the longest descriptions of Mary in the *New Testament* and have such only-in-*Luke* accounts as:

- The Angel Gabriel's role. (*Luke* 1: 26-38)
- Elizabeth's role including the *Magnificat*. (*Luke* 1: 39-56)[1286]
- The Shepherds. (*Luke* 2: 8-20)
- The presentation in the Temple with Simeon's commentary. (*Luke* 2: 21-35)

This has led some to suggest that this first section of *Luke* is more of a translation of what would be the memoirs of Mary. Could it be? Again, this is speculation but if this scenario is accurate consider the deeply personal comments about both her baby and herself that she recalled from Simeon: *"He has been sent as a sign from God, but many will oppose him. As a result, the deepest thoughts of many hearts will be revealed. And a sword will pierce your very soul."* [1287] The woman (possibly) recalling this had lived through some difficulties. She had had to deal with Joseph's confusion over her pregnancy[1288] and conflicts years later when Jesus was viewed as insane.[1289] She was at the cross[1290] and in the Upper Room after the resurrection.[1291] Further, the woman (possibly) recalling this may have had a more realistic view of the future because at one point she said, "*from now on all generations will call me blessed.*"[1292] This is one of the few verses in the *New Testament* that seems to anticipate a long future. Both a long future and her honored role have proven true.[1293] Did Mary the Mother of Jesus write part of *Luke*? We'll never know but she seems to at least have been one of Luke's unnamed sources because he notes that she recalled and thought about key events, or "*treasured all these things.... in her heart.*"[1294]

The Papacy

Finally, the Institutionalists produced the most long-lasting structure in history: the papacy. What follows is a very brief summary of this structure.[1295]

Ignatius of Antioch listed the first three bishops of Rome after Peter:

- Linus 67-76
- Cletus 76-91
- Clement 91-100. [1296]

We can see possible glimmers of these popes in the pages of the *New Testament*.

Irenaeus identified Linus as the Linus of *II Timothy* 4:21 which reads: "*Make every effort to come before winter. Eubulus greets you, also Pudens and **Linus** and Claudia and all the brethren.*" (Emphasis added). Linus was probably from Tuscany and had been made a bishop by Paul.[1297] Cletus may have had the full name of Anacletus or Anencletus. The latter term is Greek for "blameless." It is noteworthy that *Titus* 1:7 required that leaders be blameless. Origen saw Clement as the Clement of *Philippians* 4:3 which reads: "*Indeed, true companion, I ask you also to help these women who have shared my struggle in the cause of the gospel, together with **Clement** also and the rest of my fellow workers, whose names are in the book of life.*" (Emphasis added). He may be the author of *I Clement* a letter addressed to the Corinthians in about 96 intervening into a church (still) experiencing dissension. He also reminded them of Paul's earlier letter. This letter was included in the canon by some.[1298]

The Catholic Church records a succession of 266 popes. The power of the popes often depended on circumstances and the demands of their followers.[1299] The popes dealt with real life problems including imperial policy, Christology, missions, forgiveness for apostates, Christians in distress, property, cemetery management, management continuity, reunion with

Eastern Church, clerical reform and even betting on papal elections.[1300] Also, they dealt with niceties. Pope John II (533-35) was the first pope to change his name. His birth name was Mercury, the name of a pagan god. (Paul - in *Acts* 14:12-16 - was once mistaken for Mercury.[1301]) Nearly a thousand years later, another Pope, Pius II (1458-64), showed no such concern and took his name from Virgil's[1302] "pious Aeneus." Pius was a writer and novelist. He wrote a refutation of the Koran to the Sultan with an appeal to convert and be baptized.

Here is a small sample of the more noteworthy popes: five from the first few centuries and three from the last century.

- Pope Stephen I (254-257). The "Monarchical episcopate," the oversight of a church by one individual rather than a group, began to emerge in Rome in the second century. Pope Stephen I was the first pope to claim Roman primacy based on *Matthew* 16:18 (*"Now I say to you that you are Peter (which means 'rock'), and upon this rock I will build my church, and all the powers of hell will not conquer it."*) As noted earlier, he did so in a controversy with Saint Cyprian over readmitting Christians in Africa who had lapsed during persecutions. Stephen was for readmissions.[1303]
- Pope Innocent I (401-417). Pope Innocent I has sometimes been called "the first Pope." He was "... a man of great ability and commanding character. At a time when the western empire was crumbling under barbarian invasions, he seized every opportunity of asserting the primacy of the Roman See, making more substantial claims for the papacy than his predecessors." Innocent was the son of a previous pope.[1304]
- Pope Leo I (440-461). Pope Leo I handled Christological issues and confronted Attila the Hun outside Rome in 452 persuading him to withdraw. In 455 he met with the Vandal Gaiseric persuading him not to burn Rome. He is one of two popes to be called "the Great" (The other is Gregory I - 590-604.)
- Pope Gelasius (492-96). The problems of the religious and the temporal orders emerged gradually. Pope Gelasius posed the view of two powers governing the world. One was the consecrated authority of the bishops centered in the Pope; the other was the emperor. Each was a trust from God. Each was sovereign and independent of the other. Spiritual authority was superior since it provided for salvation. "This teaching was to be used by canonists and others for centuries to come in their treatment of the problem of church and state." [1305]

- Pope Gregory I (590-604) is known his history as "Saint Gregory the Great." Here is Justo L. Gonzales: "The most remarkable figure among those who served as a bridge between antiquity and the Middle Ages is without any doubt Pope Gregory, who occupied the see of Rome from 590 to 604, to whom posterity has given the title of 'the Great,' and who is traditionally counted among the four great doctors of the church." (As noted: the other three are: Jerome, Ambrose and Augustine.) He is important to liturgy as seen in the Gregorian chant. He is important to canon law as his letters show the state of that law in his era. He is important to missions in that he launched missionary efforts to England.[1306] He is the patron saint of Popes.[1307] In his era, he helped the church fill a leadership vacuum in the West.[1308] Centuries later, the Protestant reformer John Calvin considered Gregory the last good Pope.[1309]

In modern times, these three Popes stand out:

- Pope Leo XIII (1878-1903) may be seen by future historians as the initiator of long-term reform in the church. In 1899 Leo issued an encyclical *Annum Sacrum* commanding the bishops of the church to consecrate the Sacred Heart of Jesus - "the image of the infinite love of Jesus Christ which moves us to love one another." George Weigel wrote: "The Sacred Heart devotion so cherished by Leo XIII was in one sense a populist answer to the ongoing problem that theology calls 'monophysitism' - the tendency to stress the divinity of Christ to the point that his humanity becomes a mere disguise."[1310] Leo XIII is also known for issuing the encyclical *Rerum Novarum* in 1891 which addressed rights for labor and social justice issues.
- Pope John XXIII (1958-63). The Council known as Vatican II climaxed this spirit of reform. Pope John XXIII died between the first and second sessions of Vatican II. The sessions went on between 1962 and 1965. Some conclusions:

A. The church is the people of God.
B. The people of God are a royal priesthood as in *I Peter* 2:10 which reads in part: "*...for you once were NOT A PEOPLE, but now you are THE PEOPLE OF GOD...*"
C. There is equal dignity for all as in *Galatians* 3:28 which reads: "*There is neither Jew nor Greek, there is neither slave nor free man, there is neither male nor female; for you are all one in Christ Jesus.*"
D. Scripture is emphasized over scholasticism.

    E.   Freedom of conscience is emphasized.

    F.   Baptized Protestants are of the Body of Christ. Jews were "the people of God." "Those also can attain to salvation who through no fault of their own do not know the gospel of Christ of his church."

Vatican II was noted for promoting the celebration of Mass in common language and the centrality of Christ which seemed to suggest the demotion of popular saints. It also opened up communications with other religions. Bible study was advocated.[1311]

Shortly before his death, Pope John XXIII issued the papal encyclical *Pacem in Terris* (*Peace on Earth*) which was the first encyclical that a Pope did not address to the Catholics only, but also to "all men of good will." It had these prescient thoughts:

    A.   Regarding women: "…the part that women are now playing in political life is everywhere evident. This is a development that is perhaps of swifter growth among Christian nations, but it is also happening extensively, if more slowly, among nations that are heirs to different traditions and imbued with a different culture. Women are gaining an increasing awareness of their natural dignity. Far from being content with a purely passive role or allowing themselves to be regarded as a kind of instrument, they are demanding both in domestic and in public life the rights and duties which belong to them as human persons."

    B.   Regarding racial discrimination: "Today, on the contrary the conviction is widespread that all men are equal in natural dignity; and so, on the doctrinal and theoretical level, at least, no form of approval is being given to racial discrimination."

    C.   Regarding war: "Consequently people are living in the grip of constant fear. They are afraid that at any moment the impending storm may break upon them with horrific violence. And they have good reasons for their fear, for there is certainly no lack of such weapons. While it is difficult to believe that anyone would dare to assume responsibility for initiating the appalling slaughter and destruction that war would bring in its wake, there is no denying that the conflagration could be started by some chance and unforeseen circumstance. Moreover, even though the monstrous power of modern weapons does indeed act as a deterrent, there is reason to fear that the very testing of nuclear devices for war purposes can, if continued, lead to serious danger for various forms of life on earth. Hence justice, right reason, and the recognition of man's dignity cry out insistently for a cessation to the arms race. The stock-piles of armaments which have been built up in various countries must be reduced all round and simultaneously by the parties concerned. Nuclear weapons must be banned."

• Pope John Paul II is cited many times in this book. He will be remembered as the first non-Italian Pope in centuries and for his world travel and humanitarian appeal. Like John XXIII he was canonized in 2014.

There are certain timeless themes of the papacy.

• The popes were often power players. After the seat of the empire moved east, "to some extent, the popes - the good ones, at least - would have no choice but to take on the role of emperor, certainly insofar as the protection of Italy was concerned." [1312] Pope Gelasius's declaration of two spheres was an astute balancing act between the distant emperor in Constantinople and Odoacer, the very-near Germanic king of Italy. Various popes dealt with Emperor Justinian (527-565) over politics and doctrine, often coming out on the losing end.[1313] The popes reached out to the Carolingians, climaxing in the crowning of Charlemagne as Holy Roman Emperor on Christmas in 800. (Napoleon attempted to ape this ceremony about a thousand years later.[1314]) Frederick II, emperor of the Holy Roman Empire, defied the popes and was in a state of excommunication at the time he took Jerusalem from the Muslims in 1228-29.[1315]

Pope Innocent XI (1676-89) contended with Louis XIV, the most powerful ruler of the era. French prelates in thrall of the government had asserted their nationalism in the Gallican Articles of 1682 which Innocent rejected. To influence him, Louis revoked the Edict of Nantes and began persecution of Protestant Huguenots. Innocent approved of the move but not the severity of the persecutions. Innocent refused to receive a French ambassador. He was the outstanding pope of the 1600s. The French government, however, held up his canonization in 1744 and it took more than two hundred years for Innocent to be beatified.[1316] Pope Pius VI (1775-1799) died a prisoner of the French radicals, deposed and within a Rome that had been declared a republic. But he left instructions for the holding of a conclave in emergency conditions. Pope Pius VII (1800-1823) was imprisoned by Napoleon but brought prestige to the papacy. He entertained the compatibility of Christianity and democracy. [1317],[1318] In 1867 the US Congress cut off ties to the papal state. As an initial step toward resuming them, some seventy years later, President Franklin Roosevelt (1882–1945) sent Catholic businessman (and father of a future president) Joseph Kennedy (1888-1969) to represent the US at Pope Pius XII's coronation. [1319]

- There have been, as with all human institutions, many imperfections. A fraudulent document, the "Donation of Constantine" from the eighth or ninth century supposedly gave Pope Sylvester (314-335) primacy over great ecclesiastical patriarchates and Rome. It was not exposed as a fake until the sixteenth century. (But before it was exposed, in 1493, the Donation of Constantine was cited by Pope Alexander VI when he divided the Americas between Portugal and Spain. The modern effect is that Portuguese is spoken in Brazil and Spanish in the rest of South America.)

In the first thousand or so years of the papacy, violence often attended papal selection. Militias, mobs, irregulars and imperial armies were frequent factors during times of papal transitions.[1320] During a famine in Rome, Sabinian (604-606) kept tight control on the papal granaries and was accused of profiteering. This made him so unpopular that his funeral procession was detoured to avoid mobs. Pope John VIII (872-882) was the first pope to be assassinated. He was poisoned and clubbed by members of his own entourage. Pope Hadrian III (884-885) blinded an official who had opposed a previous pope and whom a subsequent pope had allowed to return from exile. In one of the most macabre episodes, Pope Formosus (891-96) had once been excommunicated before ascending to the papacy. Nine months after his death, a successor, Pope Stephen VI (896-97) had his body exhumed, dressed in papal vestments and set upon a throne. A mock trial occurred. He was found guilty of perjury and coveting the papacy. His acts and ordinations were voided. The three fingers of his right hand which he had used to swear and bless were hacked off. His body was thrown in the Tiber although a hermit retrieved and reinterred it. However, under Stephen there were reports of miracles worked by the corpse of Formosus and people took the collapse of the Lateran basilica as a divine sign. Stephen was deposed, thrown in jail and strangled.

In the next few months there were two short-reigning popes. Theodore II served twenty days in 897 before dying but in that time he annulled the after-death trial of Formosus and arranged a proper burial. When imperial protection lapsed, Rome fell to party strife. Pope Leo V (903-4) was thrown in jail by a usurper Christopher (903-4). The latter was deposed by Sergius III (904-911) who marched on Rome. He threw Christopher in jail and in 904 had Christopher and Leo V murdered. He restored the "cadaver synod" and had many ordinations therefore voided, causing great confusion.

Centuries later, the rivalry between Pope Urban VI (1378-89) and anti-Pope Clement VII (1378-1394) opened up the Great Schism (1378-1417). The two had troops and fought on the battlefield. They excommunicated each other and sought diplomatic support. At one point during this era there were three competing popes and the first post-schism Pope, Martin (1417-1431), also used troops in battle. Even after the schism, rival popes emerged. One, Antipope Felix V (1439-49), negotiated his abdication and became a cardinal bishop with a pension. A later Pope, Sixtus V (1585-90), ordered the public executions of thousands of brigands plaguing the papal estates.

- There have been doctrinal issues. Pope Marcellinus (296-304) apparently apostatized during a time of persecution and gave up copies of scripture. At least two popes are regarded by most scholars to have erred theologically. Pope Liberius (352-366) refused imperial orders to condemn Athanasius which would have supported the Arian position. After two years of exile he either signed some compromise document that was disfavored by Athanasius or was set up to look like he did. Pope Honorius I (625-638) dealt with the issues of Monophysitism. He got entangled by answering a letter from Sergius the Patriarch of Constantinople in which he quoted the Council of Chalcedon of 451 which affirmed the two natures but he used the term "one-will" of Christ. This caused controversy. Honorius was condemned by the Council of Constantinople in 680-1, an action that was upheld by Pope Leo II. Honorious's intent has been debated. He may have been trying to reach out to the Monophysites and bring reconciliation. More than a thousand years later his example was used by those who opposed papal infallibility.[1321]

For all of its human imperfections, the papacy has been a constant within Christianity and it brought institutionalism to the Catholic Church. The Church in turn defined life and even afterlife for Europeans and others for centuries. As Cyprian said in about 250 AD: "He cannot have God for his father who does not have the church for his mother." As Augustine said in the fourth century: "There is no salvation outside the church." [1322]

Finally, there is other possible *New Testament* church to identify, a type of subset of the Institutionalists.

In Chapter 4 I mentioned a "between the lines" reading of the *Gospel of John* and I also offered thoughts on the *"disciple whom Jesus loved"* who is mentioned only in *John*.

At this point, I will return to these concepts to discuss a final variety of *New Testament* Christians, the Johannine community which in all likelihood eventually merged into the Institutional Church. This analysis draws from Raymond Brown. Brown attempted to trace the development of the Johannine community over a one hundred year period. A thorough scholar, he gave his reassembling of this group's history no more than "probability."[1323]

At the outset, it is critical to understand Brown's view toward the *Gospel of John*. Brown reads *John* at two levels: describing the life of Jesus and also as a metaphor describing the growth of the Christian movement.

He saw the growth of the Christian movement in these stages:

- *John* 1:35-51 – This was the period that Jews came to Christ and accepted him as the Messiah. Andrew and another disciple – both from the camp of John the Baptist - joined Jesus. Shortly later, Peter, Philip and Nathanial joined. Andrew called Jesus the Messiah. Eventually Johannine Christianity went its own way and this is portrayed symbolically as Jesus tells Nathanial in verse 51 of the first chapter: *Truly, truly, I say to you, you will see the heavens opened and the angels of God ascending and descending on the Son of Man."*
- *John* 4 – This is the period that Samaritans came to Christ. In this chapter, Jesus – and not his Jewish followers who don't come onto the scene until verse 27– converts a Samaritan village. What do we know about the relationship between Jesus's followers and the Samaritans? First, we know that there was some hostility. In *Matthew* 10:5 Jesus prohibits his followers from entering a Samaritan village. In *Luke* 9:52-55 Samaritans are hostile. Finally, we know that it took some years after the resurrection of Jesus for someone, a deacon, also named Philip, to bring Christianity to Samaria according to *Acts* 8:1-25. As noted, this Philip was a Hellenistic Jew who opposed Temple worship. Relying on a metaphorical reading of *John*, Brown concludes that the Johannine community came to include Samaritans and Jews

who opposed Temple worship. (In *John* 8:48 the Jews suggest that Jesus is a Samaritan.)

- *John* 12 –This is the period that Gentiles came to Christ. Verse 20-23 read: *"Now there were **some Greeks** among those who were going up to worship at the feast; these then came to Philip, who was from Bethsaida of Galilee, and began to ask him, saying, 'Sir, we wish to see Jesus.' Philip came and told Andrew; Andrew and Philip came and told Jesus. And Jesus answered them, saying, 'The hour has come for the Son of Man to be glorified.'"* (Emphasis added). This shows the expansion of the Johannines into the wider world.

There is a continual thread through *John* that shows that Peter and the Twelve are not representative of all the Christians. The thread is the contrast between Peter and the *"disciple whom Jesus loved."* There are several sections of *John* in which the two are compared and contrasted.

- *John* 13:23-26 – The *"disciple whom Jesus loved"* is so close to Jesus that he can literally rest on his chest but Peter is separate enough that he has to convey his question through this disciple.
- *John* 18:15-16 - The *"disciple whom Jesus loved"* went into the high priest's palace, but Peter needs his help to go there.
- *John* 19:26-27 - The *"disciple whom Jesus loved"* is at the cross. Peter is not.
- *John* 28:2-10 - The *"disciple whom Jesus loved"* runs faster than Peter to get to the Empty Tomb and only he believes on the basis of what he sees there.
- *John* 21:7 - The *"disciple whom Jesus loved"* recognizes Jesus standing on the shore and informs Peter who it is.
- *John* 21:20-23 – After Peter asks about the fate of the *"disciple whom Jesus loved,"* Jesus brushes him off in verse 22: *"If I want him to remain until I come, what is that to you?"*

From Brown's reading of *John*, we can glean at least three areas which distinguished the Johannine community.

First, the Johannines differed from the early Institutionalists in that they had a higher Christology. The prologue of *John* (*John* 1:1-18) speaks of Jesus's equality with God and *John* 5:18 reads: *"For this reason therefore the Jews were seeking all the more to kill Him, because He not only was breaking the Sabbath, but also was calling God His own Father, making Himself equal with God."* This concept is not claimed in the Synoptics and Peter talked of Jesus as a **man** attested to by God (*Acts* 2:22). (Emphasis added).

As seen in *Acts* 5:33-42 the Jewish authorities tolerated fellow Jews who held that Jesus was the Messiah returned from death. But the Jewish authorities could not tolerate a group making Jesus out be God. Their differences with the Johannines were furthered as the Johannines became a haven for Anti-Temple Jews in the mold of Stephen and other Hellenists.

Second, whereas the Institutionalist Christians created a hierarchy, the Johannine Christians saw more of a role for the Holy Spirit. *Matthew* and *Luke/Acts* show the importance of continuity with the Twelve. The Twelve are referred to even as they move off the scene. *John* makes the "*disciple whom Jesus loved*" the continuity. *John* 19:35 notes that "*he who has seen has testified, and his testimony is true; and he knows that he is telling the truth, so that you also may believe.*" *John* 21:24 notes "*This is the disciple who is testifying to these things and wrote these things, and we know that his testimony is true.*" As noted in Chapter 4, the Twelve are mentioned sparingly in *John* and are not named in any list. They are within a larger group that stays with Jesus in John 6 and later, in *John* 20, Thomas is listed as one of the Twelve.

The Twelve, and through them what I have called the Institutionalists, were considered by the Johannines to be Christians – or followers of Jesus. Jesus tells Peter, the recognized leader of the Twelve, to guide the Christians three times in *John* 21: 15-17. But he was not the "*disciple whom Jesus loved*" the most. The leader of the Johannines was. The Johannines and the Institutionalists were, what we might call today, denominations.

By the 60s leadership transitions in the Christian movement were underway. James the brother of Jesus, Paul and Peter were all martyred.[1324] The "*disciple whom Jesus loved*" was probably dead or his death was anticipated. *John* 21: 20-23 shows this disciple's death in a clumsy way:

"*Peter, turning around, saw the disciple whom Jesus loved following them; the one who also had leaned back on His bosom at the supper and said, 'Lord, who is the one who betrays You?' So Peter seeing him said to Jesus, 'Lord, and what about this man?' Jesus said to him, 'If I want him to remain until I come, what is that to you? You follow Me!' Therefore this saying went out among the brethren that that disciple would not die; **yet Jesus did not say to him that he would not die**, but only, "If I want him to remain until I come, what is that to you?*"* (Emphasis added)

In the Institutional churches, the continuity was achieved by an emphasis on clinging to the original teachings. As noted, Paul is recorded in *Acts* 20: 28-30 telling leaders at Ephesus: "*Be on guard for yourselves and for all the flock, among which the Holy Spirit has made you overseers, to shepherd the church of God which He purchased with His own blood. I know that after my departure savage wolves will come in among you, not sparing the flock; and from among your own selves men will arise, speaking perverse things, to draw away the disciples after them."* In *Titus 1:9*, "Paul" says that church leaders should be "*holding fast the faithful word which is in accordance with the teaching, so that he will be able both to exhort in sound doctrine and to refute those who contradict."*

But *John* prescribes a different way of filling the gap caused by natural death. It stressed that the Holy Spirit will guide the Johannines because it will stay forever with those who love Jesus and keep his commandments. As he was preparing to leave, Jesus told his followers as recorded in *John* 14:16-17: "*I will ask the Father, and He will give you another Helper, that He may be with you forever; that is the Spirit of truth, whom the world cannot receive, because it does not see Him or know Him, but you know Him because He abides with you and will be in you."* A short time later he told that same group: "*...the Helper, the Holy Spirit, whom the Father will send in My name, He will teach you all things, and bring to your remembrance all that I said to you."* (*John* 14:26). Still later: "*...when He, the Spirit of truth, comes, He will guide you into all the truth; for He will not speak on His own initiative, but whatever He hears, He will speak; and He will disclose to you what is to come."* (*John* 16:13).

This is a caution against institutionalism.

Third, the *Gospel of John* differs from the Synoptic Gospels and hence most of the other churches on its emphasis of the role of women.

Here are some examples from *John*

Martha - *John* 11:27 notes that Martha answers a question from Jesus as follows: "*You are the Christ, the Son of God."* This declaration is reserved for Peter in the Synoptics who answers a question from Jesus as follows:

* *Matthew 16:16: "Simon Peter answered, 'You are the Christ, the Son of the living God.'"*
* *Mark 8:29: "Peter answered and said to Him, 'You are the Christ.'"*
* *Luke 9:20 – "And Peter answered and said, 'The Christ of God.'"*

Mary Magdalene - *John* 20:17-18 records that risen Jesus first appeared to Mary Magdalene even though Peter had been nearby. She is instructed by Jesus to tell people that he was alive and she tells them: "*I have seen The Lord."* There are two points here. First, Mary Magdalene's viewing of the risen Christ seems to meet the *New Testament* requirements to be an apostle.

In *I Corinthians* 9:1, Paul wrote, *"Am I not free? Am I not an apostle?* **Have I not seen Jesus our Lord?**" In *I Corinthians* 15:8-9 Paul wrote, *"and last of all, as to one untimely born,* **He appeared to me also**. *For I am the least of the apostles,…"* (Emphases added). Second, part of Peter's claim to preeminence among the early Christians was that he was thought to be the first to see the risen Christ. Paul and Luke strongly suggest this. In *I Corinthians* 15:5 Paul lists Peter before others as a witnesses to the resurrection. Luke writes in *Luke* 24:34 that the remaining eleven disciples announce that *"The Lord has really risen and has appeared to Simon."* But *John* revises this tradition about Peter by giving first place to Mary Magdalene. (*Matthew* 28: 1-10 indicates that Mary Magdalene and "the other Mary" were the first to see the risen Jesus but there is no direct contrast with Peter.)

The Woman at the Well - *John* 4:39 notes that the Samaritan villagers believed in Christ because of this woman's word: *"From that city many of the Samaritans believed in Him* **because of the word of the woman**…" (Emphasis added). Much later, Jesus anticipates others who will believe through human preaching. In *John* 17:20 he prays at the Last Supper for his followers but also for those who will believe through his disciples's word: *"I do not ask on behalf of these alone, but for those* **also who believe in Me through their word**;" (Emphasis added). John, then, records that both a woman and Jesus's male disciples preached about him.

Mary the Mother of Jesus - Mary the Mother of Jesus appears in *John* only twice, at the first miracle in chapter 2 and at the foot of the cross in chapter 19. She is not named in either passage. As to chapter 2, there is a theory that John drew the story of the Cana miracle from a pre -ministry phase of Jesus's life when he was living with his family. This tradition was captured in the second century apocryphal gospels and possibly[1325] in *Luke* 2:41-50 in which the twelve year-old Jesus amazes teachers in the Temple in Jerusalem. In this tradition Jesus spoke of his mission and did miracles. At Cana his mother expects him to do a miracle to help her friends and he does so. This miracle would be curious on at least two levels. First, it is rather petty. (His mother's friends had run out of wine.) Second, it might at first be inconsistent with a *New Testament* tradition of Jesus not privileging his own earthly family.[1326]

Let's focus on that second level.

The writer of *John* honors the distancing-from-the-family tradition by adding verse 4 to the account in *John* 2. In response to his mother's request to solve this problem Jesus said to her: *"Woman, what does that have to do with us? My hour has not yet come."* The author of *John*, then, reports that Jesus fulfilled his mother's request but by the insertion of verse 4 kept him aligned with the general distancing from his own family.

But let's examine another side to the distancing-from-the-family tradition by redacting an incident reported in the Synoptics and then referring to two other sections of *John*.

First, the Synoptics:

Mark 3:31-35: "Then His mother and His brothers arrived, and standing outside they sent word to Him and called Him. A crowd was sitting around Him, and they said to Him, 'Behold, Your mother and Your brothers are outside looking for You.' Answering them, He said, 'Who are My mother and My brothers?' Looking about at those who were sitting around Him, He said, 'Behold My mother and My brothers! For whoever does the will of God, he is My brother and sister and mother.'" (Emphasis added).

Matthew 12: 46-50: "While He was still speaking to the crowds, behold, His mother and brothers were standing outside, seeking to speak to Him. Someone said to Him, 'Behold, Your mother and Your brothers are standing outside seeking to speak to You.' But Jesus answered the one who was telling Him and said, 'Who is My mother and who are My brothers?' And stretching out His hand toward His disciples, He said, 'Behold My mother and My brothers! For whoever does the will of My Father who is in heaven, he is My brother and sister and mother.'" (Emphasis added).

Luke 8:19-21: "And His mother and brothers came to Him, and they were unable to get to Him because of the crowd. And it was reported to Him, 'Your mother and Your brothers are standing outside, wishing to see You.' But He answered and said to them, 'My mother and My brothers are these who hear the word of God and do it.'"

Of note, the emphasized comment was redacted by Luke. Whereas Mark and Matthew seem to exclude the family from the group of followers, Luke includes them —or at the very least, does not exclude them. Luke saw a role for Jesus's earthly family and particularly Mary in Jesus's true family which is made up of whoever "*does the will of God*" (*Mark*), "*does the will of My Father who is in heaven*" (*Matthew*) or *hear(s) the word of God and do(es) it* (*Luke*). If there are doubts about Luke's intentions, they should be resolved in *Acts 1:14* which, as we have noted, lists "*Mary the mother of Jesus, and with His brothers*" in the Upper Room.

John adheres to this Lukan tradition about Mary. He finds a role for her even if, as Jesus said at Cana, *"My hour has not yet come."* That time did come a few years later as noted in *John* 13:1: "…*"Now before the Feast of the Passover, Jesus knowing that His hour had come that He would depart out of this world to the Father,…"* A day or so later, Mary the Mother of Jesus was at the foot of the cross standing next to the *"disciple whom Jesus loved."*

Here are the words of *John* 19:25-26: *"But standing by the cross of Jesus were His mother, and His mother's sister, Mary the wife of Clopas, and Mary Magdalene. When Jesus then saw His mother, and the disciple whom He loved standing nearby, He said to His mother, 'Woman, behold, your son!' Then He said to the disciple, 'Behold, your mother!' From that hour the disciple took her into his own household."*

Some observations:

- Mary the Mother of Jesus is not mentioned by name in *John*. Like the *"disciple whom Jesus loved"* she is important here as a symbol of a disciple.
- At the cross, she is placed on an equal footing with the *"disciple whom Jesus loved."*

To summarize this section, the Johannines honored a tradition of women preachers like the Samaritan Woman at the Well. If other Christian groups saw Peter as the one who first recognized whom Jesus was and who first saw him risen from the dead, the Johannines linked these traditions with two women: Martha and Mary Magdalene. The Johannines recalled that Jesus saw a man and a woman – whom John does not even name - as models for a new community. If the institutionalists went for a hierarchy in the early decades after Jesus, the Johannines relied on the *"disciple whom Jesus loved"* and after him on the Holy Spirit.

What happened to the Johannines as time went on? It appears that in the second generation after Christ, the Johannine churches struggled with both Christology and church leadership. These issues were the occasion of the epistles *of I, II* and *III John.*

I John deals with people who had left the Johannine community. *I John* 2:19 reads *"They went out from us, but they were not really of us; for if they had been of us, they would have remained with us; but they went out, so that it would be shown that they all are not of us."* These Secessionists may have been the majority and were getting a great deal of attention in the wider society. *I John* 4:5 says of them: *"They are from the world; therefore they speak as from the world, and the world listens to them."* Both the Secessionists and those represented by the writer of the epistles[1327] probably knew the Fourth Gospel. The difference was in how they were interpreting it.

Here are two examples.

<u>Christology</u>: The Secessionists' views of Christ may have lowered his human nature in favor of his divine nature. *I John* 4:2-3 may reflect this. It reads as a warning and a condemnation: *"By this you know the Spirit of God: every spirit that confesses that Jesus Christ has come in the flesh is from God; and every spirit that does not confess Jesus is not from God; this is the spirit of the antichrist, of which you have heard that it is coming, and now it is already in the world."* The Secessionists's view may have been a plausible interpretation of *John* 1:14 and 2:11 both of which speak of Jesus having the glory of God.[1328] This is admittedly a difficult concept to understand. The Synoptics talk of the glory of God primarily at the Transfiguration and even then the leading disciples are confused. As we seen, the human and divine nature of Jesus Christ was debated by Christians for centuries. In essence, in the Johannine community, the epistles were a corrective to a misinterpretation of the Gospel by the Secessionists and drove home the humanity of Jesus.

<u>Church leadership</u>. The Secessionists and the writer of *I John* may also have been divided over authority structures. We have seen that verses like *John* 14:16, 14:26 and 16:7 speak of the guidance by the Holy Spirit. They can be read to disfavor human leadership, especially after the death of the *"disciple whom Jesus loved."*[1329] *I John* does not dwell much on the Holy Spirit other than these instances:

- To show how convictions that the Spirit is providing real guidance can be tested against the doctrine of the humanity of Jesus: *I John* 3:24-4:6 reads: *"We know by this that He abides in us, by the Spirit whom He has given us. Beloved, do not believe every spirit, but test the spirits to see whether they are from God, because many false prophets have gone out into the world. By this you know the Spirit of God: **every spirit that confesses that Jesus Christ has come in the flesh is from God;** and every spirit that does not confess Jesus is not from God; this is the spirit of the antichrist, of which you have heard that it is coming, and now it is already in the world. You are from God, little children, and have overcome them; because greater is He who is in you than he who is in the world. They are from the world; therefore they speak as from the world, and the world listens to them. We are from God; he who knows*

God listens to us; he who is not from God does not listen to us. By this we know the spirit of truth and the spirit of error." (Emphasis added).

- To tie the Holy Spirit to the historical occurrences, that Jesus was baptized and later died. *I John* 5: 5-6 reads *"Who is the one who overcomes the world, but he who believes that Jesus is the Son of God? **This is the One who came by water and blood,** Jesus Christ; not with the water only, but with the water and with the blood. It is the Spirit who testifies, because the Spirit is the truth."* (Emphasis added).

In *II* and *III John* we may see the emergence of a leadership structure. *II John* is addressed to a "chosen lady" who may be a church leader.[1330] *III John* is addressed to another church leader named Gaius and in it there is a warning about another church leader named Diotrephes. This last church leader may not have been a Secessionist since his main drawback seems to be not doctrinal but merely barring traveling missionaries. One can empathize: with the Secessionists about and getting a big following, Diotrephes may have decided to hunker down and admit no outsiders to his group.[1331]

This recognition of a new crop of leaders is a caution against over-reliance on interpretations of the Spirit.

In a generation, then, it is likely that a leadership structure symbolized by the author of the epistles plus Gaius plus (possibly) Diotrephes and plus (possibly) the "chosen lady" took root. It is highly likely that the minority of the Johannine movement, the non-Secessionists, merged with the Institutional Church. They brought with them the *Gospel of John* and the three epistles which help with the interpretation. Indeed, it is quite probable that a stronger statement can be made, that the epistles with their anti-heretical tone helped the Institutionalists accept the *Gospel of John* as an inspired book, eligible for the canon.[1332]

To summarize Christianity's debt to the Institutionalists: "...(W)hatever Christianity was at its beginning, in the course of time it became the church of popes and cardinals, of prime ministers and kings, of priests blessing cannons in battle, of crusades and wars of religion, the paintings of Giotto, the sculpture and architecture of Bernanini, and the music of Bach. The tiny house churches of the first years of Christianity did become the institutions we today know as the Episcopal, Methodist, Roman Catholic, and Orthodox Christian churches." [1333]The establishment by Constantine is evidence of the convictions of early Christians of the family of humans under God. Their belief in the unity of humans gave us a western civilization shaped by Christian ideals for 1500 years. [1334]

In conclusion to this chapter, the Institutionalists along with the overlapping categories of the Johannines, the Pietists, the New Deal Christians and the Red-Letter Christians represent a sample of the variety of *New Testament* Christians. Their existence in the pages of the *New Testament* along with the different Christians represented by Paul, the Pillars, the Q people, the Thomas people, the Way, the Saints, the Christians, Apollos and John the Baptist all attest that there is more than one Biblical way to be a Christian.

In the next chapter, we will look at two of the more serious errors committed by the different varieties of Christians.

CHAPTER 9

The Second Coming and
The Kingdom of God

Having made a case that the New Testament recognizes different types of Christians, we move toward recommending one variety. However, in this chapter we issue two warnings. A practical, portable Christianity for the twenty-first century will avoid extremes around two concepts: The Second Coming of Christ and the kingdom of Heaven. The first is a conceit mostly on the political right, the second mostly on the political left.

French Statesman Charles De Gaulle (1890 – 1970) said he was a Christian "by reason of history and geography."[1335] But what exactly is a Christian or what is essential to being one? In the final three chapters of this book we move toward promotion within the diversities of Christianity of one variant which we will label monotheistic Christianity. Chapter 9 begins this process by dealing with two interrelated errors to avoid. Both are as harmful to the Christian faith as the error of inerrancy discussed in Chapter 2 of this book. These two errors are closely interrelated. The common denominator is an anticipation of a utopian society far different than the one in which we now live. The right sees this primarily in terms of the Second Coming of Jesus Christ. The left sees it primarily as the building of the kingdom of God.[1336] Both see the utter transformation of society.

Chapter 9 deals with these errors. Chapter 10 revisits the role of the Apostle Paul in a new context. Chapter 11 recommends monotheistic Christianity.

The Second Coming of Jesus Christ

The early Christians thought that Jesus would return soon. Paul seemed to contemplate a return while some of the Thessalonians to whom he wrote were still alive.[1337] Mark records a parable of Jesus's return which concludes with the words: *"I say to you what I say to everyone: Watch for him!"*[1338] The first Christians tended to celebrate Easter every Sunday.[1339]

But over time cooler heads had to account for a postponement and in later centuries Christians developed a different understanding.[1340] Indeed, from our vantage point, nearly two thousand years later, the importance of the early Second Coming lies in the fact that it didn't happen.[1341]

But the idea of end times has always been part of the Christian religion and particularly so in the US. Millennialism had been seen as heretical in Europe or at least associated with heresies and was driven by persecution to America where it was tolerated. The founders of Massachusetts saw their territory as a refuge for those that God was going to save. Increase Mather (1639 – 1723) saw a comet in 1680 as a sign of the end. Over centuries, groups like the Shakers, the Adventists, the Mormons and others saw a Second Coming or an end to history.[1342]

Fawn Brodie observed, "In no other period in American history were 'the last days' felt to be so imminent as in that between 1820 and 1845."[1343] William Miller (1782 - 1849) used the *Old Testament's Daniel* and the *New Testament's Revelation* to predict the end of the world between March 21 1843 and March 21 1844. Then it was adjusted to October 22, 1844. Historians have called that date the Great Disappointment. Miller's followers had left jobs and businesses and confessed to unsolved crimes. Afterwards, some filed lawsuits to reclaim property they had given away. Millerism eventually evolved into the Seventh Day Adventist movement, a well-respected church stressing health and wellness in the twenty-first century.[1344]

Some of the end times obsession abated after William Miller. In the fifty years following the Civil War, most Americans who thought about the end saw it as a time of greater human perfection toward which society was gradually progressing. They could dismiss the date-setting of the Millerites as marginal.[1345] Most Protestant theologians by 1900 believed that Christ would come again after a thousand year period called the Millennium which they inferred from *Revelation* 20:1-3: *"Then I saw an angel coming down from heaven with the key to the bottomless pit and a heavy chain in his hand. He seized the dragon*[1346]—*that old serpent, who is the devil, Satan—and bound him in chains for a thousand years. The angel threw him into the bottomless pit, which he then shut and locked so Satan could not deceive the nations anymore until the thousand years were finished. Afterward he must be released for a little while."*

This was a positive view because it assumed that Christians would continue throughout history to work to improve society and convert people to Christianity. However, some Christian thinkers in the late 1800s began to tack back toward the Miller model. Christ was to come before the thousand-year period. This was a more negative view of history in which Christ would take the believers away from Earth, warfare would become worldwide, centered in the Middle East and a figure known as the Anti-Christ would emerge to take political control. A final battle called Armageddon would take place.

This is when the concept of the Rapture took root among evangelical Christians. The Rapture is a belief that Christians who are alive at a time when Jesus comes again will rise up into the atmosphere to meet him. It derives, primarily, from the sixteenth and seventeenth verses in the fourth chapter of *I Thessalonians*: *"For the Lord Himself will descend from heaven with a shout, with the voice of the archangel and with the trumpet of God, and the dead in Christ will rise first. Then we who are alive and remain will be caught up together with them in the clouds to meet the Lord in the air, and so we shall always be with the Lord."* In addition to these verses written by Paul, a section relied on by those who believe in the Rapture is *Matthew* 24:40-41 in which Jesus says, *"Then there will be two men in the field; one will be taken and one will be left. Two women will be grinding at the mill; one will be taken and one will be left."*

The notion of Rapture was apparently first promoted by British evangelical John Nelson Darby (1800- 1882) in the mid 1800s. Darby probably even coined the term.[1347] The Scofield Reference Bible published in 1909 popularized Darby's system. In the 1930s, prophecy novels emerged at the level of popular literature. A 1937 novel called *Be Thou Prepared, For Jesus is Coming* showed how the Rapture affected a fictionalized American town. It showed unbelievers wondering about the disappearance of Christians and noted sadly that "many pets were found dead, shut in the houses of departing saints." It had other vignettes.[1348]

In the late twentieth century, the Rapture became very popular. The American evangelist Hal Lindsey (1929 -) promoted it with his book, *The Late Great Planet Earth*[1349] which according to the *New York Times* was the best-selling nonfiction book of the 1970s.[1350] Lindsey acknowledged John Nelson Darby.[1351] Further, he claimed that he followed the "literal meaning" of scripture. What were Lindsey's central teachings? In view of his great popularity with evangelical Christians in the last third of the twentieth century, we will take some time with them.

In general, Lindsey taught that in the future there would be a seven-year period concluding by the return of Jesus Christ.[1352] He stated that this would be a terrible time with mankind on the verge of destruction.[1353] But Christ will come again "to put an end to the war of wars called Armageddon." He was very specific about the events that he thought would lead up to this.

First, he was very clear about the modern nation of Israel's significance. Three interrelated events would take place. The Jewish nation would be reborn in the land of Palestine.[1354] This was accomplished in 1948. The Jews would repossess Old Jerusalem and the sacred sites.[1355] This was accomplished in the Six-Day war of 1967. The Jewish nation would rebuild the ancient Temple upon its historic site.[1356] This has not been accomplished yet although, as noted, Julian the Apostate attempted it more than 1600 years ago.

Second, Lindsey saw a role for Russia or, when he wrote, the Soviet Union. According to him, Russia was "Gog" of *Ezekiel* 38. From that chapter he analyzed the words "Rosh" which he tied to Russia and "Meshech" which he then tied to Moscow.[1357] He asserted that Israel's enemy will come from the north.[1358]

Third, from the seventh chapter of *Daniel* and other parts of the *Bible*, Lindsey predicted the rise of a European political entity centered in Rome. This political entity would be a ten-nation confederacy. It was important to Lindsey that this alignment would have ten member countries because of his take on a "beast" described in *Daniel* that had ten horns.[1359] He talked of how Charlemagne[1360], Napoleon and Hitler tried to revive the Roman empire but did not have a ten-nation confederacy. Lindsey wrote, "We believe the Common Market and the trend toward unification of Europe may well be the beginning of the ten-nation confederacy predicted by *Daniel* and the *Book of Revelation*." He asserted that these factors were driving European unification:

- Fear of communism.
- The economic threat of the US.
- Concern that the US would not help against Communism.
- The waning of US military power with the US in some way becoming a part of the new European polity.
- The great potential of a united Europe.[1361]

Fourth, Lindsey saw this revived Roman Empire led by a figure called the Anti-Christ, assisted by Satan and a false prophet. Lindsey wrote that at a time of crisis the Anti-Christ would emerge.[1362] In *Revelation* 13, Lindsey saw a man who will recover from a mortal wound taking power.[1363] *Revelation* 13 also mentions a dragon who according to *Revelation* 12:9 is Satan.[1364] (An historical note: Frederick II [1194 - 1250] of the Holy Roman Empire was three when his father died. He was legendary for surviving and gaining his crown. He was a skeptic and was accused by the papacy of being the "beast." Frederick returned the compliment, saying that Pope Innocent IV was "the dragon."[1365] In such a halting fashion what we call separation of church and state in Western Civilization slowly moved forward six centuries before the US Constitution.) A false prophet is cited in *Revelation*.[1366] The mortal wound is a play on the resurrection and the false prophet is a play on John the Baptist.

Lindsey believed, with most of his school, that life was getting worse in the world and he believed that this very worsening prepared the way for the Anti-Christ who would lead the ten-nation confederacy. To demonstrate this devolution, he talked of rising crime rates and wars, overpopulation and more.

All this analysis was very superficial. He cited an article from the *Columbus Dispatch* of August 21, 1969 quoting "Chairman of the Genetics Department at Ohio State University J. Bruce Griffingal" that "unless mankind acts immediately, there will be a worldwide famine in 1985, and the extinction of man within 75 years." According to Lindsey, mankind cannot stop war due to a sinful nature and the only cure is to accept Jesus. The Anti-Christ will make great political progress for three-and-a-half years but will be opposed by Christians. Then, he will come to Jerusalem to be recognized as God.[1367] Believers will flee. [1368](These will be mostly new believers because the Rapture will have already occurred as will be explained shortly.)

Fifth, Lindsey predicted World War III with some interesting specifics. Russia will invade the Middle East.[1369] The Anti-Christ's army will destroy the Russian army.[1370] Apparently, there will be nuclear attack on Russia.[1371]

Finally there will be war between the revived Roman Empire under the Anti-Christ and "the vast hordes of the orient probably united under the Red Chinese war machine."[1372] The Chinese army will total two hundred million troops.[1373] This battle - Armageddon - will be in Israel. The Chinese will have to be moved to Israel across land.[1374] The fighting will take place in and around Jerusalem.[1375] All the cities of the world will be destroyed[1376]and at least one-third of the world's population. (Remember, this book was an off-the-charts best-seller and not in the fiction category.)[1377] Lindsey added on page 166, "Imagine, cities like London, Paris, Tokyo, New York, Los Angeles, Chicago - obliterated!" As Armageddon reaches its peak, Jesus Christ will return and save mankind "from self-extinction."[1378] (This type of "reasoning" is not new. One hundred years before Lindsey, the Utah Mormons initially thought the American Civil War would lead to war and the destruction of all countries and the Second Coming of Jesus Christ.[1379])

Lindsey placed three major qualifiers to this scenario. First, the Christians at the time all this starts will not be there. They will have experienced the Rapture and view this from Heaven. Here was Lindsey's reasoning. He distinguished between the Rapture and the second coming of Christ (but conceded that some Christians do not). He believed that God would be dealing again with the Jews during this crisis.[1380] He thought that evil people at the end of the age would be given free hand because the restraining power of Christians would be removed due to the Rapture.[1381] He also claimed that the second coming would be seen by all but the Rapture would be secretive.[1382]

Like the novelists of the 1930s, Lindsey offered several Rapture vignettes:

Here's one:

"It was puzzling - very puzzling. I was teaching my course in the Philosophy of Religion when all of a sudden three of my students vanished. They simply vanished! They were quite argumentative - always trying to prove their point from the Bible. No great loss to the class. However, I do find this disappearance very difficult to explain."[1383]

A second qualifier to all this is that Lindsey was coy – at least in his earlier writings - about the timing of the end times. He wanted to avoid the type of specific date-setting of William Miller of the previous century. He told people that when Christ comes again it would be a time of war but that the Rapture, a preceding event, could be any time. He built excitement, though. He said, "Since the restoration of Israel as a nation in 1948, we have lived in the most significant period of prophetic history. We are living in the times which *Ezekiel* predicted in chapters 38 and 39." He said, "The time is ripe and getting riper for...the Anti-Christ." He cited in *Matthew* 24:32-34, the parable of the fig tree, and applied it in this way: When Israel became a nation on May 14, 1948 the "'fig tree put forth its first leaves." Jesus's comment that *"this generation will not pass from the scene until all these things take place"* then took on twentieth century geopolitical significance. Lindsey asserted: "A generation in the *Bible* is something like forty years. If this is a correct deduction, then within forty years or so of 1948, all these things could take place. Many scholars who have studied Bible prophecy all their lives believe that this is so."[1384] In talking about the revived Roman Empire (again, which he linked it to the European Common Market) Lindsey quoted an official from the European Economic community, Dr. Walter Hallstein, that at "about 1980 we may fully expect the great fusion of all economic, military and political communities together into the United States of Europe." Lindsey: "Hallstein cited 1980. The timetable may be accelerating."[1385]

In sequels, Lindsey tantalized his fans with statements like these:

- 1980 - "The decade of the 1980s could very well be the last decade of history as we know it."
- 1980 - "... there is a time coming, and I believe absolutely that time will be during this generation, when suddenly and without warning, every true believer in Jesus will disappear from Earth. The event's speed and suddenness will leave the nonbelieving world mystified." One page later, Lindsey strengthened this statement: "We are the generation that will experience this incredible event."[1386]
- 1983 - In a section entitled "THE RAPTURE MEANS NO DEATH" there is this: "The truly electrifying fact is that many of you who are reading this will experience this mystery. You will never know what it is to die physically."[1387] (Because they would be Raptured.)
- 1999 – "What will war look like ten years from now... Does it even seem *possible* that we can survive as a society long enough to find out?" (Emphasis in the original).[1388]

Finally, as an evangelical Christian, it is not surprising the Lindsey qualified his view of end times with a very Christian role for Israel. It is centered upon Armageddon taking place in that country and a significant conversion of Jews to Jesus.[1389] The catastrophic things that will happen to Israel in this seven-year countdown, the "Tribulation," are designed to lead them to accepting Christ as the Messiah according to *Ezekiel* 38 and 39.

In summary, writing in 1970, Lindsey took the age-old[1390] notions of an Anti-Christ and the Second Coming of Jesus Christ and he worked in the Rapture and Armageddon to define a central tenet for a large movement. He did this by interpreting isolated verses of scripture written over hundreds of years from different books of the *Bible*. He was not alone. Support for these notions has held steady over the past generation. According to a 1983 Gallup Poll 62% of Americans had "no doubts" that Jesus will come to earth again.[1391] Here is Billy Graham in 1984: "The whole world is hurtling toward a war greater than anything known before."[1392] According to Bill Moyers, a 2002 Time-CNN poll revealed that over half of Americans believed that the prophecies found in the *Book of Revelation* are going to come true.[1393] By 2006 Lindsey-like views on the end times were said to be "the dominant view among conservative evangelical as well as charismatic believers today."[1394] The Rapture is the foundation for the Christian fictional series *Left Behind* by Tim LaHaye and Jerry Jenkins.[1395] Schools training evangelical pastors teach about the Rapture or have doctrinal statements supporting it.[1396]

I think several factors underscore Lindsey's success. He could not have done this in any culture that did not prize Biblical inerrancy. He avoided specific date setting but, indeed, may have caught the spirit of the *New Testament* in that the early followers of Jesus did expect his early return. Lindsey and others brought this back and with the notion of the Rapture taught that it could happen at any time. The Rapture, then, is a kind-of Second Coming, when Christ meets the believers in the air. His real Second Coming comes later, at the beginning of a millennium of peace, according to the Rapturists.

None of this makes sense. There is no significance to the end of the forty year period after the establishment of Israel. Lindsey's reference to "many scholars" should have been seen as a dodge. Claiming in 1980 that the current "generation" – a particularly vague word – would not die but fly up into the sky is idiocy. Let's go to the scriptures.

It is worth noting that "Armageddon" is mentioned only once in the *New Testament*, in *Revelation* 16:16: *"And the demonic spirits gathered all the rulers and their armies to a place with the Hebrew name **Armageddon**."* (Emphasis added).

It is further worth noting that the term "Anti-Christ" does not appear in scripture in that exact form. These are they closest references:

- *I John* 2:18- 22: *"Children, it is the last hour; and just as you heard that **antichrist** is coming, even now many **antichrists** have appeared; from this we know that it is the last hour. They went out from us, but they were not really of us; for if they had been of us, they would have remained with us; but they went out, so that it would be shown that they all are not of us. But you have an anointing from the Holy One, and you all know. I have not written to you because you do not know the truth, but because you do know it, and because no lie is of the truth. Who is the liar but the one who denies that Jesus is the Christ? This is the **antichrist**, the one who denies the Father and the Son."* (Emphasis added).
- *I John* 4:2-4: *"By this you know the Spirit of God: every spirit that confesses that Jesus Christ has come in the flesh is from God; and every spirit that does not confess Jesus is not from God; this is the spirit of the **antichrist**, of which you have heard that it is coming, and now it is already in the world. You are from God, little children, and have overcome them; because greater is He who is in you than he who is in the world."* (Emphasis added).
- *II John* 7: *"For many deceivers have gone out into the world, those who do not acknowledge Jesus Christ as coming in the flesh. This is the deceiver and the **antichrist**."* (Emphasis added).

Here are related references

- *Daniel* 11:21 - *"The next to come to power will be a despicable man who is not in line for royal succession. He will slip in when least expected and take over the kingdom by flattery and intrigue."*
- *Revelation* 13, 17:12,17 – These sections have many references to the *"Beast"* and at least one to the number 666 which is known as the *"mark of the Beast"* and a supposed requirement for people living at that time to do any kind of business.
- *II Thessalonians 2:3* – This verse refers to *"the man of sin, the son of perdition."*

The idea of an Anti-Christ has fascinated a large cohort of modern believers. Yet, what are the scriptures actually teaching here? The letters of *I, II* and *III John* were probably written by the same individual. These letters lay a basis for what in another context might be universalism with this magnificent statement in *I John* 4: 7-8: *"Beloved, let us love one another, because love is from God; everyone who loves is born of God and knows God. Whoever does not love does not know God, for God is love."*

Yet the writer is critical about other types of Christians – specifically, people who deny that Jesus Christ was both human and wholly God. He wrote: *"By this you know the Spirit of God: every spirit that confesses that Jesus Christ has come in the flesh is from God."*[1397] As we have noted earlier, he calls those who do not do this "antichrists" and makes clear that they had once been in the local church but had left.[1398] They left over this Christological issue and probably because of a control issue.

These three small *New Testament* books draw us into the complex debates over the nature of Christ. From them we can infer that a schism had occurred and another diverse Christian group had developed. We covered these issues in Chapter 8. All this richness is lost by the modern sensationalistic notion that we are really learning about an end times political dictator rather than just a faction that was on the outs with a leader in the Johannine community two thousand years ago.

The *Old Testament Book of Daniel* was probably written to bolster the morale of devout Jews when Judaism was under attack during the reign the Greek conqueror Antiochus Epiphanes (175-164 BC) who may have been the *"despicable man"* of *Daniel* 11:21.[1399] The *Book of Revelation* may also have had a very contemporary Anti-Christ in sight. The emperor Nero who according to Tacitus had burned Christians to death had committed suicide some thirty years before *Revelation* was written. But there was a myth circulated in the eastern part of the Empire that he would return to life, a view that if given credence would have terrorized Christians. There may be references to Nero in *Revelation*. The Beast with a wounded head that healed or the Beast as one *"who was, and is not, and yet is,"*[1400] the references to a seventh and eighth king (the Beast) following the present one all may be complex references to Nero. The emperor at the time of *Revelation* was the sixth after Nero. Some scholars link the number 666 to Nero. Others have been identified as the Antichrist (or the Beast, sometimes there is confusion) throughout history including various Popes, Martin Luther, Mohammed, George III, Hitler, Benito Mussolini, Mikhail Gorbachev, Henry Kissinger and others.[1401]

The" *man of sin, the son of perdition"* is not linked to a leader of a small-church faction like the Secessionists or a tyrant like Antiochus Epiphanes or Nero. The author of *II Thessalonians* addressed the issue that the end of time - however it would be styled by Christians - had not happened yet. Some of his readers apparently had worried that Jesus had returned in another place. Since travel and communications were essentially at the speed of walking, possibly Christ had come again in Jerusalem and they did not know it in Asia Minor (Turkey). *II Thessalonians*, written late in the first century, urged people not to become *"easily unsettled or alarmed by some prophecy, report or letter supposed to have come from us, saying that the day of the Lord has already come."*[1402] This letter, allegedly from the Apostle Paul, was written to refute another letter that we don't have allegedly forged in Paul's name, that the kingdom had come. There may have been concern that some people had quit working in anticipation of Jesus's kingdom.[1403] To calm anxieties the writer set out certain prerequisites. Moreover, he may be promoting Rome as a restrainer of evil.[1404]

From these scant references, references that are susceptible to other interpretations, Lindsey moved large segments of a religion. Politically, this all led to a type of passivity and an obsession with certain signs. The major sign was the formation of Israel in 1948. After that, some came to look back on the establishment of the Soviet Union and read it as the kingdom of the north, ready to attack Israel. Lindsey quoted Israeli Defense Minister Moshe Dayan in 1968 that "the next war will not be with the Arabs, but with the Russians."[1405]

Even the atomic bomb was seen as a sign predicted in the scriptures. *II Peter* 3:10 reads *"But the day of the Lord will come as unexpectedly as a thief. Then the heavens will pass away with a terrible noise, and the very elements themselves will disappear in fire, and the earth and everything on it will be found to deserve judgment."* Prior to 1945, apocalyptic Christians had predicted this fiery end of the world in terms of the earth's molten core exploding outward or by comets or some miracle. The advent of atomic weapons in 1945 led to a new and seemingly much more logical explanation of Armageddon. *II Peter* 3:10 began to be cited in articles, books and conferences as prophecy for the times.[1406] As noted in Chapter 3 even President Harry Truman speculated on the subject. However, ignoring the context of *II Peter* leads to misreading the entire letter. *II Peter* was not widely known or accepted by the early church. It may date from about 120 AD.[1407] Like *II Thessalonians* it dealt with the ongoing non-return of Jesus and pointed out that we should remind scoffers that *"with the Lord a day is like a thousand years, and a thousand years are like a day."*[1408] In other words, we don't know God's timing, so don't worry about it. That is the message of this small book – not that atomic weapons will destroy the earth.

Will there be Rapture and will Christ come again? Perhaps, but nowhere in the *New Testament* are these concepts developed in any detail and nowhere is belief in either required as a condition of salvation. I am about where Mark Twain was who wrote, upon arriving in Palestine in the late 1800s: "Christ has been here once. Will never come again."[1409] Was Lindsey crazy? I am not prepared to so label him. It is probably more appropriate to say that Lindsey wrote some pretty crazy things.[1410]

However, the era in which Hal Lindsey wrote *The Late Great Planet Earth* is important. If we spotlight him and black out the stage on which he performed in the 1970s we have a distortion. His ideas can best be understood in the context of the times. We will briefly note two secular authors of the 1960s and 1970s who also were very popular and who also made fantastic end times claims. Paul Ehrlich (1932 -) and Carl Sagan (1934 - 1996) like Lindsey predicted world-transforming change and their scenarios were every bit as imaginative as his.

Ehrlich wrote *The Population Bomb* in 1968. It was an instant best seller. It warned in millenialist terms of overcrowding due to population growth on earth. Its prologue read: "The battle to feed all of humanity over. In the 1970s the world will undergo famines - hundreds of millions of people are going to starve to death in spite of any crash program embarked upon now. At this late date nothing can prevent a substantial increase in the world death rate although many lives could be saved through dramatic programs to 'stretch' the carrying capacity of the earth by increasing food production. But these programs will only provide a stay of execution unless they are accompanied by determined and successful efforts at population control..... Population control is the only answer." (Ehrlich was cited by Lindsey to bolster his own claims about the coming world crisis.)[1411]

Ehrlich outlined three scenarios for the fifteen years after 1968. He made a caveat that these would not be true as stated but then he was quite specific describing a war in Thailand and a coup in Mexico, etc. He wrote that these "describe the kinds of disasters that *will* occur as mankind slips into the famine decades."[1412] (Emphasis in the original). Two of these scenarios involve nuclear war. The "cheerful" scenario involves death by starvation of one-fifth of the world's population and papal blessing of abortion.[1413]

All of this has proved false. But it was very popular in its time and so was the teaching of Carl Sagan.

In 1966 Sagan a professor of astronomy co-authored with a Soviet scientist, I. S. Shklovskii, *Intelligent Life in the Universe*.[1414] The book made some remarkable suggestions.

Sagan defined advanced technical civilizations in outer space as those having "a technical capability substantially in advance of our own." Sagan followed certain assumptions embodied in a formula known as the Drake Equation. The Drake Equation was developed in 1960 by astronomer Frank Drake, Sagan and other scientists to attempt to estimate the number of technical civilizations in our galaxy.[1415] From this foundation, Sagan asserted that the number of technical civilizations depends heavily on whether or not they tend to self-destruct. Then he estimated the number of the civilizations in our galaxy to be about one million. This would make them, on the average, several hundred light years apart. He assumed a lifetime of such a civilization to be 10 million years.[1416] Sagan also assumed that technical civilizations would be interested in sending and receiving radio signals.

Sagan speculated about direct contact between technical civilizations. "I believe that interstellar spaceflight to the farthest reaches of our Galaxy is a feasible objective for humanity. If this is the case, other civilizations, aeons more advanced than ours, must today be plying the spaces between the stars." Sagan conjectured that technical civilizations might send out one space probe per year. He estimated that each civilization has between 1000 and 10000 space ships on patrol per year, that each communicative technical civilization will be visited once every thousand years and that, on the average, each technical civilization that sends out ships will have them gone between 1000 and 10000 years and have them return once per year. Then, "the wealth, diversity and brilliance of this commerce, the exchange of goods and information, of arguments and artifacts, of concepts and conflicts, must continuously sharpen the curiosity and enhance the vitality of the participating societies." Closer to Earth, Sagan speculated that the moons of Mars might be artificial satellites.

Have spacemen visited Earth? I doubt it but Sagan reviewed a Sumerian legend and Mesopotamian art to speculate on a visitation.[1417]An image of a piece of artwork from ancient Sumeria which was pictured in a Soviet film *Planeta Zagadok* is re-produced in *Intelligent Life in the Universe*.

Sagan was one of the iconic figures of the 1970s and 1980s. He was on the "Tonight Show With Johnny Carson" innumerable times. He was a prolific writer and self-promoter. But his estimates of the number of extraterrestrial technical civilizations have been severely questioned. Other, non-celebrity scientists, have listed many more factors than are included in the Drake Equation and which drive down the speculation about the number of technical civilizations in the galaxy (although they allow that life at the microbial level may be more common).[1418]

Lindsey wanted Christians to participate in the Rapture. Sagan wanted people to be on the side of the heroes of history. As he put it, "one of the major intellectual revolutions of the Renaissance, one for which Copernicus and Galileo[1419] fought, and for which Giordano Bruno lost his life, was the idea that the Earth was but one of many planets in our solar system and beyond."[1420]

Lindsey, Ehrlich and Sagan all thought, as the modern phrase goes, "outside the box." Their titles - *The Late Great Planet Earth*, *The Population Bomb* and *Intelligent Life in the Universe* - caught the spirit of the 1970s.[1421] The portentous speculations that they made are oddities, however, forty years later. Lindsey talked of a European super-state stronger than the US established before 1980. He talked of the rebuilding of the "Temple" in Israel before 1988 (and assured us that "many scholars" agreed). He talked of one-third of the world dying, of a two-hundred million-troop Chinese army[1422] marching from China to Israel to fight the Europeans. Ehrlich spoke of nuclear war, about a billion people dying by famine and popes supporting abortion. Sagan entranced millions with the idea that ancient astronauts had been here and would return.

As Yogi Berra and others are quoted to have said, "It's tough to make predictions, especially about the future."[1423]

It is not our point to be too critical of predictions made two generations ago. However, there are two points to be made. The smaller one is that Lindsey and other Christians were not alone in the 1970s in seeing drastic end times changes in the near future. The larger one is that in whatever guise, a large percentage of humans may be inclined to look for a force or a messiah who will bring history to an end.

However, the error around the end times, although it may be damaging, probably does less harm than its fraternal twin: a belief in the earthy kingdom of God on Earth. We turn now to that error.

The Kingdom of God

Monotheism in concept unified the human experience as part of a process toward the fulfillment of God's plan and purposes. A kingdom on Earth is the logical conclusion in this play. The Jews had come to believe and teach that God was a loving parent shaping history as evidenced by progress. This idea of progress has been the foundation of a utopian tradition in the West. Monotheism also brought an inherently political message: since humanity was created by the one God, people are all each other's brothers and sisters.[1424] There is much that is both sublime and practical in such an outlook. Human progress over time is awe-inspiring. But it is the thesis of the rest of this chapter that a utopian view of the concept of the kingdom of God is a dangerous illusion.

In the Synoptic Gospels Jesus taught about how to prepare for a coming kingdom, which he initially said was at hand.[1425] In both *Matthew* and *Luke*, Jesus promised his immediate followers that though they had left normal lives for him, they would rule in this new kingdom, that they would sit on *"thrones, judging the twelve tribes of Israel."*[1426] He rated the kingdom as more important that normal familial relationships. He separated a fisherman named Zebedee from his wife and sons.[1427] He also separated Joanna from her husband Cuza who worked for Herod Antipater.[1428] He even seemed to tell a man to skip his own father's funeral to follow him.[1429] Jesus saw his kingdom as replacing the establishment to which he exhibited little respect. The story cited in Chapter 4 about him paying his Temple Tax shows almost a flippancy.[1430] This attitude shifts beyond this tax to authority in general. Herod Antipater, the Roman-supported leader of Galilee, was a figure mentioned dozens of times in the *New Testament*. Jesus criticized him [1431], at least once sarcastically[1432], and then ignored him during his "trial." [1433] Jesus's agenda seemed to expect divine intervention to expel the Romans and their local representatives like Herod Antipater and to create a new type of kingdom which would be governed by his followers but through the paradoxical approach of loving enemies, forgiving debts, true religion over process and caring for the poor. When his disciples argued among themselves about which of them was the greatest, he taught about being like a servant or a child.[1434]

He saw his kingdom as all-inclusive of the Jewish people and possibly beyond.[1435] In his first sermon in his home town, as recounted in *Luke,* he read sections of the *Old Testament* which seemed to provide for God's outreach to Gentiles. That's why his townspeople tried to throw him off a cliff.[1436]

The concept of the kingdom of God on Earth has endured in the centuries since Jesus. In the history of the United States many Americans saw this country as an opportune place to establish the kingdom or have talked in similar Christian utopian terms.

Thomas Paine wrote in *Common Sense* that: "The reformation was preceded by the discovery of America, as if the Almighty graciously meant to open a sanctuary to the persecuted in future years, when home should afford neither friendship nor safety." In 1821 Secretary of State John Quincy Adams submitted a report on weights and measures that called for establishment of the metric system. He thought it could become a universal unit of measure, a step toward "that universal peace which was the object of a Savior's mission, the trembling hope of the Christian."[1437] In 1859 Brigham Young (1801 – 1877) said from Salt Lake City: "Our faith must be concentrated in one great work - the building up of the kingdom of God on Earth." The Mormons thought Christ's millennial reign depended on the building of an acceptable nucleus. This was behind all the efforts of colonizing, missionary work and summoning Mormons to the American West.[1438] Harriet Beecher Stowe (1811 – 1896) in *Uncle Tom's Cabin* saw a war to end slavery as connected to the Second Coming of Christ.[1439] By 1856 the Republican Party emerged for northern evangelical Christians as an expression of the attempt to create the kingdom of God.[1440] In a similar vein, future secretary of State John Hay (1838 – 1905) an aide of President Lincoln considered him "the greatest character since Christ."[1441]

The Social Gospel of the late 1800s and early 1900s held that the millennium or "the Kingdom" was near and that it would be brought in by human agency. It was a Christianity that assumed the culture would become Christian, an exceedingly optimistic view influenced by the great Protestant missions throughout the world of the nineteenth century in which the United States took the leading part.[1442] Its most famous spokesperson, Walter Rauschenbusch (1861 – 1918), wrote "Each Christian has his own inner Bible"[1443] and that "the medium through which the people shall co-operate in their search for the kingdom of God and its righteousness" was the state.[1444] In a political convention that nominated him for President in 1912, Theodore Roosevelt said, "We stand at Armageddon, and we battle for the Lord."

The American radical Henry George (1839 – 1897) devised a "single tax" scheme which he promoted in his novel *Progress and Poverty* (1879). Near the end of the book, he said of the transformation that the single tax would usher in: "It is the glorious vision which has always haunted men with gleams of fitful splendor. It is what he saw whose eyes at Patmos[1445] were closed[1446] in a trance. It is the culmination of Christianity - the City of God on earth, with its walls of jasper and its gates of pearl! It is the reign of the Prince of Peace!"[1447] (Remember, this is all about a tax plan.) American socialist Eugene V. Debs rooted his Marxism in American and Christian terms. In 1914 he said Christ was "the master proletarian revolutionist and sower of the social whirlwind" and the descendant of "poor working people."[1448] Earlier he said, "What is socialism? Merely Christianity in action. It recognizes the equality in men."[1449]

Lincoln Steffens (1866 – 1936) wrote in 1918 that: "the revolution in Russia is to establish the kingdom of Heaven here on Earth now; in order that Christ may come soon; and, coming, reign forever."[1450] While campaigning in 1919 for American acceptance of the League of Nations and slightly before he suffered a massive stroke, President Woodrow Wilson was introduced to an audience as a "twentieth century Paul...the greatest prophet of peace." [1451] In the 1930s, activist priest Father Charles Coughlin (1891 – 1979) said the New Deal was "Christ's Deal."[1452]

Jimmy Carter worked "behind the scenes" with the head of the Southern Baptist Convention to develop a program called Bold Mission Thrust, "designed to expand the global evangelistic effort of Baptists."[1453] Barack Obama ran successfully for president asserting that: "I am confident that we can create a kingdom right here on earth."[1454] His wife Michelle Obama (1964-) said that he was the only person who understood that "before we can work on the problems, we have to fix our souls. Our souls are broken in this nation."[1455]

These sorts of Christian utopian visions have had opponents throughout American history. At the Constitutional Convention of 1787, Alexander Hamilton - thinking the proceedings were confidential - said: "The voice of the people has been said to be the voice of God (but) it is not true in fact..."[1456] Abraham Lincoln dismissed the utopians of his day saying "after all, their faces are set Zionwards."[1457] Socialist Norman Thomas (1884 - 1968) was born into a fundamentalist home. He was jaundiced toward Woodrow Wilson's utopianism saying "to disagree with Wilson was to take a great risk..... all his public life he was inclined to take strong opposition or criticism as a sin against the Holy Ghost...."[1458] Theodore Roosevelt, like Hamilton, once said that *vox populi* was "the voice of the devil, or what is still worse, the voice of a fool."[1459]Later in the twentieth century, Dwight Eisenhower (channeling Hamilton and Roosevelt) told a friend: "Even though we agree with the old proverb, 'The voice of the people is the voice of God,' it is not always easy to determine just what that voice is saying."[1460]

A less-political Christianity is skeptical of efforts to build a kingdom of God in society. A close look at the *New Testament* teachings of the kingdom lends support to this view. Jesus seemed to have progressively postponed the kingdom. Note the change: He said that his followers would not have time to preach in all the villages of Israel before the advent of the kingdom.[1461] After that, he said that the present generation would not pass away before the kingdom arrived.[1462], [1463]Still later he resorted to parables because "*the people thought that the kingdom of God was going to appear at once.*"[1464] At one point, he acknowledged that he did not know when the kingdom would come.[1465]

There are approximately eighty-one references in the Synoptics to the "kingdom of God" or the "kingdom of Heaven." However, the *Gospel of John* written later contains only two references to the "kingdom of God." They are both in Jesus's famous nighttime conversation with a Pharisee named Nicodemus recorded in the third chapter of *John* in which Jesus tells him that he must be born again to enter the kingdom of God. Jesus in *John* does not talk about a kingdom on Earth with the forces of evil subdued. He teaches that individuals can find eternal life in heaven through faith in Jesus. Those who believe in Jesus will live with God forever; those who do not are lost. As *John* 3:36 teaches: "*anyone who believes in God's Son has eternal life. Anyone who doesn't obey the Son will never experience eternal life but remains under God's angry judgment.*"[1466]

Although Luke places within *Acts* comments about the kingdom of God by Jesus himself, Philip, Paul and Barnabas and concludes *Acts* by asserting that Paul proclaimed the kingdom of God in Rome,[1467] Paul spoke of the kingdom of God less and less frequently as he wrote his letters.[1468] Paul employed a phrase "*in Christ*" which appears over a hundred times in his letters which could be a related concept.[1469] However, being "*in Christ*" appears more portable and adaptable to normal life in a variety of circumstances. It does not, for example, have apocalyptic notions and it does not envision a theocracy ruled over by Jesus's twelve disciples.

As we have seen, Paul brought to his work urgency, perceiving that he was living in the end times. Much as Jesus had spoken of a future kingdom of God, Paul saw the return of Jesus as imminent and the end of history but Paul's politics were in a sense otherworldly. He saw Jesus returning "*...to defeat every authority...*"[1470] But this was a turning point that did not turn and more of his attention was focused on defusing millennial situations: believers who thought that the end was so near that they didn't have to work or follow traditional sexual mores or who were confused about some who had died. It is not conceivable that he imagined that his letters would be canonical, intensely studied for doctrine, meaning and direction some nineteen centuries later.[1471] The Christians of the first few centuries, however, were wise enough to defer the kingdom of God and to edit and compile a *New Testament*, a surpassing wonder. Since the 400s, official Christianity has downplayed millennialism.[1472]

As it has balanced the strictures of piety with the practical needs of growing a community, the Mormon church has established a healthy balance between daily living and expectations about the kingdom of God. Clearly Joseph Smith anticipated the end times. He wrote in 1835 that another "56 years should wind up the scene." In *Doctrines and Covenant* 130:15 he wrote a revelation that if he lived to be 85 he would "see the face of the Son of Man" although he hedged that he believed it would not be any sooner (*Doctrines and Covenant* 130:17). Many Mormons viewed the polygamy crisis after Brigham Young's death when this practice brought them into conflict with the US government in terms of apocalypticism. They saw Independence, Missouri as both the site of the Garden of Eden and Christ's Second coming. Early Mormon leaders emphasized such *Bible* verses as *Revelation* 3:12 and 21:2.[1473] Mormonism developed in a larger environment that included millennial hopes and the restoration of some form of *New Testament* Christianity.[1474] But times changed and so did the Mormon Church. Continuing revelation is a central Mormon tenet. New understandings emerged. In the twentieth century millennialism, visions and speaking in tongues all waned. In the twenty-first century the kingdom is not a territory, but a world-wide church. It is optimistic, ready to do good.[1475]

The average person will not be motivated either by being assured that he/she will be lifted into the air to join Jesus or to a future, utopian state gained by politics. They will be motivated by a transcendent vision, however. As Robert Louis Wilken wrote: "The Christian vision springs from Jesus's proclamation of the kingdom of God, and the Christian hope in this kingdom rests on the Resurrection of Jesus from the dead. Jesus's Resurrection did not usher in the kingdom of God on earth, but it began something new in human experience and gave men reason to believe that their hope in the kingdom was not misplaced Because Jesus's Resurrection did not establish the Kingdom, there is no warrant for Christians to look back and say, 'Lo here' or 'Lo there.' All historical forms, ideas, or expressions are at best 'penultimate.' The kingdom reveals itself again and again as a still unrealized future that confronts every present and that will confront a, hopefully, better future situation. The futurity of the kingdom opens new possibilities for action while still denying any human institution the glory of perfection that might warrant its making an absolute claim on the obedience of individuals."[1476]

To summarize, there are two extremes to avoid. The first to avoid is the idea of a Second Coming preceded by a descent into worldwide chaos and destruction. Dwight L. Moody's statement in the nineteenth century that "I find that the earth is to grow worse and worse" is rebutted by common sense. As church historian Shirley Jackson Case put it in 1918: "It is sheer nonsense to talk dolefully about the gradual deterioration of society to a student of history. .... Viewed in the long perspective of the ages, man's career has been one of actual ascent. Instead of growing worse, the world is found to be growing constantly better..."[1477] The opposite temptation is to glamorize progress, to think we can build heaven on earth. President, Woodrow Wilson sermonizing that our task is to "Christianize the world"[1478] is representative of this viewpoint. But there is a middle path. It has to do with gradual improvement.

Thomas Jefferson, the exemplar of the American enlightenment put it this way: "If fifty years hence the average man shall invariably argue from two ascertained premises where he now jumps to a conclusion from a single supposed revelation - that is progress! I expect it to be made here, under our democratic stimulants, on a great scale, until everyman is potentially an athlete in body and an Aristotle in spirit."[1479]

By the end of Jefferson's time estimate, the American statesman Daniel Webster saw things as moving more slowly than had Jefferson although he still saw progress. He criticized people who thought that right and wrong could be distinguished "with the precision of an algebraic equation." He said they were too much in a hurry to wait for "the slow progress of moral causes in the improvement of mankind" and forgot that "the doctrines and miracles of Jesus...have, in eighteen hundred years, converted only a small portion of the human race."[1480] At whatever speed though, these are views that progress is possible, maybe inevitable.

A long-held view of history was that creation was recent and the end times were imminent.[1481] That may have changed in our era as we look at both the beginning and the end as removed from us by eons. If so, as we look to the future, people may see a vision of imperfect but steady progress. This view, combined with a portable Christianity, able to address life's problems, can also be attractive to many. Chapter 11 will cover this area. Again, the *New Testament* will be our guide. However, first we will look at one of the most misunderstood figures of history, the Apostle Paul.

CHAPTER 10

Redeeming Paul

Paul was the apostle to the Gentiles which in that context meant the apostle for freedom. By the end of the first century, Paul's more law-free gospel triumphed.[1482]

This is a world still heavily influenced by the first century figure, Paul of Tarsus.

What was he like? His initial fame came from his switch from persecutor of Christians to a chief evangelist for the new religion. Before joining the Christians, Paul may in fact have been a ringleader of persecutors from his home region. According to *Acts* 6:9, some of the Martyr Stephen's accusers were from Cilicia which is a region in modern Turkey. Its capital was Tarsus, the home of the Apostle Paul whom we know was at the scene of Stephen's murder (*Acts* 7:58). Was he also one of the accusers? That would require speculation but these two verses are evidence that he was. Yet, he became Christianity's most famous missionary.

There were complexities in his lifestyle and his character. Paul knew how to use a secretary[1483] but he prided himself in being able to work in construction or some related field telling the Corinthians that *"we work wearily with our own hands to earn our living."*[1484] He was, to say the least, an individualist but he typically headed up some type of team that could travel together or break-up and re-join.[1485] He lived in deprivation at times. In *I Corinthians* 4:11 and *II Corinthians* 11:27 he talked of going hungry, being ill-clad and homeless and having sleepless nights. But he also had a patroness as indicated in *Romans* 16:2 and he instructed Philemon to prepare a guest room for him (verse 22).

II Corinthians 4:10 talks of personal suffering (*"Through suffering, our bodies continue to share in the death of Jesus ..."*). *II Corinthians* 12:7-8 talks of some sort of ailment that so tormented him that (three times) he begged God to take it away. (*"I was given a thorn in my flesh..."*) In *Galatians* 4:13 he alludes again to this unspecified ailment writing, *"You know that it was because of a physical infirmity that I first announced the gospel to you."* Some speculation holds that

Paul may have suffered from malaria.[1486] But he wrote in what we would call sports analogies. This style possibly stemmed from his time at Ephesus where he probably witnessed annual games in honor of the goddess Diana.[1487] In an exhortation to the Corinthians he wrote in his first letter, chapter nine verses 24-27: *"Don't you realize that in a race everyone runs, but only one person gets the prize? So run to win! All athletes are disciplined in their training. They do it to win a prize that will fade away, but we do it for an eternal prize. So I run with purpose in every step. I am not just shadowboxing. I discipline my body like an athlete, training it to do what it should. Otherwise, I fear that after preaching to others I myself might be disqualified."* To the Philippians he wrote in the third chapter verse 13 that: *"I press on towards the goal for the prize…"* There are other sports analogies in the Pauline corpus either written by Paul or by those trying to imitate him. In *I Timothy* 6:12 the author urged a younger man to persist in his ministry or to *"fight the good fight…"* In *II Timothy* 2:5 after urging the reader to be strong in Christ Jesus the author reminds: *"…in the case of an athlete, no one is crowned without competing according to the rules."* In *II Timothy* 4:7, recognizing that the end of his life may be near, "Paul" asserted, *"I have fought the good fight, I have finished the race,…"*[1488]

What did Paul look like? He said that he had an unimpressive appearance[1489] and possibly the ailment he had was disfiguring because he wrote the Galatians that his condition *"put you to the test, (but) you did not scorn or despise me."*[1490] A second century writer named Onesiphoros described Paul in *Acts of Paul and Thecla* as "rather small in size, bald-headed, bow-legged, with eyebrows that met, and with a large, red and rather hooked nose. Strongly built, he was full of grace, for at times he looked like a man, at times like an angel."[1491]

In history, he has been attacked. Porphyry in the third century said, "Paul shows the ignorant person's habit of constantly contradicting himself, feverish in mind and weak in reasoning."[1492] John Locke saw the letters of Paul and others in scripture as unnecessary for salvation because - as he showed through quoting the greetings - they were written to Christians. They were "holy writers…yet every sentence of theirs must not be taken up and looked on as a fundamental article necessary to salvation…."[1493] Thomas Jefferson said Paul was "a corrupter" of the doctrines of Jesus[1494] and Nietzsche wrote that Paul killed the Christianity of Jesus and falsified history. He called Paul's depiction of Jesus the "original betrayal."[1495] Thomas Paine wrote that the character of Paul showed "a great deal of violence and fanaticism."[1496]

But Paul thought he was both a good Pharisee[1497] and a good apostle – or at least one that as we noted in Chapter 5 worked harder than the rest.[1498]

Let's examine some of the specific complaints against Paul.

Paul's seeming indifference to government, which effectively amounted to support of the status quo, has been used to marginalize opposition to governments throughout the last two thousand years. It may have been grounded in the reality of the Empire, however, particularly as it affected Jews and Jewish-Christians living in Rome. As noted, the expulsion of Jews from Rome in 49AD, about a decade prior to Paul's letter to the Romans which most clearly calls for obedience to the government is mentioned in the *Book of Acts. Acts* 18:2 records that Paul *"met a Jew named Aquila, a native of Pontus, who had recently come from Italy with his wife Priscilla, because Claudius had ordered all the Jews to leave Rome."* This expulsion may have been due to riots breaking out in the synagogues between Jews and other Jews who were followers of Jesus. Their absence may have furthered Gentile Christianity but the Jewish-Christians returned. Paul's letter addressed concerns that this mixture may have caused. Paul knew from Prisca and Aquila how brutal the expulsion had been and may have wanted to prevent another.[1499] In short, Paul may have wanted to stay on placid terms with Rome.

Pauline Christianity did not point to an earthly kingdom of Heaven. It was designed to get along with governmental authority with very little in the way of a political agenda. Paul wrote to the Romans to pay taxes and to obey the authorities. But it had a nuance that is often missed. He, like other *New Testament* writers, may have offered support to the government in the form of urging the payment of taxes and good behavior[1500] but his support for government was conditioned. His constant references to Jesus Christ as "our Lord" and "the Lord"[1501] were an affront to the Romans, a casual dismissal of the imperial system which recognized the emperor as the Lord.[1502] Over time, Paul's religion won. In three centuries time, the Empire was ungovernable without Christians and shortly after that the church survived the Empire. We number the years from the birth of Jesus Christ. The greatest Roman Emperor[1503] who presided at the time of the birth of Jesus merely has a month named for him.

In modern times Paul has been called anti-woman and anti-Semitic. A case can easily be made, however, that his promotion of women was unique in the era.

He wrote nearly two thousand years ago that in Christ there is not "male of female."[1504] He also wrote, *"...in the Lord, neither is women independent of man, nor is man independent of woman. For as the woman originates from the man, so also the man has his birth through the woman; and all things originate from God."*[1505] He relied on women to carry out his ministry as co-workers. He talked of working with "Chloe's household" in Corinth.[1506] As noted earlier, he refers to someone named Junias (along with Andronicus, possibly her husband, who is mentioned first) as relatives, as people who served prison time with him, as senior to him in the Christian faith and as *"outstanding among the apostles."* [1507] The import of this is that we know that Paul put apostles before: *"prophets, third teachers; then deeds of power, then gifts of healing, forms of assistance, forms of leadership, various kinds of tongues."*[1508] Apparently, Paul's first European convert was a woman named Lydia in Philippi.[1509] Later he was concerned about discord between two female church members there, possibly because of their leadership roles.[1510] He understood that women will pray and prophesize in church (although he felt that they should cover their heads).[1511]

His letter to the Romans was delivered by a woman named Phoebe whom he refers to as a deacon in the church in Cenchrea[1512] and his patron.[1513] The Aquila and Priscilla team is mentioned several times, sometimes listing her before him.[1514] All of this is nearly unprecedented in the ancient world. More typical is this comment found at the very end of the *Gospel of Thomas*: "Simon Peter said to them, 'Make Mary leave us, for females don't deserve life.' Jesus said, 'Look, I will guide her to make her male, so that she too may become a living spirit resembling you males. For every female who makes herself male will enter the domain of Heaven.'"[1515]

One proof text often used to discourage the involvement of women in the churches is *I Corinthians 14:34-35* which reads: *"Women should be silent during the church meetings. It is not proper for them to speak. They should be submissive, just as the law says. If they have any questions, they should ask their husbands at home, for it is improper for women to speak in church meetings."* I find convincing Bart Ehrman's view that this may have been a scribal add-on decades after Paul wrote the letter.[1516] Another possibility is suggested by Elisabeth Schussler Fiorenza who wrote that Paul adapted his views toward social norms during a time of attacks on Christians.[1517] Donald Harman Akenson is close to this view and sees these verses as ambiguous and as possibly showing Paul's concerns over syncretistic tendencies in Corinth.[1518] Amy-Jill Levine sees them as out-of-sync with Paul's overall message.[1519] Or, Paul may have unambiguously meant what is expressed here. However, I discount that possibility because it is in contrast to Paul's other comments on women and his reported experience.[1520], [1521]

With regard to his perceived anti-Semitism, a major point of this book is that this is chiefly a misreading of his rivalry with Christian Jews like James and the hard-liners who wanted him dead.[1522] In fact, his teachings were universal. He taught that as in Adam all died, in Christ all live.[1523]

Did the Apostle Paul promote slavery? He did only if one regards as his authentic views, portions of later letters which were probably not written by him. *Titus*, for example has this passage: *"Slaves must always obey their masters and do their best to please them. They must not talk back or steal, but must show themselves to be entirely trustworthy and good. Then they will make the teaching about God our Savior attractive in every way."*[1524] *I Timothy* contains this injunction: *"All slaves should show full respect for their masters so they will not bring shame on the name of God and his teaching. If the masters are believers, that is no excuse for being disrespectful. Those slaves should work all the harder because their efforts are helping other believers who are well loved."*[1525] However, as noted earlier, many scholars believe that these letters were not written by Paul but by anonymous church leaders a generation later, striving to fit the church into the mores of the Roman world.

The letter of *Philemon* was written by Paul and it concerns a runaway slave named Onesimus. Paul was writing to the owner of Onesimus, a Christian named Philemon. There are commentators who perceive that Paul was merely admonishing Philemon to refrain from punishing Onesimus but was not telling him to free his slave.[1526] This view would hold that Paul, writing in the mid-50s, had a lack of concern for social inequities because he thought the world was going to end soon. This view might cite as evidence Paul's thoughts in *I Corinthians* 7:24: *"Let each man remain in that condition in which he was called."*

There are others[1527] – and to me they are persuasive - that hold that this small book eloquently captures Paul's more abolitionist views toward slavery and that Paul admonished a Christian owner to receive back a runaway slave and free him. Paul, in his only known letter to an individual, writes Philemon that the runaway Onesimus *"is no longer like a slave to you. He is more than a slave, for he is a beloved brother, especially to me."*[1528] He used various unsubtle arguments to pressure for Onesimus's freedom. He makes the letter public by the "copying in" others: after addressing Philemon in verse 1, he notes in verse 2: *"our sister Apphia, and to our fellow soldier Archippus, and to the church that meets in your house."* In a final twist of the knife, he tells Philemon that he would be there to check on him: in verses 21 and 22 Paul writes, *"I am confident as I write this letter that you will do what I ask and even more! One more thing—please prepare a guest room for me, ..."* This view might cite as evidence Paul's thoughts in *Galatians* 3:28 that in Christ there is not *"slave nor free."*

There is a charming possibility about Onesimus's later career. He may have become a leader in the church. *Colossians* 4: 9 mentions someone with that name and "scholarly speculation has suggested that he became bishop of Ephesus, and that there he gathered together Paul's surviving letters and wrote the epistle to the Ephesians as an introduction to the collection."[1529] Perhaps Onesimus was responsible for the survival of Paul's letters into the canon. The Onesimus was who was the Bishop of Ephesus received a letter from the jailed Ignatius formerly Bishop of Antioch.[1530] Ignatius requested that some friends whom Onesimus had sent to visit him be allowed to stay. The letter is similar to the letter of Paul to Philemon.[1531] *Philemon* in any event is a very human letter. It is not a side dish in the *New Testament*; it is an entrée.[1532]

Paul also should also be credited with questioning class differences. Paul wrote the Corinthians that *"few of you were wise in the world's eyes or powerful or wealthy when God called you"*[1533] implying that some were. These were some of the problems of the better-off that he addressed: law suits over financial disputes,[1534] a stepson marrying his widowed stepmother possibly in order to protect the financial status or the patrimony of the family,[1535] going to dinners at pagan temples and buying the meat sacrificed there[1536] and the inequality they were practicing at the Lord's Supper.[1537] In all this, his emphases were on breaking down class distinctions, keeping matters out of the law courts and honoring the Lord's Supper.

There is, it must be noted, one legitimate criticism of this proponent of freedom. Paul can justly be labeled anti-gay. In *I Corinthians* the sixth chapter the ninth and tenth verses he wrote: *"Don't you realize that those who do wrong will not inherit the kingdom of God? Don't fool yourselves. Those who indulge in sexual sin, or who worship idols, or commit adultery, or are male prostitutes, or practice homosexuality, or are thieves, or greedy people, or drunkards, or are abusive, or cheat people—none of these will inherit the kingdom of God."* Later, in *Romans* 1:18, he began a description of *"wicked people"* and, then, in the twenty-sixth and twenty seventh verses of that chapter he wrote words that have brought no end of divisiveness within society and within Christian groups over the many centuries: *"For this reason God gave them over to degrading passions; for their women exchanged the natural function for that which is unnatural, and in the same way also the men abandoned the natural function of the woman and burned in their desire toward one another, men with men committing indecent acts and receiving in their own persons the due penalty of their error."*

There are those who explain these injunctions in a more positive light. The Reverend McLennan: "In the *New Testament*, homosexuality is referred to in three[1538] letters of Paul in which it's likely that he was referring to pagan practices of prostitution and sex with children. In none of these cases was anything vaguely contemplated along the lines of a lifelong monogamous commitment between same-sex partners."[1539]

This defense is unpersuasive. Paul's statements are uncompromising. I have rebutted charges against Paul concerning slaves and women. But even if my analysis is wrong, there is at least the fallback argument that in these two areas Paul was a man of his time, living within certain mores. There is no such excuse with regard to homosexuality, however, since homosexuality was widely tolerated in the Mediterranean world in his time.[1540] What then? For some this will be a deal-breaker on Paul's reputation. That's understandable. For others, it is impeachable but does not detract from his farsightedness in most other areas.[1541] These might say that he was not one dimensional but clearly an alloy of good and bad.[1542]

On slavery, on the role of women, on class differences and on the role of government, there is more to Paul than many are taught. He stood for equality and freedom and his views on these issues have twenty-first century ramifications. But there is another matter in which Paul stood for freedom which, though mostly symbolic in our era, looms as large as these others. That was the topic of dietary laws.

Paul's last word on the topic is the letter to the Romans, the one church that he wrote before having visited. In this letter we can see how Paul may have walked back from his earlier strife with Jewish-Christians to lay the basis for universalism. Whereas in the dispute within the Galatian community Paul was absolutely clear that there should be no separate table for those who wanted to observe Jewish dietary laws, two-three years later to the Romans he changed direction and, in modern terms, went about managing diversity.[1543]

There are two related factors that might have brought about this greater tolerance: the Jews in Jerusalem where Paul was about to go and the audience in Rome to whom he was writing. In *Romans* he showed that he was worried about how he would be seen by both the Jews and the Jewish-Christians in Jerusalem. He asked the Romans to: *"pray that I will be rescued from those in Judea who refuse to obey God. Pray also that the believers there will be willing to accept the donation I am taking to Jerusalem"*[1544] His subsequent trip to Jerusalem (where he was bringing money) is recounted by Luke and it is apparent that Paul was accompanied by delegates from various places where he had raised money for Jerusalem.[1545] Also, Paul was writing to an audience that doubtless included a far greater percentage of Jews than his audience in his letter to the Galatians since Jews had been readmitted to Rome after their expulsion by Claudius.[1546] (The diversity represented by the Jews and the Gentiles within the Roman church may have grown after Paul's time and by the second century, Irenaeus was distressed by it.[1547]) Paul urged a unity by accepting differences over dietary practices and the observances in the Roman congregations writing:

"I know and am convinced on the authority of the Lord Jesus that no food, in and of itself, is wrong to eat. But if someone believes it is wrong, then for that person it is wrong. And if another believer is distressed by what you eat, you are not acting in love if you eat it. Don't let your eating ruin someone for whom Christ died. Then you will not be criticized for doing something you believe is good. For the kingdom of God is not a matter of what we eat or drink, but of living a life of goodness and peace and joy in the Holy Spirit. ... Remember, all foods are acceptable, but it is wrong to eat something if it makes another person stumble....You may believe there's nothing wrong with what you are doing, but keep it between yourself and God. Blessed are those who don't feel guilty for doing something they have decided is right." [1548]

For Paul the dietary laws were just the wedge issue. His real issue was the comity he wanted between Christians and Jews. Here's some of the evidence. Paul felt compelled to assure these Christians that he did not preach a gospel that led to lawless behavior.[1549] Indeed, he made a point of correcting a misperception that his teaching encouraged lawlessness by writing, *"... some people even slander us by claiming that we say, 'The more we sin, the better it is!' Those who say such things deserve to be condemned."* [1550] As we will explore below, he was also clear that God had not abandoned Israel. As he put it: *"I ask then: Did God reject his people? By no means! I am an Israelite myself, a descendant of Abraham, from the tribe of Benjamin. God did not reject his people..."*[1551] This is from the same person who had once attacked the Jewish-Christians by likening their headquarters, *"the present city of Jerusalem"*, to the *Old Testament* figure of Hagar adding that *"she is in slavery with her children."*[1552] This is also from the same person who wrote that the Jews *"both killed the Lord Jesus and the prophets, and drove us out. They are not pleasing to God, but hostile to all men,..."*[1553]

But the later Paul instructed Gentiles in the intricacies of Jewish history and tied them to Abraham in *Romans* 4. He even writes in *Romans* 15:8 *"For I say that Christ has become a servant to the circumcision on behalf of the truth of God to confirm the promises given to the fathers."* This echoes one of Jesus's most famous parables, the Prodigal Son.[1554] The father, God, welcomes back a dissolute son. The elder son is perturbed but the father says to him in *Luke* chapter 15 verse 31, *"Son, you are always with me, and all that is mine is yours."*

What is this, if not a commitment to the Jewish people? The picture becomes more complete in the *Book of Romans* where Paul makes Jesus's point about the elder brother[1555]even more forcibly. Like the prodigal's older brother, the Jews according to Paul are always with God. For Paul this is a conviction, not a pose. He writes of the Jews in chapter 11 verses 28-29, that they are *"beloved, for the sake of their ancestors; for the gifts and the calling of God is irrevocable."* Only through Jesus as a Jew could universalism - the covenant of God with Israel made available to all - be achieved.[1556] As Paul wrote in *Romans* 15:9 after describing Christ's role to the Jews in the previous verse, Christ was also a servant to the Gentiles so that they would *"glorify God for His mercy."*

All of this is critically important to the topic of inclusive Christianity. To emphasize: Paul is changing the position that he wrote to the Galatians that they should not tolerate those who followed dietary laws (James's followers told them the opposite) to tell the Romans now that it did not matter. Only *"Goodness and peace and joy in the Holy Spirit"*[1557] mattered. The Jews and the Christians were branches of the same tree.[1558] In essence, Paul emphasized that through Jesus the God of Israel was including Gentiles as full participants in Judaism.[1559]

Romans has been described as the "Gospel According to Paul."[1560] It is the last of his surviving letters. It teaches salvation by faith and has changed the lives of people – Augustine, Martin Luther, John Wesley (1703 – 1791), Karl Barth (1886 – 1968) - who have changed societies and ways of thinking.[1561]

Augustine - He is regarded by many Protestants as a precursor to the Reformation because of his teachings on God's grace.[1562]Augustine's own conversion was prompted in Milan in the late 300s where, in a garden, he heard a child's voice urging him to read a passage in *Romans*.[1563] As the Western Roman Empire slowly collapsed, Augustine wrote the City *of God*. He saw that the real importance of the world was as the staging ground for the City of God. He saw the City of God as eternal and unrealizable on earth, brought into being by God's love and the Church. The Church and the City of God were related in Augustine's view but not identical in the present era. Eventually, however, the "Church Triumphant" would emerge with Christ's reign on earth. Augustine essentially relegated the state to a subordinate position to God and thereby made Western notions of political freedom conceivable.[1564],

Luther - Martin Luther at age 34 was angered by the selling of indulgences by Archbishop Albert of Mainz. Indulgences were a guarantee of a remission of the punishment for sins. Albert had a large collection of relics that were part of his business. These included a supposed bone of the *Old Testament* patriarch Isaac, manna, a piece of the burning bush through which God communicated to Moses, one of the rocks thrown to kill Stephen the Martyr, and assorted other junk to sell to the naive. Luther had become a popular preacher by that year saying: "Nobody will go to hear a lecture now unless the lecturer is teaching my theology, the theology of the *Bible* and St. Augustine and all true theologians of the church...." He was reading *Romans* when he first understood - as he put it through the Holy Spirit - the phrase: *"the just shall live by faith."* On October 31, 1517 he nailed his 95 theses, protesting conditions in the Catholic Church to the door of Wittenberg Castle and history changed.[1565]

Wesley - John Wesley's conversion was recorded in his diary on May 24, 1738: "In the evening, I went very unwillingly to a society in Aldersgate Street, where one was reading Luther's preface to the *Epistle to the Romans*. About a quarter before nine, while he was describing the change which God works in the heart through faith in Christ, I felt my heart strangely warmed. I felt I did trust in Christ, Christ alone for my salvation; and an assurance was given me that He has taken away *my sins*, even *mine* and saved *me* from the law of sin and death." This was not instantaneous; Wesley had been under the influence of the Moravians since his journey to Georgia in 1735. Following his conversion, Wesley took the gospel to the open air. He lived to age 88, traveling perhaps a quarter of a million miles mostly by horseback and preaching incessantly – he gave eighty sermons in eight weeks at age 85. Wesley greatly influenced Christianity in England and America, helping to create a whole new Christian denomination and several off-shoots. He came to see holiness or perfection as the essence of religion with faith as the door. (In this particular he moved away from Augustine, Luther and Calvin.) This eventually gave birth to Pentecostalism.[1566] Wesley inspired the Universalism movement and the Salvation Army in the century after his death.[1567]

Wesley also greatly affected the social life of England. In the early nineteenth century large numbers of Britain's urban and industrial masses converted to Methodism. Within one hundred years, Methodist laymen were often the most effective local union leaders and in the forefront of the rising Labour Party.[1568]

Barth - Karl Barth a Swiss pastor published a commentary on *Romans* in 1918. It was a reaction to the optimistic tenets of nineteenth century liberal theology. Barth reported later a "joyful sense of discovery" as he studied Paul's writing. He saw it as a message of God's faithfulness to people. Barth became the leading and most controversial Protestant of his time with his views of the separation of people from God and justification by faith. "Barth's ideas would become known as 'neoorthodoxy,' although that conservative-sounding term fails to capture the startling nature of the underlying thought (Barth himself hated the term). This was no mere return to fundamentalism. The neoorthodox were open to scholarly approaches to the *Bible* and rejected notions of inerrancy,.... But on occasion, particularly during the horrible years when the Swiss almost literally lived within the sound of the cannon, Barth's reactions sounded as if they came from a more primitive age, a prophetic time."[1569] An American contemporary and intellectual ally was Reinhold Niebuhr (1892 – 1971) who saw the flaws in human nature in the difficult labor situation in the 1920s Detroit.[1570]

Paul's vision of Jewish-Christian alliance was eventually trampled by history. In modern times, though, could it be revived? After the long and tortured relationship between Christians and Jews is rapprochement possible? I think it is and again there are arguments for this in the *New Testament*. For the first argument, consider the role of the Pharisees.

In Jerusalem, facing a mob of angry Jewish-Christians and then on trial for his life, Paul split the opposition between the Sadducees whom history regards as Quislings with a first loyalty to Rome, and the Pharisees who were in many respects much like the followers of Jesus. This account in *Acts* 23 verses 6-9 shows Paul citing his own belief in an afterlife and immediately dividing the Pharisees who agreed with him from the party of the Sadducees who did not accept an afterlife. (The Sadducees's more materialistic view of death must have been unusual in that time because it is called out by both the *New Testament* and Josephus. [1571]) The Pharisees in this instance in *Acts* 23 sided with Paul.[1572]

In fact, a close study of the Gospels and *Acts* shows a complex relationship between the Pharisees and Christianity. There is clear-cut evidence of a great enmity toward Jesus. We see Pharisees seeking to trap him with questions[1573] and even plotting to kill him.[1574] But they were divided about him. *John* records that, *"Some of the Pharisees said, 'This man Jesus is not from God, for he is working on the Sabbath.' Others said, 'But how could an ordinary sinner do such miraculous signs?' So there was a deep division of opinion among them."*[1575] Further, there is a stream of verses in the Gospels and *Acts* that link the Pharisees to the Christians, at least the Jewish-Christian branch.

Some Pharisees sought the Baptism of John.[1576] The Pharisees also apparently sought converts.[1577] *Luke* records three separate dinners for Jesus hosted by

Pharisees. [1578]Pharisees warned Jesus of Herod Antipater's plots against him. [1579] Jesus advised people to obey the Pharisees even when the Pharisees did not live up to their own ideals[1580] and his statement, *"The Sabbath was made for man, not man for the Sabbath"* was a Pharisaic statement. [1581] Pharisees included in their ranks Nicodemus to whom Jesus taught the need to be born again.[1582] Nicodemus later defended both Jesus and various police who were in awe of him and as a result was called a Galilean – *"You are not also from Galilee, are you?"*[1583] Nicodemus eventually buried Jesus.[1584] Paul was also a Pharisee[1585] and never directly criticized them. The writer of *Acts* also has Paul claiming to have been trained by the Pharisees's icon, Gamaliel [1586]who is described as a good Pharisee.[1587] Paul claimed according to *Acts* to be a son of a Pharisee.[1588] (Only two people in history, Paul and the ancient Jewish historian Josephus, left direct commentary that they were Pharisees.[1589])

The writer of *Acts* also suggests that some Pharisees had joined the Jesus movement inasmuch as they were present at the Council of Jerusalem.[1590]Judas of Galilee[1591] who founded the Zealot Party in the tax revolt was a Pharisee and one of his descendants, Eleazar ben Simon, led the Jews at Masada in 73 where the Jews committed mass suicide rather than surrender to the Romans. Many Pharisees were crucified in the Jewish Wars of 66-70 and 132-35. Josephus saw the Pharisees as dangerously radical. [1592] Conversely, some of the Pharisees may have been attracted to Jesus as an alternative to Roman rule.

The Pharisees were concerned that Jesus associated with "sinners,"[1593] compromising the purity of Judaism. They also objected that he claimed to be able to personally forgive sins[1594] which they saw as the prerogative of God. These concerns may have been reflected in later decades by some of the separatism of the Jewish-Christians and their anti-Pauline stance toward Jesus's divinity. The *New Testament* is edited in such a way as to marginalize the Pharisees as Christianity de-connected from its Jewish roots. Once again, we can see this process by studying a redaction - in this case the redaction of the Great Commandment to love God and love one's neighbor. This story is recorded in *Mark* 12, *Matthew* 22 and *Luke* 10.[1595]

This simple message has encouraged millions if not billions. But in the telling and re-telling we can observe Jesus's relationships with Pharisees going through change. The common elements of the story are that Jesus is asked a question by a Pharisee and either answers or with Socratic[1596] means elicits an answer that the greatest commandment is *"'You must love the Lord your God with all your heart, all your soul, all your strength, and all your mind.' And, 'Love your neighbor as yourself.'"* *Mark* covers this story in straightforward manner. The Pharisee asks Jesus what the greatest commandment is, Jesus answers and *"realizing how much the man understood"* added, *"You are not far from the kingdom of God."*[1597] But in the years after the writing of *Mark* material changes took place. *Matthew* asserts that the Pharisee *"tried to trap him with this question"*[1598] and *Luke* says that the Pharisee had a follow-up question because he *"wanted to justify his actions."*[1599] (Note: His follow-up question led to the story of the Good Samaritan.)

For the second argument that a Jewish-Christian reconciliation is possible, consider the words of Samuel Taylor Coleridge (1772 – 1834) who called *Romans* "the profoundest piece of writing in existence."[1600] *Romans* shows Jesus Christ as a redeemer offering the whole world love.[1601] In this treatise of his mature thinking, Paul goes past Pauline Christianity to be an Apostle to the Jews.[1602] He writes about preaching in Jerusalem itself and beyond.[1603] Ultimately, this *"Hebrew born of Hebrews"*[1604] comes home a universalist. This is symbolized in *Acts* which moves from Jesus's command to his disciples to stay in Jerusalem[1605] to Paul's statement, *"and so we came to Rome."*[1606] There are signs of Paul's universalism in *Acts* and in his earlier letters. Paul's sermon at Mars Hill (*Acts* 17: 22-31) stresses that the Athenians had some notion about the true God and tried to build upon that belief. That monotheistic view can be compared with Paul's short speech in Lystra when he was confronted with people who regarded him as a god: *"Men, why are you doing these things? We are also men of the same nature as you, and preach the gospel to you that you should turn from these vain things to a living God, WHO MADE THE HEAVEN AND THE EARTH AND THE SEA AND ALL THAT IS IN THEM. In the generations gone by He permitted all the nations to go their own ways; and yet He did not leave Himself without witness, in that He did good and gave you rains from heaven and fruitful seasons, satisfying your hearts with food and gladness."* (*Acts* 14: 15-17). The essence of the Mars Hill speech was also distilled in his letter to the Thessalonians: *"For (others) report about us what kind of a reception we had with you, and how you turned to God from idols to serve a living and true God, and to wait for His Son from heaven, whom He raised from the dead, that is Jesus, who rescues us from the wrath to come."* (*I Thessalonians* 1:9-10). Finally, Paul's view of God and people can be seen in this verse in the first chapter of *Romans*: *"For since the creation of the world His invisible attributes, His eternal power and divine nature, have been clearly seen, being understood through what has been made,..."* (*Romans* 1:20).

Paul, then, preached about the Jewish God. We will touch on this now in an elaboration of Paul's view of the complex relationship between Christians and Jews.

Paul shows true universalism in *Romans* because he seems to find salvation for the Jews and other non-Christians.[1607] How did Paul get to this view? There are several points to consider but it seems obvious that Paul's views changed over time. Here are some of the possible reasons for these changes of opinion.

First, Paul understood that the Christian communities consisted of Jews and Gentiles. For example:

- *Romans 15:25-17 - "For Macedonia and Achaia have been pleased to make a contribution for the poor among the saints in Jerusalem. Yes, they were pleased to do so, and they are indebted to them. For if the Gentiles have shared in their spiritual things, they are indebted to minister to them also in material things."*
- *Galatians 1:22-23 - "I was still unknown by sight to the churches of Judea which were in Christ; but only, they kept hearing, 'He who once persecuted us is now preaching the faith which he once tried to destroy.'"*

The collections for the Jewish- Christian church that we discussed in Chapter 7 also show this. Paul operated, we would say today, in a diverse environment, perhaps uniquely among the early apostles.

Second, we see evidence earlier in *Romans* that he had thought about the non-Christians Jews often. *Romans 3:1-4* has this question/answer: *"Then what advantage has the Jew? Or what is the benefit of circumcision? Great in every respect. First of all, that they were entrusted with the oracles of God. What then? If some did not believe, their unbelief will not nullify the faithfulness of God, will it? May it never be! Rather, let God be found true, though every man be found a liar, as it is written, 'THAT YOU MAY BE JUSTIFIED IN YOUR WORDS, AND PREVAIL WHEN YOU ARE JUDGED.'"*

But he quickly drops the topic until the beginning of chapter 9 where he takes up the subject again in a very abrupt transition. The previous verse holds that nothing *"will be able to separate us from the love of God, which is in Christ Jesus our Lord."* Paul then talks of his fellow Jews with great concern saying that he would be willing to be separated from Christ on their behalf. *Romans 9:3* holds: *"For I could wish that I myself were accursed, separated from Christ for the sake of my brethren, my kinsmen according to the flesh."*

The next three chapters cover the status of non-Christian Jews but are quite complicated and it is hard to track Paul's views. I will break this into three sections that more-or-less match up with the chapter divisions.

The greater part of chapter 9 deals with two large concepts. The key verses are:

- *Romans 9: 6-9* in which it is said that somehow the Christians have replaced the Jews as the chosen people: *"But it is not as though the word of God has failed. For they are not all Israel who are descended from Israel; nor are they all children because they are Abraham's descendants, but:* 'THROUGH ISAAC YOUR DESCENDANTS WILL BE NAMED.' *That is, it is not the children of the flesh who are children of God, but the children of the promise are regarded as descendants."*

- *Romans 9: 14-15* in which it is said that God is not to be questioned: *"What shall we say then? There is no injustice with God, is there? May it never be! For He says to Moses,* 'I WILL HAVE MERCY ON WHOM I HAVE MERCY, AND I WILL HAVE COMPASSION ON WHOM I HAVE COMPASSION.'"

There is nothing in these concepts that would surprise many Christians today.

From *Romans 9:30* and through much of chapter 10 Paul contrasts the Gentiles and the Jews. The key verses are:

- *Romans 9:30* in which it is said that Gentiles have found salvation by faith: *"What shall we say then? That Gentiles, who did not pursue righteousness, attained righteousness, even the righteousness which is by faith."*

- *Romans 9:31-33* in which it is said that the Jews have stumbled: *"But Israel, pursuing a law of righteousness, did not arrive at that law. Why? Because they did not pursue it by faith, but as though it were by works. They stumbled over the stumbling stone, just as it is written,* 'BEHOLD, I LAY IN ZION A STONE OF STUMBLING AND A ROCK OF OFFENSE, AND HE WHO BELIEVES IN HIM WILL NOT BE DISAPPOINTED.'"

There is nothing in these concepts that would surprise many Christians today.

The surprises come in chapter 11 of *Romans* where it is seen that God's rejection of the Jews is not final. The key verses are:

- *Romans 11:1* which is a declaration of support: *"I say then, God has not rejected His people, has He? May it never be! For I too am an Israelite, a descendant of Abraham, of the tribe of Benjamin."*

- *Romans 11:5-6* in which it looks like the Jews are made up of a chosen remnant and a resistant majority. After discussing an *Old Testament* event in which the Jews were hard pressed, Paul writes: *"In the same way then, there has also come to be at the present time a remnant according to God's gracious choice. But if it is by grace, it is no longer on the basis of works, otherwise grace is no longer grace."*

- *Romans* 11:11 in which it looks like the Jews' stumbling did not mean that they fell but was somehow to the benefit of the Gentiles: *"I say then, they did not stumble so as to fall, did they? May it never be! But by their transgression salvation has come to the Gentiles, to make them jealous."*

- *Romans* 11:12 in which there is this assertion: *"Now if their transgression is riches for the world and their failure is riches for the Gentiles, how much more will their **fulfillment** be!"* (Emphasis added). By "fulfillment" Paul refers to the remnant of Jewish-Christians and the majority of the other Jews.

- *Romans* 11:15 in which Paul speaks of the salvation of the Jews at the end of time when the resurrection of the dead occurs: *"For if their rejection is the reconciliation of the world, what will their acceptance be but **life from the dead?"*** (Emphasis added).

- *Romans* 11:16 in which Paul uses metaphors of dough/whole lump and roots/ branches to show the Christians's dependence on the Jews: *"If the first piece of dough is holy, the lump is also; and if the root is holy, the branches are too."*

- *Romans* 11:17-24 in which Paul uses the metaphor of a tree and branches to talk about salvation, noting that although (Jewish) branches were broken off and (Gentile) branches grafted in, that God could easily reverse that process.

- *Romans* 11:25-27 in which Paul seems to be saying that the resistance of the majority of the Jews will last until the right number of Gentiles are saved. Then, all the Jews will be saved: *"For I do not want you, brethren, to be uninformed of this mystery—so that you will not be wise in your own estimation—that a partial hardening has happened to Israel until the fullness of the Gentiles has come in; and so **all Israel will be saved**; just as it is written, 'THE **DELIVERER** WILL COME FROM ZION, HE WILL REMOVE UNGODLINESS FROM JACOB. THIS MY COVENANT WITH THEM, WHEN I TAKE AWAY THEIR SINS.'"* (Emphases added) In these verses in *Romans*, Paul supports his opinion that ethnic Jews will be saved by apparent references to *Isaiah* 59:20 and *Jeremiah* 31:33–34. It is significant that allusions to the new covenant of *Jeremiah* 31:33–34 elsewhere in the *New Testament* refer to Christians or the church and not, as here, to Jews.[1608] In the context of this passage, the Apostle to the Gentiles can arguably be heard to be saying that being a Jew is just as good as faith in Christ as a route to salvation. The salvation of "all Israel" is assigned to the "Deliverer" which is this context means

God. That means it is beyond Paul's mission which focused on faith in Christ. A reasonable conclusion is that Jesus Christ has no role in the salvation of ethnic Jews - at least in the end times.

Paul then expands the concept. In verses 32 and 36, Paul brings out a message that the *"all Israel"* of verse 26 applies to all people and all of creation:

- *Romans* 11:32: *"For God has shut up all in disobedience so that He may show mercy to all."*
- *Romans* 11:36: *"For from Him and through Him and to Him are all things. To Him be the glory forever. Amen."*

Let's summarize: Although, as we have noted, Paul has been critical of Jews, in *Romans* 9-11 he harkens back to his Judaism and sees that God will save them;[1609] Moreover, this view of God coheres with Paul's views as expressed In *I Corinthians* 15:24-28[1610] and discussed in Chapter 4 of this book. His views drive toward monotheism and he believes that God will save the Jews. We will discuss monotheism more in the Chapter 11, the final chapter of this book.

This view that Paul saw salvation for the Jews apart from Jesus Christ is, admittedly, a non-mainline view of Pauline thought. I put it out now as a plausible interpretation of *Romans* 9-11 and as an indication of a universalistic strain in Christian thought. That outlook may be buttressed by two obscure passages of scripture. The first we have touched upon. The second we will mention in Chapter 11:

- *I Peter* 3:18-20 and 4:6 which describes Jesus visiting Hell to save people. (As noted, this Epistle has Pauline connections.)
- *I Corinthians* 15:29 which allows for the baptism of people already dead.

Admittedly again, these passages are in the more outer areas of *New Testament* teachings. But they may stand for this: Within Christianity there is a universalistic tendency.

Christianity and Judaism have always been closely related religions. A Roman official of the early Christian era is recorded as saying about the Jewish leaders's views toward Paul: *"They simply had some points of disagreement with him about their own religion and about a dead man, Jesus, whom Paul asserted to be alive."*[1611] The Jewish sage, Maimonides (1135 – 1204), pointed out over 800 years ago, that it was primarily Christianity which has spread knowledge of the Jews's *Bible* to the human race.[1612] Without the destruction of Jerusalem in 70AD the two religions might have remained one.[1613] But that first century slaughter changed everything. Donald Harman Akenson called it almost apocalyptic and compared it to a "direct hit by a meteor," a "nuclear blast" and a "nuclear explosion."[1614] How either Christianity or Judaism would have developed together or independently aside from that catastrophe cannot be known. History does not disclose its alternatives.

This is not a simple issue. The conventional Jewish view is that Jesus was a good Jew and that Paul was an anti-Semite who developed Christianity. Hyam Maccoby[1615] portrays Paul as an adventurer who took Christianity out of "normal Judaism." This is countered by some Jewish scholarship which holds that in the pre-Destruction era Paul was "this amazing Jew, who so strongly emphasized his Jewish (indeed Pharisaic) background."[1616] The compromise is the Pauline answer that, although Judaism and Christianity remain two different religions, they are of the same branch.

Let's end this chapter by focusing what we know and what we do not know of Paul of Tarsus. Paul's missionary activity took place roughly between 33 and 64. But we only know about approximately seven years of that period. His letters and even the *Book of Acts* written some fifteen or more years after his death, concentrate on the years between 50 and 57. Here, primarily from Martin Hengel and Anna Maria Schwemer,[1617] is an analysis of the longer time period:

- Abt.30 – Crucifixion of Jesus Christ.
- Abt. 32/33 – Murder of Stephen – *Acts* 7.
- Abt. 33 - Conversion of Paul – *Acts* 9, 22 and 26. Paul covers his conversion in a more restrained fashion in: 1.) *Galatians* 1:15-16 where he writes: *"But even before I was born, God chose me and called me by his marvelous grace. Then it pleased him to reveal his Son to me···"* From this, the reader of *Galatians* might conclude that Paul was in Damascus at the time of his conversion as no "Damascus Road" is specified as it is by Luke but Damascus is implied by Paul.[1618] 2.) *I Corinthians* 15:8 where he writes: – *"last of all, as to one untimely born, He appeared to me also.."*)

Here is how we calculate to about the year 33: According to *Acts* 18: 12-17 Paul was in Corinth when Gallio was there as governor of Achaia and we know that Gallio was governor in 51-2. We can subtract back from that date 17 years - 3 from *Galatians* 1:18 and 14 from *Galatians* 2:1. Assuming another 2 years for travel, that 19 years gets to about 33. [1619] Note: Paul was probably under thirty at the time of his conversion because he is described as a "young man" at the stoning of Stephen in *Acts* 7:58. As noted in Chapter 5, Paul Johnson estimates that he was born in about 9AD making him about 12 years younger than Jesus.[1620]

- Abt. 33-36 - Paul in Damascus and Arabia – *Acts* 9:19-23 and *Galatians* 1:17-18. Luke writes that Paul stayed there for "many days" and does not mention time in "Arabia." Paul writes of this as a three year[1621] period including time in "Arabia."

- Abt. 36 - Flight of Paul from Damascus – *Acts* 9: 23-25 and *II Corinthians* 11:32ff. Both of these accounts assert that the city was under guard to watch for Paul and that he escaped through some type of opening or window in the wall in a basket. The difference is that Luke writes that the Jews were after Paul and Paul writes that an official of Aretas the king was pursuing him In Chapter 2 of this book, I put these two accounts into the Inconsistent but Reconcilable category but I prefer Paul's version because it was more contemporaneous and first-hand.

- Abt. 36 - Visit of Paul with Peter in Jerusalem and journey to Tarsus - *Acts* 9:26-30 and *Galatians* 1:18-20. Luke has Barnabas taking Paul to "the Apostles." Paul writes that he stayed at Peter's house for two weeks and did not see any other apostles except for James the brother of Jesus. Verse 20 makes this emphasis: *"Now in what I am writing to you, I assure you before God that I am not lying."* I have found these sections to be Inconsistent, Irreconcilable and Insignificant but can understand that others will find them reconcilable at some level. In any event, we should assume that these two weeks with Peter constituted one of the world's more important meetings and they must have reached some level of consensus. Paul must have learned something about the life of Jesus. Peter, for his part, must have learned something about Paul's more universal views. The evidence for this is seen in that Peter had already had an outreach to the Samaritans (*Acts* 8), later had his own mission to the non-Jews (*Acts* 10-11) and still later was supportive of Paul at the Council of Jerusalem (*Acts* 15). Moreover, Paul assumed Peter had knowledge of the inclusion of the non-Jews in *Galatians* 2; and, *I Peter*[1622] shows affinity for Paul. In short, the two weeks were critical. They came some six years after the crucifixion and about thirteen years before the Council of Jerusalem. Without this initial meeting between Paul and Peter, the Council may not have been a success. It also is the basis for *I Corinthians* 15:11 in which Paul asserts that with all the diversity there was still a core unity: *"Whether then it was I or they, so we preach and so you believed.*" This is a is a fabulous statement to come from the pen of someone as controversial as Paul. The thesis of this book is that *New Testament* Christianity has a healthy amount of diversity. It also has an underlying unity.

- Abt. 36/37 to 39/40 - Paul in Tarsus and Cilicia. During this time the mission of the Hellenists in Antioch began – *Acts* 11:19-24. This is a critical period and the length suggests that much of Paul's theology may have been developed apart from the Antiochene church. Certainly the dispute he had there later adds weight to this possibility.

- Abt 38/39 - Journey of Barnabas from Jerusalem to Antioch - *Acts* 11:25.

- Abt. 39/40 - Barnabas brings Paul from Tarsus to Antioch - *Acts* 11:26. Paul may have been working as a missionary in and around Tarsus and it might have taken up to a year to make contact.

- Abt. 41 to 46/47 – Paul's mission in Antioch. During the first part of this time several events occurred: 1.) Paul's "heavenly journey" would have occurred because he wrote about it fourteen years later (*II Corinthians* 12:2ff). 2.) Agabus the prophet comes from Jerusalem and the Antioch Christians send a collection of money to Jerusalem with Barnabas and Paul (*Acts* 11:27-30). (This trip is difficult to reconcile with *Galatians* and as noted earlier, at least one commentator suggests that it is reported in *Acts* out of order and actually denoted some of the collections Paul made.) 3.) James the brother of John is murdered in Jerusalem and Peter is imprisoned and escapes on Passover (*Acts* 12: 1-17).

- Abt. 46/47 - First journey of Paul and Barnabas to Cyprus, Cilicia and southern Galacia. This is usually called Paul's **first missionary journey** - *Acts* 13:3-14:28. (Emphasis added).

- Abt. the end 48/early 49 - Council of Jerusalem - *Acts* 15: 1-29 and *Galatians* 2:1-10.

- Abt. the Spring of 49 - Paul sets out for Asia Minor and the Aegean. He has his first break with Barnabas over the exclusion of John Mark - *Acts* 15:36-41. He starts what is usually called his **second missionary journey**. (Emphasis added). Before this we really don't know much about Paul's missionary activities in "Arabia," Tarsus, Cilicia and other places. It might be covered by a statement that he wrote years later: "*from Jerusalem and round about as far as Illyricum I have fully preached the gospel of Christ.*" (*Romans* 15:19). Paul is without a doubt the best known figure within Christianity for at least the first hundred and fifty years of its existence but our knowledge about him really stems from the next seven to ten years.[1623]

- Abt. 49/50 - Paul in Thessalonica - *Acts* 17:1-9.
- Abt. 50-52 - Paul in Corinth - *Acts* 18: 1-17.
- Abt. 52/53 - Journey of Paul to Ephesus, from there to Caesarea and apparently Jerusalem and then Antioch where he had his second break with Barnabas over the exclusion of non-Jews. Paul returns to Ephesus through Galatia - *Acts* 18:18-23 and *Galatians* 2:13. There is a lot packed in here.[1624] Luke makes no mention of this break with Barnabas which must have been more painful than the first. Paul starts what is usually called his **third missionary journey**. (Emphasis added).
- Abt. 53-55 - Paul in Ephesus – *Acts* 19 verse 10 states that he was there for two years. He wrote *I Corinthians* there (*1 Corinthians* 16:8). As noted earlier, while living in Ephesus, Paul also may have written *Galatians* and *II Corinthians*.
- Abt. 56/57 - Paul in Corinth again. *Acts* 20:2-3 reports that he spent three months in Greece from which we may infer Corinth. Paul probably wrote *Romans* there. The evidence: 1.) In *1 Corinthians* 1:14 he mentions that he baptized someone named Gaius and in *Romans* 16:23 he assert that he is staying at Gaius's house. [1625]2.) He was getting ready to head to Jerusalem as seen in *Acts* 20:16 and the letter to the Romans mentions this Jerusalem trip. – *Romans* 15:25, 31. 3.) According to *Romans* 16:1 Phoebe delivered the letter to the Romans and, as noted, she lived near Corinth.
- Abt. 57 –Paul visits with the deacon Philip in Caesarea on his way to Jerusalem. Luke says little about Philip although as evidenced by the hospitality that Philip showed Paul in *Acts* 21: 8-14, it is likely that they were philosophically on the same page and did similar work.
- Abt. 57 - Paul in Jerusalem – *Acts* 21:17- 23:30.
- Abt. 57-59 - Paul in prison in Caesarea and his trial before King Agrippa and Bernice and the governor Festus– *Acts* 23:33 – 26:31. *Acts* 24:26-27 asserts that he was imprisoned there for two years while the Roman official Felix was hoping for a bribe. Paul may have written *Philemon* there.
- Abt. 62 - Martyrdom of James the brother of the Lord in Jerusalem[1626]; Possible martyrdom of Paul in Rome.
- Abt. 62/63 – Possible journey of Paul to Spain.
- Abt. 64 – Possible martyrdom of Peter and Paul in Rome.[1627]

In conclusion, Paul preached with an urgency, to get the word to everyone before what he considered the "end" - that is why he needed to get to Spain[1628], which in a flat-earth era was the end of the world and maybe he got there. His basic teaching was that love of others was more important than everything else – even faith and knowledge were nothing by comparison as he wrote in the timeless language of *I Corinthians* 13. He also summarized all laws to loving other people, not mentioning God.[1629] He advised that *"carrying one another's burdens"* fulfilled the law of Christ.[1630]

But he kept having conflicts with Jewish-Christians and these conflicts led to the negotiations at the Council of Jerusalem, Here his views were tentatively accepted with the understanding that he would contribute money for some purpose. In the *Book of Romans*, he is preparing somewhat apprehensively[1631] to deliver this aid even though the Jewish-Christians were worrying whether this *"all things to all men"* evangelist was fulfilling the commitments he made at the Council. Their concern was grounded in this fact: Pauline Christianity severed the message about Jesus from nationalism and thereby may have made it possible for Christianity to survive. Paul was a religious inventor, a genius in the field. He had a synthetic mind. He was willing – as we have seen – to examine, interpret and add to the words of Jesus Christ. As Albert Schweitzer (1875 – 1965) reported, Paul established the right to think within Christianity and could be called "the patron saint of thought in Christianity."[1632] His Christianity was not in any new code of moral rules but in the power of Christ to empower us to follow good conduct. Albert Schweitzer again on Paul's version of Christianity: "Ethics are brought in a natural way into connection with the idea of the forgiveness of sins and of redemption in general…"[1633]

The church as described in *Acts* which began in and around the Jerusalem Temple reached its launching pad for universalism from Paul's rented apartment[1634] in Rome.

This universalism is emphasized by Luke in the *Book of Acts* with characteristic artistry. As noted, the details of Paul's Damascus Road experience vary and there is a deliberate evolution of Paul's commission to take the good news to the world. The commission is given greater and greater emphasis throughout the book as follows:

- *Acts* 9:15 - Jesus to Ananias. One verse.
- *Acts* 22:14-15 - Ananias to Paul. Two verses.
- *Acts* 26:16-18 - Jesus to Paul. Three verses.[1635]

In a generation or two, Paul's brand of the gospel began to sweep away all or most of the competitors and even the Protestant Reformation stayed within Pauline bonds - in fact it strengthened those bonds. Paul's prominence in history is therefore assured. Moreover, he may be the most "authentically defined" of all the figures in the Bible. In this regard, "(h)is only rival is King David."[1636]

By the end of his life, Paul saw that the saving promise that God had made to Abraham was fulfilled in Christ for all of humanity. In *Galatians* 3:8 he described it as *"the gospel (preached) beforehand."* Paul, then, saw the gospel as the welcome news of God's grace now covering the Gentiles. He saw the gospel as Israel's message to the world.[1637]

To summarize, the religion of Paul is a river so deep, that it might be called an ocean and he would have been surprised to see it systematized. Yet the essentials could be grasped by ordinary people:

- The certainty of human sinfulness before God.
- The atoning sacrifice of Christ on the cross for all.
- The promise of resurrection and eternal life.
- Christ in us.[1638]

How then should we live? The concluding chapter of this book modestly offers one variation of Christianity.

CHAPTER 11

What then?
(The afterlife. Love and universalism)

What is the most efficient way to be a Christian? It is this: to be a good person and to believe in God. Jesus's life and death hold out for us a hope of life after death. Can we prove that? Of course not. It is only a hope and may not, in the end, be all that important.

So what do we know about Christianity and what does it mean?

From Josephus, who wrote in the 90s and who was the first non-Christian to write about Jesus we find:

- A mention of John the Baptist as a major pre-Jesus religious leader.
- Affirmation that one of Jesus's brothers was named James and that he supported his brother's goals.
- Affirmation that Jesus of Nazareth was indeed a significant religious figure in the first one-third of the first century, that he did something to trouble the Jewish religious establishment and therefore the local Roman authorities and that he was crucified.

Josephus's credibility is enhanced by his neutral approach. We also learn from Josephus that Jesus:

- Was a wise man.
- Did startling deeds.
- Gained a following among Jews and Gentiles.
- Was crucified by the order of the Roman governor after being accused by Jewish leaders.
- Was loved by his followers after his death who became known as Christians and still existed at the time of Josephus's writing.[1639],[1640]

We have more from antiquity. It is established in the four Gospels and by the second century Roman historian Tacitus[1641] that Jesus was put to death.[1642] A modern consensus is that "the fact of the death of Jesus as a consequence of crucifixion is indisputable, despite hypotheses of a pseudo-death or a deception which are sometimes put forward."[1643] The question of Jesus's nonexistence is "effectively dead as a scholarly question."[1644]

But after his crucifixion there is abiding mystery that must be noted. All four Gospels report of a man named Barabbas. *Matthew* reports that the Roman governor tried to release Jesus rather than a *"notorious prisoner named Jesus Barabbas"* (although some early manuscripts omit the word "Jesus" before "Barabbas"[1645]). *Mark* calls him Barabbas and reports that he was in prison with rebels and *"committed murder during the insurrection."*[1646] *Luke* reports that Barabbas was *"a man who had been put in prison for an insurrection that had taken place in the city, and for murder."*[1647] *John* reports that Barabbas was a *"bandit."*[1648]

This story about Barabbas has elements of legend. *Mark* notes that *"at the feast he (Pilate) used to release for them one prisoner for whom they asked."*[1649] *Matthew* records that *"at the feast the governor was accustomed to release for the crowd any one prisoner whom they wanted."*[1650] *Luke* implies the same[1651] and finally, up to seventy years after the event, the *Gospel of John* has Pilate saying to the Jewish leaders that *"you have a custom that I should release one man for you at the Passover."*[1652] However, there is no historical record that there was anything like a Passover amnesty.[1653] But, the story of the offered pardon may fit an anti-Jewish agenda. Pilate is presented as a weak pawn to the Jewish leaders and eventually, by *Matthew's* rendering *"all"* the people said about Jesus, *"his blood be on us and on our children"*[1654] while Barabbas walked free.[1655]

Further, Barabbas's name, especially when rendered in *Matthew* as "Jesus Barabbas," is very curious. The name means Son of God. "Bar" means "son" as when Peter is called Bar-Jonah in *Matthew* 16:17. Abba is a word for God as used in *Mark* 14:36, *Romans* 8:15, and *Galatians* 4:6.[1656] It is likely that this choice of names is very significant. Is it reasonable that the name Barabbas is no more significant than - for example – Sosipater, one of Paul's relatives mentioned in *Romans* 16:21? Lena Einhorn speculates that the insurrection that Barabbas engaged in was the confrontation on the Mount of Olives and that Jesus Christ was in league with him.[1657]

All this is of course speculative. A counter argument is that Jesus was not involved in the uprising because if he was, Peter, James and John and the other disciples would probably have been arrested and crucified alongside him. Instead, it appears that Peter lived on for a generation and as the historian Eusebius wrote was crucified upside down in Rome, probably in the 60s.[1658],[1659] This is what we can be sure of from history and the *New Testament*: that there was some sort of uprising in Jerusalem during what we now call Holy Week and that one of the leaders had a name meaning Son of God or even Jesus Son of God and that Jesus Christ was also crucified at the order of the Roman authorities.

So we know that Jesus Christ lived and that he was crucified. That means that he was nailed to a cross and left to die of shock. In the earliest account that we have of his crucifixion, Jesus died a relatively quick death – but it still took several hours - after calling out *"My God, my God, why have you forsaken me?"*[1660] From this execution, the greatest social movement in history arose.[1661] His followers started a movement in his name based on the conviction that he was somehow still alive.

In modern times, the story of Jesus can lead us to a belief in God. We don't have to believe that Jesus was God - just that, as the early Jewish-Christians believed, he pointed to God. The story of Jesus also suggests tantalizing possibilities – just possibilities – about a life beyond death. Finally, Jesus's teachings have stood for the ages as a guide. It is a thesis of this book that within this mix is a *New Testament* form of Christianity, shorn of inerrancy, the church, the deification of Jesus, the Second Coming and an earthly kingdom of God. Let's look at three elements of this.

Belief in God

Does God exist? I don't know but I do know that he *could* exist and that many are convinced that he[1662] does. James Madison wrote late in life, "The belief in a God All Powerful wise and good, is so essential to the moral order of the world and to the happiness of man, that arguments which enforce it cannot be drawn from too many sources nor adapted with too much solicitude to the different characters and capacities impressed with it."[1663]

For the most part, belief in God is intuitive. Justice William O. Douglas (1898 – 1980) wrote that "we are a religious people whose institutions presuppose a Supreme Being." President Eisenhower described himself as "the most intensely religious man I know."[1664] It may be that the concept of infinity – there is always something greater – suggests a god. There is also the very fact of our life and consciousness – it too may suggest a god to some. It may be, as Marcus Borg has said, that "...broadly speaking, worldviews fall into two main categories: religious and secular. For the secular worldview there is only 'this' - and by 'this' I mean the visible world of our ordinary experience. For a religious worldview, there is 'this' and 'more than this.'" [1665]

Francis Collins (1950 -) a leader of the Human Genome Project believes that the very improbability of existence argues for a creator God. For example, if gravity was off by just "one part in a hundred million million, then the expansion of the universe after the Big Bang would have not occurred in the fusion that was necessary for life to occur. A creator becomes a rather plausible explanation for what is otherwise an exceedingly improbable event - namely, our existence."[1666] As Albert Einstein once said, "The most incomprehensible thing about the world is that it is comprehensible." [1667] This may be what NT Wright called a form of Deism - an "absentee-landlord (whose) god keeps clear of historical involvement" – but it is still monotheistic.[1668]

There are some different and very legitimate notions of God. For at least a century many have held to a "high-minded, evolution-friendly theism."[1669] As a poet said in 1908,

"Some call it Evolution,
And others call it God."[1670]

Ulrich Zwingli (1484 – 1531) the leader of the Protestant Reformation in Switzerland wrote: "What God is is perhaps above human understanding, but not that God is."[1671] For Carl Sagan, "Darwin's insight that life evolved over the eons through natural selection was not just better science than *Genesis*, it also afforded a deeper, more satisfying *spiritual* experience." Sagan admired William James's definition of religion as a "feeling of being at home in the Universe."[1672] John Wayne reportedly said: "I don't much like God when he gets under a roof."[1673]

While we cannot prove or disprove God, we can know the effects of atheism which in our time have tended toward a degrading of human rights. "Without God," Dostoevsky famously wrote, "all is permitted"[1674] or as John Adams surveying the French Revolution declaimed, "I know not what to make of a republic of thirty million atheists."[1675] Here is the future of the French Revolution that Adams, a different kind of revolutionary, was sensing but could not yet know. The French Revolution ushered in two decades of "revolutionary and Napoleonic struggles, which would encompass all the great powers, leave the continent choking on its own blood - with a toll of over two million dead or maimed - realign boundaries, topple rulers, kill a pope, weaken empires, divide America, and presage the ghastly bloodshed of the twentieth century's two world wars." In August of 1792 a violent mob ...arrested the French royal family and murdered nine hundred Swiss Guards. "...(C)orpses of Swiss guards, what was left of them, were stripped naked and mutilated; gobbets of human flesh were mounted on pikes and carried in triumph through the streets; other corpses were piled on bonfires and then lit." This was after the king had ordered the Swiss Guards to cease firing.[1676]This is what Thomas Paine foresaw when he said "the people of France were running headlong into atheism."

If in France atheism was attended by a reign of terror, in America monotheism was attended by political progress. "America's Founders wrote in the Declaration of Independence that we are endowed 'by our Creator' with certain inalienable rights. Rights depend upon a moral source, a rights giver." That is a why a generation removed from the American and French Revolutions, Tocqueville observed that in America the "boldest" political ideas of the Enlightenment were "more fully applied" then in any other country. "It was only the anti-religious doctrines that never were able to make headway."[1677]

In history, non-events that were expected are sometimes more astonishing than actual events. A surprising non-event in the twentieth century was the failure of God to die.[1678] Good can come out of that fact because for all the harm that religion has done, atheism has done far more. The Soviet Gulag, the Cultural Revolution in China of the 1960s and the Cambodian genocide of the 1970s were all linked to atheistic regimes.

There is little more that I can say on the topic. People have learned to believe or disbelieve in a prime mover or first cause or God independent of scientific advance and despite such human suffering as the horrors of war in the twentieth century during which more than 150 million people were killed by state violence. Some turn from God when they see suffering. More turn toward God.

Doing good

Paul and Christians ever since have had to deal with a point of view that goes something like this: "Since we're saved by grace we can live free of the moral laws." Often, as in Corinth, that had something to do with sex but as we have seen, this view covered other areas as well. The authors and editors of the *New Testament* worked to blunt this line of reasoning. One of their rhetorical tools was reference to the *Old Testament* figure of Abraham.

Abraham may or may not be an historical person but three billion of the world's people descend, spiritually from him. If he lived, the time estimates are generally between 2100 BC and about 1000 BC. According to *Genesis* 11:31 and 15:7 he came from the land of Ur which is in present day Iraq. Abraham was an important figure or persona in the ancient world. He was seen as the first figure of civilization. As noted, there was a tradition based on *Genesis*

14:15[1679] and 15:2[1680] that he had been king of Damascus. Josephus wrote of Abraham that "He was a man of ready intelligence on all matters, persuasive with his hearers." *Genesis* 12:10 records that Abraham went to Egypt to escape a famine. Josephus said he went there to share and essentially compete with the religious leaders there.[1681] He is a person of *Genesis*, the *New Testament* and the *Koran*.[1682] A *Book of Abraham* that Joseph Smith said he translated in about 1835 has been scripture for the Mormon church (since 1880).[1683] Abraham's move toward monotheism - or at least the story of someone called Abraham doing so - changed the world. It made it easier to envision a universal code. In 1818, John Adams wrote: "It has pleased the Providence of the first Cause, the Universal Cause, that Abraham should give religion not only to the Hebrews but to Christians and Mahomitans, the greatest part of the modern civilized world."[1684]

As noted, Paul and James the brother of Jesus had fundamental differences. But in Abraham there is common ground. Both cite Abraham has an exemplar - Paul of faith[1685] and James of good conduct - and they draw that conclusion from the same *Old Testament* verse, Genesis 15:5 which says of Abraham: "*Then he believed in the* LORD*; and He reckoned it to him as righteousness.*" Paul makes the point of Abraham's great faith, writing in both *Romans* 4:3 and *Galatians* 3:6 that "*Abraham believed God, and God counted him as righteous because of his faith.*" The position of James is captured in the *New Testament* letter that bears his name. It makes the point of Abraham's good conduct in *James* 2:23 by the exact same words as cited by Paul and then adding in the next verse, "*So you see, we are shown to be right with God by what we do, not by faith alone.*" The message of the life of Abraham is monotheism and good conduct. To this, Jesus and the *New Testament* added: access to God and an afterlife.

This opens vistas for us. Paul taught that a Christian, if indeed he used that term, believed that Jesus had died for our sins and rose from the dead. But as we have been attempting to illustrate, there are other types of Christians. James represents one of those types, but even as we have talked of the differences, let us stress the similarities.

Both Paul and James saw good conduct similarly. As noted earlier, both summarized what appears to be Jesus's Great Commandment this way:

- Paul in *Galatians* 5:14: "*For the whole law can be summed up in this one command: 'Love your neighbor as yourself.'*"[1686]
- James in *James* 2:8: "*Yes indeed, it is good when you obey the royal law as found in the Scriptures: 'Love your neighbor as yourself.'*"[1687]

Moreover, even the supposed doctrinal differences may be less than meets the eye. The great historical critic of the Jamesian version of Christianity was Martin Luther. Luther found *James* so troubling to the Pauline doctrine of justification by faith that he called it the "epistle of straw"[1688] and often tore it from Bibles.[1689] He suggested at one point that it was forged.[1690] However, Luther eventually came to accept its canonicity.[1691] He may have recognized that the differences from Pauline doctrine were significant but not necessarily contradictory.

When the author of *James* downplayed faith, he certainly did not mean a trusting relationship with Jesus Christ. Instead, he meant mere intellectual assent of which he noted even "demons" are capable.[1692] In other words, *James* offers a different but compatible-to-Paul version of Christianity. It was compatible not only because *James* also recognized faith but the Pauline churches recognized the importance of doing good. We know this because of warnings about a very human and predictable problem – free-loaders. Evidence that sharing occurred in the Pauline communities can be seen in the admonitions of *II Thessalonians* 3:10-12 which required the able-bodied to work and *I Timothy* 5:3-16 which stipulated that only widows who were *"truly alone"* should receive assistance.[1693]

CS Lewis (1898-1963) wrote that "Christians have often disputed as to whether what leads the Christian home is good actions, or Faith in Christ."[1694] It would seem that it is both - although different Christian groups will have different emphases. The Jamesian approach may well appeal to people who want to be Christians not because of Paul's surviving letters from 50AD - 60AD to small bands of people in ancient Turkey and Greece but because they try to follow Jesus's teachings. In that regard, they may be closer to the Roman centurion at the cross who proclaimed the dying Jesus an innocent man[1695] symbolizing no more than that people should all try to do better with our lives. They may be fascinated with the Sermon on the Mount, by Jesus's memorable one-liners, by his memory. They may be more in line with Peter who said in the first break-out of the Jesus movement in Jerusalem that Jesus was *"a man singled out by God"*[1696] or Paul on Mars Hill who described Jesus as *"the man he (God) has appointed."*[1697] They can claim a pedigree from John the Baptist, Q, Apollos, the Sermon on the Mount or the *Epistle of James* or the *Epistle of Jude*.[1698] They might take such a simple approach as outlined in *III John* verse 11 which reads in part: *"Whoever does good is from God; whoever does evil has not seen God."*

There are connections to others in world history.

Justin Martyr wrote in about 150AD: "We are taught that Christ is the first born of God, and we have shown that He is the reason (word) of whom the whole human race partake. And those who live according to reason are Christians, even though they are counted atheists. Such were Socrates and Heraclitus among the Greeks, and those like them...."[1699] This view was never completely submerged. It manifested in others and more than one thousand years later had an articulate spokesperson. Erasmus of the Netherlands (1466/69 – 1536) was a contemporary of Martin Luther. Erasmus did not leave the Catholic Church.[1700] The printing press (the Internet of that time) made the *Bible* more accessible to the average person in his lifetime and Erasmus approved: "Let us consider who the hearers of Christ himself were. Were they not a promiscuous multitude? ... Is Christ offended that such should read him as he chose for his hearers? In my opinion the husbandman should read him, with the smith and the mason, and even prostitutes, bawds and Turks...."[1701] He thought that through education he could purify the Church. He wrote, "I endure the church till the day I see another (better) one." He urged reform:

- Tolerance.
- Turning over of church lands to those who farmed them.
- Allowing priest to marry.
- Alternate forms of communion.
- Reform of monasteries away from promiscuity. He said that "many convents" had become "public brothels." [1702]

Erasmus revived study of the Christian classics. He was the most influential intellectual of his time and was known as the "prince of humanists." He was persuaded to move from literary pursuits to the study of the *Bible*.[1703] Erasmus thought that Christianity was fully expressed through Christ, particularly in the Sermon on the Mount. He saw it as an ethical religion, prefigured by classic philosophers. "A universal ethical theism having its highest illustration in Christ was his idea."[1704] To the common people of his time he wrote this common sense message: "You will not be damned if you do not know whether the Spirit proceeding from the Father and the Son had one or two beginnings, but you will not escape damnation if you do not cultivate the fruits of the spirit: love, joy, peace, patience, kindness, goodness, long-suffering, mercy, faith, modesty, continence and chastity."

Erasmus asked rhetorically: "Is it not possible to have fellowship with the Father, Son and Holy Spirit, without being able to explain philosophically the distinction between them, and between the Nativity of the Son and the procession of the Holy Spirit?"[1705] He would have eliminated *I John*

5:7-8 (*"For there are three that testify: the Spirit and the water and the blood; and the three are in agreement.."*) since this passage was not in the Greek manuscripts.

These meanings can be ascribed to Erasmus's life:

- As the Middle Ages ended, a biblically based Christian Humanism was the center of religious thought in northern Europe, facilitated by the invention of the printing press. [1706]
- "The reformation that Erasmus advocated was in the field of ethics rather than dogmatics. This was so, not because he believed the church and its late medieval theologians to be right on every point, but rather because he felt that correct theological affirmations were of secondary importance when it came to the actual practice of Christian life." Erasmus thought that true Christian doctrine was uncomplicated but that academics had made it complicated. He saw that truth was one. He drew from the idea of the Logos.[1707]
- A century and a half later, John Locke's view that Christianity was a religion of reason and common sense was Erasmusian.[1708]

Monotheism and good conduct are evocative of the program of the Jewish-Christians of the first century and may be a typically American form of Christianity. Robert Frost (1874 – 1963) intriguingly called his religion a form of *Old Testament* Christianity and Lincoln referred to Americans as the "almost chosen people."[1709] The *"Old Testament* Christianity" is continuous throughout American history. "Protestant philo-Semitism got off the Mayflower."[1710] Jonathan Edwards (1703-1758) wrote of America as "the principal kingdom of the Reformation."[1711] The Puritans called themselves "God's American Israel."[1712] They compared their arrival in Massachusetts to Moses's Red Sea crossing. Thomas Paine compared King George III to the pharaoh. In 1776 Thomas Jefferson, John Adams and Benjamin Franklin proposed an image of Moses leading the Red Sea crossing as the seal of the United States. In the antebellum South slaves sung of Moses leading the Israelites out of slavery as a metaphor for their yearnings for freedom and Harriet Tubman of the Underground Railroad was known as the Moses of the slaves.[1713] Tubman said she was guided on the rescue trips by an "invisible pillar of cloud by day, and of fire by night" - a clear reference to the help that Moses received from God while leading the Children of Israel to the Promised Land according to *Exodus* 13:21-22.[1714] Brigham Young in 1850 said: "We feel no fear. We are in the hands of our Heavenly Father, the God of Abraham and Joseph, who guided us to this land..."[1715]

George Washington who seldom referred to Jesus often referred to God in monotheistic and philosophical terms. In a letter after the Revolutionary War he called God, the "great Searcher of human hearts." In his inaugural address, he described God as "that Almighty Being who rules over the universe, who presides in the councils of nations, and whose providential aids can supply every human defect" and, later to Congress, as the "Great Arbiter of the Universe" and "the Supreme Ruler of Nations."[1716] George Washington's view of God was of a being who is watchful, all seeing, but who seldom interferes. Abraham Lincoln's concept of God was similar. In the middle of the Civil War, Lincoln said, "God is not on our side - but I hope we are on God's side."[1717] Both Lincoln and Frederick Douglas (1818 – 1895) quoted *Hamlet* to explain their destiny: "There's a divinity that shapes our ends, Rough-hew them as we will."[1718] This remoteness is not altogether foreign to the *New Testament* where God only speaks three times - at Jesus's baptism, at his Transfiguration and in a scene in *John* 12 after Gentiles first began to ask about Jesus.[1719]

Thomas Jefferson, with scissors, removed the miracles from the *New Testament*.[1720] What was his purpose? The *Jefferson Bible* "grew out of his desire to reconcile Christianity with the Enlightenment and at the same time answer all those critics who said that he was an enemy of all religion. Jefferson discovered that Jesus, with his prescription for each of us to love our neighbors as ourselves, actually spoke directly to the modern enlightened age. Jefferson's version of the *New Testament* offered a much-needed morality of social harmony for a new republican society."[1721] Jefferson criticized John Calvin, the orthodox church father Athanasius of the fourth century, the Trinity,[1722] predestination and salvation by faith. He referred to Calvin and Athanasius as "false shepherds foretold as to enter not by the door into the sheepfold, but to climb up some other way" alluding to Jesus's teachings about false prophets in *John* 10:1.[1723] In a letter written to a friend on January 26, 1824 Jefferson wrote that he hoped that all Christians "would rally to the Sermon in the mount, make that the central point of Union in religion, and the stamp of genuine Christianity." He thought that would defeat dogmatism, a label under which he included such views of Jesus Christ as:

- "He is a member of the God-head."
- "He is a being of eternal pre-existence."
- "He was a man divinely inspired."

He also asked that his thoughts on this matter be kept confidential responding to a request to publicize his views by paraphrasing scripture: "You press me to consent to the publication of my sentiments and suppose they might have effect even on Sectarian bigotry. But have they not the Gospel? If they hear not that, and the charities it teacheth, neither will they be persuaded though one rose from the dead."[1724]

John Adams, wrote to his wife that although abilities and privilege differed between people, "the precept, however, do *as you would be done by*, implies an equality which is the real equality of nature and Christianity..."[1725] In 1813 Adams wrote Jefferson that "the great result of all my researches has been a most diffusive and comprehensive charity. I believe with Justin Martyr, that all good men are Christians."[1726] In 1816 Adams wrote him that "the Ten Commandments and the Sermon on the Mount contain my religion."[1727] At about the same time, he wrote Benjamin Rush, "Ask me not then whether I am a Catholic or Protestant, Calvinist or Armenian. As far as they are Christians, I wish to be a fellow disciple with them all."[1728]

Some moderns wanting to be Christians may also agree with Adams's son John Quincy Adams, the sixth President of the United States, who confided to his diary late in life that he could not believe that Christ died for the sins of humans: "It is not true. It is hateful. But how shall I contradict St. Paul?"[1729] (Contrast this statement with that of the forty-second President Bill Clinton who wrote in his memoirs about his childhood conversion: "In 1955, I had absorbed enough of my church's teachings to know that I was a sinner and to want Jesus to save me..." Decades later as president, Clinton referred to Jesus Christ in his public speeches more often than did his successor, President George W. Bush who was a favorite of conservative Christians.[1730]) John Quincy Adams went on to say, "I reverence God as my creator. As creator of the world. I reverence him with holy fear. I venerate Jesus Christ as my redeemer; and, as far as I can understand, the redeemer of the world. But this belief is dark and dubious."[1731] They may find full expression for their beliefs in the writings of one of the forgotten founding fathers, Thomas Paine: "My country is the world and my religion is to do good."[1732]

Benjamin Franklin may also be an inspiration. A month before he died Franklin said: "I believe in one God, creator of the universe. That he governs it by his Providence. That he ought to be worshipped. That the most acceptable service we render to him is doing good to his other children." He added that the system of morals that Jesus provided was "the best the world ever saw or is likely to see." On whether Jesus was divine, he employed Franklin wit: "I have some doubts as to his divinity; though it is a question I do not dogmatize upon, having never studied it, and think it needless to busy myself with it now, when I expect soon an opportunity of knowing the truth with less trouble."[1733]

Abraham Lincoln knew the *Bible* well and quoted it often although he modestly said that he was "a poor hand to quote Scripture."[1734] Here is Lincoln in one of his answers as to why he never joined a church: "When any church will inscribe over its alter as its sole qualification for membership the Savior's condensed statement of the substance of both the law and the Gospel, 'Thou shall love the Lord thy God will all thy heart, and with all thy soul, and with all thy mind, and thy neighbor as thyself,' [1735]- that Church will I join with all my heart and soul."[1736] Lincoln, incidentally, is the president who put "In God We Trust" on coins during the Civil War and established Thanksgiving as the fourth Thursday in November in 1864.[1737],[1738]

This form of Christianity is exemplified by President Franklin Roosevelt's comment when he was accused of having Jewish ancestors: "(I)n the dim distant past (my family) may have been Jews or Catholics or Protestants. What I am more interested in is whether they were good citizens and believers in God. I hope they were both."[1739] Eleanor Roosevelt (1884 – 1962) once asked FDR if he believed in the basics of the Episcopalian faith in which he had been raised. He said, "I really never thought about it. I think it is just as well not to think about things like that too much." When asked about his creed, FDR said: "I am a Christian and a Democrat - that's all."[1740] President Harry Truman (1884 – 1872) thought "every problem in the world would be solved if only men would follow the Beatitudes."[1741]

These statements are a type of Jeffersonian Christianity. The assumption is that those who try to follow Jesus's life and teachings are Christians. Their inspirational books might be *James* or the *Gospel of Thomas* or *Q*. They may be closer to the original followers of Jesus and his family than those whose faith derives from Paul's writings. In terms of *New Testament* authority, they would interpret *John* 14: 6 – *"Jesus told him, 'I am the way, the truth, and the life. No one can come to the Father except through me'"* – metaphorically: They might see that coming "through" Jesus would mean doing good to others as required for salvation in *Matthew* 25.[1742] In that passage, Jesus distinguished the sheep from the goats because they fed the hungry.

It is likely that these types of Christians will not be believers in any kind of fundamentalism and will look with dismay on the debates over evolution. But in that they are in good company. Many Christian leaders have tried to reconcile Darwinism with Christianity. Pope John Paul II proclaimed evolution "more than a hypothesis."[1743] CS Lewis seemed to have had no problem with it.[1744] Francis Collins is a Christian[1745] and describes himself as a "theistic evolutionist."[1746],[1747]

These types of Christians will also uphold the ideal of religious liberty. Again, this is a theme of American history. In its essence, America was religious from its beginning. American colonies were settled by Puritans who were dissenters and saw the new land as an escape from persecution. The new Constitution guaranteed "free expression" of religion. This led to competition among churches which fueled their growth in the 1800s. The American founding with its lack of an anticlerical base, its separation of church and state and its division of power made possible the survival of religion in modernity. Other revolutions - the French, the Russian and the Mexican - vigorously attacked religion.[1748]

At the start of the American Revolution, all the states established official state churches but there was a tradition of dissent seen in Roger Williams (abt. 1603 – 1683), Anne Hutchinson (1591 - 1643), and William Penn (1644 – 1718). Maryland had been established as a haven for Catholics. Immigration by nonconformists Germans, French, Dutch, Swiss and Swedes proceeded throughout the seventeenth and eighteenth centuries.[1749] The religious diversity in the American colonies distinguished them from Britain and helped define what America meant. The *Bible* and a broad understanding of Christianity were unifying influences.[1750] When the country did not live up to this promise of religious freedom, the religious (like the early dissenters, or Baptists or the Mormons) could move. That explains the origins of cities as far flung as Hartford, Connecticut, Providence, Rhode Island or Salt Lake City, Utah.[1751]

The ethos of the Founders toward religious liberty had a very modern tone. James Madison was a delegate to the Virginia state convention in May of 1776 drafting the Virginia Declaration of Rights. In the legislative history he effected a change from "all men should enjoy the fullest toleration the exercise of religion" to "all men are entitled to the free exercise of religion."[1752] In 1790, George Washington went to Rhode Island and wrote to a Jewish congregation in Newport. He told it: "It is now no more that toleration is spoken of as if it was by the indulgence of one class of people, that another enjoyed the exercise of their inherent natural rights. For happily the government of the United States which gives bigotry no sanction, to persecution no assistance, requires only that they who live under its protection should demean themselves as good citizens..."[1753] Thomas Paine in *Rights of Man in* 1791 wrote: "Toleration is not the opposite of intoleration, but is the counterfeit of it. Both are despotisms. The one assumes to itself the right of withholding liberty of conscience, and the other of granting it."[1754]

The Declaration of Independence makes no mention of any specific religions. In a very religious era, here is how it referred to God:

- "Nature's God"
- "Creator"
- "Supreme Judge of the world"
- "Divine Providence"

The Constitution makes no mention of God.[1755] (Alexander Hamilton joked that the reason that God wasn't mentioned in the Constitution is that the Founders forgot to put in a reference.[1756]) At the time of the ratification debates some thought that the Constitution's ban on religious tests would bring "Popery," the "Inquisition," office holders swearing support to "Jupiter, Juno, Minerva, or Pluto," "Mahometans, who ridicule the doctrine of the trinity,"... "Jews, Turks & Infidels."[1757] These allegations could be seen as direct responses to Washington who, amazingly for the era, said that America should be "open to receive...the oppressed and persecuted of all nations and religions; whom we shall welcome to a participation of all our rights and privileges.... They may be Mohametans, Jews or Christians of any sect, or they may be atheist."[1758]

In Federalist No. 10 Madison counted on republicanism (delegated power) and large distances (the extended Republic) to curb excesses and check interests. He referred to religious diversity and hoped that checks and balances and the size of the new country would keep extreme causes from overwhelming the common good. Thus America became the first nation to disestablish religion and to protect the free exercise of religion by law. In short the Founders got it right on religion.

Here are examples of how a religious country practiced religious liberty. George Washington and John Adams concluded a treaty with Tripoli (modern Libya) which included the claim that the United States was "not, in any sense, founded on the Christian religion."[1759] In the election of 1800 Thomas Jefferson was excoriated by his political enemies for supposed unorthodox religious views. His party responded that Jefferson was a champion of religious liberty. He was portrayed as standing for "the equal brotherhood of the Moravian, the Mennonist, and the Dunker."[1760] His supporters said that he "does not think that a Catholic should be banished for believing in transubstantiation or a Jew from believing in the God of Abraham, Isaac and Jacob." John Adams was reportedly distressed by the attacks on Jefferson and was quoted as saying: "What does that have to do with the public?" This was consistent with his 1797 inaugural which he said was addressed to all who "call themselves Christians" and an 1812 letter to Benjamin Rush stating: "Nothing is more dreaded than the national government meddling with religion."[1761]

As a new faculty member in 1805, John Quincy Adams asked for and got an exception to a requirement to declare religious conformity with Harvard, saying that he objected in principle and believed in "reserving my confession of faith for my Maker."[1762] One of Andrew Jackson's supporters, the Reverend Ezra Stiles Ely (1786 – 1861), attempted to start a Christian political party. Jackson wrote to dissuade him: "Amongst the greatest blessings secured to us under our Constitution is the liberty of worshipping God as our conscience dictates." Ely attempted to end federal mail delivery on Sundays. A congressional committee under Richard M. Johnson (1780/1781 -1850)[1763] responded: "It is not the legitimate province of the Legislature to determine which religion is true, or what is false. Our government is a civil, and not religious institution." In 1832 Henry Clay proposed a day of prayer and fasting in response to a cholera epidemic. Andrew Jackson opposed it. He said he believed in "the efficacy of prayer" but felt that the official day would violate the Constitution. Jackson: "I could not do otherwise without transcending those limits which are prescribed by the Constitution for the President and without feeling that I might in some degree disturb the security which religion now enjoys in this country in its complete separation from the political concerns of the General Government....It is the province of the pulpits and the state governments to recommend the mode by which the people may best attest their reliance on the protecting arm of the almighty in times of great public distress."[1764]

President John Tyler (1790 – 1862) in 1843 asserted that "No religious establishment *by law* (Emphasis in the original) exists among us. The conscience is left free from all restraint to worship his Maker after his own judgment.... The Mohammedan, if he were to come among us, would have the privilege guaranteed to him by the Constitution to worship according to the Koran; and the East Indian might erect a shrine to Brahma if it so pleased him."[1765] At that same time, Joseph Smith wrote thirteen articles of the Mormon Statement of Faith. The eleventh: "We claim the privilege of worshiping Almighty God according to the dictates of our conscience, and allow all men the same privilege, let them worship how, where, or what they may."[1766] Tyler's successor James Knox Polk (1795 – 1849) was asked to prevent the Mormon move west. Polk had an evangelical heritage. His mother descended from the family of John Knox (1510 – 1572) who brought the Reformation to Scotland. His reply to the "Mormon question" was: "If

I could interfere with the Mormons, I could with the Baptists or any other religious sect."[1767] This anticipated Lyndon Johnson more than a century later as John F. Kennedy's running mate when the latter's Catholicism was an issue: "If...people do apply a religious test as a qualification for office, then we tear up the Bill of Rights and throw our Constitution into the wastebasket. In the next election, the Baptists will be out, and next a Jew or a Methodist or a Christian cannot be President, and soon we will disqualify everyone who believes in God and only the atheists will be left as eligible, and that's not the American way."[1768]

The Founders were afraid of religious majorities. Jefferson's statement: "Divided we stand. United we fall" spoke for religious liberty.[1769] Madison wrote that conscience was a form of property deserving government protection.[1770] Their views have stood. In a classic restatement of religious liberty in 1951, Justice Douglas wrote: "...We have above all else feared the political censor. We have wanted a land where our people can be exposed to all the diverse creeds and cultures of the world."[1771] This calls to mind Eisenhower in 1954: "Our government makes no sense unless it is founded on a deeply felt religious faith - and I don't care what it is."[1772] In America religious liberty is a strength.

A broader and more inclusive approach will not weaken Christianity if fundamentalists and liberals apply tolerance.[1773] Both need to recognize that the US is, as Reinhold Niebuhr said, the most secular and the most religious of western nations.[1774] Both need to remember Tocqueville's observation in a prior century that "religion...must be regarded as the foremost of the political institutions of that country; for if it does not impart a taste for freedom, it facilitates the use of free institutions."[1775]

The hope is that fundamentalists can accept as equal those Christians who base their religion on the teachings of Jesus even if they see Jesus as a great teacher rather than as God and that the latter group can respect the Christian convictions of the fundamentalists. Now we are on shaky ground. This may be a deal-breaker for fundamentalists. Consider CS Lewis: "I am trying to prevent anyone saying the really foolish thing that people often say about Him: 'I'm ready to accept that Jesus was a great moral teacher, but I don't accept His claim to be God.'" Lewis reckoned that a great moral teacher would not have claimed to be God if he was not.[1776] I cautiously and respectfully disagree because I don't think that CS Lewis gave weight to the contradictions in the *New Testament* and the many different types of Christians that are represented in its pages. This of course is an issue of many centuries. The Nicene Creed (325) held that Christ was "one in being" with God. As we noted, Arius of Alexandria opposed this and taught that Christ was a creature, inferior to God. He had a high view of Jesus. He saw Jesus "as the most perfect person in the world - with unquestioned moral authority." Yet, he still saw him as created by God and not co-equal with God.[1777] As he wrote: "There was a time when Christ was not."[1778]

Arius's view lost out - although he received a pardon from Constantine[1779] who regarded the controversy leading up to the Nicene Creed as "extremely trivial"[1780],[1781] - but related controversies caused bloodshed and then later arguments for centuries.[1782] However, if diversity is not managed to at least a minimum degree, it is difficult to see that a deified, Jesus-centered form of Christianity, clinging to inerrancy can thrive in the decades ahead. In 1822, Thomas Jefferson wrote that "I trust that there is not a young man now living in the United States who will not die a Unitarian." [1783] He was wrong. In fact, he said this at that very time evangelical Christianity was surging in the Second Great Awakening. In 1880 Robert Ingersoll wrote that "the churches are dying out all over the land"[1784] and he was also wrong. In 1929 Charles Francis Potter founder of the Humanist Society of New York and later a signer of the *Humanist Manifesto* wrote, "The next great 'Life of Jesus' will forever dispose of the myth that the Man of Galilee was a god who came down to earth, a deity incarnate, bringing an absolutely new revelation to mankind."[1785] That belief has by no means become the dominant one in Christianity. But are Arius, Jefferson, Ingersoll and Potter directionally correct for the twenty-first century?[1786] I don't know.

What is it to do good? There is a lot of room for maneuvering on this question. People, trying to do good, may be on opposite sides of the ballot, the picket line or even a war. In a time and place of religious liberty, such as the modern United States, doing good might simply mean caring for each other as Jesus taught and thinking about the way he is recorded to have lived and trying to emulate those principles. As we have emphasized, these are themes less common to Paul and more common to Q, the Jewish-Christians, the Epistle of James or the teachings of John the Baptist. Yet Paul is not completely left our either. As noted, he followed Jesus's example and showed a willingness to pare down the Ten Commandments and he twice cited the once-obscure commandment found in *Leviticus* to love one another as a summary of the law. (See footnotes 681 and 710.)

What could the cross of Jesus mean to such believers? It could be a message that Jesus would live and die for others.

For those interested, *New Testament* Christianity also offers an additional possibility: living past the grave. The resurrection of Jesus Christ is a message that death does not end life permanently and that evil does not win out in the end.[1787] Is there life after death? Again, I don't know and no one else does either. But let me offer a *New Testament* basis for that belief and hope.

The afterlife

It is possible that advances in science in the next few centuries will prolong life or even preserve some semblance indefinitely. But for all of us now living our eventual death is a certainty. Much of what we do and deem important will be picked up by others or neglected. As Charles de Gaulle said, "the cemeteries of the world are full of indispensable men."[1788]

Here, I think, is the reality. Among the world's billion Christians, confidence that there is a life after death is shaky. Christians want to believe and often persuade themselves that they do but doubts persist. A strong faith that there was an afterlife soothed generations before modernity but is probably gone forever.[1789]

In a high school English class in 1968 I read a short story, "The Jilting of Granny Weatherall" by Katherine Anne Porter (1930). It recounts the thoughts of an eighty year old woman dying at home in bed. It is the very last day of her life and as she approaches the moment of death, she recalls that years before she was jilted, literally at the altar, when her husband-to-be had not appeared. She wonders if she is to be disappointed again. The story ends with her thoughts as follows: "'God, give a sign!' For a second time there was no sign. Again no bridegroom and the priest in the house. She could not remember any other sorrow because this grief wiped them all away. 'Oh, no, there's nothing more cruel than this – I'll never forgive it.' She stretched herself with a deep breath and blew out the light."

That story is my oldest recollection that possibly there is no afterlife. My grandfather and a peer of his who lived near my family in those years each separately told me that they did not believe that they would in any way survive death. Both have been dead for nearly forty years. I cannot argue myself or anyone else into a different point of view.

However, I can analyze what the *New Testament* says about the subject as a way of giving us hope that there *might* be a life beyond the grave although I unambiguously acknowledge that this hope is shaky. We don't know. George Washington referred to life after death as "...that country whence no Traveler ever returns."[1790] However, it is one of the great strengths of Christianity that it has always brought people to terms with death.[1791] Thomas Jefferson in 1817 wrote to Abigail Adams that: "Our next meeting must then be in the country to which (others) have flown, a country, for us, not now very distant."[1792] Six years later Jefferson, still ruminating on Christianity, wrote to John Adams that although he anticipated that one day soon the notion of Jesus's virgin birth "will be classed with the fable of the generation of Minerva in the brain of Jupiter" he also looked forward to an afterlife "with more readiness than reluctance. May we meet there again...."[1793]

For all of the *New Testament* diversity that we have been discussing, NT Wright finds a great deal of consensus among the early Christians on both the resurrection of Jesus and the afterlife of humans.[1794] They are inextricably linked. We move toward the conclusion of this book by thinking about the resurrection of Jesus of Nazareth and what it tells us.

There is pressure within some groups of modern Christians to accept the physical resuscitation of Jesus's corpse. This brand holds that if the resurrection of the physical body of Jesus Christ is not a literal fact, we are left in despair and futility in an awful world. It is not difficult to find examples of this point of view. Here is one issued by an evangelical study center located near the University of Oregon: "... if Jesus was not raised from the dead, then this life is all there is; and this life stinks."[1795] This view derives from the heart of Pauline Christianity. Paul wrote that if Christ had not been raised from the dead, the Christians's faith is useless and the Christians are to be pitied more than everyone.[1796] To this I would make these three points:

- Proponents of this brand of Christianity have accomplished much good in the world and have powerful intellectual advocates.[1797]
- But it is not the only lane on the Way as the pages of the *New Testament* illustrate.
- Paul's concept of the resurrection may not have included a physical resuscitation of Jesus's corpse. Moreover, certain of the other accounts may be intended as metaphorical.

What does the *New Testament* say about Jesus's resurrection?

The accounts that we have of the resurrection of Jesus were written by Paul in *I Corinthians* 15 about twenty years after the event, then in *Mark* about forty years after the event and then in *Matthew* about fifty to sixty years after the event, then in *Luke* and *Acts* about sixty to seventy years after the event and finally in *John* about seventy years after the event.[1798] There is a great deal of variety in these accounts.

Paul's encounter with the risen Jesus is covered, as we have seen, in *Acts* 9, 22 and 26 and is described as a great light and a voice. Paul writes in *I Corinthians*

15 that Jesus appeared to Peter, the Twelve, James the brother of Jesus and himself. We assume that the "Twelve" is a reference to the eleven remaining disciples after the death of Judas. No detail is given for any of this except possibly in an account in *II Corinthians* 12 in which Paul says he was "*caught up into the third heaven*" and he didn't know if he was in or outside his body and he heard things that neither he nor any human could tell. At this point we are up to thirteen people who saw the risen Jesus - the eleven disciples plus James plus Paul. Then Paul adds that Jesus appeared to over five hundred people at one time but again he provides no details. However, this could be a reference to Pentecost described in *Acts* 2. This experience was remembered as a mighty wind and what appeared to be tongues of fire.[1799]

The Synoptic Gospels add two more witnesses, both named Mary and John agrees that one Mary was a witness. That makes fifteen identified individuals aside from the five hundred. *Luke* adds Joanna who as noted he had earlier described as the estranged wife of one of Herod Antipater's key staff members. *Luke* adds several other unnamed women. *Luke* also adds two more witnesses, Cleopas and an unnamed colleague. Together they may – as we speculated in Chapter 6 - have been Jesus's uncle and aunt. That makes eighteen individuals plus several unnamed women aside from the five hundred.[1800]

John adds no new people to the list unless the "*disciple whom Jesus loved*" is considered outside the eleven remaining disciples. For our purposes, we will assume that he was. So the apparent total of those who saw the risen Christ was nineteen plus several others plus more than five hundred. (The figure of five hundred probably included many of the nineteen plus several others although not Paul.)[1801],[1802]

Peter later explained that the risen Jesus "*was not seen by all the people, but by witnesses whom God had already chosen—by us who ate and drank with him after he rose from the dead.*"[1803]

In the account of the *Gospel of Mark*, no one saw him. In *Matthew* there are two appearances of the resurrected Jesus. One is outside the Empty Tomb.[1804] It is to Mary Magdalene and the "other Mary." They had "*fear and joy*" and they worshipped him and - *contra Mark* - may (or may not) have followed his instructions to tell his followers to meet him in Galilee. The second is with the "eleven" on a mountain in Galilee that he had "designated." They also worshipped him but some doubted.[1805] These two accounts bracket a strange story about the Roman soldiers who were guarding Jesus's tomb and the religious authorities conspiring to create a rumor that Jesus's body was stolen.

Luke and *John,* written later, begin to give concrete examples of appearances of Jesus in Jerusalem. In *Luke* 24 there are two direct appearances of the resurrected Jesus and one indirect one. Jesus appeared to two of his followers on the road between Jerusalem and the village of Emmaus, a trip of about seven miles. They did not recognize him. Later, when they did recognize him he vanished. Still later that day, these two followers joined the eleven disciples back in Jerusalem. Jesus suddenly appeared to them. The story goes on that some thought he was a ghost and he disabused them of that by showing them his hands and feet and inviting them to touch him. They still didn't believe but were filled with joy. Then he ate a fish as they watched. Then he walked out with them and *"was taken up into heaven,"* an occurrence that Luke repeats in *Acts* 1.[1806] The third account is indirect. The eleven disciples told the Emmaus travelers that Jesus had appeared to Peter but they provide no details.

In *John* 20-21, there are four appearances of the resurrected Jesus. One is outside the Empty Tomb. It is to Mary Magdalene. She does not initially recognize him and when she does, he tells her not to cling to him because he first needs to ascend to God.[1807] Second, he later came through locked doors to appear to his remaining disciples (minus Thomas). He showed them his wounds from the crucifixion. Third, he appeared a week later to the same group including Thomas and showed Thomas his wounds. Thomas confessed his belief and Jesus responded that people who believe without seeing are more blessed.[1808] Finally, he appeared in Galilee to some of his disciples who had apparently gone back to their fishing business. At first - and it is from a distance - they did not recognize him.

The story of the stolen body,[1809] the lack of confidence that they were seeing Jesus, the fear, the worship of Jesus by these seventeen people plus several others (I'm not counting James and Paul who may have come later), a Jesus who is not easily recognized, not always believed, able to appear and vanish, the earlier accounts by Paul and Mark that do not recognize a risen human body are all consistent with a vision. A similar experience occurred at the Transfiguration at which Peter, James and John saw Elijah and Moses and were terrified, an experience that in one account Jesus termed a *"vision."*[1810] The concept of a vision is particularly evident in the first accounts of the risen Jesus which Paul said had *"been passed on"* to him.[1811] The flexibility of the resurrection is underscored best in the earliest Gospel, *Mark.* Although no appearances are listed, the resurrection – in some form – seems to be an accepted fact in that Jesus predicts it several times[1812] and the angels told the women at the Empty Tomb on the first Easter: *"He is risen from the dead!"*[1813]

So what did the resurrection mean for Paul? It meant something very specific, that we too could survive death. Before looking at what he wrote to the Corinthians, however, let's reflect on his earliest letter – *I Thessalonians*. The fourth chapter of that letter, verses thirteen through eighteen contains these words:

*"But we do not want you to be uninformed, brethren, about those who are asleep, so that you will not grieve as do the rest who have no hope. **For if we believe that Jesus died and rose again, even so God will bring with Him those who have fallen asleep in Jesus**. For this we say to you by the word of the Lord, that we who are alive and remain until the coming of the Lord, will not precede those who have fallen asleep. For the Lord Himself will descend from heaven with a shout, with the voice of the archangel and with the trumpet of God, and the dead in Christ will rise first. Then we who are alive and remain will be caught up together with them in the clouds to meet the Lord in the air, and so we shall always be with the Lord. Therefore comfort one another with these words."*

NT Wright has said that *I Thessalonians* 4:14 (highlighted above) is "a succinct summary of virtually the whole of *I Corinthians* 15."[1814] The entire passage has a Gospel parallel. *Matthew* 16:27-28 and 24:30-31 read as follows:

Matthew 16 - "For the Son of Man will come with his angels in the glory of his Father and will judge all people according to their deeds. And I tell you the truth, some standing here right now will not die before they see the Son of Man coming in his Kingdom."

Matthew 24 – "And then at last, the sign that the Son of Man is coming will appear in the heavens, and there will be deep mourning among all the peoples of the earth. And they will see the Son of Man coming on the clouds of heaven with power and great glory. And he will send out his angels with the mighty blast of a trumpet, and they will gather his chosen ones from all over the world—from the farthest ends of the earth and heaven."

So there were stories dating from Jesus's ministry of a Son of Man coming. Paul, faced with the concern of his church in Thessalonica about Christians who had died, took this story and made modifications – one might call them redactions:

1. He speaks of "we" rather than "you" - an editorial change.
2. He speaks of the Lord's return rather than the return of the Son of Man.
3. He considers those who have already died.
4. He talks of Christians meeting the Lord in the clouds.

But the trumpet and the angel(s) and the descent are there.

His key point is not about some type of Rapture, discovered by Christians some nineteen centuries later, but about people having hope for an afterlife for themselves and others because Jesus had risen.

In *I Corinthians* Paul develops this thought further where he was dealing with some who thought their own resurrection or at least the new life had already taken place.[1815] Paul taught that it was in the future and that we would be transformed like Jesus was.[1816] It was difficult to explain but the core point probably was that Paul had seen the risen Christ[1817] who was both visible and identifiable. Jesus was not a mortal body since "*flesh and blood cannot inherit the kingdom of heaven.*"[1818] and mortal bodies are perishable.[1819] So, Paul saw the risen Jesus neither as a revived corpse nor as a ghost that had left the body. Instead he saw the risen Jesus as transformed into a "*spiritual*" body.[1820] Here is the key: he saw this as the future for Christians, calling Jesus the "*first fruits.*"[1821]

Our transformation is admittedly less than perfectly clear but there does appear to be some continuity, like a plant (our eventual spiritual body) grown from a seed (our mortal body).[1822] Yet Paul also appears to have thought our transformation was underway.[1823] He talks of Christians undergoing change into his likeness "*from one degree of glory to another*"[1824] and day-by-day renewal of our inner nature even though our body is wasting away.[1825] Paul did not write all his thoughts down in one paper but rather responded to circumstances in his churches. But from these responses we can conclude that Paul taught that the resurrection of Jesus Christ gives us hope for an afterlife and that hope has some manifestation in our daily lives although not in our physical capabilities.[1826], [1827]

I am convinced that the story of the resurrection is not about the resuscitation of a corpse. I can go so far as to say that the story of the resurrection may be a parable and its truth does not depend on its factuality. Note:

- No appearance stories are in more than one Gospel even though many pre-Easter stories are the same - although as noted earlier the controversial resurrection section of *Mark* 16:9-20 shows some knowledge of *Luke* and *John*.
- It is hard to see the appearance on the road to Emmaus as objective history. Jesus is not recognized and then he is.[1828] He disappears. The story is laden with allegory - the breaking of the bread equals the

opening of scripture's meaning. Isn't it teaching us that he is with us even if we don't know it?

- My doubts have a *New Testament* base as noted earlier. (See *Matthew 28:16-19.)* There are other instances in which Jesus's disciples doubted that Jesus had risen from the dead. In *Luke* 24:37-43 Jesus needed to prove who he was by having them handle him and by eating. In *John* 20:20 and 24-28 Jesus had to show the disciples his wounds. Thomas wasn't there but when he came back to the group he too needed to see the wounds. Finally, in what is one of the strangest concepts about the resurrection, in *Acts* 1:3 Jesus spent forty days with them and showed them "*many proofs.*" Why would he need to show proofs over a forty day period?
- Jesus ascends in both *Luke* and *Acts.* He is seen apparently still later by Paul. This casts doubt on the literalness of forty days.[1829]

Additionally, consider the life and death of John the Baptist. As we have noted, *Mark* chapter 6 reports that after John the Baptist's judicial murder, Herod Antipater was concerned that John the Baptist had risen from the dead. However there is no record that he ordered a checking of John the Baptist's grave. That is because he was not thinking about a decapitated corpse being resuscitated. But he still thought it was possible that John the Baptist had returned to life. This shows that in the culture of the time one could think of someone being resurrected in a new body with their former body left in the tomb.[1830]

No matter. It is as Marcus Borg has said that "'Jesus is a figure of the present and not just of the past. He continued to be experienced by his first followers after his death and continues to be experienced to this day...In short, Jesus lives."[1831] I add that Paul wanted his followers to know that this meant they could have hope for another life. I know that many hold for the resuscitation of Jesus's corpse, basing this view on some of the Gospel accounts. This view is to be respected. But let's close out this section by looking at the concept of Jesus's resurrection as it progresses in a simple Gospel story.

We know that the early Christians were burdened by the fact that their founder had been brutally executed. Paul recognized that for most of the world the message of the cross was "*foolishness.*"[1832] The followers of Jesus had to deal with the fact that Jesus had been killed and buried. This was intellectual baggage. By redacting one of the key people involved with Jesus's burial, we can see a progressive elevation of what had to be a very difficult event to explain. The person to look at is Joseph of Arimathea.

Mark 6:29 shows that after the execution of John the Baptist, his followers buried him. The writer of *Mark* probably would have preferred a similarly dignified burial for Jesus. He tries to show that there was one by mentioning that Joseph of Arimathea was respected and that he bought a new shroud.[1833] The later writers take this further. Joseph of Arimathea becomes both rich and a disciple of Jesus.[1834] He is a good and just man who did not participate in the trial in the Sanhedrin.[1835] He becomes a secret disciple of Jesus, secret due to his fear of the Jews and he was assisted by the respected Nicodemus.[1836] The burial place is elevated also from *Mark*. It belonged to Joseph of Arimathea according to *Matthew* 27:60. *John* 20:15 has it in a garden. It is new according to *Matthew* 27:60, *Luke* 23:53 and *John* 19:41.[1837] The point of all this is that despite the embarrassment of his death, Jesus got a dignified burial by a prominent man and then later physically came back to life.[1838]

Fine. Maybe he did and maybe he did not. But the central teaching of the resurrection is that in some sense Jesus escaped death and so can we.[1839] That theme emerged early. In *Acts*, Sadducees in the neighborhood of the Temple in Jerusalem were annoyed at the apostles Peter and John who were preaching about the risen Jesus and its implication. Or, to quote directly: "*These leaders were very disturbed that Peter and John were teaching the people that through Jesus there is a resurrection of the dead.*"[1840]

Let me sum up. Are we going to live past death? I hope we are but I don't know and I don't know how any conclusion on this question could be verified or falsified.[1841] We may exist past death but, on the other hand, it may be as Russian novelist Vladimir Nabokov (1899-1977) thought, that human existence "is a brief crack of light between two eternities of darkness."[1842] But I don't think it is crucial that we know the answer or that we harbor strong beliefs on this point. In this, I part from the *New Testament* teaching of Paul that if this life is all there is, then much of it such as taking risks for others or baptizing for the dead(!)[1843] doesn't make sense. He writes memorably that if this life ends at the grave, "*Let's feast and drink, for tomorrow we die!*"[1844] John Adams made a similar point in 1816 at the age of 81 that "if it should be revealed or demonstrated that there is no future state, my advice to every man, woman, and child would be...to take opium."[1845] His son felt pretty much the same way. John Quincy Adams wrote that he was a Christian and believed in life after death. "If the existence of man were limited to this life, it would be impossible for me to believe the universe made any moral sense." He was also content, with respect to evil people to be patient with "the delays of divine justice."[1846] I disagree with all of them. Life is to be lived whatever we think of our chances for an afterlife. For both skepticism and optimism,

Benjamin Franklin is a good spokesman. In 1764 he wrote to the evangelist George Whitefield about God: "...if he loves me, can I doubt that he will go on to take care of me, not only here but hereafter?"[1847] He speaks for me. I am a monotheist and I hope for an afterlife based on doing good.

Final Conclusion

Justice Sandra Day O'Connor (1930 -) once wrote: "at the heart of liberty is the right to define one's own concept of existence, of meaning, of the universe, and of the mystery of human life."[1848] I have tried to do that in the context of the *New Testament*. Let me conclude.

We live in a time not only unrecognizably different than the era in which the *New Testament* was written but also barely connected with all the eras that came after for many hundreds of years. What was life like for our ancestors during fifty or sixty generations after Jesus and Paul? For the most part, it was a dirt floor, a single garment, early marriage, and early death. For most of that time people thought in terms of a flat earth. Even as the modern age dawned in the sixteenth century, both Luther and Calvin mocked the very idea that the earth revolved around the sun. Luther wrote in reaction to Copernicus: "People give ear to an upstart astrologer who strove to show that the earth revolves, not the heavens or the firmament, the sun or the moon.....This fool wishes to reverse the entire scheme of astrology; but sacred Scripture tells us that Joshua commanded the sun to stand still, not the earth."[1849] Calvin chimed in, referring to *Psalm* 93: "The world also is stabilized, that it cannot be moved."[1850] He asked a variation of that conversation-stopping question prevalent in all eras: "Who will venture to place the authority of Copernicus above that of the Holy Spirit?"[1851]

We only recently know that the universe began about 14 billion years ago in a blaze of light from an infinitesimally small point that rapidly expanded: the Big Bang.[1852] We know that the Earth formed about 9 billion years later, and the first life on Earth began less than a billion years after that. Our ancestors who came out of Africa so long ago were late comers. In our generation, we have discovered well over 1700 planets (by 2014) orbiting stars other than our sun. Although none are Earthlike in character, we expect to identify several in the next decade with telescopes now under development. Perhaps we will even detect life on some of them.[1853]

In much of what I have written in this book, I acknowledge that I am hardly walking in fresh snow. I understand my viewpoint to be a variant of such schools of thought that we mentioned in Chapter 8 as:

- <u>Arianism.</u> In the fourth century this view denied Jesus's true divinity on the principle that if he was begotten of the father there was a time when he did not exist.[1854] To refine a point, I might be closer to the views of Paul of Samosata who prefigured Arianism and was an Adoptionist, seeing Jesus as a human infused with the Holy Spirit at a certain time in his life.

- <u>Monarchianism.</u> In the second and third centuries Monarchianism was in support of the unity of God versus the polytheism advocated by Gnostics. Two systems of Monarchianism emerged. Dynamic Monarchianism taught that the power of God lived in the man Jesus. This view was close to the Ebionites. It was condemned by Rome in AD 195. Modalist Monarchianism so closely identified Christ with God that it held that the God suffered in Christ. It is sometimes called "Patripassianism." In the 200s its teacher was Sabellius and therefore it is sometimes called "Sabellianism." I resonate with the denial of the distinctions within the Godhead, and the Modalist Monarchianism's view that Son and the Spirit were merely modes in which God appeared.[1855]

My views were anathematized by different church councils in those centuries working to define the relationships between God, Jesus Christ and the Holy Spirit. But I live many centuries later and don't care about these councils. My views resonate more with historical figures we have discussed in this book such as Arius, Pelagius (who stressed freedom in the 400s), Erasmus (who stressed tolerance in the 1500s), Calixtus (who called for Christian unity in the 1600s) and John Wesley (who inspired good conduct and eventually universalism in the 1700s).

My views may also be a variant of early American liberal Christianity which, following Enlightenment principles, demanded simplicity and reasonableness in religion and emphasized God's role as the Architect and Governor of the universe. This was a God without wrath who did not send people to heaven or hell because of their actual belief. This grew to become Unitarianism. It held that Jesus was a man with a special divine mission, not God. An archetypical figure of this early period of Unitarianism was John Quincy Adams.

At one point in the *Book of Acts* as the Christian message was beginning to be shared with non-Jews, Peter exclaimed:" *I now realize how true it is that God does not show favoritism but accepts men from every nation who fear him and do what is right.*"[1856] This should be marked carefully. It is monotheistic, it is universal and it is conduct-based and hints at a form of Christianity that is distinct - at least in its emphases - from modern evangelicalism. A dialog between President Truman and a young Billy Graham in 1950 captured this dichotomy. Graham asked Truman about his faith. Truman answered: "Well, I try to live by the Sermon on the Mount and the Golden Rule." Graham replied, "I just don't think that's enough."[1857]

Well, what is enough? In 1822 Thomas Jefferson summarized his creed as follows:

- That there is one God, and he is all perfect.
- That there is a future state of rewards and punishments.[1858]
- That to love God with all thy heart and thy neighbor as thyself, is the sum of religion."[1859]

And this is what he wrote to his namesake in the last full year of his life: "Adore God. Reverence and cherish your parents. Love your neighbor as yourself, and your country more than yourself. Be just. Be true. Murmur not at the ways of Providence. So shall the life into which you have entered be the portal to one of eternal and ineffable bliss."[1860] It is the central thesis of this book that this is enough or, as John Adams closed an 1825 letter to Jefferson on the subject of free inquiry: "The substance and essence of Christianity, as I understand it, is eternal and unchangeable, and will bear examination forever, but it has been mixed with extraneous ingredients, which I think will not bear examination, and they ought to be separated. Adieu."[1861]

In Paul's time there were God-fearers, the Gentiles who respected monotheism but not the strictures of Judaism. Peter converted a group of God-fearers in *Acts* 10. Paul preached to another group attending services in a synagogue at Psidian Antioch in modern-day Turkey. According to *Acts* 13 verse 16: "... *Paul stood, lifted his hand to quiet them, and started speaking. 'Men of Israel,' he said, 'and you God-fearing Gentiles, listen to me.'*" According to *Acts* 17:17, when Paul was in Athens: "*He went to the synagogue to reason with the Jews and the God-fearing Gentiles...*"

The God-fearers represented a third way between Judaism and the Roman world. [1862]They supported the synagogues[1863] and protected the Jews in alien cultures. They included many prominent women: *Acts* 16 (Lydia, in Philippi), *Acts* 17:4 (Thessalonika), *Acts* 17:12 (Berea). There is a hint in the *Gospel of Luke* about the God-fearers. Once more, a type of redacting is highly relevant. The Gospels present three accounts of Jesus healing the servant (or son) of a Roman official from a distance: *Matthew* 8: 5-13; *Luke* 7:1-10 and *John* 4:46-53. Only in *Luke* does the official not come himself to ask for Jesus's help. Instead, "*When the officer heard about Jesus, he sent some respected Jewish elders to ask him to come and heal his slave. So they earnestly begged Jesus to help the man. 'If anyone deserves your help, he does,' they said, 'for he loves the Jewish people and even built a synagogue for us.'"*[1864] *Luke* and *Acts* were addressed to Theophilus who was either a real person or a symbol, but in either case represented the God-fearers.[1865]

The Ethiopian converted by Philip noted in Chapter 7 is a type of as a God-fearer. He *"had gone to Jerusalem to worship"* and *"was reading aloud from the book of the prophet Isaiah"* at the time of his meeting with Philip.[1866],[1867] Others included Jason of Thessalonica[1868] and Titius Justus of Corinth.[1869]

The God-fearers were Paul's natural constituency and he may have met many of them initially in the synagogues he visited in urban centers. He won an agreement for them at the Council of Jerusalem, stood up for them at Antioch, paid money for them and died for them trying to get to Spain. The world is filled with such people today who, like Thomas Jefferson, have little patience for the trappings of Christianity but for whom the *New Testament* was written.

I have quoted or referenced all twenty-seven *New Testament* books. I have quoted or referenced thirty-three of the forty-four American Presidents. Although a Protestant, I have cited saints, three of whom - James of the Twelve, Peter and most stupendously the Blessed Virgin Mary - sprang from their *New Testament* roots into the next twenty centuries of history. I have cited Popes with special respect for John Paul II and John XXIII who are also saints. I have relied on many Christian heroes including two very different ones with the same name who lived centuries apart: Martin Luther and Martin Luther King Jr. I have carefully analyzed a collectively bargained agreement referred three times in the *New Testament*. I have identified Paul's Christian adversaries, some of whom were mortal enemies. I have restated with my own enthusiasm Jesus's teachings and tried to explain why his resurrection can be accepted by a broad base.

By listing many who have come before us and the immensity of time and space I have underscored the brevity of our lives because as a Psalmist taught, recognizing our own mortality is the path to wisdom.[1870]

I have done all this to drive home these points.

- There is a diversity of Christianity in the pages of the *New Testament*.
- One variety - close to the Jewish-Christians – is God-centered good living.
- There is hope of life beyond.

If Christianity is to be a religious basis for twenty-first century life, I believe it needs to shed many of its accoutrements and embrace a broad message, symbolized in the Council of Jerusalem, the teachings of Paul and the teachings of Jesus.

SOURCES

Sydney E. Ahlstrom *A Religious History of the American People* (New Haven and London: Yale University Press, 1972. Fourth Printing, 1974)

Donald Harman Akenson, *Saint Saul: A Skeleton Key to the Historical Jesus* (Oxford: Oxford University Press, 2000)

Donald Harman Akenson, *Surpassing Wonder: The Invention of the Bible and the Talmuds* (New York, San Diego, London: Harcourt Brace & Company, 1998)

Charlotte Allen, *The Human Christ The Search for the Historical Jesus* (Oxford: Lion Publishing plc, 1998)

John L. Allen Jr. *The Global War on Christians Dispatches From the Front Lines of Anti-Christian Persecution* (New York: Image an imprint of the Crown Publishing Group, a division of Random House LLC, a Penguin Random House Company, Kindle Edition, 2013)

Richard Bauckham *Jude and the Relatives of Jesus in the Early Church* (Edinburg: T&T Clark, 1990)

Richard Bauckham *Jesus and the Eyewitnesses The Gospels as Eyewitness Testimony* (Grand Rapids, Michigan and Cambridge UK: William R. Eerdmans Publishing Company, Kindle Edition, 2006)

Pope Benedict XVI. *The Apostles and Their Co-Workers* (Huntington, Indiana: Our Sunday Visitor Publishing Division Our Sunday Visitor, inc, 2007)

Pope Benedict XVI *Jesus of Nazareth The Infancy Narratives* Translated by Philip J. Whitmore (New York: Image, 2012)

Craig L. Blomberg and Stephen E. Robinson *How Wide the Divide A Mormon & an Evangelical in Conversation* (Downers Grove, Illinois: InterVarsity Press, 1997)

Marcus Borg *The Heart of Christianity* (San Francisco: Harper, 2003)

Marcus J Borg *Jesus: Uncovering the Life, Teachings, and Relevance of a Religious Revolutionary* (New York: HarperCollins, 2006)

Marcus Borg, "An Emerging Christian Way" in Michael Schwartzentruber, editor, *The Emerging Christian Way: Thoughts, Stories and Wisdom for a Faith of Transformation* (Canada: Copperhouse, 2006)

Marcus Borg, editor and Ray Riegert, Co-Editor Jesus and Buddha: The Parallel Sayings (Berkeley: Seastone, Ulysses Press, 1997, 1999)

Marcus J. Borg and John Dominic Crossan *The First Paul: Reclaiming the Radical Visionary Behind the Church's Conservative Icon* (New York: HarperOne An Imprint of HarperCollins Publishers, 2009)

Marcus J Borg and John Dominic Crossan *The Last Week: What the Gospels Really Teach About Jesus's Final Days in Jerusalem* (New York: HarperSanFrancisco A *Division of* HarperCollins*Publishers*, 2006)

Marcus J. Borg and NT Wright *The Meaning of Jesus Two Visions* (New York: HarperCollins Publishers, 1999 First HarperCollins Paperback Edition Published In 2000)

Paul Boyer *When Time Shall Be No More: Prophecy Belief in Modern American Culture* (Cambridge and London: The Belknap Press of Harvard University Press, 1992)

Fawn Brodie *No Man Knows my History* (New York: Vintage Books, A division of Random House, Inc. 1945. First Vintage Books Edition, 1995)

Raymond E. Brown, SS *The Community of the Beloved Disciple The Life, Loves and Hates of an Individual Church in New Testament Times* (New York, Mahwah: Paulist Press, 1979)

Matthew Bunson *The Pope Encyclopedia An A to Z of the Holy See* (New York: Crown Trade Paperbacks, 1995)

Thomas Cahill *Desire of the Everlasting Hills: The World Before and After Jesus* (New York, London, Toronto, Sydney, Aukland: Nan A. Talese Doubleday, 1999)

Earle E. Cairns *Christianity Through The Centuries A History of the Christian Church Revised and Enlarged Edition* (Grand Rapids, Michigan: Zondervan Publishing House, 1954, 1981)

Eugene E. Campbell *Establishing Zion The Mormon Church in the American West, 1847-1869* (Salt Lake City: Signature Books, 1988)

Joel Carmichael *The Birth of Christianity* (New York: Dorset Press,1989)

James Carroll *Christ, Actually The Son of God for the Secular Age* (New York: Viking Published by the Penguin Group, 2014)

Paolo Cesaretti *Theodora Empress of Byzantium* Translated from the Italian by Rosanna M. Giammanco Frongia, Ph.D. a Mark Magowan Book (New York: The Vendome Press, 2001, 2004)

Christianity The Illustrated Guide to 2000 Years of the Christian Faith Chief Consultant Ann Marie B. Bahr Australia: Millennium House

Father Michael Collins and Matthew A. Price *The Story of Christianity* (London: DK Publishing, Inc., 1999)

Harvey Cox *The Future of Faith* (New York: HarperOne *An Imprint of* HarperCollins*Publishers,* 2009)

John Dominic Crossan and Jonathan L. Reed, *In Search of Paul How Jesus' Apostle Opposed Rome's Empire with God's Kingdom A New Vision of Paul's Words & World* (New York: HarperOne *An Imprint of* HarperCollins*Publishers,* 2004)

John Dominic Crossan *The Birth of Christianity: Discovering What Happened in the Years Immediately After the Death of Jesus* (New York: HarperSanFrancisco a Division of HarperCollinsPublishers, 1998)

Daniel C. Dennett and Lisa LaScola *Caught in the Pulpit Leaving Belief Behind* Foreword by Richard Dawkins (Durham, North Carolina: Pitchstone Publishing, Kindle Edition,2015)

Sally Denton *Faith and Betrayal: A Pioneer Woman's Passage in the American West* (New York: Alfred A. Knopf, 2005)

Sally Denton *American Massacre The Tragedy at Mountain Meadows, September 1857* (New York: Alfred A. Knopf, 2003)

John Dillenberger and Claude Welch *Protestant Christianity Interpreted Through its Development* (New York: Charles Scribner's Sons, 1954)

Karen Dockery, Johnnie Godwin, Phyllis Godwin, *The Student Bible Dictionary* (Ulrichville, OH: Barbour Books, an imprint of Barbour Publishing, Inc:, 2000. Originally published by Holman Bible Publishers, 1993)

Documents of the Christian Church second edition Selected and Edited by Henry Bettenson (London, Oxford and New York: Oxford University Press) First published, 1943. Second edition, 1963. First issued as an Oxford University Press paperback, 1967

Dinesh D'Souza *What's So Great About Christianity* (Washington DC: Regnery Publishing Company An Eagle Publishing Company, 2007)

James DG Dunn *Did the First Christians Worship Jesus? The New Testament Evidence* (London: Society for Promoting Christian Knowledge; Louisville, KY: Westminster John Knox Press, 2010 Kindle Edition, 2010)

James DG Dunn *Jesus, Paul, and the Gospels* (Grand Rapids, Michigan and Cambridge UK: Eerdmans Publishing Co., Kindle Edition, 2011)

Bart D. Ehrman *Did Jesus Exist? The Historical Argument for Jesus of Nazareth* (New York: HarperOne *An Imprint of* HarperCollins*Publisher*, Kindle Edition, 2012)

Bart D. Ehrman *Forged Writing in the Name of God Why the Bible's Authors Are Not Who We Think They Are* (New York: HarperOne *An Imprint of* HarperCollins *Publishers*, 2011)

Bart D. Ehrman *God's Problem: How the Bible Fails to Answer Our Most Important Question - Why We Suffer* (New York: HarperOne a Division of HarperCollins Publishers, 2008)

Bart D. Ehrman *Jesus Interrupted: Revealing the Hidden Contradictions in the Bible (And Why We Don't Know Them)* (New York: HarperOne *An Imprint of* HarperCollins*Publishers*, 2009)

Bart D. Ehrman *Misquoting Jesus The Story Behind Who Changed the Bible and Why* (San Francisco: Harper, 2005)

Bart D. Ehrman *Peter, Paul and Mary* (Oxford: Oxford University Press, 2006)

Bart D Ehrman *The Lost Gospel of Judas Iscariot* (Oxford: Oxford University Press, 2006)

Bart Ehrman *The New Testament,* (New York: Oxford, 2000)

Bart D. Ehrman *Truth and Fiction in the DaVinci Code: A Historian Reveal What We Really Know About Jesus, Mary Magdalene, and Constantine* (Oxford: Oxford University Press, 2004)

Lena Einhorn *The Jesus Mystery: Astonishing Clues to the True Identities of Jesus and Paul* (Guilford, Connecticut: The Lyons Press and Imprint of The Globe Pequot Press, 2007)

Bruce Feiler Abraham *A Journey to the Heart of Three Faiths* (New York: Wm. Morrow *An Imprint of* HarperCollins*Publishers*, 2002)

Bruce Feiler *America's Prophet Moses and the American Story* (New York: William Morrow *An Imprint of* HarperCollins*Publishers*, 2009)

Justo L. Gonzales *A History of Christian Thought From the Beginnings to the Council of Chalcedon* Volume 1 Revised Edition (Nashville, Abingdon Press, Kindle Edition, 1970, 1987)

Justo L. Gonzales *A History of Christian Thought Volume II* Revised Edition From Augustine to the Eve of the Reformation (Nashville: Abingdon Press, Kindle Edition, 1972, 1987)

Justo L. Gonzales *A History of Christian Thought Volume III Revised Edition From the Protestant reformation to the Twentieth Century* (Nashville: Abingdon Press, Kindle Edition, 1975)

Justo L. Gonzales, *Acts The Gospel of the Spirit* (Maryknoll, New York: Orbis Books, 2001)

Justo L. Gonzales, *The Story of Christianity Volume 1 The Early Church to the Dawn of the Reformation* (New York: HarperCollins e-books, 1984, 2010)

Ondina E. Gonzales and Justo L. Gonzales *Christianity in Latin America A History* (Cambridge, New York, Melbourne, Madrid, Cape Town, Singapore, Sao Paulo, Delhi: Cambridge University Press, Kindle Edition, 2008)

Edgar J. Goodspeed *A Life of Jesus* (New York, Evanston, and London: Harper & Row, Publishers, Harper Torchbook The Cloister Library, 1950)

Michael Grant, *Constantine the Great: The Man and His Times* (USA: Barnes & Noble, Inc., 1993)

Michael Grant *History of Rome* (New York: Charles Scribner's Sons, 1978)

Michael Grant *Jesus: An Historian's Review of the Gospels* (New York: Charles Scribner's Sons, 1977)

Michael Grant *Saint Paul* (New York: Barnes and Noble Books, 2005)

Michael Grant *Saint Peter A Biography* Michael Grant Publications Ltd. 1994 (New York: Barnes & Noble, 2009)

Andrew Greeley and Michael Hout *The Truth About Conservative Christians: What They Think and What They Believe* (Chicago and London: The University of Chicago Press, 2006)

Robin Griffith-Jones *The Gospel According to Paul: The Creative Genius Who Brought Jesus To The World* (New York: HarperSanFrancisco A Division of HarperCollinsPublishers, 2004)

Paul C. Gutjahr, *The Book of Mormon A Biography* (Princeton and Oxford: Princeton University Press, Kindle Edition, 2012)

Martin Hengel and Anna Maria Schwemer *Paul Between Damascus and Antioch The Unkown Years* (Louisville, Kentucky: Westminster John Knox Press, 1997 Translation by Jown Bowden, 1997)

James Hitchcock *History of the Catholic Church From the Apostolic Age to the Third Millenium* (San Francisco: Ignatius Press, 2012)

Hubert Jedin, Editor *History of the Church Volume I From the Apostolic Community to Constantine* by Karl Baus *A Crossroad Book* (New York: The Seabury Press, 1962, English Translation, 1965)

Philip Jenkins *Jesus Wars: How Four Patriarchs, Three Queens, and Two Emperors Decided What Christians Would Believe for the Next 1,500 Years* (New York: HarperOne *An Imprint of* Harper*Collins Publishers*, 2010)

Philip Jenkins *The Great and Holy War How World War I Became a Religious Crusade* (New York: HarperOne *An Imprint* of HarperCollins*Publishers*, Kindle Edition, 2014)

Philip Jenkins *The Lost History of Christianity: The Thousand Year Golden Age of the Church in the Middle East, Africa, and Asia - and How it Died* (New York: HarperCollins Publishers HarperOne An Imprint of HarperCollins*Publisher*, 2007)

Philip Jenkins *The Next Christendom The Coming of Global Christianity* Third Edition (Oxford Oxford University Press, Kindle edition, 2011)

Paul Johnson *A History of Christianity* (New York, London, Toronto, Sydney: Simon and Schuster, A Touchstone Book, 1976)

Paul Johnson *Jesus A Biography From a Believer* (New York: Viking. Published by the Penguin Group, Kindle Edition, 2010)

Paul Johnson *The Quest For God: A Personal Pilgrimage* originally published in Great Britain in 1996 by Weidenfeld & Nicolson, Orion House (New York: HarperCollins*Publishers*,1996)

Werner Keller. *The Bible as History* Translated by William Neil (New York: William Morrow and Company, 1956)

JND Kelly *The Oxford Dictionary of Popes* (Oxford and New York: Oxford University Press, 1986)

David Klinghoffer *Why The Jews Rejected Jesus: The Turning Point in Western History* (New York, London, Toronto, Sydney, Aukland: Doubleday, 2005)

Jon Krakauer *Under the Banner of Heaven: A Story of Violent Faith* (New York: Anchor Books a Divison of Random House, Inc., 2003,2004)

Herbert Krosney *The Lost Gospel: The Quest for the Gospel of Judas Iscariot* (Washington DC: National Geographic, 2006) Foreword by Bart D. Ehrman

Michael J. Kruger *The Question of Canon Challenging the Status Quo in The New Testament Debate* (Downers Grove, Illinois: IVP Academic an imprint of InterVarsity Press, 2013)

Amy-Jill Levine *The Misunderstood Jew: The Church and the Scandal of the Jewish Church* (New York: HarperCollins, 2006)

Bernard Lewis. *What Went Wrong?* (Oxford: Oxford University Press, 2002)

CS Lewis, *Mere Christianity* (New York: Macmillan Publishing Company, a division of Macmillan, Inc., 1943, 1945, 1953)

John Locke *The Reasonableness of Christianity with A Discourse of Miracles and Part of A Third Letter Concerning Toleration* Edited, Abridged and Introduced by IT Ramsey A Library of Modern Religious Thought (Stanford: Stanford University Press, 1958. Written by John Locke (1632-1704) in 1695

Rich Lowry *Lincoln Unbound How An Ambitious Young Railsplitter Saved The American Dream And How We Can Do It Again* (New York: Broadside Books *An Imprint of* HarperCollins*Publishers*, 2013)

Gerd Ludemann, *The Earliest Christian Text I Thessalonians* (Salem, Oregon: Polebridge Press, Willamette University, Kindle Edition, 2013, Revised and expanded from the original German)

Gerd Ludemann in collaboration with Alf Ozen Translated by John Bowden *What Really Happened to Jesus A Historical Approach to the Resurrection* (Louisville, Kentucky: Westminster John Knox Press, 1995)

Hyam Maccoby *Revolution in Judaea: Jesus and the Jewish Resistance* New York: Taplinger Publishing Company, Inc.,1973)

Hyam Maccoby *The Mythmaker Paul and the Invention of Christianity* (New York: Barnes & Noble Books 1998 by arrangement with HapersSanFrancisco, a division of HarperCollins Publishers, Inc. Published by Hyam Maccoby, 1986)

Diarmaid MacCulloch, *Christianity: The First Three Thousand Years* (New York: Viking published by the Penguin Group, Kindle Edition, 2009)

Burton L Mack *The Lost Gospel: The Book of Q & Christian Origins* (San Francisco: HarperSanFrancisco, 1993)

Burton L. Mack *Who Wrote The New Testament?: The Making of the Christian Myth* (New York: HarperCollins and HarperSanFrancisco, 1995). First HarperCollins paperback, 1996

Martin Marty *The Christian World: A Global History* (New York: The Modern Library an Imprint the Random House Publishing Group, A Division of Random House, Inc. A Modern Library Chronicles Book, 2007)

Rev. Scotty McLennan *Jesus Was a Liberal* (New York: Palgrave MacMillan a division of St. Martin Press) 2009)

John P. Meier *A Marginal Jew Rethinking the Historical Jesus Volume One The Roots of the Problem and the Person* ABRL (New York, London, Toronto, Sydney, Aukland: Doubleday, 1991).

John P. Meier *The Vision of Matthew: Christ, Church and Morality in the First Gospel* (New York: Crossroads, 1991)

John P. Meier *A Marginal Jew Rethinking the Historical Jesus Vlm III Companions and Competitors* (New York, London, Toronto, Sydney, Auckland: The Anchor Bible Reference Library Doubleday a Division of Random House, Inc., 2001)

Jean Milet *God or Christ* (London: SCM Press, 1980) Translated by John Bowden from the French

Niels C. Nielson *God in the Obama Era Presidents Religion and Ethics From George Washington to Barack Obama* (New York: Morgan James Publishing, LLC, 2009)

WOE Oesterley, LittD., D.D. (Camb.) and Theodore H. Robinson, Litt.D. (Camb.), D.D. (Lond.) *Hebrew Religion: Its Origin and Development* (London: S.P.C.K, 1952)

Bob O'Gorman, Ph.D., and Mary Faulkner, M.A. *The Complete Idiot's Guide to Understanding Catholicism*, Third Edition (New York: Alpha Books Published by the Penguin Group, 2006)

Richard N. Ostling and Joan K. Ostling; *Mormon America: The Power and the Promise The Beliefs, Rituals, Business Practices, and Well-Guarded Secrets of One of the World's Fastest Growing and Most Influential Religions* (New York: HarperSanFrancisco A *Division of* HarperCollins*Publishers*, 1999)

The Oxford Illustrated History of Christianity Edited by John McManners Oxford and New York: Oxford University Press, 1992)

Elaine Pagels *Beyond Belief* (New York: Random, 2003)

Elaine Pagels *Revelations Visions, Prophecy and Politics in the Book of Revelation* (New York: Viking Published by the Penguin Group, 2012)

Elaine Pagels and Karen L. King *Reading Judas: The Gospel of Judas and the Shaping of Christianity* (New York: The Penguin Group, 2007)

Jaroslav Pelikan *Jesus Through The Centuries: His Place in the History of Culture* (New York, Cambridge, Philadelphia, San Francisco, Washington, London, Mexico City, Sao Paulo, Singapore, Sydney: Harper & Row, Publishers Reprinted by arrangement with Yale University Press, 1985, 1987)

Jaroslav Pelikan *Mary Through the Centuries Her Place in the History of Culture* (New Haven and London: Yale University Press, 1996)

J Phillips *The Disciple Whom Jesus Loved Take Another Look The Bible Has The Answers* (Austell, GA: Waymaker Communications, Fifth Edition 2011 First Edition Copyright 2000)

Robert Pinsky *The Life of David* (New York: Schocken Books a division of Random House, Inc. and Toronto: Random House of Canada Limited, Kindle Edition, 2005)

Charles Francis Potter *The Story of Religion As Told In The Lives Of Its Leaders* (Garden City, New York: Garden City Publishing Company Star Books, Simon and Schuster, Inc., 1929)

Stephen Prothero *American Jesus How the Son of God Became a National Icon* (New York: Farrar, Straus and Giroux, 2003)

Stephen Prothero *Religious Literacy What Every American Needs to Know and Doesn't* (New York: HarperOne a Division of HarperCollinsPublisher, 2007)

Reader's Digest *After Jesus: The Triumph of Christianity* (Pleasantville, New York and Montreal: Reader's Digest Association, Inc., 1992)

Reader's Digest *Atlas of the Bible: An Illustrated Guide to the Holy Land* (Pleasantville, New York and Montreal, The Reader's Digest Association, Inc., 1981)

Reader's Digest *Jesus and His Times* (Pleasantville, New York and Montreal: The Readers Digest Association, Inc., 1987)

The Reliability of the New Testament Bart D. Ehrman & Daniel B. Wallace In Dialogue Robert B. Stewart, Editor (Minneapolis: Fortress Press, 2011)

Yves Renouard *The Avignon Papacy 1305-1403* Originally published by Presses Universitaires de France, Paris as La Papaute a Avignon, 1954 translated by Denis Bethell (Hamden, Connecticut: Archon Books, 1970) Printed in Great Britain by Latimer Trend & Co Ltd Plymouth

Don Richardson *Eternity in Their Hearts* Ventura, California: Regal Books from Gospel Light, 1981 Kindle Edition, 1981)

James M. Robinson *The Secrets of Judas The Story of the Misunderstood Disciple and His Lost Gospel* (New York: HarperCollins*Publisher*s HarperSanFrancisco *A Division of* HarperCollins*Publishers*, 2006)

Joan Roughgarden *Evolution and Christian Faith Reflections of An Evolutionary Biologist* (Washington DC, Covelo, London: Island Press, 2006)

Josiah Royce *Race Questions, Provincialism, and Other American Problems* (New York: The Macmillan company, 1908)

Culbert Gerow Rutenber *The Dagger and the Cross An Examination of Christian Pacifism* (Nyack, New Fellowship Publications, 1958. First Published November 1950. Second Printing, January, 1953. Fellowship Paperback Edition, February 1958. Forward by John C. Bennett.

Carl Sagan *The Varieties of Scientific Experience: A Personal View of the Search for God* Edited by An Druyan (New York: Penguin Press, 2006)

EP Sanders *Paul: A Brief Insight* (New York and London: Sterling, 1991)

Annette Sandoval *The Directory of Saints: A Concise Guide To Patron Saints* (New York, London, Victoria, Toronto, Aukland: Penguin, 1996)

Wolfgang Schrage, *The Ethics of the New Testament* (Philadelphia; Fortress Press, 1988) First Published in German in 1982. Translated by David E. Green

William Smith, LLD A Dictionary of the Bible Revised and Edited by Rev. F. N. and M. A. Peloubet (Grand Rapids: Zondervan Publishing House, 1948. Copyright 1884 by Porter and Coates. First Grand Rapids printing 1967. Sixteenth printing December 1979.)

John Shelby Spong *Jesus For the Non-Religious: Recovering the Divine at the Heart of the Human* (New York: HarperSanFrancisco A Division of HarperCollins Publishers, 2007)

Donald Spoto *The Hidden Jesus A New Life* (New York: St. Martin's Griffin, 1998)

Donald Spoto *Reluctant Saint The Life of Francis of Assisi* (New York: Penguin Group Penguin Compass, 2002)

Rodney Stark *Discovering God: The Origins of the Great Religions and the Evolution of Belief* (New York: HarperOne a division of HarperCollins*Publishers*, 2007

Rodney Stark *God's Battalions The Case for the Crusades* (New York: HarperOne *An Imprint of* HarperCollins*Publishers*, 2009)

Rodney Stark *One True God: Historical Consequences of Monotheism* (Princeton and Oxford: Princeton University Press, 2001)

Rodney Stark. *The Rise of Christianity A Sociologist Reconsiders History* (Princeton: Princeton University Press, 1996)

Rodney Stark *The Rise of Mormonism* Edited by Reid L. Neilson (New York: Columbia University Press, 2005)

Rodney Stark *The Triumph of Christianity How the Jesus Movement Became the World's Largest Religion* (New York: HarperOne *An Imprint of* HarperCollins*Publishers,* 2011)

Rodney Stark *The Victory of Reason: How Christianity Led to Freedom, Western Capitalism, and Western Success* (New York: Random House, 2005)

Lee Strobel *The Case for The Real Jesus: A Journalist Investigates Current Attacks on the Identity of Christ* (Grand Rapids: Zondervan, 2007)

Jon M. Sweeney *The Pope Who Quit: A True Medieval Tale of Mystery, Death and Salvation* (New York: Image Books, an imprint of the Crown Publishing Group, a division of Random House, Inc., Kindle Edition, 2012)

James D. Tabor *The Jesus Dynasty* (New York: Simon & Schuster, 2006)

Samuel Tadros *Motherland Lost The Egyptian and Coptic Quest for Modernity* (Stanford: Hoover Institution Press, Kindle Edition, 2013)

Jason Thompson *A History of Egypt From Earliest Times to the Present* (New York: Anchor Books, A division of Randomhouse, Inc., 2008)

Burton H. Throckmorton, Jr. ed., *Gospel Parallels: A Synopsis of the First Three Gospels* (Toronto, New York and Edinburg: Thomas Nelson and Sons, 1949, 1957, reprinted April, 1960)

Greg Tobin *The Good Pope The Making of a Saint and the Remaking of the Church – The Story of John XXIII and Vatican II.* (New York: HarperCollins Publishers, Inc, 2012, Kindle Edition)

The Novels and Other Works of Lyof N. Tolstoi My Confession. My Religion. The Gospel in Brief (New York: Charles Scribner's Sons, 1913 Thomas Y. Crowell & Co. Copyright 1899)

Rev. John Trigilio, ThD and Rev. Kenneth Brighenti, *The Saints for Dummies* (Hoboken, New Jersey: Wiley Publishing, Inc., 2010)

Robert E. Van Vorst, *Jesus Outside the New Testament: An Introduction to the Ancient Evidence* (Grand Rapid, Michigan and Cambridge UK: William B. Eerdmans Publishing Company, 2000)

Richard S. Van Wagoner *Sidney Rigdon: A Portrait of Religious Excess* (Salt Lake City: Signature Books, 1994 Paperbound printing 2006 Signature Books)

Williston Walker *A History of The Christian Church* (New York: Charles Scribner's Sons, 1940, Written 1919.)

George Weigel *God's Choice: Pope Benedict XVI and the Future of the Catholic Church* (New York: HarperCollins, 2005)

L. Michael White *From Jesus to Christianity* (San Francisco Harper Collins, 2004)

L. Michael White *Scripting Jesus The Gospels in Rewrite* (New York: HarperCollins e-books, 2010)

Robert Louis Wilken *The Christians as the Romans Saw Them* (New Haven and London: Yale University Press, 1984)

Robert Louis Wilken *The First Thousand Years A Global History of Christianity* (New Haven and London: Yale University Press, 2012)

Robert Louis Wilken *The Myth of Christian Beginning: History's Impact on Belief* (Garden City, New York: Doubleday & Company, Inc.,1971)

Garry Wills *Head and Heart: American Christianities* (New York: The Penguin Press, 2007)

Garry Wills *What Jesus Meant* (Penguin Books: New York and London, 2006)

Garry Wills *What Paul Meant* (New York: Penguin, 2006)

Garry Wills *What the Gospels Meant* (New York: Viking Published by the Penguin Group, 2008)

Garry Wills *Why I Am A Catholic* (Boston and New York: Houghton Mifflin Company, 2002)

AN Wilson *CS Lewis A Biography* (London and New York: WW Norton & Company, Inc., 1990)

AN Wilson *Jesus A Life* (New York and London: WW Norton & Company, inc and WW Norton & Company, Ltd., 1992)

AN Wilson *Paul: The Mind of the Apostle* (New York: W.W. Norton & Company, 1997)

Ben Witherington III *New Testament History A Narrative* Account (Grand Rapids, Michigan: BakerAcademic a division of *Baker Publishing Group,* Kindle Edition, 2001)

Ben Witherington III *The Jesus Quest The Third Search For the Jew of Nazareth* (Downers Grove, Illinois: InterVarsity Press, 1995)

David Wolpe *David The Divided Heart* (New Haven and London: Yale University Press, Kindle Edition, 2014).

Thomas E. Woods Jr. *How the Catholic Church Built Western Civilization* (Washington DC: Regnery Publishing, Inc., 2005)

NT Wright *How God Became King The Forgotten Story of the Gospels* (Sydney, Toronto, Aukland, London, New York: HarperOne *An Imprint of* HarperCollins*Publishers*, Kindle Edition, 2012)

NT Wright *Simply Jesus A New Vision of Who He Was, What He Did, And Why He Matters* (New York: HaperOne *An Imprint* of HarperCollins*Publishers*, 2011)

NT Wright *The Resurrection of the Son of God Christian Origins and the Question of God* Volume Three (Minneapolis: Fortress Press, 2003)

ENDNOTES

[1] I have not italicized the names of the (traditional) authors of the *New Testament* Books. In the cases of the four traditional Gospel writers I have tried to make a distinction between the person and the book with the latter earning the italics. For example, in Chapter 4, in speaking about the differences between the Gospels I have this sentence: "If Matthew or Luke redacted a story from *Mark* it was because they wanted to say it differently and possibly address different types of Christians." In this, I am referring to the presumed writers, Matthew and Luke and the *Gospel of Mark*.

[2] James Shreeve, *National Geographic* March 2006. (Some more recent estimates push this exodus from Africa back to about 125,000 years ago. See Marc Kaufman, *Washington Post San Francisco Chronicle* January 28, 2011.)

[3] I owe this ruminating of the last century to Michael Crichton's (1942 – 2008) eloquent Introduction to his 1999 novel *Timeline*. Source for water on Mars: John Johnson Jr., *Los Angeles Times Oakland Tribune* August 1, 2008. Source for water on the Moon: Alicia Chang Associated Press *Honolulu Star Bulletin* November 14, 2009 and Michio Kaku *Opinionjournal.com* November 17, 2009. This is a big deal. First, we didn't know water was on the Moon. Second, it can help sustain future astronauts. Water has hydrogen, which might be used in rocket fuels. It also has oxygen to fill air tanks. (The Moon is airless.) Once purified, this could be drinking water. Additional note: Volcanic samples from the Moon that were collected in the 1970s now show that the Moon's interior holds more water than we previously thought. See David Perlman, *San Francisco Chronicle* May 24, 2011.

[4] Paul Johnson, A History *of Christianity* (New York, London, Toronto, Sydney: Simon and Schuster, A Touchstone Book, 1976) 334ff.

[5] It is not that I care particularly for animals. Rather, the "explanation" often proffered that suffering somehow has redemptive value does not seem to apply to an animal caught in a steel trap or in the jaws of a predator. (Nor can I see it applying in most human situations.)

[6] *II Corinthians* 4:8.

[7] George Will, *Oregonian* May 8, 2006.

[8] Edward J. Larson, *A Magnificent Catastrophe: The Tumultuous Election of 1800, America's First Presidential Campaign* (New York, London, Toronto, Sydney: Free Press, A Division of Simon & Schuster, Inc., 2007) 171. Note: Jefferson - and John Adams - communicated frequently with Rush. Rush was a signer of the Declaration of Independence and attended the Continental Congress. He helped reconcile Jefferson and Adams late in their lives, a reunion that produced a corpus of American letters. In 1812 Rush wrote Adams of Jefferson: "I consider you and him as the North and South Poles of the American Revolution. Some talked, some wrote, and some fought to promote and establish it, but you and Mr. Jefferson *thought* for us all." See Jon Meacham, *Thomas Jefferson The Art of Power* (New York: Random House, Kindle Edition, 2012) Location 2114. Rush described his own religious views in his later years in a letter to Adams as "a compound of the orthodoxy and heterodoxy of most of our Christian churches." He is considered the "Father of American Psychiatry." Rush University Medical Center in Chicago is named for him. See http://en.wikipedia.org/wiki/Benjamin_Rush (Accessed May 1, 2012). As a very young man in 1773 he wrote, "Patriotism is as much a virtue as justice, and is as necessary for the support of societies as natural affection is for the support of families." See *PatriotPost.US* November 14, 2008. Upon the ratification of the US Constitution in 1787, Rush wrote to a friend, "Tis done. We have become a nation." See *PatriotPost.US* April 11, 2008. Jefferson wrote Rush's son a line in 1820 often found in public places today: "The boisterous sea of liberty is never without a wave." See *PatriotPost.US* December 21, 2007. (This son, Richard Rush, ran as John Quincy Adams's running mate in a losing effort in 1828.) Rush was also an advocate for temperance. See Daniel J. Flynn *A Conservative History of the American Left* (New York: Crown Forum, an imprint of the Crown Publishing Group, a division of Random House, Inc., New York 2008) 71. In the 1790s Benjamin Rush was a leader in the Universalist religious sect. See Susan Dunn, *Jefferson's Second Revolution The Election Crisis of 1800 and the Triumph of Republicanism* (Boston and New York: Houghton Mifflin Company, 2004) 36. Benjamin Rush was also considered the father of veterinary medicine in America and taught medicine at the University of Pennsylvania where one of his students was the future US president, William Henry Harrison. Rush was a protégé of Benjamin Franklin. See James Humes, *Which President Killed a Man?: Tantalizing Trivia and Fun About Our Chief Executives and First Ladies* Illustrations by William Bramhall (New York: MJF Books, 2003) 126.

[9] Indeed, in 1822, he wrote, "Had the doctrines of Jesus been preached always as pure as they came from his lips, the whole civilized world would now have

been Christian." See Steven Waldman, *Founding Faith: Providence, Politics and the Birth of Religious Freedom in America* (New York: Random House, 2008) 80.

[10] Although for centuries, Christians thought that a man named Luke wrote *Luke* and *Acts* and that a man named Matthew wrote *Matthew* and Mark wrote *Mark* and John wrote *John*, modern scholars question these claims. I will deal with some of these questions in this book. However, for the sake of convenience, I will use the traditional names for the authors of these Biblical books. Note: All of the *New Testament* writers were Jewish with the possible exception of Luke who, if he was a Gentile, knew Judaism well. See Marcus J Borg, *Evolution of the Word The New Testament in the Order the Books Were Written* (New York: HarperOne *An Imprint of* HarperCollins *Publishers*, Kindle Edition, 2012) 7.

[11] Early in his *New Testament* career as recounted in the *Book of Acts*, Paul was known as Saul. I will consistently refer to him as Paul. Why did he change to Paul? We don't know but there is one hint. In *Acts* chapter 13 verses 4 through 12, the writer reports that Saul as he was then known made a convert of an important Roman official on the island of Cyprus. The *New Testament* account is that this official was *"a man of intelligence"* but may have been influenced by a *"magician"* opposing the Christian message. However, Saul condemned this magician to his face and the magician was even struck blind for a time. The Roman official then *"believed when he saw what had happened, being amazed at the teaching of the Lord."* The official's name was Sergius Paulus and after that Saul is consistently referred to as Paul except in those instances when his own earlier conversion is recounted. He may have taken Sergius Paulus's name in a token of respect for this important person who had joined the Christian movement.

[12] Stephen Prothero, *Religious Literacy What Every American Needs to Know and Doesn't* (New York: HarperOne a Division of HarperCollinsPublisher, 2007) 24. Another study showed that "(w)ell over 80 percent" of Americans pray quite regularly. See Rodney Stark, *The Rise of Mormonism* Edited by Reid L. Neilson (New York: Columbia University Press, 2005) 38.

[13] Nancy Haught, *Oregonian* February 10, 2008.

[14] Stark, *The Rise of Mormonism* 38. Yet another study showed that a fifth of the "atheists" in a Pew Survey said that they believed in God. See John Micklethwait and Adrian Wooldridge *OpinionJournal.com* April 7, 2009. These people also might also be "ready" – but ready for what?

15 http://www.gallup.com/poll/141044/americans-church-attendance-inches-2010.aspx (Accessed May 3, 2012).

16 I am a little uncertain on whether Jesus's death is substitutionary or exemplary - an example of divine love. *Mark* 10:45 indicates that Jesus's death was a ransom for many. *Luke* doesn't include that verse. In early sermons in *Acts* - 2:36-28 and 3:17-19 - Peter seems to be saying that the death of an innocent man can drive people to repentance. In this sense, redemption is in the power of Jesus's example rather than in an act where God is appeased. To put it another way, Marcus J Borg and John Dominic Crossan have suggested that Jesus died not for the sins of the world but because of the sins of the world. See Borg and John Dominic Crossan, *The Last Week: What the Gospels Really Teach About Jesus's Final Days in Jerusalem* (New York: HarperSanFrancisco A *Division of* HarperCollins*Publishers*, 2006) 162. I regret it if I have misstated Borg's and Crossan's point of view.

17 But, to be clear, I stand in awe of the *New Testament* as an historical document and a guide for life. I just think that claiming that it is error-free is inaccurate and diversionary.

18 Paul C. Nagel, *John Quincy Adams: A Public Life, A Private Life* (New York: Alfred A. Knopf, 1997) 230-1.

19 [http://www.gallup.com/poll/148427/Say-Bible-Literally.aspx?utm_source=alert&utm_medium=email&utm_campaign=syndication&utm_content=morelink&utm_term=Religion+-+Religion+and+Social+Trends](http://www.gallup.com/poll/148427/Say-Bible-Literally.aspx) (Accessed November 2, 2011). See also Borg, *The Heart of Christianity (San Francisco: Harper, 2003)* 4. Borg reports that Gallup found the percentage agreeing with this statement in 1963 to be 65%. It is interesting to note the differences between the percentages of Americans who give the *Bible* high stature and the percentage with basic knowledge of it. Only half of U.S. adults know the title of even one Gospel (*Matthew, Mark, Luke* or *John*). Most can't name the *Bible's* first book (*Genesis*). The trend extends even to evangelicals; only 44% of teenage evangelicals could identify a particular quote as coming from the Sermon on the Mount. Polls show that nearly two-thirds of Americans believe the *Bible* holds the answers to "all or most of life's basic questions," but pollster George Gallup has dubbed us "a nation of biblical illiterates." See David Van Biema *Time* April 2, 2007. To take a final example: 83% of Americans regard the *Bible* as the word of God but half of them do not know who preached the Sermon on the Mount (Jesus). See Micklewaith, Special Report *The Economist* November 3, 2007.

20 http://www.dts.edu/about/doctrinalstatement/ (Accessed May 3, 2012).

[21] http://www.westernseminary.edu/AboutWS/ftp.htm. (Accessed May 1, 2012).

[22] http://www.intervarsity.org/about/#/our/doctrinal-basis (Accessed May 1, 2012).

[23] http://home.earthlink.net/~ronrhodes/Inspiration.html (Accessed May 1, 2012).

[24] Garry Wills, *Why I Am A Catholic* (Boston and New York: Houghton Mifflin Company, 2002) 198ff. Note: In 1943 a Papal encyclical issued by Pope Pius XII called *Divino Afflante Spiritu* ("Inspired by the Holy Spirit") qualified this approach. It called for new translations of the *Bible* from the original languages. It permitted literary criticism of the *Bible*. The Catholic scholar Raymond E. Brown whom we will refer to later described it as a "Magna Carta for biblical progress." See http://en.wikipedia.org/wiki/Divino_Afflante_Spiritu (Accessed May 2, 2012).

[25] It is not at all clear that these Christians are credulous people by nature. In a 2008 study by the Baylor Institute for Studies of Religion, Americans were polled on whether they believe in the lost continent of Atlantis, UFOs, Bigfoot, the Loch Ness monster, astrology, palm readers and psychics. The results reaffirmed a few earlier surveys: Those embracing traditional Christian beliefs were less likely to believe in Big Foot, palm readers, etc. "Traditional Christian religion greatly decreases credulity, as measured by beliefs in the occult and paranormal," the study reports. See Mike Licona, *Baptist Press TownHall.com* February 23, 2009.

[26] In 2011, the organization changed its name to "Cru." One of the leaders explained that the word "Crusade" had "a negative connotation for lots of people across the world, especially in the Middle East." See http://www.christianitytoday.com/ct/2011/julyweb-only/campus-crusade-name-change.html (Accessed November 24, 2014).

[27] http://www.campuscrusadeforchrist.com/aboutus/statementoffaith.htm (Accessed May 1, 2012). Note: Evangelical institutions such as Multnomah University, a school training pastors in Portland Oregon, follows this line with a doctrinal statement reading: "We believe in the verbal, plenary inspiration of Scripture. This means the Holy Spirit dynamically superintended the verbal expressions of the human authors of Scripture so that the very thoughts God intended were accurately penned in the wording of the **original manuscripts**." (Emphasis added). See http://www.multnomah.edu/about/doctrinal-statement/ (Accessed May 3, 2012). Dallas Theological Seminary's full statement has a similar provision. Mormon leader Joseph Smith said something very similar in 1843: "I believe the *Bible* as it ought to be, as it came from the pen of the original writers." See Benjamin E. Park, "'Build, Therefore Your Own World': Ralph Waldo Emerson, Joseph Smith, and

American Antebellum Thought" *Journal of Mormon History*" Winter 2010 63. Note: Joseph Smith revised the *Bible* by deleting the *Song of Solomon* and adding chapters to *Genesis*. See Alex Beam, *American Crucifixion The Murder of Joseph Smith and the Fate of the Mormon Church* (New York: PublicAffairs, a Member of the Perseus Books Group, Kindle Edition, 2014 Location 280.

[28] http://www.fuller.edu/page.aspx?id=7381&terms=Inerrancy Note: Fuller's statement on inerrancy is over eleven hundred words. (Accessed May 1, 2012).

[29] *Acts* 17: 15-16 and 18:5.

[30] This disconnect is complicated and we will return to it.

[31] Although this is an *Old Testament* example, Reverend Graham's experience described herein clearly applied for him to the *New Testament* as well. Note: This story is in the *Book of Jonah* and it asserts that *"a great fish"* swallowed Jonah (chapter 1 verse 17). The story of Jonah is referred to in the *New Testament* where in *Matthew* Jesus calls the fish a *"sea monster"* (chapter 12 verse 40) and labeled the incident the *"sign of Jonah."* Jesus referred to the *"sign of Jonah"* on two other occasions without mentioning the sea monster (*Matthew* 16:4 and *Luke* 11:29-32). The account of Jonah became one of the most well-known Biblical stories. In history, people have often assumed the fish or the sea monster to be a whale. Additional note: In 2014 the purported tomb of Jonah in Iraq was attacked by the Islamic Terrorists, ISIS. See Janine Di Giovanni and Connor Gaffey *Newsweek* April 3, 2015.

[32] Collin Hansen, *Christian History* Fall 2004. Some half a century later, Graham told an interviewer: "I'm not a literalist in the sense that every single jot and tittle is from the Lord…This is a little different in my thinking through the years." The article went on to say that Graham believed that parts of the *Bible* are figurative and that Christians could disagree. One part that was figurative, according to Graham, was the meaning of "day" in *Genesis*. (Treating "day" as figurative allowed Graham to evade the evolution debate.) One that was precise was that the whale did swallow Jonah. See Meacham, *Newsweek*, August 14, 2006. Since accepting that the *Bible* uses metaphors in no way damages the point of inerrancy, I would hold that Graham's late-in-life views are essentially the same as when he was a young evangelist.

[33] Grover Cleveland, president of the United States from 1885-89 and 1893-1897, for example, kept a *Bible* inscribed by his mother: "My son, Stephen Grover Cleveland, from his loving Mother." See Henry F. Graff, *Grover Cleveland The American Presidents* Arthur M. Schlesinger, Jr., General Editor (New York: Henry Holt and Company Times Books, 2002) 31.

[34] In this book, we will focus nearly all comments on the *New Testament*.

[35] L. Michael White, *From Jesus to Christianity* (San Francisco: Harper Collins, 2004) 94-99, 172, 414-417, 425.

[36] *Mark* 13:1 and *Luke* 21: 20-2.

[37] Bart D. Ehrman *Jesus Interrupted: Revealing the Hidden Contradictions in the Bible (And Why We Don't Know Them)* (New York: HarperOne *An Imprint of* HarperCollins*Publishers,* 2009) 144ff. White, *From Jesus to Christianity* 94-99 dates *Luke* (and *Acts*) between 90AD-100AD. Note: I have found one modern scholar who argues for the possibility of earlier datings of the Gospels. See Richard Bauckham, *Jesus and the Eyewitnesses: The Gospels and Eyewitness Testimony* (Grand Rapids: Wm. B. Eerdmans Publishing Co., Kindle Edition, 2006).

[38] Ehrman, *Misquoting Jesus The Story Behind Who Changed the Bible and Why* (San Francisco: Harper, 2005) 48, 72.

[39] Ehrman, *The New Testament* (New York: Oxford, 2000) 480 and AN Wilson, *Paul: The Mind of the Apostle* (New York: W.W. Norton & Company, 1997) 251.

[40] *The Reliability of the New Testament Bart D. Ehrman & Daniel B. Wallace In Dialogue* Robert B. Stewart, Editor (Minneapolis: Fortress Press, 2011) 16-17, 19.

[41] Ehrman, *The New Testament* 480 and Ehrman, *Misquoting Jesus The Story Behind Who Changed the Bible and Why* 88-90.

[42] It was not until the Middle Ages, about 800, that scribes began inserting spaces between words, making reading for comprehension much easier. See Nicholas Carr *San Francisco Chronicle* E2 June 20, 2010.

[43] Ehrman, *Misquoting Jesus The Story Behind Who Changed the Bible and Why* 48.

[44] It is worth noting that some scholars would assert that by studying variations in the manuscripts we can arrive at a very close approximation of the original texts. That sort explanation has not, to my knowledge, been offered by Campus Crusade in defense of its position and in any event concedes sufficient ground that it is probably incompatible with any view of inerrancy. (So what if we can get closer to the original documents? The innerantists need to prove that those documents or their derivatives contain no errors.)

[45] *Revelation* 22:18-9.

[46] Ehrman, *The New Testament* 377, 385. See also http://www.earlychristianwritings.com/2thessalonians.html which estimates that *II Thessalonians* was written between 80 and 100 AD. (Accessed May 2, 2012).

[47] White, *From Jesus to Christianity* 425. Some date it as late as the 150. See Borg, *Evolution of the Word The New Testament in the Order the Books Were Written* 587.

[48] Ehrman, *Misquoting Jesus The Story Behind Who Changed the Bible and Why* 52. More on Origen: Origen (185-254) was the greatest Christian scholar before Augustine of the fourth century. *See* Reader's Digest *After Jesus: The Triumph of Christianity* (Pleasantville, New York and Montreal: Reader's Digest Association, Inc., 1992) 158. Note: *Matthew* 19:12 reads: "*Some are born as eunuchs, some have been made eunuchs by others, and some choose not to marry for the sake of the kingdom of Heaven. Let anyone accept this who can.*" Origen followed this scripture to the point of castrating himself. However, he later came to teach against literalism and in favor of an allegorical view of scripture. See Paul Boyer, *When Time Shall Be No More: Prophecy Belief in Modern American Culture* (Cambridge and London: The Belknap Press of Harvard University Press,1992) 47-48.

[49] Ehrman, *Misquoting Jesus The Story Behind Who Changed the Bible and Why* 40.

[50] Literacy has been a problem over much of the life of Christianity. In the "Dark Ages" - a term historians apply to, roughly speaking, the period from 476 AD-1000 AD - the Church built its education around the seven sacraments of Baptism, Confirmation, Eucharist, Penance, Anointing of the Sick, Holy Orders and Matrimony. (For the Eucharist, the priests were afraid the Eucharist wine which they saw as the blood of Christ would be spilled, so the laity only received the bread.) The "Middle Ages" is seen by historians to encompass the Dark Ages and continuing until the 1500s. In that era, cathedrals with mosaic tapestries and illustrative windows were "books" for the illiterates, teaching about the life of Jesus and the Virgin Mary. See Martin Marty, *The Christian World: A Global History* (New York: The Modern Library an Imprint the Random House Publishing Group, A Division of Random House, Inc. A Modern Library Chronicles Book, 2007) 82-3, 97. In the 700s the Eastern church based in Constantinople (modern Istanbul) was wracked for over a century by the Iconoclastic Controversy in which the religious and civil authorities intermittently banned the use of icons or images, viewing them as idols. John of Damascus known as the last of the "Fathers" of the Eastern church defended images and icons with, among other arguments, "...seeing that not everyone has a knowledge of letters nor time for reading, the Fathers gave their sanction to depicting these events on images, as being acts of great heroism, in order that they should form a concise memorial of them." See Justo L. Gonzales, *A History of Christian Thought From Augustine*

to the Eve of the Reformation Volume II Revised Edition (Nashville: Abingdon Press, Kindle Edition, 1972, 1987) Location 3907.

[51] For a full discussion of this possibility see Ehrman, *The New Testament* 326-31 and Robin Griffith-Jones, *The Gospel According to Paul: The Creative Genius Who Brought Jesus To The World* (New York: HarperSanFrancisco A Division of HarperCollinsPublishers, 2004) 285ff.

[52] Forgeries of this letter were detected by early Christians trying to establish a canon. See Ehrman, *Jesus Interrupted: Revealing the Hidden Contradictions in the Bible (And Why We Don't Know Them)* 206. Note: There actually is a "letter" to the Laodiceans embedded in the *New Testament* but it is not written by Paul. The *Book of Revelation* 3: 14-21 contains its text. Within it, two verses contain concepts familiar to modern evangelicals and possibly other Christians:

- Verse 16 introduces the idea of "lukewarm" Christians.
- Verse 20 introduces the idea of Christ seeking out people and reads in its entirety: *"Behold, I stand at the door and knock; if anyone hears My voice and opens the door, I will come in to him and will dine with him, and he with Me."*

[53] *II Timothy* 4:13 reads: *"When you come bring the cloak which I left at Troas with Carpus, and the books, especially the parchments."* Michael J. Kruger writes: "What did these notebooks contain? There are a number of possibilities, such as excerpts of Jesus' teachings, or early Christian *testimonia* (*Old Testament* proof texts supporting Messianic claims about Jesus), or even copies of Paul's own letters." See Michael J. Kruger *The Question of Canon Challenging the Status Quo in The New Testament Debate* (Downers Grove, Illinois: IVP Academic an imprint of InterVarsity Press, 2013) 93-94.

[54] *Luke* 1: 1-4.

[55] *Luke* 10: 29-37.

[56] *Luke* 15:11-32.

[57] *Luke* 17: 11-19. Note: President Calvin Coolidge (1872 – 1933) heard a sermon based on this text and later remarked that he was not sure that the one leper that thanked Jesus was any more grateful than the others. "When I appoint a man to office I don't want him to thank me. I want him to go and make good." See Donald R. McCoy, *Calvin Coolidge The Quiet President* (New York: The Macmillan Company and London: Collier-Macmillan Limited, 1967) 284. This is not offered as transcendent wisdom but only as

an example of how the *New Testament* has permeated American life, a topic we will take up in Chapter 3.

[58] *Luke* 19:1-9.

[59] *Luke* 10:38-42. In this account, Mary is listening to Jesus's teaching and Martha is preparing a meal. Ultimately, Martha comes to Jesus to complain that the situation is unfair. Jesus responds, *"Martha, Martha, you are worried and distracted by many things; here is need of only one thing. Mary has chosen the better part, which will not be taken away from her."* In later centuries, the Catholic Church made Martha the patron saint of cooks. She is also the patron saint of dieticians, servants and waitpersons. Her feast day is July 29. See Annette Sandoval, *The Directory of Saints: A Concise Guide To Patron Saints* (New York, London, Victoria, Toronto, Aukland: Penguin, 1996) 62.

[60] Robert E. Van Vorst, *Jesus Outside the New Testament: An Introduction to the Ancient Evidence* (Grand Rapid, Michigan and Cambridge UK: William B. Eerdmann Publishing Company, 2000) 137.

[61] Ehrman, *The New Testament* 455-6. White, *From Jesus to Christianity* 423 puts *Jude* as written from Rome abt. 90 AD -110 AD. For a discussion about an earlier possible date for *Jude* see Bauckham, *Jude and the Relatives of Jesus in the Early Church* (Edinburgh: T&T Clark, 1990).

[62] Borg, *Evolution of the Word The New Testament in the Order the Books Were Written* 401. *II Peter*, then, is probably the last chronological book of the *New Testament*. Besides the ways in which in incorporates *Jude*, there are these additional reasons for a late dating of this book:

- *II Peter* 3: 1 contains a reference to *I Peter*: *"This is now, beloved, the second letter I am writing to you in which I am stirring up your sincere mind by way of reminder,"*
- *II Peter* 3: 15-16 refer to Paul's letters: *"....regard the patience of our Lord as salvation; just as also our beloved brother Paul, according to the wisdom given him, wrote to you, as also in all his letters,..."*
- *II Peter* 3: 3-10 offers up a rationale for why Jesus hasn't come again yet: *"The Lord is not slow about His promise, as some count slowness, but is patient toward you, not wishing for any to perish but for all to come to repentance."* (Verse 9) Moreover, that section quotes unnamed scoffers who were saying: *""Where is the promise of His coming? For ever since the fathers fell asleep, all continues just as it was from the beginning of creation'"(Verse 4)* which may indicate a multi-generational time frame. It is at this point that the author of *II Peter* asserts that *"with the Lord one day is like a thousand years, and a thousand years like one day."* (Verse 8)

[63] The idea that Luke wrote the "we" sections –and not someone else - is given some credence by Luke's willingness to insert the first person "me" into his text in *Luke* 1:3 and "I" into *Acts* 1:1 showing that he is not inhibited from referring to himself when appropriate. See Ben Witherington III, *New Testament History A Narrative* Account (Grand Rapids, Michigan: BakerAcademic a division of *Baker Publishing Group*, Kindle Edition, 2001) Location 4894.

[64] Donald Harman Akenson, *Saint Saul: A Skeleton Key to the Historical Jesus* (Oxford: Oxford University Press, 2000) 137-142.

[65] Martin Hengel and Anna Maria Schwemer, *Paul Between Damascus and Antioch The Unknown Years* (Louisville, Kentucky: Westminster John Knox Press, 1997 Translation by John Bowden, 1997) 18-19. Here is a slightly variant view: "To narrate this saga that ranges from Jerusalem to Rome, Luke seems to have relied on three sources: The presumed diary which he kept when he traveled with Paul some thirty or forty years earlier, one or two written accounts of the earliest days of Christianity, and oral tradition. As (in *Luke*), he was able to weave his diverse materials into a graphic story. Luke's artistry shows itself especially in the speeches which he, like the Greek historians, inserts into the mouths of his chief personages, and in his ability to transmit the excitement of the marvelous and the miraculous." See *Literature from the Bible*, selected by Joseph Frank (Boston and Toronto: Little, Brown and Company, 1963) 384.

[66] *John* 21:24. Note: There is another point of view which we will mention in Chapter 4. It is that this verse does not indicate a source of *John* but is instead evidence that the "*disciple whom Jesus loved*" wrote the *Book of John* in its entirety.

[67] In 1687 August Herman Franke (1663-1727) had what he viewed as a new birth while preparing a sermon on *John* 20:31. Franke became of the great leaders of German Pietism, a reform movement in German Lutheranism. Pietism was a reaction to orthodoxy. It held for a rediscovery of a personal Christian life. Features of pietism included small-group house meetings to study scripture, the priesthood of all believers and simple doctrine. Franke emphasized that believers should have a personal "struggle of repentance," contending with the law and sin and a time of conversion. He wrote: "We may safely assure those who read the word with devotion and simplicity, that they will derive more light and profit from such a practice, and from connecting meditation with it...than can ever be acquired from drudging through an infinite variety of unimportant minutiae." Franke established educational foundations, orphanages and a foundation for the publication of the *Bible*. He promoted foreign missions and Pietism's interest in missions is seen in that it

has influences now in churches throughout the world. See Williston Walker, *A History of The Christian Church* (New York: Charles Scribner's Sons, 1940, Written 1919) 498-500 and *Justo L. Gonzales A History of Christian Thought From the Protestant Reformation to the Twentieth Century* Volume III Revised Edition (Nashville: Abingdon Press, Kindle Edition, 1975) Locations 5656ff, 5709.

[68] The idea that a written or oral account of Jesus's miracles was extant before 70 AD in Palestine and reflected a view of Jesus as a wonder worker was first suggested by the German theologian Rudolf Bultmann (1884 - 1976) in 1941. Heresy proceeding were initiated against him. See http://en.wikipedia.org/wiki/Signs_gospel. (Accessed May 2, 2012).

[69] This point is also made earlier in John's Gospel. Between the miracles of turning water into wine in Cana of Galilee recorded in *John* 2:1-11 and the healing of the son of a government official, also in Cana of Galilee, recorded in *John* 4:46-54 and explicitly called *"the second sign that Jesus did after coming from Judea to Galilee"* (*John* 4:54), there is this verse: *"When he was in Jerusalem during the Passover festival, many believed in his name because they saw the signs that he was doing."* (*John* 2:23). It should be noted that the sign recorded as the second sign is not necessarily a mistake in the Gospel since it is listed at the second sign in Galilee and the ones in Jerusalem were not being tabulated in this list.

[70] "The Gospels preserve only selections of the Jesus tradition, and when one considers the extensive overlap in contents, they are slender selections at that. *John* 21:25 makes this selectivity explicit..." See Van Vorst 179-80.

[71] Ehrman, *The New Testament* 13.

[72] Ehrman, *Jesus Interrupted: Revealing the Hidden Contradictions in the Bible (And Why We Don't Know Them)* 210.

[73] I have read a Kindle version of Eusebius *History of the Church*. Eusebius lived from abt. 263 – abt. 339. He was bishop of Caesarea and has been called the "Father of Church History." Whenever I have referred to Eusebius in this book I have cited the relevant Book and Chapter.

[74] Eusebius Book III Chapters 3 and 25.

[75] Burton L Mack, *The Lost Gospel: The Book of Q & Christian Origins* (San Francisco: HarperSanFrancisco, 1993) 230-1.

[76] Justo L. Gonzales, *A History of Christian Thought From the Beginnings to the Council of Chalcedon* Volume 1 Revised Edition (Nashville, Abingdon Press, Kindle Edition, 1970, 1987) 149. Here is Philip Jenkins: "Christians

have an ancient fascination with the book of *Revelation*, which portrays a sequence of world-destroying catastrophes culminating in a perfect age of divine rule on earth. In both Protestant and Catholic versions of the Bible, *Revelation* appears as the final book, suggesting that it is in a sense the ultimate point of the story." See Philip Jenkins, *The Great and Holy War How World War I Became a Religious Crusade* (New York: HarperOne *An Imprint* of HarperCollins*Publishers*, Kindle Edition, 2014) 139.

[77] Paul wrote in *Romans* 16:14: *"Salute Asyncritus, Phlegon,* **Hermas**, *Patrobas, Hermes, and the brethren which are with them."* (Emphasis added). Irenaeus, Tertullian and Origin all attributed the *Shepherd of Hermas* to this Hermas. This seems unlikely because as noted above most scholars date the *Shepherd of Hermas* in the middle of the second century. It appears to have been written by a Christian in Rome named Hermas who may have been the brother of Pope Pius I (abt. 140- abt. 155). See Matthew Bunson *The Pope Encyclopedia An A to Z of the Holy See* (New York: Crown Trade Paperbacks, 1995) 275. Note: Tradition holds that Hermas of *Romans* 16:14 may have been one of the seventy followers whom Jesus sent on a mission trip as referred to in *Luke* 10: 1-8 and that later he was Bishop of Dalmatia – a Roman province and a region in modern Croatia. See William Smith, LLD, *A Dictionary of the Bible* Revised and Edited by Rev. F. N. and M. A. Peloubet (Grand Rapids: Zondervan Publishing House, 1948. Copyright 1884 by Porter and Coates. First Grand Rapids printing 1967. Sixteenth printing December 1979) 242 and Ehrman, *The New Testament* 474-76. The *Codex Sinaiticus* from the fourth century includes the *Shepherd of Hermas*. See Ehrman, *Jesus Interrupted: Revealing the Hidden Contradictions in the Bible (And Why We Don't Know Them)* 211.

[78] Most scholars believe that only seven of the *New Testament* letters traditionally ascribed to the Apostle Paul were actually written by him, a point I will discuss in Chapter 4.

[79] However, most modern scholarship holds that *Revelation* was written by a different John, not the Apostle John.

[80] Ehrman, *US News & World Report Special Collectors Edition Mysteries of Faith "Scripture's Imposters."*

[81] Jerome was born in Dalmatia. He was a scholar and an ascetic. In Rome he was the spiritual guide of several wealthy women. He traveled to Bethlehem in 386 and with financial help from one of the noblewomen built monasteries. He also built a hospice "remembering Mary and Joseph who had found no room there." With later collaborators he put together the Latin translations of the scripture - the *Vulgate* or "official" text. Jerome sounds like a modern with

this view: "Should an argument on the *New Testament* arise between Latins because of interpretations of the manuscripts fail to agree, let us turn to the original; that is, to the Greek text in which the *New Testament* was written." He wrote: "ignorance of the Scriptures is ignorance of Christ." This was quoted in the Second Vatican Council. See Pope Benedict XVI, *The Fathers* (Huntington, Indiana: Our Sunday Visitor Publishing Division, 2008) 140ff.

[82] Father Michael Collins and Matthew A. Price, *The Story of Christianity* (London: DK Publishing, Inc.) 1999) 35, 61. Note: The *New Testament* was sub-divided into chapters by the English Archbishop Stephen Langdon (died 1228). Verses were introduced in the 1500s. See WRF Browning Oxford *Dictionary of the Bible* (New York: Oxford University Press, Kindle Edition, 1996) Location 1103ff.

[83] Johann Eck (1486-1543), a Catholic theologian who opposed the Protestant Reformation added another argument. He frequently cited *John* 21:25 - *"I suppose that if all the other events in Jesus's life were written, the whole world could hardly contain the books."* - to oppose the Reformers stance of *sola scriptura*, reasoning from this verse that there was more to Christianity than what is covered in the *Bible*. See James Hitchcock, *History of the Catholic Church From the Apostolic Age to the Third Millennium* (San Francisco: Ignatius Press, 2012) 261 and *Justo L. Gonzales, A History of Christian Thought From the Protestant Reformation to the Twentieth Century* Volume III Revised Edition Location 732.

[84] *Matthew* 19:16ff; *Mark* 10: 17ff; *Luke* 18:18ff. To make matters slightly more confusing, *Mark* and *Luke* seem to describe a man possibly past youth. In answer to Jesus's comment of the importance of keeping commandments the man said:

- *Mark* 10:20 *"Teacher, I have kept all these things from my youth up."*
- *Luke* 18: 21 *"All these things I have kept from my youth."*

[85] *Matthew* 13:55-6.

[86] *Luke* 4:22.

[87] *John* 6:40.

[88] *Matthew* 2: 1-12 and *Luke* 2: 1-20. *Mark* does not record the birth of Jesus nor does *John*. *John* 7:40-2 seems to discount the possibility that he was born in Bethlehem as people who wonder if he is the Messiah say: *"... Surely the Christ is not going to come from Galilee, is He? Has not the Scripture said that the Christ comes from the descendants of David, and from Bethlehem, the village where David was?"* More on Bethlehem: One of Jesus's non-Jewish ancestors,

Ruth, lived in Bethlehem (*Ruth* 1:19; 4:11). King David was born there. (*I Samuel* 17:12). *Micah* 5:2 is a prophecy that Judah would be revived through a ruler born there. It reads: *"But as for you, Bethlehem Ephrathah, Too little to be among the clans of Judah, From you One will go forth for Me to be ruler in Israel. His goings forth are from long ago, From the days of eternity."* Jerome worked on the *Vulgate* while living there. See Browning Location 1061ff.

[89] Who were the wise men? "Legend has placed their number variously from 3 to 12..... Most believe that they came from Persia or Babylon..." *Matthew* seems to be interested in letting readers know that the birth of Jesus attracted experts in prophecy. See Reader's Digest *Jesus and His Times* (Pleasantville, New York and Montreal: The Reader's Digest Association, Inc.) 1987) 26-30.

[90] December 25 is held dear by Christians. Originally, it was a day for a pagan feast linked to the mystery-cult figure of Mithra. By the late 200s or early 300s the day was taken over by Christians to observe the birth of Christ. The relatively late date of this co-option suggests that the impact of mystery cults on Christianity may have been marginal. See Justo L. Gonzales, *A History of Christian Thought From the Beginnings to the Council of Chalcedon* Volume 1 Revised Edition 58. Here is Ben Witherington III: "The first real witness to the tradition that Jesus was born on December 25 is Hippolytus (A.D. 165–235), a date that John Chrysostom (abt. 349–407) supports as well. All we can say is that such a date is possible, but we have no compelling early evidence in the Gospels or elsewhere that points definitely in this direction." See Witherington, *New Testament History A Narrative Account* Location 1062.

[91] *Matthew* 2: 9-11.

[92] *Luke* is the only Gospel which mentions a manger – *Luke* 2: 7, 12 and 16. Note: The Christian writer Justin Martyr (abt. 100- abt. 165) was born in a town about forty miles from Bethlehem called Flavia Neapolis. This town was built on the site of the Biblical city of Shechem after Shechem was destroyed by the Romans in the 70s. Shechem is mentioned dozens of times in the *Old Testament* and once in the *New Testament* in *Acts* 7:15- 16 in words attributed to the Martyr Stephen in his speech recounting Jewish history that led up to Christ: *"And Jacob went down to Egypt and there he and our fathers died. From there they were removed to Shechem and laid in the tomb which Abraham had purchased for a sum of money from the sons of Hamor in Shechem."* Justin visited Bethlehem and said that the manger was a cave. See Paul Johnson, *Jesus A Biography From a Believer* (New York: Viking. Published by the Penguin Group, Kindle Edition, 2010) 20. Note: "In the area around Bethlehem, rocky caves had been used as stables since ancient times." See Joseph Ratzinger Pope Benedict XVI *Jesus of Nazareth The Infancy Narratives* Translated by Philip

J. Whitmore (New York: Image, 2012) 67. Further note: Justin Martyr was converted to Christianity in Ephesus. See Charlotte Allen, *The Human Christ The Search for the Historical Jesus* (Oxford: Lion Publishing plc, 1998) 51.

[93] *Matthew* 2:22-23. They thought it would be safer because Joseph had "*heard that Archelaus was reigning over Judea in place of his father Herod.*"

[94] *Matthew* 2:13-15. Joseph's and Mary's and Jesus's flight to Egypt is honored by the Coptic Church which has a tradition that the family was there for three-and-a-half years. See Samuel Tadros *Motherland Lost The Egyptian and Coptic Quest for Modernity* (Stanford: Hoover Institution Press, Kindle Edition, 2013) Location 286.

[95] Here is Ben Witherington III on the differences: "It needs to be remembered that the Matthean and Lukan birth accounts share certain fundamental notions, including the betrothed couple Mary and Joseph, the virginal conception, the Davidic descent of Joseph, the birth in Bethlehem during Herod's reign, the angelic revelation of the name Jesus, and Jesus's upbringing in Nazareth. This is true even though the majority of material in these two birth narratives is not common to both." See: Witherington, *New Testament History A Narrative* Account Location 1130.

[96] I owe these accounts of the arrest to Borg and Crossan, *The Last Week: What the Gospels Really Teach About Jesus's Final Days in Jerusalem* 125 and regret it if I have misstated Borg's and Crossan's point of view.

[97] *Matthew* 27: 57-61; *Mark* 15: 42-47; *Luke* 23: 50-56; and *John* 19:38-42.

[98] *Mark* 15: 42-47.

[99] *Matthew* 27:57.

[100] *Luke* 23: 50-1.

[101] *John* 19:38.

[102] Here is a note on a Christian legend: In the sixteenth and seventeenth centuries most English people believed that their country had received Christianity directly from Christ's disciple Joseph of Arimathea, that the Emperor Constantine was British (his mother Helena being the daughter of the British King Coilus), and that he had Christianized the whole civilized world, as John Foxe (who wrote *Book of Martyrs* in 1563) put it, "by the help of the British army." See Paul Johnson *First Things* June/July 2006.

[103] The Synoptic Gospels are the first three in the canon: *Matthew, Mark* and *Luke*. They are so named because of their similarity. In Greek, the term means "seeing together." Note: All of the events in Jesus's public ministry

in the Synoptics can be placed within one year. In *John*, the period of time is longer. See Borg *Jesus: Uncovering the Life, Teachings, and Relevance of a Religious Revolutionary* (New York: HarperCollins, 2006), 137ff.

[104] *Mark* 15:39.

[105] *Matthew* 27:54.

[106] *Luke* 23:47.

[107] *Matthew* 12:30 - "*He who is not with Me is against Me....*" *Mark* 9:40 – "*For he who is not against us is for us.*"

[108] However, at least one commentator has suggested that Lydia was the financial backer behind Paul's remarks in *Philippians* chapter 4 verses 15-16: "*As you know, you Philippians were the only ones who gave me financial help when I first brought you the Good News and then traveled on from Macedonia. No other church did this. Even when I was in Thessalonica you sent help more than once.*" He may also have alluded to her in *II Corinthians 11:9*: "*and when I was present with you and was in need, I was not a burden to anyone; for when the brethren came from Macedonia they fully supplied my need, and in everything I kept myself from being a burden to you, and will continue to do so.*" See Justo L. Gonzales, *Acts The Gospel of the Spirit* (Maryknoll, New York: Orbis Books, 2001) 189. Note: Philippi corresponds with a town of about eleven thousand in modern Greece called Filippoi. It is where the assassins of Julius Caesar had been vanquished about a century before Paul got there. See Hitchcock 35.

[109] Galatia derives its name from the Gallic or Celtic tribes who came into Macedonia and Thrace in about 280 BC. It later became a Roman province. It was the "Gaul" of the East. It is in modern Turkey. See William Smith 202.

[110] Roman citizenship was of great benefit. Moreover, it could have stressed a theological point to Paul. As Diarmaid MacCulloch puts it: "It may have been his pride in this status of universal citizen which first suggested to Paul that the Jewish prophet who had seized his allegiance in a vision had a message for all people and not just the Jews." See Diarmaid MacCulloch, *Christianity: The First Three Thousand Years* (New York: Viking published by the Penguin Group, Kindle Edition, 2009) 43.

[111] If indeed Paul was taught by Gamaliel a time to so indicate might have been in the context of *Galatians* 1: 14 in which he wrote, "*I advanced in Judaism beyond many among my people of the same age, for I was far more zealous for the traditions of my ancestors*" or *Philippians* 3: 4-6 in which he wrote, "*If anyone else has reason to be confident in the flesh, I have more: circumcised on the eighth day, a member of the people of Israel, of the tribe of Benjamin, a Hebrew*

born of Hebrews; as to the law, a Pharisee; as to zeal, a persecutor of the church; as to righteousness under the law, blameless." If he was a Roman citizen, then the punishments that he described in *I Corinthians* 11:25 and which Luke himself describes in *Acts* 16:22 were illegal. See Borg and John Dominic Crossan *The First Paul: Reclaiming the Radical Visionary Behind the Church's Conservative Icon* (New York: HarperOne *An Imprint of* HarperCollins *Publishers*) 2009) 68.

[112] *Galatians* 1:17.

[113] Borg and Crossan, *The First Paul: Reclaiming the Radical Visionary Behind the Church's Conservative Icon* 75-77.

[114] The six Herods that appear in this book were Judean rulers in the *New Testament* period:

- Herod the Great (74/73 BC – 4 BC). His ancestors converted to Judaism. He is known in the *New Testament* for the Massacre of the Innocents according to *Matthew* 2:10-23.
- Archelaus (23 BC – 18 AD). He could also be called Herod Archelaus and was a son of Herod the Great and appears in the *New Testament* only in connection with Joseph's realization that it was unsafe to return from Egypt to Judea as recounted in *Matthew* 2. He was deposed in 6 AD.
- Philip the Tetrarch (Died 34 AD). He was a son of Herod the Great and appears in the *New Testament* in *Matthew 14* and *Mark 6* as the first husband of Herodias who had left him for his brother Herod Antipater which in turn led step-by-step to the judicial murder of John the Baptist. But there is some confusion here. Josephus asserts that Herodias was not initially married to Philip but to a different son of Herod the Great (*Antiquities* Book XVIII Chapter 5). This point is given some credence in that when the story of Herodias is told in *Luke* 3, the name of the first husband is omitted. In other words, this line of reasoning is that the writers of *Mark* and later *Matthew* got the name wrong. Philip is listed in *Luke* 3 in connection with the dating of the rise of John the Baptist.
- Herod Antipater (Before 20 BC – After 39 AD) known by the nickname Antipas was another son of Herod the Great and ruled in Galilee. He is known in the *New Testament* for his role in the beheading of John the Baptist and the crucifixion of Jesus Christ.
- Herod Agrippa, also known as Agrippa I, (11 BC – 44 AD) was the grandson of Herod the Great and the nephew of Herod Antipater. He is known in the *New Testament* for his role in the judicial murder of

James the son of Zebedee, the imprisonment of Peter, the execution of the guards after Peter's prison break, and his own ghastly death in *Acts* 12.

- Herod Agrippa II (27/28 AD – abt. 90 AD) was the last king of the Herodian line. The *New Testament* only identifies him as Agrippa. He was the son of Herod Agrippa I. He was also the brother of Bernice and Drusilla the wife of the Roman procurator Felix all of whom appear in *Acts* in chapters 23 through 26.

In Roman circles, rumors persisted that Agrippa II had an incestuous relationship with his sister Bernice. She later appealed to Roman soldiers to cease violence during the civil disturbances in Jerusalem before the Jewish War and still later became the mistress of Titus, the victorious Roman general of that war.

Agrippa II is known in the *New Testament* for his role in Paul's trial during the course of his appeal to Rome in *Acts* 25 and 26. Agrippa II had this exchange with Paul after the latter's testimony as recorded in *Acts* 26:

- Verse 27: Paul to Agrippa – *"King Agrippa, do you believe the Prophets? I know that you do."*
- Verse 28: Agrippa to Paul - *"In a short time you will persuade me to become a Christian."*
- Verse 29: Paul to Agrippa – *"I would wish to God, that whether in a short or long time, not only you, but also all who hear me this day, might become such as I am, except for these chains."*

In verse 31 Agrippa met with his inner circle including Bernice and they seemed to reach a consensus on Paul: *"This man is not doing anything worthy of death or imprisonment."* In verse 32 Agrippa added: *"This man might have been set free if he had not appealed to Caesar."*

Note: In his trial before Agrippa, Paul experienced a prophecy that Jesus had once made about him as reported in *Acts* 9:15: *"He is a chosen instrument of Mine, to bear My name before the Gentiles and **kings**..."*(Emphasis added).

In order to distinguish the Herodians we will refer to them as Herod the Great, Archelaus, Philip, Herod Antipater (or Herod Antipas), Herod Agrippa and Agrippa.

[115] Hengel and Schwemer 111-118, 181, 428. John the Baptist's murder is recorded in *Matthew* 14:1-12; *Mark* 6:14-29 and *Luke* 3:19 and 9:7-9. John was probably killed in 27 or 28 AD. The defeat of Herod Antipater by Aretas was probably in about 35 or 36 AD.

[116] I am sure that there are those who would say that this inconsistency is significant. After all, Matthew (who wrote later) changes a private revelation to a public one and thereby shows Mark's tendency toward secret revelation. I put it in this category on a close call only because I don't think it challenges a Christian doctrine. But I could be wrong.

[117] John P. Meier, *The Vision of Matthew: Christ, Church and Morality in the First Gospel* (New York: Crossroads, 1991) 21-22, 144.

[118] St. Augustine whom I will mention often in this book tried to reconcile the discrepant times of when Jesus was crucified. He came to the view that when Mark said the third hour he meant that that was the time Jesus was **delivered** to be crucified (Emphasis mine). Augustine went on: "For to make a frank acknowledgement, we cannot get over the statement of the sixth hour in John's narrative; and Mark records the third hour; and, therefore, if both of us accept the testimony of the writers, show me any other way in which both of the notes can be taken as literally correct. If you can do so, I shall most cheerfully acquiesce..." Augustine went on further: "Only don't consider it an inevitable conclusion that any of the four evangelists has stated what is false,..." See Charlotte Allen, *The Human Christ The Search for the Historical Jesus* 86.

[119] Borg and Crossan, *The Last Week: What the Gospels Really Teach About Jesus's Final Days in Jerusalem 110.*

[120] Can there be a more reviled person in history than Judas? In modern times, there have been iconoclasts stepping forward to ask us to see another side. Some point out that Judas must have been a trusted member of the Twelve as evidenced by his responsibility for the group's money (*John* 13:29) and that he was practical enough to deplore what he saw as the waste of money for oils to anoint Jesus but concerned enough to suggest that it could have been given to the poor (*John* 12: 4-5). One scholar asserts that Judas is the only person to whom Jesus addresses as "friend" (*Matthew* 26:50), that he was sitting next to Jesus at the Last Supper (*John* 13:26) and that Jesus tells him "*What you are about to do, do quickly.*" (*John* 13:27). Others also note that there was rivalry amongst the disciples (*Luke* 22:24) and that Judas may have been trying to force Jesus's hand to lead an uprising. When he saw that Jesus was to die instead, this reasoning goes, he committed suicide in despair. Finally, it is pointed out that Jesus may have seen Judas as fulfilling scripture (*John* 17:12) and that his final actions were preceded by Satan entering him (*John* 13:27). Some add that Paul makes no unambiguous reference to Judas and, in fact, reports that the risen Jesus appeared to "the Twelve." (*I Corinthians* 15: 3-8). Garry Wills goes so far as to call Judas "our Patron Saint Judas." See Wills, *What Jesus Meant* (Penguin Books: New York and London, 2006) 104. Other

references to the revisionist view on Judas include: Herbert Krosney, *The Lost Gospel: The Quest for the Gospel of Judas Iscariot* (Washington DC: National Geographic, 2006) Foreword by Bart D. Ehrman; Elaine Pagels and Karen L. King, *Reading Judas: The Gospel of Judas and the Shaping of Christianity* (New York: The Penguin Group, 2007); Ehrman, *The Lost Gospel of Judas Iscariot* (Oxford: Oxford University Press, 2006). It seems to me that the revisionist view of Judas overlooks Judas's petty thievery and the statement that he was not at all concerned with the poor (*John*12:6).

[121] The death of Judas in *Acts* may not be a suicide. See Borg and Crossan *The Last Week: What the Gospels Really Teach About Jesus's Final Days in Jerusalem* 126.

[122] *Matthew* 28:2.

[123] *Mark* 16:5. Note: He told them that Jesus had risen from the dead and according to this account, they were so afraid, they ran away and told no one.

[124] *John* 20: 12. Note: In this account, these two angels only met Mary Magdalene.

[125] *Luke* 24:4. Note: These two men sound very much like the two men whom Luke identified as the *Old Testament* figures of Moses and Elijah at the Mount of Transfiguration in *Luke* 9:30-1 and the two men dressed in white who addressed Jesus's followers as he ascended into Heaven in *Acts* 1: 10-11.

[126] Actually no horse is mentioned in *Acts*, but others, including artists, have made it a reasonable supposition.

[127] In this book the term Jewish-Christians refers to those Jews in and around Palestine, and especially Jerusalem, who followed Jesus after the first Easter. The most recognizable of this group are Peter and James the brother of Jesus.

[128] *Acts* 9: 26-30. As noted earlier, Luke has Paul reprising this episode in *Acts* 22:17-21 but this time he saw Jesus Christ there.

[129] *Acts* 11:27-30 and 12:25. As we will see, the collecting of money for the Christians in Jerusalem was a constant in Paul's career.

[130] *Galatians* 1:18-19.

[131] *Galatians* 1:15 – 2:1.

[132] Justo L. Gonzales, *Acts The Gospel of the Spirit* 125. I regret it if I have misstated Gonzales's point of view.

[133] Hellenistic Jews were a category within Judaism in ancient times that mixed historic Jewish religious beliefs with parts of Greek culture. They had

centers of influence in Alexandria and Antioch. In the *New Testament* their response to the Jesus movement varied:

- *Acts* 6:1 - Controversy between the Hellenists and the Jerusalem Jews within the Jerusalem church led to the establishment of the seven proto-deacons. The most famous in this group was Stephen the Martyr.
- *Acts* 9:29 - Paul argued in Jerusalem with Hellenists who attempted to kill him.
- *Acts* 11:19-26 – This is more by inference but it appears that some of the Hellenists dispersed by persecution in Jerusalem helped develop the Christian movement in Antioch.

[134] Hengel and Schwemer *47*, 133ff, 242. I regret it if I have misstated Hengel's and Schwemer's point of view. Dieter Georgi writes that Luke backdated the trip described in *Acts* 11:27-30 and 12:25 and that it actually happened later, after the Council of Jerusalem described in *Acts* 15 and *Galatians* 2. See Dieter Georgi, *Remembering The Poor: The History of Paul's Collection for Jerusalem* (Nashville: Abingdon Press, 1965, 1992) 44-45.

[135] See Burton H. Throckmorton, Jr. ed., *Gospel Parallels: A Synopsis of the First Three Gospels* (Toronto, New York and Edinburgh: Thomas Nelson and Sons, 1949, 1957, reprinted April, 1960) vi. Bart D. Ehrman has said something similar: "...the first thing to say about these 300,000 or 400,000 differences is that most of them don't matter for anything. They are absolutely irrelevant, immaterial, unimportant, and a lot of them you can't even reproduce in English translations from the Greek." See *The Reliability of the New Testament Bart D. Ehrman & Daniel B. Wallace In Dialogue* Robert B. Stewart, Editor (Minneapolis: Fortress Press, 2011) 21. Further note: The variations between the manuscripts of the *New Testament* were apparently first noted by the British theologian John Mill (1645 – 1707). See http://en.wikipedia.org/wiki/John_Mill_(theologian) (Accessed May 2, 2012).

[136] Lee Strobel, *The Case for the Real Jesus: A Journalist Investigates Current Attacks on the Identity of Christ (Grand Rapids: Zondervan, 2007). Strobel is also the author of The Case for Faith: A Journalist Investigates the Toughest Objections to Christianity* (Zondervan), *The Case for a Creator: A Journalist Investigates Scientific Evidence that Points Toward God* (Zondervan) and *The Case for Christ: A Journalist's Personal Investigation of the Evidence for Jesus* (Zondervan).

[137] This verse will be further discussed in Chapter 10.

[138] Some scholars believe an ending was lost or Mark did not have time to finish it and that this section may reflect a perception of second century Christians that the earlier period had great miracles. See Borg and Crossan, *The Last Week: What the Gospels Really Teach About Jesus's Final Days in Jerusalem* 219 and Reader's Digest *After Jesus: The Triumph of Christianity* 48. According to Gerd Ludemann in collaboration with Alf Ozen Translated by John Bowden, *What Really Happened to Jesus A Historical Approach to the Resurrection* (Louisville, Kentucky: Westminster John Knox Press, 1995) 34 and footnote on 140, *Mark* 16: 9-20 probably was not an ending written specially for *Mark* but existed as type of catechism, a "kind of a summary of the Easter reports known to the author." It shows some knowledge of *Luke*, *John* and *Acts*:

- Verse 9-10: *"After Jesus rose from the dead early on Sunday morning, the first person who saw him was Mary Magdalene, the woman from whom he had cast out seven demons. She went to the disciples, who were grieving and weeping, and told them what had happened."* See *Luke* 8:2, *John* 20:1, 11-19.

- Verse 11: *"But when she told them that Jesus was alive and she had seen him, they didn't believe her."* See *Luke* 24:11.

- Verse 12-13: *"Afterward he appeared in a different form to two of his followers who were walking from Jerusalem into the country. They rushed back to tell the others, but no one believed them."* See *Luke* 24:13-35.

- Verse 14: *"Still later he appeared to the eleven disciples as they were eating together. He rebuked them for their stubborn unbelief because they refused to believe those who had seen him after he had been raised from the dead."* See *Luke* 24:36-43, *Acts* 1:4.

- Verse 15-16: *"And then he told them, 'Go into all the world and preach the Good News to everyone. Anyone who believes and is baptized will be saved. But anyone who refuses to believe will be condemned.'"* See *Luke* 24:47.

- Verse 17-18: *"These miraculous signs will accompany those who believe: They will cast out demons in my name, and they will speak in new languages. They will be able to handle snakes with safety, and if they drink anything poisonous, it won't hurt them. They will be able to place their hands on the sick, and they will be healed."* See *Acts* 16:16-18; 2:1-11; 28:3-6; 3:1-10; 9:31-35; 14:8-10; 28:1-10.

- Verse 19:" *When the Lord Jesus had finished talking with them, he was taken up into heaven and sat down in the place of honor at God's right hand."* See; *Acts* 1:9; *Luke* 24:51.

- Verse 20: *"And the disciples went everywhere and preached, and the Lord worked through them, confirming what they said by many miraculous signs."* See the entire *Book of Acts.*

[139] The preceding six examples are in Strobel 85ff.

[140] Strobel 80.

[141] Strobel 75.

[142] Stark, *Discovering God: The Origins of the Great Religions and the Evolution of Belief* (New York: HarperOne a division of HarperCollins*Publishers*, 2007) 294.

[143] Strobel 83.

[144] Akenson, *Surpassing Wonder: The Invention of the Bible and the Talmuds* (New York, San Diego, London: Harcourt Brace & Company, 1998). Note: John Quincy Adams wrote in his journal in the late 1830s: "Our religion is the religion of a book...man must be educated upon earth for heaven." See Nagel 374.

[145] Paul Johnson, *A History of Christianity* 377.

[146] Harry Emerson Fosdick, "Shall the Fundamentalists Win?" *Christian Work* 102 (June 10, 1922): 716–722.

[147] Ehrman, *Misquoting Jesus The Story Behind Who Changed the Bible and Why* 35.

[148] As the canon came into being, "quite possibly the various gospels were included in order to show that the faith of the church was not based on the witness of single apostles, ..." See Justo L. Gonzales *A History of Christian Thought From the Beginnings to the Council of Chalcedon* Volume 1 Revised Edition 149. Moreover, although the discrepancies in the Gospel accounts were well known to the early Christians and Tatian's work may well have been an attempt to reconcile them, these discrepancies were apparently not enough of a concern to the early Christians to go with one harmonized gospel. They stuck with four. Note: Irenaeus's comment may not have as been silly in its time as it is too modern ears. The number four had a certain symbolism of completeness:

- *Revelation* 4:6-8 –Mentions four creatures around the throne.
- *Revelation* 7:1 – Mentions four angels.
- *Revelation* 7:1 – Mentions four winds.
- *Revelation* 7:1 and 20:8 – Mentions four directions.

- *Revelation* 4:5; 8:5; 11:19.; 16; 18 -There is a fourfold pattern of "every tribe, tongue, people, and nation" and there are four occurrences of the pattern of thunder, rumblings and lightning.

See Kruger 160.

[149] Reader's Digest *Jesus and His Times* 8, 11.

[150] Michael Grant, *Jesus: An Historian's Review of the Gospels* (New York: Charles Scribner's Sons, 1977) 183.

[151] Meier, *The Vision of Matthew: Christ, Church and Morality in the First Gospel* 72.

[152] Rev. Scotty McLennan, *Jesus Was a Liberal* (New York: Palgrave MacMillan a division of St. Martin Press, 2009) 79.

[153] Micklethwait and Wooldridge, *OpinionJournal.com* April 7, 2009.

[154] Walker 501, 504. The story of Jesus's birth is covered in *Matthew* 1:23 and 2:1-23 and *Luke* 1:27 and 2: 1-39. From it we learn that Jesus was born in Bethlehem to a virgin named Mary. But he mostly grew up in Nazareth. Nazareth is about 100 miles north of Jerusalem. Bethlehem is five or so miles from Jerusalem. Bethlehem was a more important town than Nazareth.

But there are many questions associated with all of this.

1. As noted, *Matthew* has Joseph and Mary living in Bethlehem, in fact having a house there where the wise men visited them and the baby Jesus. *Matthew* gives the impression that Jesus and Mary and Joseph may have stayed in Bethlehem for about two years since Herod eventually killed male infants two years and under when the wise men did not return to him.

2. *Luke* has them living in Nazareth but going to Bethlehem for tax purposes. But consider: *Luke* says the tax-related census causing Mary and Joseph to be in Jerusalem was ordered by Caesar Augustus when Quirinius was governor of Syria. But: according to *Luke* 1:5 - Jesus was born when Herod was still king and we know that Herod died in 4 BC and Quirinius did not become governor until 6-7 AD. That's a ten to eleven year discrepancy. See White, *From Jesus to Christianity* 11-13, 33 and Lena Einhorn, *The Jesus Mystery: Astonishing Clues to the True Identities of Jesus and Paul* (Guilford, Connecticut: The Lyons Press and Imprint of The Globe Pequot Press, 2007) 5 and

Reader's Digest *Jesus and His Times* 14 and John Shelby Spong *Jesus For the Non-Religious: Recovering the Divine at the Heart of the Human* (New York: HarperSanFrancisco A Division of HarperCollins Publishers, 2007) 22.

3. Moreover, is *Luke's* tax-collecting narrative credible? "No ancient historian... ever made the slightest reference to this universal census supposedly conducted by the Emperor Augustus. Josephus in *Antiquities* mentions a census in Judea in 6 CE, and says that its purpose was to count heads before the imposition of a poll tax. The unpopularity of the tax, and of the census, led to the insurrection led by one Judas of Galilee (mentioned by Luke himself in the *Acts of the Apostles*.) The purpose of the census was purely statistical. There is no reason to suppose that anyone who took part in it would have been required to return to a village where some

putative ancestor had lived more than a thousand years previously." See Wilson, *Jesus A Life* (New York and London: WW Norton & Company, inc. and WW Norton & Company, Ltd., 1992) 75. Note: According to *Luke* 3:23-31, Joseph was of the house of David separated by forty-one generations from David.

4. As noted earlier *John* 7:42 hints that there were questions about the place of Jesus's birth a couple of generations after his death: *"Has not the Scripture said that the Christ comes from the descendants of David, and from Bethlehem, the village where David was?"* This seems to discount the possibility of a birth in Bethlehem and an ancestry of David. Note: Apart from the birth stories in *Matthew* and *Luke*, Bethlehem, Jesus's birthplace, is not mentioned again in the *New Testament*.

[155] Donald Spoto, *Reluctant Saint The Life of Francis of Assisi* (New York: Penguin Group Penguin Compass, 2002) xviii.

[156] *Luke* 1:11-21.

[157] *Luke* 1: 26-38.

[158] *Daniel* 8:16 and 9:21.

[159] According to the Catholic Church, the angel Gabriel is the patron saint of broadcasters. He is also the patron saint of clerics, diplomats, messengers, postal workers, stamp collectors, telecommunication workers and television workers. See Sandoval 39. According to Islam,

Gabriel visited Muhammad (570-632) in 610. See David Levering Lewis, *God's Crucible: Islam and the Making of Europe, 570-1215*(New York and London: WW Norton) 2008.There was an American who should be famous named Gabriel and his story reflects poorly on members of the American pantheon. In 1800 Virginia Governor James Monroe wrote Thomas Jefferson about rumors of a slave revolt - "a negro insurrection" - in Virginia. The revolt fizzled as some slaves betrayed it. Monroe called out the militia and hunted down the leaders. He wrote James Madison that "this alarm has kept me much occupied." As trials and executions ensued and more were waiting trial Monroe wrote Jefferson again: "It is unquestionably the most serious and formidable conspiracy we have ever known of the kind." He went on that he was not sure "whether mercy or severity is the better policy in this case" but he allowed that "when there is cause for doubt it is best to incline to the former." Jefferson's advice: "Whether to stay the hand of the executioner is an important question. There is strong sentiment that there has been hanging enough. The other states and the world at large will forever condemn us if we indulge a principle of revenge." But Jefferson added: "I hazard these thoughts for your own consideration only, as I would be unwilling to be quoted in this case." This from Jefferson of the Declaration in 1776 and who applauded Shay's Rebellion in 1787, telling John Adams: "I like a little rebellion now and then." Monroe issued some pardons but in the end twenty-seven men were hanged including the leader Gabriel. Gabriel appears to have been an intelligent and daring man skilled enough so that his owner had allowed him to work on certain days for other whites to earn extra money for himself (and no doubt his owner). He had had some undefined trouble with the law before his decision to instigate a slave revolt. The response by the American exemplars of the Enlightenment was merciless. See Susan Dunn 155ff. Gabriel's full name was Gabriel Prosser. In 2007 the Governor of Virginia pardoned Prosser and his followers.

[160] The Biblical names are ironic because California got its own name from a fictional work by an early 15th century Spanish writer who imagined an "Amazon" race that he called Californians led by a Queen Califia who was, as this best-selling author of his era wrote, "a queen of majestic proportions, more beautiful than all others, and in the very vigor of her womanhood. She was not petite, nor blond, nor golden-haired. She was large, and black as the ace of clubs. But the prejudice of color did not then exist even among the most brazen-faced or the most copper-headed. For, as you shall learn, she was reputed the most beautiful of women; and it was she,... who accomplished great deeds, she was valiant and courageous and ardent with a brave heart, and had ambitions to execute nobler actions than had been performed by any other ruler ..." The Californians fought with golden weapons on behalf of Europeans against Turks at Constantinople and eventually became Christians.

A 23-minute film narrated by Whoopi Goldberg as Califia is shown at Disneyland in California. See Kevin Starr, California: A History (New York: The Modern Library A Modern Library Chronicles Book, 2005, 5 and http://en.wikipedia.org/wiki/Queen_Califia [Accessed May 2, 2012]). The Christian place names in California are also juxtaposed with classical paganism: the state seal features Minerva, the Roman goddess of wisdom. The seal of the University of California, however, echoes a Biblical theme: Fiat Lux - "Let There Be Light."

[161] The ancient Philadelphia, located in modern Turkey has fewer than forty thousand inhabitants. It survived for centuries in the Byzantine Empire but fell to the Turks after 1390, then to the Mongol Timur the Lame who built a wall of corpses to celebrate his victory. It soon returned to the Ottoman empire. It is now named Alaşehir. The Greeks who once lived there fled to Greece and founded *Nea Filadelfeia*. Philadelphia, Pennsylvania has about 1.4 million inhabitants although the surrounding area boosts the population to over five million.

[162] Meredith Mason Brown, *Frontiersman: Daniel Boone and the Making of America* (Baton Rouge: Louisiana State University Press, 2008) 3ff. Note: Daniel Boone (1734 – 1820) was born into a Quaker family in Pennsylvania. His father was expelled from the Quakers when Boone was fourteen on the grounds that two of his children had married outside the Quaker fellowship. My ancestor Thomas Prewitt was born in Salisbury, England in 1616 and came to Virginia, probably as a Quaker. On July 25 1648 he was found guilty of committing fornication by a court in Virginia (I believe York County) inasmuch as he and his wife were not married by the rules of the established church but in a Quaker ceremony.

[163] *Acts* 7:11.

[164] *Acts* 13:19. He mentions that God destroyed seven nations in the land of Canaan.

[165] See *Mark* 7: 24-30 and *Matthew* 15: 21-28.

[166] *Acts* 11:26-27 and 13:1.

[167] After 500 Damascus and Alexandria also lost influence. This decline was due to changes in trade routes, plague, perhaps climate change and the arrival of Islam. See Philip Jenkins, *The Lost History of Christianity: The Thousand Year Golden Age of the Church in the Middle East, Africa, and Asia - and How it Died* (New York: HarperCollins Publishers HarperOne *An Imprint of* HarperCollins*Publisher*, 2007) 234-36.

[168] They are in California, South Carolina, Alabama, Alaska, Arkansas, Colorado, Florida, Georgia, Idaho, Illinois, Kansas, Louisiana, Missouri, Mississippi, North Carolina, Ohio, Tennessee, Texas, Virginia.

[169] *Revelation* 1:11 and 2:8.

[170] Collins and Price 41, 44.

[171] Saint Anselm (1033 - 1109) was possibly the earliest of the Scholastics. Scholasticism was a commitment to the use of reason. He wrote a practical definition of God: "that than which nothing greater can be conceived." He went on that "that than which nothing greater can be conceived" could not exist only in our minds and not in reality because, if so, it would not be the greatest conceivable thing since we could imagine something greater, that actually existed. Got that? See Thomas E. Woods, Jr. *How the Catholic Church Built Western Civilization* (Washington DC: Regnery Publishing, Inc., 2005) 58-59. Anselm read the scripture "*The fool has said in his heart, 'There is no God.'*" (*Psalm* 14:1) to mean that atheism was a failure of reason not belief. He thought that people did not "believe" in God. They knew him to exist. See Hitchcock 176. More on Anselm: Aside from his arguments on the existence of God, Anselm is known for his argument that the work of Christ was to pay humans's debt to God, not to the Devil. This reasoning has been accepted in the West. But it is not the oldest view of the work of Christ "nor does it appear to be the main thrust of the *New Testament.*" See Justo L. Gonzales, *A History of Christian Thought From Augustine to the Eve of the Reforma*tion Volume II Revised Edition Location 3172.

[172] San Bernardino was named by the Spanish in 1810 for Bernardino of Siena (1380 - 1444) who helped lead a religious revival. He was canonized in 1450. In an only-in-America twist, the first Anglo settlers to the area were Mormons in the late 1840s.

[173] Junipero Serra (1713-1784) was the Spanish Franciscan who founded the chain of missions in California. In 1988 Pope John Paul II beatified Serra which is a step on the way to sainthood. It also is recognition that the one who is beatified has entered Heaven and has the ability to intercede for individuals who pray in his/her name. Someone who is beatified is given the title "Blessed." In modern times, Serra's relationship to the Native Americans of California has come under significant criticism for the missions's reliance on forced labor and beatings. One argument is that he should be judged by the standards of his time. Even so, the counter-argument runs, these Indians were unaccustomed to beatings in their culture. In 2015 Pope Francis (2013-) made Junipero Serra a saint.

[174] San Juan Capistrano is a city of about thirty-five thousand in Southern California. It has been nationally known since the 1930s for the annual return of the Swallows, a migratory bird. The city grew up around the mission by that name founded by Father Serra in 1776. John of Capistrano (1386-1456) was an Italian saint and a Franciscan. He was a one-time general of the

Franciscans and a diplomat. He led a successful crusade against the Turks in
Serbia. See Hitchcock 205.

[175] Santa Rosa of Lima, Peru was among the most revered of saints in Latin
America. She was born in1586 and came to devote her life to the Christ Child
and his mother. Rosa made her own crown of thorns with nails which she
wore hidden under a veil and her hair. She died in 1617. Within 70 years she
became the first American-born saint of the Catholic Church. See Ondina
E. Gonzales and Justo L. Gonzales *Christianity in Latin America A History*
(Cambridge, New York, Melbourne, Madrid, Cape Town, Singapore, Sao
Paulo, Delhi: Cambridge University Press, Kindle Edition, 2008) 86ff.

[176] Named for the Protestant reformer John Calvin (1509-1564).

[177] Named for the Mormon leader Brigham Young (1801-1877).

[178] "It is a conspicuous, if seldom noted, historical detail that during the first
millennium of Christian history the Church attracted many of the most gifted
thinkers in the ancient world. The parade of luminaries is impressive: Clement
and Origen of Alexandria, Eusebius of Caesarea, Athanasius of Alexandria,
Hilary of Poitiers, Gregory of Nyssa, Basil of Caesarea, Gregory Nazianzus,
Maximus the Confessor, John of Damascus, and of course the four Latin
doctores ecclesiae (teachers of the Church), Jerome, Ambrose, Augustine,
Gregory the Great. Yet Augustine towers above all. It is not hyperbolic to
say during his lifetime he was the most intelligent man in the Mediterranean
world. From the time of Plato and Aristotle, the great philosophers of ancient
Greece, across more than fifteen centuries until Thomas Aquinas in the High
Middle Ages, he has no equal." Augustine wrote one of the most quoted lines
of all time: "You have made us for yourself, Oh Lord, and our heart is restless
until it rests in you." See Robert Louis Wilken, *The First Thousand Years A
Global History of Christianity* (New Haven and London: Yale University Press,
2012) 183, 184.

[179] Clovis, king of the Franks, won a military victory in 496 which brought
the Franks into Christianity. The Papacy was advantaged by gaining a military
ally in Europe two centuries before the coming of the Muslims. Clovis also
eliminated the Goths in France. Later Popes came to call Frankland (France)
the "eldest daughter of the Church." See David Levering Lewis, 140, 228. It
took Clovis some time before he understood the complete Christian message.
When told the story of Jesus's crucifixion, the warrior king is said to have
remarked: "Oh, if only I had been there with my Franks!" See Woods 13.
Taking the long view in the next century, Gregory of Tours (538-594), a
bishop in Gaul, wrote on the baptism of Clovis: "This is not the kingdom
of God but only the first step on the path leading to it." See "Inside the

Medieval World," *National Geographic,* 2014 29. According to Wikipedia, Clovis New Mexico may have gotten its name because the daughter of the settlement's railroad stationmaster was studying French at the time of the town's naming and suggested the new name. Its previous name was Riley's Switch. Artifacts found in the 1930s near Clovis have led to a description of a prehistoric culture, which anthropologists call the Clovis culture. The artifacts included stone spear points and several cutting tools made of stone flakes. Sites containing these types of artifacts have been found in other locales in the Americas, but the name Clovis Culture has stuck. This culture existed for several hundred years about thirteen thousand years ago. See http:// en.wikipedia.org/wiki/Clovis, New Mexico (Accessed May 2, 2012).

[180] Lawrence of Rome (abt. 225 – 258) was born in what is modern day Spain and died in Rome as a martyr, grilled over an open fire. Lawrence was a Roman deacon who refused to turn over church treasure, instead showing the authorities the poor and saying, "This is our treasure." Roasting on a gridiron he reportedly said, "Turn me over, I'm done on this side." See Hitchcock 51.

[181] According to the Catholic Church the patron saint of lost articles is this Anthony of Padua (1195-1231). His feast day is June 13. He is also the patron saint of barren women, the poor, Portugal, shipwrecks and travelers. He is invoked against starvation. See Sandoval 144-45. He was an intellectual who joined the Franciscans. See Spoto, *Reluctant Saint The Life of Francis of Assisi* 165-6.

[182] Erasmus(1466/69 – 1536) of the Netherlands is an important figure in Christian history and possibly as a model for a more God-centered Christianity that we will cover in Chapter 11.

[183] In 1804 these two fought the most famous duel in American history. In preparing for the duel with Burr - the sitting Vice President - forty-nine year old Hamilton who had been at the Constitutional Convention in 1787 and was the first Secretary of the Treasury under George Washington told his wife that "the scruples of a Christian" required him to waste his shot against Burr. He then proceeded to draw up his will. Burr killed him. See Susan Dunn 252. Note: Even at that time, the Catholic Church had long opposed dueling. The Council of Trent which met in the mid- 1500s primarily to deal with Church reform in the aftermath of the Protestant Reformation included penalties against dueling, asserting that "the detestable custom of dueling which the Devil had originated, in order to bring about at the same time the ruin of the soul and the violent death of the body, shall be entirely uprooted from Christian soil." See http://www.newadvent.org/cathen/05184b.htm (Accessed December 9, 2012).

[184] According to the Catholic Church, Michael is the patron saint of battle. His feast day is September 29. He is also the patron saint of the dead, grocers, mariners, paratroopers, police officers and radiologists. He is often shown in art with scales as if weighing souls. See Sandoval 29-30. According to the Jehovah's Witnesses when the *Bible* mentions Michael, it is referring to Jesus Christ. See *What Does the Bible Really Teach?* (Brooklyn, New York: Watchtower Bible and Tract Society of New York, Inc. 2009 Printing) 218-19. Among the reasons is that *Revelation* 12:7 has Michael leading an army of angels and *Revelation* 19:14-16 and *II Thessalonians* 1:7 have Jesus leading angels. The tract points out: "...God's Word nowhere indicates that there are two armies of faithful angels in heaven..."

[185] *Luke* 1:19-26 and *Jude* 1:9. However, a reading of *John* 5:1-17 has led some to conclude that there was another angel named Raphael. This scripture recounts the Bethesda pool in Jerusalem in Jesus's day that ill people gathered around, hoping that immersion would bring a healing. Some of the ancient *New Testament* manuscripts add this as verse 4: "*for an angel of the Lord went down at certain seasons into the pool and stirred up the water; whoever then first, after the stirring up of the water, stepped in was made well from whatever disease with which he was afflicted.*" According to the Catholic Church, the angel Raphael is the patron saint of the blind. His name means "God heals." Because of the healing role assigned to Raphael, he is associated with this miracle. He is also the patron saint of lovers, nurses, physicians, and travelers. His feast day is September 29. See Sandoval 33. A town in California is named for him – it is spelled San Rafael. Note: The pool in this account has been identified by modern archaeology. See Browning Location 682.

[186] Santa Fe is yet another city named in St. Francis's honor. The Franciscans who founded it in 1610 named it Villa Real de la Santa Fe de San Francisco de Asis. ("The Royal Village of the Holy Faith of St. Francis of Assisi.") See Justo L. Gonzales, *The Story of Christianity Volume 1 The Early Church to the Dawn of the Reformation* (New York: HarperCollins e-books, 1984, 2010) Location 7668ff.

[187] Randall Balmer, *Redeemer The Life of Jimmy Carter* (New York: Basic Books, A Member of the Perseus Books Group, Kindle Edition, 2014) 1.

[188] Stark, *God's Battalions The Case for the Crusades* (New York: HarperOne *An Imprint of* HarperCollins*Publishers, 2009)* 36-44.

[189] At least one historian attributes the Muslim failure to take France to internecine struggles as much as the Christian victory in 732. See David Levering Lewis 178.

[190] But it sometimes hints. Many of the months of the year are named after Roman figures. January is named after Janus, the god of the doorway. July and August are named for Roman Caesars. Northern non-Biblical deities are commemorated in the days of the week: Tiw (Tuesday), Woden (Wednesday), Thor (Thursday), and Fridd (Friday). See Hitchcock 72, 131. The day which the Jews of Jesus's time called the Sabbath came to be known instead after a Roman god, Saturn.

[191] Additional note: *New Testament* sounding names do not always trace there. Virginia was named after Queen Elizabeth the "Virgin Queen." Marysville, California after an early settler. Joseph, Oregon and San Quentin, California after Native American leaders. Mars Hill, Maine which has a population of about 1500 is not named after the locale in Athens where Paul is supposed to have given an important sermon recorded in *Acts* 17: 22-31. It is named after an early settler named Hezekiah Mars.

[192] David Levering Lewis 286, 320.

[193] *II Thessalonians* 3:10. See *The General History of Virginia* by Captain John Smith Book III. Three hundred years later, the Communist Vladimir Lenin made this the first principle of socialism. See http://en.wikipedia.org/wiki/ He who does not work, neither shall he eat (Accessed May 2, 2012).

[194] Charles C. Mann, *1491: New Revelations of the Americas Before Columbus* (New York: Alfred A. Knopf) 2005 Tenth printing December 2005. 54-5. This is a reference to these three verses which describe the place of Jesus's crucifixion:

- *Matthew* 27:33 – "*And when they came to a place called Golgotha (which means Place of a Skull).*"
- *Mark* 15:22 – "*And they brought him to the place called Golgotha (which means Place of a Skull).*"
- *John* 19:17 – "*and he went out, bearing his own cross, to the place called The Place of a Skull, which in Aramaic is called Golgotha.*"

[195] According to scripture, this Beast will be pretty terrible. It will rise out of a bottomless pit. (*Revelation* 11:7). It will have ten horns and seven heads and blasphemous names on its heads. (*Revelation* 13:1). It's going to give everyone a mark and "*no one can buy or sell unless he has the mark.*" (*Revelation* 13: 16-17).

[196] Waldman 41, 42. Paine was referring to *I Samuel* 8: 4-9 where elders within ancient Israel come to their leader Samuel who was a judge and asked for a king. This is what follows starting in verse 6: "*But the thing was displeasing in the sight of Samuel when they said, 'Give us a king to judge us.'*

And Samuel prayed to the LORD. The LORD said to Samuel, 'Listen to the voice of the people in regard to all that they say to you, for they have not rejected you, but they have rejected Me from being king over them. Like all the deeds which they have done since the day that I brought them up from Egypt even to this day—in that they have forsaken Me and served other gods—so they are doing to you also. Now then, listen to their voice; however, you shall solemnly warn them and tell them of the procedure of the king who will reign over them.'" But things are never so clear cut. An *Old Testament* writer noted about an earlier time: *"In those days there was no king in Israel. Everyone did what was right in his own eyes."* (*Judges* 17:6).

¹⁹⁷ *Job* is an *Old Testament* book. It recounts the story of a man who stood up to many trials visited upon him by God after a discussion with the Devil as a test of Job's faith. In the King James version of the *Bible, James* 5:11 reads: *"We count those blessed who endured. You have heard of the endurance of Job and have seen the outcome of the Lord's dealings, that the Lord is full of compassion and is merciful."*

¹⁹⁸ Thomas Fleming, *The Perils of Peace: America's Struggle for Survival After Yorktown* (New York: HarperCollins, Smithsonian Books Collins *An Imprint of* HarperCollins *Publishers,* 2007) 66.

¹⁹⁹ Fleming 247. Benjamin Franklin was referring to *Matthew* 5:9: *"Blessed are the peacemakers…"*

²⁰⁰ Fleming 266. This was a conscious or unconscious evocation of verses like *Matthew* 16:6 in which Jesus said, *"… Take heed and beware of the leaven of the Pharisees and of the Sadducees."* Similar verses are *Mark* 8:15, *Luke* 12:1 and *I Corinthians* 5:7-8.

²⁰¹ Fleming 292. The Sanhedrin refers to assembly of Jewish judges which constituted the supreme court and legislative body of ancient Israel. The Sanhedrin is mentioned twenty-three times in the *New Testament.* Jesus (*Matthew* 26 and *Mark* 14), Peter and John (*Acts* 4), the "Apostles" and Peter (*Acts* 5), Stephen (*Acts* 7) and Paul (*Acts* 22) all appeared before it.

²⁰² This was a reference to one of Jesus's remarks quoted in *Matthew* 10:29-31 and closely quoted in *Luke* 12:6-7. Jesus used God's concern for sparrows to remind his listeners of God's greater concern for humans. This metaphor appears in *Matthew* and *Luke* but not in *Mark* (or *John*). It is an example of what scholars theorize was one saying in a book of sayings in circulation during the first century which if it existed may have pre-dated the Gospels. This will be covered more in Chapter 6.

²⁰³ *Psalm* 127:1.

[204] The story of the Tower of Babel is recounted in *Genesis* 11:1-9. People congregated in a city and decided to build a tower to show their greatness. God, who had told them to scatter throughout the earth, regarded this as disobedience and pride. He responded by confusing their languages so that they were forced to congregate with others who spoke the same language and thus were divided.

[205] But the convention did not go along with Franklin's (pious?) suggestion. Different objections included that it might alarm people, that different faiths were represented in the Convention, that they had no money to pay a chaplain and that public prayer would offend Quaker delegates. See Carl Van Doren, *The Great Rehearsal: The Story of the Making and Ratifying of the Constitution of the United States*, With a New Introduction by DW Brogan (New York: Time Reading Program, Time Incorporated, 1965 Original Copyright, 1948, Viking Press) 123-4. Note: Thomas Jefferson called the Quakers the Protestant Jesuits possibly of the opinion that the Quakers showed clannishness and martyrdom. See Richard Norton Smith, *An Uncommon Man: The Triumph of Herbert Hoover* (New York: Simon and Schuster, 1984) 61. Two Presidents were raised in Quaker homes: Herbert Hoover and Richard Nixon. Hoover said about the experience: "I came of Quaker stock. I never worked very hard at it." Nixon was a complex figure. Hoover saw Nixon as a preacher pretending to be a politician. In the Cold War Nixon said: "I'm not necessarily a respecter of the *status quo* in foreign affairs. I'm a chance taker in foreign affairs; I would take chances for peace. The Quakers have a passion for peace, you know." See Niels C. Nielson *God in the Obama Era Presidents Religion and Ethics From George Washington to Barack Obama* (New York: Morgan James Publishing, LLC, 2009) 126, 218.

[206] *Exodus* 14.

[207] *Exodus* 20. As a child, I heard more than one Baptist minister intone that God didn't call them the ten *suggestions*.

[208] Van Doren 231. See also Meacham *American Gospel* (Random House, 2006), 95. Gouverneur Morris's modesty was noteworthy. He wrote these immortal words as the Preamble to the Constitution: "We the People of the United States, in Order to form a more perfect Union, establish Justice, insure domestic Tranquility, provide for the common defence, promote the general Welfare, and secure the Blessings of Liberty to ourselves and our Posterity, do ordain and establish this Constitution for the United States of America." Late in life, Madison saw it differently: "Whatever may be the judgment pronounced on the competency of the architects of the Constitution, or whatever may be the destiny of the edifice prepared by them, I feel it a

duty to express my profound and solemn conviction ... that there never was an assembly of men, charged with a great and arduous trust, who were more pure in their motives, or more exclusively or anxiously devoted to the object committed to them." See *PatriotPost.US* April 6, 2010. (Incidentally, Gouverneur Morris was ambassador to France in 1792. At a public meeting in that country he called the French Constitution a "wretched piece of paper" and said that popular government was "good for nothing in France." The French demanded his recall saying that he had provoked "great disgust." See Harlow Giles Unger *The Last Founding Father James Monroe And A Nations Call To Greatness* [Philadelphia: De Capo Press, A Member of the Perseus Books Group, 2009] 96-7.)

[209] *Jonah,* especially the first two chapters, recounts this story. In the *New Testament,* Jonah's experience is seen as a prefigurement of the death and resurrection of Jesus Christ. See *Matthew* 12: 38-41 and *Luke* 11: 29-32. Jesus uses the phrase "Sign of Jonah." As noted, the *Bible* does not say that Jonah was swallowed by a whale but by a great fish or a sea monster.

[210] The *Bible* has lots of verses talking about sowing and reaping, using this agricultural activity as metaphor. This particular quote is possibly a reference to *Ecclesiastes* the third chapter with its famous litany around the theme that in life there is a place for everything. The first two verses of that chapter read: *"There is an appointed time for everything. And there is a time for every event under heaven—A time to give birth and a time to die; A time to plant and a time to uproot what is planted."*

[211] Van Doren 243, 246.

[212] Van Doren 272 (possibly a reference to *Luke* 10:18).

[213] Susan Dunn 63. Most Americans probably know that according to *Genesis* Adam and Eve were the first two people. Adam is mentioned five times in the *New Testament*:

- *Luke* 3:38 – In the genealogical list of Jesus's ancestors.
- *Romans* 5:12-21 – A figure by which sin came into the world.
- *I Corinthians* 15:22, 45 – A symbol of mortality.
- *I Timothy* 2:13-14 – A reference to make a sexist point – that Adam was created before Eve and was not deceived into sin but Eve was and that therefore women should not teach but be silent.
- *Jude* 14 – A genealogical reference point for Enoch, a prophet.

Eve is only mentioned in *I Timothy* 2:13 which reads: *"For Adam was first formed, then Eve."*

[214] Jay Winik, *The Great Upheaval: America and the Birth of the Modern World 1788-1800* (New York: HarperCollins, 2007) 561.

[215] This was a portion of the "Mazzei letter" which was written to a foreign friend Philip Mazzei in 1796 and made public in 1797. See Larson 39. Jefferson was criticizing members of Congress from his own party who had backed down from a Constitutional fight with George Washington and Alexander Hamilton over the release of state papers pertinent to the negotiations of the controversial Jay Treaty. See Michael Beschloss, *Presidential Courage Brave Leaders and How They Changed America 1787-1989* (New York, London, Toronto, Sydney: Simon & Schuster, 2007) 27. Samson was an *Old Testament* figure whose story is told in *Judges* 13-16. The reference "heads shorn by the Harlot" is an allusion to the *Old Testament* figure of Delilah who cut Samson's long hair which apparently was the source of his great strength, weakening him and exposing him to his enemies. She appears in *Judges* 16 and there is no evidence that she was a prostitute except that the same chapter does talk about Samson visiting prostitutes. This does not keep Samson out of receiving mention in *Hebrews* 11:32 along with other Hebrew heroes as examples of faith, defined in that context as the *"assurance of things hoped for, the conviction of things not seen"* (*Hebrews* 11:1). The Samsonite luggage company is named for this strongman.

Solomon was the third king of Israel, successor to his father David. He is mentioned 273 times in the *Old Testament* and ten times in the *New Testament*. In *I Kings* 3: 1-10 he is granted one wish by the Lord and Solomon asks for wisdom. As a result, God gave him both wisdom and wealth as recounted in *I Kings* 4. This same account appears in *II Chronicles* 1.

Note: - On April 16, 1945 President Truman, a few days into his presidency after the death of Franklin Roosevelt, addressed Congress. In his conclusion he said: "As I have assumed my duties, I humbly pray Almighty God, in the words of King Solomon: *'Give therefore Thy servant an understanding heart to judge Thy people, so that I may discern between good and bad: for who is able to judge Thy so great a people?'* I ask only to be a good and faithful servant of my Lord and my people." See David McCullough, *Truman* (New York, London, Toronto, Sydney, Tokyo, Singapore: Simon and Schuster, 1992) 360. Truman was quoting from *I Kings* 3: 9. In *Matthew* 6:29 Jesus asserts that the lilies of the field are more beautiful than Solomon was in all his glory, making the point that God cares for these flowers and, by implication, will also care for humans.

[216] Jack Shepherd, *The Adams Chronicles: Four Generations of Greatness* (Boston and Toronto: Little, Brown and Company, Prepared by arrangement

with the Massachusetts Historical Society, The Adams Papers, and Harvard University Press. Introduction by Daniel J. Boorstin, 1975) xxv. It seems that she was paraphrasing *Proverbs* 15:30: *"A cheerful look brings joy to the heart, and good news gives health to the bones."* Abigail Adams had the ability to be very amusing. Her father was an ultra-orthodox minister who had hoped that she would marry a minister and was disappointed in her choice of John Adams. After her wedding he allowed her –as was apparently his custom with his children upon their marriages – to select the Biblical text from which he would preach the following Sunday. Abigail chose *Matthew* 11:18. Jesus's words about John the Baptist as recorded in that verse are: *"For John came neither eating nor drinking, and they say, 'He has a demon.'"* See Alf J. Mapp, Jr. *The Faith of Our Fathers What America's Founders Really Believed* (Rowman & Littlefield, 2003 New York: Fall River Press, 2006 by arrangement with Rowman & Littlefield Publishing Group, Inc.) 59-60.

[217] David McCullough, *John Adams* (New York: Simon & Schuster, 2005) 488.

[218] *II Corinthians* 11:26 and *Galatians* 2:4.

[219] Susan Dunn 86. The Lion and the Lamb are not conjoined in any verses but two verses in Isaiah are often cited:

- *Isaiah* 11:6 - *"And the wolf will dwell with the lamb, And the leopard will lie down with the young goat, And the calf and the young lion and the fatling together; And a little boy will lead them."*
- *Isaiah* 65:25 - *"The wolf and the lamb will graze together, and the lion will eat straw like the ox; and dust will be the serpent's food. They will do no evil or harm in all My holy mountain,' says the LORD."*

This predicts a millennium time with harmony and no aggressors.

[220] David O. Stewart, *The Men Who Invented the Constitution: The Summer of 1787* (New York, London, Toronto, Sydney: Simon & Schuster, 2007) 237-38. This is a Biblical reference but probably not an obvious one to modern readers. It alludes to the story of Moses freeing the Hebrew people from bondage in Egypt. God told Moses that his rod could be used to perform miracles and thereby he could impress the Egyptian pharaoh (*Exodus* 4:17). Moses and his brother used the rod that way and it helped him to perform the most famous of all his miracles, the parting of the sea as recounted in *Exodus* 14: 16-21.

[221] Nagel 260-2. Adams was quoting Paul's famous statement in *I Corinthians* 1:25: *"For the foolishness of God is wiser than men, and the weakness of God is stronger than men."*

²²² Nagel 285. Adams was quoting or closely paraphrasing *Matthew* 26:39, *Mark* 14:36 and *Luke* 22: 42. In addition, there are three other instances in which Jesus spoke of his coming ordeal using the metaphor of a cup: *Matthew* 20: 22-23, *Mark* 10: 38-39 and *John* 18:11. In *Matthew* and *Mark* he indicates some confidence that his followers will also be able to drink of this "cup." In *John* he disarms his followers, asking them, about the "cup": *"shall I not drink it?"*

²²³ Jackson sprang to national prominence by defeating the British at the Battle of New Orleans in 1815. An ally, the pirate Jean Lafitte, received a pardon from President James Madison in return for his heroic service at that battle. Knowingly or unknowingly, Lafitte invoked one of Jesus's parables found in *Luke* 15 stating, "I am the Lost Sheep who desires to return to the flock." See Patrick J. Buchanan, *A Republic, Not an Empire Reclaiming America's Destiny* (Washington DC: Regnery Publishing, Inc. An Eagle Publishing Company, 1999) 84.

²²⁴ David E. Johnson and Johnny R. Johnson, *A Funny Thing Happened on the Way to the White House: Foolhardiness, Folly and Fraud in Presidential Elections, from Andrew Jackson to George W. Bush* (New York: Barnes & Noble, 2007) 10. In this election, Jackson had received more electoral votes than Adams, but not a majority. As required by the Constitution, the election was then decided in the House of Representatives, where Clay used his influence to secure Adams's victory. Subsequently, when Adams picked Clay to be the Secretary of State – which for the past four presidents had been a stepping stone to the presidency - the Jackson partisans were outraged, or at least feigned outrage. We know this in history as the "Corrupt Bargain." Years later, Adams invoked Christianity to declare his innocence of any deal with Clay, declaring that when he died, "should those charges have found their way to the throne of Eternal Justice, I WILL, IN THE PRESENCE OF OMNIPOTENCE, PRONOUNCE THEM FALSE" (Emphasis in the original). See Richard J. Carwardine, *Evangelicals and Politics in Antebellum America* (Knoxville, The University of Tennessee Press, 1997) 73. Adams knew how to make phrases. He had run-ins with his contemporary Daniel Webster (1782 - 1852) and once referred to "the gigantic intellect, the envious temper, the ravenous ambition, and the rotten heart of Daniel Webster." See Holman Hamilton, *Zachary Taylor Soldier in the White House* (Indianapolis and New York: The Bobbs-Merrill Company, Inc.,1951) 57. (Clay may have backed Adams only because he saw him as the lesser of evils with respect to other candidates and because he was close to Adams on such issues as strengthening the country through higher tariffs and federal expenditures for roads, canals and manufacturing - the heart of what Clay and historians called the "American

System." Moreover, Clay was a logical choice for the Secretary of State post because he had foreign experience as a negotiator reaching the peace treaty which ended the War of 1812.)

[225] The reference to Judas is, of course, a staple. Jackson's Vice President and successor, Martin Van Buren, was defeated when he ran for re-election in 1840. Eight years later he ran as a candidate for President on the ticket of the Free Soil party. The opposition Whigs mocked him as a "Judas Iscariot." See Carwardine 91. Some newspapers called him "...the Judas Iscariot of the nineteenth century" and erstwhile ally President James K. Polk called Van Buren "the most fallen man" he had ever known. See Ted Widmer, *Martin Van Buren* The American Presidents Arthur M. Schlesinger, Jr., General Editor Times Books (New York: Henry Holt and Company, LLC, 2005) 459. The reference to Judas is not only a staple, it is also cross-cultural. In the 1930s one of the more disgusting creatures of the twentieth century, Nikita Khrushchev, was an up-and-coming Communist in the Soviet Union, firmly on the side of Joseph Stalin who is probably in a tie with Adolf Hitler as the most heinous creature of that era. In the bloody internecine battles in the USSR, Khrushchev denounced Stalin's arch-enemy Leon Trotsky as the "Judas-Trotsky." See Robert Gellately, Lenin, *Stalin and Hitler: The Age of Social Catastrophe* (New York: Vintage Books A Division of Random House, Inc., 2007) 273.

[226] Beschloss 88. The *New Testament* references are: *Matthew* 21:12-13, 23; *Mark* 11:15-17, 26-28; *Luke* 19:45-46, 20:1-2; *John* 2:14-18. Note: There is, however, some confusion here. *Matthew, Mark* and *Luke* all placed this event in the last week of Jesus's life – after what we traditionally call his triumphal entry into Jerusalem on what we call Palm Sunday. *John* placed it much earlier in Jesus's ministry. *John* described Palm Sunday in *John* 12: 12-16. It is possible that Jesus dispersed the money changers in the Temple twice although no Gospel makes that claim.

[227] Widmer 64.

[228] Robert W. Winston, *Andrew Johnson Plebian and Patriot* (New York: Henry Holt and Company, 1928) 33-34. Knowingly or not, Johnson was referring to *Genesis* 3:7 although he left out Eve as part of that verse makes it clear that both Adam and Eve did the sewing: "...*So they sewed fig leaves together to cover themselves.*" As noted, from *Mark* 6:3 we hear that Jesus was a carpenter. From *Acts* 18:3 we learn that Paul was a tentmaker. In *I Corinthians* 4:12, Paul says of himself and his companions, "*we work wearily with our own hands to earn our living....*" In the 1850s in defending his constituents who

were poor whites, Johnson said: "Laboring with the hands does not make one a slave." If so, "Paul was a slave...." See Winston 137.

229 This is certainly a core teaching of Jesus, recorded in *Matthew* 19:30; 20:16; *Mark* 9:35; 10:31 and *Luke* 13:30.

230 Meacham, *American Lion: Andrew Jackson in the White House* (New York: Random House Large Print Edition, 2008) 362.

231 According to the *Old Testament Book of Esther*, Esther was a Jewish woman who saved her coreligionists from the evil designs of Haman, a counselor to a king. In a turnabout, Haman was hanged on a gallows that he had built for Esther's uncle Mordecai. The gallows were about 75 feet off the ground according to *Esther* 7: 9-10. Note: Andrew Jackson was familiar with this passage. In a letter that years later was shown to Abraham Lincoln, Andrew Jackson said that rebels starting civil wars "should be sent to Haman's Gallows." See Beschloss 102. Additional note: Mordecai John Pruitt (1849-1918) was born in Kentucky and was my Great Grandfather.

232 *Luke* 8:1-3 shows women traveling with Jesus. All four gospels report that women were present at the crucifixion (*Matthew* 27:55-56, *Mark* 15: 40-41, *Luke* 23:49 and *John* 19:25) and the Empty Tomb (*Matthew* 28:1-10, *Mark* 16:1-7, *Luke* 24:1-8 and *John* 20: 1-17). The account in *Luke*, verses 5-7, contains this statement by the two men whom the women encountered at the Empty Tomb: *"Why are you looking among the dead for someone who is alive? He isn't here! He is risen from the dead!* **Remember what he told you back in Galilee,** *that the Son of Man must be betrayed into the hands of sinful men and be crucified, and that he would rise again on the third day."* (Emphasis added). Verse 8 adds: *"Then they remembered that he had said this."* This is a clear indication that Jesus shared his mission directly with the women throughout his ministry just as he did with his male disciples (although there is no indication that they comprehended it any better than the men did).

233 Meacham, *American Lion: Andrew Jackson in the White House* 532.

234 Nagel 360. In the *Old Testament*, *Exodus* 32 records the terrifying story of the Israelites abandoning the true God and making an idol, a Golden Calf. It was a sign of their faithlessness and they were punished. In *Acts* 7:41, the Martyr Stephen cites that story in his trial as a prefigurement of the Jewish leadership of his time rejecting Jesus Christ.

235 Nagel 380-1. Note: This is a quote from Jesus in a parable that he told in *Matthew* 25: 14-30. The quotes are in verses 21 and 23. There is a nearly identical story in *Luke* 19: 11-27 without this specific quote.

²³⁶ Buchanan, *A Republic, Not an Empire Reclaiming America's Destiny* 115 and Meacham, *American Lion: Andrew Jackson in the White House* 578. This was a reference to *Luke* 2: 25-35 wherein Simeon who would not "*see death before he had seen the Lord's Christ*" (verse 26) blessed the baby Jesus in the Temple. Andrew Johnson, an admirer of Andrew Jackson, used the same metaphor in 1866 to describe his hope to see national unity in the immediate aftermath of the Civil War. See Lately Thomas, *The First President Johnson The Three Lives of the Seventeenth President of The United States of America* (New York: William Morrow & Company, Inc., 1968) 488.

²³⁷ Hamilton, Zachary *Taylor Soldier in the White House* 270.

²³⁸ Hamilton, Zachary *Taylor Soldier in the White House* 318, 322. Note: There are two Lazaruses mentioned in the *New Testament*. The more famous one was the brother of Mary and Martha and was raised from the dead by Jesus as described in *John* 11 and 12. The less famous Lazarus was a character in a story by Jesus recorded in *Luke* 16: 19-31 who had died and "*was carried by the angels into Abraham's bosom.*" (verse 22). A rich man who had known Lazarus in life also died but was sent to Hell where he was still able to see Abraham and Lazarus "afar off." (verse 23). The rich dead man talked with Abraham and tried unsuccessfully to get Abraham to send Lazarus back to earth to warn his family about Hell. Seward's critics were likening him to this Lazarus. President Franklin Roosevelt alluded the more famous Lazarus in 1942 when he was asked to place former President Herbert Hoover into a responsible position dealing with manpower shortages on the home front as the US had entered World War II. FDR and Hoover were bitter rivals and Hoover was marginalized at that time in American public life. FDR declined, saying: "Well, I'm not Jesus Christ, I'm not going to raise him from the dead." See Richard Norton Smith 309. Final Note: I have read one analysis that suggests that the Lazarus in the story was a reference to the Lazarus who was later raised from the dead by Jesus. If so, Jesus may have been referring in the story not to his own resurrection but to that of Lazarus. See J Phillips, *The Disciple Whom Jesus Loved Take Another Look The Bible Has The Answers* (Austell, GA: Waymaker Communications, Fifth Edition 2011 First Edition Copyright 2000) 128ff.

²³⁹ *Mark* 3:24-27. Lincoln was talking about a country, one portion of which allowed slavery. Jesus was giving evidence that he himself was not allied with Satan. He opposed Satan and, "*If Satan has risen up against himself and is divided, he cannot stand, but he is finished!.*" (verse 26). Note: This is not a book about whether or not Satan is a real figure or a metaphor but it is important to acknowledge that Jesus and the writers of the *New Testament*

took the existence or at least the concept of Satan and evil very seriously. From the perspective of the *New Testament,* Jesus defeated Satan in his temptations (*Matthew* 4:1-11; *Mark* 1:12-13; *Luke* 4:1-13), his exorcisms and his death (*I Corinthians* 2:8; *Colossians* 2:15). There will be a final victory (*Revelation* 20) but for Christians the fight continues (*Ephesians* 6:10-20). See NT Wright, *Simply Jesus A New Vision of Who He Was, What He Did, And Why He Matters* (New York: HaperOne *An Imprint* of Harper*CollinsPublishers*, 2011) 120. Evil, from this perspective then, might not be looked at as focused on individual people but may be broader and – although it is difficult to acknowledge - have a spiritual side. At least that may be the perspective of the *New Testament.* Pope John Paul II may have exemplified this point. In 1981 a man named Mehmet Ali Agca shot and gravely wounded John Paul. During the trial people kept trying to find out who had sent the would-be assassin. The Soviet Communists and the Turkish Fascists both had motives. Later, however, the Pope forgave his attacker and said privately that the human origin of the attack did not matter. "I know well that the responsible one was the devil," the Pope said. "And whether he used the Bulgarian people or the Turkish people, it was diabolical." Life then is a struggle sometimes against evil in the effort to do good. See Peggy Noonan, *WallStreetJournal. com* December 17, 2012.

[240] John Staffer, *Time* July 4, 2005. *Proverbs* 25:11 reads: *"A word fitly spoken is like apples of gold in pictures of silver."* Here is more background: As the break-up of the union loomed and the Civil War drew near in late 1860, President-elect Abraham Lincoln corresponded with a former Whig colleague Senator Alexander Stephens of Georgia later vice president of the Confederacy. They could not find common ground. Lincoln wrote him: "You think slavery is *right* and ought to be extended while we think it is *wrong* and ought to be restricted. That I suppose is the rub. It certainly is the only substantial difference between us." Stephens urged Lincoln to speak out for national reconciliation: "A word fitly spoken by you now would be like 'apples of gold in pictures of silver.'" Lincoln didn't go along with Stephens because he thought any comment from him before he took office would encourage secession. But he loved the quote from *Proverbs* 25:11 and began to use it himself. See Harold Holzer, *Lincoln President-Elect: Abraham Lincoln and the Great Secession Winter* of 1860-61 (New York, London, Toronto, Sydney: Simon & Schuster, 2008) 178.

[241] Wills, *Head and Heart: American Christianities* (New York: The Penguin Press, 2007) 283. Note: In 1856 the territory of Kansas erupted into a kind of civil war between pro-slavery and free-soil partisans. On May 24 as retaliation

for violence in Lawrence two days earlier John Brown and his sons attacked three isolated cabins and chopped five pro-slavery men and boys to pieces "as declared by Almighty God" according to Brown. The five had no connection to the attack on Lawrence. See McCullough, *Truman* 27.

[242] Holzer 17. Lincoln was quoting from the Lazarus story that Jesus told in *Luke* 16: 19-31, specifically verse 13.

[243] *New Testament* references in "The Battle Hymn of the Republic" are:

- The winepress of God's wrath (*Revelation* 14:19)
- The terrible sword (*Revelation* 18:15)
- An all-fulfilling trumpet (*Revelation* 10:7)

[244] Meacham, *American Gospel* 116-7.

[245] Humes 109. This was a near-quote of *Matthew* 8:22 and *Luke* 9:60.

[246] Doris Kearns Goodwin, *Team of Rivals: The Political Genius of Abraham Lincoln* (New York: Simon & Schuster, 2005) 722.

[247] A couple of generations earlier, Andrew Jackson claimed that he read three chapters of the *Bible* every day. See Meacham, *American Lion: Andrew Jackson in the White House* 29. John Quincy Adams also read several chapters a day of the *Bible* throughout his life. See Nagel 181.

[248] Edwin P. Hoyt, *James A. Garfield* (Chicago: Reilly & Lee Co) 1964) 6, 36. Garfield was paraphrasing *Hebrews* 9:22: "...*almost all things are by the law purged with blood; and without shedding of blood is no remission.*" Garfield was a serious Disciples of Christ preacher, though never ordained. His first sermon in 1853 or 1854 compared Jesus Christ to Napoleon. Both rose from obscurity and were defeated and Napoleon's return to Paris was like the resurrection. See James M. Perry, *Touched With Fire: Five Presidents and the Civil War Battles That Made Them* (New York: Public Affairs) 2003) 5. In his mature years, as a candidate for President, Garfield said, "I would rather be defeated than make capital out of my religion." See Arthur Schlesinger Jr. *Los Angeles Times* October 26, 2004.

[249] Winston 366.

[250] Paul F. Boller, Jr., *Presidential Campaigns From George Washington to George W. Bush* Oxford, New York, Aukland, Bangkok, Buenos Aires, Cape Town, Chennai, Dar es Salaam, Delhi Hong Kong, Istanbul, Karachi, Kolkata, Kuala Lumpur, Madrid, Melbourne, Mexico City, Mumbai, Nairobi, Sao Paulo, Shanghai, Taipei, Tokyo, Toronto) 1984, 1985, 1996, 2004) 147.

[251] Rome has remained the capital of Catholic Christianity through the centuries. However, it was looted by the Muslims in 843 and again in 846. See Stark, *God's Battalions The Case for the Crusades* 12ff.

[252] Boller 146.

[253] The crown of thorns placed on Jesus by Roman soldiers at the time of his crucifixion is mentioned in *Matthew* 27:29, *Mark* 15:17 and *John* 19:2, 5. Bryan was something of an ignoramus. He did not actually understand the issue he was addressing in this famous speech which was called bimetallism and meant more coinage of silver, shortened to "free silver." He wrote: "The people of Nebraska are for free silver and I am for free silver. I will look up the arguments later." See Jonah Goldberg, *Oregonian* April 28, 2007. He was also somewhat of a bigot. William Howard Taft had written that he did not believe "in the divinity of Christ." (See James Chace, 1912 *Wilson, Roosevelt, Taft & Debs - The Election That Changed the Country* (New York: Simon & Schuster Paperbacks, 2004) 24. In the 1908 election, Taft's Unitarianism was attacked by Bryan: "Think of the United States with a President who does not believe that Jesus Christ was the Son of God, but looks upon our immaculate savior as a ...low cunning imposter." Theodore Roosevelt counseled Taft: "The same attack was made upon Lincoln as being a nonorthodox Christian as upon you, and far severer attacks upon Jefferson." See Meacham, *American Gospel* 147. Bryan, however, is probably best remembered for arguing against evolution in a Tennessee court room in 1925. Here is another use of the Crown of Thorns metaphor: Pope Paul VI (1963-78) called the priests leaving the priesthood to marry his personal Crown of Thorns. He had written that celibacy would actually be a recruitment incentive. See Wills, *Why I Am A Catholic* 242,244. King Louis IX of France (1214 – 1270) acquired what he assumed was the authentic Crown of Thorns on a crusading adventure. This eventually helped promote him to sainthood. This "Crown of Thorns" is now in a vessel in the Notre Dame Cathedral in Paris. St. Louis, Missouri is named for him. See http://en.wikipedia.org/wiki/Crown_of_Thorns (Accessed May 2, 2012).

[254] Johnson and Johnson 79. Ananias was a *New Testament* figure put to death for lying as recorded in *Acts* 5: 1-11.

Note: I assume it was this Ananias to whom Roosevelt was referring but there are two other *New Testament* Ananiases. One lived in Damascus and, according to the *Book of Acts* (but not *Galatians*), figured prominently in the conversion of Paul (then known as Saul). Paul was blinded on the road to Damascus where he had intended to persecute followers of Jesus. His conversion is described in *Acts* 9, 22 and 26. The first two accounts mention a man named Ananias. *Acts* 9, verses 10 through 19 records that *"Now there was a disciple at Damascus named **Ananias**; and the Lord said to him in a vision, 'Ananias.' And he said, 'Here I am, Lord.' And the Lord said to him, 'Get up and go to the street called Straight, and inquire at the house of Judas for a man from Tarsus named Saul, for he is praying, and he has seen in a vision a man named **Ananias** come in and lay his hands on him, so that he might regain his sight.' But **Ananias** answered, "Lord, I have heard from many about this man, how much harm he did to Your saints at Jerusalem; and here he has authority from the chief priests to bind all who call on Your name.' But the Lord said to him, 'Go, for he is a chosen instrument of Mine, to bear My name before the Gentiles and kings and the sons of Israel; for I will show him how much he must suffer for My name's sake.' So **Ananias** departed and entered the house, and after laying his hands on him said, 'Brother Saul, the Lord Jesus, who appeared to you on the road by which you were coming, has sent me so that you may regain your sight and be filled with the Holy Spirit.' And immediately there fell from his eyes something like scales, and he regained his sight, and he got up and was baptized; and he took food and was strengthened."* (Emphasis added).

Acts 22, verses 12 through 16 then records in words attributed to Paul that: *"A certain **Ananias**, a man who was devout by the standard of the Law, and well spoken of by all the Jews who lived there, came to me, and standing near said to me, 'Brother Saul, receive your sight!' And at that very time I looked up at him. And he said, 'The God of our fathers has appointed you to know His will and to see the Righteous One and to hear an utterance from His mouth. For you will be a witness for Him to all men of what you have seen and heard. Now why do you delay? Get up and be baptized, and wash away your sins, calling on His name.'"* (Emphasis added).

Note: In the first instance Ananias is a follower of Jesus. In the second he is a devout, well-respected Jew. The account of Paul's conversion in *Acts* 26 does not mention Ananias.

Acts 23 verses 1 through 5 mentions a third Ananias, the high priest who ordered Paul struck during a trial in the Sanhedrin. Paul retorted aggressively as recorded in verse 3 with this: *"God is going to strike you, you whitewashed wall! Do you sit to try me according to the Law, and in violation of the Law order me to be struck?"* When called to account for this response, Paul claimed not to know that this Ananias was the high priest. (Is it plausible that Paul, an educated man, who had worked with a previous high priest - see *Acts* 9:1 - actually did not know that this Ananias was the high priest or was Paul using sarcasm?) This Ananias is mentioned one more time in the *New Testament* in *Acts* 24:1. In this instance he is represented by a lawyer at one of Paul's trial-type appearances. According to Josephus he was killed by the Jewish rebels in 66. See Justo L. Gonzales, *Acts The Gospel of the Spirit* 255.

Final note: Long before Roosevelt used the allusion to Ananias, it was commonplace in the American lexicon. It was cited by the Puritan authorities against a dissenter, Anne Hutchinson, although she was not executed. (Other dissenters including Mary Dyer were.) See Wills, *Head and Heart: American Christianities* 59-60. During the 1876 presidential election, Democrat candidate Samuel Tilden was attacked as "Slippery Sam", "Soapy Sam", and "Ananias Tilden." See Boller 134.

[255] Edmund Morris, *The Rise of Theodore Roosevelt* (New York: Modern Library Paperback Edition 2001 Copyright 1979 by Edmund Morris) 178. *John* 1: 35-51 recounts the beginning of the formation of Jesus's immediate followers. The day after he is baptized he attracts to his group Andrew and an unnamed person. They had been disciples of John the Baptist. Andrew promptly brought in his brother Peter and Jesus himself brought in Philip. Philip after joining up went to (his friend?) Nathaniel and told him, "*We have found the very person Moses and the prophets wrote about! His name is Jesus, the son of Joseph from Nazareth.*" Nathanial uttered these biased words: "*Can anything good come from Nazareth?*" Jesus called him a "*man of complete integrity*" and soon told him he would "*see heaven open and the angels of God going up and down on the Son of Man, the one who is the stairway between heaven and earth.*" (verse 51). Nathaniel is not in the lists of the twelve disciples unless he is the same person who is named Bartholomew. In fact, he is not mentioned elsewhere in the *New Testament* except for once in *John* 21:2 which asserts that he was with Peter, Doubting Thomas, James and John and two other of Jesus's disciples at the Sea of Tiberias to witness one of Jesus's post-resurrection appearances. This may be intended as fulfillment of *John* 1:51.

[256] Johnson and Johnson 82. As noted, Roosevelt liked to quote from the *Bible*. In accepting the nomination of the Progressive Party a few months earlier, he had stated that he was in the fight for principles "and the first and foremost of these goes back to Sinai, and is embodied in the commandment, *Thou Shalt Not Steal.*" See Chace 123. The reference to "loaves and fishes" could apply to several *New Testament* sections. There are six accounts of feedings of multitudes from a small amount of bread and fish and a large amount left over:

- *Mark* 6:30-44 and 8: 1-10
- *Matthew* 14:13-21 and 15:32-39
- *Luke* 9:10-17
- *John* 6:1-14

Polycarp of Smyrna held that the boy who offered Jesus the loaves and fishes that Jesus multiplied to feed the people was later bishop of Tours in France. See Collins and Price 41, 44. Note: The boy is only mentioned in one of the accounts, *John* 6: 8-9.

Note: On May 11, 330 the emperor Constantine dedicated his new capital, Constantinople on the grounds of the ancient Greek city of *Byzantium* which is a Latinized version of the original name Byzantion. (Constantinople is modern Istanbul.) Constantine honored classical paganism, Jewish history and Jesus. Beneath a column with a statue of himself he buried drums, a cloak of Athena the Greek goddess of wisdom, an axe used by Noah and the baskets from the feeding of the thousands by Jesus. See Lars Brownworth, *Lost to the West: The Forgotten Byzantine Empire That Rescued Western Civilization* (New York: Crown Publishers 2009) 22-23.

[257] Johnson and Johnson 78-9. The term "Holy Roller" refers to an exuberant Pentecostalism derived from *Acts* 2 where the audience that received the Holy Spirit after a sermon by Peter on the Day of Pentecost was so enthusiastic that they were mistakenly thought to be inebriated. Note: Taft also called Theodore Roosevelt a "fakir," a "juggler," a "green goods man," and a "gold brick man."

[258] David Pietrusza, *1920 The Year of the Six Presidents* (New York: Carroll & Graf Publishers, an Imprint of Avalon Publishing Group, 2007) 269. Broun's readers would have known that this was a reference to the Day of Pentecost. (Debs was convicted in that case, went to prison but was subsequently pardoned by President Warren G Harding, the twenty-ninth president of the United States. Harding's middle name was Gamaliel.)

[259] Murray B. *Seidler, Norman Thomas Respectable Rebel* Copyright 1961 Syracuse University Press Manufactured in the United States of America by the Vail-Ballou Press, Inc., Binghamton, New York) 29. This is a time-honored metaphor which refers to Paul's conversion as recounted in *Acts* 9, 22 and 26.

[260] John W. Dean, Warren *G. Harding The American Presidents* Arthur M. Schlesinger, Jr., General Editor Times Books (New York: Henry Holt and Company, LLC) 2004) 131. Note: There are two versions of the Lord's Prayer:

- *Matthew* 6: 9-14: *"Pray, then, in this way:*
  'Our Father who is in heaven,
  Hallowed be Your name.
  Your kingdom come.
  Your will be done,
  On earth as it is in heaven

> *Give us this day our daily bread.*
> *And forgive us our debts, as we also have forgiven our debtors.*
> *And do not lead us into temptation, but deliver us from evil.*
> *For Yours is the kingdom and the power and the glory forever. Amen'"*
- *Luke 11:1-4: "It happened that while Jesus was praying in a certain place, after He had finished, one of His disciples said to Him, 'Lord, teach us to pray just as John also taught his disciples.' And He said to them, 'When you pray, say:*
> *"Father, hallowed be Your name.*
> *Your kingdom come.*
> *Give us each day our daily bread.*
> *And forgive us our sins,*
> *For we ourselves also forgive everyone who is indebted to us.*
> *And lead us not into temptation."'"*

James D. Tabor believes that the wording in verse 1 - *"teach us to pray **as John taught his disciples*** (Emphasis added) – is evidence that this was a prayer taught by John the Baptist prior to Jesus teaching it. See James D. Tabor, *The Jesus Dynasty* (New York: Simon & Schuster, 2006) 137.

[261] Boller 228. As noted, from *I Kings* 3:12 one could infer that Solomon was the wisest person who has ever lived.

[262] Boller 257.

[263] The Beatitudes are found at the beginning of the Sermon on the Mount in *Matthew* 5: 3-11 (*Matthew* 5:1 describes this sermon as taking place *"on the mountain"*) and in what some call the Sermon on the Plain in *Luke* 6: 20-26. (*Luke* 6:17 describes this sermon as taking place when *"Jesus came down with them and stood on a level place."*) These sayings follow a well-know formula *"Blessed are…"* and are often used in figures of speech, much as Hoover did.

[264] *PatriotPost.US* April 15, 2009.

[265] Nielson 44. FDR, of course, was drawing from Jesus's confrontation with authorities at the Temple in Jerusalem.

[266] http://www.dickb.com/articles/bible_roots_dsb.shtml (Accessed May 2, 2012).

[267] According to the Catholic Church the patron saint of alcoholism is Monica (331-387), the mother of St. Augustine. Her feast day is August 27. Her son is the patron saint of brewers. His feast day is August 28. He is also the patron saint of printers and theologians. See Sandoval 14, 37-38.

[268] Elise Soukup, *Newsweek* October 17, 2005.

269 http://www.pbs.org/americanprophet/joseph-smith.html (Accessed May 2, 2012).

270 It is only inferentially a *New Testament* reference, but Smith's successor Brigham Young once was quoted to say about Zachary Taylor, the twelfth President of the US who served from 1849-1850, "Dead and in hell, and I am glad of it." See Johnson and Johnson 227. Note: Brigham Young denied saying this. See Ronald W. Walker, "'The Affair of the Runaways': Utah's First Encounter with the Federal Officers, Part 1", *Journal of Mormon History*, Fall 2013, Volume 39, No. 4. pp. 1-43.

271 Stark, *The Rise of Mormonism* 30-31.

272 Noting that Halley's Comet had appeared in 1835, Twain wrote in his biography, "I came in with Halley's Comet in 1835. It is coming again next year (1910), and I expect to go out with it. It will be the greatest disappointment of my life if I don't go out with Halley's Comet. The Almighty has said, no doubt: 'Now here are these two unaccountable freaks; they came in together, they must go out together.'"

273 Jesus in an apocalyptic discourse in *Matthew* 24 asserts in verse 31 that: *"And he shall send his angels with a great sound of a trumpet, and they shall gather together his elect from the four winds, from one end of heaven to the other."* Paul in a discourse about the resurrection of Jesus Christ and life after death in *I Corinthians* 15 asserts in verse 52 that: *"In a moment, in the twinkling of an eye, at the last trumpet. For the trumpet shall sound, and the dead shall be raised incorruptible, and we shall be changed."* The word "trumpet" appears seven times in *Revelation* and only five times in the rest of the *New Testament*.

274 Roy Morris, Jr. *Fraud of the Century Rutherford B. Hayes, Samuel Tilden and the Stolen Election of 1876* (New York, London, Toronto, Sydney, Singapore) 2003, 143. Here is religious language typical of that era: In 1877 during the bitter election aftermath of the presidential contest between Samuel Tilden and Rutherford B. Hayes, the US congress met as an electoral commission and gave the election to Hayes in what most historians believe was a fraudulent decision. A Tilden supporter Congressman Joseph C. Blackburn said: "Today is Friday. Upon that day the savior of the world suffered crucifixion between two thieves. On this Friday, constitutional government, justice, honesty, fair dealing, manhood, and decency suffer crucifixion amid a number of thieves." See Roy Morris 237.

275 *Matthew* 4:16 uses this phrase in connection with Jesus's ministry beginning after the arrest of John the Baptist. In this statement Jesus is understood to be quoting *Isaiah* 9:2. *Luke* 1:79 has Jesus's uncle, Zechariah, using this phrase in a poem addressed to his infant son John the Baptist in a clear reference to Jesus.

276 http://books.google.com/books?id=iiPZq_dE6MwC&pg=PA227&lpg=
PA227&dq=acheson+hiss+matthew&source=bl&ots=wxreLTbFYY&sig=U-
oLOp80Hx2PQhO-vKJG23QP24I&hl=en&ei=F60IS7HrH4KutQPNkKD
rDA&sa=X&oi=book_result&ct=result&resnum=1&ved=0CAgQ6AEwAA#
(Accessed May 2, 2012).

277 Gellately 592. This is a possible reference to *II Peter* 3:7-10.

278 Richard Norton Smith 357. This is a reference to the Four Horsemen of
the Apocalypse described obscurely in *Revelation* 6: 1-8. These horses have
different colors – white, red, black and pale green - and tradition has assigned
them different interpretations.

279 Tom Wicker, *Dwight D. Eisenhower* The American Presidents Arthur M.
Schlesinger, Jr., General Editor Times Books (New York: Henry Holt and
Company, LLC) 2002) 23. Note: David Dwight Eisenhower was named for
the famous American Evangelist Dwight L Moody (1837-1899.) See Nancy
Gibbs and Michael Duffy, The *Preacher and the Presidents: Billy Graham
in the White House* (New York: Center Street a division of Hatchette Book
Group USA, 2007) 35. Eisenhower later changed the order of his first two
names.

280 Boller 315. LBJ was quoting *Isaiah* 1:18. *Isaiah* 43:26 has a related comment
"...*let us argue our case together; State your cause, that you may be proved right.*"
In another, less reverent example of *Bible* quoting, President Johnson liked to
quote Jesus from the Sermon on the Mount with a twist: "Cast your bread
upon the waters and the sharks will get it." See Johnson and Johnson 137.
Note: Billy Graham was close to LBJ and said that "he was always a little bit
scared of death." Graham spent the last weekend of LBJ's term in the White
House, offered the invocation at Richard Nixon's inauguration the next day
and spent the first night of Nixon's term at the White House. See Gibbs and
Duffy 123, 154.Note: One author has said that Billy Graham was also afraid
of dying. See Frank Schaeffer, *Crazy for God How I Grew Up as one of the
Elect, Helped Found The Religious Right, And Lived to Take All (Or Almost All)
Of It Back* (New York: Carroll & Graf Publishers, 2007) 101.

281 JFK said this in 1961. See James Pierson, *Commentary* May 2006; Ronald
Reagan said it often including in his farewell address to the nation in 1989. It is
an analogy associated with Puritan John Winthrop (1587/8– 1649) who used
it in 1630 in a sermon entitled "A Model of Christian Charity" given aboard
ship advising the Massachusetts Bay colonists that their settlement would be
watched by the world. See http://history.hanover.edu/texts/winthmod.html
(Accessed May 2, 2012).

[282] David Pietrusza, *1960 LBJ vs. JFK vs. Nixon: The Epic Campaign That Forged Three Presidencies* (New York and London: Union Square Press An Imprint of Sterling Publishing Co. Inc.) 2008) 414.

[283] http://en.wikipedia.org/wiki/Dies_Irae (Accessed May 2, 2012).

[284] Beschloss 325. According to three of the Gospels, Jesus walked on water. The earliest account is recorded by in *Mark* 6:45-51. The disciples thought he was a ghost and were terrified. *Matthew* 14: 22-27 recounts that the boat was "*far away from land.*" *John* 6:15-21 reports that the disciples had rowed for three to four miles when they saw Jesus walking on the water. In other Gospel accounts, Jesus was in the boat asleep in a storm, woke up and calmed the storm. See *Mark* 4: 35-40; *Matthew* 8: 23-27 and *Luke* 8: 22-25. Paul came close to replicating this storm-calming miracle when he was in custody and in transfer to Rome as described in *Acts* 27:13-41. In this instance, Paul reported a message of assurance from "*an angel of the God to whom I belong*" (verse 23) and loss of life was prevented, although the ship was destroyed. Note: "Walking on water" has in our time and perhaps in earlier eras become a commonplace metaphor for accomplishing a very difficult task.

[285] Boller 346-7.

[286] http://mednews.stanford.edu/stanmed/2006summer/carter.html (Accessed May 2, 2012).

[287] Beschloss 284.

[288] This is a reference to Jesus's conversation with Nicodemus as recorded in *John* 3.

[289] Boyer 142-3.

[290] Ann Coulter, *Guilty: Liberal "Victims" and Their Assault On America* (New York: Crown Forum, 2008) 46-7. According to *Matthew* 2:1 and *Luke* 1:5, Herod the Great was ruler of Judea at the time of Jesus's birth. According to *Matthew* 2:16, Herod in a fit of rage ordered the murder of all male children in the area of Bethlehem in an attempt to kill Jesus. Jackson liked the Republicans-as-Herod theme. Eight years later, criticizing President-elect George W. Bush's budget priorities, he noted that it was the Christmas season and then said, "That's why Mary and Joseph had to pay tax and do the census count. But when Herod got the money, he wanted to invest in the shepherds having more land and more sheep, not invest in at-risk babies. Jesus was an at-risk baby, you know, in the manger, in the stable." See *Talk of the Nation*, December 27, 2000 quoted in Rod Dreher *National Review Online* August 16, 2002.

[291] Quayle (1947 -) earlier that year had given a speech criticizing a popular sit-com for in his view promoting single-motherhood as a life style choice. Jesse Jackson took off on this one too saying that Mary was a single mother - which she was not according to *Matthew* 1:24 although according to *Luke* 2:5, she may still have been the fiancée of Joseph at the exact time of Jesus's birth. This sort of stuff catches on. In the 2006 Democrat Senate primary in Virginia, James Webb called his Jewish opponent the "Anti-Christ of outsourcing." He won the primary and later the general election. See Coulter 169.

[292] *Galatians* 6:9.

[293] Jeff Gerth and Don Van Natta *Her Way: The Hopes and Ambitions of Hillary Rodham Clinton* (New York, Boston, and London: Little Brown and Company, 2007) 193.

[294] Gerth and Van Natta 203.

[295] *Matthew* 6:21 quotes Jesus: *"For where your treasure is, there your heart will be also."* Gore reversed that: "In my faith tradition, it's written in the *Book of Matthew*, where your heart is, there is your treasure also." See http://www.gargaro.com/algore.html (Accessed May 2, 2012).

[296] *James* 2: 26.

[297] Rich Lowry *Townhall.com* March 24, 2005.

[298] John Micklethwait and Adrian Wooldridge, *God is Back How The Global Revival of Faith is Changing the World* (New York: The Penguin Press 2009) 130.

[299] Hell is not a subject of this book but there are references to it in the *New Testament*. Here is one: *"For if God did not spare the angels when they sinned, but cast them into Hell and committed them to chains of deepest darkness to be kept until the judgment..."* (*II Peter* 2:4). This verse is a predecessor comment to say that if that is so, then God knows how to punish unrighteous people. Some Christian believers infer from *Revelation* 20: 14-15 that Hell is a *"lake of fire"* into which all those all those whose names are not *"found recorded in the Book of Life"* will be *"thrown."* They infer from *Revelation* 9:1-2 that it is a *"bottomless pit"* where *"smoke pour(s) out as though from a huge furnace..."* They hear in *Matthew* 22:13 in one of Jesus's parables that people in Hell will *"be weeping and gnashing (their) teeth."* They reason from *Luke* 16:23-24 which is a statement in one of Jesus's stories that people in Hell will be able to see those in Heaven but will know that they themselves can never be relieved from their torture. The never-ending nature of this punishment is reinforced

in *Revelation* 14:11 which reads: "*The smoke of their torment will rise forever and ever, and they will have no relief day or night, ...*" From *Jude* 13, some Christians infer that Hell is the "*blackness of darkness forever.*"

Is Hell a hopeless place? If it exists, it probably is. However, one reference in the *New Testament* seems to say that Christ went on a mission to save the "*spirits*" there. See *I Peter* 3:18-20 and 4:6. There was a tradition in the early church that Judas's suicide (*Matthew* 27:2-10 and possibly *Acts* 1:18-19) was based on his hope that although a just God would send him to Hell, a God that was also merciful would have Jesus there too as a last chance to save souls. See Frederick Buechner, *Peculiar Treasures A Biblical Who's Who* with illustrations by Katherine G. Buechner (San Francisco: HarperSanFrancisco *A Division of* HarperCollins*Publishers*, 1979) 93.

Note: American presidents have referred to Hell. During a time in 1862 when his party was suffering political defeat, the Union armies had had large losses and England seemed close to recognizing the Confederacy, Abraham Lincoln said, "if there is a worse place than Hell, I am in it." See Rich Lowery, *Portland Oregonian* December 31, 2008. When Herbert Hoover was president in 1929 his wife was criticized in the southern press and elsewhere for inviting a black woman to an official White House function. The woman was the wife of a congressman. Hoover told his wife that one of the advantages of being an orthodox Christian was "that it included a hot hell" adding that her critics would find "special facilities in the world to come." See Richard Norton Smith 111. In 1960 former President Harry Truman told Southerners that if they voted for Richard Nixon for President over John F. Kennedy, they deserved to go to Hell. Nixon protested Truman's language. JFK said he would tell Truman "that our side" should "try to refrain from raising the religious issue." See Boller 300. JFK, the first (and so far only) Roman Catholic President (the current Vice-President Joseph Biden is also Catholic) wore his religion lightly. A writer once told one of JFK's sisters that he wanted to write a book about JFK's personal religion. Her reply: "That will be a very short book." See Meacham, *American Gospel* 182. JFK was once asked: "What kind of Catholic are you?" He answered: "I go to church on Sundays." See Pietrusza, *1960 LBJ vs. JFK vs. Nixon: The Epic Campaign That Forged Three Presidencies* 258. Two authors have written: "Like so many presidents, Kennedy and Nixon were raised by devout mothers who tried, with mixed success, to shape their sons's spiritual lives." See Gibbs and Duffy 79.

I grew up in a church going family. The two churches that were most prominent in my family were the First Baptist Church of Alameda California and the First Baptist Church of Santa Clara California. I attended these churches from age six through 22 (1957 -74). Our doctrines included original sin and the need to accept Christ as one's savior but I don't recall a single sermon about Hell in the terms described above. I took these references from a tract produced by The Gospel Tract and Bible Society, PO Box 700, Moundridge Kansas 67107. The tract's caption indicates that it was produced by the Church of God in Christ, Mennonite. It was given to me by a woman outside the National Zoo in Washington DC on July 26, 2009.

Note: Napoleon claimed that he had had no religion since he was nine and had heard a preacher say that his hero Julius Caesar was in Hell. See Paul Johnson, *Napoleon* (New York: Viking Published by the Penguin Group, 2002) 30. Further note: After the killing in 2011 of the terrorist leader Osama bin Laden, the majority of people in United States said bin Laden was in Hell. See *CNN* May 4, 2011.

[300] *John* 2: 10.

[301] Brent Bozell III, *TownHall.com* September 11, 2008.

[302] *I Corinthians* 13:11 reads, *"When I was a child, I spoke and thought and reasoned as a child. But when I grew up, I put away childish things."*

[303] The title is a reference to the Hebrew patriarch Joseph who was sold into slavery as recounted in *Genesis 37.*

[304] Sewall also weighed-in on an end times debate going on in his lifetime. New England Puritan minister Cotton Mather (1663-1728) predicted an end-time at various dates in the late 1600s and early 1700s. Samuel Sewall thought the year 2000 might be right. See Boyer 69-71.

[305] Hamilton, Zachary *Taylor Soldier in the White House* 289-308. Webster may have been quoting *Luke* 4:18 which in the King James Version of the *Bible* has Jesus saying at the outset of his ministry: *"The Spirit of the Lord is upon me, because he has anointed me to proclaim good news to the poor. He has sent me to proclaim liberty to the captives and recovering of sight to the blind, to set at liberty those who are oppressed."*

[306] Wills, *Head and Heart: American Christianities* 87-93, 152, 189-91.

[307] Herbert S. Parmet, *George Bush The Life of a Lone Star Yankee* (New York: a Lisa

Drew Book Scribner) 1997) 193. This is taken from *John* 8:32.

[308] Stark, *The Victory of Reason: How Christianity Led to Freedom, Western Capitalism, and Western Success* (New York: Random House, 2005) 24.

[309] *Romans* 7:19.

[310] Madison seemed to accept human sin. He once said: "[T]here is a degree of depravity in mankind which requires a certain degree of circumspection and distrust." See *PatriotPost.US Wednesday Chronicle* Vol. 09 No. 37 September 16, 2009. He was educated at Princeton, then an evangelical institution. In 1821 (at age 70) he referred to the "genius and courage of Luther." In 1832 (at age 81) he referred to Christianity as the "best & purest" religion." See Waldman 95ff, 99. Here is Madison even later, in 1833: "It has been said that all Government is an evil. It would be more proper to say that the necessity of any Government is a misfortune. This necessity however exists; and the problem to be solved is, not what form of Government is perfect, but which of the forms is least imperfect." See PatriotPost.US May 15, 2009.

[311] *PatriotPost.US* April 8, 2009.

[312] I have quoted sections of Madison's and Hamilton's writing that stress the limitations. But the worth of people was also recognized by Madison in Federalist 51 when he called the legislature, elected by the people, the supreme power in a republic.

[313] The concept of checks and balances on the power of government may have come from Charles-Louis de Secondat, baron de La Brède et de Montesquieu (1689-1755) whose work greatly influenced Madison. Montesquieu also looked at government from the same perspective of human fallibility as he wrote, that "government should be set up so that no man need be afraid of another." See http://en.wikipedia.org/wiki/Charles_de_Secondat,_baron_de_Montesquieu (Accessed May 2, 2012). Alternatively it could have come from John Calvin through John Witherspoon (1723-1794) a Presbyterian leader who was president of the College of New Jersey, now Princeton, and a signer of the Declaration of Independence. In his *Institutes of the Christian Religion* which he wrote and revised starting in 1536 Calvin said: "The vice or imperfection of men therefore renders it safer and more tolerable for the government to be in the hands of many, that they may afford each other mutual assistance and admonition, and that if any one arrogate to himself more than is right, the many may act as censors and masters to restrain his ambition." See John Dillenberger and Claude Welch, *Protestant Christianity Interpreted Through its Development* (New York: Charles Scribner's Sons, 1954) 56, 146.

[314] Daniel Schorr, *Portland Oregonian* November 26, 2006 and Josiah Bunting III, *Ulysses S. Grant* The American Presidents Arthur M. Schlesinger, Jr., General Editor Times Books (New York: Henry Holt and Company, LLC, 2004) xvii.

[315] All three Synoptics include the famous account of Jesus's discussion on taxes – *Matthew* 22: 19-22; *Mark* 12:15-17; and *Luke* 20:23-26. Here is the account in *Mark*: *"But He, knowing their hypocrisy, said to them, 'Why are you testing Me? Bring Me a denarius to look at.' They brought one. And He said to them, 'Whose likeness and inscription is this?' And they said to Him, 'Caesar's.' And Jesus said to them, 'Render to Caesar the things that are Caesar's, and to God the things that are God's.'"* Note: The Roman emperor Tiberius was born in 42 BC. He reigned from 14AD – 37AD. He was a large and strong man. "It was during Tiberius's reign that Jesus Christ undertook his mission in Galilee (part of Herod Antipas's client-princedom of Galilee-Peraea), and was subsequently crucified in Jerusalem (in the Roman province of Judaea). When, according to the Evangelists, Jesus requested that a 'penny' should be brought to him, and, after asking whose image and inscription it bore, pronounced that people should 'Render to Caesar the things that are Caesar's and to God the things that are God's', the coin must have been a *denarius* bearing the portrait and titles of Tiberius." See Grant, *The Roman Emperors A Biographical Guide to the Rulers of Imperial Rome 31BC - AD 476* (New York: Barnes & Noble, 1997 Originally published 1985. The 1997 edition published by Barnes & Noble, Inc. by arrangement with Scribner, an imprint of Simon & Schuster) 24.

[316] *John* 18:36.

[317] Again, the Americans built on a concept with deep roots in Europe. Thomas More (1478-1573) went to his death rather than assent to the divorce of the Henry VIII, declaring, "I am the King's good servant, but God's first." See Patrick J. Buchanan *TownHall.Com* July 1, 2008.

[318] *PatriotPost.US* August 26, 2008.

[319] Bernard Lewis, *What Went Wrong?* (Oxford: Oxford University Press, 2002) 96-98.

[320] Hitchcock 110, 141-2.

[321] Dinesh D'Souza, *TownHall.com* December 15, 2008.

[322] Stark, *One True God: Historical Consequences of Monotheism* (Princeton and Oxford: Princeton University Press, 2001) 221.

[323] *Mark* 10:43: *"But among you it will be different. Whoever wants to be a leader among you must be your servant."* *Luke* 22:27: *"Who is more important, the one who sits at the table or the one who serves? The one who sits at the table, of course. But not here! For I am among you as one who serves."*

[324] *John 3:16: "For God loved the world so much that he gave his one and only Son, so that everyone who believes in him will not perish but have eternal life."*

[325] *Romans 5:8: "But God showed his great love for us by sending Christ to die for us while we were still sinners."*

[326] *Galatians 3:28: "There is no longer Jew or Gentile, slave or free, male and female. For you are all one in Christ Jesus."*

[327] Meacham, *American Lion: Andrew Jackson in the White House* 79.

[328] L. Michael White holds for a date of authorship of *I Thessalonians* of about 50-51 AD. See White, *From Jesus to Christianity* 172. EP Sanders suggests an earlier date, possibly as early as 41 AD. See EP Sanders, *Paul: A Brief Insight* (New York and London: Sterling,1991) 34.

[329] Akenson, *Saint Saul: A Skeleton Key to the Historical Jesus* 125 and White, *From Jesus to Christianity* 94-99. Letters written decades later and attributed to Paul emphasize living upright conventional lives: holding jobs (*II Thessalonians* 3: 10, 11), family values (*Ephesians* 5: 22-23) and church structure (*I Timothy* 3: 1-13). Other letters attributed to Paul include *Colossians, II Timothy* and *Titus. Hebrews* is not typically attributed to Paul but some have viewed it that way. In 1546, the Council of Trent, probably reacting to Martin Luther's relegation of *Hebrews* to an appendix in his German translation of the *Bible* and as non-Pauline, declared all 14 letters historically attributed to Paul to be so. See Akenson, *Saint Saul: A Skeleton Key to the Historical Jesus* 125. But the matter was not settled. In 1807 Friedrich Schleiermacher who defended the Christian faith against what he called its "cultural despisers" wrote that *I Timothy* could not have been written by Paul. In the next two centuries scholars have come to the view the six letters - *I* and *II Timothy* and *Titus, II Thessalonians, Ephesians* and *Colossians* – as "deutero-Pauline" which means that they have secondary standing in the Pauline corpus. They have used word studies and analysis of doctrine to reach this conclusion. In regard to doctrine, the teachings about women, the nature of salvation and end times seem to be more the product of second century debates than Paul's thinking. See Ehrman, *Forged Writing in the Name of God Why the Bible's Authors Are Not Who We Think They Are* (New York: HarperOne *An Imprint of* HarperCollins *Publishers*: 2011) 92ff. When one considers these fourteen letters attributed to Paul and the fact that *Acts* is largely written *about* Paul - one begins to see the influence of the Pauline version of Christianity on the *Bible*. See Ehrman, *God's Problem: How the Bible Fails to Answer Our Most Important Question - Why We Suffer* (New York: HarperOne a Division of HarperCollins Publishers, 2008) 236. Additional note: There is some scholarly support

that can be cited in favor of Paul writing *II Thessalonians* and *Colossians* See Ehrman, *The New Testament* 378-81.

330 *Romans* 13: 5-6.

331 *I Corinthians* 14: 26-40.

332 *Romans* 6: 1-2.

333 Borg, *Evolution of the Word The New Testament in the Order the Books Were Written* 17.

334 The reasoning here is that according to *Matthew* 8 Jesus was in Capernaum and then crossed over the sea on a trip in verses 23 through 34 and then apparently returned in *Matthew* 9:1 which reports that Jesus *"came to His own city."*

335 *Matthew* 17:24-27.

336 *Matthew* 2:23.

337 *Mark* 1:24 and *Luke* 4:34.

338 *Mark* 10:47 and - probably, although Bartimaeus is not named - *Luke* 18:37.

339 *Matthew* 26:71 and *Mark* 14:67. The same girl made no such reference according to *Luke.* See *Luke* 22:56.

340 *John* 18: 5-7 - They answered *"Jesus of Nazareth,"* then fell to the ground when Jesus identified himself and he had to ask a second time.

341 According to *John* 19:19, Pilate wrote an inscription that was placed on the cross that read: *"JESUS THE NAZARENE, THE KING OF THE JEWS."* The other Gospels all note the sign but do not attribute it to Pilate and recall different wordings:

   • *Mark* 15:26 - *"THE KING OF THE JEWS"*
   • *Matthew* 27:37 - *"THIS IS JESUS THE KING OF THE JEWS"*
   • *Luke* 23:38 - *"THIS IS THE KING OF THE JEWS"*

342 *Mark* 16:6 – The other Gospels have other greeters and no mention of Nazareth.

343 *Luke* 24:19.

344 *Acts* 2:22.

345 *Acts* 3:6: *"I have no silver or gold...but what I have, I give you. In the name of Jesus Christ the Nazarene – walk."*

[346] *Acts* 4:10.

[347] *Acts* 6:14.

[348] *Acts* 22:8 in response to his question, *"who are you, Lord?"*

[349] *Acts* 26:9.

[350] Richard Bauckham suggests that the move to Capernaum may have been because of a rift with his family in Nazareth. See Bauckham, *Jude and the Relatives of Jesus in the Early Church* 46-7.

[351] Edgar J. Goodspeed, *A Life of Jesus* (New York, Evanston, and London: Harper & Row, Publishers, Harper Torchbook The Cloister Library, 1950) 45.

[352] Bauckham, *Jude and the Relatives of Jesus in the Early Church* 46-7.

[353] "... (T)he synagogue where Jesus is said to have taught has been found at Capernaum, ... Remains of its foundation have been found below the present ruins of a later Roman synagogue." See Amy D. Bernstein "Decoding Christianity" in *US News and World Report Special Edition* "Mysteries of Faith Secrets of Christianity" 2010 p. 10.

[354] Diaa Hadid, *Associated Press* December 21, 2009.

[355] Ehrman, *Did Jesus Exist? The Historical Argument for Jesus of Nazareth* (New York: HarperOne *An Imprint of* HarperCollins*Publisher*, Kindle Edition, 2012) 295.

[356] Johnson, *Jesus A Biography From a Believer* 15.

[357] Matthew may not have known that Joseph and Mary were originally from Nazareth although Luke clearly does. Matthew has them going there after their stay in Egypt to avoid the violence in Judaea: *"So Joseph got up, took the Child and His mother, and came into the land of Israel. But when he heard that Archelaus was reigning over Judea in place of his father Herod, he was afraid to go there. Then after being warned by God in a dream, he left for the regions of Galilee, and came and lived in a city called Nazareth. This was to fulfill what was spoken through the prophets: 'He shall be called a Nazarene.'"* (Matthew 2:21-23.) Note: There is something rather strange in this linkage to *"the prophets"* since Matthew does not refer to any particular scripture. Luke has them leaving Nazareth before Jesus's birth (*Luke* 2:4-5) and then returning to *"their own city of Nazareth"* after he was born (*Luke* 2:39). See Pope Benedict XVI, *Jesus of Nazareth The Infancy Narratives* 65,66, 115.

[358] *Matthew* is the favorite Gospel of most Americans followed by *John*, then *Luke*, then *Mark*. See Prothero, *Religious Literacy What Every American Needs*

to Know and Doesn't 151. In the fourth century, St. Augustine called *Mark* the "drudge and condenser" of *Matthew*. In Gary Wills's words, *Matthew* "has been the most influential Gospel, the one most used in Christian instruction, the one put first in the canonical collection." See Wills, *What the Gospels Meant* (New York: Viking Published by the Penguin Group, 2008) 11,107. Note: *Matthew* is the most Jewish of the Gospels. See Grant, *Jesus: An Historian's Review of the Gospels* 186.

[359] Peter and possibly his point of view suffuse this Gospel. He is mentioned as the first disciple called (*Mark* 1:16). He is also in *Mark* 16:7 the last of the Twelve mentioned when, after the resurrection, a young man tells the women at the Empty Tomb: "..go, tell His (Jesus's) disciples and **Peter**, He is going ahead of you to Galilee; there you will see Him, just as He told you." (Emphasis added). See also *Acts* 12:12-17 where Peter went to the house in Jerusalem of Mark's mother and *I Peter* 5:13 where Mark is linked with Peter.

[360] It is conceivable, however, that he contributed to the development of this Gospel. There are certain passages – for example the first two chapters - which appear only in *Mathew*. These possibly were derived from the tax man who was Matthew of the Twelve. If that is the case, then the Gospel might have been named after its best-known contributor. See Witherington, *New Testament History A Narrative Account* Location 7403.

[361] According to the Catholic Church Matthew is the patron saint of accountants and security guards. His feast day is September 21. See Sandoval 10.

[362] Buechner 109-10. From these sources – Peter, Barnabas, the Christians who met at his mother's house and, conceivably as an eye witness in Gethsemane - Mark could have gathered the materials for *Mark*. See Witherington, *New Testament History A Narrative Account* Location 7148.

[363] White, *From Jesus to Christianity* 94-99.

[364] White, *From Jesus to Christianity* 94-99. Note: St. Augustine held for a chronological order of *Matthew-Mark-Luke*, a view that prevailed for centuries and still has supporters. See Meier, *The Vision of Matthew: Christ, Church and Morality in the First Gospel* 10.

[365] In *Mark* some key words have been left in the Aramaic, the language Jesus spoke, and the author who wrote the Gospel in Greek had to translate, showing an oral or written tradition behind his work:

- *Mark* 5 - In the account of the healing of Jairus's daughter, verse 41 reads: *"Taking the child by the hand, He said to her, 'Talitha kum!' (which translated means, 'Little girl, I say to you, get up!'").*
- *Mark* 15 – In the account of Jesus on the cross, verse 34 reads: *"At the ninth hour Jesus cried out with a loud voice, 'ELOI, ELOI, LAMA SABACHTHANI?' which is translated, 'MY GOD, MY GOD, WHY HAVE YOU FORSAKEN ME?'"*

See Ehrman, *Did Jesus Exist? The Historical Argument for Jesus of Nazareth* 87ff.

[366] *Luke* 1: 1-4.

[367] *John* 21: 25.

[368] Justo L. Gonzales, *The Story of Christianity Volume 1 The Early Church to the Dawn of the Reformation* 213ff.

[369] *Mark* 4:35-41. Matthew and Luke writing later make no mention of other boats. See *Matthew* 8:23-27 and *Luke* 8:22-25. Note: As to more detail, all three of these Gospels include in the story that Jesus was initially asleep as the storm grew but only *Mark* records that he was asleep on a *"cushion."* Additional note: All of the Gospels report that Jesus had the power to calm storms and one can take literal and/or metaphorical lessons from these stories. The details occasionally vary and the reactions of the disciples also vary between instances. Here is the breakdown:

On at least one occasion, Jesus was asleep in the boat, the disciples awakened him and he quieted the storm:

- *Matthew* 8:23-27 – Reaction: the disciples were amazed.
- *Mark* 4:35-41 – Reaction: they were afraid.
- *Luke* 8:22-25 – Reaction: they were amazed and afraid.

On another occasion, Jesus walked on the water to get to the boat and he quieted the storm:

- *Matthew* 14: 22-33. Reaction: In this account, Peter attempts the same thing but his faith fails and Jesus rescues him. When it was over the disciples worshipped Jesus and said: *"You are certainly God's son!"* The account in *Matthew* is a redaction of *Mark*. It bolsters Peter as the leader of the apostles.
- *Mark* 6: 47-52 Reaction: They were afraid because they did not recognize Jesus and he was going to pass by the boat. When they figured out it was Jesus and he got into the boat they were astonished but did not learn anything.
- *John* 6: 16-21. Reaction: They were afraid.

Note: In 1986 a severe drought in the Sea of Galilee revealed an ancient 27-foot long boat dating to approximately Jesus's time. It showed that boats big enough to accommodate Jesus and his twelve apostles were present in the *New Testament* era. See "Jesus and the Apostles Christianity's Early Rise," *National Geographic,* 2014 62.

[370] See Wilson, Jesus *A Life* 68-9. We infer that she was hungry. *Mark* 5: 43 reports that Jesus *"said that something should be given her to eat." Luke* 8:55 reports something substantively the same: *"He gave orders for something to be given her to eat."* The account in *Matthew* 9:18-26 makes no mention of food.

[371] *Acts,* written by a Gospel writer, also has mundane details. Here are two examples:

- *Acts* 18: 12-16 summarizes a short trial of Paul before Gallio, the Roman proconsul in the area of Corinth. Gallio dismissed the charges. Then verse 17 reads as follows: *"And they all took hold of Sosthenes, the leader of the synagogue, and began beating him in front of the judgment seat. But Gallio was not concerned about any of these things."* Who was Sosthenes and why was he seized before Gallio? The name is mentioned only one other time in the *Bible* in *I Corinthians* 1:1 as an author with Paul of that letter but this might or might not be the same person. Sosthenes may be the same person as the Crispus mentioned in *Acts* 18:8 because in both instances they are called *"the leader of the synagogue."*
- In *Acts* 21 Paul was attacked in a Temple riot. When a Roman military contingent intervened, he was permitted to address the mob as recorded in *Acts* 22. The next day the commander assembled some of the religious leaders to hear Paul more formally as recorded in *Acts* 23. However, that broke down into acrimony as well and the military again had to extricate Paul. The following day – as also recorded later in chapter 23 – Paul's enemies conspired to kidnap him from the Roman authorities. This in turn was foiled as Paul's nephew learned of the plot and informed the commander who ordered 200 soldiers to escort Paul out of Jerusalem from which he went on to be tried in a safer location in a non-religious setting. The scripture records that the nearby town where Paul and his military escort spent the first night out of Jerusalem was called Antipatris (*Acts* 23:31), the only time this place is mentioned in scripture Antipatris was built by Herod the Great and named after his father, Antipater. See Browning Location 542. Note: Earlier in this episode, when Paul was first rescued by the soldiers he was taken to the barracks (*Acts* 21: 34, 37). Although it is

not mentioned in scripture, these barracks were also built by Herod the Great and named for the Roman general Mark Antony (83BC – 30BC). See Browning Location 555 and Johnson, *Jesus A Biography From a Believer* 14. Paul's unnamed nephew accounts for two verses of Holy Scripture. They constitute his report to the Roman military officer: "*The Jews have agreed to ask you to bring Paul down tomorrow to the Council, as though they were going to inquire somewhat more thoroughly about him. So do not listen to them, for more than forty of them are lying in wait for him who have bound themselves under a curse not to eat or drink until they slay him; and now they are ready and waiting for the promise from you.*" (*Acts 23*: 20-21)

[372] For example, it was noted earlier that the writers of the Synoptics place the crucifixion on the day before the Passover but John places it on the Passover to emphasize that he saw Jesus as the Passover lamb. Since all four Gospels acknowledge that the crucifixion occurred on a Friday (*Matthew* 27:62; *Mark* 15:42; *Luke* 23:54; *John* 19:31, 42) this difference could shift the events of that week by a year if one examines whether Passover was on Thursday (the Synoptics) or Friday (*John*). Is this just a mistake? Michael L. White comes down this way: "We may start by assuming with recent *New Testament* scholarship that the *Gospel of John* shows direct awareness of the Synoptics, especially *Mark* and/or *Luke*. In other words, we may also assume that the audience of the *Gospel of John* knew the synoptic Passion narrative in which the Last Supper was the Passover meal. Rather than an alternative history, however, the *Gospel of John* has given a creative retelling of the story that redeploys the Passover symbolism in a new way....Neither is it the case that the Johannine shift constitutes a wildly new theological idea. We have other, earlier allusions to Passover symbolism in *1 Corinthians* 5:7 ('*For our paschal lamb, Christ, has been sacrificed*'), but with no reference to a historical event. The Johannine story has simply 'narrativized' this long-standing theological interpretation by turning it into a dramatic retelling of the events surrounding the crucifixion of Jesus." See L. Michael White *Scripting Jesus The Gospels in Rewrite* (New York: HarperCollins e-books, 2010) Locations 490, 499, 542, 551. Note: "In a favorite metaphor of the church fathers, the Gospels are a river in which an elephant can drown and a gnat can swim." See Jaroslav Pelikan, *Jesus Through The Centuries: His Place in the History of Culture* (New York, Cambridge, Philadelphia, San Francisco, Washington, London, Mexico City, Sao Paulo, Singapore, Sydney: Harper & Row, Publishers Reprinted by arrangement with Yale University Press, 1985. First Perennial Library edition published 1987) 5.

373 Wilson, *Jesus A Life* 43.

374 *Mark* 15:2.

375 *Mark* 15:5.

376 *Mark* 15:34.

377 *Luke* 23:3.

378 *Luke* 23: 28-31.

379 *Luke* 23:34. In 1960 Lyndon Johnson running for Vice President was confronted with aggressive demonstrators at a Dallas hotel. The next day he told a crowd: "I looked at them and thought of what the Good Book says: 'Forgive them Lord, for they know not what they do.'" See Pietrusza, *1960 LBJ vs. JFK vs. Nixon: The Epic Campaign That Forged Three Presidencies* 387.

380 *Luke* 23:43.

381 *Luke* 23: 46.

382 *Luke* 22:44.

383 *Mark* 14: 3-9. Some argue that the Dead Sea Scrolls found in 1947 present evidence that Bethany was a leper colony. See Browning Location 1049.

384 *Matthew* 26:6-13.

385 *Luke* 7:36-50.

386 *John* 12: 1-8. This home may have been where Jesus stayed in the evenings during the last week of his life.

387 *John* had some precedent for this. Both Mark and Matthew, while not overtly linking Judas to this event, immediately follow-up their story with an account of Judas approaching the authorities to make a deal to betray Jesus. See *Mark* 14:10-11 and *Matthew* 26:14-15.

388 It is important to distinguish between two Caesareas. This city, Caesarea Philippi, is in modern Israel, the area now known as the Golan Heights. Herod the Great had built a temple there dedicated to Caesar Augustus. The city previously had been named Panion and was re-named in honor of the emperor by Herod's son, Philip the tetrarch, who vainly added "Philippi" to avoid confusion with the other Caesarea. The other Caesarea was built on the Mediterranean coast also by Herod the Great to honor Caesar Augustus. It is also in modern Israel. Caesarea was the residence of Roman prefects. Its population included Jews and Gentiles. Christianity was brought there by Philip (*Acts* 8:40; 21:8). Peter first became aware of the equality of Jews

and Gentiles in the Church by being summoned to Caesarea by Cornelius, a centurion and a Gentile God-fearer. (*Acts* 10:1-2ff). Paul was taken to Caesarea for trial (*Acts* 23:23). See Browning Location 1343-47.

[389] Jesus often called himself the "Son of Man" and it is frequently noted that the writer of the *Old Testament Book of Daniel* used that term to describe an end times figure. Some think that by applying the phrase to himself Jesus stressed both his role in the end times and also his humanness. See Witherington, *New Testament History A Narrative Account* Location 2215ff. I regret it if I have misstated Witherington's point of view and it should be acknowledged that he states that the Son of Man in *Daniel* is "in a particular eschatological role as the representative standing between Israel and God. The representative is to be given a dominion, or kingdom by God - indeed, an everlasting dominion." It is hard to understand this as a description of any kind of ordinary human. Nevertheless, Witherington, to emphasize, sees the term as also denoting humanness.

Here is an alternative view on the meaning of the Son of Man.

Although James Carroll acknowledges that the early Church understood the term Son of Man as an affirmation of humanness and that a great deal of historical Jesus scholarship agrees, he dissents.

Carroll also goes to *Daniel,* writing of that book: "It looks forward… to a Messiah who transcends David, transforms the hope of Israel—and is somehow divine. Daniel's ecstatic rendition of this personage is quite explicit." Carroll then quotes *Daniel* 7:13:

"I kept looking in the night visions,
And behold, with the clouds of heaven
*One like a **Son of Man** was coming,*
And He came up to the Ancient of Days
And was presented before Him." (Emphasis added)

Then he concludes: "The 'Ancient of Days' referred to here is the enthroned figure, aged and sovereign, who becomes lodged in the religious imagination of Jews, and ultimately Christians, as the Father in heaven, the High God. He will one day be pictured paradigmatically by Michelangelo on the ceiling of the Sistine Chapel—flowing white beard and all. But the lesser 'Son of Man,' also showing up in this vision, has a divine character, too."

Carroll, then, ties Jesus's divinity, not his humanity, to the term Son of Man. See: James Carroll, *Christ, Actually The Son of God for the Secular Age* (New York: Viking Published by the Penguin Group, 2014) 82, 99. I regret it if I have misstated Carroll's point of view.

Does the term Son of Man denote divinity or humanness? This matter is too deep for a non-specialist like me and I will leave it as a controversy in Christology except to give my view that with very little effort one could find a significant overlap between the views of Ben Witherington III and James Carroll on this topic.

390 *Mark* 8: 27-30 with *Matthew* 16:13-20. Regarding the passage in *Matthew*: "Few passages from the *Bible* have been more controversial than this one, especially since the Reformation, yet it comes into play in the early Church only gradually. It is first cited in the third century by Stephen, bishop of Rome (254-257), in his dispute with Cyprian over rebaptism." See Wilken, *The First Thousand Years A Global History of Christianity)* 164-5. See also JND Kelly *The Oxford Dictionary of Popes* (Oxford and New York: Oxford University Press, 1986) 13-21.

Additional note: The concept of Saint Peter being the gatekeeper at the "Pearly Gates" stems from Jesus giving him the "keys to the kingdom" in *Matthew* 16:19: *"And I will give you the keys of the kingdom of Heaven. Whatever you forbid on earth will be forbidden in heaven, and whatever you permit on earth will be permitted in heaven."* See Sandoval 144.

391 *Mark* 8:31-33 and *Matthew* 16: 21-23.

392 *Matthew* 17:24-27.

393 See *Mark* 9:30-32 and 9:33-37 and *Luke* 43-45 and *Luke* 9:46-48.

394 *Matthew* 17:27.

395 I owe this thought to Meier, *The Vision of Matthew: Christ, Church and Morality in the First Gospel* 125-27 and regret it if I have misstated Meier's point of view. Meier draws other points from the Temple Tax story. These include:

- Jesus showing his authority to the church.
- The special position of Peter in the church.
- The relationship of the church to Judaism - it is free but it does not have license and it should not give offense.
- The opposition of Jewish officials.

396 *Matthew* 26:57-27:10, *Mark* 14:53-72, *Luke* 22:54-71 and *Acts* 1:18-19.

397 *Matthew* 22; 1-14.

398 *Luke* 14:11.

399 *Luke* 14:23.

[400] Paul Johnson, A History *of Christianity* 116 and Marty 79-80. Here is another view: Augustine only reluctantly accepted forced conversions under some pressure from the warlike Christian Donatists in his area of North Africa. Donatism had risen up there during a time of persecution in the early 300s. The Donatists held after the persecution ended that Christian leaders who had complied with governmental dictates to turn in copies of the scripture lost their authority to consecrate bishops. Although condemned by Rome, the Donatists persisted in North Africa into the 500s and possibly until the Islamic invasion. Augustine reasoned that even if the first generation was forced, the second might go to the faith sincerely. He justified mass baptisms in the *City of God* arguing that the Church was not elite but a place where wheat and weeds grew together until the harvest. He also came to develop his doctrine of a just war in the context of the struggles with the Donatists. See Hitchcock 59 and Wilken, *The First Thousand Years A Global History of Christianity)* 187-89 and Justo L. Gonzales *A History of Christian Thought From Augustine to the Eve of the Reformation* Volume II Revised Edition Locations 332ff, 374. Also, in New Spain in the 1500s the Dominican Bartolome de las Casas explicitly rejected this argument that coercion was justified. See MacCulloch 692-3.

[401] Burton L Mack, *Who Wrote The New Testament? The Making of the Christian Myth* (New York: HarperCollins and HarperSanFrancisco, 1995 First HarperCollins paperback, 1996) 2.

[402] Did the writer of the *John* have access to the Synoptics? Ehrman says that it is a difficult question but comes down on the negative because *John* is so different that the Synoptics. However, Ehrman thinks that the writer of *John* at least knew some of the same traditions that the Synoptic writers did, especially about the death of Jesus. See Ehrman, *The New Testament* 163-4. Borg and Crossan and Bauckham all think that the writer of *John* did have access to at least some of the Synoptics. See Borg and Crossan *The Last Week: What the Gospels Really Teach About Jesus's Final Days in Jerusalem* IX and Bauckham, *Jesus and the Eyewitnesses: The Gospels and Eyewitness Testimony* Location 6967. I regret it if I have misstated Ehrman's, Borg's, Crossan's or Bauckham's points of view.

[403] During his ministry, Jesus accompanied by Peter, James and John climbed a mountain to pray. Jesus was transfigured: his face and his clothes glowed. The *Old Testament* figures of Moses and Elijah appeared and conversed with Jesus. See *Mark* 9: 2-13, *Matthew* 17: 1-13 and *Luke* 9: 28-36. Note: *Mark* and *Matthew* record that Jesus was transfigured as Peter, James and John watched but *Luke* records that they were asleep while he was being transfigured.

Note: All the Synoptics place the Transfiguration right after an announcement by Jesus that is very similar:

- *Mark 9:1: "I tell you the truth, some standing here right now will not die before they see the kingdom of God arrive in great power!"*
- *Matthew 16:28: "And I tell you the truth, some standing here right now will not die before they see the Son of Man coming in his Kingdom."*
- *Luke 9:27: "I tell you the truth, some standing here right now will not die before they see the kingdom of God."*

Mark and *Matthew* then time the Transfiguration six days later. *Luke* times it *"about eight days later."*

[404] The first chapter of *John*, the fourteenth verse, reads: *"…we have seen his glory, the glory as of a father's only son, full of grace and truth."*

[405] Wilson, *Jesus A Life* 156. As I will repeat, that is the specific reason for his miracles as reported in *John* 20:30-31.

[406] *Mark* 2: 23-27.

[407] *I Samuel* 21: 1-6.

[408] Here is another redaction: when Matthew and Luke wrote up this story they left out the erroneous reference to Abiathar. See *Matthew* 12:1-4 and *Luke* 6:1-5.

[409] *I Samuel* 13: 13-14 reads: *"Samuel said to Saul, 'You have acted foolishly; you have not kept the commandment of the LORD your God, which He commanded you, for now the LORD would have established your kingdom over Israel forever. But now your kingdom shall not endure. The LORD has sought out for Himself **a man after His own heart**, and the LORD has appointed him as ruler over His people, because you have not kept what the LORD commanded you.'"* (*Emphasis added*).

[410] *I Samuel* 16:1-13. Verse 13 reads: *"Then Samuel took the horn of oil and anointed him in the midst of his brothers; and the Spirit of the LORD came mightily upon David from that day forward…"* This is referred to in *Psalm* 89:20: *"I have found David My servant; With My holy oil I have anointed him."*

[411] One example is in *I Samuel* 20:1 in which Saul is still in power and David is on the run and comes to Saul's son: *"Then David fled from Naioth in Ramah, and came and said to Jonathan, 'What have I done? What is my iniquity? And what is my sin before your father, that he is seeking my life?'"*

[412] Wright, *Simply Jesus A New Vision of Who He Was, What He Did, And Why He Matters* 42. I regret it if I have misstated Wright's point of view.

[413] *Mark* contains "immediately" seventeen times. *Matthew, Luke* and *John* which are longer books contain it six, thirteen and five times.

[414] Ehrman, *Jesus Interrupted: Revealing the Hidden Contradictions in the Bible (And Why We Don't Know Them)* 42.

[415] The first Passover is mentioned in *John* 2:13 and 2:23. It is in that time that *John* mentions the cleansing of the Temple. *John* notes that Jesus gained converts because they saw the miracles that he performed but he does not list those miracles. The second Passover is mentioned in *John* 6:4 and is in the context of Jesus feeding five thousand up in Galilee. The third Passover is mentioned in *John* 11:55 and introduces the last week of Jesus's life.

[416] Tabor, *The Jesus Dynasty* 138ff.

[417] Eusebius Book III Chapter 24. See also See Bauckham, *Jesus and the Eyewitnesses: The Gospels and Eyewitness Testimony* Location 7243.

[418] I use the words "Lord's Supper" to be synonymous with Eucharist.

[419] *John* 20:30-31.

[420] *Mark* 5: 21-43.

[421] *John* 11:1-44.

[422] In about the year 200 Clement of Alexandria described *John* as a "spiritual gospel." He thought that John knew that the historical facts "had been made clear in the [prior] Gospels..." See Borg *Evolution of the Word The New Testament in the Order the Books Were Written* 303 and White, *Scripting Jesus The Gospels in Rewrite* Location 10356ff..

[423] Jesus may have distinguished the feeding of the multitudes from the other signs and made the point that for at least some people the signs were not enough. See *John* 6:26: "*I tell you the truth, you want to be with me because I fed you, not because you understood the miraculous signs.*"

[424] This story of healing involved a pool in Jerusalem named Siloam. As with the Bethesda pool in *John* 5 cited earlier, modern archaeology has indentified this pool. See Browning Location 682.

[425] Ehrman, *The New Testament* 171ff.

Note: As to the early communal struggles between Jews who followed Jesus and those who did not, Donald Spoto has written:

"It is critical to recall, first of all, that the followers of Jesus were Jews for decades after his death: Jesus himself, after all, never founded a new religion —much less did he advocate defection. To be Christian meant to be a Jew who believed in Jesus, and a Christian still observed the Mosaic Law, went to the synagogue, was bound by religious practices such as fasting, prayer, the requirement of the visiting the Jerusalem temple and so forth.

"The rift between mainstream Judaism and the Christian sect within it had several causes and took a period of time to be final (from the early 50s until perhaps as late as 150), but by the middle of the second century, Christianity was seen to represent an entirely new and different religion.

"First of all, a few years after his death, the disciples and other Jews who came to believe in Jesus through their preaching began to accept Gentiles without requiring them to convert first to Judaism. Jews who did not believe in Jesus would have been understandably offended when Gentile Christians, freely mingling with Jewish-Christians, claimed to be part of the New Israel because they proclaimed faith in Jesus. In addition, there were some Jewish-Christians who formed their own local synagogues, and in some places entire synagogues of Jews came to believe in Jesus. All these were seen as encouraging disunity in Judaism and further weakening a faith already threatened by political dissent, Roman imperialism and widespread variations in belief.

"But the definitive break between Christianity and Judaism occurred as a result of two specific developments - one in Christian faith about Jesus and one in the crisis of Judaism itself.

"By the end of the first century, as the implications of the life and death and (most of all) the Resurrection of Jesus became clearer, Christians came to express their firm belief in his divinity. The community from which came the *Gospel According to John*, for example, proclaimed the fully developed faith that Jesus was both Lord (which means reigning Messiah of the universe, and this by virtue of his Resurrection) and God (by virtue of what would later, in a philosophical term, be called his 'nature'). For Jews this was apostasy, and their leaders had to react unambiguously and severely: such a Christian belief was misunderstood by Jews as affirming 'two Gods,' and this threatened the heart of Jewish monotheism ('The Lord our God is one.').

"Related to this development of Christian faith was the second factor, the crisis in Judaism. After the failure of the Jewish revolt against Rome in the 60s and the destruction of the Jewish temple on order of the Emperor in 70, it was necessary for Jewish people throughout the Empire and beyond it to describe and define themselves. With the simultaneous rise of the rabbinic movement and the gradual dominance of the Pharisees, pluralism was held suspect – and the first people to be challenged and expelled from synagogues for their unorthodox views were Jewish-Christians....

"And so Jews who came to accept him (Jesus) were banned from the synagogue. Without the protection of their identity as Jews – who had civil rights in the Roman Empire and so were excused from the duty of worshiping the gods – these expelled Christians were now exposed to Roman scrutiny and persecution. It is easy, then, to understand Christian resentment against Jews, and this attitude colored the composition of the Gospels in the last third of the first century: they are the works of disenfranchised outcasts liable to subjugation and death. This is the source of the anti-Judaic strain in the *New Testament*. On the other hand, growing Christian anti-Semitism was countered by an equally virulent Jewish anti-Christianity, as stories circulated in which Jesus of Nazareth was portrayed as a wicked, adulterous magician, the illegitimate son of an adulteress who had cohabited with a Roman Jew.

"When Constantine became emperor in the fourth century, however, Christians won political clout, and the hatred solidified on one side." See Spoto, *The Hidden Jesus A New Life* (New York: St. Martin's Griffin, 1998) 221-223.

Note: A verse in the last book of the *Bible* may evoke this early communal bitterness between Jews and followers of Jesus. *Revelation* 2:9 refers to *"a synagogue of Satan"* in Smyrna.

[426] According to *Luke* 3:23 at his baptism Jesus was *"about thirty years of age."* This would have placed his ministry in the late 20s AD.

[427] *Luke* 1:29.

[428] *Luke* 2:19 reports that she "pondered."

[429] *Luke* 2:33.

[430] *Luke* 2:49.

[431] *Luke* 2:50.Note: The truth behind this story may be a recollection that he was a very precocious youth.

[432] *Luke* 2:52.

[433] *Luke* 4:16.

[434] *Luke* 23:26 records that he was too weak to carry his own cross. *Mark* 15:44 asserts that Pilate was surprised how quickly he died.

[435] *John* 7:5.

[436] *Mark* 3:21.

[437] *Luke* 4:29.

[438] *Mark* 3:31-35. Note: The church father Tertullian who lived 160-220 viewed this section of scripture as Jesus's effort to teach the kinship of faith, not to deny family. See Stark, *Discovering God: The Origins of the Great Religions and the Evolution of Belief* 305-6.

[439] *Acts* 5:36 - Theudas is also mentioned by the ancient historian Josephus who said he led masses out to the Jordan River. Josephus called him an imposter. See White, *From Jesus to Christianity* 37.

[440] *Acts* 5:37 - Judas the Galilean is also mentioned by Josephus who said he was the "founder" of the Zealots who led rebellions after the death of Herod the Great and during the unrest of the tax census. See White, *From Jesus to Christianity* 37. His grandson later led revolutionary Jews against the Romans in the Jewish War of the late 60s. See Witherington, *New Testament History A Narrative Account* Location 6672.

[441] *Acts* 21: 38 The "Egyptian" is also mentioned by Josephus. See White, *From Jesus to Christianity* 37. The "Egyptian" insurrectionist had never been caught. An arresting Roman officer apparently thought he had him when he only had the Apostle Paul, who was, moreover, a Roman citizen. It is hard to tell in the reading of the account but the officer must have been shocked and disappointed.

[442] *Luke* 13: 1-2.

[443] There is a significant factual error in *Acts*. Luke in *Acts* 5:36-37 has Gamaliel in the 30s "remembering" Theudas who actually formed his following in the 40s. He says that "after" Theudas, Judas the Galilean was active "*in the days of the census.*" The location of Judas during the census is correct but that occurred in 6AD. See Meier, *A Marginal Jew Rethinking the Historical Jesus Vlm III Companions and Competitors* (New York, London, Toronto, Sydney, Auckland: The Anchor Bible Reference Library Doubleday a Division of Random House, Inc., 2001) 298 and as previously noted: Wilson, *Jesus A Life* 75.

[444] One interpretation of *John* 18:3-12 which describes Jesus's arrest on the Mount of Olives holds that approximately a thousand Roman soldiers were deployed. See Einhorn 133. Another reading is that John describes the arresting party as six hundred imperial soldiers. (Mark describes the party arresting Jesus as a crowd from the chief priests, scribes and elders.) See Borg

and Crossan, *The Last Week: What the Gospels Really Teach About Jesus's Final Days in Jerusalem* 124.

[445] *Matthew* 16:20, *Mark* 8:30.

[446] *John* 8:1-11. Although this is one of Jesus's most famous encounters containing a quote that has come down through the centuries – paraphrased as "he who is without sin, throw the first stone" - it a difficult passage since it does not appear in the most reliable manuscripts. As noted earlier, many consider it inauthentic. It may have been part of the oral or written traditions and picked up by a later copyist. See Van Vorst 179ff. Also, it is inserted in other parts of the *New Testament* in other manuscripts: after *John* 21:25 or after *Luke* 21:38. See Ehrman, *Misquoting Jesus The Story Behind Who Changed the Bible and Why* 63-65 and *The Reliability of the New Testament Bart D. Ehrman & Daniel B. Wallace In Dialogue* Robert B. Stewart, Editor (Minneapolis: Fortress Press, 2011) 58. Note: There is another encounter in *John* 4 with a possibly adulterous woman – one who had had five husbands and was then living with another man. Jesus was nonjudgmental. However both Jesus and Paul placed prohibitions against adultery in their summaries of the commandments (*Matthew* 19:18; *Mark* 10:19; *Luke* 18:20 and *Romans* 13:9.)

The stance of the early Christian communities against adultery was actually a stand for women primarily because the prohibition covered not only the unfaithful wife but also the unfaithful husband. The latter was a relatively novel idea in the Roman world. See Woods 214.

[447] *Leviticus* 20:10.

[448] Jesus, after all, went to parties at:

- Matthew's house - *Matthew* 9:9-13.
- Zacchaeus's house - *Luke* 19: 1-10.

[449] Meier, *A Marginal Jew Rethinking the Historical Jesus Vlm III Companions and Competitors* 79-80.

[450] These first century critics of Jesus were, of course, the same who found John the Baptist too ascetic. See Meier, *The Vision of Matthew: Christ, Church and Morality in the First Gospel* 76-7.

[451] The Essenes were a sect living in Israel at the time of Jesus. They were devoted to asceticism and ritual purity. They withdrew from the cities. Although they are not mentioned in the *Bible* we know about them from the

writings of Josephus and the Dead Sea Scrolls found in 1947. See Ehrman, *Did Jesus Exist? The Historical Argument for Jesus of Nazareth 279-80.*

[452] Wilson, *Jesus A Life* 157-8.

[453] *Luke* 4:31-2.

[454] The Synoptics report that the Roman soldiers gambled with dice for the clothes - *Matthew* 27:35; *Mark* 15: 24 and *Luke* 23:34. The Fourth Gospel simply says that the soldiers divided Jesus's clothes among themselves and adds the detail that there were four Roman soldiers present (*John* 19:23).

[455] *Luke* 2:41 reads: *"Now His parents went to Jerusalem every year at the Feast of the Passover."* This showed a high level of piety on the part of Joseph and Mary. The names that they chose for their sons implies the same: James/Jacob (the patriarch), and three of the names of the patriarch's sons: Joses/Joseph, Judas/Judah, Simon/Simeon. (*Mark* 6:3). See James DG Dunn *Did the First Christians Worship Jesus? The New Testament Evidence* (London: Society for Promoting Christian Knowledge; Louisville, KY: Westminster John Knox Press, Kindle Edition, 2010) 94.

[456] *Matthew* 8:19; 9:11; 12:38; 17:24; 19:16, 22:16; 22:24; 22:36; 26:16; *Mark* 4:38; 5:35; 9:17; 9:38; 10:17; 10:20; 10:35; 12:14; 12:19; 12:32; 13:1; 14:14; *Luke* 3:12; 7:40; 8:49; 9:38; 10:25; 11:45; 12:13; 18:18; 19:39; 20:21; 20:28; 20:39; 21:7; 22:11; *John* 8:4; 11:28; 13:13; 13:14; 20:16.

[457] *John* 1:38; 1:49; 3:2; 3:26; 6:25.

[458] *Luke* 4:16-20.

[459] *Mark* 1:19-20 reads: *"Going on a little farther, He saw James the son of Zebedee, and John his brother, who were also in the boat mending the nets. Immediately He called them; and they left their father Zebedee in the boat with the hired servants."*

[460] *Luke* 5:10 refers to Peter's amazement at one of Jesus's miracles and reads in part: *"His partners, James and John, the sons of Zebedee, were also amazed...."*

[461] *John* 1:44. Bethsaida was in a Gentile-dominated area and Peter may well have grown up bilingual, speaking Aramaic and Greek. (The Apostle Philip was also from Bethsaida and he apparently spoke Greek according to *John* 12:20-21.) See Bauckham, *Jesus and the Eyewitnesses: The Gospels and Eyewitness Testimony* Location 3269.

[462] *Matthew* 8:5-14, *Mark* 1:21-29 and *Luke* 4:31-38. There is a site today in Capernaum which is reputed to be the house where Peter lived. It is a Byzantine church built over a first-century dwelling. See Tabor, *Paul and Jesus How*

the Apostle Transformed Christianity (New York, London, Toronto, Sydney, New Delhi: Simon and Schuster, 2012 Location 3483. Note: According to *Galatians* 1:18-19, Peter may also have had a house in Jerusalem. In those verses Paul reports that he stayed with Peter in Jerusalem for two weeks and saw no other apostle, except James, the brother of Jesus.

463 *Matthew* 27:57.

464 *Luke* 8:3.

465 *Mark* 5: 21-43 and *Luke* 8:40-56.

466 *Luke* 19:1-10.

467 Browning Location 888.

468 Stark, *The Triumph of Christianity How the Jesus Movement Became the World's Largest Religion* 89. I regret it if I have misstated Stark's point of view.

469 I owe this thought to Tabor, *The Jesus Dynasty* 87 and regret if I have misstated Tabor's view.

470 *Luke* 10: 1. Note: Some ancient manuscripts record that seventy-two disciples were sent out.

471 Wright, *Simply Jesus A New Vision of Who He Was, What He Did, And Why He Matters* 85. It is often noted that the Jewish people were nearly destroyed in 70 AD by the Romans and in the Second World War by the Nazis. It is sometimes overlooked that ten of the twelve Jewish tribes were destroyed seven centuries before Christ by the Assyrians. There are legends and mysteries surrounding the fate of these ten tribes. Many centuries later some thought that these lost Hebrews might be the ancestors of the American Indians. In the early 1800s as the Lewis and Clark expedition to explore the American West was setting up, a question written for them by Benjamin Rush at the request of President Thomas Jefferson was: "What [is the] affinity between their [the Indians's] religious Ceremonies & those of the Jews?" See Charles Krauthammer *Things That Matter Three Decades of Passions, Pastimes and Politics* (New York: Crown Forum an imprint of the Crown Publishing Group, a division of Random House LLC, a Penguin Random House Company, Kindle Edition, 2013) Location 3618. Certain tiny fringe groups in Israel claim to be descendants of one or more of these ten lost tribes. See Joshua Muravchik, *Liberal Oasis The Truth About Israel*, Kindle Edition, 2014 Location 467ff.

472 *Matthew* 26:20-29 and *Mark* 14: 12-26. *Luke* 22: 14-38 do not mention that all twelve were there but that is a reasonable inference since verse 14 reports that "the Apostles" were there.

[473] The British missionary to China, Hudson Taylor (1832 – 1905), popularized the phrase "The Great Commission" to characterize Jesus Christ's call in *Matthew* 28:19-20: "*Go therefore and make disciples of all the nations, baptizing them in the name of the Father and the Son and the Holy Spirit, teaching them to observe all that I commanded you; and lo, I am with you always, even to the end of the age.*" See Jenkins, *The Next Christendom The Coming of Global Christianity* Third Edition (Oxford Oxford University Press, Kindle Edition, 2011) 46.

[474] *Matthew* 28:16-20.

[475] *Luke* 24: 9, 33-52.

[476] *Acts* 1:13 describes the eleven remaining disciples going to the Upper Room. It seems to have been the same place where Jesus had the Last Supper with his disciples before the crucifixion. See *Mark* 14:12-16 and *Luke* 22: 7-13 which both have Jesus telling two of his disciples (*Luke* identifies them as Peter and John) how to find an "upper room" to prepare the Passover meal. (Note: There may have been a change in location by verse 14 of *Acts* 1 when some women including Jesus's mother Mary joined them. At that point the apostles needed to accommodate a bigger crowd which was listed as 120 people in verse 15.) A later tradition identified the house owned by Mary, the mother of John Mark, to which Peter went after a jail escape (*Acts* 12:12-17) with the Upper Room. See Justo L. Gonzales, *Acts The Gospel of the Spirit* 27, 146.

[477] *Acts* 1:13-26.

[478] *Acts* 6:2. Perhaps it was delegation of authority although as I will note later it may have been the setting up of a separate governing structure.

[479] *Revelation* 21:14. Note: Two small *New Testament* books invoke the "apostles" against heretics:

- *Jude* 17: "*But you, beloved, ought to remember the words that were spoken beforehand by the **apostles of our Lord Jesus Christ**,*" (Emphasis added).
- *II Peter* 3:2ff - "*that you should remember the words spoken beforehand by the holy prophets and the commandment of the Lord and Savior spoken by your **apostles**.*" (Emphasis added).

[480] This James is never mentioned in the *New Testament* apart from his brother John. In the listing of the twelve disciples of Jesus, the brothers James and John are always listed in the first group. Moreover, James is always listed before John except in the list in *Acts*. Why the change in order? Here are the two possible interrelated reasons: John was closer to Peter as evidenced by

them working together in Jerusalem and Samaria and James was executed relatively early in the life of the Jerusalem Church.

[481] *Matthew* 4:21; *Matthew* 10:2; *Mark* 1:19; *Mark* 3:17; *Mark* 10:35 and *Luke* 5:10. Note: It appears that their mother was also a follower of Jesus as she was at the cross according to *Matthew* 27:56.

[482] *Mark* 10: 35-37. James and John ask Jesus for a "favor" which turns out to be: "*When you sit on your glorious throne, we want to sit in places of honor next to you, one on your right and the other on your left.*" The Synoptic Gospels treat this event differently. *Mark* records James and John asking for first seats in the kingdom. According to *Matthew* chapter 20 verse 20, their mother makes this request. *Luke* omits it all together. Since Matthew and Luke undoubtedly had *Mark* before them as they wrote, this re-write raises interesting issues. Was Mark determined to downgrade some of the inner circle? Did Matthew want to cover up this embarrassment? Did Luke go even further? I owe this thought to Crossan, *The Birth of Christianity: Discovering What Happened in the Years Immediately After the Death of Jesus* 349-50 and regret it if I have misstated Crossan's point of view by the questions I pose. There is another interesting possibility that arises from this interaction as recounted in *Mark* 15:27 at the crucifixion: "*They crucified two robbers with Him, one on His right and one on His left.*" NT Wright links this section with the earlier request from James and John and he asserts that Jesus on the cross was in his glory with the spots that James and John had sought taken. See Wright, *How God Became King The Forgotten Story of the Gospels* (Sydney, Toronto, Aukland, London, New York: HarperOne *An Imprint of* HarperCollins*Publishers*, Kindle Edition, 2012) 227. I regret it if I have misstated Wright's point of view.

[483] *Mark* 1:20.

[484] *Mark* 1: 29-31.

[485] *Mark* 5: 21-43. In this rather long account, Jairus, an official at a synagogue, approaches Jesus to ask for his help with his sick daughter. Jesus starts for Jairus's house but gets interrupted. Others come with news that the girl has died and that it is too late. Jesus went on anyway to the house and he "*allowed no one to accompany Him, except Peter and James and John the brother of James.*" (*verse 37*). He healed the girl. This story is told substantially the same in *Luke* 8:40-56. It is told in abbreviated form in *Matthew* 9: 18-26. *Matthew* does not name the synagogue official or mention Peter, James and John.

[486] *Luke* 5:8-11.

[487] *Matthew* 17: 1-8; *Mark* 9: 2-8 and Luke 9: 28-36.

488 *Mark* 13:3

489 *Matthew* 26:36-46 and *Mark* 14:32-42. In both accounts Peter, James and John could not stay awake.

490 *John* 21. Note: In this instance Jesus appeared to several people, not just to an inner circle of Peter, James and John. Also, the brothers are not named but are referred to as the "sons of Zebedee."

491 *Galatians* 2:9.

492 *Acts* 3:1 – 4:31 – the scripture quoted is from *Acts* 4:18-20.

493 *Acts* 2:1-10.

494 *Mark* 3:17.

495 *Luke* 9:54.

496 *Acts* 8:14-25.

497 My reading of *John* 20-21 is that John went back to his fishing business *after* the resurrection of Jesus. *John* 20: 19-29 records two appearances of Jesus apparently to the Twelve - minus Judas and, for the first appearance, Thomas (verse 24) - apparently in Jerusalem. In *John* 21 Jesus appears to several disciples including the "sons of Zebedee" (verse 2) while they were fishing in the Sea of Galilee about a hundred miles away.

498 Bauckham *Jesus and the Eyewitnesses The Gospels as Eyewitness Testimony* Location 7049.

499 *John* 21:24 reads *"This is the disciple who is testifying to these things and wrote these things, and we know that his testimony is true."*

500 According to *John* 19: 26-27, while Jesus was on the cross, he *"saw His mother, and the disciple whom He loved standing nearby, He said to His mother, 'Woman, behold, your son!' Then He said to the disciple, 'Behold, your mother!' From that hour the disciple took her into his own household."*

501 *John* 6:66-71.

502 *Matthew* 17:1-9; *Mark* 9:2-9; *Luke* 9:28-36.

503 *Matthew* 9:18-36; *Mark* 5:21-43; *Luke* 8:40-56. As noted, Jairus is not named in *Matthew*.

504 *Matthew* 26:36-46; *Mark* 14:32-42; *Luke* 22:39-46. *John* 18:1-11. Note: "Gethsemane" is mentioned in *Matthew* and *Mark*. *John* provides the detail that it was a "garden." All four Gospels indicate that this scene was near or on the Mount of Olives. These are differences that I would put in the

"Inconsistent but Reconcilable" category described in Chapter 2. Additional note: There may have been trees in the Garden of Gethsemane as according to Josephus, the Romans cut down trees there in 70AD to build siege equipment for the attack on Jerusalem. See Special Newsweek Edition "Jesus His Life After Death" Collector's Edition Easter 2015 49.

[505] The expectation of early Christians that Christ was coming again in their lifetimes may have focused on this disciple. See Bauckham, *Jesus and the Eyewitnesses: The Gospels and Eyewitness Testimony* Location 7154-7159.

[506] Wills, *What the Gospels Meant* 190. Bauckham disagrees that the "*disciple whom Jesus loved*" was a latecomer. He asserts that the this disciple was with Jesus from the beginning of Jesus's ministry reasoning from this section and others that he was the anonymous disciple of John the Baptist who joined Jesus's group early: "*...the next day John was standing with two of his disciples, and he looked at Jesus as He walked, and said, 'Behold, the Lamb of God!' The two disciples heard him speak, and they followed Jesus. And Jesus turned and saw them following, and said to them, 'What do you seek?' They said to Him, 'Rabbi (which translated means Teacher), where are You staying?' He said to them, 'Come, and you will see.' So they came and saw where He was staying; and they stayed with Him that day, for it was about the tenth hour. One of the two who heard John speak and followed Him, was Andrew, Simon Peter's brother.*" (*John* 1:35-40). See Bauckham, *Jesus and the Eyewitnesses: The Gospels and Eyewitness Testimony* Location 6623ff.

[507] Griffith-Jones 238-40.

[508] Lazarus was ill and his sisters Mary and Martha wanted to contact Jesus. According to *John* 11:3-5: "*So the sisters sent word to Him, saying, 'Lord, behold, he whom You love is sick.' But when Jesus heard this, He said, 'This sickness is not to end in death, but for the glory of God, so that the Son of God may be glorified by it.' Now Jesus loved Martha and her sister and Lazarus.*"

I can find only one other reference to Jesus loving another individual. According to *Mark* 10:21 Jesus loved the rich young ruler – although that is not in the other Synoptic accounts of this event.

[509] *Mark* 14: 51-52 reads: "*A young man was following Him, wearing nothing but a linen sheet over his naked body; and they seized him. But he pulled free of the linen sheet and escaped naked.*"

[510] Einhorn 109-110. Here is some of the reasoning used by Einhorn and others:

- Lazarus who had apparently been resurrected from the dead by Jesus about a week earlier (*John* 11) was a wanted man according to *John* 12:10 because he was leading people to follow Jesus.

- Lazarus's identity still needed to be kept from the authorities in the time that the stories which came to be the *Gospel of Mark* were first told.

- Accordingly, the story of his resurrection was not told in *Mark*. It was natural, however, that he would have been in Gethsemane and that the police would have attempted to arrest him. It was also natural that, again, his identity was muted. But in the Jerusalem church which was pretty small and where everybody knew everybody, the story of Jesus bringing Lazarus back to life and of him being the young man in Gethsemane would have been well-known.

[511] Tradition holds that Saint John of Ephesus opposed Gnosticism, a heresy with which the early church contended. *I John* seems to be directed against it. See Justo L. Gonzales, *A History of Christian Thought From the Beginnings to the Council of Chalcedon* Volume 1 Revised Edition 132.

[512] Bauckham relies in part on second century Christian leaders Papias (Estimated 70-155) and Polycrates (abt.130-abt. 196). Neither Papias's nor Polycrates's major works have survived except in fragments quoted by others. Papias was the Bishop of Hierapolis which was a Roman province and is in modern Turkey. Papias wrote that he heard information that came from an unwritten, oral tradition of the church leaders, a "sayings" tradition that had been passed on. In his words: "And if by chance anyone who had been in attendance on the elders should come my way, I inquired about the words of the elders – [that is,] what [according to the elders] Andrew or Peter said, or Philip, or Thomas or James or John or Matthew or any other of the Lord's disciples, and whatever Aristion and the **elder John**, the Lord's disciples, were saying." (Emphasis added). (It is noteworthy that two of the Johannine letters come from "the Elder" as noted in *II John* 1 and *III John* 1.) Polycrates was Bishop of Ephesus. He is the best source that the Fourth Gospel was written in that city. Polycrates wrote of "John" in a clear reference to *John* 13:23 as "he who had leaned back on the Lord's breast."

Additionally: Bauckham offers speculation about the "*disciple whom Jesus loved*" that derives from an exegetical tradition. This goes back to the instance in which Peter and John of the Twelve were arrested in Jerusalem for preaching and then taken before the high priest. *Acts* 4:6: reads that "*Annas the high priest was there, and Caiaphas and **John** and Alexander, and all who were of high-priestly descent.*" (Emphasis added). From this there arose a tradition that the "*disciple whom Jesus loved*" was this John with a connection to the high priest. This case is bolstered by *John* 18:15 in which the high priest may indeed have known this disciple. See Bauckham, *Jesus and the Eyewitnesses: The Gospels* *and Eyewitness Testimony* Locations 420ff, 6092, 6673, 6765, 7490ff, 7707. I regret if I have I misstated Bauckham's point of view.

[513] *Mark* 6:3.

[514] *Matthew* 13:55. However, this conclusion may be contradicted in a still later account that bears some similarities that identifies Joseph. See *John* 6: 41-59 especially verse 42.

[515] *Luke* 1:48.

[516] Van Vorst 117.

[517] *Matthew* 10:5. The Samaritans were the local people who were not taken into Babylonian exile in the sixth century BC, an epochal event in Jewish history. When the exiles returned later that century and took to rebuilding the Temple, they looked down on those who had remained. These in turn resented the condescension and built a rival temple in the territory known as Samaria. The tension with the Jewish people lasted for centuries, well into Jesus's time. See MacCulloch 62.

[518] *Luke* 10: 25-37. This Gospel also contains two other stories that reach out to Samaritans: *Luke* 9:51-56 has Jesus rebuking his disciples James and John for offering to call down fire on a Samaritan village. *Luke* 17:11-19 has Jesus healing ten lepers but only one returned to thank him and he was identified as a Samaritan. The writer of *John* also recounted that Jesus visited a Samaritan village and brought about a significant conversion with *"many of the Samaritans"* saying, *"We have heard for ourselves and know that this One is indeed the Savior of the world."* See *John* 4: 1-42.

[519] Prothero, *Religious Literacy What Every American Needs to Know and Doesn't* 13. Here is an example: In 2002, Senator Jesse Helms who had been viewed by AIDS advocates as an enemy said that he would ask for an extra $500 million to prevent mother-to-child transmission of AIDS overseas, contingent on matching funds from the private sector. He wrote: "Some may say that this initiative is not consistent with some of my earlier positions..... In the end our conscience is answerable to God. Perhaps, in my 81st year, I am too mindful of soon meeting Him, but I know that, like the Samaritan traveling from Jerusalem to Jericho, we cannot turn away when we see our fellow man in need." *The New York Times* called Helms an "AIDS Savior." See *New York Times* March 26, 2002.

[520] *Luke* 15: 11-32.

[521] *Matthew* 15:14; *Luke* 6:39.

[522] *Matthew* 5:9.

[523] *Matthew* 17:20; *Luke* 17:6.

[524] *Matthew* 5:15.

[525] *Matthew* 7:7, *Luke* 11:9 Note: In the second century the church father Irenaeus, faced with persecutions from without and schisms from within, sought to build a unified church. His internal opponents countered with this saying of Jesus, in an effort to keep heterodoxy alive. See Pagels, *Beyond Belief* (New York: Random, 2003) 129-30.

[526] Some form of this saying exists in all four Gospels:

- *Matthew* 13:57 - "But Jesus said to them, 'A prophet is not without honor except in his hometown and in his own household.'"
- *Mark* 6:4 - "Jesus said to them, 'A prophet is not without honor except in his hometown and among his own relatives and in his own household.'"
- *Luke* 4:24 - "And He said, 'Truly I say to you, no prophet is welcome in his hometown.'"
- *John* 4: 43-44 – "After the two days He went forth from there into Galilee. For Jesus Himself testified that a prophet has no honor in his own country."

[527] *Matthew* 6: 28-31.

[528] *Matthew* 5:41.

[529] *Matthew* 5:43.

[530] *Matthew* 7: 3-5.

[531] *Matthew* 23:24.

[532] *Mark* 12:13-17 and *Matthew* 22:15-22.

[533] *Mark* 4:13, 7:17; *John* 10:6 and 16:29.

[534] Grant, *Jesus: An Historian's Review of the Gospels* 91. Also: "Seven parables appear in all three Synoptics: the new cloth in the old coat, the new wine in old wineskin, the sower and the different soils, the lamp under the bushel, the mustard seed, the fig tree and the tenants." The two most memorable – "The Good Samaritan" and "The Prodigal Son" - are only in *Luke*. See Paul Johnson, *Jesus A Biography From a Believer* 108.

[535] *Matthew* 13: 34-35.

[536] This is a theory that emerged in the early 1900s and applied primarily to *Mark* which asserts that Jesus commanded his followers to be silent about

his status as the Messiah during his lifetime. Also, Ben Witherington III has written: "In a volatile environment outsiders would have a hard time penetrating the parables and deciphering his speech. This may have made it possible for Jesus's ministry to go on longer than it would have if he had been as direct in his critique of the powers that be as John the Baptist was." See Witherington, *New Testament History A Narrative Account* Location 2206ff.

[537] Galilee was the northern province of Palestine. In Jesus's time Palestine was divided into three provinces - Galilee, Samaria and Judea. See *Luke* 17:11 and *Acts* 9:31. All of the Apostles - at least after Judas's departure - were Galileans. See *Acts* 1:11. They may have had an accent occasioned by contact with their non-Jewish neighbors. See *Matthew* 26:73. For the suggestion that Judas may not have been Galilean, see Krosney, *The Lost Gospel: The Quest for the Gospel of Judas Iscariot* 52.

[538] I owe this thought to Meier, *The Vision of Matthew: Christ, Church and Morality in the First Gospel* 89-90 and regret it if I have misstated Meier's point of view.

[539] Indeed, the Good Shepherd theme in *John* 10 echoes the Synoptics:

- *Matthew* 18:12-14 - To his disciples: *"What do you think? If any man has a hundred sheep, and one of them has gone astray, does he not leave the ninety-nine on the mountains and go and search for the one that is straying? If it turns out that he finds it, truly I say to you, he rejoices over it more than over the ninety-nine which have not gone astray. So it is not the will of your Father who is in heaven that one of these little ones perish."*
- *Luke* 15:4-7 - To Pharisees and scribes as sinners and tax collectors were gathering around him: *"What man among you, if he has a hundred sheep and has lost one of them, does not leave the ninety-nine in the open pasture and go after the one which is lost until he finds it? When he has found it, he lays it on his shoulders, rejoicing. And when he comes home, he calls together his friends and his neighbors, saying to them, 'Rejoice with me, for I have found my sheep which was lost!' I tell you that in the same way, there will be more joy in heaven over one sinner who repents than over ninety-nine righteous persons who need no repentance."*
- *Mark* 6:34 - *"When Jesus went ashore, He saw a large crowd, and He felt compassion for them because they were like sheep without a shepherd; and He began to teach them many things."*
- *Matthew* 10: 5-6 - *"These twelve Jesus sent out after instructing them: 'Do not go in the way of the Gentiles, and do not enter any city of the Samaritans; but rather go to the lost sheep of the house of Israel.'"*

- *Matthew* 15:24 - To a Canaanite women: *"But He answered and said, 'I was sent only to the lost sheep of the house of Israel.'"*
- *Luke* 12:32 - To his followers: *"Do not be afraid, little flock, for your Father has chosen gladly to give you the kingdom."*

[540] Contained in *Matthew* chapters 5-7, the Sermon on the Mount may be a collection of Jesus's sayings that he pronounced in various locales in his ministry. (As noted earlier, Luke records many of these saying as part of Jesus's comments *"on a large, level area"* in *Luke* 6:17.) The Sermon on the Mount is the most quoted part of the *New Testament*. The Sermon on the Mount has been referred to as the *Magna Carta* of the Kingdom. See Meier, *The Vision of Matthew: Christ, Church and Morality in the First Gospel* 47. Martin Luther King said that the Sermon on the Mount was foundational to the American civil rights movement. See McLennan 5.

Matthew 7: 12 – *"So in everything, do to others what you would have them do to you…"* - acquired the label, the "Golden Rule", in the Middle Ages. See Wills, *What the Gospels Meant* 76, 91, 92. Note: The *Didache* was an early Christian text containing guidance for Christian groups. Scholars date it from the late first or early second century. Some church fathers considered in canonical; others did not. It had been lost for centuries but was found in Istanbul in 1875. The *Didache* 1:2 puts the Golden Rule in the negative. "Whatever you would not have done to yourself, do not do to another." See John Dominic Crossan *The Birth of Christianity: Discovering What Happened in the Years Immediately After the Death of Jesus* (New York: HarperSanFrancisco a Division of HarperCollinsPublishers, 1998) 364 and Justo L. Gonzales, *A History of Christian Thought From the Beginnings to the Council of Chalcedon* Volume 1 Revised Edition 67ff and Throckmorton 29.

[541] *Matthew* 19:30; 20:16; *Mark* 9:35; 10;31; *Luke* 13:30.

[542] I owe this concept to Borg, *Jesus: Uncovering the Life, Teachings, and Relevance of a Religious Revolutionary* 167 and regret it if I have misstated Borg's point of view.

[543] *Matthew* 7:13; *Luke* 13:24.

[544] The only one of Jesus's miracles in *John* that is in all the Synoptics is the feeding of the five thousand. As noted earlier, it appears in *John* 6: 1-15 and in the Synoptics as follows:

- *Matthew* 14: 13-21
- *Mark* 6: 30-44
- *Luke* 6: 1-17

In *Matthew*, *Mark* and *John* the feeding miracle is followed by the walking on water miracle.

As noted *Matthew* and *Mark* recount an additional feeding miracle - this time of four thousand in *Matthew* 15:32-39 and *Mark* 8: 1-10.

There is a certain amount of precision in these stories. The feeding of the five thousand contains this identical detail in all four accounts: the food all came from five loaves and two fishes. This makes it a different story than the feeding of the four thousand in which the food all came from seven loaves and a few fish.

[545] *John* 21:25.

[546] The story of Jesus healing a woman with a hemorrhage is told in *Matthew* 9: 20-22; *Mark* 5: 25-34; *Luke* 8: 43-48. The woman merely touched Jesus's cloak. In *Mark* and *Luke*, Jesus is recorded as saying that he recognized that power had gone out of him. Eusebius writing three hundred years later claimed that this woman came from Caesarea Philippi and: "Since I have mentioned this city I do not think it proper to omit an account which is worthy of record for posterity. For they say that the woman with an issue of blood, who, as we learn from the sacred Gospel, received from our saviour deliverance from her affliction, came from this place, and that her house is shown in the city, and that remarkable memorials of the kindness of the Saviour to her remain there. For there stand upon an elevated stone, by the gates of her house, a brazen (bronze?) image of a woman kneeling, with her hands stretched out, as if she were praying. Opposite this is another upright image of a man, made of the same material, clothed decently in a double cloak, and extending his hand toward the woman. At his feet, beside the statue itself is a certain strange plant, which climbs up to the hem of the brazen cloak, and is a remedy for all kinds of diseases. They say that this statue is an image of Jesus. It has remained to our day, so that we ourselves also saw it when we were staying in the city." See Eusebius Book VII Chapter 18.

[547] It has been noted that the virgin birth is explicitly mentioned in two of the four Gospels: *Matthew* 1: 18-20 in which the pregnancy by the Holy Spirit is noted and an angel assures Joseph not to worry in a dream and *Luke* 1: 31-37 in which the angel Gabriel notifies Mary and there is no record of Joseph's concern. Some commentators have noted Joseph's absence in a verse which asserts that the wise men *"going into the house ...saw the child with Mary his mother, and they fell down and worshiped him." (Matthew 2:11).* These commentators draw the inference that it is Matthew's way of emphasizing the virgin birth. See Pope Benedict XVI, *Jesus of Nazareth The Infancy Narratives* 102. There is a minority opinion that a verse in the prologue of the *Gospel of*

John which seems to refer to Christian believers actually is a poor translation and refers to Jesus. *John* 1:13 talks of those: *"who were born, not of blood nor of the will of the flesh nor of the will of man, but of God."* The argument goes that if it refers to Jesus it is an oblique reference to the virgin birth. See Pelikan, Mary *Through the Centuries Her Place in the History of Culture* (New Haven and London: Yale University Press, 1996) 11-12.

[548] Stark, *Discovering God: The Origins of the Great Religions and the Evolution of Belief* 285.

[549] *Mark* 6: 1-6.

[550] *Matthew* 13: 54-58.

[551] I owe this thought to Spong 63, 71 and regret it if I have misstated Spong's point of view.

[552] Pelikan *Jesus Through The Centuries: His Place in the History of Culture* 183-84, 193.

[553] Eusebius also cited this verse in describing Jesus. See Eusebius Book I Chapter 3.

[554] Much of this and my conclusions are drawn from: James DG Dunn *Did the First Christians Worship Jesus? The New Testament Evidence* 102-111 and I regret it if I have misinterpreted Dunn's point of view.

[555] Bart D. Ehrman *Did Jesus Exist? The Historical Argument for Jesus of Nazareth* 111ff. Note: Peter's *Acts* 3 speech covered in verses 11 through 26 of that chapter shows signs of having some of the very early Christian influence perhaps a half century before *Acts* was written. There is a reference to *"The God of Abraham, Isaac and Jacob, the God of our fathers"* (*Acts* 3:13). He calls his listeners *"the sons of the prophets and of the covenant."* (*Acts* 3: 25) See Justo L. Gonzales, *Acts The Gospel of the Spirit* 57.

[556] For more analysis of how scholars view some of the speeches in *Acts* to be part of a pre-Lukan tradition see Kruger 132-33.

[557] See also: James DG Dunn *Did the First Christians Worship Jesus? The New Testament Evidence* 136-37.

[558] According to Robert Louis Wilken, this verse was a point of dispute between Christian rivals Arius and Athanasius in their Christological disputes of the 300s which we will cover in Chapter 8. Arius believed Jesus was created by God and tended to see this verse as a proof text that Jesus matured as did other humans. Athanasius emphasized that Jesus was God as described in the

Nicene Creed. See Wilken, *The Myth of Christian Beginning: History's Impact on Belief* (Garden City, New York: Doubleday & Company, Inc., 1971) 92.

[559] Wright, *Simply Jesus A New Vision of Who He Was, What He Did, And Why He Matters* 4.

[560] Wilson, *Jesus A Life* 167.

[561] *Mark* 16:1-2.

[562] *Matthew* 27:56; 27:61; 28:1; *Mark* 15:40; 15:47; 16:1; 16:9; *Luke* 24:10; *John* 19:25; 20:1; 20:18. *Luke* 8:2 is the one reference of Mary Magdalene apart from the crucifixion and resurrection. She is quite likely included in the group gathering in the Upper Room with the now-eleven Apostles after Jesus's ascension. The group is described in *Acts* 1:14: *"These all with one mind were continually devoting themselves to prayer, **along with the women**, and Mary the mother of Jesus, and with His brothers." (Emphasis added).*

[563] Reader's Digest *After Jesus: The Triumph of Christianity* 25 and McLennan 71. This name may have come from her role in delivering to the Apostles the news that Jesus had risen as recounted in *Matthew* 28:1-10 where according to verse 1 she is with *"the other Mary,"* *Luke* 24:1-10 where according to verse 10 she is with *"Joanna and Mary the mother of James; also the other women with them"* and *John* 20:1-18 where she is alone. *Mark* 16:1-8 recounts that she told no one because she was afraid and has her, according to verse 1, with *"Mary the mother of James, and Salome."*

[564] http://en.wikipedia.org/wiki/Mary_Magdalene. (Accessed May 2, 2012).

[565] Wilson, *Jesus A Life* 152.

[566] In modern popular culture Mary Magdalene has been fictionalized as the wife of Jesus by Dan Brown in the best-seller, *The Da Vinci Code*. The movie version was directed by Ron Howard and starred Tom Hanks. This has given high profile to her but scholars like Thomas Cahill are scathingly critical: "The description of Christianity in the popular thriller *The Da Vinci Code* as a fraud perpetrated by Constantine not only is preposterous to any reader with a modicum of historical knowledge but rests on melodramatically anti-Christian assumptions. The book's further premise that the Catholic Church sends out Opus Dei hit men to murder anyone who has stumbled on the truth is a straight-forward anti-Catholic libel. And its notion that Jesus fathered progeny by Mary Magdalene is a fantasy lacking the least historical support." See Thomas Cahill, *Mysteries of the Middle Ages The Rise of Feminism, Science and Art from the Cults of Catholic Europe* (New York: Nan A. Talese an imprint of The Doubleday Broadway Publishing Group, a division of Random House, Inc., 2006) 45-6.

Bart D. Ehrman writes that he liked *The Da Vinci Code* as a work of fiction and recommended it to friends but also writes that: "Even though he (Dan Brown) claims that his 'descriptions of ...documents...are accurate,' in fact they are not." See Ehrman, *Truth and Fiction in the DaVinci Code: A Historian Reveal What We Really Know About Jesus, Mary Magdalene, and Constantine* (Oxford: Oxford University Press, 2004) 189-90. However, even if Mary Magdalene was not his wife, did Jesus have a wife? In 2012, Harvard professor, Karen L. King, announced the discovery of a piece of papyrus smaller than a business card. It was written in the ancient Coptic language, probably in the 300s. The script is readable under magnifications and contains this phrase: "Jesus said to them, 'My wife ...'" The text beyond "My wife" is cut off. King noted that this relic should not be seen as proof that Jesus was married but added that it "suggests that some early Christians had a tradition that Jesus was married. There was, we already know, a controversy in the second century over whether Jesus was married, caught up with a debate about whether Christians should marry and have sex." But Dr. King said she wants nothing to do with the *DaVinci Code*: "At least, don't say this proves Dan Brown was right." See Laurie Goodstein *New York Times* September 18, 2012. However, in 2014, many specialists in ancient manuscripts denounced this piece of papyrus as a forgery saying that King had been tricked. See Jerry Pattengale *Wall Street Journal* May 1, 2014. My conclusion: If Jesus had a wife, it would be pretty odd that the *New Testament* does not mention her since it mentions other members of his immediate family – his parents, his brothers and, in some manuscripts, his sisters and his cousin. See also Wright, *Simply Jesus A New Vision of Who He Was, What He Did, And Why He Matters* 6. Note: Christian tradition identified Mary Magdalene as the woman in *Luke* 7 who washed Jesus's feet with her tears at the banquet put on by Simon the Pharisee. See Charlotte Allen, *The Human Christ The Search for the Historical Jesus* 185-6.

[567] This woman is described in *Mark* as the mother of James. Since James was Jesus's brother, this may have been Mary the mother of Jesus. What is clear is that Mary and Jesus's brothers were in Jerusalem with the disciples after the resurrection. *Acts* 1:14 in its entirety reads: *"They all met together and were constantly united in prayer, along with Mary the mother of Jesus, several other women, and the brothers of Jesus."*

[568] *Mark* 16: 5-8.

[569] As I have explained earlier even evangelical scholars contest the authenticity of the latter part of *Mark* 16.

[570] *John* 20:15 (a gardener), *Luke* 24:37 (a ghost), or *Luke* 24: 16 (simply not recognized or, as the scripture actually says, *they were kept from recognizing him*.")

[571] *John* 21:15.

[572] *Luke* 24:31.

[573] *Matthew* 28: 19-20.

[574] *John* 20: 24-9.

[575] *Matthew* 28: 10. 16-20.

[576] *Luke* 24: 33-53.

[577] *Acts* 1: 3.

[578] *I Corinthians* 15:6.

[579] *Acts* 1: 9.

[580] The abrupt ending in *Mark* should not, however, be taken to mean that Mark or his readers did not accept the resurrection. *Mark* 14:28 records Jesus's promise that after rising he would meet his followers in Galilee. Moreover, Jesus predicted his death and resurrection in *Mark* 8:31; 9:31 and 10:32-34. Note the disciples's responses:

- Peter tried to talk him out of it – *Mark* 8:32.
- The Twelve talked of their relative worth – *Mark* 9: 32-34. Verse 34 witheringly reports: "...*they had been arguing about which of them was the greatest.*"
- As noted, James and John schemed. – *Mark* 10: 35-37.

[581] *Matthew* 3:3; *Mark* 1:3; *Luke* 1:76; 3:4; 7:27 and *John* 1:23.

[582] *John* 14:5-6.

[583] *Acts* 9:1-2; *Acts* 19:23; *Acts* 22:4, *Acts* 24:22.

[584] *Acts* 22:4.

[585] *Acts* 14:27. Note: A standard search for the term "Door of Faith" yields these types of organizations by that name: orphanages, Pentecostal churches and broadcast ministries.

[586] We will have more discussion on this James in Chapter 7. The key point here is that this James was the earthly brother of Jesus and not one of the twelve disciples.

[587] *Acts* 6:1.

[588] However, as we will see in Chapter 10, although Paul's Christian ministry lasted about thirty years, all we know about is, at most, a decade.

[589] Paul Johnson, *Jesus A Biography From a Believer* 21. As noted, *Acts* 7:58, which is the first mention of Paul (Saul), calls him a *"young man."*

[590] It is not surprising that *Acts* 21:39 has Paul referring to Tarsus as "no insignificant city." \

[591] *Galatians* 1:14.

[592] *Philippians* 3:5-6.

[593] *II Corinthians* 11:22.

[594] *I Corinthians* 9:22.

[595] According to *Galatians* 1:14, he was *"more extremely zealous for my ancestral traditions."*

[596] According to *I Corinthians* 15:10, he *"labored even more than all of them, yet not I, but the grace of God with me."*

[597] According to *I Corinthians* 14:8, he thanked God that *"I speak in tongues more than you all."*

[598] I owe this thought to Wilson, *Jesus A Life* 24ff and regret it if I have misstated Wilson's point of view.

[599] *Galatians* 2:8.

[600] *Acts* 21: 20-21. They may have known him only by reputation. Paul claims he was not known in Christian gatherings in Judea – *Galatians* 1:22. However as has been noted this point is controversial and cannot be easily squared with the accounts in *Acts* which have Paul present at the murder of Stephen (*Acts* 7:58-8:1), in consultation with the High Priest (*Acts* 9:1), and as, shortly after his conversion, moving *"about freely in Jerusalem, speaking boldly in the name of the Lord."* (*Acts* 9:28).

[601] *II Corinthians* 10:10.

[602] *Acts* 21: 20-31. Note: According to *Acts* 9:29, Jewish Hellenists tried to kill Paul early in his Christian career also. The role of the Jewish Hellenists in *Acts* needs more consideration. Their numbers in Jerusalem were considerable. Many Diaspora Jews in that era came to Jerusalem, some to live out their lives. Therefore, they tended to be elderly people with a sufficiently fervent religious conviction to cause them to emigrate. Some of the Hellenists had converted to Christianity as described in *Acts* 6. The development of Christian Hellenists may have put pressure on the non-Christian Hellenists to show their Jewish orthodoxy. (There is one modern suggestion that the conflict described here over food distribution was in the wider community and that

the church raised its profile with the Hellenists by siding with them in it. All the deacons had Greek names indicating that they might be Hellenists. It has also been suggested that the selection of the deacons was actually the emergence of a separate governing structure to oversee the Hellenists who had converted to Christianity.)

The opposition to Stephen came from other Hellenists according to *Acts* 6:9, presumably among the unconverted. The persecution after the murder of Stephen was of Hellenistic Christian Jews and not the "Hebrews." Hence the Twelve could stay in Jerusalem for the time being. See Justo L. Gonzales *Acts The Gospel of the Spirit* 35, 88-91, 95, 100, 101.

[603] *Philippians* 1: 17.

[604] *II Corinthians* 11:4.

[605] *Philippians* 3:2.

[606] *Galatians* 5:15.

[607] *Galatians* 3:1.

[608] *Galatians* 5:4.

[609] *II Corinthians* 11:13.

[610] *II Corinthians* 11:5.

[611] Paul Johnson, *A History of Christianity* 62.

[612] *Galatians* 5:12.

[613] In light of all this, what are we to make of the Catholic Church's designation of Paul as the patron saint of public relations? One can understand that he is also the patron saint of Malta (*Acts* 28:1) and tentmakers (*Acts* 18:3) and that he is invoked against snake bites (*Acts* 28:3-6). But public relations? See Sandoval 192.

[614] Martin Luther, Paul's great admirer, labeled *Revelation* as "neither apostolic nor prophetic" and placed it in an appendix to his *New Testament*. See Boyer 60-61.

[615] *Revelation* 2:14.

[616] *Revelation* 2:2,9; 3:9. Verses like these show an anti-Pauline slant on what it meant to be a follower of Jesus within the pages of the *New Testament*. Although the language is extreme, Paul – as we have seen – could play in that polemical league. But these verses are also somewhat of an historical artifact.

The view that these Pauline churches were apostate could not withstand the tides of history.

[617] Ehrman, *Peter, Paul and Mary* 163. Justin wrote of topics that Paul had covered but did not mention Paul:

- Gentiles and the rejection of the Jews, but no mention of *Romans* 9-11.
- Christians paying their taxes, but no mention of *Romans* 13 although at least one other ancient writer did in this context.
- The resurrection of humans, but no mention of *I Corinthians* 15 although, again, at least one other ancient writer did in this context. See Walter Bauer, Orthodoxy *and Heresy in Earliest Christianity* Mifflintown, PA: Sigler Press, 1996, fortress press, 1971, second German edition with added appendices, by George Strecker translated by a team from the Philadelphia Seminar on Christian Origins and edited by Robert A. Kraft and Gerhard Krodel. Originally published in 1934. 215-6.

Note: Justin Martyr also quoted from the *New Testament* Gospels but he did not name them. He referred to them as "Memoirs of the Apostles." See Ehrman, *Truth and Fiction in the DaVinci Code: A Historian Reveal What We Really Know About Jesus, Mary Magdalene, and Constantine* 84. Further Note: In defending that Jesus was born in Bethlehem, Justin Martyr suggested that the critics check the census data from the time of Quirinius. See Charlotte Allen, *The Human Christ The Search for the Historical Jesus* 52. There is no record of any follow-up. Further note: Justin seemed to have based his Christian faith upon the *Old Testament*, the Synoptic gospels, and the *Book of Revelation*. See Bauer 87.

[618] There were two important Christian Clements in the first two centuries of the Christian era and both have been mentioned in this book. Clement of Alexandria (abt. 150 – 215) was an important Christian philosopher often associated with Origen. Clement of Rome lived earlier, in the late first century, and was Bishop of Rome (i.e., a Pope) after Peter and wrote at least one letter that bears his name. He is considered by the Catholic Church to be an Apostolic Father. Who were the Apostolic Fathers? Here is Justo L. Gonzales: "The earliest surviving Christian writings apart from those which now form part of the *New Testament* canon are those of the so-called Apostolic Fathers. They have been given this title because at the time it was thought they had known the apostles. In some cases this seems quite possible, but in others it was a mere product of imagination. The name 'Apostolic Fathers' appeared in the seventeenth century, when it was applied to five writings or bodies of

writings. But through the years three other members have been added to the group, so that now the Apostolic Fathers are eight: Clement of Rome, the *Didache*, Ignatius of Antioch, Polycarp of Smyrna, Papias of Hierapolis, the *Epistle of Barnabas*, the *Shepherd of Hermas*, and the *Epistle to Diognetus*." See Justo L. Gonzales, *A History of Christian Thought From the Beginnings to the Council of Chalcedon* Volume 1 Revised Edition 61. Pope Clement served from about 88 to 97 and was identified by Origen to be the Clement cited by Paul in *Philippians* 4:3 as someone with whom Paul worked. *I Clement* is considered the most important Christian writing of the first century outside of the *New Testament* and the *Didache*. See Bunson 81-2.

[619] Wills, *Why I Am A Catholic* 73-4. *I Clement* reports that Peter died at the same time for the same reason. See also Grant, *History of Rome* 345 which goes so far as to say that Paul's trial or trials and subsequent execution in Rome were instigated by Jewish-Christians.

[620] *II Timothy* 1:15.

[621] Grant, *Saint Paul* 167-9. Clement's writing suggests that Paul got to Spain and then returned to Rome where he was executed in 64 AD. See Reader's Digest *Atlas of the Bible: An Illustrated Guide to the Holy Land* (Pleasantville, New York and Montreal, The Reader's Digest Association, Inc., 1981) 199.

[622] Walker 524ff.

[623] Wright, *The Resurrection of the Son of God Christian Origins and the Question of God* Volume Three (Minneapolis: Fortress Press, 2003) 30.

[624] Ehrman, *Misquoting Jesus The Story Behind Who Changed the Bible and Why* 21. See *I Thessalonians* 1: 9-10 and *I Corinthians* 15: 3-4.

[625] The simple formula on how to get saved spelled out in *Romans* 10:9 has certainly been challenged over the millennia. Here is one example. When popes in the 200s - Calistus (217-222), Cornelius (251-3) and Stephen (254-257) - dealt leniently on issues of forgiveness and salvation they were challenged by other church leaders. These issues included the status of Christians who committed serious sins after baptism, the status of Christians who committed apostasy during persecutions and then sought re-admittance to the churches and the validity of death-bed reconciliations in such cases. See Kelly 13-21.

[626] The liberal theologians of the 1800s saw a difference even in the *New Testament* between the "gospel of Jesus and the gospel of Paul, the 'religion of Jesus' and the 'religion *about* Jesus.'" See Dillenberger and Welch 221 and Walker 19. Some have seen a contrast within Christianity as a religion "of Jesus or about Jesus." See Charles Francis Potter *The Story of Religion As Told*

In The Lives Of Its Leaders (Garden City, New York: Garden City Publishing Company Star Books, Simon and Schuster, Inc., 1929) 227.

[627]   *I Corinthians* 15:3.

[628]   *Galatians* 4:4.

[629]   *I Corinthians* 9:15.

[630]   *Galatians*1:19.

[631]   *Romans* 15:7.

[632]   *I Corinthians* 11:23 reads: *"For I received from the Lord that which I also delivered to you, that the Lord Jesus in the night in which He was **betrayed** took bread;"* (Emphasis added). However, there is some ambiguity here. The matter is unclear because the same Greek word which is rendered "betrayed" here is rendered in *Romans* 8:32 as "gave him up": *"He who did not spare his own Son, but **gave him up** for us all—how will he not also, along with him, graciously give us all things?"* (Emphasis added). *I Corinthians* 11:23 may be the first reference to Judas in history although Judas is not named and there is no other possible reference in Paul's letters to Judas. See Ehrman, *The Lost Gospel of Judas Iscariot* (Oxford: Oxford University Press, 2006) 15-16.

[633]   *I Corinthians* 2:2.

[634]   *I Corinthians* 15:5. There is no record that Jesus appeared to Judas. Possibly the "Twelve" was for Paul a figure of speech.

[635]   One historian has suggested that modern people may know more about the life of Jesus than Paul did since we have the written Gospels and he did not. See Paul Johnson, *A History of Christianity* 23. It should be noted that whoever wrote *Hebrews* seemed to know:

- That Jesus was of the tribe of Judah as *Hebrews* 7:14 reads in part, *"For it is evident that our Lord was descended from Judah,..."*
- Something about Jesus's prayer in Gethsemane as *Hebrews* 5:7 reads, *"In the days of His flesh, He offered up both prayers and supplications with loud crying and tears to the One able to save Him from death, and He was heard because of His piety."* Compare this, for example, to *Mark* 14:36: *"And He was saying, 'Abba! Father! All things are possible for You; remove this cup from Me; yet not what I will, but what You will.'"*

[636]   *I Corinthians* 5: 1, 11. As I will note later, there is a minority view that Paul was not dealing here with incest *per se* but a stepson contracting a marriage with his widowed stepmother possibly in order to protect family finances.

637 In one of history's coincidences, the conquistador Hernan Cortes who did at least as much to transform the world as Martin Luther had a nearly identical lifespan: (1485-1547).

638 George Weigel, *God's Choice: Pope Benedict XVI and the Future of the Catholic Church* (New York: HarperCollins, 2005) 27. Note: It may be unfair to add that a couple of years later when Billy Graham's wife Ruth Graham (1920-2007) died Graham said that, "She was the greatest Christian I ever knew." (Cathy Lynn Grossman, *USA Today* June 15-17, 2007).

639 *Galatians* 5:19-20.

640 *I Corinthians* 1:23-25. Writing in about 170AD, Celsus criticized Christians who cited this saying of Paul for credulousness. He wrote that some Christians "do not even want to give or to receive a reason for what they believe, and use such expressions as 'Do not ask questions; just believe' and 'Your faith will save you.' Others quote the Apostle Paul. 'The wisdom in the world is evil and foolishness is a good thing.'" See Wilken, *The Christians as the Romans Saw Them* (New Haven and London: Yale University Press, 1984) 97.

641 *Acts* 9, 22 and 26.

642 *Galatians* 1:12.

643 *Galatians* 1:16.

644 *Galatians* 2:2: "*I went up in accord with a revelation.*"

645 That is the interpretation I give *II Corinthians* 5:16: "*Therefore from now on we recognize no one according to the flesh; even though we have known Christ according to the flesh, yet now we know Him in this way no longer.*"

646 *II Corinthians* 12:2-4. Note: It is difficult to reconcile this claim with Jesus's statement as recorded in *John* 3:13: "*No one has ascended into heaven, but He who descended from heaven: the Son of Man.*"

647 *Acts* 16:9.

648 *Acts* 22:17-21.

649 *Galatians* 1:16.

650 *I Corinthians* 2: 7-8.

651 I Corinthians 11:23.

652 *I Thessalonians* 4:15.

[653] His trip to the Jerusalem Council was actually the second time he had visited with leaders there - Peter and James - to confer over doctrine. They met (negotiated?) for two weeks some fourteen years before the Council. See *Galatians* 1:18-19 and 2:1.

[654] *I Corinthians* 15: 3-8. His note that Christ appeared to him *"as to one untimely born..."* perhaps obliquely conceded that his message was different than the others. See Wilson, *Jesus A Life* 22.

[655] *Luke* 2:46.

[656] *Acts* 22:3.

[657] *Matthew* 27:19.

[658] *Acts* 26: 30-31.

[659] Note: *Matthew* 2:11 records about the wise men at Jesus's birth that ..."*they fell to the ground and worshiped Him. Then, opening their treasures, they presented to Him gifts of gold, frankincense, and **myrrh**."* (Emphasis added). Church tradition associates myrrh with Jesus's crucifixion. (The gold is associated with his kingship and the incense to his divine sonship.) See Pope Benedict XVI *Jesus of Nazareth The Infancy Narratives* 107.

[660] Here is James D. Tabor: "Whether Paul was born in Tarsus, one has to doubt because Jerome, the fourth century Christian writer, knew a different tradition. He says that Paul's parents were from Gischala, in Galilee, a Jewish town about twenty-five miles north of Nazareth, and that Paul was born there. According to Jerome, when revolts broke out throughout Galilee following the death of Herod the Great in 4 BC, Paul and his parents were rounded up and sent to Tarsus in Cilicia as part of a massive exile of the Jewish population by Romans to rid the area of further potential trouble. Since Jerome certainly knew Paul's claim, according to the *Book of Acts*, to have been born in Tarsus, it is very unlikely he would have contradicted that source without good evidence." See Tabor, *Paul and Jesus How the Apostle Transformed Christianity* Location 3750ff.

[661] Einhorn 111, 133, 158, 160, 161, 175-76, 180, 189-90. For more on Paul's family coming from Galilee see Hubert Jedin, Editor *History of the Church Volume I From the Apostolic Community to Constantine* by Karl Baus *A Crossroad Book* (New York: The Seabury Press, 1962, English Translation 1965) 99.

[662] *Matthew* 20:1-16. See verse 16.

[663] *Matthew* 6:1-18. See verse 1.

[664] *Romans* 3:20.

[665] WOE Oesterley, LittD., D.D. (Camb.) and Theodore H. Robinson, Litt.D. (Camb.), D.D. (Lond.) *Hebrew Religion: Its Origin and Development* (London: S.P.C.K, 1952) 406-8.

[666] *Romans* 14:20.

[667] *Mark* 7:15.

[668] *Matthew* 17:20; *Matthew* 21: 21; *Mark* 11: 23.

[669] *I Thessalonians* 5:2. The writer of *II Thessalonians* may have been dealing with fallout from the notion of the imminent and unheralded return of Jesus because he emphasized that certain events needed to occur before the Lord returned. These included the appearance of a *"man of lawlessness."* See *II Thessalonians* 2: 3-4. The writer's immediate concern may have been with people who thought the Lord would come soon and in the meantime were, as verse 11 of the third chapter says, *"living idle lives, refusing to work."*

[670] *Luke* 12:39. See also *Matthew* 24:43 which is nearly the same: *"But be sure of this, that if the head of the house had known at what time of the night the thief was coming, he would have been on the alert and would not have allowed his house to be broken into."* This metaphor is picked up in three other instances:

- *II Peter* 3:10 – *"But the day of the Lord will come like a thief,..."*
- *Revelation* 3:3 – In the words of Jesus Christ: *"So remember what you have received and heard; and keep it, and repent. Therefore if you do not wake up, I will come like a thief, and you will not know at what hour I will come to you."*
- *Revelation* 16:15 - In the words of Jesus Christ: *"Behold, I am coming like a thief...."*

[671] *I Thessalonians* 5:6.

[672] *Matthew* 25: 1-13.

[673] *Matthew* 16:6, *Mark* 8:15, *Luke* 12:1 and *I Corinthians* 5:7-8.

[674] *I Corinthians* 5: 9-13 and *Matthew* 18: 15-18. From the Pauline corpus, *I Timothy* 1:20 and *Titus* 3:10 also speak of expulsions. Paul, of course, claimed the right to exercise discipline over his converts. See *II Corinthians* 1:23 and 13:10. *Matthew* 18: 15-18 reads:

"If your brother sins, go and show him his fault in private; if he listens to you, you have won your brother. But if he does not listen to you, take one or two more with you, so that BY THE MOUTH OF TWO OR THREE WITNESSES EVERY FACT MAY BE

CONFIRMED. *If he refuses to listen to them, tell it to the church; and if he refuses to listen even to the church, let him be to you as a Gentile and a tax collector. Truly I say to you, whatever you bind on earth shall have been bound in heaven; and whatever you loose on earth shall have been loosed in heaven.*" As noted earlier the Essenes were a religiously strict group living at the time of Jesus and may provide the context for this type of enforcement of group norms. See Justo L. Gonzales, *A History of Christian Thought From the Beginnings to the Council of Chalcedon* Volume 1 Revised Edition 36.

[675] *Romans* 12:14.

[676] *Romans* 12:17. He wrote the Thessalonians the same message: "*See that no one repays another with evil for evil, but always seek after that which is good for one another and for all people.*" (*I Thessalonians* 5:15). The writer of *I Peter* echoed this urging his reader to be "*humble in spirit; not returning evil for evil or insult for insult, but giving a blessing instead; for you were called for the very purpose that you might inherit a blessing.*" (*I Peter* 3:8-9).

[677] *Romans* 12: 19.

[678] *Matthew* 5: 44.

[679] *Matthew* 22:21; *Mark* 12: 17; and *Luke* 20:25. However, Jesus's statement on taxes is cryptic enough to allow for other interpretations. One of the charges lodged against him in his trial was that he forbade "*giving tribute to Caesar.*" (*Luke* 23:2).

[680] *Galatians* 5:14.

[681] *Matthew* 22: 36-40. Note: Jesus summed up the law with two commandments. The first was to love God. It was familiar to his listeners and drawn from *Deuteronomy* 6:4-5. The second was "*You shall love your neighbor as yourself.*" This one may have been a surprise. It quotes *Leviticus* 19:18 but it is in a list of rulings in *Leviticus* 19 and was in effect pulled out of its context by Jesus and given great significance. Some of the context of *Leviticus* 19 includes prohibitions against cursing a deaf man (verse 14) and against wearing a garment with two kinds of material mixed together (verse 19). There are no explicit references to *Leviticus* 19:18 in Jewish literature before Jesus. Paul cites it in *Romans* 13:9 and *Galatians* 5:14 as summing up the commandments. It appears in *James* 2:8 as the "*royal law.*" Paul (and James) must have taken this from Jesus. See James DG Dunn, *Jesus, Paul, and the Gospels* (Grand Rapids, Michigan and Cambridge UK: Eerdmans Publishing Co., Kindle Edition, 2011) Location 2391ff.

[682] Thomas Cahill, *Desire of the Everlasting Hills: The World Before and After Jesus* (New York, London, Toronto, Sydney, Aukland: Nan A. Talese Doubleday, 1999) 108. Note: Some divinity school graduates are unaware of the disconnect between Jesus and the teachings of Paul. One pastor has written about his seminary experiences: "We were not taught that Paul never mentions any of Jesus's teachings, or miracles, or birth narrative. Paul doesn't quote Jesus, except one time. We did learn that Paul's letters came way before the Gospels were written. So there are many times, reading through Paul's letters, where he's making a point, and you think he could really buttress his point here by quoting something Jesus said, but somehow he doesn't know about it." See Daniel C. Dennett and Lisa LaScola, *Caught in the Pulpit Leaving Belief Behind* Foreword by Richard Dawkins (Durham, North Carolina: Pitchstone Publishing, Kindle Edition, 2015) Location 1978.

[683] *I Corinthians* 15:7 and *Galatians* 2: 9-12.

[684] *I Corinthians* 9:5.

[685] As noted, in *I Corinthians* 15:3-8 Paul wrote that the risen Christ appeared to the "Twelve" although at the time of Jesus's appearances, there were actually eleven disciples. The betrayer Judas had abandoned Jesus and died. *Matthew* 28:16 and *Luke* 24:33-6 are very clear that eleven disciples were present. The *New Testament* avers that his replacement Matthias, who is only mentioned once in the entire *New Testament*, was not selected until after Jesus ascended to Heaven – *Acts* 1: 12-26. Again, Paul's reference to the "Twelve" was possibly a figure of speech.

[686] *I Corinthians* 9:5 (He had a believing wife who accompanied him and Paul asserted that he himself should also have that right.), *I Corinthians* 15:5 (Peter saw the resurrected Christ.) and *Galatians* 2: 9-21 (He acted hypocritically and was rebuked by Paul. We don't know Peter's side of the story.) Here an important assumption must be disclosed. I assume that Peter and Cephas were the same person. That is the position of the majority of scholars, but not all. See Ehrman *The New Testament* 335. Note: There are others in the *New Testament*, both in the Pauline corpus and out of it who get criticized but we really don't know their side of the story: *I Timothy* 1:19-20 lists two who have gone against their conscience and ruined their faith and who blaspheme whom "Paul" has given over to Satan for their own good: Hymenaeus and Alexander. *II Timothy* 1:15 lists two people who have abandoned "Paul": Phygelus and Hermogeneus. *II Timothy* 2:16-18 lists two who have become impious and/or perhaps led others into impiety and confusion by saying the resurrection has already taken place: Hymenaeus and Philetus. *II Timothy* 4:10 talks of a Demas who is too worldly and has deserted "Paul." *II Timothy*

4:14-15 warns of an Alexander the Coppersmith who has been very harmful to "Paul" and who opposed his message whom the Lord will take care of. *III John* 9-10 lists a Diotrephes who does not acknowledge authority and rejects emissaries. We will mention Alexander the Coppersmith in Chapter 7 in connection with how Paul's message may have conflicted with his economic interest and in connection with punishment. We will mention Diotrephes in Chapter 8 in connection with the growth of the church.

687 *Galatians* 2:9.

688 *I Corinthians* 7: 2 and 5 warn about temptation to sexual immorality. *Galatians* 6:1 talks of temptation more generally.

689 *I Corinthians* 10:13.

690 *I Thessalonians* 3:5.

691 *Hebrews* says about Jesus's temptations:

- 2:18 - *"For since He Himself was tempted in that which He has suffered, He is able to come to the aid of those who are tempted."*
- 4:15 - *"For we do not have a high priest who cannot sympathize with our weaknesses, but One who has been tempted in all things as we are, yet without sin."*

692 Note the sermon by the American Harry Emerson Fosdick in 1922 quoted earlier. http://historymatters.gmu.edu/d/5070/ (Accessed May 2, 2012).

693 I owe the concepts in this section to Ehrman *The Lost Gospel of Judas* 123-4 and regret it if I have misstated Ehrman's point of view.

694 However, Ben Witherington III has noted that certain Pauline verses may support the Virgin Birth:

- *Romans* 1:3 - (Jesus) *"was born of a descendant of David **according to the flesh.**"* (Emphasis Added).
- *Galatians* 4:4 - (Jesus was) *"born of a woman."*
- *Philippians* 2:7 – (Jesus was) *"made in the likeness of men."*

See Witherington, *New Testament History A Narrative Account* Location 1163. I regret it if I have misstated Witherington's point of view.

695 Ehrman, *The New Testament* 363-65.

696 *II Corinthians* 5:16. I owe this thought to Wilson, *Jesus A Life* 33 and regret it if I have misstated Wilson's point of view.

[697] *Galatians* 1:18. We will spend more time on the chronology of Paul's life in Chapter 10.

[698] Here is Marcus Borg: "There is an obvious reason that Paul did not often refer to what Jesus said and did. He wrote to communities that he had taught in person and so he would already have told them about Jesus. The one exception is his letter to Christians in Rome, but they also already knew about Jesus. The purpose of Paul's letters was not to tell people about Jesus but to stay in touch with his communities and to address issues that had arisen in his absence. They are about applications of Paul's understanding of life 'in Christ' – one of his most important phrases – to particular circumstances." Borg also notes that since Paul was a persecutor of Christians as seen in *Acts* 7 and 9 and *Philippians* 3 he at least knew something about Jesus since he had concluded that the Jesus movement should be opposed. See Borg, *Evolution of the Word The New Testament in the Order the Books Were Written* 11, 21. Note: It is possible that Christianity was carried to Rome by some Romans who had been at Pentecost. *Acts* 2:10 records that "*visitors from Rome*" had been present there.

[699] *I Corinthians* 2:2.

[700] *I Corinthians* 11:23-5.

[701] *Matthew* 10:10 and *I Corinthians* 9: 1-14.

Note: The requirement to pay preachers in *Matthew* comes from Jesus's instructions to his twelve apostles when he sent them out to preach, telling them not to take provisions because the "*laborer deserves his food.*" Although the accounts in *Mark* and *Luke* also instruct the apostles not to take provisions, there is no similar passage about the laborer deserving food. See *Mark* 6:8-11 and *Luke* 9: 3-4. However, Luke later records an account of Jesus sending out seventy (or seventy-two) of his followers. He tells them not to take provisions and to stay in the first house they visit. He says that if a "*son of peace*" is in the house, they should stay there and eat and drink what is provided for "*the laborer deserves his wages.*" See *Luke* 10: 1-8. The *Didache* furthered this theme: "But every true prophet who wants to live among you is worthy of his support. So also a true teacher is himself worthy, as the workman, of his support. Every first-fruit, therefore, of the products of wine-press and threshing-floor, of oxen and of sheep, you shall take and give to the prophets, for they are your high priests." *I Timothy* 5: 17-18 from the Pauline corpus, probably written later than the *Didache* asserts, "*Let the elders who rule well be considered worthy of double honor, especially those who labor in preaching and teaching; for the scripture says, 'YOU SHALL NOT MUZZLE THE OX WHILE HE IS THRESHING,' and, 'The laborer deserves to be paid.'*" This thought is echoed in *III John* 6-8, a letter written around the late first century to someone named

Gaius who has met some missionaries and is advised that *"You will do well to send them on in a manner worthy of God; for they began their journey for the sake of Christ, accepting no support from non-believers. Therefore we ought to support such people, so that we may become co-workers with the truth."* All of this suggests that many churches – at least by the second century – included a paid clergy. Indeed, Origen, writing in the early 200s, said that Paul's use of this *Old Testament* verse showed that Paul, and by implication other church leaders, had the right to be supported by the church. See Justo L. Gonzales, *A History of Christian Thought From the Beginnings to the Council of Chalcedon* Volume 1 Revised Edition 213. We will have occasion to consider this verse in later chapters dealing with it both as an example of "scripture" (Chapter 8) and of the use of allegory (Chapter 10).

[702] *Mark* 10:2-12; *Matthew* 19:3-12; *Matthew* 5:31-32; *Luke* 16:18 and *I Corinthians* 7: 10-11.

[703] I owe this thought to Crossan *The Birth of Christianity: Discovering What Happened in the Years Immediately After the Death of Jesus* 424-5 and regret it if I have misstated Crossan's point of view. Note: Earlier in his ministry Paul wrote to the Thessalonians: *"For you recall, brethren, our labor and hardship, how working night and day so as not to be a burden to any of you."* (*I Thessalonians* 2:9).

[704] Here are two points of context about Jesus's prohibition on divorce:

- The question Jesus was asked about divorce in *Mark* 10:1-12 and *Matthew* 19:1-12 was in a politically charged atmosphere. Both sections put the locale in *"the region of Judea (and) beyond the Jordan..."* (*Matthew* 19:1 and *Mark* 10:1). This was where John the Baptist had operated. He had been murdered for calling into question the divorce of Herod Antipas. See Wright, *Simply Jesus A New Vision of Who He Was, What He Did, And Why He Matters* 102-3.
- His condemnation of divorce was very likely out of a concern for women. It is noteworthy that the wife of Pilate was intrigued by him. See Paul Johnson, *Jesus A Biography From a Believer* 142ff.

[705] *I Corinthians* 7:10-11.

[706] For a discussion on this expansion see Wolfgang Schrage, *The Ethics of the New Testament* (Philadelphia: Fortress Press, 1988), 124 First published in German in 1982. Translated by David E. Green.

[707] Jesus questioned laws limiting activity on the Sabbath by performing healings and claiming to be Lord of the Sabbath. See, for example, *Mark*

3:2 and *Mark* 3:4. In the US, laws and mores restricting certain activities on Sundays were in place for many years. These were often questioned. Grover Cleveland, president of the United States from 1885-89 and 1893-1897, often played cards on Sundays. He joked that his minister father had thought it was sinful to fish on Sundays but "he never said anything about draw-poker." See Graff 38. Cleveland was a highly intelligent and sophisticated man. Yet, his response to the higher criticism of the *Bible* in his era was dismissive: "The *Bible* is good enough for me, just the old book under which I was brought up. I do not want notes or criticisms or explanations about authorship or origins or even cross-references. I do not need them or understand them, and they confuse me." See McLennan 86. (Quoted from Peter J. Gomes *The Good Book: Reading the Bible with Mind and Heart* (New York: Avon Books, 1996) 8.

[708]   *I Corinthians* 7:12-17.

[709]   It is worth noting that Paul was operating in a different environment than Jesus. He was dealing with Christians who were married to non-Christians. See Meier, *A Marginal Jew Rethinking the Historical Jesus Volume One The Roots of the Problem and the Person* ABRL (New York, London, Toronto, Sydney, Aukland: Doubleday, 1991) 46. This context was more complex than that which Jesus faced. Even though Paul could permit divorce to a Christian deserted by a non-Christian spouse he clearly saw the value in maintaining these mixed marriages if the non-Christian wanted to do so. This acceptance of mixed marriage may have had a lot to do with church growth over the first few centuries as spouses converted in increasing numbers and also the children raised in such unions often became Christians. See Stark, *The Triumph of Christianity How the Jesus Movement Became the World's Largest Religion* 134ff. Note: The approval of mixed marriages also appears in *I Peter* 3:1-2: "… *you wives must accept the authority of your husbands. Then, even if some refuse to obey the Good News, your godly lives will speak to them without any words. They will be won over by observing your pure and reverent lives.*"

[710]   There is also an example of Paul possibly showing a willingness to modify *Old Testament* teachings. In *Romans* chapter 13 verse 9 as noted he shortened what appear to be the Ten Commandments to four and added a summary: "…*You shall not commit adultery, You shall not murder, You shall not steal, You shall not covet, and if there is any other commandment, it is summed up in this saying, "You shall love your neighbor as yourself."*

This leaves out these six commandments from *Exodus* 20:

- *"You shall have no other gods before Me"* (verse 3).
- *"You shall not make for yourself an idol"* (verse 4).

- *"You shall not take the name of the LORD your God in vain"* (verse 7).
- *"Remember the Sabbath day, to keep it holy"* (verse 8).
- *"Honor your father and your mother"* (verse 12).
- *"You shall not bear false witness against your neighbor"* (verse 16).

This should not surprise us because again, as noted, Jesus himself made similar – but not identical - summaries to the Rich Young Ruler in *Matthew* 19: 18-20; *Mark* 10: 17-20; and *Luke* 18:18-21. In the *Mark* account Jesus lists the prohibitions against murder, adultery and stealing, adds the prohibition about bearing false witness and the command to honor parents and one that isn't in the Ten Commandments against defrauding. In *Matthew* Jesus's list is the same as in *Mark* except that he doesn't mention defrauding and he does add: YOU SHALL LOVE YOUR NEIGHBOR AS YOURSELF." In the *Luke* account Jesus's list is the same as in *Matthew* except that he doesn't mention the one to love your neighbor as yourself. Note: Centuries passed and in the 1600s Roger Williams (abt. 1603 – 1683) emigrated from England to the Massachusetts Bay Colony where he refused an invitation to preach in the established churches because the civil authorities were required to enforce the Ten Commandments and Williams objected to those commandments that had to do with people's relationship to God because he found them to be exclusionary toward other religions including Islam. See Potter 509.

711 *Matthew* 5: 44-45.

712 *Romans* 12:20.

713 Paul also said this about loving enemies:

- *I Thessalonians* 5:15. - *"See that no one repays another with evil for evil, but always seek after that which is good for one another and for all people."*
- *I Corinthians* 4:12 – *"...when we are reviled, we bless; when we are persecuted, we endure."*

The writer of *I Peter* said something very similar in the third chapter the ninth verse: *"Don't repay evil for evil. Don't retaliate with insults when people insult you. Instead, pay them back with a blessing.*

714 *Acts* 1:14.

715 Grant, *Jesus: An Historian's Review of the Gospels* 179. See also Grant, *History of Rome* (New York: Charles Scribner's Sons, 1978) 347-8. Note: *Acts* 28: 17-22 reports that when Paul was a prisoner in Rome he met with *"leading men of the Jews."* They told him that they had not heard of him but that they had heard of the sect that he represented. (They noted that it was it *"spoken*

against everywhere.") This is a reminder that the Christian movement was bigger than Paul.

[716] Walter Laqueur, *The Dream That Failed Reflections on the Soviet Union* (New York and Oxford: Oxford University Press) 1994 vii.

[717] We will have more discussion on this James in Chapter 7. Again, the key point here is that this James was the earthly brother of Jesus and not one of the twelve disciples.

[718] *Galatians* 2:9: *"and when James and Cephas and John, who seemed to be pillars…"* It is a safe assumption that the "Pillars" were very important in the early church. As James DG Dunn writes: "The fact that three of the central figures in the earliest Christian community were regarded as 'pillar' apostles suggests that they were thought of as pillars in the temple of God as envisaged in *Revelation* 3:12." That verse addressed to the angel of the church of Philadelphia reads: *"He who overcomes, I will make him a pillar in the temple of My God, and he will not go out from it anymore; and I will write on him the name of My God, and the name of the city of My God, the new Jerusalem, which comes down out of heaven from My God, and My new name."* See James DG Dunn *Did the First Christians Worship Jesus? The New Testament Evidence* 44.

[719] *Galatians* 1:18-19 and 2:1ff.

[720] *Mark* 6: 47-52 and *Matthew* 14:26-33.

[721] It is interesting to note the different descriptions of the ascension of Jesus Christ in *Luke* and *Acts*, both presumably written by the same author (*Luke* 24:50-2 and *Acts* 1:9-11). Some examples:

- *Luke* seems to say that it occurred on the day of the resurrection; *Acts* says that it occurred after "forty days." This can be reconciled because the Gospel account does not explicitly say that it occurred on the day of the resurrection.
- The Gospel account says that it occurred in Bethany and the *Acts* account on the Mount of Olives. This can also be reconciled because Bethany is on the Mount of Olives.
- The Gospel account does not mention the *"two men in white clothing"* that the *Acts* account does. These were not just bystanders. They said to the disciples as Jesus had ascended: *"Men of Galilee, why do you stand looking into the sky? This Jesus, who has been taken up from you into heaven, will come in just the same way as you have watched Him go into heaven."* However, as noted earlier, the *Luke* account has these two announcing Jesus' resurrection (*Luke* 24:5). See Justo L. Gonzales, *Acts The Gospel of the Spirit* 23-24.

Good News for Moderns

722 *Acts* 1:6.

723 Mack, *Who Wrote The New Testament?: The Making of the Christian Myth* 67ff.

724 *Luke* 3:23.

725 *Matthew* 1:19.

726 *Mark* 3:32, 6:3, *John* 2:12 and after the resurrection, *Acts* 1:14.

727 Marty 6.

728 Pagels, *Revelations Visions, Prophecy and Politics in the Book of Revelation* (New York: Viking Published by the Penguin Group, 2012) 14.

729 *Acts* 2:9, 6:9, 18:25 and 19:3.

730 William Smith 175.

731 In the *New Testament*, "Asia" refers to a Roman province in modern western Turkey with an administrative capital in Ephesus. See Browning Location 767.

732 *Revelation* 2: 1-7.

733 Johannine writing - a gospel, three letters, and *Revelation* probably originated at the end of the first century on the west coast of Asia Minor. The gospel's purpose was to persuade people to believe in Jesus (*John* 20:31) and to criticize the Jews in the Diaspora that disagreed with this. Hubert Jedin notes that "…no generally accepted solution to the question of authorship of the Johninne writings has been found …" See Jedin 119-23.

734 *I Corinthians* 16:8.

735 *Acts* 19:19 reads: *"And many of those who practiced magic brought their books together and began burning them in the sight of everyone; and they counted up the price of them and found it fifty thousand pieces of silver."* Pope Gregory XVI (1831-46) cited *Acts* 19:19 to oppose freedom of the press. See Wills, *Why I Am A Catholic* 194.

736 Remains of this temple have been discovered in Ephesus. See Browning Location 687.

737 That is possibly contradicted by *Acts* 19: 29-31 which, in describing a riot in Ephesus, goes on to say that his friends protected him: *"The city was filled with the confusion, and they rushed with one accord into the theater, dragging along Gaius and Aristarchus, Paul's traveling companions from Macedonia. And when Paul wanted to go into the assembly, the disciples would not let him. Also*

some of the Asiarchs who were friends of his sent to him and repeatedly urged him not to venture into the theater." Some two hundred years later, Cyprian of bishop of Carthage went into hiding during a time of persecution and continued to govern through a network. He compared his actions to Paul at Ephesus. See Hitchcock 52.

[738] Collins and Price 34.

[739] *I* and *II Timothy* and *Titus* have been called the "Pastoral epistles" since the 1700s. See Ehrman, *Forged Writing in the Name of God Why the Bible's Authors Are Not Who We Think They Are* 92ff.

[740] Borg and Crossan, *The First Paul: Reclaiming the Radical Visionary Behind the Church's Conservative Icon* 55. *I Timothy* 1: 3 reads: *"When I left for Macedonia, I urged you to stay there in Ephesus..."* The church father Ignatius of Antioch [abt 35-50 – abt. 98-117] wrote that Paul mentioned the Ephesians "in every letter" although we know of only two cites and they are in only in one letter: *I Corinthians* 15:32 and 16:8. See Bauer 218.

[741] Tradition also has John, the apostle living a long life in Ephesus and buried there. More on Ephesus: A future pope, Hilarus I (461-468) was Pope Leo I's representative at the Second Council in Ephesus in 449 dealing with the Christological controversy of Monophysitism (the belief that Christ had only one nature and that it was divine). The council ended up condemning Bishop Flavian of Constantinople who had opposed Monophysitism. Hilarus opposed the condemnation and escaped only with difficulty. He attributed his escape to the Apostle John in whose burial chamber he had hid. See Kelly 43, 45. In the sixth century the eastern emperor built a basilica in John's honor. See Pope Benedict XVI, *The Apostles and Their Co-Workers* (Huntington, Indiana: Our Sunday Visitor Publishing Division Our Sunday Visitor, Inc., 2007) 78. However, there is a considerable amount of uncertainty here. As noted earlier, Richard Bauckham has made the case that it was not John of the Twelve but another John, the *"disciple whom Jesus loved"* who lived in Ephesus. Note: The Second Council of Ephesus was repudiated by the Council of Chalcedon two years later.

[742] This remarkable comeback began from the point in which she is first (obliquely) referred to in history. It is in Paul's letter to the Galatians (Remember, the Gospels and *Acts* were written later.) In that letter, Paul adds to a description of Jesus that he was *"born of a woman"* (*Galatians* 4:4), a probable figure of speech merely to say that he was human. See Pelikan, *Mary Through the Centuries Her Place in the History of Culture* 14-15. To sum up, there is this possibility: Paul, living in Ephesus, knows Mary and refers

to her in this letter and from that humble start she becomes the most famous woman in history.

743 Sandoval 5, 31.

744 Wilson, *Jesus A Life* 83.

745 http://bibleresources.bible.com/passagesearchresults2. php?passage1=Mark+3&book_id=48&version1=51&tp=16&c=3 (Accessed May 2, 2012).

746 Stark *The Rise of Mormonism* 49 and http://www.jesusdynasty.com/blog/2006/08/30/getting-our-jameses-straight/. (Accessed May 2, 2012.)

747 Bauckham, *Jude and the Relatives of Jesus in the Early Church* 8-9.

748 Bauckham, *Jude and the Relatives of Jesus in the Early Church* 16.

749 http://www.biblicalstudies.org.uk/article_relatives_bauckham.html (Accessed May 2, 2012).

750 But would Joseph's brother Clopas be married to Mary's sister, also named Mary? Perhaps. Or: "sister" in *John* 19:25 might have meant "sister-in-law." See http://en.wikipedia.org/wiki/Mary_of_Clopas (Accessed May 2, 2012).

751 *Luke* 24:18.

752 I will note that there is speculation back to Origen that Peter was one of the travelers on the Road to Emmaus. See Grant, *Saint Peter A Biography* (Michael Grant Publications Ltd. 1994. New York: Barnes & Noble, 2009) 100. However, that possibility seems contradicted by *Luke* 24:33 which states that the two Emmaus travelers returned to Jerusalem where they found *"the eleven disciples."* (Judas was dead.)

753 *Jude* 1:1.

754 Jude is not included in the lists of the twelve apostles in *Matthew* 10:3 and *Mark* 3:18, but there is a Thaddeus which has caused some to conflate the two as "Jude Thaddeus." Note: The modern writer Hyam Maccoby speculates that Jude and the traitor Judas were the same person. See Charlotte Allen, *The Human Christ The Search for the Historical Jesus* 307.

755 John P. Meier says no. See Meier, *A Marginal Jew Rethinking the Historical Jesus Vlm III Companions and Competitors* 200. James D. Tabor says yes. See Tabor, *The Jesus Dynasty* 138ff. Ben Witherington III says possibly, writing that "Recent scholarship has shown that a very good case can be made for this document actually being from Jude the brother of James the Just and of Jesus. It is unlikely that a later Christian writer would have adopted the name of

so obscure a figure for the sake of lending authority to his pronouncements."
See Witherington, *New Testament History A Narrative Account* Location 5750.

756 White, *From Jesus to Christianity* 423.

757 Stark *The Rise of Mormonism* 49-52. See also Bauckham, *Jude and the Relatives of Jesus in the Early Church* 82-106.

758 http://en.wikipedia.org/wiki/Jewish_Christians. (Accessed May 2, 2012).

759 Bauckham, *Jude and the Relatives of Jesus in the Early Church* 74-106. It may be that the elders mentioned here in *Acts* are the "seventy" (or seventy-two) that Luke refers to in *Luke* 10. See Tabor, *Paul and Jesus How the Apostle Transformed Christianity* Location 690.

760 The transition of the leadership of the Jerusalem Christians from James the brother of Jesus to Simon (or Symeon) his cousin is described by Eusebius as follows: "After the martyrdom of James and the conquest of Jerusalem which immediately followed, it is said that those of the apostles and disciples of the Lord that were still living came together from all directions with those that were related to the Lord according to the flesh (for the majority of them also were still alive) to take counsel as to who was worthy to succeed James. They all with one consent pronounced Symeon, the son of Clopas, of whom the Gospel also makes mention; to be worthy of the episcopal throne of that parish. He was a cousin, as they say, of the Saviour. For Hegesippus records that Clopas was a brother of Joseph." See Eusebius Book III Chapter 11. Eusebius goes on to say that Simon "suffered a death similar to that of the Lord." See Eusebius Book III Chapter 32.

761 Some traditions hold that members of Jesus's extended family may have returned from Jerusalem to Galilee and influenced Christian believers during the first century, possibly even in Nazareth. See Witherington, *New Testament History A Narrative Account* Location 3446ff.

762 Kelly 35.

763 The historian Josephus actually said more about James than he did about Jesus. See *Crossan The Birth of Christianity: Discovering What Happened in the Years Immediately After the Death of Jesus* 463-4.

764 "The *New Testament* is so remarkably silent on the subject of the family of Jesus that it seems quite likely that the early texts were expurgated. Even Mary is seldom mentioned, and her portrait is further obscured by confusing references to several 'other' Marys, who sometimes might not be 'others' at all." See Stark *The Rise of Mormonism* 49.

765 *I Corinthians* 15:7.

766 Catholic tradition holds that "despite its name, the *Acts of the Apostles* recounts the activities of only a few of the Twelve, probably because the rest had departed on long missionary journeys from which they never returned." See Hitchcock 27-8.

Also by tradition the Twelve, before they left Jerusalem, made assignments to themselves as well as other *New Testament* heroes of the countries of the known world so that the Gospel would be preached to "every creature." Some included;

- Spain – to James the brother of John.
- England – to Joseph of Arimathea.
- Persia- to Bartholomew. (As noted, this may be the same person as Nathanial.)
- India – to Thomas.
- Mesopotamia (modern Iraq) – to Jude Thaddeus.

Also churches in the large cities in the Mediterranean world pointed to early Christian leaders among their supposed founders: Rome to Peter and Paul; Alexandria to Mark; Constantinople to Andrew; Athens to a character mentioned in *Acts* 17:34 called Dionysius the Areopagite.

Note: In the Inca creation story the chief god Viracocha disguised himself as a wandering beggar. In 1613 a native Andean man of noble birth Don Felipe Guaman Poma de Ayala wrote a letter to King Philip III of Spain. It was an argument for more self-rule and it claimed that the beggar was the Apostle Bartholomew who came to the Andes and brought the pre-Incan people to Christianity.

See MacCulloch 164-5. Hitchcock 35, Ondina E. Gonzales and Justo L. Gonzales 1, 64.

767 *Acts* 12:17. It may well be that Peter's wife who is alluded to in *I Corinthians* 9:5 left with him and that most of the Twelve also fled along with their wives, also alluded to in *I Corinthians* 9:5. This latter possibility is supported in that some years later, Paul visited Jerusalem and only reported seeing two of the Twelve – Peter and John. - *Galatians* 2:9.

768 *I Corinthians* 1:12; 3:22; 9:5; 15:5.

769 Peter is the legendary author of the epistles that bear his name toward the end of the *New Testament* but most scholars discount this possibility. See, for example, White, *From Jesus to Christianity* 425; Ehrman, *Peter, Paul and Mary* (Oxford: Oxford University Press, 2006), 77ff. Also Peter, according

to *Acts* 4:13, was "unschooled." These are additional possible *New Testament* references to Peter:

- *John* 21:18-19 - A possible reference to his own crucifixion.
- *I Peter* 5:13 locates him in "Babylon," a reference to Rome as seen in *Revelation* 14:8; 16ff and 18:2. See Browning Location 862. Note: The Church of the East – see Chapter 8 - regards this verse as a reference by the Apostle Peter to the actual Mesopotamian city of Babylon. See http://en.wikipedia.org/wiki/Assyrian_Church_of_the_East (Accessed May 2, 2012).

The church fathers Clement of Rome writing to the Corinthians in the late first century and Ignatius Bishop of Antioch write of Peter being in Rome. See Jedin 112 - 114.

770 *Matthew* 16: 16-19; *Mark* 8:29; *Luke* 9:20.

771 All four gospels record that one of Jesus's followers in Gethsemane cut off the ear of one of the assailants of Jesus. Only John records that it was Peter. Only Matthew records the famous quote contained above. Mark has Jesus saying nothing to his would-be protector. Luke has Jesus saying: *"Stop! No more of this."* John has Jesus saying to Peter: *"Put the sword into the sheath; the cup which the Father has given Me, shall I not drink it?"* See *Matthew* 26: 51-53, *Mark* 14: 47-48, *Luke* 22: 50-51, and *John* 18: 10-11.

772 *I Corinthians* 15: 5. However, this primacy is contradicted in:

- *Matthew* 28:9 – which cites the women in the garden as the first to see the risen Jesus.
- *Luke* 24:13-35 – which indicates that Cleopas and a fellow traveler on the road to Emmaus may have been the first. It is not established if this appearance preceded the one to Peter cited in verse 34 or not.
- *John* 20:11-18 which cites Mary Magdalene as first.

However, whether or not he was the first, the Gospel record supports *I Corinthians* 15 that Peter saw the risen Christ:

- *Mark* 16: 7 – As noted earlier, a young man at the Empty Tomb told the women who had gone there: *"..go, tell His (Jesus's) disciples **and Peter**, He is going ahead of you to Galilee; there you will see Him, just as He told you."* (Emphasis added).
- *Luke* 24:34 – The disciples told other followers: *"The Lord has really risen. He appeared to **Peter**."* (Emphasis added).

[773] This order was actually repeated three times in slightly varying form at the end of the *Gospel of John*, chapter 21 verses 15-17: "*So when they had finished breakfast, Jesus said to Simon Peter, 'Simon, son of John, do you love Me more than these?' He said to Him, 'Yes, Lord; You know that I love You.' He said to him, 'Tend My lambs.' He said to him again a second time, 'Simon, son of John, do you love Me?' He said to Him, 'Yes, Lord; You know that I love You.' He said to him, 'Shepherd My sheep.' He said to him the third time, 'Simon, son of John, do you love Me?' Peter was grieved because He said to him the third time, 'Do you love Me?' And he said to Him, 'Lord, You know all things; You know that I love You.' Jesus said to him, 'Tend My sheep.'*" (Emphases added).

[774] *Acts* 2: 1-41.

[775] Apparently, at about the same time, Peter and John were preaching to the Samaritans, Philip continued the outreach to Gentiles by converting the Ethiopian Eunuch in *Acts* 8:26-39.

[776] *Acts* 10:1 – 11:18. Note: As with the story of Paul's conversion, Luke uses repetition to emphasize the significance of Cornelius's conversion – in this instance he tells the story "only" two times. The message to Peter was a vision in which he was commanded to eat animals deemed "unclean" under Jewish religious laws with a voice telling him, "*What God has cleansed, no longer consider unholy.*" *(Acts* 10:15 and 11:9*)* Martin Luther's comment on these sections was: "As he pronounced these animals clean, which according to his own law were still unclean, so he pronounces the Gentiles and all of us righteous, although as a matter of fact we are sinners just as those animals were unclean." See *Justo L. Gonzales, A History of Christian Thought From the Protestant Reformation to the Twentieth Century* Volume III Revised Edition Location 861.

[777] *Mark* 1:30 and I *Corinthians* 9:5. Note: Here is one other non-celibate Pope. Pope Hormisdas (514-23) was married and had a son before his ordination. That son became Pope Silverius (536-37). Both father and son were eventually canonized. Additional note: In 1967 Pope Paul VI promoted priestly celibacy in *Sacerdotalis Caelibatus*. It is a twelve thousand-word document with 152 footnotes, many of them references to the *New Testament*. But he omitted reference to I *Corinthians* 9:5 which comes from Paul and reads in its entirety: "*Don't we have the right to a Christian wife with us as the other apostles and the Lord's brothers do, and as Peter does?*" See Kelly 239ff. Note: Peter may have had at least one daughter: Pope Paul I (757-767) is known in Catholic history for restoring the catacombs of Rome, transferring the bodies to chapels. One of the bodies was the supposed daughter of Peter, Petronilla, whom the Frankish royal house revered. See Kelly 90-93.

[778] *James* 2: 14-17.

[779] *James* 2: 26.

[780] *James 1:1.*

[781] *James* 2:1.

[782] *James* 5:12 - compare to *Matthew* 5:33-37.

[783] *James* 2:8 - compare to *Matthew* 22:39-40.

[784] *James* 5:1-6 - compare to *Matthew* 19:23-24.

[785] *James* 4:13-15- compare to *Luke* 12:16-21.

[786] *James* 1:26. This is very similar to Jesus's teachings in the Sermon on the Mount. *Matthew* 7:21 reads: *"Not everyone who says to Me, 'Lord, Lord,' will enter the kingdom of heaven, but he who does the will of My Father who is in heaven will enter."*

[787] *James* 2:2.

[788] *James* 2:21.

[789] *James* 2:25.

[790] *James* 5:11. Job was a figure of endurance under great pressure as described in the *Old Testament Book of Job*. This verse in *James* reads: *"We count those blessed who endured. You have heard of the endurance of Job and have seen the outcome of the Lord's dealings, that the Lord is full of compassion and is merciful."* Note: During the American Civil War in the 1860s Abraham Lincoln may have turned more to the reading of the *Bible*. At one point, Mary Todd Lincoln's seamstress, curious about what portion of the scriptures he was reading, walked quietly behind where Lincoln was sitting and noticed that he was engrossed in the *Book of Job*. See Richard Carwardine, "Religion and National Construction in the Age of Lincoln," *Journal of Mormon History*, Spring 2010, 49.

[791] *James* 5:16-18 uses Elijah to make the point that prayer can work. Note : Elijah is referred to one other time in the *New Testament* outside of the Gospels. *Romans* 11:2-4 uses Elijah to make the point that God has not abandoned Israel.

[792] http://www.zianet.com/maxey/Elders8.htm (Accessed May 2, 2012).

[793] *Luke* 1: 5-10.

[794] *Luke* 2: 22-38.

795 Acts 3: 1-10.

796 *Acts* 5:42.

797 *Acts* 21:23-26.

798 *Matthew* 21: 12-17; *Mark* 11: 15-19; *Luke* 19: 45-48; *John* 2: 13-17. In the Synoptics, the phrase "*den of robbers*" was used. *John* records Jesus's criticism that the officials have turned the Temple into a "market."

799 I owe this concept to Amy-Jill Levine, *The Misunderstood Jew: The Church and the Scandal of the Jewish Church* (New York: HarperCollins, 2006) 154ff and regret it if I have misstated Levine's point of view.

800 It is accepted in this book that his mission was directed to the Jews. But it is not that simple. He went to the districts around Tyre and Sidon (*Matthew* 15:21 and *Mark* 7:31) and people from those districts came to him (*Mark* 3:8). Also, he often spoke favorably of those areas, at least in comparison to his Jewish base. (*Matthew* 11: 21-22; *Luke* 4:26; 10:13-14). Not surprisingly, people of Sidon later showed hospitality to Paul (*Acts* 27:3).

801 *Matthew* 15:26 and *Mark* 7:27. There are other anti-Gentile comments of Jesus in the *New Testament*. For example:

- *Matthew* 5:47 – "*If you greet only your brothers, what more are you doing than others? Do not even the Gentiles do the same?*"
- *Matthew* 6: 7-8: "*And when you are praying, do not use meaningless repetition as the Gentiles do, for they suppose that they will be heard for their many words. So do not be like them…*"
- *Matthew* 18:17 - (In the context of people who refuse to listen to the church): "*If he refuses to listen even to the church, let him be to you as a Gentile.*"
- *Matthew* 20:25-26 – "*You know that the rulers of the Gentiles lord it over them, and their great men exercise authority over them. It is not this way among you,…*" See also *Mark* 10:30, 42 and *Luke* 22:25.

802 *Matthew* 15:24; *Mark* 7: 27; *Matthew* 10:5. See also *John* 4:9.

803 *Mark* 5:17; *Luke* 8:37-8; *Luke* 9:52-3.

804 According to the last verse in the *Book of Luke* (Remember, the same author wrote *Luke* and Acts), after Jesus departed from Bethany the apostles returned to Jerusalem and "*stayed continually at the temple, praising God.*"

805 *Acts* 2:42-6 and *Acts* 6:9. Note: Jesus had prophesized that his followers would be excluded from the synagogues. See *John* 16:2.

[806] Joel Carmichael, *The Birth of Christianity* (New York: Dorset Press,1989) 59 and

Griffith-Jones 153.

[807] *Acts* 24:5.

[808] James DG Dunn *Jesus, Paul, and the Gospels* Location 2474.

[809] *Galatians* 4: 9-10.

[810] *Colossians* 2:16.

[811] *Acts* 9:26-30 and *Galatians* 1:18-19.

[812] *Acts* 15: 4.

[813] Georgi *The Opponents of Paul in Second Corinthians*, 1964 English Translation, Fortress Press, 1986. Printed in the UK by Billing & Sons, Worcester. Bound by Hunter & Foulis Ltd. Edinburg, for T & T Cl, 167ff. ark LTD., Edinburg First Printed in the UK, 1987 39, 41ff, 45, 49, 52, 83ff, 85, 152, 164. I regret it if I have misstated Georgi's point of view.

[814] Tabor, *Paul and Jesus How the Apostle Transformed Christianity* Location 3524ff.

[815] *Acts* 2: 38.

[816] *Matthew* 21:23-27; *Mark* 11: 27-33; *Luke* 20: 1-8.

[817] William Smith 30.

[818] In early Christianity the Septuagint was crucial. It "was the *Bible* of the first known Christian authors, the *Bible* that almost all the writers of the *New Testament* used." (The writer of *Revelation* may have quoted from a different version of Jewish scriptures.) See Justo L. Gonzales, *A History of Christian Thought From the Beginnings to the Council of Chalcedon* Volume 1 Revised Edition 42, 60.

[819] Cahill, *Mysteries of the Middle Ages The Rise of Feminism, Science and Art from the Cults of Catholic Europe* 5ff.

[820] There is an Alexandria in the state of Virginia in the United States. It is an old city by United States standards. It is a point of historical interest with tours of preserved homes like that of the family of Confederate General Robert E. Lee (1807 – 1870) which was later owned by the American labor leader, John L. Lewis (1880 – 1969).

[821] Witherington, *New Testament History A Narrative Account* Location 3714ff.

822 In the 800s when Alexandria was under Muslim control, Venetian travelers brought what they assumed was Mark's body to Venice where St. Mark's Basilica was built to preserve it. See Hitchcock 190. In 1968, at least part of this relic was returned to Egypt. See Tadros Location 692.

823 Reader's Digest *After Jesus: The Triumph of Christianity* 95-6.

824 *Acts* 18: 24-28.

825 *I Corinthians* 3: 4-5.

826 *Acts* 19: 1-7.

827 *I Corinthians* 3:6.

828 *Acts* 19:3. How did the adherents of John the Baptist get to Ephesus? Here's one possible explanation: "Jewish visitors from western providences joined the crowds that went out to hear (John the Baptist), and carried his message back to cities like Ephesus, where Paul twenty-five or thirty years later found groups of John's disciples.....While John seems to have made no effort to organize his followers, it is clear that many of them organized themselves in Johannist circles out in the great centers of the Roman world, far beyond the limits of Palestine." See Goodspeed 40-41.

829 *I Corinthians* 2:1.

830 Herein is a useful criterion for weighting the possibility that a particular scripture is authentic: If it is somewhat at variance to another part of scripture or to the mission of the church and yet is still included, it may have a higher chance of being authentic. For example, the Gospels make it clear that Jesus was the friend of sinners. This must be correct since it is at variance with the teachings of the early church. I owe this thought to Wilson, *Jesus A Life* 155-6 and regret it if I have misstated Wilson's point of view.

831 There is another type of baptism in the *New Testament* that makes the whole issue of baptism more confusing. Therefore, like the "Baptism of John," the primary reason for including it would be the (very praiseworthy) motive of accuracy. It is baptism "in the name of the Lord Jesus" or "in Jesus's name." As noted, the Apostles sent Peter and John to Samaria to check on Philip's ministry there (*Acts* 8:14-17). They discovered that the Samaritans had only been "*baptized in the name of the Lord Jesus*" and had not received the Holy Spirit. Peter and John placed hands on them and they received the Spirit. This seems to indicate an incompleteness in only being "*baptized in the name of the Lord Jesus.*" However, this is not clear because in other sections of *Acts* people are baptized in Jesus's name and still received the Holy Spirit:

- *Acts* 2:38 – Peter told a crowd gathering at Pentecost who asked what they should do: *"Repent and each of you be baptized in the name of Jesus Christ for the forgiveness of your sins; and **you will receive the gift of the Holy Spirit**."* (Emphasis added).

- *Acts* 10:47-48 – Peter had finished speaking to Cornelius and the crowd at his house in Caesarea. He saw that the Holy Spirit had come upon them and said: *"'Surely no one can refuse the water for these to be baptized **who have received the Holy Spirit** just as we did, can he?' And he ordered them to be baptized in the name of Jesus Christ."* (Emphasis added).

- *Acts* 19:1-6. This concerns Paul and should be quoted in full to cast doubt on any claim based on the Samaritan account of *Acts* 8 that baptism only in the name of Jesus was somehow incomplete: *"It happened that while Apollos was at Corinth, Paul passed through the upper country and came to Ephesus, and found some disciples. He said to them, 'Did you receive the Holy Spirit when you believed?' And they said to him, 'No, we have not even heard whether there is a Holy Spirit.' And he said, 'Into what then were you baptized?' And they said, 'Into John's baptism.' Paul said, 'John baptized with the baptism of repentance, telling the people to believe in Him who was coming after him, that is, in Jesus.' When they heard this, they were baptized in the name of the Lord Jesus. And when Paul had laid his hands upon them, **the Holy Spirit came on them**, and they began speaking with tongues and prophesying."* (Emphasis added).

In summary, there appears to be a significant inconsistency between the *Acts* 8 account and the accounts in *Acts* 2, 10 and 19 over whether baptism in the name of the Lord Jesus is sufficient or not to bring about the Holy Spirit in the believer's life. This is the conclusion of Justo L. Gonzales: "One thing is clear, and that is that if any of these texts is taken as a rigid norm that the Spirit must follow, or as an absolute and essential practice in the life of the Church, this contradicts Luke's wider understanding of the freedom of the Spirit." See Justo L. Gonzales *Acts The Gospel of the Spirit* 108-109.

[832] *I Corinthians* 2:1-2. I owe this thought to Akenson, *Saint Saul: A Skeleton Key to the Historical Jesus* 153-58 and regret it if I have misstated Akenson's point of view.

[833] *Luke* 1:36 reports that their mothers were relatives.

[834] "...(T)he Dispersion (Diaspora) was the general title applied to those Jews who remained settled in foreign countries after the return from the Babylonian exile..." See William Smith 146. At the time of Jesus, Jews in the Diaspora

outnumbered Jews in Palestine four million to one million. They read the *Old Testament* in Greek. The Martyr Stephen, Barnabas and Paul were from the Diaspora. The Greek names of the deacons selected in *Acts* 6:1-6 are near-proof that Jews from the Diaspora were in the Jerusalem community at that time. See Stark, *The Rise of Christianity A Sociologist Reconsiders History* (Princeton: Princeton University Press, 1996) 49-71 and Jedin 75, 99.

[835] In this he quoted *Mark* 1:7, *Luke* 3:16 and *John* 1:27. This quote was in a sermon in Antioch in Psidia preached in a synagogue. Paul was talking about Jesus and here is the context contained in verses 24-25: *"Before he (Jesus) came, John the Baptist preached that all the people of Israel needed to repent of their sins and turn to God and be baptized. As John was finishing his ministry he asked, 'Do you think I am the Messiah? No, I am not! But he is coming soon—and I'm not even worthy to be his slave and untie the sandals on his feet.'"* Note: This Antioch is different than the Antioch mentioned more prominently in the *New Testament*. The remains of a Byzantine church are the traditional location of the synagogue where Paul preached. Seventeen ancient cities in Turkey were named Antioch. http://www.allaboutturkey.com/yalvac.htm (Accessed May 2, 2012).

[836] *John* 1: 26-33; *Acts* 1:5 and 11:16.

[837] I owe these thoughts to Jedin 119-23 and regret it if I have misstated Jedin's point of view.

[838] The early Christians adapted pagan customs with the dates for Christmas and Easter as the most prominent examples. The Summer Solstice (June 21) when the days start to become shorter became the Feast of St. John the Baptist because he had said: *"He must increase, but I must decrease."* (*John* 3: 30)

[839] *Acts* 1:22.

[840] *Luke* notes that average people as opposed to their leaders had been baptized by John. See *Luke* 7:28-30.

[841] *Mark* 2:18.

[842] *Luke* 9:7.

[843] Tabor, *The Jesus Dynasty* 137.

[844] Grant, *Jesus: An Historian's Review of the Gospels* 47 and note on 213.

[845] Ehrman, 215.

[846] Josephus did not note any nexus between Jesus and John the Baptist. He did write that John was noted for his baptizing. In reporting on John's

preaching, Josephus put more emphasis than the Gospels did on ethics and righteousness and less on apocalypticism. He also reported that John the Baptist was arrested because of concerns that he might start a rebellion rather than his criticism of a royal marriage. See Witherington, *New Testament History A Narrative Account* Location 1722ff and Wilson, *Jesus A Life* 114.

847 Paul Johnson, *A History of Christianity* 21.

848 *Luke* 3:11.

849 *Luke* 3: 12-13.

850 *Luke* 3: 14.

851 *Matthew* 11:12.

852 *Luke* 3: 10-20. Verses 19-20 state: *"But when Herod the tetrarch was reprimanded by him because of Herodias, his brother's wife, and because of all the wicked things which Herod had done, Herod also added this to them all: he locked John up in prison."*

Note: If indeed the ill-starred second marriage led to the brutal murder of John the Baptist, it may have been the first of two *New Testament* consequences. The second could be the near capture of Paul then Saul in Damascus at the very beginning of his career. See Chapter 2 above.

853 *Matthew* 14: 1-13, *Mark* 6: 14-32. See also Grant, *History of Rome* 341.

854 *Mark* 1: 4, 9. To repeat a concept, the conclusion that John baptized Jesus for the remission of sins is thought to be authentic because it is so paradoxical to our view of Jesus Christ as sinless and as the Lord of the universe that the early editors of the *New Testament* would not have included it unless it actually happened. See among others: Witherington, *The Jesus Quest The Third Search For the Jew of Nazareth* (Downers Grove, Illinois: InterVarsity Press, 1995) 201 analyzing the scholarship of John P Meier.

855 *John* 10:41 suggests that John the Baptist did no miracles: *"Many came to Him (Jesus) and were saying, 'While John performed no sign, yet everything John said about this man was true.'"*

856 Tradition has him Bishop of Caesarea. See William Smith 45.

857 Akenson, *Saint Saul: A Skeleton Key to the Historical Jesus* 83. It is my view that the first two of these versions had a great deal in common and I have tended to treat them as one.

858 Additionally, if a sufficient number of Paul's epistles had not been preserved the result might have been the same as if he had not written them.

[859] Wilson, *Jesus A Life* 102-3.

[860] To summarize some of the foregoing, it might have taken off this way: John's baptism was connected to repentance and forgiveness of sins. Those baptized were responding to his call to be part of an apocalyptic end- times group. Apparently Peter and John were baptized this way (*Acts* 1:22 and *John* 1:35–42.) Toward the end of his life Jesus said that anyone who had rejected John's baptism rejected God. (*Mark* 11:29–33 and *Luke* 7:26–30.) However in *Acts* which is heavily influenced by Paul, Peter and the others as we have noted, begin talking about baptizing in the name of Jesus Christ in order to receive the Holy Spirit. See *Acts* 2:38. Of course, we see that this remains a matter of controversy. In *Acts* 18:24–25, we see that Apollos is unfamiliar with any baptism other than the baptism of John. Then, in *Acts* 19:1–7 there is a similar group in Ephesus. There is no record of whether Apollos was rebaptized. However, he did go on to Corinth where the issue of baptism and his own role became controversial in Paul's eyes.(*I Corinthians* 1:10-17). This is some 25 years after the crucifixion and is evidence of a Christianity before Paul. Since it was written some years after that, it is also evidence of the authors' need to reject that other form of baptism. See Tabor, *Paul and Jesus How the Apostle Transformed Christianity* Location 2262ff.

[861] *Mark* 6:14; *Luke* 9:7

[862] *Matthew* 16:14; *Mark* 8:28; *Luke* 9:19.

[863] *Mark* 6:15; *Luke* 9:8.

[864] *II Kings* 2:11 reports that Elijah had been taken to Heaven in chariots and horses of fire or a whirlwind. Note: Since Elijah had allegedly never died, many Jewish people in that era thought he was an important presence who would could one day return. In this they were bolstered by the very last words of the *Old Testament, Malachi* 4:5-6: *"Behold, I am going to send you Elijah the prophet before the coming of the great and terrible day of the* Lord. *He will restore the hearts of the fathers to their children and the hearts of the children to their fathers, so that I will not come and smite the land with a curse."* The conviction that Elijah was still alive and cared for the Jewish people, then, was powerful. It was manifested at the cross. It is evident from *Mark* 15: 34-36 that the bystanders there thought that Jesus was crying out to Elijah. (Although it is equally clear that they were mistaken.) See James DG Dunn *Did the First Christians Worship Jesus? The New Testament Evidence* 35.

[865] *Matthew* 11:14. See also *Matthew* 17:11-12 and *Mark* 9:12-13.

[866] *John* 1:21.

867 *Matthew* used about 90 percent of *Mark*. *Luke* used about 50 percent of *Mark*. See Spong 27. More specifically, *Matthew* reproduces about 600 of *Mark's* 661 verses "in language largely identical." *Matthew* in addition has *Q* (about 250 verses), and 400 more verses. *Luke* reproduces about half of *Mark*, plus *Q* plus about 500 more verses. *Luke* is for Gentile Christians. See Grant, *Jesus: An Historian's Review of the Gospels* 186, 187. Note: Notwithstanding his reliance on *Mark*, the writer of *Luke* may have at least some reservations about it since his stated purpose, as we have noted, was to write out the Gospel *"in consecutive order" (Luke*1:3).

868 *Matthew* 8:5-13 and *Luke* 7:1-10. *Q* alludes to other miracles. See *Luke* 7:21-23, 10:13 and 11:30. These match M*atthew* 11:2-11, 11:21-23 and 10:40 and 12:38-42.

869 However, "(T)he eschatology of *Q* presumes Jesus's death and resurrection.....Jesus's death is presupposed most prominently in the saying that his disciples must pick up their own cross and follow after him."(*Luke* 14:27). This matches with *Matthew* 10:37-8. See Van Vorst 173-4. See also *Luke* 13:35 in which Jesus states, *"Behold, your house is left to you desolate; and I say to you, you will not see Me until the time comes when you say, 'BLESSED IS HE WHO COMES IN THE NAME OF THE LORD!'"* This matches with *Matthew* 23:38-39 in which Jesus states *"Behold, your house is being left to you desolate! For I say to you, from now on you will not see Me until you say, 'BLESSED IS HE WHO COMES IN THE NAME OF THE LORD!'"*

870 Mack, *Who Wrote The New Testament?: The Making of the Christian Myth* 47ff, 63. Note: Here are two scriptures common to *Matthew* and *Luke* but not in *Mark* and hence part of any *Q* analysis and may therefore be of an older tradition showing how some followers viewed Jesus in non-Pauline terms. *Luke* 7:35 quotes Jesus, *"···wisdom is vindicated by all her children."* A similar comment made by Jesus is found in *Matthew* 11:19 and in the same context of comparing himself with John the Baptist. This may show an understanding of Jesus as a prophet and as one, like John the Baptist, with sagely wisdom. See L. Michael White *Scripting Jesus The Gospels in Rewrite* Location 1229.

871 *I Thessalonians* 4:15.

872 *I Corinthians* 11: 23-26 and *I Corinthians* 15: 1-8.

873 Pelikan, *Jesus Through The Centuries: His Place in the History of Culture* 9.

874 Akenson, *Saint Saul: A Skeleton Key to the Historical Jesus* 111.

875 Charlotte Allen, "The a Search For A No-Frills Jesus" *The Atlantic Online* December 1996.

876 http://www.answers.org/bible/missing_q.html (Accessed May 2, 2012) and Akenson, *Saint Saul: A Skeleton Key to the Historical Jesus* 279.

877 There is further evidence of this in the disparate accounts of Judas's death in *Matthew* and *Acts* noted in Chapter 2. The *Acts* account shows a Palestinian origin which would likely go back to the time right after the crucifixion. This origin is shown in that an important word is left in Aramaic: "Akeldama" - which means "field of blood." See Bart D. Ehrman *Did Jesus Exist? The Historical Argument for Jesus of Nazareth* 108.

878 William Smith 105. Who was Enoch? Enoch was an *Old Testament* figure. He lived for 365 years and on the basis of this verse: *"And Enoch walked with God and he was not; for God took him"* (*Genesis* 5:24), the *New Testament* writer of *Hebrews* concluded that he did not die and was an example of faith. (*Hebrews* 11:5). Incidentally, living for 365 years seems like quite a feat, but according to the *Old Testament* it's really nothing for that era. Enoch's father lived for 962 years and Enoch's son Methuselah lived for 969 years. How did Methuselah, the man who according to the *Bible* lived the longest human life, die? We don't know but we do know from a careful analysis of the scriptures that he died in the year of the Great Flood. See *Genesis* 5:18-27, *Genesis* 7:11 and *Hebrews* 11:7. Enoch is mentioned two other times in the *New Testament*:

- *Luke* 3:37 as an ancestor of Joseph the father *"as was supposed"* of Jesus (*Luke* 3:23).
- As previously noted in *Jude* 14 as a descendant of Adam. However, there is a problem. The *Luke* account would have Enoch fourteen generations from Abraham as determined through the listing of the ancestors but this verse introduces the Enochian quote here with this: *"It was also about these men that Enoch, in the **seventh** generation from Adam, prophesied,..."* (Emphasis added).

Enoch is only mentioned once in the *Talmud* and in a somewhat negative manner. See Hyam Maccoby *Revolution in Judaea: Jesus and the Jewish Resistance* New York: Taplinger Publishing Company, Inc., 1973) 91.

Several books written between the *Old* and *New Testaments* bear the name *Enoch*. *I Enoch* achieved the status of being quoted by *Jude* and thereby appeared in the *Bible*. *I Enoch* was never considered part of the orthodox canon but is considered inspired scripture by the Ethiopian Orthodox church and by some early church fathers. The book deals with fallen angels who ask Enoch to intercede for them. In addition to the direct quote in *Jude*, *I Enoch* may also be the basis for a passage in *I Peter* cited earlier which asserts that Jesus, after his death, *"went and made a proclamation to the spirits in prison,* who in former times did not obey, when God waited patiently in the days of Noah, during the building of the ark, in which a few, that is, eight people, were saved through water." (*I Peter* 3:19-20). See MacCulloch 68, 279 and http://en.wikipedia.org/wiki/1_Enoch (Accessed May 2, 2012). (I wonder if those spirits included Methuselah.) *I Enoch* may also be the basis for:

- *Luke* 10:17-18 - "*The seventy returned with joy, saying, 'Lord, even the demons are subject to us in Your name.' And He said to them, 'I was watching Satan fall from heaven like lightning.'*" (Note: "In the 1600s, the Sorbonne professor Edmond Richer had the view that parish priests, as the direct successors of these seventy (or seventy-two) disciples, had authority independent of their bishops. See Hitchcock 331.
- *II Peter 2:4* - "*For God did not spare even the angels who sinned. He threw them into hell, in gloomy pits of darkness, where they are being held until the day of judgment.*"

See White, *From Jesus to Christianity* 71-73.

Finally, Jesus himself may have quoted from at least one of the *Books of Enoch*. These statements may derive from Enochian writings:

- *John* 14:2 – "*In My Father's house are many dwelling places; if it were not so, I would have told you; for I go to prepare a place for you.*"
- *Matthew* 5: 34-35, 37 – "*But I say to you, make no oath at all, either by heaven, for it is the throne of God, or by the earth, for it is the footstool of His feet, … But let your statement be, 'Yes, yes' or 'No, no'; anything beyond these is of evil.*" See Potter 218-220.

Note: Centuries later, to deal with his hard-pressed followers in the early 1830s, the Mormon leader Joseph Smith set up a redistribution plan called the "United Order of Enoch." The idea was to give property to the church, work the land as stewards and have the bishop distribute the surplus. It did not succeed. See Richard N. Ostling and Joan K. Ostling, *Mormon America: The Power and the Promise The Beliefs, Rituals, Business Practices, and Well-Guarded Secrets of One of the World's Fastest Growing and Most Influential Religions* (New York: HarperSanFrancisco A *Division of* HarperCollins*Publishers*, 1999) 30.

Additional note: There is another less famous Enoch in the *Bible*. In one of the best-known stories ever, the first humans, Adam and Eve, had two sons, Cain and Abel. The former killed the latter and was sent by God to live "East of Eden." There he and his wife (where did she come from?) had a son named Enoch for whom they named a "city." See *Genesis* 4:1-17.

Final note: A distant cousin of mine Enoch Pruitt (1840-1912) was born in Kentucky.

[879] The Devil was calling Moses a murderer. Here are the facts. The story is told in the second book of the *Bible*, *Exodus*. Moses was born as a Hebrew slave in Egypt but was taken from his home at birth for his own safety and raised within the Egyptian master class. When he was an adult, he went to visit the Hebrews. He saw an Egyptian beating a Hebrew slave and "*after looking in all directions to make sure no one was watching, Moses killed the Egyptian and hid the body in the sand.*" Later, he was accused by other Hebrews and knew he had to flee. See *Exodus* 2: 11-15. Was it murder or some form of justifiable homicide? You be the judge.

[880] This text is also called the *Assumption of Moses*. It appears to have been written about 90 AD. See Browning Location 796.

[881] Bauckham, *Jude and the Relatives of Jesus in the Early Church* 235ff, 270-80.

[882] There is also a rather humorous example of a writer of the scripture relying on other literature. Whoever wrote the *Book of Titus* warned his readers about the people in Crete with this verse of scripture: "*One of themselves, a prophet of their own, said, 'Cretans are always liars, evil beasts, lazy gluttons.'*" (*Titus* 1:12). He appears to be quoting Epimenides of the city of Knossos on Crete, a semi-mythical 6th century BC Greek seer. See http://en.wikipedia.org/wiki/1_Enoch and http://en.wikipedia.org/wiki/Epimenides (Both accessed on May 2, 2012). Note: In his lifetime, Jesus himself was called a "glutton." See *Matthew* 11:19. Further Note: This Epimenides has been associated with the establishment in Athens of the altar "to the unknown god" described in the *New Testament* in *Acts* 17. See Don Richardson *Eternity in Their Hearts* Ventura, California: Regal Books from Gospel Light, Kindle Edition, 1981) 9-23. In this respect, it is noteworthy that the writer of *Titus* called Epimenides a "prophet."

[883] Books attributed to Enoch and Moses were controversial. Athanasius's letter of 367 cited earlier which is the first list of the 27 *New Testament* books condemns writings supposedly derived from Moses and Enoch. He wrote that they were "filled with myths." See Pagels, *Revelations Visions, Prophecy and Politics in the Book of Revelation* 66.

[884] Benjamin Franklin felt the same way. As a young man in Philadelphia he was angry at a group of Presbyterian ministers due to their emphasis on scripture over virtue and referred to them as "grave and dull animals." See Waldman 21.

[885] Ehrman, *Jesus Interrupted: Revealing the Hidden Contradictions in the Bible (And Why We Don't Know Them)* 199-200.

[886] Pagels, *Beyond Belief* 70ff.

[887] Incidentally, the Catholic Church has made "Doubting Thomas" the patron saint of architects for the many churches he was said to have built on his pilgrimages. Tradition holds that he went to India. His feast day is July 3. See Sandoval 18-19. Indian and Catholic traditions also hold that Thomas died in India and was buried there. In the 1500s Spanish Jesuit St. Francis Xavier (1506 – 1552) was thought to have prayed at the tomb of St. Thomas. See Hitchcock 399.

[888] http://www.beliefnet.com/story/128/story_12865_4.html. (Accessed May 2, 2012).

[889] Strobel 42.

[890] Meier, *A Marginal Jew Rethinking the Historical Jesus Vlm III Companions and Competitors* 10. In this context, it should be noted that not only the *Gospel of Thomas* but also other books that the western church views as noncanonical were also excluded by the eastern church from the canon even though they were outside the control of Rome. "Throughout the Middle Ages, neither Nestorians nor the Jacobites were under any coercion from the Roman/ Byzantine Empire or church, and had they wished, they could have included any alternative Gospels or scriptures they wanted to. But instead of adding to the canon, they chose to prune. The Syriac *Bible* omits several books that are included in the West (*II Peter, II and III John, Jude* and the *Book of Revelation.*) ....The deep conservatism of these churches, so far removed from papal or imperial control, makes nonsense of claims that the church bureaucracy allied with empire to suppress unpleasant truths about Christian origins." See Jenkins, *The Lost History of Christianity: The Thousand Year Golden Age of the Church in the Middle East, Africa, and Asia - and How it Died* 88. Note: Meier is not a believer in inerrancy. Based on criteria that he follows, for example, he opines that Jesus's famous statement in *Matthew* 16: 18-19 ("*Thou are Peter...*") has only a plausible case for being historical. See Meier, *A Marginal Jew Rethinking the Historical Jesus Vlm III Companions and Competitors* 231-2.

[891] Ehrman, *Lost Christianities*, (New York: Oxford University Press) 2003 13.

[892] Mack, *Who Wrote The New Testament?: The Making of the Christian Myth* 61.

[893] Ehrman, *Lost Christianities* 58-9.

[894] Pagels and King, *Reading Judas: The Gospel of Judas and the Shaping of Christianity* xix.

895 Ehrman, *The Lost Gospel of Judas Iscariot* (Oxford: Oxford University Press, 2006) 53.

896 I am moving quickly here but should not leave the impression that somehow Q and *Thomas* are seamlessly related. Robert E. Van Vorst: "The genre of *Thomas* ...cannot convincingly be pressed to support reconstructions of Q that make Jesus a sage only. Q's John the Baptizer material, its clear reference to the miracles of Jesus and its narration of one miracle, and its stronger references to the death and coming of Jesus distinguish Q from *Thomas.*" See Van Vorst 216.

897 Eric Reece, *Harpers* December 2005. Note: Reece explicitly ties *Thomas's* approach to Christianity to Thomas Jefferson.

898 *I Corinthians* 2:2

899 One modern scholar, Helmut Koester has said: "The *Gospel of Thomas* and Q challenge the assumption that the early church was unanimous in making Jesus's death and resurrection the fulcrum of Christian faith. Both documents presuppose that Jesus's significance lay in his words, and in his words alone." See Helmut Koester, *Ancient Christian Gospels: Their History and Development.* (London: SCM Press and Philadelphia: Trinity Press International, 1990) 86 quoted in Crossan, *The Birth of Christianity: Discovering What Happened in the Years Immediately After the Death of Jesus* 408.

900 Wilson, *Paul: The Mind of the Apostle* 15.

901 Ehrman, *The New Testament* 138.

902 *Luke* 1 1-4.

903 "Theophilus" means "lover of God." In this instance, it may have been a figure of speech or an individual. If the latter, who might it be? One who has been suggested is a man named Flavius Clements a Roman aristocrat who died in the first century as a Christian martyr. See Justo L. Gonzales, Acts *The Gospel of the Spirit* 13-14.

904 *Acts* 1: 1-3.

905 Ehrman, *The New Testament* 138.

906 However, Martin Hengel and possibly Anna Maria Schwemer believe this to be the case: "I regard *Acts* as a work that was composed soon after the Third Gospel by Luke 'the beloved physician' (*Colossians* 4:14), who accompanied Paul on his travels from the journey with the collection to Jerusalem onwards." See Hengel and Schwemer 7. Note: "The journey with the collection to Jerusalem" is covered in *Acts* 11:27-30 and 12:25. Further

note: Eusebius wrote that Luke was a physician from Antioch, close to Paul and author of two "inspired books" which he specified were the *"Gospel"* and *"Acts of the Apostles."* See Eusebius Book III Chapter 4. Further note: Some have adduced from a comparison of two verses that Luke was more sympathetic to physicians than Mark. This is an account of Jesus healing the woman with a hemorrhage noted earlier:

- *Mark 5:25-26 reads: A woman who had had a hemorrhage for twelve years, and had endured much at the hands of many physicians, and had spent all that she had and was not helped at all, but rather had grown worse.*

- Luke 8:43 reads: *And a woman who had a hemorrhage for twelve years, and could not be healed by anyone*

(The account in *Matthew* is doesn't mention any efforts of healing, merely stating in the ninth chapter verse 20 that the woman had *"been suffering from a hemorrhage for twelve years."*)

[907] There are other evidences of Africa in the *New Testament*:

- Joseph, Mary and the baby Jesus fled to Egypt (*Matthew* 2).
- At Pentecost, in addition to the Cyrenians, there were people from Egypt (*Acts* 2).
- Stephen asserted that Moses was taught all the wisdom of the Egyptians (*Acts* 7).
- Philip met an Ethiopian (*Acts* 8).
- One of the listed prophets and teachers at Antioch with Paul was *"Simeon who was called Niger." (Acts 13)*
- Apollos was of Alexandria (*Acts* 18).

Note: "During several centuries Africa, rather than Rome, was the center of Latin Christian thought." Tertullian was an early figure. Others included Cyprian and Augustine. See Justo L. Gonzales *A History of Christian Thought From the Beginnings to the Council of Chalcedon* Volume 1 Revised Edition 171. Further Note: In the modern era, the Christian churches are growing dramatically in Africa. That is beyond the scope of this book. For further information see Jenkins, *The Next Christendom The Coming of Global Christianity* Third Edition (Oxford Oxford University Press, Kindle Edition, 2011). For example:

- "About a third of the world's Christians by 2050 will be African, and those African Christians will outnumber Europe's by more than two to one." (112)

- One African country, Uganda, will by 2025 have many more self identifying Christians than countries such as Germany or England. (114)

908 *Matthew* 27:32; *Mark* 15:21 and *Luke* 23: 26. *John* 19:17 records that Jesus carried his cross *"by himself."*

909 Bauckham, *Jude and the Relatives of Jesus in the Early Church* 9.

910 *Romans* 16:13.

911 *Acts* 2:10.

912 *Acts* 6:9.

913 *Acts* 11:20.

914 *Acts* 11: 21-31.

915 Sandoval 21-22.

916 *Acts* 2:41; 4:4; 4:21; 5:14 and 5:26.

917 *Acts* 5: 1-11.

918 *Acts* 12: 19.

919 *Acts* 1: 18.

920 *Acts* 12: 23.

921 *Acts* 5: 15.

922 *Acts* 19: 11-12.

923 *Acts* 5 and throughout.

924 *Acts* 14: 19-20. It was Lystra.

925 *Acts* 9: 36-42.

926 *Acts* 20: 7-12. In this story, Paul was preaching in a crowded house and a young man named Eutychus was seated in a third-story window. He (Eutychus) fell asleep, fell to the ground and died. Paul went outside and resurrected him. "Eutychus" means fortunate. See Karen Dockery, Johnnie Godwin and Phyllis Godwin, *The Student Bible Dictionary* (Ulrichville, OH: Barbour Books, an imprint of Barbour Publishing, Inc:, 2000. Originally published by Holman Bible Publishers, 1993) 88.

[927] *Acts* 28: 3-6. Paul did this on the island of Malta which became an important Christian center. It fell to the Muslims in 835. See Stark, *God's Battalions The Case for the Crusades* 12ff.

[928] *Acts* 8:9-24. Christian tradition labeled this sorcerer Simon Magus, the founder of Gnosticism, a heresy as noted that the ancient church combated in the second and early third centuries. See Walker 55-6. Justo L. Gonzales goes farther: "According to a very ancient tradition, whose first component is Justin (Martyr), Simon Magus was the founder of Gnosticism. The historical truth seems to be, not that Simon founded this type of religion, but that in Chapter 8 of *Acts* we have a record of one of the earliest encounters between Christianity and Gnosticism." This story shows the syncretistic element in Gnosticism. Note: Justin Martyr saw a statue in Rome built to honor a god. He erroneously thought it was a statue in honor of Simon Magus. His mistake was discovered centuries later when the Roman inscription was uncovered in 1574. See Justo L. Gonzales, *A History of Christian Thought From the Beginnings to the Council of Chalcedon* Volume 1 Revised Edition 131, 156. Further note: The sin of simony - the gaining church office through bribery - was named for Simon Magus because the eighteenth and nineteenth verses of this account read *"Now when Simon saw that the Spirit was bestowed through the laying on of the apostles' hands, he offered them money, saying, 'Give this authority to me as well, so that everyone on whom I lay my hands may receive the Holy Spirit.'"* (His entreaty was rejected.) See Hitchcock 98.

[929] *Acts* 13:6.

[930] *Acts* 8:26 and other places.

[931] Here are the instances:

- *Acts* 5:18-19 - Peter and John assisted by an angel.
- *Acts* 12:6-11 - Peter assisted by an angel.
- *Acts* 16:25-40 - Paul and Silas assisted by an earthquake and yet waiting around to get legal satisfaction.

[932] *Acts* 13: 9-11.

[933] *Acts* 14: 8-18. We learn from this account that Paul may have been a more visible speaker than Barnabas as one verse reads, in part, that they called Paul *"Hermes, because he was the chief speaker."* (verse 12).

[934] *Acts* 10: 25-6.

[935] *Acts* 16: 16-18.

[936] *Acts* 11:27-30 and *Acts* 21:8-14. One has to note: Predicting a future famine somewhere and that someone with Paul's personality would get in some degree of trouble would not be a difficult forecast to make. Further note: According to the Catholic Church Agabus is the patron saint of clairvoyance. He is also the patron saint of psychics. His feast day is February 13. See Sandoval 55.

[937] *Acts* 19: 13-17. This is a great story. Like so many others, it occurred in Ephesus. The priest was named Sceva. His sons were trying to cast out evil spirits. Here is the passage: *"But also some of the Jewish exorcists, who went from place to place, attempted to name over those who had the evil spirits the name of the Lord Jesus, saying, 'I adjure you by Jesus whom Paul preaches.' Seven sons of one Sceva, a Jewish chief priest, were doing this. And the evil spirit answered and said to them, 'I recognize Jesus, and I know about Paul, but who are you?' And the man, in whom was the evil spirit, leaped on them and subdued all of them and overpowered them, so that they fled out of that house naked and wounded. This became known to all, both Jews and Greeks, who lived in Ephesus; and fear fell upon them all and the name of the Lord Jesus was being magnified."* Note: In a weird way the American divine Cotton Mather (1663-1728) explored the concept of exorcism by non-Christian means many centuries later. He once tried to exorcize demons from a woman using expressions and incantations in the local Indian language. He was pleased to see that Indian magic had no effect. See Mann 55-6.

[938] *Acts* 26: 10-11.

[939] *Acts* 2:40 comes at the end of a sermon and indicates that the foregoing is just a summary of the whole sermon: *"**And with many other words** he solemnly testified and kept on exhorting them, saying, 'Be saved from this perverse generation!'"* (Emphasis added). See also *Acts*: 2:42; 4:32-35; 5:12-16; 6:7; 9:31; 19:20; 28:31. As Justo L. Gonzales puts it: "Luke seeks a balance between simply telling particular instances and a more generalized overview of what is in fact taking place." See Justo L. Gonzales, *Acts The Gospel of the Spirit* 43, 49-50, 217. Here is Ben Witherington III: "Even a cursory glance at the speeches in *Acts* shows that at most they are summaries of speeches, not transcripts of whole speeches, for with rare exception they take only a minute or two to recite." See Witherington, *New Testament History A Narrative Account* Location 350.

[940] It is also striking that none of Paul's letters are quoted in the *Book of Acts* since the book – at least the second half – celebrates his ministry.

[941] *Romans* 15: 18-19.

[942] *I Thessalonians* 1:5.

943 *I Corinthians* 2:3-4.

944 *II Corinthians* 12: 1-12.

945 *II Corinthians* 11:30. 12:5 and 12:9.

946 Some of the tales in *Acts* remind one of Robert Ingersoll's (1833-1899) comment that the reason everyone in the United States believes in the *Bible* is that no one actually reads it. See Prothero, *Religious Literacy What Every American Needs to Know and Doesn't* 145. Note: There was a *New Testament* allusion in *Sports Illustrated* in 2008 which demonstrated Biblical illiteracy. In the letters-to-the-editor section in the February 18 issue, a reader commented about the brothers Eli and Peyton Manning in the context of Eli's role as the quarterback on the winning the Super Bowl team. Peyton had been the winning quarterback in the previous year's Super Bowl. *SI* headlined this letter: "Get Behind Me, Peyton." That is a casual reference to *Matthew* 16: 21-23 and *Mark* 8: 31-33. In these accounts Jesus explained to his disciples that his true mission was rejection by the authorities and death and resurrection. According to *Mark*, Jesus spoke "plainly." Peter, however, strongly objected to this definition of Jesus's cause. Jesus responded, *"Get behind me, Satan!"* In 2008 I asked ten randomly selected middle age American adults in Portland, Oregon if they understood the reference in *SI*. None did.

947 Private ownership of a home in Jerusalem by a follower of Jesus does not in my view contradict the ethos called out early in *Acts*: *Acts* 2: 44-45 and 4:32 talks of *"all the believers"* engaged in sharing *"everything they had."* I think we can assume that private ownership continued in the early church. Ananias and Saphira were struck dead by Peter for lying, not for possessing wealth. They collaborated in holding back some of the proceeds of the sale of some property while turning over some of the profit to the Apostles. Peter said to Ananias: *"While it remained unsold, did it not remain your own? And after it was sold, was it not under your control? Why is it that you have conceived this deed in your heart? You have not lied to men but to God."* (*Acts* 5: 4). The sharing of material goods by certain early Christians in Jerusalem, however, has been cited throughout the centuries by radicals seeking redistributionist policies. One twentieth century example: In 1913-15 the Industrial Workers of the World organized unemployed workers in big cities to seek government relief and jobs. It confiscated food at warehouses and even restaurants. One of the IWW's supporters said that this activity "expose(d) the irreligion of capitalism" which, "based on private ownership, is hostile to the communism of the early church,..." See Philip S. Foner, *History of the Labor Movement in the United States Volume 4 The Industrial Workers of the World 1905-1917* (New York: International Publishers, 1965) 449. This is no doubt a simplistic

reading of the economy of the early Christian movement. However, a high degree of sharing of private property probably occurred throughout the *New Testament* era as we will note in Chapter 11.

[948] *Acts* 12:13-16.

[949] *Acts* 4: 6 notes that a man named Alexander was a relative of Annas the high priest and was present during a trial of Peter and John. *Acts* 19:33 mentions a Jew named Alexander as attempting to quell the riot in Ephesus during Paul's ministry. *Mark* 15:21 lists an Alexander as a son of the man who carried Jesus's cross. *I Timothy* 1:20 labels an Alexander along with someone named Hymenaeus as blasphemous. *II Timothy* 4:14-15 reads, purportedly from the Apostle Paul: *"Alexander the coppersmith did me great harm; the Lord will pay him back for his deeds. You also must beware of him, for he strongly opposed our message."* This may be the same Alexander mentioned in *I Timothy*. (Incidentally, Paul may have had problems with these trades. According to *Acts* 19:24-31 a silversmith named Demetrius in Ephesus incited the riot against him. Coppersmiths and silversmiths undoubtedly saw Paul's message as a threat to their businesses of producing what some would call idols.)

[950] *Acts* 17:22-31. Paul's open-air preaching on Mars Hill does not appear to have been very successful. People sneered at him. But he converted at least a few and, improbably, this spawned a Christian legend that persisted for a thousand years. *Acts* 17:34 reads: *"But some men joined him and believed, among whom also were **Dionysius the Areopagite** and a woman named Damaris and others with them."* (Emphasis added). Toward the end of the 400s or in the early 500s, a Christian theologian, probably living in Syria, wrote under a pseudonym which came to be called Dionysius the Areopagite and in that credulous era it was assumed that these writings came from the hand of Paul's Athenian follower mentioned in *Acts* 17:34. That belief persisted for centuries – apparently until the 1400s - but was eventually discredited.

These writings were the first thorough exploration of Christian mysticism, the root of which went to Paul's comments in *II Corinthians* 12: 2-4 noted earlier in which he tells of a man (undoubtedly himself) taken temporarily into the "third heaven":

I know a man in Christ who fourteen years ago—whether in the body I do not know, or out of the body I do not know, God knows—such a man was caught up to the third heaven. And I know how such a man—whether in the body or apart from the body I do not know, God knows— was caught up into Paradise and heard inexpressible words, which a man is not permitted to speak.

"Pseudo-Dionysius" described the mystical condition as one of exalted prayer in which the soul of a person goes beyond normal existence. The writer thought that the normal world of appearances hid but also partly showed the real world of the spirit. This theology had great influence. In the 800s Johannes Scotus Erigena (abt. 815 – abt. 877) an Irish theologian translated and commented on *Pseudo-Dionysius*. He saw that it was impossible to know God and that everything that the scriptures say about God must be understood not literally but figuratively. As Paul said in *I Corinthians* 3:2: *"I gave you milk to drink, not solid food; for you were not yet able to receive it. Indeed, even now you are not yet able,…."* He saw God as the end toward which all things were headed, meaning that after a series of stages all things will return to God who becomes *"all in all,"* referring to *I Corinthians* 15: 28: *"When all things are subjected to Him, then the Son Himself also will be subjected to the One who subjected all things to Him, so that God may be all in all."* See Justo L. Gonzales, *A History of Christian Thought From Augustine to the Eve of the Reformation* Volume II Revised Edition Locations 1721ff, 2390ff and Hitchcock 125, 236. Note: *Acts* 17:34 also refers to *"a woman named Damaris."* Chrysostom, Archbishop of Constantinople, thought that Dionysius and Damaris were husband and wife. See Justo L. Gonzales, *Acts The Gospel of the Spirit* 203.

Note: Besides Dionysius, there were others in the crowd including some from the group called "Epicureans." *Acts* 17:18 reads in part: *"And also some of the Epicurean and Stoic philosophers were conversing with him. Some were saying, 'What would this idle babbler wish to say?'"* Who were the Epicureans? They were followers of the philosophy of Epicurus who lived from about 341BC – 270BC. He held that the purpose of philosophy was to live a happy life with freedom from fear, to live self-sufficiently with friends and to avoid pain. Thomas Jefferson once wrote, "I am an Epicurean." See Tevi Troy *What Jefferson Read, Ike Watched, and Obama Tweeted 200 years of Popular Culture in the White House* (Washington DC: RegneryPublishing, Inc., 2013) 9-10. Further note: Epicurus held such theories as "(1) that matter is composed of atoms, (2) that the present state of nature is the result of a long evolutionary process, (3) that life exists elsewhere in the universe, and (4) that there is no God, or at least no personal God." See Michael J. Crowe *The Extraterrestrial Life Debate* 1750-1900 (Mineola, New York: Dover Publications, Inc., Kindle Edition, 1999. Copyright 1986 Cambridge University Press) 3.

[951] *Acts* 18: 4-8.

[952] *Acts* 19:9.

[953] *Acts* 20:4. Tychicus is mentioned four other times in the *New Testament*, each time in letters not usually attributed to Paul and believed to have been

written in the second generation of Christianity. He is always associated with Paul:

- *Ephesians 6:21 – "But that you also may know about my circumstances, how I am doing, **Tychicus**, the beloved brother and faithful minister in the Lord, will make everything known to you."* (Emphasis added).
- *Colossians 4:7 – "As to all my affairs, **Tychicus**, our beloved brother and faithful servant and fellow bond-servant in the Lord, will bring you information."* (Emphasis added).
- *II Timothy 4:12 - "But **Tychicus** I have sent to Ephesus."* (Emphasis added).
- *Titus 3:12 - "When I send Artemas or **Tychicus** to you, make every effort to come to me at Nicopolis, for I have decided to spend the winter there."* (Emphasis added).

Note: The first two references are evidence that *Ephesians* and *Colossians* were written about the same time since Tychicus is cited as a deliverer of the letters. See Browning Location 2791.

[954] *Acts 20:4 and 21:9.* Trophimus is significant because the attack on Paul by the Jewish-Christians was caused by suspicion that Paul had brought Trophimus, an Ephesian Gentile, into the Temple. See *Acts 21: 27-36.* Trophimus is considered by some to have accompanied Titus in bringing a letter from Paul to the Corinthians. See *II Corinthians 8:16-24.* In this scripture, Paul refers to a *"brother who is famous among all the churches for his proclaiming of the good news; and not only that, but he has also been appointed by the churches to travel with us while we are administering this generous undertaking"* See William Smith 714. According to *II Timothy 4:20,* Trophimus was ill at Miletus. Miletus in Paul's era was a wealthy city near Ephesus. Today it is a ruin. It appears that when Paul was in Ephesus as described in *Acts 19* the whole region heard the Christian message. *Acts 19:10* reports that *"all who lived in Asia heard the word of the Lord, both Jews and Greeks."* (Recall: In the *New Testament*, "Asia" refers to a Roman province in modern western Turkey with an administrative capital in Ephesus. See Browning Location 767.) Moreover, in *I Corinthians 16: 9* Paul reports that *"I will remain in Ephesus until Pentecost; **for a wide door for effective service has opened to me**..."* (Emphasis added). We can assume, therefore, that a Christian community had developed in Miletus. In *Acts* 20, Paul met with leaders of the church in Ephesus at Miletus on a journey in which Trophimus was a companion. This was not the time that Trophimus could have been left there because, as *Acts 21:29* indicates, Trophimus was with Paul on this journey all the way to Jerusalem. If, according to *II Timothy 4:20,* Trophimus

was left there by Paul, it would appear to be a different time. Although there is skepticism that Paul wrote *II Timothy* it may be that the core truth here is that Paul was in Miletus more than once.

Note on *II Timothy* 4:20: This verse raises interesting questions. Why didn't Paul heal him? If it was not really Paul who wrote *II Timothy* was Trophimus by that era a respected elder or even a celebrity, mentioned in this epistle to add authenticity? Further note: Miletus is an unincorporated community in West Virginia.

[955] I have often wondered why people like Tychicus, Trophimus, or Tertius the scribe in *Romans* 16:22 are named but other more important *New Testament* figures go unnamed. *Mark* 14:3-9 (and *Matthew* 26:6-13 and *Luke* 7:36-39) and *Mark* 14:47 (and *Matthew* 26:51 and *Luke* 22:50) mention people who probably should have been named due to the significance of what they did. The first is an instance of a woman anointing Jesus. The second is a case of someone wounding one of those who came for Jesus at Gethsemane. One reason for the lack of naming is that these two people might have been forgotten when the *Gospel of Mark* was written. Another is that these people might have been at risk and, if so, given anonymity. I owe this thought to Stark, *Discovering God: The Origins of the Great Religions and the Evolution of Belief* 299 and regret it if I have misstated Stark's point of view. If anonymity was key in Mark's time it may not have been when *John* was written a generation later. *John* 12 describes a story similar to the anointing story in *Mark* 14 and identifies the anointer as Mary, the sister of Martha and Lazarus. *John* 18:10 identifies the would-be defender of Jesus as Peter and the victim as Malchus. Note: At least in the case of the anointing it is only fair to say that there might be more at play here than simply the impulse toward protecting identities. As noted earlier, there are enough differences in these accounts that they may reflect more than one such similar incident or there may have been other purposes such as showing Judas in a bad light as the account in *John* does. Note: AN Wilson suggests that Malchus is Paul. Malchus was the *"servant of the high priest"* and might have been as recognizable to the Markan community which originally heard this story as the *"disciple whom Jesus loved"* was to Johannine community. See Wilson, *Jesus A Life* 205.

[956] *Acts* 23:16. He also referred to a couple named Andronicus and Junias as relatives, and not merely relatives but also apostles, people with whom he had done jail time and who were senior to him. (*Romans* 16:7). This couple may have founded the church or one of the churches in Rome. See James DG Dunn, *Jesus, Paul, and the Gospels* Location 3495. Note: Martin Hengel and Anna Maria Schwemer speculate that the Roman Christian community was

founded from Jerusalem. They note that Paul mentions Jerusalem four times in *Romans* 15. See Hengel and Schwemer 287. Further note: There are others whom the *New Testament* lists as having served jail time with Paul:

- *Philemon* 1:23 - Epaphras who is also mentioned in *Colossians* 1:7 and 4:12.
- *Acts* 16:25 – Silas in Philippi.
- *Acts* 27:1, 45 – "[S]ome other prisoners" in the transport to Rome.
- *Colossians* 4:10 – Aristarchus.

The writer of *Hebrews* advised his readers to "*Remember the prisoners, as though in prison with them...*" *Hebrews* 13:3

[957] *Acts* 23: 27.

[958] *Acts* 24:17.

[959] *Acts* 24: 26. As this verse indicates, Felix would spend time talking with Paul during his captivity in hopes to get a bribe. By contrast, Herod Antipater's talks with the incarcerated John the Baptist, as mentioned in *Mark* 6:20, were because Antipater enjoyed the conversation.

[960] Here is Ben Witherington III on this period: "We may be wondering where Luke is during the two years that Paul spends in custody. I suggest that he probably was with Paul a good deal bringing him sustenance and necessities, but also using the time to gather a great deal of data from James and the Jerusalem church, and from Philip and his family in Caesarea, about the earliest period." See Witherington, *New Testament History A Narrative Account* Location 5982.

[961] William Smith 191 and Justo L. Gonzales, *Acts The Gospel of the Spirit* 259ff.

[962] *Acts* 24:22.

[963] *Acts* 28: 30-31.

[964] *Acts* 6:5.

[965] *Acts* 13:1

[966] *Acts* 13:1. One wonders if he was a spy. If he was not a spy, it is worth noting that the gospel had penetrated Herod Antipater's inner circle through the wife of one of his staff as called out in *Luke* 8:3 as noted earlier and here as one of the leaders of the church at Antioch.

⁹⁶⁷ *Matthew* 14:3 and *Mark* 6:17. *Luke* 3:1 cites this Philip in connection with the dating of John the Baptist's ministry.

⁹⁶⁸ *Matthew* 10:3; *Mark* 3:18; *Luke* 6:14 and *Acts* 1:13.

⁹⁶⁹ *John* 1: 35-49.

⁹⁷⁰ *John* 12: 20-22.

⁹⁷¹ Note:

- At his trial, the charges against Stephen included that he said that the Temple would be torn down. See *Acts* 6:13-14 – "*They put forward false witnesses who said, 'This man incessantly speaks against this holy place and the Law; for we have heard him say that this Nazarene, Jesus, will destroy this place and alter the customs which Moses handed down to us.'*"
- Luke does not mention this as one of the charges against Jesus although other Gospel writers do. See *Matthew* 26:61 and 27:40; *Mark* 14:58 and 15:29. See also *John* 2:19.

In the end, Stephen essentially accepted a charge of reducing the Temple in importance. See his comment in *Acts* 7:48 - "*... the Most High does not dwell in houses made by human hands;*"

⁹⁷² *Acts* 8: 26-39.

⁹⁷³ *Acts* 8:40 and 21: 8-14. Here is a speculative question: Just as Philip prepared the way for Peter to go to Samaria in *Acts* 8, did he also prepare the way for Peter to meet with Cornelius who resided on Caesarea according to *Acts* 10:1? Here is more speculation: Did Luke learn from Philip and/or his four daughters about Philip's early ministry and the selection of the seven deacons of *Acts* 6? See Justo L. Gonzales, *Acts The Gospel of the Spirit* 138.

⁹⁷⁴ In the *New Testament* era the church was very small. Traditions and stories were passed on by actual eyewitnesses. One possible example may fit in with this Philip. According to Eusebius, Papias was the bishop of Hierapolis in the first third of the second century. Also according to Eusebius, Papias knew the daughters of Philip (mentioned in *Acts* 21:9) as a boy and may have learned from them. Papias's assumed line span – before 70 – abt. 155 - makes this plausible. (Papias's writings only survive in fragments quoted by others.) See Bauckham, *Jesus and the Eyewitnesses: The Gospels and Eyewitness Testimony* Location 301-385. I regret it if I have misstated Bauckham's point of view. Eusebius discusses the death of Philip by quoting a letter from Polycrates, who was bishop of Ephesus, to Victor, bishop of Rome: "For in Asia also great lights have fallen asleep which shall rise again on the last day, at the coming

of the Lord, when he shall come with glory from heaven and shall seek out all the saints. Among these are Philip, one of the twelve apostles, who sleeps in Hierapolis, and his two aged virgin daughters, and another daughter who lived in the Holy Spirit and now rests at Ephesus…" See Eusebius Book III Chapter 31. Note: In 2011 archaeologists in Hierapolis discovered what they think is Philip's tomb. See "Jesus and the Apostles. Christianity's Early Rise," *National Geographic*, 2014 112.

[975] Wilson, Jesus *A Life* 246-9.

[976] Gallio found him innocent. Gallio was the brother of the philosopher Seneca. He was a friend of Nero but fell out of favor and was coerced to commit suicide at Nero's order. See Justo L. Gonzales, *Acts The Gospel of the Spirit* 208.

[977] Stark, *Discovering God: The Origins of the Great Religions and the Evolution of Belief* 296-7.

[978] It is more likely that only those somehow involved in the riots were expelled. The population of Jews in Rome probably numbered in the tens of thousands at the time. See Stark, *The Triumph of Christianity How the Jesus Movement Became the World's Largest Religion* 29.

[979] Coincidentally, according to *Acts* 8:26-40 the Ethiopian Eunuch converted by Philip on the road from Jerusalem to Gaza was also a treasurer - to Candace the Queen of Ethiopia. And, of course Judas was the treasurer within the Twelve – *John* 12: 4-7, although a dishonest one. This last instance raises a point: Jesus picked Judas over Matthew to be the person in the group handling the money even though Matthew, as a tax man, had financial qualifications. Why? Who knows? Who cares?

[980] Stark, *Discovering God: The Origins of the Great Religions and the Evolution of Belief* 296-7. More on this inscription: "An inscription from the middle of the 1st century AD on paving near the theatre (in Corinth) names a certain Erastus as an aedile." An aedile was a higher rank than Paul assigned to Erastus but still an official position with responsibility for civic financial matters. Erastus was not a common name. Perhaps Paul called him a treasurer as a general statement or perhaps Erastus was later promoted. See Browning Location 2855. Note: In the United States, the National Council of Churches opened a nineteen story building in New York in 1958. The cornerstone was taken from ancient Corinth and laid by President Dwight Eisenhower. See Ross Douthat, *Bad Religion How We Became a Nation of Heretics* (New York: Free Press, 2012) 31.

[981] *Acts* 11:19-20.

982 Pelikan, *Jesus Through The Centuries: His Place in the History of Culture* 222.

983 At this point two important caveats must be made.

- First, The story in the *Book of Acts* is about the westward expansion of Christianity. But, to quote Pope Benedict XVI (2005-2013): "(Christianity's) expansion in the first centuries was both toward the West - toward the Greco-Latin world, where it later inspired European culture - and in the direction of the East, as far as Persia and India." See Pope Benedict XVI, *The Fathers* 157. The Christian churches of the Middle East and the East survived independent of Rome and Constantinople for hundreds of years. Indeed one could say Europe became the home of Christianity primarily because by the 1400s Christianity had been destroyed elsewhere by the Muslims. See Stark, *The Triumph of Christianity How the Jesus Movement Became the World's Largest Religion* 211. In Chapter 8, we will very briefly touch on these churches.

- Second, Belloc's quote may now be decades out of date and there were doubts even before that. As Philip Jenkins has written: "As Europe was tearing itself apart during the Thirty Years War, St. Vincent de Paul recalled Jesus's promise that his church would continue until the end of days - but he also noted that Jesus had said nothing about the faith necessarily surviving in Europe. The Christian future might well lie in Africa, or South America, in China or Japan. Such an insight became all the more probable when set against the religion's long history: the 'Christian heartland' has repeatedly shifted as time went on. Syrians and Mesopotamians had once believed that their lands would always be solidly Christian, just as modern Europeans imagine that Christianity will survive on their continent." In this light, the selection in 2005 of Pope Benedict XVI from a pool that included many qualified Third World possibilities in the College of Cardinals could be seen as a last-minute effort to shore up the Catholic Church in Europe before the decline was irreversible. See Jenkins, *The Next Christendom The Coming of Global Christianity* Third Edition 237, 243.

This all is a reminder that, although I write from an American perspective, Christianity is a worldwide religion with great variation.

984 John Adams and Thomas Jefferson wrote a lot about future generations. So did Thomas Paine who wrote in *Common Sense* in 1776: "As parents, we can have no joy, knowing that this government is not sufficiently lasting to ensure any thing which we may bequeath to posterity: And by a plain method

of argument, as we are running the next generation into debt, we ought to do the work of it, otherwise we use them meanly and pitifully. In order to discover the line of our duty rightly, we should take our children in our hand, and fix our station a few years farther into life; that eminence will present a prospect, which a few present fears and prejudices conceal from our sight." A European Enlightenment figure Denis Diderot (1713 – 1784) picked up this theme: "Posterity is for the philosopher what the next world is for the religious man." See Paul Johnson, *A History of Christianity* 350.

[985] Wilken, *The Myth of Christian Beginning: History's Impact on Belief* 32-33.

[986] John Dominic Crossan and Jonathan L. Reed, *In Search of Paul How Jesus's Apostle Opposed Rome's Empire with God's Kingdom A New Vision of Paul's Words & World* (York: HarperOne An Imprint of HarperCollins*Publishers*, 2004) 32-34. Note: Luke also records that Pilate thought Jesus innocent and stated so three times: *Luke* 23: 4, 14 and 22. In *John*, Pilate also declares Jesus innocent three times: *John* 18:38, 19:6 and possibly, 19:12. In *Mark* he never declares him innocent. In *Matthew*, his wife declares Jesus innocent but Pilate just washes his hands of the matter in *Matthew* 27: 19, 24. *Luke* in general tends to exonerate Roman authorities. *Matthew* 27:37-31 and by implication *Mark* 15: 16-20 have Roman soldiers mocking Jesus. *Luke* 23:11 has Herod Antipater and his soldiers mocking him.

[987] Reader's Digest *After Jesus: The Triumph of Christianity* 51, 52. Claudius is mentioned in *Acts* 11:28 and 18:2.

[988] *Acts* 12:2 records tersely that Herod Agrippa "*had James, the brother of John, put to death with the sword.*" Eusebius, the church historian, wrote in the early 300s that James was beheaded. See Eusebius Book II Chapter 9.

[989] *John* 18:10.

[990] Sandoval 21.

[991] David Levering Lewis 315-316.

[992] Near the outbreak of the Mexican-American War, in 1845-46 General Zachary Taylor of the US was camped at Corpus Christi, which as we have noted earlier means Body of Christ. He received warning that General Francisco Mejia of Mexico might attack from Matamoros. See Hamilton, *Zachary Taylor Soldier of the Republic* 165. So, the English version would be that an army camped at "Body of Christ" faced a foe camped at "Muslim Killer."

[993] Or is it a paradox? Jesus's description of his ministry in *Luke* 12:49, 51 and 53 and *Matthew* 10:34-36 and the description of Jesus returning to earth in

II Thessalonians 1:6-9 speak of strife and violence. The Gospel accounts have Jesus bringing fire and sword. *II Thessalonians* has him returning with angels and fire to bring vengeance on those that don't know God or obey Jesus's Gospel. In *Revelation* 19: 11-16, Jesus Christ is again a warrior. He is seen in some future state on a *"white horse"* waging *"righteous war."* His eyes are like *"flames of fire."* His armies also ride on *"white horses."* Moreover, out of his mouth comes *"a sharp sword to strike down the nations."* He plans to rule over them *"with an iron rod."* In summary, *"(he) will release the fierce wrath of God, the Almighty, like juice flowing from a winepress."* For a more prosaic version of identifying Jesus of Nazareth with punishment of opponents of Christianity consider *11 Timothy* 4:14-15 cited earlier and purportedly written by the Apostle Paul: *"Alexander the coppersmith did me great harm;* **the Lord will pay him back** *for his deeds."* (Emphasis added).

[994] Ostling and Ostling 29. Joseph Smith did not announce this meeting with these *New Testament* figures until several years after 1829 and it came as a surprise to many who had followed him since 1829. See Dan Vogel, "Evolution of Early Mormon Priesthood Narratives" *The John Whitmer Historical Association Journal* Spring/Summer 20-4 Volume 34 Number 1 58.

[995] Finally, there is yet another James that was associated with Jesus - James the son of Alphaeus. He is listed among the Twelve in the Synoptics: *Matthew* 10:3, *Mark* 3:18 and *Luke* 6:15. He is also listed among the Twelve in *Acts* 1:13, present in the Upper Room. Pope Benedict XVI identifies this James as the James of the Council, the brother of Jesus, although he says that he was probably only loosely related to Jesus and by Semitic custom called "brother." He seems to acknowledge that some experts recognize two individuals. See Pope Benedict XVI, *The Apostles and Their Co-Workers* 69ff.

But to confuse things, *Mark* 2:14 records that as Jesus was *"walking along, he saw Levi son of Alphaeus sitting at the tax booth, and he said to him, 'Follow me.' And he got up and followed him."* Later, Jesus was criticized for socializing with Levi and his friends and responded with one of his most memorable statements: *"Those who are well have no need of a physician, but those who are sick; I have come to call not the righteous but sinners."* (*Mark* 2:17). *Luke* 5:27-32 also tells this story. *Matthew* 9: 9-13 also tells this story but refers to the tax man as Matthew, not Levi. Like James the son of Alphaeus, Matthew is listed among the Twelve in all four lists. The most logical explanation: Matthew and Levi were the same person and therefore this James and Matthew/Levi were brothers. If so, fully half of the Twelve were brother pairs: Peter and Andrew, James and John and James the son of Alphaeus and Matthew/Levi.

[996] See, for example, *John* 7:5.

[997] *Acts 4:32: "And the congregation of those who believed were of one heart and soul; and not one of them claimed that anything belonging to him was his own, but all things were common property to them."*

[998] *Acts* 6:7. P. 51ff - However, there is no suggestion that they acted as priests within the churches. The early Christians did not need priests.

[999] Wilson, *Paul: The Mind of the Apostle* 50. The decades between the 30s and the 60s were complicated. Consider:

- There were early persecutions as described in *Acts* and the dispersing of the Hellenists.
- However, there is evidence that the Jerusalem Christians enjoyed some stability. *Acts* 9:31 describes this time: *"...the church throughout all Judea and Galilee and Samaria enjoyed peace, being built up; and going on in the fear of the Lord and in the comfort of the Holy Spirit, it continued to increase."* (See James DG Dunn *Did the First Christians Worship Jesus? The New Testament Evidence* 114.)
- But the execution of the Apostle James, the brother of the Apostle John in *Acts* 12 revealed danger.

By the early 60s their situation had worsened enough so that the execution of James the brother of Jesus could take place although - to make matters somewhat more complicated – this execution was still very unpopular: The Roman authorities threatened to put the Sadducean high priest Annas II on trial for it. See Hengel and Schwemer 225. Note: In 2002 *Biblical Archaeology Review's* editor announced the finding of a burial box with an inscription indicating that it had contained the bones of "James, the son of Joseph, brother of Jesus." Some experts who studied the artifact believed it was genuine and probably referred to James the brother of Jesus. This remains a matter of controversy. See Tabor, *Paul and Jesus How the Apostle Transformed Christianity* Location 525.

[1000] This provides another example of a Christian place name turning up in America but it is quite a stretch. Here is the story. Under continuous pressure during the Roman Wars, the Jewish-Christians in Jerusalem relocated to the town of Pella less than one hundred miles away in modern Jordan. Pella is not listed in the *New Testament* but it was part of the Decapolis, a group of ten cities that is mentioned. These cities were in a predominantly Gentile area.

Matthew 4:25 informs that great multitudes from that area followed Jesus. In the fifth chapter of *Mark* we learn that Jesus healed a demon-possessed man and sent the demons into a herd of swine. The man then, according to the twentieth verse of that chapter, spread the word about Jesus throughout the Decapolis. In the seventh chapter of *Mark* we hear of Jesus going into the area of the Decapolis and healing a deaf man who also had trouble speaking. Jesus used his own saliva in this cure.

When the Jewish-Christians, then, repaired to Pella, they were going into an area that had known Jesus in his lifetime. Jerome observed surviving Christian communities in the Pella area in the fourth century. See MacCulloch 107. Many centuries roll by. The Jewish-Christian form of Christianity disappears into history, losing out to the Pauline versions. Yet, in 1847 Dutch immigrants to the US seeking religious freedom, established a town in Iowa and named it Pella. It now has about ten thousand inhabitants.

1001 Tabor, *The Jesus Dynasty* 301.

1002 Witherington, *The Jesus Quest The Third Search For the Jew of Nazareth* 252, quoting Raymond E. Brown.

1003 Today it is a ruin in modern Turkey.

1004 *Acts* 9: 2-27; 22: 5-11; 26: 12-20; Also, *Galatians* 1:17 implies that Christians were in Damascus.

1005 Reader's Digest *After Jesus: The Triumph of Christianity* 50-1.

1006 *Acts* 11:19-21. Cyprus is thus an important locale in Christian history. It fell to the Muslims in 653. See Stark, *God's Battalions The Case for the Crusades* 12ff.

1007 *Acts* 4:36.

1008 William Smith 44.

1009 *Acts* 11:22-25. (This arguably qualified Barnabas as the most significant talent scout of all time.) It may have taken Barnabas some time to find Paul because Paul was preaching in the regions of Syria and Cilicia (*Galatians* 1:21). Tarsus was the capital of Cilicia. See Justo L. Gonzales, *Acts The Gospel of the Spirit* 138. Note: Earlier Barnabas had apparently seen Paul preaching boldly in Damascus. See *Acts* 9:27.

1010 It is worth noting, therefore, that although Paul was the "Apostle to the Gentiles", Barnabas also preached to the Gentiles as did Apollos and as did Peter both at Pentecost (*Acts* 2) and to Cornelius (*Acts* 10:1 – 11:19). These accounts may have been an attempt to link the branches of early Christianity. See Grant, *Saint Paul* (New York: Barnes and Noble Books, 2005) 152.

There is plenty of other *New Testament* evidence that Paul was not the only one to bring Christianity to the Gentiles:

- *Romans* 15:19-20 - Paul wrote that he would not preach where Christ was already known or *"build on another man's foundation."*
- *Acts* 15:40 - After his break from Paul, Barnabas went back to Cyprus.
- *Acts* 28:13-14 - There apparently was a Christian community near Puteoli in Naples because *Acts* talks of Paul meeting "brethren" there.
- *I Peter 1* speaks of Christians in several areas: Pontus, Galatia, Cappadocia, Asia and Bithynia. Pontus, Cappadocia and Bithynia are never mentioned by Paul and, in fact, according to *Acts* 16:7 when he was traveling with Silas, *"they were trying to go into Bithynia, and the Spirit of Jesus did not permit them."* *Acts* 2:9ff makes it clear that Jews from Pontus and Cappadocia were at Pentecost and may have been the first missionaries in those areas. See Jedin 111-12.

[1011] Wilson, *Paul: The Mind of the Apostle* 113 and Carmichael 59.

[1012] *Acts* 11:26.

[1013] *Galatians* 2: 11-21. I have noted earlier Luke's tendency in *Acts* to summarize. Here is a case in point. Verses 22 and 23 of *Acts* 18 follow a section in which Paul left Ephesus and read in their entirety as follows:

- Verse 22: *"When (Paul) had landed at Caesarea, he went up and greeted the church, and went down to Antioch."*
- Verse 23: *"And having spent some time there, he left and passed successively through the Galatian region and Phrygia, strengthening all the disciples."*

Martin Hengel and Anna Maria Schwemer speculate that these verses pack in a lot of events. They offer that this is the one instance in *Acts* which covers the break-up in Antioch described by Paul in *Galatians* 2 and shows Luke's tendency to smooth over difficult matters. If so, this might have been the chain of events:

Paul goes to Jerusalem on a visit not otherwise mentioned in *Acts* or any of his letters: *Acts* 18:22 - *"he went up and greeted the church."*

While there, Paul hears that Peter and some others from the Jewish-Christian cohort have gone to Antioch: *Galatians* 2: 11-12 - Peter and some of James's colleagues were in Antioch.

Paul hurries to Antioch: *Acts* 18: 22 - "(Paul) *went down to Antioch.*"

Paul has the confrontation in Antioch and then leaves: *Acts* 18:23 —*"And having spent some time there he left and passed successively through the Galatian region and Phrygia.*" This starts what is often called Paul's third missionary journey. See Hengel and Schwemer 215.

[1014] This confrontation was cited two centuries later in a church father's polemics. Cyprian of Carthage was born in the early 200s. He was born into wealth and converted to Christianity at age 40. He sold his properties to distribute his wealth. He became bishop of Carthage in 248 or 249. Cyprian used the account in *Galatians* of the criticism of Peter by Paul as a way to deny the authority of the bishop of Rome over church affairs in Carthage. See Justo L. Gonzales, *A History of Christian Thought From the Beginnings to the Council of Chalcedon* Volume 1 Revised Edition 238, 244.

[1015] *Acts* 26:28.

[1016] Ehrman, *Peter, Paul and Mary* 74. See also *II Peter* 3:16.

[1017] *I Peter* 4: 16.

[1018] These should not be confused with Christians living since apostolic times in India who trace their origin to the Apostle Thomas and are known as the Thomas Christians.

[1019] Yes, others. Yet another name for the followers of Jesus was a "peculiar people." This term, found in *I Peter* 2:9, echoes *Deuteronomy* 14:2. Pope Gregory III (731-741) sought a pact with Charles Martel asking him to defend "the church of God and His peculiar people." This was probably a reference to *I Peter* 2:9. Many centuries later, Vatican II linked the idea of the church as the "people of God" to *I Peter* 1:2, 2:5-6 and, especially, 2:9-10. These passages were neglected by the future Pope Benedict in his mid-1980s criticism of the concept which he read as having Marxist overtones. See Wills, *Why I Am A Catholic* 261-2. In modern America, Mormons have liked to call themselves a peculiar people. See Ostling and Ostling 36.

[1020] Mack, *The Lost Gospel: The Book of Q & Christian Origins* 234.

[1021] In the *New Testament* "the Twelve" receded in importance but as a concept it resurfaced often in history. In one example, Brigham Young in 1847 pronounced to the Salt Lake Mormons that they would not work on Sunday and that "no one should buy any land that came here, that he had none to sell;...but for every man land would be issued to him for city and farming purposes, whatever they could till. He might till it as he pleases, but he must be industrious and take care of it." This of course required some oversight and later that year Young cited the authority of a group he called the Twelve: "It is the right of the Twelve to nominate the officers and the people to receive them." Much of the time of the Twelve "was spent in granting permits to build

mills and cut timber and attending to the economic welfare of individuals."
On June 26, 1865 he said: "Tomorrow it will be twenty-one years since Joseph
Smith was killed, and from that time to this the Twelve have dictated, guided
and directed the destinies of this great people." See Eugene E. Campbell,
Establishing Zion The Mormon Church in the American West, 1847-1869 (Salt
Lake City: Signature Books, 1988) 5ff, 149. Note: Brigham Young once said
of Joseph Smith: "He took heaven, figuratively speaking, and brought it down
to earth." In another context Young said of Smith: "He had all the weaknesses
a man could have when the vision was not upon him, when he was left to
himself." See Beam Locations 280, 519.

[1022] *Acts* 1: 15-26. Note: Although Matthias is not mentioned again in the
Bible after his selection to join the Twelve, according to tradition he died in
Judaea, a martyr stoned to death. See Justo L. Gonzales, *Acts The Gospel of
the Spirit* 30.

[1023] When I was a boy I heard a sermon on the selection of Matthias and how
there was no further mention of him after that. The preacher tried to make
the point that the apostles had not asked the Holy Spirit for guidance and
that therefore they had picked someone who deserved no further mention. To
a boy this seemed profound. Now it seems like one of the dumber sermons I
heard. (And I heard a lot of dumb ones.)

[1024] Paul Johnson, *A History of Christianity* 3.

[1025] *Acts* 15: 1-33.

[1026] *Galatians* 2: 1-10.

[1027] *Galatians* 2: 1, 3.

[1028] James had lost Jesus. John had lost the other James. The Jesus movement
caused martyrs: John the Baptist, Jesus, Stephen, James and probably Peter
and Paul. Peter's martyrdom is suggested by Jesus's quote in *John* 21:18-19 -
words undoubtedly written long after Peter had died: "'*Truly, truly, I say to
you, when you were younger, you used to gird yourself and walk wherever you
wished; but when you grow old, you will stretch out your hands and someone
else will gird you, and bring you where you do not wish to go.' Now this He said,
signifying by what kind of death he would glorify God.*"

[1029] *Galatians* 2:6. Paul's apparent aside here in *Galatians* is to emphasize that
the Jerusalem church was not superior. Later in *Galatians* he metaphorically
attacked Jerusalem. *Galatians* 4: 21-26 reads: "*Tell me, you who want to be
under law, do you not listen to the law? For it is written that Abraham had
two sons, one by the bondwoman and one by the free woman. But the son by*

the bondwoman was born according to the flesh, and the son by the free woman through the promise. This is allegorically speaking, for these women are two covenants: one proceeding from Mount Sinai bearing children who are to be slaves; she is Hagar. Now this Hagar is Mount Sinai in Arabia and corresponds to the present Jerusalem, for she is in slavery with her children. But the Jerusalem above is free; she is our mother." See Georgi, *Remembering The Poor: The History of Paul's Collection for Jerusalem* 31.

[1030] It did have elements of a summons but the *Acts* account also makes it plain that Paul's views had widespread support even outside of Antioch. *Acts* 15:3: *"Therefore, being sent on their way by the church, they were passing through both Phoenicia and Samaria, describing in detail the conversion of the Gentiles, and were bringing great joy to all the brethren."*

[1031] Barnabas was indeed a "dear friend":

- He had sold property and given the proceeds to the early church in Jerusalem (*Acts* 4:36-37).
- He introduced Paul when he was still called Saul to the Apostles in Jerusalem, shortly after Paul's conversion when they had reason to fear him (*Acts* 9:27).
- The Apostles sent him to investigate the new church in Antioch (*Acts* 11:22).
- He then *"went to Tarsus to look for Saul* (Paul)" and brought him to Antioch (*Acts* 11: 25).
- He (and Paul) had brought money from Antioch to Jerusalem (*Acts* 11:29-30).
- He became one of the Christian leaders in Antioch and an early missionary (*Acts* 13 and 14).
- He was at the Council of Jerusalem (*Acts* 15).
- After a *"sharp disagreement"* with Paul over whom to take on a missionary journey, they parted and Barnabas *"sailed away to Cyprus,"* his native land and that is the last mention of him in *Acts*. (*Acts* 15:39).

Barnabas is mentioned in two of Paul's letters. To the Corinthians, Paul indicated that unlike other missionaries, both he and Barnabas worked for a living (*I Corinthians* 9:6). Paul later wrote to the Galatians as he was in conflict with the Jewish-Christians that *"even Barnabas was carried away by their hypocrisy."* (*Galatians* 2:13).

Although he became an offstage personality in comparison to his more famous protégé, Barnabas may have been very impressive. He was once identified as

Zeus the king of the gods by a crowd in the city of Lystra in what is modern Turkey (*Acts* 14: 8-18). Paul was identified as a lesser god, Hermes. In our era, Lystra is a mound. Barnabas may have been related to John Mark (*Colossians* 4:10) and, as such, may also have been related to the Mary who owned a house to which Peter repaired after his prison break (*Acts* 12:12).

Note: Barnabas may have been one of the seventy (or seventy-two) of *Luke* 10:1. See Hengel and Schwemer 205 and Eusebius Book I Chapter 12.

[1032] This is the first time Silas is mentioned in *Acts*. He is then mentioned nine more times in the next three chapters during which he becomes Paul's traveling companion on what is counted as Paul's second missionary journey. He is thought to be the same person as Silvanus who is listed as a coauthor of *I Thessalonians* and *II Thessalonians* and who preached in Corinth. See *I Thessalonians* 1:1; *II Thessalonians* 1:1; and *II Corinthians* 1:19. *I Peter 5:12* refers to him a "*faithful brother*."

Note: The incident in Lystra ties in well with the local culture of that time. Ovid (43 BC – 17/18 AD), was one of the great Roman poets. *Metamorphoses*, a multi-volume collection of mythological stories, is his best known writing. One story is about a couple named Baucis and Philemon. They were an elderly married couple who, without knowing it, hosted the gods Zeus and Hermes. Ovid situated this tale near Lystra. Further note: *Hebrews* 13:2 reads: "*Do not neglect to show hospitality to strangers, for by this some have entertained angels without knowing it.*"

Further Note: The people of Lystra were like the people of Malta in that they came to regard Paul as a god. In the latter instance, this belief came about because Paul survived with aplomb a poisonous snake bite as recorded in *Acts* 28:1-6. (When the snake first bit Paul everyone thought it was punishment because that they thought he was a murderer.)

[1033] Pelikan, *Jesus Through The Centuries: His Place in the History of Culture* 209.

[1034] *Matthew* 11:30.

[1035] I owe this concept to: Stark, *The Rise of Christianity A Sociologist Reconsiders History* 213 and regret it if I have misstated Stark's point of view.

[1036] The sexual behavior prohibited in *Leviticus* is incestuous sex which could be the Council's emphasis in *Acts* 15 and the same word - *porneia* - also appears in *I Corinthians* 5:1 referring to incestuous sexual activity. See Meier, *The Vision of Matthew: Christ, Church and Morality in the First Gospel* 255-6.

[1037] John Mark was a major figure only slightly below the elites of Paul, Barnabas and Peter:

- He was related to Barnabas – *Colossians* 4:10.
- He appears several other times in scripture: as Paul's companion in Rome (*Colossians* 4:10; *Philemon* 24; *II Timothy* 4:11) and as noted Peter's companion in Rome (*I Peter* 5:13).) Note: II Timothy 4:11 reads: "*Only **Luke** is with me. Pick up **Mark** and bring him with you, for he is useful to me for service.*" Emphases added). James D. Tabor suggests that the presumed Gospel authors Mark and Luke were associates of Paul. See Tabor, *Paul and Jesus How the Apostle Transformed Christianity* Location 282.
- According to Papias the bishop of Hierapolis Mark was the "interpreter" of Peter.

Whether any of these accounts are historically accurate, they at least show John Mark's importance in the early church. Note: John Mark may also have had an indirect role in the Council of Jerusalem. According to *Acts* 13:13, John Mark had left Paul and Barnabas during the early stages of their first missionary trip and had returned to Jerusalem. He might have brought word to the leaders there about Paul's activities. That could have caused sufficient concern for them to commission a trip of reviewers to visit the church in Antioch as mentioned in *Acts* 15:1 which in turn precipitated the Council.

[1038] *Acts* 15:36-41 covers the break over John Mark. *Galatians* 2:13 covers the break in Antioch. Martin Hengel and Anna Maria Schwemer estimate that these two events were about two-and-a-half years apart. See Hengel and Schwemer 216.

[1039] *Galatians* 2:11-14.

[1040] *Acts* 6:9.

[1041] See Throckmorton xvi.

[1042] Eusebius Book III Chapter 27. Note: John Toland (1670-1722) an early Deist wrote that the Ebionite doctrines were consistent with the Unitarianism of his time. Modern writers like AN Wilson, John Dominic Crossan, Hyam Maccoby and Gerd Ludemann have all seen Ebionitism, or "Jewish Christianity," as the religion of Jesus. See Charlotte Allen, *The Human Christ The Search for the Historical Jesus* 103-4, 308.

[1043] White, *From Jesus to Christianity* 430.

[1044] *Titus* 1: 10-11.

[1045] *Acts* 15:5.

[1046] James Madison wrote: "The States were divided into different interests not by their difference of size but principally from their having or not having slaves..." See Joseph J. Ellis, *Founding Brothers: The Revolutionary Generation* (New York: Vintage Books, 2000) 90.

[1047] Ideas have consequences. James Madison's compromise probably launched the United

States but led to the Civil War in 74 years. James of Jerusalem's compromise launched Christianity but probably doomed the Jewish-Christian variety.

[1048] *Galatians* 2:4.

[1049] *Galatians* 2:6, 9.

[1050] *Galatians* 2:10.

[1051] It is silent here but on another occasion Paul and Barnabas collected money to take to Jerusalem in response to a famine. See *Acts* 11: 27-30. As noted, Dieter Georgi supposes that this account may be a carrying out of the agreement to "remember the poor" cited in *Galatians*, but entered out of order in *Acts* and somewhat obscured: "When Luke wrote this text, ... the motivation behind (the collection) and the exact date of the collection had simply been forgotten." Georgi, *Remembering The Poor: The History of Paul's Collection for Jerusalem* 44. Georgi also notes that the *Galatians* account does not include the decree concerning the Gentiles (the four prohibitions: eating animals sacrificed to idols, eating meat with its blood, eating animals killed by strangulation and *porneia*) and that in fact Paul wrote that the Pillars did not add any burden on him beyond remembering the poor. Georgi holds that this puts some doubt on whether there was a decree concerning the Gentiles. See Georgi, *Remembering The Poor: The History of Paul's Collection for Jerusalem* 31.

[1052] Crossan, *The Birth of Christianity: Discovering What Happened in the Years Immediately After the Death of Jesus* 473-4.

[1053] *Acts* 11: 27-30. (Again, Dieter Georgi suggests that this is out of order. See above.)

[1054] *Romans* 15:25-6; *I Corinthians* 16: 1-3; *II Corinthians* 8: 1-8; *Acts* 24:17. The last shows a very matter-of-fact conclusion to all these efforts: "*Now after several years I came to bring alms to my nation and to present offerings.*"

[1055] *Matthew* 17: 24. Jesus himself paid it as noted.

[1056] See, for example, Justo L. Gonzales *Acts The Gospel of the Spirit* 176.

[1057] Marty 15.

[1058] Borg and Crossan, *The First Paul: Reclaiming the Radical Visionary Behind the Church's Conservative Icon* 217-18. We must also bear in mind that this was money for the most part from Gentiles delivered by Paul, a figure of some controversy at a time, when tensions were building that would ultimately break out in war with the Romans.

[1059] *I Corinthians* 10: 25-26.

[1060] This assumes that Dieter Georgi is wrong and that there actually was the decree concerning the Gentiles. See above.

[1061] *Acts* 21: 18-26.

[1062] *Acts* 15:28.

[1063] This downgrading of the status of the prohibitions between Acts 15 and Acts 21 lends credence to Dieter Georgi's skepticism about their very existence. See above.

[1064] It certainly took centuries for Paul's version of Christianity to become orthodox. But Jewish Christianity may have been nearly wiped out in the Roman Wars of 66-70 and the 130s.

[1065] David Klinghoffer, *Why The Jews Rejected Jesus: The Turning Point in Western History* (New York, London, Toronto, Sydney, Aukland: Doubleday, 2005) 98.

[1066] Hyam Maccoby, *The Mythmaker Paul and the Invention of Christianity* (New York: Barnes & Noble Books, 1998 by arrangement with HapersSanFrancisco, a division of HarperCollins Publishers, Inc. Published by Hyam Maccoby, 1986) 144.

[1067] *Acts* 21: 20-25.

[1068] Stephen's role as a principal in an intra-Christian dispute is largely forgotten. He is remembered as the earliest of Christian martyrs and as the patron saint of bricklayers. His feast day is December 26. He is also the patron saint of deacons and stonemasons. See Sandoval 38.

[1069] Ben Witherington III's view of the events around the Council of Jerusalem differs from those presented in this book. Witherington holds that the meeting that Paul describes in *Galatians* 2 refers to the meeting described in *Acts* 11: 27-30, not the Council of Jerusalem described in *Acts* 15. He acknowledged that this is a "scholarly debate."

Witherington also looks at the four proscriptions issued by James the brother of Jesus in *Acts* 15:20 - eating animals sacrificed to idols, eating meat with its blood, eating animals killed by strangulation and *porneia* - and substantively restated by James and other elders in *Acts* 21:25 in a different way: "...(W)hat needs to be asked about the decree is this: Where might one find all four of these things in one venue? The answer is, in a pagan temple." Witherington adds: "Thus, at the end of the day, it does not appear that James is imposing Jewish food laws on Gentiles so much as he is urging them to break completely with all that went on in pagan temples, including sacred prostitution."

Witherington's views are worthy of great respect from specialists and, in my case, non-specialists. The view that *Galatians* 2 is not directly connected to the Council seems to contain the additional view that the Council affirmatively decided not to require circumcision of the Gentile Christians which is different than the point advanced in this book.

There is a point of commonality, however, and it is seen in this concluding point of Witherington when he writes of the Council that "a great turning point in church history had transpired, and the church survived intact..." See Witherington, *New Testament History A Narrative Account* Location 4656ff. I regret it if I have misstated Witherington's point of view.

[1070] *I Corinthians* 15:7.

[1071] *Acts* 9:31.

[1072] Luke is the *only* historian of Christianity until the time of Eusebius in the fourth century with the possible exception of Hegesippus of the second century. His writings are quoted in other works and support Luke's idealization of the early period by developing lists of bishops in important locales. See Wilken, *The Myth of Christian Beginning: History's Impact on Belief* 52-76.

[1073] Wilken, *The Myth of Christian Beginning: History's Impact on Belief* 34ff.

[1074] "Some *New Testament* scholars now believe that the author of the *Gospel of Luke* and the *Acts of the Apostles* modeled it on Virgil's *Aeneid* in an attempt to compose a Christian epic." See Harvey Cox, *The Future of Faith* (New York: HarperOne *An Imprint of* HarperCollins*Publishers* 2009) 168.

[1075] *Ephesians* 2:3.

[1076] *Philippians* 3:6.

[1077] *Ephesians* 2:6.

[1078] *Romans* 6: 3-4.

[1079] *I Thessalonians* 4:17 and *I Corinthians* 15:35-39. I owe this thought to Ehrman, *Peter, Paul and Mary* 157 and regret it if I have misunderstood Ehrman's point of view.

[1080] Ehrman, *Peter, Paul and Mary* 155-56. Note: *Colossians* 1:15-20 (like *Philippians* 2:6-11) may be an early hymn. See Reader's Digest *After Jesus: The Triumph of Christianity* 50. We know that the early Christians must have sung hymns from several pieces of evidence:

Mark 14:26 – Before going to the Mount of Olives, the night he was arrested, Jesus and his disciples sang a hymn.

Acts 16:25 - When they were in jail in Philippi, Paul and his colleague Silas were *"singing hymns of praise to God"* for an audience of other prisoners.

Colossians 3:16 – The order of church worship called for hymns.

It is outside of scripture but, as we will see, a Roman official writing in about 111 about Christians in modern Turkey said that they sang hymns. See James DG Dunn *Did the First Christians Worship Jesus? The New Testament* 37-38.

[1081] *Colossians* 2:16.

[1082] *Colossians* 2:18-19.

[1083] *Colossians* 2:13.

[1084] *Colossians* 3: 1-4.

[1085] Ehrman, *The New Testament* 378-8. I regret it if I have misstated Ehrman's point of view.

[1086] Ehrman, *The New Testament* 381.

[1087] Schrage 128ff.

[1088] *Galatians* 3:28.

[1089] Jon Krakauer, *Under the Banner of Heaven: A Story of Violent Faith* (New York: Anchor Books a Division of Random House, Inc. 2003,2004) 68.

[1090] Sally Denton, *American Massacre The Tragedy at Mountain Meadows, September 1857* (New York: Alfred A. Knopf, 2003) 9. It is probably true, as a future Vice President of the United States Henry Wallace said in 1937, that "of all the American religious books of the nineteenth century, it seems probable that the *Book of Mormon* was the most powerful. It reached perhaps only one percent of the people of the United States, but it affected this one percent so powerfully and lastingly that all the people of the United States have been affected, especially by its contribution to opening up one of our great frontiers." Note: In 1861 President Abraham Lincoln borrowed the *Book of Mormon* from the Library of Congress. He kept it for eight months. The *Book of Mormon* talks of post-resurrection appearances of Jesus in the ancient Americas. In 1982, Mormon authorities began adding a subtitle to the *Book of Mormon*: "*Another Testament of Jesus Christ.*" See Fawn Brodie, *No Man Knows my History* New York: Vintage Books, A division of Random House, Inc. 1945. First Vintage Books Edition, 1995) 67-8, Mary Jane Woodger and Wendy Vardeman White, "The *Sangamo Journal's* 'Rebecca' and the 'Democratic Pets': Abraham Lincoln's Interaction With Mormonism" *Journal of Mormon History* Fall 2010 119 and Prothero, *American Jesus How the Son of God Became a National Icon* (New York: Farrar, Straus and Giroux, 2003) 309. Paul C. Gutjahr has written: "Some scholars have noted that had Mormonism adhered to the teachings found in the *Book of Mormon*, it would have differed little on central doctrinal issues from the country's other Protestant denominations. The *Book of Mormon* is Trinitarian in nature and is a strong proponent of monogamy; it contains none of the more aggressive revelations about the plurality of gods and marrying more than one woman that came to mark Mormonism in the later part of Joseph's life." See Paul C. Gutjahr, *The Book of Mormon A Biography* (Princeton and Oxford: Princeton University Press, Kindle Edition, 2012) Location 835.

[1091] Campbell 37.

[1092] Ehrman, *The New Testament* 411. According to Tertullian writing in the late 100s, Barnabas wrote *Hebrews*. *See* Justo L. Gonzales, *Acts The Gospel of the Spirit* 182.

[1093] *Hebrews* 2:1.

[1094] *Hebrews* 3:7-8.

[1095] *Hebrews* 6:4-6.

[1096] *Hebrews* 8:10-12.

[1097] *Hebrews* 8:13.

[1098] Habakkuk was a prophet whose era was about six hundred years before the time of Christ. See William Smith 225.

[1099] Or *her* thinking if the writer was Priscilla or some other woman.

[1100] In that instance we will see how both Paul and the writer of *James* draw different meanings from *Genesis* 15: 6 which says about the patriarch Abraham: "*Then he believed in the* LORD; *and He reckoned it to him as righteousness.*"

1101 Daniel B. Wallace has calculated that it would take two hours to read through the words of Jesus in the *New Testament*. See *The Reliability of the New Testament Bart D. Ehrman & Daniel B. Wallace In Dialogue* Robert B. Stewart, Editor (Minneapolis: Fortress Press, 2011) 52.

1102 Stan Guthrie, *Christianity Today* March 4, 2008 http://blog. christianitytoday.com/ctliveblog/archives/2008/03/is_barack_obama.html (Accessed May 2, 2012).

1103 *Matthew* 5:3.

1104 *Luke* 6:20.

1105 *Matthew* 5:6.

1106 *Luke* 6:21.

1107 *Luke* 6:24-26.

1108 *Matthew* 19:16ff; *Mark* 10: 17ff; *Luke* 18:18ff.

1109 There is some support for monasticism in the *New Testament*: *I Corinthians* 7:29 – *"But this I say, brethren, the time has been shortened, so that from now on those who have wives should be as though they had none;"*

1110 Reader's Digest *After Jesus: The Triumph of Christianity* 179 and

Sandoval 15, 40. See also Jason Thompson, *A History of Egypt From Earliest Times to the Present* (New York: Anchor Books, A division of Randomhouse, Inc., 2008) 152.

1111 Monasticism grew up separate from the church hierarchy and monks came to support themselves with work - often either crafts or farming. It grew steadily in the fourth through sixth centuries and also in medieval times. It was vital to Christianity. Further:

- Monks were some of the first missionaries into northern Europe.
- After the success of Islam in the East, monasteries translated the Bible into Arabic. See Wilken, *The First Thousand Years A Global History of Christianity* 107-8.

1112 This quote is attributed to St. Anthony: "Whoever knows himself, knows God." See Pagels *Revelations Visions, Prophecy and Politics in the Book of Revelation* 155.

1113 Walker 251ff. and Justo L. Gonzales, *A History of Christian Thought From Augustine to the Eve of the Reformation* Volume II Revised Edition Location

3495ff. In 1996 Pope John Paul II met with a group of Waldenses, talked about composing any differences and blessed them. See Cox 109-10.

[1114] Walker 255.

[1115] Marty 93-4, Sandoval 16 and Hitchcock 153-4, 164 - Interestingly, Francis was originally given the name John at his baptism after John the Baptist. His father who had been away in France on business rejected the name and insisted that he be called Francesco or, in English, Francis. He was named, then, for France. See Spoto, *Reluctant Saint The Life of Francis of Assisi* xv, 5-6, 27, 36ff,88,98, 154ff, 200.

[1116] Pelikan, *Jesus Through The Centuries: His Place in the History of Culture* 212-13.

[1117] *The Novels and Other Works of Lyof N. Tolstoi My Confession. My Religion. The Gospel in Brief* (New York: Charles Scribner's Sons, 1913 Thomas Y. Crowell & Co. Copyright 1899) 76ff, 106, 107, 120-21.

[1118] Purgatory is an exclusively Catholic concept. It is a place where souls who are not damned to Hell go after death for purification or purging before entering Heaven. It was taught as far back as Augustine and seems to be based on the custom of praying for the dead. A figure of the late Middle Ages, Pope John XXII (1316-1334), cast the question of purgatory into confusion for a brief period. He preached a doctrine of "soul sleep" which held that at death souls fall into a sleep to be awakened at judgment day. John later recanted this opinion. See Hitchcock 90, 215.

[1119] In 1415 Pope Gregory XII resigned to end a schism in the Church. This followed a great deal of maneuvering on Gregory's part including the appointment of four of his nephews to the College of Cardinals. He was succeeded by Pope Martin V. In 2013 Pope Benedict XVI resigned due to advanced age. He was 85. He was succeeded by Pope Francis who was then 76.

[1120] http://www.newadvent.org/cathen/15126a.htm (Accessed November 13, 2012), Spoto, *Reluctant Saint The Life of Francis of Assisi* 88 and Hitchcock 212. The *Unam Sanctam* quoted:

- *I Corinthians 2:15 - "But he who is spiritual appraises all things, yet he himself is appraised by no one."*
- *Matthew 16:19 - "I will give you the keys of the kingdom of heaven; and whatever you bind on earth shall have been bound in heaven, and whatever you loose on earth shall have been loosed in heaven."*

It also ruled that salvation was impossible outside the church. See Jon M. Sweeney, *The Pope Who Quit: A True Medieval Tale of Mystery, Death and Salvation* (New York: Image Books, an imprint of the Crown Publishing Group, a division of Random House, Inc., Kindle Edition, 2012) 227-228.

1121 Yves Renouard, *The Avignon Papacy 1305-1403* Originally published by Presses Universitaires de France, Paris as La Papaute a Avignon, 1954 translated by Denis Bethell (Hamden, Connecticut: Archon Books, 1970, Printed in Great Britain by Latimer Trend & Co Ltd Plymouth)13 and http://en.wikipedia.org/wiki/Pope_Celestine_V (Accessed May 2, 2012), Sweeney 137ff, 164-5, 237 and Sandoval 35. French domination and perceived domination of the Avignon popes hurt the Church and Rome. See Hitchcock 215. To lay the disasters of the next hundred years on Celestine, however, may be unfair. This view is offered by AN Wilson: "I bend my knee to the unwilling holy man who knew there was no meeting place between the pursuit of power and the worship of God." See Wilson, "Best Pope: The Pontiff Who Quit," *New York Times* April 18, 1999.

1122 Micklethwait and Wooldridge, *God is Back How The Global Revival of Faith is Changing the World* 97.

1123 Pelikan, *Jesus Through The Centuries: His Place in the History of Culture* 213ff, 216-218.

1124 Moreover, there are allies to the Red-Letter Christians. In the 1980s Joseph Cardinal Bernardin (1928-1996) of the US developed an ideology he called the "Consistent Ethic of Life" in response to the modern era which had technologies that threatened the sanctity of human life. Bernardin's philosophy has been called the "seamless garment" which is an allusion to *John* 19:23 which describes a scene at the cross: "*Then the soldiers, when they had crucified Jesus, took His outer garments and made four parts, a part to every soldier and also the tunic; now the tunic was seamless, woven in one piece.*" This philosophy holds that various threats to life including abortion, capital punishment, euthanasia, militarism, social injustice and economic injustice require consistent response that gives value to the sacredness of human life. See Joseph Cardinal Bernardin "Consistent Ethic of Life: Continuing the Dialogue" The William Wade Lecture Series St. Louis University March 11, 1984.

Also: There is a take on pacifism that holds that it is the correct Christian response to violence even if humanity's sinful nature is viewed as a given and even if it will not lead to a reduction in violence. Writing in the 1950s Professor Culbert Rutenber, a pacifist himself, noted that many commentators thought that the pacifism of his time was a natural development of the

404

Social Gospel which is discussed in Chapter 9. He wrote that: "In an effort to make it appear that pacifism is practical and relevant to the modern scene, pacifists exhibit a trust in the essential goodness of human nature that historical reality seems to belie." Professor Rutenber quoted favorably others who saw this type of pacifism as "cheap utopianism" but still argued for pacifism even if it did not lead to worldwide peace. See Culbert Gerow Rutenber *The Dagger and the Cross An Examination of Christian Pacifism* (Nyack, New Fellowship Publications, 1958. First Published November 1950. Second Printing, January, 1953. Fellowship Paperback Edition, February 1958. Forward by John C. Bennett. 28-32.

[1125] An additional note on Red-Letter Christians: Their guiding principles are derived from most – but not all – of the words of Jesus in the *New Testament*. For example, I doubt seriously if they point to either of the following words of Jesus which are drawn from a larger sample:

- *Revelation 3:9: "Behold, I will cause those of the synagogue of Satan, who say that they are Jews and are not, but lie—I will make them come and bow down at your feet, and make them know that I have loved you."*
- *Revelation 21:6-8: "I am the Alpha and the Omega, the beginning and the end. I will give to the one who thirsts from the spring of the water of life without cost. He who overcomes will inherit these things, and I will be his God and he will be my son. But for the cowardly and unbelieving and abominable and murderers and immoral persons and sorcerers and idolaters and all liars, their part will be in the lake that burns with fire and brimstone, which is the second death."*

A caveat is important, however. All this was probably meant to by symbolic. *Revelation* is an apocalyptic text and as James DG Dunn writes: "Apocalyptic visions major on the grandiose and the bizarre, on startling symbolism and hyperbole." See James DG Dunn *Did the First Christians Worship Jesus? The New Testament Evidence* 131.

A Final Note: The words of Jesus in the *New Testament* are not limited to the Gospels and *Revelation*. The *Book of Acts* quotes Jesus talking to Paul in the process of his conversion in *Acts* 9, 22 and 26 and in each case he asked Paul why he was persecuting him. *Acts* 1 records that after Jesus was asked by his followers if he was restoring the kingdom of Israel he told them, according to verses 7 and 8: *"It is not for you to know times or epochs which the Father has fixed by His own authority; but you will receive power when the Holy Spirit has come upon you; and you shall be My witnesses both in Jerusalem, and in all Judea and Samaria, and even to the remotest part of the earth."* *Acts* 22 verses

17-21 record an additional conversation between Jesus and Paul when Jesus warned him to leave Jerusalem.

[1126] Woods, 135ff.

[1127] Marty 147.

[1128] Ondina E. Gonzales and Justo L. Gonzales 145ff.

[1129] Ondina E. Gonzales and Justo L. Gonzales 260ff.

[1130] *Matthew* 5: 27-28. See also *Matthew* 5: 21-22; 31-32; 33-34; 38-39; 43-44.

[1131] *I Timothy* 5:18. ("*For the Scripture says, 'YOU SHALL NOT MUZZLE THE OX WHILE HE IS THRESHING.' And in another place, 'Those who work deserve their pay!'*") The first quote in verse 18 is of *I Corinthians* 9:9 (which itself is identified as from Moses (*Deuteronomy* 25:4); the second quote could be a close approximation of *Matthew* 10:10 (the Twelve) or *Luke* 10:7 (the seventy [or seventy-two]) or *I Corinthians* 9:14 but it is identified as scripture.

[1132] *II Peter* 3:16.

[1133] *II Peter* 1:20.

[1134] Now known as Sinop, it is a city in Turkey near the Black Sea.

[1135] Ehrman, *Peter, Paul and Mary* 162.

[1136] However, Marcion thought that the letter that we call *Ephesians* was actually the letter to the Laodiceans referred to in *Colossians* 4:16. (Some of the early manuscripts as noted omit the words "*in Ephesus*" in *Ephesians* 1:1.) See Browning Location 2799.

[1137] Wills, *What the Gospels Meant* 206. As noted, as the *New Testament* canon formed, it is likely that four gospels were included in order to show that the Christian message was not based on the word of a single apostle as asserted by Marcion. See Justo L. Gonzales *A History of Christian Thought From the Beginnings to the Council of Chalcedon* Volume 1 Revised Edition 149.

[1138] Ehrman, *Jesus Interrupted: Revealing the Hidden Contradictions in the Bible (And Why We Don't Know Them)* 194 and Reader's Digest *After Jesus: The Triumph of Christianity* 131-2.

[1139] Ehrman *Lost Christianities* 103ff.

[1140] Even though we recognize *Philemon* as Paul's one personal letter, it was still meant to be read to the larger congregation. Verse 2 includes among the addressees: "*and to the church in your house.*"

[1141] Bauer 221-222. To make this as complete a picture as possible, it is important to note that during the centuries before Athanasius's list of 367, many of the twenty-seven texts that eventually became the *New Testament* canon steadily gained acceptance as "scripture." Some of the evidence as noted by the examples in this chapter is internal to the texts themselves. There is additional internal evidence. Whoever wrote *Colossians* wanted that letter read in at least one other church as shown by the sixteenth verse of the fourth chapter of that letter. As noted previously, several of the Pauline letters contain commands that they should be read aloud. Beyond the need to do so because of widespread illiteracy, this may have conveyed an authority. Also, some of the *New Testament* writing has a farewell aspect to it as though the writer was trying to preserve information for the believers after his death. Here are two instances:

- *II Peter* 1:13–15: *"I consider it right, as long as I am in this earthly dwelling, to stir you up by way of reminder, knowing that the laying aside of my earthly dwelling is imminent, as also our Lord Jesus Christ has made clear to me."*
- *Acts* 20:17–35 contains a speech attributed to Paul as he leaves Ephesus for the last time. It includes this in verses 29-31: *"I know that after my departure savage wolves will come in among you, not sparing the flock; and from among your own selves men will arise, speaking perverse things, to draw away the disciples after them. Therefore be on the alert..."*

Finally, it is worth noting that long before the canon was certified, some of the early Christian leaders such as Irenaeus, Clement of Alexandria, Justin Martyr, Papias, and Polycarp appeared to cite from or mention texts that became part of the evolving canon. See Kruger 63, 74, 159-97.

[1142] The records are unclear but Marcion's excommunication may have come under Pope Pius I (abt. 142 - abt. 155) who lived in a time when the Monarchical episcopate - the oversight of a church by one individual rather than a group - began to emerge in Rome. If so, this Pope may have been flexing his muscles. See Kelly 10. But serious issues were involved. Justo L. Gonzales writes:

"Among the many varying interpretations of its message which the early Christian church had to face, none were so dangerous as that proposed by Marcion, a native of Sinope..."

"In summary, one may say that Marcion's doctrine is an exaggerated Paulinism." See Justo L. Gonzales *A History of Christian Thought From the Beginnings to the Council of Chalcedon* Volume 1 Revised Edition 137, 141.

1143 Stark, *The Triumph of Christianity How the Jesus Movement Became the World's Largest Religion* 175. Note. Marcion may have found Christians outside of Roman influence who appreciated his take on Christianity. Here is Walter Bauer: "One final point. The reckless speed with which from the very beginning, the doctrine and ideology of Marcion spread can only be explained if it had found the ground already prepared. Apparently, a great number of the baptized, especially in the East, inclined toward this view of Christianity and joined Marcion without hesitation..... No one can call that a falling away from orthodoxy to heresy." See Bauer 194.

1144 Ehrman, *Lost Christianities* 109ff and Justo L. Gonzales *A History of Christian Thought From the Beginnings to the Council of Chalcedon* Volume 1 Revised Edition 141.

1145 Akenson, *Surpassing Wonder: The Invention of the Bible and the Talmuds* 220. *Revelation* inspired Montanus and his movement. See Pagels, Revelations *Visions, Prophecy and Politics in the Book of Revelation* 103.

1146 The Gnostics were a force in their own right and may also have influenced Marcion. See Walker 56-57.

1147 Throckmorton xiv. The *Codex Sinaiticus* from the fourth century includes the *Letter of Barnabas*. See Ehrman, *Jesus Interrupted: Revealing the Hidden Contradictions in the Bible (And Why We Don't Know Them)* 211.

1148 Collins and Price 43.

1149 *Jude* 1:3.

1150 *Titus* 1:13. See also *I Timothy* 1:10 and *Titus* 1:9.

1151 *II Thessalonians* 2:15 and 3:6.

1152 *I John* 4: 1-3.

1153 As noted, there is no historical reference to *II Peter* until 220 AD and it does not seem to have been widely distributed for another century after that time. See Ehrman, *The New Testament* 455-6.

1154 *II Peter* 1:1.

1155 *II Peter* 1:16-18: "*For we were not making up clever stories when we told you about the powerful coming of our Lord Jesus Christ. We saw his majestic splendor with our own eyes when he received honor and glory from God the Father. The voice from the majestic glory of God said to him, 'This is my dearly loved Son, who brings me great joy.' We ourselves heard that voice from heaven when we were with him on the holy mountain.*" Note: Ben Witherington III has suggested that, although this letter was probably written well after the life of Peter, the passage on the Transfiguration could be "a genuine Petrine fragment." See Witherington, *New Testament History A Narrative Account* Location 6768.

[1156] According to White, *From Jesus to Christianity* 423-30, *Jude* was written from about 90-110, *II Peter* was written in the 120s - 130s, *I* and *II Timothy* and *Titus* were written from about 120 – 130. According to Ehrman, *The New Testament* 377, 385 435, *I Peter* was written near the end of the first century as was *II Thessalonians*.

[1157] *I Timothy* 1: 2-3 reads: "*I am writing to Timothy, my true son in the faith. ….When I left for Macedonia, I urged you to stay there in Ephesus and stop those whose teaching is contrary to the truth.*" More on Ephesus: In 431 the First Council of Ephesus, under Augustinian influence, ratified an earlier condemnation of "Pelagianism," the belief that Jesus was not atonement for the sins of humans but merely a good example. See http://en.wikipedia.org/wiki/Pelagianism (Accessed May 2, 2012). That is fitting as *Ephesians* has been called the "Alps of the *New Testament*" because of its mountain top views of Christ. See Dockery, Godwin and Godwin 85-6.

[1158] *Titus* 1: 4-5 reads: "*I am writing to Titus, my true son in the faith that we share. … I left you on the island of Crete so you could complete our work there and appoint elders in each town as I instructed you.*" Crete was a Christian center. It fell to the Muslims in 624. See Stark, *God's Battalions The Case for the Crusades* 12ff. Note: If *Titus* was not written by Paul, there is no reason to link the origin of Christianity in Crete with Paul. In that case, this letter would have been an attempt to bring the Crete church into a Pauline environment. Possibly the effort would have drawn on a tradition covered in *Acts* 27:7-21 of Paul's presence in Crete. See Bauer 76.

[1159] Ehrman, *The New Testament* 385 and Ehrman, *Jesus Interrupted: Revealing the Hidden Contradictions in the Bible (And Why We Don't Know Them)* 130.

[1160] Borg, *Evolution of the Word The New Testament in the Order the Books Were Written* 563. Note: Timothy and Titus were in Paul's inner circle. What do we know about them?

Timothy was the son of a Jewish-Christian woman and a Gentile father. Paul apparently met him in Lystra (*Acts* 16:1). Timothy's mother's name was Eunice and his grandmother who appears to have also been a Christian was named Lois. Timothy is cited twenty-five times in the *New Testament*. He served as Paul's envoy to the trouble spot of Corinth. (*I Corinthians* 4:17). He is even listed as a joint author with Paul of *II Corinthians, Philippians, Colossians, I Thessalonians* (along with Silvanus who is mentioned before him),

II Thessalonians (again along with Silvanus who is mentioned before him), and *Philemon*. There may some link to the author of the letter to the Hebrews as seen in *Hebrews* 13:23: *"Take notice that our brother Timothy has been released, with whom, if he comes soon, I will see you."*

Titus was a Gentile. It is unclear where Paul met him but a careful reading of *II Corinthians* chapters 7 and 8 suggests that he helped mediate between Paul and the Christians in Corinth. He was also at the Council of Jerusalem. *Galatians* 2: 1, 3 reads: *"Then after an interval of fourteen years I went up again to Jerusalem with Barnabas, taking Titus along also. But not even Titus, who was with me, though he was a Greek, was compelled to be circumcised."* Dieter Georgi writes: "(I)n Jerusalem, Titus became the living illustration of what the freedom of Gentile believers was all about. Apparently, someone demanded his circumcision... We know that Paul and Barnabas remained adamantly opposed to the proposition." See Georgi, *Remembering The Poor: The History of Paul's Collection for Jerusalem* 25. Titus is cited twelve times in the *New Testament*.

II Timothy is far more personal than *I Timothy*. It is a farewell letter. It has memories (1:5). It talks of prison (1:8; 16-17). It talks of Paul's sense of abandonment (1:15; 4:9-16). He anticipates death (4:6). It talks of "last days" (3:2-5). Marcus Borg writes: "This is not Paul. But it is not far from Paul." See Borg, *Evolution of the Word The New Testament in the Order the Books Were Written* 563, 575ff, 583.

[1161] *I Peter* 5:5.

[1162] *Acts* 6:3.

[1163] *Titus* 1:9. See also Reader's Digest *After Jesus: The Triumph of Christianity* 104.

[1164] *I Timothy* 2: 14-15.

[1165] *II Timothy* 3: 2-4.

[1166] *I Timothy* 1:4 and *Titus* 1:10-16 and 3:9. See Ehrman, *The New Testament* 386-88.

[1167] *Romans* 3:8.

[1168] *Hebrews* 13:9

[1169] See *Philippians* 2:5-11; *Colossians* 1:15-20; *Revelation* 5:11,13.

[1170] See *I Corinthians* 12:3.

[1171] Van Vorst 24-29.

[1172] *II Corinthians* 11:25 and *Acts* 16:22 - not to mention Pilate.

[1173] For example, a century after Christ, one estimate of the number of Christians in Rome was between one hundred and one hundred and fifty people. See Wilson, *Jesus A Life* 40.

[1174] *Acts* 7:54-60; 13:48-51; 14:19-21; 21:27-36; *I Thessalonians* 2:13-16.

[1175] *Matthew* 10:34-37.

[1176] *Romans* 16:16 and *I Peter* 5:14.

[1177] Walker 49.

[1178] Wilken, *The Christians as the Romans Saw Them* 24-25. Note: When Pliny the Younger reported that a Christian group in Bithynia sang hymns to Christ as God and pledged to live a moral life, it isn't clear whether these were heretics, an Orthodox group (that we are calling Institutionalists) or some type of mixed group. We know that Marcion was active in that area soon after. See Bauer 90-91.

[1179] The Pliny/Trajan correspondence can be found at http://www9. georgetown.edu/faculty/jod/texts/pliny.html. (Accessed November 2, 2012). Trajan's advice on how to handle the problem of Christians came down to an ancient equivalent of the "Don't Ask Don't Tell" approach often favored by leaders: "They are not to be sought out; if they are denounced and proved guilty, they are to be punished,..." About eighty-five years later the legal scholar and church father Tertullian condemned the inherent contradiction in this guidance. See Justo L. Gonzales, *A History of Christian Thought From the Beginnings to the Council of Chalcedon* Volume 1 Revised Edition 172.

[1180] *I Peter* 1:1.

[1181] *I Peter* 2:12.

[1182] *I Peter* 2:12.

[1183] *I Peter* 2:13-14.

[1184] *I Peter* 3: 13-17.

[1185] *Acts* 1:12-26.

[1186] *Acts* 15:4.

[1187] Browning Location 520 and Borg, *Evolution of the Word The New Testament in the Order the Books Were Written* 218.

[1188] *Matthew* 10:5-6.

[1189] *Mark* 7: 24-30 and *Matthew* 15: 21-28.

[1190] *Matthew* 5:17.

[1191] *Galatians* 2:16.

[1192] *Matthew* 5:18.

[1193] *I Corinthians* 8:20-21.

[1194] *Matthew* 28: 18-20.

[1195] *Matthew* 27: 51-54. This was quite an earthquake. Tombs were opened and "*many bodies of the saints who had fallen asleep were raised. After his (Jesus's) resurrection they came out of the tombs and entered the holy city and appeared to many.*" (verses 52-53). Matthew adds the earthquake to Mark's version to account for the resurrection of other martyrs. See Borg and Crossan, *The Last Week: What the Gospels Really Teach About Jesus's Final Days in Jerusalem* 175-76.

[1196] *Matthew* 28:2.

[1197] Luke and Mark have Jesus predicting earthquakes as a sign of end times (*Mark* 13:8 and *Luke* 21:11). Luke possibly alludes to an earthquake or a tremor in *Acts* 4:31when he describes a reunion of Peter and John with their colleagues after the two had been released from custody. He writes: "*And when they had prayed, the place where they had gathered together was shaken, and they were all filled with the Holy Spirit and began to speak the word of God with boldness.*" Luke cites an earthquake as destroying a prison in Philippi that held the Apostle Paul and his co-worker Silas resulting in the conversion of the jailer (he became "*a believer in God*") and an apology from the city authorities when they learned that Paul was a Roman citizen (*Acts* 16: 25-40). In the *Book of Revelation*, earthquakes are mentioned frequently in an apocalyptic context (*Revelation* 6:12, 8:5, 11:13, 11:19 and 16:18). Matthew, in keeping with all this, recounts that after Jesus's triumphal entry a week before his crucifixion, the city is shaken. The word he uses is like an earthquake (*Matthew* 21:10).

[1198] I owe this thought to Meier, *The Vision of Matthew: Christ, Church and Morality in the First Gospel* 15-33 and regret it if I have misunderstood Meier's point of view. Meier goes on to point out that even though Matthew waited until the very end of the gospel to proclaim the universalism of Jesus he supplies predictions of it throughout his narrative of Jesus's life:

Matthew 2:1-12 - The adoration by the wise men.

Matthew 4:12-17 - The change of residence to Capernaum with the prophecy of Isaiah about "*Galilee of the Gentiles.*"

Matthew 5:46-47 and 18:17 - Association with tax collectors and sinners.

Matthew 8:5-13 - The healing of the centurion's servant into which Matthew inserts a Q statement about many coming from the east and west to feast in the kingdom.

Matthew 8:28-34 - The exorcism of the Gadarene demoniacs.

Matthew 15: 21-28 - The healing of the daughter of the Canaanite woman.

[1199] Crossan, *The Birth of Christianity: Discovering What Happened in the Years Immediately After the Death of Jesus* 3-14.

[1200] Grant, *Jesus: An Historian's Review of the Gospels* 182 and Ehrman, *The New Testament* 212.

[1201] Wilken, *The Christians as the Romans Saw Them* 94.

[1202] Collins and Price 38.

[1203] Note that in this account Tacitus referred to Pilate as the "procurator." However, a coin discovered in 1961 in Caesarea Maritima (an ancient port associated with the city of Caesarea in modern Israel) shows that Pilate as governor had the title of "prefect" which meant he also had a military command. This may show that Tacitus didn't look up any records if any existed but had heard the information. Did he hear it from Christians or others? Who knows? See Ehrman, *Did Jesus Exist? The Historical Argument for Jesus of Nazareth* 44, 56.

[1204] Van Vorst 29, 37ff. There is an intriguing possibility of another mention. An ancient historian named Thallos wrote an account of the eastern Mediterranean area around 55 AD. Most of his book perished but it was quoted by a Christian writer Sextus Julius Africanus in about 220 AD in a book, *History of the World*. This book was also lost but one quote was picked up by Byzantine historian Georgius Syncellus in about 800 AD. According to Syncellus, when Julius Africanus mentioned the darkness at the time of the death of Jesus, he wrote: "In the third (book) of his histories, Thallos called this darkness an eclipse of the sun, which seems to me to be wrong." The evidence, then is that Thallos knew of Jesus's death and the portent of darkness referred to in *Matthew* 27:45; *Mark* 15:33; and *Luke* 23:44. See Vorst 20-21.

[1205] Stark, *The Rise of Mormonism* 3, 22. Note: In the late 1800s, Friedrich Engels (1820-1895) the source along with Karl Marx (1818-1883) for Marxism wrote that the growth of socialism would be like this steady growth of

Christianity until it dominated the world. See Michael Harrington, *Socialism Past and Future* (New York Arcade Publishing 1989, 2011) 42.

[1206] Wilson, *Paul: The Mind of the Apostle* 69.

[1207] Stark, *The Rise of Christianity A Sociologist Reconsiders History* 135.

[1208] *James* 1:1 and *I Peter* 1:1.

[1209] Stark, Discovering God*: The Origins of the Great Religions and the Evolution of Belief* 312.

[1210] Reader's Digest *Atlas of the Bible: An Illustrated Guide to the Holy Land* 204-6. So why did Rome win out as the "capital of Christianity?" It may owe its status to the sack of Jerusalem by the Romans in 70 AD which scattered the Jewish-Christians and the executions and burials of Peter and Paul in Rome. It still took more than two centuries. See MacCulloch 110.

[1211] Wilken, *The Christians as the Romans Saw Them* 45, 98, 100, 124-30, 136, 145, 153, 166, 178, 204.

[1212] One of these refutations was by Origen. See Wilken, *The Christians as the Romans Saw Them* 94. Origen's refutation may have preserved up to ninety percent of Celsus's original writing. See Van Vorst 64ff.

[1213] Wilken, *The Christians as the Romans Saw Them* 106. As noted, Pliny the Younger reported this deification of Jesus to Trajan.

[1214] Hitchcock 47.

[1215] Charlotte Allen, *The Human Christ The Search for the Historical Jesus* 54.

[1216] The name Porphyry was a pun bestowed on him by a mentor. It meant purple and was an imperial color.

[1217] Tyre was an ancient Phoenician city. It is mentioned dozens of times in the *Bible*. Jesus visited there or at least near there (*Matthew* 15:21; *Mark* 7:24-31). People from Tyre came to hear Jesus give his "Sermon on the Plain" (*Luke* 6:17) and possibly on one other occasion (*Mark* 3:8). Jesus compared them favorably to the Jews. (*Matthew* 11:21-22; *Luke* 10: 13-14). Paul visited a Christian group in Tyre for about a week (*Acts* 21: 3-7). Tyre is about one hundred miles north of Jerusalem. There are towns named Tyre in the US in New York and Michigan.

[1218] http://en.wikipedia.org/wiki/Porphyry_(philosopher). (Accessed May 2, 2012). Note: Writing seventeen hundred years after Porphyry, the American Thomas Paine in his 1793 *Age of Reason* raised some of the same objections to the *New Testament* that Porphyry had – the discrepancies around the genealogical lists, the birth stories and time of day that Jesus died – and he reached a similar conclusion. He advocated a "plain, pure, and unmixed belief of one God, which is deism..." See Thomas Paine *The Age of Reason* (Barnes & Noble: New York) 151.

[1219] Grant, *History of Rome* 418.

[1220] Brownworth 34-35.

[1221] Klinghoffer 146. According to legend, Julian the Apostate called out as he died on the battlefield: "O pale Galilean, you have conquered." See Hitchcock 59. Julian was buried in Tarsus, the home of the Apostle Paul. See Brownworth 37. Note: Julian was a schoolmate with two brothers who became leading Christian thinkers of that era. Basil of Caesarea and his brother Gregory of Nyassa along with Gregory of Nazianzus came to be known as the Cappadocian Fathers and lived in what is now eastern Turkey. They taught that in Christ there is a union of two natures (*hypostases*) - the "hypostatic union." They were supportive of the Nicene Creed and helped develop the doctrine of the Trinity. See Hitchcock 84 and Reader's Digest *After Jesus: The Triumph of Christianity* 247-8.

[1222] Some writers have attributed the fall of Rome in part to the influence of Christians. In the late 1700s, Edward Gibbon wrote in the *Decline and Fall of the Roman Empire*, that Christianity's pacifistic ethic drained Rome's military spirit. He also linked the diversion of resources to convents and monasteries and theological disputes to increasing divisions in Roman society. See John L. Allen Jr. *The Global War on Christians Dispatches From the Front Lines of Anti-Christian Persecution* (New York: Image an imprint of the Crown Publishing Group, a division of Random House LLC, a Penguin Random House Company, Kindle Edition, 2013) 246. Note: Although Rome fell within a century of Constantine, the Byzantine Empire persisted under his successors for a thousand years - until 1453. I will be unsubtle here. One of the lessons of history is that immense spans of time are involved in comparison with how short our lives are. This is a *New Testament* message. The *Epistle of James* urges humility by reminding people:

"Come now, you who say, 'Today or tomorrow we will go to such and such a city, and spend a year there and engage in business and make a profit.' Yet you do not know what your life will be like tomorrow. You are just a vapor that appears for a little while and then vanishes away." (James 4: 13-14).

[1223] Paul Johnson, *A History of Christianity* 127. Conversion to Christianity in Western Europe in the Dark Ages (400-1000) meant encouraging such behavior as monogamy, observing Lent, burial rather than cremation and abandoning other gods. It was during the 500s that the practice of dating years from the birth of Jesus Christ took hold. By medieval times, the Catholic Church permeated every aspect of life in Europe. In James Hitchcock's words: "The entire culture was organized in such a way that at every turn people were reminded of divine realities and drawn toward them. Thus church spires were the tallest structure in every town, and churches and outdoor shrines were everywhere. The hours of the day, announced by church bells, were organized according to the Divine Office, and the year was organized according to the liturgical feasts that reenacted the cycle of Christ's life and that of His saints." See Hitchcock 110, 131, 141.

[1224] Samosata was an ancient Greek city in modern day Turkey.

[1225] The Great Commission of *Matthew* 28:18-19 (*"…baptizing them in the name of the Father and the Son and the Holy Spirit…"*) guided the Council of Nicaea in the formation of the doctrine Trinity. See Pelikan, Mary *Through the Centuries Her Place in the History of Culture* 9-10.

[1226] Justo L. Gonzales, *A History of Christian Thought From the Beginnings to the Council of Chalcedon* Volume 1 Revised Edition 293, 294, 297. Why did Athanasius think that? The Nicene Council affirmed that Jesus Christ and God were "of the same substance" – the Greek word was "homoousios." Others argued that Jesus Christ and God were "of a similar substance" - the Greek word is nearly identical with only one additional letter which I have emphasized by bolding it: "homoiousios." Athanasius and others worried that if Jesus Christ had a similar – and not same - divine substance, monotheism would be compromised. Athanasius's party won the day. In later centuries, many who took the cause of the Arians gravitated to the position that Jesus Christ was a human. But the original dispute was whether he was some type of lesser God. Note: In old age Athanasius came to accept an interpretation in the Nicene formula from homoousios (of the same substance) to homoiousios (of a similar substance). He recognized the needs of Christians who were not Arians but saw distinctions between the Father and the Son. "Through a series of negotiations, Athanasius convinced many of these Christians that the formula of Nicea could be interpreted in such a way as to respond to the concerns of those who would rather say, 'of a similar substance.'" In 362 at a synod in Alexandria, Athanasius and his supporters held that people could talk of the three members of the Trinity as "one substance" as long as distinctions weren't destroyed or "three substances" as long as they understood there weren't three gods. See Justo L. Gonzales *The Story of Christianity Volume 1 The Early Church to the Dawn of the Reformation* 3654ff.

[1227] In his own time Origen complained about the gap between Christian intellectuals and common people who knew nothing *"except Jesus Christ and Him crucified."* In the 200s - 400s the monastic movement in Egypt and Syria produced monks who could be directed in violent demonstrations in doctrinal disputes. Athanasius came to use them this way. See Paul Johnson, *A History of Christianity* 94. Charlotte Allen has said that Athanasius had the toughness of a street thug. See Charlotte Allen, *The Human Christ The Search for the Historical Jesus* 62.

[1228] Athanasius wrote the *Life of Anthony* which helped promote the monastic movement. With the age of martyrs for the most part in the past, the faithful sought out stories of unusual acts of spirituality. According to Athanasius, Anthony of Egypt was influenced to go toward asceticism by:

- *Acts* 4:32 and following. *Acts* 4:32 reads: *"And the congregation of those who believed were of one heart and soul; and not one of them claimed that anything belonging to him was his own, but all things were common property to them."*
- *Matthew* 19:21 – *"Jesus said to him, 'If you wish to be complete, go and sell your possessions and give to the poor, and you will have treasure in heaven; and come, follow Me.'"* (Again, the Rich Young Ruler)

Athanasius's *Life of Anthony* became popular. It was translated into Latin and Syriac and read throughout the Empire. It influenced Augustine. See Justo L. Gonzales, *A History of Christian Thought From the Beginnings to the Council of Chalcedon* Volume 1 Revised Edition 292 and Wilken, *The First Thousand Years A Global History of Christianity* 100, 102, 106. As noted, Anthony lived to age 100. According to the *Life of Anthony,* Anthony was told by God when he was to die. Later, in the 500s, people believed that only saints could know the day and hour of their deaths. See Paolo Cesaretti, *Theodora Empress of Byzantium* Translated from the Italian by Rosanna M. Giammanco Frongia, Ph.D. a Mark Magowan Book (New York: The Vendome Press, 2001, 2004) 207,364.

[1229] Collins and Price 60. Athanasius was also sometimes called "the black dwarf" because he was so short and dark. See Justo L. Gonzales, *The Story of Christianity Volume 1 The Early Church to the Dawn of the Reformation* 3534ff.

[1230] Cesaretti 44, 356. That is a street version of Arius's position. More elaborately, in the words of Jean Milet: "Like many others (and doubtless with the majority of believers at this time), Arius could not bring himself to accept that this Jesus could be called 'God born of God, true God of true God.' He had too much feeling for the oneness of God, for his unalterable transcendence, to go so far as this 'mental confusion' which could lead to seeing God in Christ. He was certainly willing to allow that Jesus was inhabited by a kind of 'divine personality', but it was understood that this divine personality was not God himself but one of his 'creations.' In this case the 'polarization' of the faith around the oneness of the divine being would not be altered. There would be a predominant belief, belief in God, and a belief subordinate to the first, the content of which was still to be defined, belief in Christ. However, as is well known, this theory was contested at the Council of Nicaea (325) and then the Council of Constantinople (381)." See Jean Milet *God or Christ* (London: SCM Press, 1980) Translated by John Bowden from the French 12.

[1231] MacCulloch 222. Note: As we will cover in Chapter 11, Arianism persisted in the Germanic tribes in Europe for another century or more. Charlotte Allen has written: "For many Christians, it was easier to comprehend a numinous superhero who was rather like Hercules than the puzzling Jesus of Christian orthodoxy whose precise measure of humanity and divinity was so troublesome." See Charlotte Allen, *The Human Christ The Search for the Historical Jesus* 61.

[1232] Hitchcock 84.

[1233] Justo L. Gonzales, *A History of Christian Thought From the Beginnings to the Council of Chalcedon* Volume 1 Revised Edition 353-4. Here is how Jean Milet describes Nestorius: "Nestorius... was unable to bring himself to accept the 'mental confusion' which consisted in identifying Jesus purely and simply with God. He contented himself with considering Jesus to be a privileged 'messenger' of God, a kind of super-prophet, who will have had exceptional relations with the deity. He, too, maintained a single pole for faith: there is only one belief that counts, belief in God; belief in Christ is no more than an aid to that. Nestorius...had to be challenged ...at the Council of Ephesus (431)."

See Milet 12.

[1234] Here is how this controversy was described by Pope Benedict XVI some sixteen centuries later:

"(Nestorius was) a severe and authoritarian monk trained in Antioch. The new Bishop of Constantinople, in fact, soon provoked opposition because he preferred to use as Mary's title in his preaching 'Mother of Christ' (*Christotokos*) instead of 'Mother of God' (*Theotokos*), already very dear to popular devotion.

"One reason for Bishop Nestorius's decision was his adherence to the Antiochene type of Christology, which, to safeguard the importance of

Christ's humanity, ended by affirming the division of the Divinity. Hence, the union between God and man in Christ could no longer be true, so naturally it was no longer possible to speak of the 'Mother of God.'

"The reaction of Cyril - at that time the greatest exponent of Alexandrian Christology, who intended on the other hand to stress the unity of Christ's person - was almost immediate, and from 429 he left no stone unturned, even addressing several letters to Nestorius himself." See Pope Benedict XVI, *The Fathers* 113-114.

[1235] Hitchcock 85ff.

[1236] A thousand years after Chalcedon, Lutheran George Calixtus (1585-1656) called for a unity among Christian traditions. He taught a difference between fundamental and secondary articles of faith with only the first category necessary for salvation. He taught, in other words, that the *Bible* itself is the true source of doctrine and has everything needed for salvation but also has sound doctrines that are not needed for salvation. When asked how one would know the distinction between the two categories he referred to what he called the *consensus quinquasaecularis* or the councils of the first five centuries. The appeal to tradition and his distinction of categories was an outreach. The ideas of Calixtus can be traced to the ecumenism of the 1900s. See *Justo L. Gonzales A History of Christian Thought From the Protestant reformation to the Twentieth Century* Volume III *Revised Edition* Location 4795ff.

[1237] MacCulloch 240, 245. The Ethiopian church has stayed Monophysite for centuries. See Hitchcock 211. Unlike Syria and Egypt it was not conquered by the surging Islam of the 600s. Its canon includes in addition to certain *New Testament* books, *Enoch*, the *Shepherd of Hermas* and *I* and *II Clement*. See Wilken, *The First Thousand Years A Global History of Christianity* 218, 219.

[1238] Jenkins, *Jesus Wars: How Four Patriarchs, Three Queens, and Two Emperors Decided What Christians Would Believe for the Next 1,500 Years* 13-14. See also Hitchcock 210.

[1239] In 1973 Coptic Pope Shenouda (1923 – 2012) and Pope Paul VI issued a joint statement on christology that resolved a fifteen hundred year break: "We confess that our Lord and God and Savior and King of us all, Jesus Christ, is perfect God with respect to His divinity, perfect man with respect to his humanity. In Him His divinity is united with His humanity in a real, perfect union without mingling, without commixtion, without confusion, without alteration, without division, without separation. His divinity did not separate from His humanity for an instant, not for the twinkling of an eye. He who is God eternal and invisible became visible in the flesh, and took upon Himself the form of a servant. In Him are preserved all the properties of the divinity and all the properties of the humanity, together in a real, perfect, indivisible and inseparable union." See Tadros Locations 2831, 3004ff.

[1240] Christians in the East could trace their lineage back to Pentecost. In *Acts* 2 we read that devout Jews from *"every nation"* (verse 5) heard the Christians speaking in their native languages and were amazed. *Acts* 2: 9 lists: *"Parthians, Medes, Elamites, people from Mesopotamia."* These represent territories east of Judea in modern Iran, Iraq and Syria. Some of these Diaspora Jews were no doubt among the three thousand who were baptized that day according to *Acts* 2:41. If, as I have suggested, *Acts* 16:9 denotes the movement of Christianity westward, *Acts* 2:9 shows that it moved east also.

[1241] There is a Nineveh, Indiana in the United States. It has a population of about four thousand. Some of the scenes from the basketball movie *Hoosiers* (1986) were filmed there.

[1242] MacCulloch 247-52

[1243] Jenkins, *The Lost History of Christianity: The Thousand Year Golden Age of the Church in the Middle East, Africa, and Asia - and How it Died* ixff, 33-34, 64. Here is Justo L. Gonzales: "The Mongols took Baghdad in 1258, and the Nestorian community never recovered from that blow. ... In more recent times, the persecutions that the Nestorians have suffered in the Near East have reduced their numbers to a few thousand." *Justo L. Gonzales A History of Christian Thought From the Protestant Reformation to the Twentieth Century* Volume III Revised Edition Location 7964. See also Hitchcock 210.

[1244] Christianity *The Illustrated Guide to 2000 Years of the Christian Faith* Chief Consultant Ann Marie B. Bahr Australia: Millennium House 20.

[1245] http://en.wikipedia.org/wiki/Assyrian_Church_of_the_East (Accessed May 2, 2012). Note: Throughout the Middle East the Christian Church in all its forms is in decline. As the Catholic Patriarch of Jerusalem put it in 2011, the Holy Land might become "a spiritual Disneyland" - full of attractions but devoid of its indigenous Christian populations. See John L. Allen Jr. 124.

[1246] Christianity *The Illustrated Guide to 2000 Years of the Christian Faith* 20. Due to these complexities and because of the significance of the Council of Chalcedon of 451 I will offer another summary of its aftermath. Here are the words of Robert Louis Wilken:

"The controversies of the fifth century shattered the tenuous unity of Christianity in the East, and the one Church confessed in the Nicene Creed ('in one holy catholic and apostolic Church') was on its way to division into several distinct communions, each with its own hierarchy:

"1. Those who held to the Council of Chalcedon. In the Middle East these Christians, many of whom spoke Syriac, came to be called Melkites, from the Syriac word for king or emperor, because they were in communion with the emperor in Constantinople. There was also another Chalcedonian community, the Maronites, named after a Monk called Maro who died in the early fifth century. After his death a monastery was founded in northern Syria, and during the controversy over Christ these monks and their followers accepted the Council of Chalcedon.

"2. The Copts of Egypt. These Christians now had their own patriarch, distinct from the Chalcedonian patriarch. The Copts were joined by the West Syrians, those living in the vicinity of Antioch, in the early sixth century. They came to be called Jacobites, because Jacob Baradeus, bishop of Edessa (543-578) traveled through the region consecrating bishops and establishing an independent hierarchy in Syria. With the Copts they formed the second major grouping, the non-Chalcedonians, or miaphysites." (i.e., Monophysites).

"3. The Syriac speaking Christians in the Sassanid Persian Empire and Central Asia. They are often called Nestorians, because they rejected the Council of Ephesus in 431, where Nestorius was deposed, but the proper term for this large body of Christians is the Church of the East. Their patriarch, or *catholicos*, resided at Seleucia-Ctesiphon, a city occupying both sides of the Tigris, and later at Baghdad." See Wilken, *The First Thousand Years A Global History of Christianity* 225.

[1247] The Muslim Dome of the Rock was built in Jerusalem between 685-691. On the side facing the Church of the Holy Sepulcher was this inscription: "God has no son." See Stark, *God's Battalions The Case for the Crusades* 86.

[1248] Paul Johnson, *A History of Christianity* 242-3 and Brownworth 130. In the words of Robert Louis Wilken:

- "No event during the first thousand years of Christian history was more unexpected, calamitous, and consequential than the rise of Islam. Few irruptions in history have transformed societies as rapidly and irrevocably as did the conquest and the expansion of the Arabs of Islam in the seventh century. And none came with greater swiftness."
- "Once the Mediterranean had been a western lake joining the deserts of Egypt with the cities of Italy and North Africa, but with the coming of Islam it became an immense moat dividing the Muslim East from the Christian West. In two hundred years many of the

Christians of the region would be speaking Arabic, and territories that were once provinces of the Roman Empire would be ruled from Baghdad, not Constantinople."

- "By the middle of the eighth century more than fifty percent of the Christian world had fallen under Muslim rule. In the span of less than a hundred years, the Arabs had conquered greater Syria (including the Holy Land and Jordan) and Egypt, and made their way from the western edge of Egypt along the North African littoral until they reached the Atlantic Ocean. From the Arabian peninsula they advanced northeast through Persia and across the Asian steppes to India. In 711 they reached Sind, today a province in Pakistan. Within the same decade, they crossed the Strait of Gibraltar into Spain and in midcentury established an independent Muslim kingdom in the peninsula." See Wilken, *The First Thousand Years A Global History of Christianity* 288, 294, 307.

[1249] Jerusalem's history over the centuries has been marked by attacks:

- 70 AD - In the war with the Romans, Jewish-Christians suffered along with other Jews. Some went to Pella across the Jordan River. Others stayed in Jerusalem. The city was largely ruined but partially rebuilt over the next several decades.
- 135 AD - After the last Jewish revolt, the Romans renamed Jerusalem Aelia Capitolina after the emperor and the god Jupiter. In the early Christian era Jerusalem was less important than such other Christian cities as Alexandria, Antioch, Rome and Carthage. But by the 400s Jerusalem had been promoted to the status of a Patriarchate with supervision over churches in the area. It also had a supposed fragment of the Cross.
- 614 AD - The Persians sacked Jerusalem. This was a calamity for the Christian world. We have moving poetry from the Patriarch Sophronius as he was led into exile. The Eastern Christians recovered Jerusalem from the Persians but lost it to the Arabs in 636. By the end of the 600s at least some Arab coins bore the verse from the Koran: "He is God, one, eternal; he does not beget nor is he begotten." Also in the mosque of the Dome of the Rock are such inscriptions as: "O ye people of the book, overstep not bounds in your religion; and of God speak only truth. The Messiah Jesus, son of Mary, is only an apostle of God, and his Word which he conveyed into Mary, and a Spirit proceeding from him. Believe therefore in God and his apostles, and say not 'Three.' It will be better for you. God is only

one God." See Wilken *The First Thousand Years A Global History of Christianity* 110f, 279ff, 288ff.

- 1099 – The Crusaders recovered Jerusalem in 1099 and lost it back to the Muslims in 1187. In 1244, Jerusalem was overrun by the Tartars who killed the Christian inhabitants and dispossessed the Jews.
- 1250 - The Mamluks took the city and held it for more than two hundred and fifty years.
- 1517 – The Ottoman Turks took Jerusalem and held it until World War I.
- 1917 – British General Edmund Allenby took Jerusalem during World War I and the League of Nations recognized a British mandate over the city and related territories that lasted until 1948.
- 1948 – The City was divided between Israel and Jordan.
- 1967 – The Israelis reunited the city following the Six-Day War.

[1250] Brownworth 130-8, 174. Note: Antioch stayed in Christian hands until 1085 when it fell to the Seljuk Turks. The Crusaders recovered it in the late 1090s and then lost it.

[1251] Quoted in Sydney E. Ahlstrom, *A Religious History of the American People* (New Haven and London: Yale University Press, 1972. Fourth Printing, 1974) 994.

[1252] Justo L. Gonzales, *A History of Christian Thought From Augustine to the Eve of the Reforma*tion Volume II Revised Edition Location 2347.

[1253] In 1204 during the Fourth Crusade which was intended to retake Jerusalem from the Muslims, the Crusaders of Western Europe invaded and sacked Constantinople. Large scale murder, rape, looting and the destruction of works of art followed and much of the city was burned. The Byzantine Empire retook the city in 1261. In 1453 it finally fell to the Muslims and today is known as Istanbul. Regarding the events of 1204, Pope John Paul II wrote in the twenty-first century: "It is tragic that the assailants, who set out to secure free access for Christians to the Holy Land, turned against their brothers in the faith. The fact that they were Latin Christians fills Catholics with deep regret." In 2004 he noted to Bartholomew I, Patriarch of Constantinople, during a Vatican visit: "How can we not share, at a distance of eight centuries, the pain and disgust." This was regarded as an apology to the Greek Orthodox Church which the Patriarch accepted: "The spirit of reconciliation is stronger than hatred." See http://en.wikipedia.org/wiki/Fourth_Crusade (Accessed May 2, 2012).

¹²⁵⁴ Brownworth 221-24, MacCulloch 973, Cox 110-11. Justo L. Gonzales *A History of Christian Thought From Augustine to the Eve of the Reforma*tion Volume II Revised Edition Location 2347.

¹²⁵⁵ For another perspective, here is Philip Jenkins's description of the *filioque* controversy: "Innovations from the fringe become normal. To take one example, a majority of Christians around the world regularly recite a version of the Nicene Creed, which proclaims belief 'in the Holy Spirit, the Lord and Giver of Life, who proceeds from the father *and the Son*' (my emphasis). The phrase 'and the Son,' *filioque,* is not part of the original text, and is condemned by the Eastern Orthodox churches. The *filioque* originated in the distant borderlands of Christianity as it existed in the sixth and seventh centuries, as Catholics in Spain and Gaul confronted missionary issues unfamiliar to the mainstream church of the day, which was centered in Constantinople. Being forced to deal with Arians, who rejected the equality of Father and Son, local Catholics asserted the dignity of Christ, and they did so by taking what seems like a breathtakingly bold step. They simply altered the creed in order to reflect local needs and realities. By the eighth century, the *filioque* spread across Western Europe, and Charlemagne and his heirs popularized it as part of their campaign to spread Christianity throughout the Germanic world. Only in the eleventh century, though, was this weird border practice accepted by the papacy. By that time, this explosive word had become a proud symbol of the emerging Western church, and an assertion of its distinctiveness from the ever-more distant church of the East." See Jenkins, *The Next Christendom The Coming of Global Christianity* Third Edition (Oxford Oxford University Press, Kindle Edition, 2011) 148.

¹²⁵⁶ Collins and Price 59.

¹²⁵⁷ Wills, *Why I Am A Catholic* 57ff.

¹²⁵⁸ *Galatians* 2:9.

¹²⁵⁹ *Galatians* 2:13.

¹²⁶⁰ *II Corinthians* 11:15.

¹²⁶¹ *Mark* 8:33.

¹²⁶² *John* 18:10.

¹²⁶³ *Matthew* 16:23.

¹²⁶⁴ *Matthew* 17:1-8, *Mark* 9:2-8; *Luke* 9:28-36.

¹²⁶⁵ *I Corinthians* 1:12.

[1266] *I Corinthians* 9:5.

[1267] Meier, *A Marginal Jew Rethinking the Historical Jesus Vlm III Companions and Competitors* 159.

[1268] *Acts* 8:14-25.

[1269] *Galatians* 2:11-14.

[1270] *I Corinthians* 1:12; 3:22.

[1271] I owe this thought to Akenson, *Saint Saul: A Skeleton Key to the Historical Jesus* 153-58 and regret it if I have misstated Akenson's point of view. Note: Martin Hengel and Anna Maria Schwemer speculate that the deep hurt Paul experienced in Antioch (documented in *Galatians*) may have caused this subtle criticism of Peter. See Hengel and Schwemer 206ff.

[1272] *I Corinthians* 10:4, *Ephesians* 2:19, *Romans* 9:33 (similar to *Acts* 4:11).

[1273] Larry Barber, *News & Views* Vol. 25, No. 6 August 2008. Note: These three parties at Antioch were represented at the Council of Jerusalem as discussed in Chapter 7 of this book.

[1274] Wills, *Why I Am A Catholic* 253.

[1275] See Jenkins, *The Lost History of Christianity: The Thousand Year Golden Age of the Church in the Middle East, Africa, and Asia - and How it Died* 48.

[1276] Brownworth 124-5.

[1277] With modern immigration patterns, the Virgin has moved beyond Mexico. "In the United States, at some point in the early twenty-first century, the membership of the Roman Catholic Church became more than half Hispanic or Latino. The Virgin of Guadalupe, until 1980 seldom seen in a North American Catholic church, was now venerated in churches as far north as Alaska and as far west as Hawaii." See Ondina E. Gonzales and Justo L. Gonzales 304.

[1278] http://en.wikipedia.org/wiki/Our_Lady_of_Guadalupe (Accessed May 2, 2012) and Sandoval 15.

[1279] The papal pronouncement *Ineffabilis Deus* by Pope Pius IX in 1854 declaring the immaculate conception of Mary was an important milestone on the road to papal infallibility sixteen years later. The issue had been the subject of heated argument for centuries. In the late 1600s Pope Sixtus IV prohibited anyone from accusing another of heresy on this issue. Pius IX settled the matter by declaring the Immaculate Conception as dogma. In 1870 Papal infallibility was declared by the First Vatican Council. See *Justo*

L. Gonzales, A History of Christian Thought From the Protestant Reformation to the Twentieth Century Volume III Revised Edition Location 7547.

[1280] Sandoval 34-5, 65, 75, 84, 99, 105, 116, 142, 163, 216, 242.

[1281] Kelly 269, 292.

[1282] Micklethwait and Wooldridge, *God is Back How The Global Revival of Faith is Changing the World* 6.

[1283] *Acts* 28:1-10 recounts when Paul and his companions were shipwrecked on Malta while he was in custody on his way to Rome. Verses 7-10 read *"Now in the neighborhood of that place were lands belonging to the leading man of the island, named Publius, who welcomed us and entertained us courteously three days. And it happened that the father of Publius was lying in bed afflicted with recurrent fever and dysentery; and Paul went in to see him and after he had prayed, he laid his hands on him and healed him. After this had happened, the rest of the people on the island who had diseases were coming to him and getting cured. They also honored us with many marks of respect; and when we were setting sail, they supplied us with all we needed."* Tradition holds that Paul founded a church on Malta and that Publius was its first bishop. See Justo L. Gonzales, *Acts The Gospel of the Spirit* 276.

[1284] Cahill, *Mysteries of the Middle Ages The Rise of Feminism, Science and Art from the Cults of Catholic Europe* 108.

[1285] In Catholic tradition the *"woman clothed with the sun, and the moon under her feet, and on her head a crown of twelve stars"* of the vision described in *Revelation* 12:1 is a reference to Mary and is sometimes cited as the theological underpinning for a view that Mary is something like the feminine face of God. Here is Philip Jenkins: "Apocalyptic expectations flourished among Roman Catholics, who in 1914 represented by far the largest segment of the Christian world, almost half the whole. Although Catholics generally lacked the Protestant obsession with biblical minutiae, they had their own clear ideas about the mysterious figures of the book of *Revelation*, which they understood in the context of the Virgin Mary. *Revelation's* chapter 12 describes the awesome figure of the Woman Clothed with the Sun, '*the moon under her feet, and on her head a crown of twelve stars,*' who gives birth to a messianic ruler. In the narrative, she is the holy and heavenly counterpart to evil female figures like the Scarlet Woman and the Whore of Babylon. Reading Mary as the Woman Clothed with the Sun— as we presumably should—neatly associates the Virgin with the end times, as her appearance in the text marks the beginning of some of the most violent and phantasmagoric portions of *Revelation*. This includes the war in heaven that pits Michael and his angels against the Red Dragon." Jenkins goes on later: "Since the 1930s, popes had been contemplating a United States of Europe. The European movement that actually emerged in the 1950s— the ancestor of today's European Union— inevitably had a strong Catholic and Christian ideology at its core. More specifically, its Catholic leaders were inspired by the Marian devotional upsurge that followed the 1950 proclamation of the Assumption. Coincidentally or not, the crucial diplomatic agreement that serves as the charter for the modern European Union is the 1957 Treaty of Rome. That emphasis is commemorated in the flag that we see today as the symbol of the European Union, twelve gold stars on a blue field. When the Council of Europe designed a new flag, it chose an assemblage that in the context of the time frankly evoked the image of the Virgin Mary, the woman crowned with twelve stars and depicted in blue garb. The flag's designer has explicitly credited the passage in the book of *Revelation* as his source for the image, which was formally adopted on December 8, 1955, the feast of the Immaculate Conception. All that is omitted in the eventual product is the Virgin herself, in a natural bow to Europe's Protestants and its other faiths. For a Catholic generation whose consciousness was formed in 1916 and 1917, how could they envision a united Europe except in Marian and apocalyptic terms? Not surprisingly, given its secular coloring, the modern-day EU strives to dismiss the Marian connection as an embarrassing myth, but the iconographic evidence leaves no doubt of the original intention." See Jenkins, *The Great and Holy War How World War I Became a Religious Crusade* 141, 232. (In *Science and Health* Mary Baker Eddy [1821 – 1910] the founder of Christian Science identified the "*woman clothed with the sun*" of *Revelation* 12:1 as herself.)

Apart from this scripture, the first known Marian apparition in the history of the Catholic Church was to St. Gregory Thaumaturgus, "the Wonder-Worker" (abt. 217 - abt. 270), a bishop in Neocaesarea, which now is the site of a town of about ninety thousand called Niksar in northern Turkey. It was apparently a powerful vision. Legend holds that when Gregory became the bishop, there were only seventeen Christians in Neocaesarea, but at his death there remained only seventeen non-Christians. During the papacy of John Paul II great attention was paid to Marian shrines. This was an outreach to the church in the Third World. Marian visions have been reported thousands of times in many cultures reaching an apex in the twentieth century with more than 200 appearances since 1930. See Richard Covington Collector's Edition *US News and World Report* "Secrets of Christianity The Real Jesus," 2012 54, Potter 570-1, Hitchcock 88, Justo L. Gonzales, *A History of Christian Thought From the Beginnings to the Council of Chalcedon* Volume 1 Revised Edition

255 and Jenkins, *The Next Christendom The Coming of Global Christianity* Third Edition 145-6.

[1286] Portions of the *Magnificat* describe radical change. Verses 52 and 53 of *Luke* 1 say of God "*He has brought down rulers from their thrones, And has exalted those who were humble. HE HAS FILLED THE HUNGRY WITH GOOD THINGS; And sent away the rich empty-handed.*" As a whole, the *Magnificat* has become a text for Third World activism. See Jenkins, *The Next Christendom The Coming of Global Christianity* Third Edition 174.

[1287] *Luke* 2: 34-35.

[1288] *Matthew* 1:19.

[1289] *John* 10:20.

[1290] *John* 19: 25-27.

[1291] *Acts* 1: 13-14.

[1292] *Luke* 1:48.

[1293] Pelikan, Mary *Through the Centuries Her Place in the History of Culture* 17- 18, 20-21. Here is another *New Testament* passage that anticipates a future of earthly existence: "*Children, obey your parents in the Lord, for this is right. 'HONOR YOUR FATHER AND MOTHER (which is the first commandment with a promise), SO THAT IT MAY BE WELL WITH YOU, AND THAT YOU MAY LIVE LONG ON THE EARTH.'*" (*Ephesians* 6: 1-3 – undoubtedly written in the generation after Paul.) This echoes the fifth of the Ten Commandments which is found in *Exodus* 20: 12: "*Honor your father and your mother, that your days may be prolonged in the land which the LORD your God gives you.*"

[1294] See *Luke* 2:19 - after the shepherds and the angels had left the scene of Jesus's birth and *Luke* 2:51 - after Jesus, at 12, had been recovered by his parents in Jerusalem.

[1295] For comparison sake, the papacy goes back two thousand years. The United States's oldest cultural institution is arguably Harvard University, established a mere four hundred years ago.

[1296] Hitchcock 41 and Kelly 6-7. Further, historians agree that Peter may have preselected two or three men to follow Linus. See Sweeney 36.

[1297] http://en.wikipedia.org/wiki/Pope_Linus (Accessed May 1, 2012).

[1298] Bunson 81-2. Note: The *Codex Alexandrinus* from the fifth century includes within the *New Testament I* and *II Clement*, allegedly written by this Clement who had been appointed by Peter bishop of Rome. See Bart D.

Ehrman, *Jesus Interrupted: Revealing the Hidden Contradictions in the Bible (And Why We Don't Know Them)* (New York: HarperOne *An Imprint of* HarperCollins*Publishers*, 2009) 211.

[1299] In 1856, Alexis de Tocqueville wrote: "The pope is driven more by the faithful to become an absolute ruler of the Church than they are impelled by him to submit to his rule." See Wills, *Why I Am A Catholic* 49.

[1300] Pope Gregory XIV (1590-91) prohibited all betting on papal elections or the length of a pontificate and Pope Gregory XV (1621-23) reorganized the papal elections requiring written secret ballots. See Kelly 273-4, 278-80.

[1301] *Romans* 16:14 has Paul greeting a "Hermes" which is the Greek form of Mercury.

[1302] The Roman poet Virgil lived from 70BC- 19BC. His *Aeneid* is considered the epic of ancient Rome and its founding myth. The hero, Aeneus, borrowed from Greek literature centuries earlier, is constantly referred to as "pious Aeneus." This Pope's choice of that name may also be a sign that he was familiar with Date's *Divine Comedy* which had been published about a hundred years earlier and which used the *Aeneid* as a source and even had Virgil as a character.

[1303] Wills, *Why I Am A Catholic* 86-8.

[1304] Kelly 39.

[1305] Gelasius was willing to defy the emperor because he was banking on the Germanic reign in Italy, begun by the Gothic ruler Odoacer, an Arian. See Wills *Why I Am A Catholic* 97-98. Here is how Donald Spoto describes the tension that lasted throughout the centuries: "In theory, the church and the empire worked together to minister to the spiritual and temporal needs of citizens; in practice, society was rent with divisions between popes and emperors, who were perpetually locked in a power struggle. Emperors wanted to control the appointment of bishops and the authority to decide doctrinal disputes, while popes anointed kings and emperors, owned armies and cities and fought for control of state affairs. The result was predictable: constant disputes, skirmishes, political maneuvering to the point of deception and murder - and the ceaseless outbreaks of war in one place or another." As noted, in 1302 Pope Boniface VIII issued the bull *Unam Sanctam*, declaring that the pope was the rightful ruler of the world. See Spoto, *Reluctant Saint The Life of Francis of Assisi* 9, 88.

[1306] Justo L. Gonzales, *A History of Christian Thought From Augustine to the Eve of the Reformation* Volume II Revised Edition Locations 1225-1231, 1432.

[1307] Sandoval 184.

[1308] Marty 77.

[1309] http://en.wikipedia.org/wiki/Pope_Gregory_I#cite_note-5 (Accessed May 2, 2012).

[1310] Weigel, Evangelical *Catholicism Deep Reform in the 21ˢᵗ-Century Church* (New York: Basic Books A Member of the Perseus Books Group, 2013) 31ff.

[1311] Ondina E. Gonzales and Justo L. Gonzales *Christianity in Latin America A History* 242, 252.

[1312] Thomas Cahill *Mysteries of the Middle Ages The Rise of Feminism, Science and Art from the Cults of Catholic Europe* 42.

[1313] Wills, *Why I Am A Catholic* 97-105.

[1314] Pius VII (1800-23) eventually excommunicated Napoleon and was in turn banished by him. After Napoleon's fall, however, Pius persuaded the British to be lenient with him and even allowed Napoleon's mother and brothers to live in Rome quietly. See Bunson 281-2.

[1315] Wills, *Why I Am A Catholic* 139-40.

[1316] Innocent XI was beatified in 1956 and has not been canonized.

[1317] Kelly 13-21, 24, 28, 32, 39, 43-45, 48, 51, 57, 58, 59, 60, 68, 88-93, 101, 110-112, 114-16, 118-19, 227, 240, 243-4, 244-5, 247-8, 271-2, 279, 287-88, 301-4. Bunson 175.

[1318] President Thomas Jefferson ordered the tiny US Navy to suppress the Muslim Barbary pirates of the Mediterranean who kidnapped European and Americans for ransom. (This action is the basis for the line in the *Marines' Hymn*, "From the Shores of Tripoli") When Pius VII heard about this he said that the US "had done more for the cause of Christianity than the most powerful nations of Christendom have done for ages." See Christopher Hitchens *City Journal* Spring 2007.

[1319] Wills, *Head and Heart: American Christianities* 438.

[1320] Wills, *Why I Am A Catholic* (Boston and New York: Houghton Mifflin Company, 2002) 157.

[1321] Papal rule and the primacy of the See in Rome were by no means accepted by all Christians over the centuries, even prior to the Protestant Reformation. For example, Photius - the Ecumenical Patriarch of Constantinople in the late 800s - wrote on the papacy and the primacy of the Roman church in his treatise *Against the Primacy*. His main points:

- Roman primacy is baseless because Peter was the bishop of Antioch before he was the bishop of Rome. Note: Tradition holds that Peter was bishop of Antioch. Although this is unlikely, the claim itself is evidence of the spreading influence of the Roman church in the second century. It was part of an effort to show a chain of succession of orthodox bishops back to Jesus. For example, Irenaeus claimed direct linkage to Jesus through Polycarp and John and Clement of Alexandria claimed that his Christian teachers had been taught by Peter, James, John and Paul. See Bauer 117-119.
- An argument could be made for the primacy of Jerusalem where not only Peter but earlier Jesus was leader.
- An argument could be made for the primacy of Byzantium where according to legend Andrew was bishop before Peter went to Rome.
- Jesus's words *"On this rock, I will build my church..."* refer not to Peter but to Peter's confession that Jesus was the Lord.
- The Romans should not limit grace to one region.
- The Pope should recall the words of Jesus, *"He who wishes to be first among you, let him become your servant."* See Gonzales, *A History of Christian Thought From Augustine to the Eve of the Reformation* Volume II Revised Edition Location 3973ff.

[1322] Father Michael Collins and Matthew A. Price, *The Story of Christianity* (London: DK Publishing, Inc.) 1999) 43.

[1323] Raymond E. Brown, SS *The Community of the Beloved Disciple The Life, Loves and Hates of an Individual Church in New Testament Times* (New York, Mahwah: Paulist Press, 1979). On page 171 of this short book, Brown wrote: "I warned the reader in the Preface that my reconstruction of Johannine community history carried at most probability."

[1324] We have noted:

- In Chapter 7 the murder of James the brother of Jesus, probably in 62.
- In Chapter 5 the murder of Paul, probably in 64.

We will note Peter's death, probably in the 60s, in Chapters 10 and 11.

[1325] But only possibly. As Ben Witherington III has pointed out, the story of the twelve year old Jesus in the Temple has these marks of authenticity:

- It puts his parents in a bad light. They neglected to keep track of him and they didn't understand him.
- There are no miracles as there are in some of the apocryphal Gospels. See Witherington, *New Testament History A Narrative Account* Location 1611ff.

[1326] Some of the ways in which Jesus says these are extreme:

- *Mark 10:29-30: "Truly I say to you, there is no one who has left house or brothers or sisters or mother or father or children or farms, for My sake and for the gospel's sake, but that he will receive a hundred times as much now in the present age, houses and brothers and sisters and mothers and children and farms, along with persecutions; and in the age to come, eternal life."*
- *Mathew 10:37: "He who loves father or mother more than Me is not worthy of Me; and he who loves son or daughter more than Me is not worthy of Me".*
- *Luke 14:26: "If anyone comes to Me, and does not hate his own father and mother and wife and children and brothers and sisters, yes, and even his own life, he cannot be My disciple."*

[1327] Brown assumes that all three epistles were written by the same person and that it was not the "*disciple whom Jesus loved*" since people like the Secessionists and people like Diotrephes mentioned in *III John* would have been unlikely to defy Him. See Brown 94-95.

[1328] *John 1:14 – "And the Word became flesh, and dwelt among us, and we saw His glory, glory as of the only begotten from the Father, full of grace and truth." John 2:11 – "This beginning of His signs Jesus did in Cana of Galilee, and manifested His glory…"*

[1329] As noted earlier in this chapter, this may have been somewhat of the problem among the Paulines at Corinth a generation earlier.

[1330] The letter of *II John* is addressed to "*the chosen lady and her children.*" Verse 5 refers to her as "*lady.*" Verse 13 closes the letter by saying: "*The children of your chosen sister greet you*" which suggests the possibility of another female leader. Here is Marcus J Borg: "For centuries, it has been taken for granted that 'elect lady' and 'elect sister' refer to Christian communities, just as 'the church' in the *New Testament* is occasionally referred to as the bride of Christ. But the natural meaning of this language in *II John* is that the author is writing to a woman who is the leader of an early Christian community. The closing greeting from the children of '*your elect sister'* suggests another Christian community headed by a woman. Thus the letter may provide evidence for women in leadership roles in Johannine communities, consistent with what we see in the genuine letters of Paul." See Borg, *Evolution of the Word The New Testament in the Order the Books Were Written* 415. Note: In 1868, Eliza Snow (1804 – 1887) who was a renowned Mormon writer and a plural wife of both Joseph Smith and, after his death, Brigham Young, wrote an article to promote the establishment of a philanthropic women's organization called the "Female Relief Society" among the Mormons in Utah. She had helped start an earlier version under Joseph Smith's guidance in 1842 in Illinois. In her article is this: "We were told by our martyred prophet, that the same organization existed in the church anciently, allusions to which are made in some of the epistles recorded in the *New Testament,* making use of the title, 'elect lady' *(II John* 1)." The Relief Society is still in existence with millions of members. See Jill Mulvay Derr and Carol Cornwall Madden, "Preserving the Record and Memory of the Female Relief Society of Nauvoo, 1842-*93 Journal of Mormon History,* Summer, 2009. More on Eliza Snow: Joseph Smith's wife Emma supposedly once saw Smith kissing Eliza Snow on a second floor landing at the Smith house in Nauvoo, Illinois, and threw her down the stairs. See Beam Location 1555. Note: The more traditional view of the "lady" - that it is a metaphor for a church community - is seen in, for example, Browning Location 2682.

[1331] Outsiders were a potential problem in this era. In *Revelation 2:2* Jesus Christ commends the church at Ephesus for testing out false apostles: *"I know your deeds and your toil and perseverance, and that you cannot tolerate evil men, and you put to the test those who call themselves apostles, and they are not..."*

[1332] In a similar way, it is likely that the pastoral epistles, *I* and *II Timothy,* and *Titus,* helped make the genuine Pauline epistles acceptable to the Institutionalists. See Bauer 224-228

[1333] The "churches" in the first century may have averaged about fifty people. See Borg, *Evolution of the Word The New Testament in the Order the Books Were Written* 12.

[1334] Wilken, *The Myth of Christian Beginning: History's Impact on Belief* 195-6.

[1335] Elie Kedourie, *Commentary* January 1993. DeGaulle was an anti-Semite. He referred to the Jews in 1967 as "an elite people, self-confident and domineering." He also said Jews had provoked "ill will in certain countries and at certain times." See Jon D. Levenson, *Commentary* December 2008. Anti-Semitism may be endemic to the French culture. Voltaire (1694 -1778) wrote that Judaism was not just another religion but the root of religious evil.

See David Horowitz *Radicals Portraits of a Destructive Passion* (Washington DC: Regnery Publishing, Inc. Distributed by Perseus Distribution, Kindle Edition, 2012) Location 565.

[1336] I will use the kingdom of God and the kingdom of Heaven interchangeably.

[1337] *I Thessalonians* 4: 14-17.

[1338] *Mark* 13:37.

[1339] Christians may have worshipped on the first day of the week since they saw it as the day of the resurrection. Note these verses:

- Covering the resurrection: *Mark 16:1-2: "When the Sabbath was over, Mary Magdalene, and Mary the mother of James, and Salome, bought spices, so that they might come and anoint Him. Very early **on the first day of the week**, they came to the tomb when the sun had risen."* (Emphasis added).

- Covering Paul's travel: *Acts 20:6-7 – "We sailed from Philippi after the days of Unleavened Bread, and came to them at Troas within five days; and there we stayed seven days. **On the first day of the week**, when we were gathered together to break bread, Paul began talking to them, intending to leave the next day, and he prolonged his message until midnight."* (Emphasis added).

- Covering Paul's guidance to the churches: *I Corinthians 16:1-2 – "Now concerning the collection for the saints, as I directed the churches of Galatia, so do you also. **On the first day of every week** each one of you is to put aside and save, as he may prosper, so that no collections be made when I come."* (Emphasis added).

- Covering the prophecies in *Revelation: Revelation 1:9-10 – "I, John, your brother and fellow partaker in the tribulation and kingdom and perseverance which are in Jesus, was on the island called Patmos because of the word of God and the testimony of Jesus. I was in the Spirit **on the Lord's day**, and I heard behind me a loud voice like the sound of a trumpet,...."* (Emphasis added).

See James DG Dunn, *Did the First Christians Worship Jesus? The New Testament Evidence* 49.

By the fourth century, a fixed date for Easter was needed to link to Passover. The Council of Nicaea settled on "the first Sunday after the full moon following the spring equinox." See William Manchester, *A World Lit Only by Fire: The Medieval Mind and the Renaissance Portrait of An Age* (New York: Little Brown and Company, Hatchette Book Group USA, 1992, 1993) 12.

[1340] Augustine's writings tended to shut down speculation about end times in favor of a heavenly "City of God" emerging in part through the work of the Church as we will note in Chapter 10. See Hitchcock 96.

[1341] In fairness to the Jehovah's Witnesses, it is my understanding that they believe that something *like* the Second Coming occurred in 1914 when "Christ became King and God's heavenly kingdom began to rule." See *What Does the Bible Really Teach?* 84-85 and 215-18.

[1342] When future president Herbert Hoover was Secretary of Commerce in 1921-29 commercial radio was in its infancy. A religious sect applied to build a radio station to warn people about the end of the world. Hoover advised them that if the world's end was imminent, it would be a wiser investment to buy time at existing stations. See http://www.hoover.archives.gov/exhibits/Hooverstory/gallery04/index.html (Accessed May 2, 2012).

[1343] Denton, *Faith and Betrayal: A Pioneer Woman's Passage in the American West* (New York: Alfred A. Knopf, 2005) 21.

[1344] Jonathan Kirsch, *US News & World Report* Special Edition 2006.

[1345] Frederic J. Baumgartner, *Longing for the End: A History of Millennialism in Western Civilization* (New York: St. Martins Press) 1999 167, 195ff.

[1346] Dragons are mentioned thirty-four times in the *Bible* with twelve *New Testament* cites, all in *Revelation*. They were also conjured up in late antiquity. Saint George (abt. 275/81 – 303) was a Greek who became a Roman officer. He was known in Christian piety as a dragon slayer. He may have been an inspirational figure centuries later in the village of Assisi, Italy as the school attended by St. Francis was named San Giorgio. See Spoto, *Reluctant Saint The Life of Francis of Assisi* 19ff. (Saint George, Utah is not named for him but for an early Mormon pioneer.)

[1347] Jonathan Kirsch *US News & World Reports* Special Edition 2006.

[1348] Boyer 106.

[1349] Hal Lindsey with CC Carlson *The Late Great Planet Earth* (Grand Rapids, Michigan: Zondervan Publishing House) 1970, Sixth printing, 1970.

[1350] Wills, *Head and Heart: American Christianities* 381. See also Barbara R. Rossing, *The Rapture Exposed: The Message of Hope in the Book of Revelation* (Boulder: Westview Press, 2004) 22-24. See also Boyer 5.

[1351] Rossing 24.

[1352] He cited *Revelation* 11:2-3 which reads: *"Leave out the court which is outside the temple and do not measure it, for it has been given to the nations; and they will tread under foot the holy city for forty-two months. And I will grant authority to my two witnesses, and they will prophesy for twelve hundred and sixty days, clothed in sackcloth."* See Lindsey, *The Late Great Planet Earth* 44.

[1353] He cited *Matthew* 24:21-22 which reads: *"For then there will be a great tribulation, such as has not occurred since the beginning of the world until now, nor ever will. Unless those days had been cut short, no life would have been saved; but for the sake of the elect those days will be cut short."* See Lindsey, *The Late Great Planet Earth* 44.

[1354] He cited *Ezekiel* 38:8 which reads *"After many days you will be summoned; in the latter years you will come into the land that is restored from the sword, whose inhabitants have been gathered from many nations to the mountains of Israel."* See Lindsey, *The Late Great Planet Earth* 51.

[1355] Lindsey on page 55: "It is clear in (*Zechariah* 12-14) that the Jews would have to be dwelling in and have possession of the ancient city of Jerusalem at the time of the Messiah's triumphant advent."

[1356] He cited *Matthew* 24:15 which reads: *"Therefore when you see the* ABOMINATION OF DESOLATION *which was spoken of through Daniel the prophet, standing in the holy place (let the reader understand),"* See Lindsey, *The Late Great Planet Earth* 55.

[1357] He cited *Ezekiel* 38: 1-2 which reads: *"And the word of the* LORD *came to me saying, 'Son of man, set your face toward Gog of the land of Magog, the prince of Rosh, Meshech and Tubal, and prophesy against him.'"* See Lindsey, *The Late Great Planet Earth* 63.

[1358] He cited *Ezekiel* 38:6 which reads: *"Gomer with all its troops; Beth-togarmah from the remote parts of the north with all its troops—many peoples with you."* and *Ezekiel* 38:15 which reads: *"You will come from your place out of the remote parts of the north, you and many peoples with you, all of them riding on horses, a great assembly and a mighty army;"* and *Ezekiel* 39:2 which reads: *"and I will turn you around, drive you on, take you up from the remotest parts of the north and bring you against the mountains of Israel."* See Lindsey, *The Late Great Planet Earth* 66. Lindsey on page 60: "There are three major prophecies on this northern sphere of political power which are to be found in *Ezekiel* 38; 39; *Daniel* 11:40-45; and *Joel* 2:20."

[1359] He cited *Daniel* 7:19-20 which reads: *"Then I desired to know the exact meaning of the fourth beast, which was different from all the others, exceedingly dreadful, with its teeth of iron and its claws of bronze, and which devoured, crushed and trampled down the remainder with its feet, and the meaning of the ten horns that were on its head and the other horn which came up, and before which three of them fell, namely, that horn which had eyes and a mouth uttering great boasts and which was larger in appearance than its associates."* He also cited *Revelation* 13: 1-3, part of which reads: *"Then I saw a beast coming up out of the sea, having ten horns and seven heads, and on his horns were ten diadems."* See Lindsey, *The Late Great Planet Earth* 92 and 103-4.

[1360] Let us put Charlemagne into historical context. Charlemagne (742-814) was one of the greatest of all medieval rulers. In the 770s and beyond, he fought against the Saxons and the Lombards who wanted territory in central Italy held by the Popes. In the Saxon wars, conversion to Christianity became a condition for survival, with forced conversions of whole tribes the result of defeat. As noted, he was crowned by Pope Leo III on Christmas Day in 800 as the first Holy Roman Emperor and that empire lasted over one thousand years. In the words of Robert Louis Wilken: "Emperors stride again and again across the pages of Christian history, and in the early centuries four of them gave particular shape to the story: Caesar Augustus during whose reign Jesus was born; Constantine, who signifies the turning of the people of the Roman Empire to Christianity; Theodosius in the late fourth century, who ruled that Catholic Christianity would be the religion of the empire; and Justinian, the great builder and lawgiver of the Eastern Roman Empire. By any measure these four emperors mark major epochs in the Church's history. But there was a fifth, no less significant, no less a shaper of events, and his name was Charlemagne, king of the Franks, who in the year 800 was crowned emperor of the new Christian society that had come into being in northern Europe in the early Middle Ages." See Wilken, *The First Thousand Years A Global History of Christianity* 333.

[1361] Lindsey, *The Late Great Planet Earth* 95, 96, 184.

[1362] He cited *II Thessalonians* 2:4 which reports that this figure will be one *"who opposes and exalts himself above every so-called god or object of worship, so that he takes his seat in the temple of God, displaying himself as being God."* See Lindsey, *The Late Great Planet Earth* 109-10.

[1363] He cited *Revelation* 13: 1-3 which reads: *"Then I saw a beast coming up out of the sea, having ten horns and seven heads, and on his horns were ten diadems, and on his heads were blasphemous names. And the beast which I saw was like a leopard, and his feet were like those of a bear, and his mouth like the mouth of a lion. And the dragon gave him his power and his throne and great authority. I saw one of his heads as if it had been slain, and his fatal wound was healed. And the whole earth was amazed and followed after the beast;"* See Lindsey, *The Late Great Planet Earth* 103, 104, 107.

[1364] He cited *Revelation* 12:9 which reads: *"And the great dragon was thrown down, the serpent of old who is called the devil and Satan, who deceives the whole world; he was thrown down to the earth, and his angels were thrown down with him."* See Lindsey, *The Late Great Planet Earth* 106.

[1365] Baumgartner 63ff. Note: Frederick II (1194-1250) epitomized the popes's view of a bad ruler; his younger contemporary Louis IX of France (1214-1270) noted earlier as the crusader and recoverer of the crown of thorns symbolized the ideal. See Hitchcock 149. (Frederick had promised to go on a crusade but failed to show, probably leading to a significant defeat in 1221 in the crusade that included Francis of Assisi noted earlier.)

[1366] He cited *Revelation* 13:11-18, 19:20 and 20:10 which read in order:

- 13:11-18 - *"Then I saw another beast come up out of the earth. He had two horns like those of a lamb, but he spoke with the voice of a dragon. He exercised all the authority of the first beast. And he required all the earth and its people to worship the first beast, whose fatal wound had been healed. He did astounding miracles, even making fire flash down to earth from the sky while everyone was watching. And with all the miracles he was allowed to perform on behalf of the first beast, he deceived all the people who belong to this world. He ordered the people to make a great statue of the first beast, who was fatally wounded and then came back to life. He was then permitted to give life to this statue so that it could speak. Then the statue of the beast commanded that anyone refusing to worship it must die. He required everyone—small and great, rich and poor, free and slave—to be given a mark on the right hand or on the forehead. And no one could buy or sell anything without that mark, which was either the name of the beast or the number representing his name. Wisdom is needed here. Let the one with understanding solve the meaning of the number of the beast, for it is the number of a man. His number is 666."* See Lindsey, *The Late Great Planet Earth* 112.
- 19:20 - *"And the beast was captured, and with him the false prophet who did mighty miracles on behalf of the beast—miracles that deceived all who had accepted the mark of the beast and who worshiped his statue."* See Lindsey, *The Late Great Planet Earth* 112.
- 20:10 – *"Then the devil, who had deceived them, was thrown into the fiery lake of burning sulfur, joining the beast and the false prophet. There they will be tormented day and night forever and ever."* See Lindsey, *The Late Great Planet Earth* 112.

^{1367} He again cited: *II Thessalonians* 2:4 which he interpreted to report that an Anti-Christ figure will be one: *"who opposes and exalts himself above every so-called god or object of worship, so that he takes **his seat in the temple of God,** displaying himself as being God"* (Emphasis added) and again *Matthew* 24: 15 which reads: *"Therefore when you see the* ABOMINATION OF DESOLATION *which was spoken of through Daniel the prophet, **standing in the holy place** (let the reader understand)"* (Emphasis added). See Lindsey, *The Late Great Planet Earth* 109, 153.

^{1368} He cited *Matthew* 24:16 which reads: *"then those who are in Judea must flee to the mountains"* and *Revelation* 12: 6, 14 which reads: *"And the woman fled into the wilderness, where God had prepared a place to care for her for 1,260 days."* (verse 6) and *"But she was given two wings like those of a great eagle so she could fly to the place prepared for her in the wilderness. There she would be cared for and protected from the dragon for a time, times, and half a time..."* (verse 14). See Lindsey, *The Late Great Planet Earth* 153.

^{1369} He cited *Ezekiel* 38:14-16 which reads: *"Therefore, son of man, prophesy against Gog. Give him this message from the Sovereign Lord: When my people are living in peace in their land, then you will rouse yourself. You will come from your homeland in the distant north with your vast cavalry and your mighty army, and you will attack my people Israel, covering their land like a cloud. At that time in the distant future, I will bring you against my land as everyone watches, and my holiness will be displayed by what happens to you, Gog. Then all the nations will know that I am the Lord."* He also cited *Daniel* 11:40-41 which reads: *"Then at the time of the end, the king of the south will attack the king of the north. The king of the north will storm out with chariots, charioteers, and a vast navy. He will invade various lands and sweep through them like a flood. He will enter the glorious land of Israel and many nations will fall, but Moab, Edom, and the best part of Ammon will escape."* See Lindsey, *The Late Great Planet Earth* 157.

^{1370} He cited *Ezekiel* 38:18-22 which reads: *"But this is what the Sovereign Lord says: 'When Gog invades the land of Israel, my fury will boil over! In my jealousy and blazing anger, I promise a mighty shaking in the land of Israel on that day. All living things—the fish in the sea, the birds of the sky, the animals of the field, the small animals that scurry along the ground, and all the people on earth—will quake in terror at my presence. Mountains will be thrown down; cliffs will crumble; walls will fall to the earth. I will summon the sword against you on all the hills of Israel, says the Sovereign Lord. Your men will turn their swords against each other. I will punish you and your armies with disease and bloodshed; I will send torrential rain, hailstones, fire, and burning sulfur!'"* and *Ezekiel* 39:3- 5 which reads: *"I will knock the bow from your left hand and the arrows from your right hand, and I will leave you helpless. You and your army and your allies will all die on the mountains. I will feed you to the vultures and wild animals. You will fall in the open fields, for I have spoken, says the Sovereign Lord."* See Lindsey, *The Late Great Planet Earth* 160, 161.

1371 He cited *Ezekiel* 39:6 which reads: *"And I will rain down fire on Magog and on all your allies who live safely on the coasts. Then they will know that I am the Lord."* See Lindsey, *The Late Great Planet Earth* 161.

1372 He cited *Revelation* 16:12-16 which reads: *"The sixth angel poured out his bowl on the great river, the Euphrates; and its water was dried up, so that the way would be prepared for the kings from the east. And I saw coming out of the mouth of the dragon and out of the mouth of the beast and out of the mouth of the false prophet, three unclean spirits like frogs; for they are spirits of demons, performing signs, which go out to the kings of the whole world, to gather them together for the war of the great day of God, the Almighty. (Behold, I am coming like a thief. Blessed is the one who stays awake and keeps his clothes, so that he will not walk about naked and men will not see his shame.) And they gathered them together to the place which in Hebrew is called Har-Magedon."* and *Joel* 3:9-14 which reads:

"Proclaim this among the nations:
Prepare a war; rouse the mighty men!
Let all the soldiers draw near, let them come up!
Beat your plowshares into swords
And your pruning hooks into spears;
Let the weak say, 'I am a mighty man.'
Hasten and come, all you surrounding nations,
And gather yourselves there.
Bring down, O LORD, Your mighty ones.
Let the nations be aroused
And come up to the valley of Jehoshaphat,
For there I will sit to judge
All the surrounding nations.
Put in the sickle, for the harvest is ripe.
Come, tread, for the wine press is full;
The vats overflow, for their wickedness is great.
Multitudes, multitudes in the valley of decision!
For the day of the LORD is near in the valley of decision.." (Lindsey, *The Late Great Planet Earth* 162, 164).

1373 He cited *Revelation* 9:16 which reads: *"I heard the size of their army, which was 200 million mounted troops."* See Lindsey, *The Late Great Planet Earth* 82, 162.

[1374] He cited *Revelation* 16:12 which reads: *"The sixth angel poured out his bowl on the great river, the Euphrates; and its water was dried up, so that the way would be prepared for the kings from the east."* Lindsey points out: "India has revealed recently an important development. It is reported that 12,000 Chinese soldiers are at work inside Pakistan-held Kashmir on the road which would give Chinese troops in Tibet a shortcut to the subcontinent." See Lindsey, *The Late Great Planet Earth* 165.

[1375] He cited *Zechariah* 12:2-3 which reads: *"I will make Jerusalem like an intoxicating drink that makes the nearby nations stagger when they send their armies to besiege Jerusalem and Judah. On that day I will make Jerusalem an immovable rock. All the nations will gather against it to try to move it, but they will only hurt themselves."* and *Zechariah* 14:1-2 which reads: *"Watch, for the day of the Lord is coming when your possessions will be plundered right in front of you! I will gather all the nations to fight against Jerusalem. The city will be taken, the houses looted, and the women raped. Half the population will be taken into captivity, and the rest will be left among the ruins of the city."* See Lindsey, *The Late Great Planet Earth* 165.

[1376] He cited *Revelation* 16:19 which reads: *"The great city of Babylon split into three sections, and the cities of many nations fell into heaps of rubble. So God remembered all of Babylon's sins, and he made her drink the cup that was filled with the wine of his fierce wrath."* See Lindsey 166.

[1377] He cited *Revelation* 9:15-18 which reads: *"Then the four angels who had been prepared for this hour and day and month and year were turned loose to kill one-third of all the people on earth. I heard the size of their army, which was 200 million mounted troops. And in my vision, I saw the horses and the riders sitting on them. The riders wore armor that was fiery red and dark blue and yellow. The horses had heads like lions, and fire and smoke and burning sulfur billowed from their mouths. One-third of all the people on earth were killed by these three plagues—by the fire and smoke and burning sulfur that came from the mouths of the horses."* See Lindsey, *The Late Great Planet Earth* 166.

[1378] Lindsey, *The Late Great Planet Earth* 168.

[1379] Campbell 290.

[1380] He cited *Revelation* 7: 1-4 which reads: *"Then I saw four angels standing at the four corners of the earth, holding back the four winds so they did not blow on the earth or the sea, or even on any tree. And I saw another angel coming up from the east, carrying the seal of the living God. And he shouted to those four angels, who had been given power to harm land and sea, 'Wait! Don't harm the land or the sea or the trees until we have placed the seal of God on the foreheads of his servants.' And I heard how many were marked with the seal of God—144,000 were sealed from all the tribes of Israel."* (What follows is 12,000 from each of the 12 tribes of Israel). See Lindsey, *The Late Great Planet Earth* 142.

[1381] He cited *II Thessalonians* 2: 6-12 which reads: *"you know what is holding him back, for he can be revealed only when his time comes. For this lawlessness is already at work secretly, and it will remain secret until the one who is holding it back steps out of the way. Then the man of lawlessness will be revealed, but the Lord Jesus will kill him with the breath of his mouth and destroy him by the splendor of his coming. This man will come to do the work of Satan with counterfeit power and signs and miracles. He will use every kind of evil deception to fool those on their way to destruction, because they refuse to love and accept the truth that would save them. So God will cause them to be greatly deceived, and they will believe these lies. Then they will be condemned for enjoying evil rather than believing the truth."* See Lindsey, *The Late Great Planet Earth* 110.

[1382] He cited *Revelation* 1:7 which reads: *"Look! He comes with the clouds of heaven. And everyone will see him— even those who pierced him. And all the nations of the world will mourn for him. Yes! Amen!"* See Lindsey, *The Late Great Planet Earth* 142-43.

[1383] Lindsey, *The Late Great Planet Earth* 136.

[1384] Lindsey, *The Late Great Planet Earth* 43.

[1385] Lindsey, *The Late Great Planet Earth* 96.Note: Hallstein was a figure of the Cold War era whose policies were that West Germany would not have any diplomatic relations with any country that recognized East Germany.

[1386] Lindsey, *The 1980s: Countdown to Armageddon* (New York, Toronto, London, Sydney, Aukland: Bantam) 1980 Bantam Trade edition 1981 Bantam rack-size edition 1982) Cover page, 170, 171. Note: This book was on the *New York Times* best-seller list for twenty weeks. See Boyer 5.

[1387] Lindsey, *The Rapture* (Toronto, New York, London, Sydney: Bantam Books, 1983) 38.

[1388] Lindsey, *Vanished Into Thin Air: The Hope of Every Believer* (Beverly Hills: Western Front.) 1999) 14. Note: This book has twenty-five chapters. Some chapters have titles and some do not. Two are either identical or nearly identical to chapters in his 1983 book: *The 1980s: Countdown to Armageddon.*

1389 He cited *Zechariah* 13: 8-9 which reads:

"*'Two-thirds of the people in the land*
will be cut off and die,' says the Lord.
'But one-third will be left in the land.
I will bring that group through the fire
and make them pure.
I will refine them like silver
and purify them like gold.
They will call on my name,
and I will answer them.
I will say, "These are my people,"
and they will say, "The Lord is our God."'" See Lindsey, *The Late Great
Planet Earth* 167.

1390 One example: Joachim of Fiore (abt. 1135 – 1202), was the founder of a
monastic order. He was a student of *Revelation*. He related the three persons
of the Trinity with three stages in history. The first was between Adam and
Jesus; the next between Jesus and 1260; the last one to commence in 1260.
He got to 1260 by reckoning that there were 42 generations between Adam
and Jesus and that 42 generations or 1260 years would get to the next stage.
(He noted that in the *Old Testament* generations were of different lengths
but saw that a more perfect setup in the *New Testament* would have each
generation at 30 years.) "Thus, Joachim's doctrine is an enthusiastic and
idealistic spiritualism that, in view of the evil that reigns in the world, finds
refuge in the hope of a new age." Later his views of the stages of history were
taken up by some of the more radical Franciscans and interpreted in a way that
saw themselves as representatives of the new spiritual age against the church.
Late in the 1200s this group of Franciscans was persecuted and eventually
disappeared from history. See Justo L. Gonzales *A History of Christian Thought
From Augustine to the Eve of the Reformation* Volume II Revised Edition
Locations 3529ff, 4478ff.

1391 Boyer 2.

1392 *Wills, Head and Heart: American Christianities* 356-82.

1393 http://www.thirdworldtraveler.com/Religion/Blind_Faith.html
(Accessed May 2, 2012).

1394 http://www.enjoyinggodministries.com/article/the-dispensational-
premillennial-view-of-the-kingdom-of-god/ (Accessed May 2, 2012).

1395 This series of books was published between 1995 and 2007.

1396 Dallas Theological Seminary holds that: "We believe that, according to the Word of God, the next great event in the fulfillment of prophecy will be the coming of the Lord in the air to receive to Himself into heaven both His own who are alive and remain unto His coming, and also all who have fallen asleep in Jesus, and that this event is the blessed hope set before us in the Scripture, and for this we should be constantly looking." See http://www.dts. edu/about/doctrinalstatement/ (Accessed May 2, 2012).

1397 *I John* 4:2.

1398 *I John* 2: 18-19 and 4:3

1399 Boyer 31.

1400 *Revelation* 17:8.

1401 Boyer 43-4, 61-3, 72, 108, 178, 207-8. Note: St. Augustine wrote in the *City of God* in the early 400s: "It is uncertain in what temple the antichrist will sit, whether in the ruin of the temple that was built by Solomon, or in the Church." The English philosopher Roger Bacon wrote in the 1200s: "All wise men believe that we are not far removed from the time of antichrist." See Sweeney 130, 131.

1402 *II Thessalonians* 2:2. Note: Several other scriptures warn against false prophets and it is, again, a thesis of this book that these may have been other sorts of Christians whose stories we don't know:

- *II Peter* 2:1 - "*But **false prophets** also arose among the people, just as there will also be false teachers among you, who will secretly introduce destructive heresies, even denying the Master who bought them, bringing swift destruction upon themselves.*" (Emphasis added).
- *I John* 4:1 – "*...because many **false prophets** have gone out into the world.*" (Emphasis added).
- *Revelation* 2:20 – "*But I have this against you, that you tolerate the woman Jezebel, **who calls herself a prophetess**, and she teaches and leads My bond-servants astray so that they commit acts of immorality and eat things sacrificed to idols.*" (Emphasis added).

1403 *II Thessalonians* 3:10-12.

1404 Grant, *Saint Paul* 171ff.

1405 Lindsey, *The Late Great Planet Earth* 59. The next war Israel fought was the Yom Kippur war in 1973 against Syria and Egypt. The USSR supplied Egypt and Syria. The US supplied Israel. As recalled by President Richard Nixon's chief of staff Alexander Haig, at a critical time Nixon asked the Secretary of State Henry Kissinger for a list of Israel's military needs. When Kissinger began to read aloud from a list, Nixon, who at the time was enmeshed in the Watergate scandal which would eventually end his presidency, ordered: "Double it. Now get the hell out of here and get the job done." Jason Maoz *JewishPress.com* August 5, 2005. In the national election less than a year before, two out of three Jews had voted for Nixon's opponent, George McGovern.

[1406] Wills, *Head and Heart: American Christianities* 356-82 and Boyer 115-6.

[1407] Ehrman, *Peter, Paul and Mary* 77.

[1408] *II Peter* 3:3-8.

[1409] Ellis, *America's Creation: Triumphs and Tragedies at the Founding of the Republic* (New York: Alfred A. Knopf, 2007) 16.

[1410] He also made some racist ones. He spoke of the "Asian horde" and the "Yellow Peril." He referred to the Russian military as a "barbarous army." See Lindsey, *The Late Great Planet Earth* 81, 82, 161.

[1411] Lindsey: "If we complain about not being able to find 'breathing space,'..... imagine what it might be like thirty years from now, if we're still around!

"Men who are studying population biology, such as Paul Ehrlich, professor at Stanford University and expert in this field, are inclined to be doomsters because of the research they have done. Ehrlich, for instance, says: 'Mankind may be facing its final crisis. No action that we can take at this late date can prevent a great deal of future misery from starvation and environmental degradation.'" See Lindsey, *The Late Great Planet Earth* 102.

[1412]

Dr. Paul R. Ehrlich, *The Population Bomb* (New York: Ballantine Books, Inc., 1968, Twelfth Printing, 1970) 72.

[1413] Ehrlich 78.

[1414] Sagan actually updated and expanded an earlier book by Shklovskii who said years later that he only found out about this when he saw a copy of the book with his name and Carl Sagan's on the cover. See David Grinspoon, Lonely *Planets The Natural Philosophy of Alien Life* (New York: Ecco *An Imprint of* HarperCollins*Publishers*, 2004) 226.

[1415] The group that formed the Drake Equation called themselves the "Order of the Dolphin." Sagan dedicated *Intelligent Life in the Universe* to "the memory of John Burton Sanderson Haldane, FRS., member of the National

Academies of Sciences of the United States and of the Soviet Union, member of The Order of the Dolphins, and a local example of what this book is about."

[1416] Note: This book is formatted in a way that allows each author to make separate comments. At this point Shklovskii adds: "In my opinion, these estimates of Sagan are slightly too optimistic."

[1417] Note: Since about 1947, we have, according to some commentators, lived in the "flying saucer" era with sightings and reports of Unidentified Flying Objects or UFOs. One evangelical response is that unexplained UFOs are actually the manifestation of demons. "The truth about UFOs can be known. Indeed, the UFO mystery is a mystery solved. Earth is not being visited by aliens from another planet, but some people are being visited by spirit beings who want everyone to *think* they are aliens from another planet." See Hugh Ross, Kenneth Samples, Mark Clark *Lights in the Sky & Little Green Men: A Rational Christian Look at UFOs and Extraterrestrials* (Colorado Springs: NavPress, 2002) 169. Carl Sagan noted that Hal Lindsey also believed that UFOs were operated by demons. See Sagan, *The Demon-Haunted World: Science as A Candle in the Dark* (New York: Ballantine Books, 1996 First Ballantine Books Edition 1997) 129.

[1418] Peter Douglas Ward and Donald Brownlee, *Rare Earth Why Complex Live is Uncommon in the Universe* (New York: Copernicus) 2000. Note: *Rare Earth* is dedicated to Carl Sagan.

[1419] Galilei Galileo (1564-1642) using a new telescope discovered four moons of Jupiter, the first new worlds discovered since antiquity. He published in support of Nicolaus Copernicus's (1473-1453) heliocentric theory that the earth revolved around the sun and was condemned by the Catholic Church in 1632. In 1992 Pope John Paul II asserted that the Church had been wrong in condemning Galileo. Subsequently, Pope Benedict XVI credited Galileo for helping people "contemplate with gratitude God's works." See Hitchcock 318.

[1420] I. S. Shklovskii and Carl Sagan, *Intelligent Life in the Universe* (New York: Dell Publishing Co., Inc. Copyright 1966 by Holden-Day, Inc. Fifth Printing) P. 357-61, 363-76, 409, 412, 449-464.

[1421] Lindsey called the Rapture "the ultimate trip." See Lindsey, *The Late Great Planet Earth* 135.

[1422] In 2009, according to Wikipedia, the Chinese army is the world's third largest military force, with approximately 3 million troops. See http://en.wikipedia.org/wiki/List_of_countries_by_number_of_servicemen (Accessed May 2, 2012).

[1423] http://www.workinghumor.com/quotes/yogi_berra.shtml. (Accessed May 2, 2012). Some do work out, but they need to be kept pretty general. Theodore Roosevelt wrote in 1897 that in the future Japan could have designs on Hawaii and in a private letter that "if Russia chooses to develop purely on her own line and resist the growth of liberalism...she will sometime experience a red terror that will make the French Revolution pale." As Assistant Secretary of the Navy, TR wrote his superior in 1898 about a "flying machine" he had witnessed along the Potomac River near Washington. He recommended further study for military purposes. "The machine worked. It seems to me worthwhile for this government to try whether it will not work on a large enough scale to be of use in the event of war." See Edmund Morris 598, 607, 636.

[1424] Maccoby *Revolution in Judaea: Jesus and the Jewish Resistance* 81-2.

[1425] *Mark* 1:15. This is Jesus's first recorded utterance.

[1426] *Matthew* 19:28 and *Luke* 22:28-30.

[1427] *Mark* 1:20 and *Matthew* 27:56. The sons were James and John.

[1428] *Luke* 8:3.

[1429] *Luke* 9:60.

[1430] Recall that in *Matthew* 17, a chapter that includes an account of the Transfiguration and a prediction of his death and resurrection, Jesus dealt with a question brought to him by Peter about whether he would pay his tax to support the Temple. His answer in *Matthew* 17: 27: "...go to the lake and throw out your line. Take the first fish you catch; open its mouth and you will find a four-drachma coin. Take it and give it to them for my tax and yours." Note: By paying the Temple Tax Jesus seemed to endorse the system that funded sacrifices for the remission of sins and yet he himself forgave sins.

[1431] *Mark* 8:15.

[1432] *Luke* 13:32.

[1433] *Luke* 23:8-12. Herod Antipater played it very cautiously during that whole episode. His judicial murder of another popular religious leader, John the Baptist, probably still gnawed at him – not pangs of conscience but rather feelings of disquiet over the possible reaction of the people and the impact on him. He also took the occasion to ally more with his Roman counterpart, Pilate.

[1434] *Mark* 9: 33-37.

[1435] In one parable – recounted in *Luke* 14: 16-24 - he used the metaphor of a formal banquet to which the invited guests made excuses. When the host could not fill up the invitee list he instructed his servants to invite outsiders and even to compel people to attend.

[1436] *Luke* 4:16-30.

[1437] Nagel 262-5.

[1438] Campbell 135.

[1439] Wills, *Head and Heart: American Christianities* 317.

[1440] Carwardine 277-78.

[1441] Beschloss 107. Why is it so tempting to deify a leader? Here is actress Susan Sarandon in 2009 on President Barack Obama: "He's a community organizer like Jesus was, and now we're a community and he can organize us." See *National Review* February 23, 2009.

[1442] Dillenberger and Welch 165, 173, 232.

[1443] Flynn 124.

[1444] Jonah Goldberg, *Liberal Fascism: The Secret History of the American Left From Mussolini to the Politics of Meaning* (New York, London, Toronto, Sydney, Aukland: Doubleday, 2007) 217.

[1445] According to *Revelation* 1:9 a man named John was on the island of Patmos. Jesus appeared to him and he wrote *Revelation*. Patmos is a small Greek island of about three thousand people. In the United States, there is a Patmos, Arkansas of about sixty people.

[1446] We don't know that his eyes were closed. *Revelation* 1:10 just indicates that he was "*in the Spirit.*"

[1447] Henry George, *Progress on Poverty: An Inquiry Into The Cause of industrial Depressions And Of Want With Increase of Wealth...The Remedy* (New York: Robert Schalkenbach Foundation, 1962) Originally published 1879.

[1448] Pietrusza, *1920 The Year of the Six Presidents* 266.

[1449] Chace 85.

[1450] Flynn 99, 104, 105, 124, 177-8. Note: Steffens was also an admirer of Benito Mussolini, asserting that God "formed Mussolini out of the rib of Italy." See Goldberg, *Liberal Fascism: The Secret History of the American Left From Mussolini to the Politics of Meaning 28*. (Going to the *Old Testament* Steffens wrote in *Moses in Red* published in 1926: "Think of Moses as the archetypical uncompromising Bolshevik..." See Bruce Feiler, *America's Prophet Moses and the American Story* (New York: William Morrow *An Imprint of* HarperCollins*Publishers*, 2009) 231.

[1451] Pietrusza, *1920 The Year of the Six Presidents* 44.

[1452] Goldberg, *Liberal Fascism: The Secret History of the American Left From Mussolini to the Politics of Meaning* 432.

[1453] Bret Stephens *OpinionJournal.com* November 2, 2005 review of Jimmy Carter's *Our Endangered Values* 2005.

[1454] Daniel Flynn *FrontpageMagazine.com* May 1, 2008.

[1455] Goldberg, *National Review* May 5, 2008. Note: Americans have often gotten carried away with this kingdom of God on Earth notion. At his inaugural for the Tennessee governorship in 1853, future President Andrew Johnson made a speech linking democracy with Christianity in an apocalyptic way. It contains these statements: "Man is not perfect, it is true, but we all hope he is approximating perfection, and that he will, in the progress of time, reach this grand and most important end in all human affairs....This I term the divinity of man...and this divinity can be enlarged, and man can become more God-like than he is....then the voice of the people will be the voice of God." See Winston 76-79. This was silly stuff and was so recognized at the time.

[1456] Stewart 94.

[1457] Beschloss 111. He also said these people were "the unhandiest devils in the world to deal with." See Lowry, *Lincoln Unbound How An Ambitious Young Railsplitter Saved The American Dream And How We Can Do It Again* (New York: Broadside Books *An Imprint of* HarperCollins*Publishers*, 2013) 228.

[1458] Seidler 8, 11-12. This is a reference to *Matthew* 12: 31-32 in which Jesus said, "*Therefore I tell you, every sin and blasphemy will be forgiven people, but the blasphemy against the Spirit will not be forgiven. And whoever speaks a word against the Son of Man will be forgiven, but whoever speaks against the Holy Spirit will not be forgiven, either in this age or in the age to come.*" *Mark* 3:28-29 makes this same point. In each case, Jesus is accused of casting out demons by a Satanic power and this is part of his defense. *Luke* 11:14-23 recounts the same accusation against Jesus but his defense does not include the injunction of *Matthew* and *Mark* about sinning against the Holy Spirit and how it is unforgivable. *Luke* 12:10, however recounts that "*and everyone who speaks a word against the Son of Man will be forgiven, but the one who blasphemes*" *against the Holy Spirit will not be forgiven."* In some parts of Christianity, this has come to mean an exception to God's grace. But it is not well-understood.

[1459] Edmund Morris 252.

[1460] Stephen E. *Ambrose Eisenhower: Soldier, General of the Army, President Elect 1890-1952* (New York: Simon and Schuster, 1983) 527.

[1461] *Matthew* 10:23.

[1462] *Mark* 13: 30 reads: *"I tell you the truth, this generation will not pass from the scene before all these things take place."* According to Ben Witherington III, John P. Meier regards *Mark* 13:30 as inauthentic, "because the emphasis on 'time limits' for the kingdom's arrival ...is a telltale sign of its origin in the early church, pressed as it was to come to terms with the passing years and the failure for the end to come." See Witherington, *The Jesus Quest The Third Search For the Jew of Nazareth* 209-10. This is a conclusion with which Witherington, who admires Meier and even dedicates this book to him, disagrees.

[1463] A close reading of two famous Pauline passages suggests a similar point: that Paul expected the Second Coming to come in his own generation. *I Thessalonians* 4:13-17 reads: *"But we do not want you to be uninformed, brethren, about those who are asleep, so that you will not grieve as do the rest who have no hope. For if we believe that Jesus died and rose again, even so God will bring with Him those who have fallen asleep in Jesus. For this we say to you by the word of the Lord, that **we who are alive and remain** until the coming of the Lord, will not precede those who have fallen asleep. For the Lord Himself will descend from heaven with a shout, with the voice of the archangel and with the trumpet of God, and the dead in Christ will rise first. Then **we who are alive and remain** will be caught up together with them in the clouds to meet the Lord in the air, and so we shall always be with the Lord."*(Emphasis added). A few years later in his first letter to the Corinthians, the fifteen chapter, verse 51 and 52 Paul seems to be writing something very similar: *"Behold, I tell you a mystery; **we will not all sleep**, but we will all be changed, in a moment, in the twinkling of an eye, at the last trumpet; for the trumpet will sound, and the dead will be raised imperishable, and we will be changed."* (Emphasis added). Gerd Ludemann perceives a difference in Paul's views in *I Corinthians* from what he wrote in *I Thessalonians*. According to Ludeman, Paul had moved from believing that no more Christians will die before the Second Coming (to the Thessalonians) to a view that not all the now living Christians will die before the Second Coming (to the Corinthians). As Ludemann puts it:

"The imminent expectation of primitive Christianity can be delineated precisely enough to enable us to say that the Christians of the first generation after the death and 'resurrection' of Jesus generally thought they would no longer have to face death, for the arrival of the Lord, or the kingdom of God, was immediately at hand.

"We find this belief in *I Thessalonians* 4:13-17, where Paul does not reckon with any more deaths until the second coming. Yet, according to *I Corinthians* 15:51-52 the majority will die and only a minority will survive. This is evident from Paul's formulation in v.51b: *'We shall not all sleep, but we shall all be changed.'* The emphasis in this prophetic declaration is clearly that *all* will be transformed, the dead as well as living. This statement assumes that the quantitative change has occurred in the proportions of the (still) living and (in the meantime) dead in Paul's circles and thus also in Corinth. This change effected the shift in Paul's formulation. Now 'the present generation of Christians can retain only certainty that not all of them will fall among the group of *nekroi.*' The wording of *I Corinthians* 15:51b thus leads to the view that most will die before the parousia." See Ludemann, *The Earliest Christian Text I Thessalonians* (Salem, Oregon: Polebridge Press, Willamette University, Kindle Edition, 2013 Revised and expanded from the original German) Location 2331ff.

[1464] *Luke* 19:11.

[1465] *Mark* 13:32.

[1466] See Ehrman, *Jesus Interrupted: Revealing the Hidden Contradictions in the Bible (And Why We Don't Know Them)* 80-81.

[1467] *Acts* 1:3, 8:13, 14:22, 19:8, 20:25, 28:23, 31.

[1468] Grant, *Saint Paul* 171ff. In those instances where Paul or the Pauline corpus mentions the kingdom it is usually in the future sense:

- *I Corinthians* 6: 9-10 – *"Or do you not know that the unrighteous will not inherit the kingdom of God? Do not be deceived; neither fornicators, nor idolaters, nor adulterers, nor effeminate, nor homosexuals, nor thieves, nor the covetous, nor drunkards, nor revilers, nor swindlers,* **will inherit the kingdom of God.**" (Emphasis added)
- *I Corinthians* 15:50 – *"Now I say this, brethren, that flesh and blood* **cannot inherit the kingdom of God***; nor does the perishable inherit the imperishable."* (Emphasis added)
- *Galatians* 5:19-21 – *"Now the deeds of the flesh are evident, which are: immorality, impurity, sensuality, idolatry, sorcery, enmities, strife, jealousy, outbursts of anger, disputes, dissensions, factions, envying,*

> *drunkenness, carousing, and things like these, of which I forewarn you, just as I have forewarned you, that those who practice such things **will not inherit the kingdom of God.**" (Emphasis added)*

- *Ephesians 5:5 – "For this you know with certainty, that no immoral or impure person or covetous man, who is an idolater, **has an inheritance in the kingdom of Christ and God.**" (Emphasis added)*
- *I Thessalonians 2:10-12 "You are witnesses, and so is God, how devoutly and uprightly and blamelessly we behaved toward you believers; just as you know how we were exhorting and encouraging and imploring each one of you as a father would his own children, so that you would walk in a manner worthy of the God **who calls you into His own kingdom and glory.**" (Emphasis added)*
- *II Thessalonians 1:5 – "This is a plain indication of God's righteous judgment so that you **will be considered worthy of the kingdom of God**, for which indeed you are suffering."*
- *Colossians 4: 10-11 – "Aristarchus, my fellow prisoner, sends you his greetings; and also Barnabas's cousin Mark (about whom you received instructions; if he comes to you, welcome him); and also Jesus who is called Justus; these are the **only fellow workers for the kingdom of God** who are from the circumcision, and they have proved to be an encouragement to me." (Emphasis added)*
- *II Timothy 4:1,18. – "I solemnly charge you in the presence of God and of Christ Jesus, who is to judge the living and the dead, and by His appearing and His kingdom…. The Lord will rescue me from every evil deed, and **will bring me safely to His heavenly kingdom**; to Him be the glory forever and ever. Amen." (Emphasis added)*

[1469] Borg and Crossan, *The First Paul: Reclaiming the Radical Visionary Behind the Church's Conservative Icon* 186-88.

[1470] *I Corinthians* 15:24 – "After that the end will come, when he will turn the kingdom over to God the Father, having destroyed every ruler and authority and power."

[1471] The letter to the Romans may be an exception since he had never been there at the time of its writing but the other letters seem highly situational. For example in *Philippians* 4:2 he urges two people - Euodia and Syntyche –to get along.

[1472] Baumgartner 4, 45ff.

[1473] R. Jean Adams "The Re-establishment and Redemption of Zion", *The John Whitmer Historical Association Journal* Volume 34 Number 1 Spring/Summer 2014 3-4. Here are the two verses:

- *Revelation 3:12 – "He who overcomes, I will make him a pillar in the temple of My God, and he will not go out from it anymore; and I will write on him the name of My God, and the name of the city of My God, the new Jerusalem, which comes down out of heaven from My God, and My new name."*
- *Revelation 21:2 – "And I saw the holy city, new Jerusalem, coming down out of heaven from God, made ready as a bride adorned for her husband."*

[1474] Other American churches were also influenced by end-times dogma and the desire to restore *New Testament* Christianity. Some examples included the Disciples of Christ with its offshoots, the Christian Church and the Church of Christ. Despite other differences, these groups shared with the Mormons an aim to pass over the Protestant Reformation of the 1500s and go back to apostolic Christianity for inspiration, viewing the Roman Catholic Church and most Protestant churches as corrupt. See Craig L. Blomberg and Stephen E. Robinson, *How Wide the Divide A Mormon & an Evangelical in Conversation* (Downers Grove, Illinois: InterVarsity Press, Kindle Edition, 1997) 26-27. Alexander Campbell (1788 –1866) one of the founders of the Disciples of Christ said early in the nineteenth century: "We neither advocate Calvinism, Arminianism, Arianism, Socianism, Trinitarianism, Unitarianism, Deism, or Sectarianism but *New Testamentism.*" (Emphasis in the original). See: Prothero, *American Jesus How the Son of God Became a National Icon* 49. The Socinians were an Arian-like group in Europe at the time. The Arminians rejected predestination and were named for Jacob Arminius a sixteenth century Dutch theologian. Note: Even within the moment started by Joseph Smith there is diversity. There were early Mormons who rejected the leadership of Brigham Young and did not go to Utah. "In the mid-19th-century, the Reorganized Latter Day Saints emerged in the American Midwest as one of the many heirs to Joseph Smith Jr.'s Restoration movement. Led from 1862 to 1914 by Joseph Jr.'s moderate and congenial namesake son, Joseph Smith III, the RLDS Church grew from a few hundred largely rural members in Wisconsin, Illinois, and Iowa to more than seventy thousand members at the time of Smith's death who were spread across the United States, French Polynesia, Australia, England, and Canada." See David J. Howler, "Eating Vegetables to Build Zion: RLDS Children in the 1920s" *Journal of Mormon History* Winter

2009 Volume 35, No. 1. 7-8. (Joseph Smith Jr. was the full name of the founder of the Mormon Church. He was named for his father.) In 2001, the RLDS changed its name to the Community of Christ and number about 250,000. At various times over the past 150 years the RLDS (or Community of Christ) has been in legal wrangles with yet another Latter Day Saint off-shoot, the Church of Christ (Temple Lot) a denomination of about two thousand members which holds title to a two-acre property in Independence, Missouri which Mormon history holds that Joseph Smith prophesied would be the site of a temple that would be built in preparation for the Second Coming of Jesus Christ.

Here is more on Mormon polygamy.

Polygamy began secretively during Joseph Smith's life when the Mormons were still primarily in Nauvoo. Joseph Smith had nearly forty plural wives. But he kept this information out of his diaries and he issued denials that he had more than one wife.

In the Illinois period, Joseph Smith had private conversations with men on plural marriage or what he called "celestial marriage." There are recollections of those conversations which were later documented. One man remembered Smith alluding to Jesus's parable of the talents in *Matthew* 25:13-30. In this parable, Jesus told of men who had been given different amounts of money measured in units called "talents" by their master. When the master returned, one man had, through wise investment, turned five talents into ten. Another, who had only originally been given one talent had not invested, but merely saved the money. The master disapproved and instructed that this one-talent man give the one talent to the one who had ten. The traditional interpretation of this parable is that Christians should use their gift and abilities to serve the kingdom of God.

However, in the conversation with Joseph Smith, this witness heard a different message. It was, as he recalled years later, that in Heaven, the man who only had one wife would lose her to a man who had ten wives.

Another man later recalled that Joseph Smith told him that monogamy "was given when the church was in its infancy, [and] then it was all right to see the people on milk, but now it is necessary to give them strong meat." This is a take-off from *I Corinthians* 3:2 which reads: "*I gave you milk to drink, not solid food; for you were not yet able to receive it. Indeed, even now you are not yet able,...*"

In 1844, while the Mormons were still in Illinois, a newspaper in Nauvoo presented evidence about Joseph Smith's multiple marriages. As mayor,

Smith urged the city council in Nauvoo to declare the paper a "nuisance." The newspaper office was attacked and its press was destroyed. State authorities arrested Smith on charges of "riot." He and his brother were jailed away from Nauvoo and a mob broke into their cell and murdered them. After Joseph Smith's death Brigham Young married many of his widows.

The Mormons announced the doctrine of plural marriage in 1852 when they were ensconced in Utah. (In another century the literary critic Harold Bloom described this as "the most courageous act of spiritual defiance in all of American history.") They made no attempt to write up the history of plural marriage in the Illinois era until Joseph Smith's sons and the RLDS denied that Smith had been involved in it. Therefore, beginning in 1869, the Church began to collect affidavits from women who had been plural wives to Smith and other men in Illinois and from other witnesses. Joseph Smith III and his mother still did not acknowledge this. In 1885 Joseph Smith III went to Salt Lake. By this time Brigham Young was dead as was his own mother. Joseph Smith III was 53 and his father had been dead for over forty years. His beliefs on polygamy were then summarized by him as follows: "Whether if [polygamy] originated with Joseph Smith or any other teacher in the church, in his lifetime and subsequently, the doctrine was false, its practice erroneous and degrading, and its acceptance wholly unwarranted by any law of God as revealed."

In 1890 the Mormon Church officially advised against any future plural marriages. This is known as the Woodruff Manifesto after the then Mormon president, Wilford Woodruff. A second manifesto was issued in 1904 and plural marriages essentially ended by attrition. See George Smith "The Forgotten Story of Nauvoo Celestial Marriage" *Journal of Mormon History* Fall 2010 129-165, Ronald E. Romig "The RLDS Church on the Pacific Slope" *Journal of Mormon History* Spring 2009 111 and Beam Location 1583 and Prothero, *American Jesus How the Son of God Became a National Icon 183.*

Note: Vincent Shurtliff (1814 – 1893) was born in Massachusetts and was my 3G Grandfather. He joined the Mormon Church in 1845, was driven out of Illinois with the Mormons and was one of the pioneers to settle in Salt Lake City.

He had five plural wives. The last four marriages were all in Salt Lake City. Here is an overview:

Her Name	Her Age at Time of Marriage	His Age at Time of Marriage	Number of Children
Elizabeth Loomis	20	22	9
Mary Elizabeth (Hadlock) Brockway	26	33	7. (Note: My ancestor, Martha Maria Shurtliff (1852-1909), was from this union. She had two half-sisters born within five months of her own birth to Vincent Shurtliff's first and third wives.")
Elizabeth Topham	17	36	10
Lydia Amanda Shurtliff	16	40	3
Sarah Ann Hewlett	19	49	Unknown

[1475] Ostling and Ostling 21, 30, 71-72, 76, 86-87, 91-93.

[1476] Wilken, *The Myth of Christian Beginning: History's Impact on Belief* 193-94.

[1477] Shirley Jackson Case, *The Millennial Hope: A Phase of Wartime Thinking* (Chicago, University of Chicago Press, 1918) 235, 237-239. Note: Case acknowledged that apocalypticism met human needs of giving hope in difficult times. He also acknowledged that certain portions of the *Bible* seemed to have "expected a catastrophic end of the world." He further said that the allegorizing approach of Origen and Augustine was at variance with the apocalypticism of the earliest Christians. Quoted in Boyer 103.

[1478] Goldberg, *Liberal Fascism: The Secret History of the American Left From Mussolini to the Politics of Meaning* 219-20.

[1479] Herbert Agar in introduction to *Henry Adams, The Formative Years*, Volume 1 Condensed and Edited by Herbert Agar (London: Collins, 1948) 94.

1480 Hamilton, *Zachary Taylor Soldier in the White House* 308.

1481 *The Oxford Illustrated History of Christianity* Edited by John McManners Oxford and New York: Oxford University Press, 1992) 2.

1482 Levine 84.

1483 *Galatians* 6:11 and *Romans* 16:22.

1484 *I Corinthians* 4:12.

1485 See *Acts* 17:14 – 18:5. For Paul's take see *I Thessalonians* 3:1-6.

1486 Borg and Crossan, *The First Paul: Reclaiming the Radical Visionary Behind the Church's Conservative Icon* 191.

1487 As noted, the temple to the goddess Diana (also called Artemis) was in Ephesus. See Dockery, Godwin and Godwin 85ff. According to WRF Browning the silversmiths of *Acts* 19 sold miniatures of Diana. See Browning Location 736.

1488 Paul and his imitators were fond of analogies. Christ is referred to as a rock (*I Corinthians* 10:4), death is analogized to sleep (*I Thessalonians* 5:10), Christ as the basis of the church is explained in the metaphor of the foundation of a house (*I Corinthians* 3:11), the apostles are also compared to the foundation of a house and Christ to the cornerstone of a house (*Ephesians* 2:20), the church's support of the truth is described as a pillar (*I Timothy* 3:15). Military analogies are used in explaining Christian qualities as part of the armor of God (*Ephesians* 6:11ff).

1489 *II Corinthians* 10:10. He also thought that he lacked what was considered a professional speaking style. In *II Corinthians* 11:6 he wrote: "*I am unskilled in speech.*" There is some irony or disconnect here in that *Acts* portrays Paul as an accomplished orator although, as noted, the words in those speeches may be Luke's, the presumed author of *Acts*.

1490 *Galatians* 4:14.See also *II Corinthians* 12:6.

1491 Collins and Price 31. John Chrysostom, Archbishop of Constantinople, speculated that the reference cited earlier where a crowd assumed that Paul was the Greek god Mercury (*Acts* 14:12) suggests that Paul, like Mercury, was small in stature. See http://bible.cc/acts/14-12.htm (Accessed May 18, 2012).

1492 Griffith-Jones 11.

1493 John Locke, *The Reasonableness of Christianity with A Discourse of Miracles and Part of A Third Letter Concerning Toleration* Edited, Abridged and Introduced by IT Ramsey A Library of Modern Religious Thought

(Stanford: Stanford University Press, 1958. Written by John Locke [1632-1704] in 1695) 71–74.

[1494] Wills, *What Paul Meant* (New York: Penguin, 2006) 1. Jefferson felt that the true principles of Jesus were in the Gospels rather than the epistles. See Mapp 16. Note: Jefferson thought the Gospels were the earliest Christian writings as did most people of his time. See Wills, *Why I Am A Catholic* 316. It is ironic that one twentieth century scholar referred to Jefferson as "the St. Paul of American democracy." See Ahlstrom 1.

[1495] Akenson, *Saint Saul: A Skeleton Key to the Historical Jesus* 11.

[1496] Thomas Paine, *The Age of Reason* (Barnes & Noble: New York) 172.

[1497] *Galatians* 1:13-15 and *Philippians* 3:4-6.

[1498] *I Corinthians* 15:9-10 and *II Corinthians* 11:5, 21-23.

[1499] Griffith-Jones 382-3.

[1500] *Romans* 13: 1-6. *I Peter* 2:13 reads: "*For the Lord's sake, respect all human authority—whether the king as head of state, or the officials he has appointed. For the king has sent them to punish those who do wrong and to honor those who do right.*"

[1501] Here are some examples of "the" Lord: *Romans* 1:7 and 13:14, *I Corinthians* 1:3, *I Thessalonians* 1:1. Here are examples of "our" Lord: *Romans* 5:1 and 5:11, *I Corinthians* 1:2, *I Thessalonians* 1:3, 5:9, 23, 28.

[1502] I owe this thought to Borg and Crossan, *The First Paul: Reclaiming the Radical Visionary Behind the Church's Conservative Icon* 109ff but it is very important to note that these two eminent scholars see this as more than casual. They see it as a "treasonous insult." NT Wright agrees and writes that Paul's message to the Philippians is "set within a more overtly counter-imperial theology than we have seen up to now: Jesus is lord and saviour, and by strong implication, easily audible to residents in a Roman colony, Caesar is not." See Wright, *The Resurrection of the Son of God Christian Origins and the Question of God* Volume Three 225.

[1503] Augustus is a world historical figure. Michael Grant: "Augustus was one of the most talented, energetic and skillful administrators that the world has ever known. The enormously far-reaching work of reorganization and rehabilitation which he undertook in every branch of his vast Empire created a new Roman Peace, in which all but the humblest classes benefited from improved communications and flourishing commerce. The autocratic regime which (learning from Caesar's mistakes) he substituted for the collapsing

Republic - although challenged, from the outset, by a number of conspiracies - was to have a very long life. It brought stability, security and prosperity to an unprecedented proportion of the population for more than two hundred years; it assured the survival and eventual transmission of the political, social, economic and cultural heritage of the classical world - Roman and Greek alike; and it supplied the framework within which both Judaism and Christianity were disseminated. (Jesus Christ was born, and Judaea converted from a client-state into a Roman province, during this reign.)" See Grant, *The Roman Emperors A Biographical Guide to the Rulers of Imperial Rome 31BC - AD 476* 15.

[1504] *Galatians* 3:28.

[1505] *I Corinthians* 11: 11-12.

[1506] *I Corinthians* 1:11.

[1507] *Romans* 16:7. As noted, she may have been a founder or co-founder of one of the Roman churches. See James DG Dunn, *Jesus, Paul, and the Gospels* Location 3495.

[1508] *I Corinthians* 12:28.

[1509] *Acts* 16: 14, 40. According to the Catholic Church, Lydia is the patron saint of cloth dyers. Her feast day is August 3. See Sandoval 56.

[1510] *Philippians* 4:2

[1511] *I Corinthians* 11: 4-6.

[1512] Paul had ties to Cenchrea (*Acts* 18:18. It was a port town near Corinth.)

[1513] *Romans* 16: 1-2.

[1514] *Acts* 18:3, *I Corinthians* 16:17, *Romans* 16: 3-5.

[1515] *Gospel of Thomas* Saying 114.

[1516] Ehrman, *The New Testament* 395-407. For one thing, these two verses contradict Paul's comments a few chapters earlier and cited above that when women did speak their heads should be covered.

[1517] McLennan 72-3.

[1518] Akenson, *Saint Saul: A Skeleton Key to the Historical Jesus* 11-13, 153-58.

[1519] Levine 84.

[1520] However, modern sensibilities may be offended by Paul's rhetorical use in *Galatians* 4:25 of an *Old Testament* figure, Hagar the Egyptian servant of

Abraham's wife, who was used and abused by Abraham as a prefigurement of the Old Covenant. We will mention more about Hagar shortly.

[1521] Raymond E. Brown notes contradictory Biblical texts on the subject of women: "If *Ephesians* 5:24 states that wives must be subject in everything to their husbands, *Ephesians* 5:21 introduces that section by commanding 'Be subject to one another.' If *I Corinthians* 12:7 says that the man (*aner*) is the image and glory of God, while the woman is the glory of man, *Genesis* 1:27 states that both man and woman are in the image of God. If *I Corinthians* 14:34 rules that women should keep silent in the churches, *I Corinthians* 12:5 recognizes the custom that women pray and prophesy - and prophecy is the charisma ranking second after apostleship (*I Corinthians* 12:28) to the extent that *Ephesians* 2:20 has the church, the household of God, built upon the foundation of apostles *and prophets*. I might continue listing contrary voices, but then we would still have the question of how to evaluate the voices that stress subordination. Once more we would have to ask: Is that purely a cultural pattern or is it divine revelation?"

Brown further notes: "It is frequently argued that *I Corinthians* 14:44b-36 is not genuinely Pauline." See Brown 185.

[1522] To restate for emphasis a point that I have made in Chapter 5: "Paul had his own ideas about Jesus which differed quite radically from those of the disciples of Jesus. He was therefore in continual conflict with the Jewish-Christians,...." See Potter 238.

[1523] *I Corinthians* 15:22 and 45.

[1524] *Titus* 2: 9,10.

[1525] *I Timothy* 6: 1-2.

[1526] See, for example: Ehrman, *The New Testament* 344 – 47. I regret it if I have misstated Ehrman's point of view.

[1527] Borg and Crossan, *The First Paul: Reclaiming the Radical Visionary Behind the Church's Conservative Icon* 31-45. I regret it if I have misstated Borg's or Crossan's points of view.

[1528] *Philemon* 16.

[1529] See Browning Location 6488 and http://www.encyclopedia.com/topic/Onesimus.aspx. (Accessed May 3, 2012). EP Sanders holds that someone(s) collected Paul's letters in about 90. See Sanders 27.

[1530] Ignatius of Antioch adopted the term "Christian" and may have been the first to use the term "Christianity." See Pagels, *Revelations Visions, Prophecy* and *Politics in the Book of Revelation* 70. More on Ignatius: As noted, Ignatius was Bishop of Antioch. Ignatius urged the Christians of Rome not to prevent his martyrdom. He said to them, "permit me to be an imitator of the Passion of my God!" Ignatius wrote to the church at Smyrna that: "Jesus Christ was *truly* of the seed of David, he was *truly* born of a virgin,' 'and was *truly* nailed [to the cross] for us." Two thousand years later, Pope Benedict XVI wrote: "One can perceive in these words on fire with love the pronounced Christological 'realism' typical of the Church of Antioch, more focused than ever on the Incarnation of the Son of God and on his true and concrete humanity." Ignatius promoted the church hierarchy and Christian unity. He was also the first in Catholic literature to use the term "catholic" or "universal." He said: "Wherever Jesus Christ is, there is the Catholic Church." See Pope Benedict XVI, *The Fathers* 13,14-16. Note: Ignatius had been born about 30 and there was a legend that he had been the little child that Jesus picked up and placed among his disciples to teach them humility as described in the Synoptics: *Matthew* 18:1-4; *Mark* 9:33-37 and *Luke* 9:46-48. The account in *Luke* reads as follows: *"An argument started among them as to which of them might be the greatest. But Jesus, knowing what they were thinking in their heart, took **a child** and stood him by His side, and said to them, 'Whoever receives **this child** in My name receives Me, and whoever receives Me receives Him who sent Me; for the one who is least among all of you, this is the one who is great.'"* (Emphases added). See Justo L. Gonzales *The Story of Christianity Volume 1 The Early Church to the Dawn of the Reformation* Location 1094ff.

[1531] Buechner 142-44.

[1532] A different take on Paul's view toward slavery as evidenced in the letter of *Philemon* is a tension that seems to recognize both slavery and the spirit which undermined it. After centuries the spirit of Christianity led to practical action. See Pelikan, *Jesus Through The Centuries: His Place in the History of Culture* 211-212.

[1533] *I Corinthians* 1:26.

[1534] *I Corinthians* 6:1-8.

[1535] *I Corinthians* 5:1-13. This is assumed by most commentators to be a moral issue not a class issue. I owe the concept of class distinction to Borg and Crossan, *The First Paul: Reclaiming the Radical Visionary Behind the Church's Conservative Icon* 197-200 and regret it if I have misstated Borg's and Crossan's point of view.

[1536] *I Corinthians* 10:14-33.

[1537] *I Corinthians* 11: 17-37.

¹⁵³⁸ Reverend McLennan cites the two passages above plus *I Timothy* 1:9-11. That section, starting in verse 8, reads: *"But we know that the Law is good, if one uses it lawfully, realizing the fact that law is not made for a righteous person, but for those who are lawless and rebellious, for the ungodly and sinners, for the unholy and profane, for those who kill their fathers or mothers, for murderers and immoral men and homosexuals and kidnappers and liars and perjurers, and whatever else is contrary to sound teaching, according to the glorious gospel of the blessed God, with which I have been entrusted."*

¹⁵³⁹ McLennan 23-24. McLennan cites John Boswell, *Christianity, Social Tolerance and Homosexuality* (Chicago: University of Chicago Press, 1980).

¹⁵⁴⁰ Akenson, *Saint Saul: A Skeleton Key to the Historical Jesus* 11-13.

¹⁵⁴¹ Despite his on-again-off-again animosity toward Jewish-Christians, Paul did accept certain theological diversities as seen from his cites of different factions in Corinth loyal to Peter and Apollos (*I Corinthians* 1:12-13; 3:4-6, 22; 4:6; 16:12). The only person he turned over to Satan was one who possibly was guilty of moral turpitude (*I Corinthians* 5:5). In this regard it is interesting that "Paul" applied that punishment in one of the pastorals to people who had "suffered shipwreck in regard to their faith" (*I Timothy* 1:19-20). See Bauer 235-236.

¹⁵⁴² In the modern era, people have pointed out that Jesus Christ did not have a direct statement condemning homosexuality. The closest I have found to Jesus addressing the subject are these three generalities:

• *Matthew* 5:17 - *"Do not think that I came to abolish the Law or the Prophets; I did not come to abolish but to fulfill."* In this instance, Jesus stood by Jewish law, part of which proscribed homosexuality – for example, *Leviticus* 18:22: *"You shall not lie with a male as one lies with a female; it is an abomination."*

• *Matthew* 15:19 – *"For out of the heart come evil thoughts, murders, adulteries, fornications, thefts, false witness, slanders."* (Emphasis added). See also *Mark* 7:2. Fornication is sex outside of marriage.

• *Matthew* 19:4-5 – Jesus: *"Have you not read that He who created them from the beginning MADE THEM MALE AND FEMALE, and said, 'FOR THIS REASON A MAN SHALL LEAVE HIS FATHER AND MOTHER AND BE JOINED TO HIS WIFE, AND THE TWO SHALL BECOME ONE FLESH?'"* This would seem to be a prohibition of same sex marriage.

Do these sections of scripture array Jesus of Nazareth with those who would oppose homosexuality in the twenty-first century? You be the judge. Pope Francis said in 2013 regarding gay priests: ""If someone is gay and he

searches for the Lord and has good will, who am I to judge?" See http://
www.nytimes.com/2013/07/30/world/europe/pope-francis-gay-priests.
html?pagewanted=all&_r=0 (Accessed June 4, 2014).

1543 Wills, *What Paul Meant* 125. and White, *From Jesus to Christianity* 172.

1544 *Romans* 15:31.

1545 *Romans* 15: 25-6. However, according to *Acts* 20:4, none of the delegates
were from Corinth despite his pleadings to that church for funds. See *II
Corinthians* 2: 1-9.

1546 *Acts* 18:2. Indeed, eventually, Jews got exemption from emperor-worship
requirements from Claudius but Christians did not. Moreover, as the Christian
movement grew it got the negative attention of the government as suggested
in *I Peter* 4:16 ("[B]ut if anyone suffers as a Christian, he is not to be ashamed,
but is to glorify God in this name.") and in later warnings from Celsus about
its lack of loyalty. See Browning Location 2765.

1547 Pagels and King, *Reading Judas: The Gospel of Judas and the Shaping of
Christianity* xxi. Irenaeus fought any kind of diversity, writing: "Outside the
church there is no salvation." See Pagels, *Revelations Visions, Prophecy and
Politics in the Book of Revelation* 139.

1548 *Romans* 14: 14-22.

1549 *Romans* 6: 1-2.

1550 *Romans* 3:8.

1551 *Romans* 11: 1-2. As noted, Paul also cites his Judaic roots by referring to
his membership in the tribe of Benjamin in *Philippians* 3 :5. To the extent
that the speech attributed to Paul in *Acts* 13 reflects his style and thoughts, it
is interesting to note that in verse 21 Paul, while giving a history of the Jewish
people, says, *"Then they asked for a king, and God gave them Saul the son of
Kish, a man of the tribe of Benjamin, for forty years."* This is the only time that
King Saul is mentioned in the *New Testament*. (He was mentioned over 300
times in the *Old Testament*.) Could it have been a source of pride for Paul
who was once known as Saul that he was of the some tribe as that king and
was named for him?

1552 *Galatians* 4:23-6. Note : this passage demonstrates that Paul was willing
to read scripture allegorically. As noted, Hagar was the Egyptian servant of
Abraham's wife Sarah. Paul treated Hagar as a symbol of the Old Covenant
and Sarah of the New Covenant. The life of Hagar can be read in *Genesis*
16: 1-16 and 21: 9-17. There is at least one more example of Paul reading

scripture allegorically. As mentioned earlier, In *I Corinthians* 9:9 Paul cited *Deuteronomy* 25:4 to give a basis for paying church workers: *"For it is written in the Law of Moses, 'YOU SHALL NOT MUZZLE THE OX WHILE HE IS THRESHING.'"* He goes on to say in the rest of verse 9 and in verse 10: *"God is not concerned about oxen, is He? Or is He speaking altogether for our sake? .."* As noted, *I Corinthians* 9:9 and *Deuteronomy* 25:4 are quoted in *I Timothy* 5:18. Origen pointed out the obvious: that Paul interpreted scriptures, at times allegorically. Here is relevant background: In the 200s-300s the school at Antioch took an historical and grammatical approach to the scriptures in contrast to the Alexandrians who took a more allegorical approach. Clement of Alexandria, like Origen, saw texts as having meaning at two levels: literal and spiritual. For example he looked at the near sacrifice of Isaac in *Genesis* 22 in that manner. He also held that scripture must be interpreted in the context of other scripture. He linked, for example, *John* 6 in which Jesus talks of drinking his blood to *Genesis* 4:10 in which God says to Cain: *"The voice of your brother's blood is crying to me from the ground."* From this, Clement said that in the *Bible* "blood" is representative of "Word" and therefore in *John* 6 Jesus is referring to the Word. See Justo L. Gonzales, *A History of Christian Thought From the Beginnings to the Council of Chalcedon* Volume 1 Revised Edition 194ff, *212-213, 260.* Note: The near sacrifice by Abraham of Isaac mentioned in *Genesis* 22 is alluded to two times in the *New Testament* - in *Hebrews* 11:17-19 and, briefly, in *James* 2:21. The account in *Hebrews* sounds like it is somewhat allegorical: *"By faith Abraham, when he was tested, offered up Isaac, and he who had received the promises was offering up his only begotten son; it was he to whom it was said, 'IN ISAAC YOUR DESCENDANTS SHALL BE CALLED.' He considered that God is able to raise people even from the dead, from which he also received him back as a type."* (Emphasis added).

[1553] *I Thessalonians* 2:15.

[1554] *Luke* 15: 11-32.

[1555] Roman Catholic doctrine holds that Jews are "elder brothers" with a covenant with God. See Daniel Johnson, *Commentary* April 2009.

[1556] Pelikan, *Jesus Through The Centuries: His Place in the History of Culture* 16-19.

[1557] *Romans 14*:17.

[1558] *Romans* 11.

[1559] Borg, *Evolution of the Word The New Testament in the Order the Books Were Written* 27.

[1560] Wilson, *Paul: The Mind of the Apostle* 193-4.

[1561] Paul Johnson, *A History of Christianity* 281, 365, 496.

[1562] Augustine was opposed in his lifetime by a British-born monk, Pelagius. Pelagius's birth date is not known but he was in Rome in 405 and reacted negatively to Augustine's doctrine of grace because he saw more of a role for human effort. He saw that Augustine's view left an insufficient role for human freedom and he was concerned that the emphasis on grace led to moral decline. Pelagius is regarded by the Catholic Church as a heretic. See Justo L. Gonzales, A *History of Christian Thought From Augustine to the Eve of the Reformation* Volume II Revised Edition Location 383ff.

[1563] Marty 63.

[1564] Hitchcock 95-96. I regret it if I have misstated Hitchcock's point of view. Note: Augustine may also have refocused people on the transcendent rather than ongoing politics. In the words of Robert Louis Wilken: "By the time Augustine became bishop it seemed that the whole world had become a chorus praising Christ. Like his contemporaries, Augustine believed that Rome had placed itself under Christ's rule. But as his thinking matured Augustine began to have doubts about this sanguine view of history, and in the *City of God* he divests the Roman Empire of religious significance." See Wilken *The First Thousand Years A Global History of Christianity* 189.

[1565] Paul Johnson, *A History of Christianity* 281. Note: Here are Roman Catholic comments about Luther:

- "Although Luther has come down in history as a champion of human freedom against institutional tyranny, he actually accused the Church of being too easygoing, of falsely assuring people of salvation and thereby short-circuiting their process of repentance. But his anxiety also stemmed from his belief that, in requiring people to confess their sins and to overcome them, the Church was imposing an impossible burden. Christians should instead accept the reality of sin and rely entirely on divine mercy, since, in Luther's view, sin is not so much specific actions as it is man's very nature, his fundamental orientation toward evil." See Hitchcock 256-7. Note: The Council of Trent (1545-1563) condemned what it regarded as Protestant heresies. It included this statement: "If anyone says the sinner is justified by faith alone, meaning that nothing else is required to cooperate in order to obtain the grace of justification, and that it is not in any way necessary that he be prepared and disposed by the action of his will, let him be anathema." More on the Council of Trent: The

Council of Trent stuck with Catholic doctrine but reformed the Church in such areas as simony, absenteeism, violation of vows of celibacy. Its spirit was the spirit of the Jesuits: traditional doctrine, a moral life, an outreach to the whole church. The Council is the start of the modern Church. In an interrelated development, the papacy was strengthened: "The pope was ... made at once the source of the council's authority and its final interpreter." See *Justo L. Gonzales, A History of Christian Thought From the Protestant reformation to the Twentieth Century* Volume III Revised Edition Locations 4468, 4508ff, 4523.

- Luther allegedly added the word "alone" to the above-quoted verse in scripture "*the just shall live by faith*" in his translation of the *New Testament*. See Hitchcock 264.

[1566] http://www.gbgm-umc.org/aldersgate-wheaton/aumcname.html (Accessed May 3, 2012.) See also Edward T. Oakes, *First Things* December, 2004.

[1567] Potter 473, 497-501. In Potter's words about the impact of *Romans*: "Paul, Augustine, Luther, Wesley; Roman Jew, Carthaginian, German and Englishman, how they clasp hands across the centuries!" See Potter 485.

[1568] Jenkins, *The Next Christendom The Coming of Global Christianity* Third Edition 196-7.

[1569] Jenkins, *The Great and Holy War How World War I Became a Religious Crusade* 224.

[1570] Dillenberger and Welch 255ff.

[1571] Levine 58. Besides this section, these *New Testament* verses remind us of the Sadducees's beliefs: *Mark* 12:18 and *Matthew* 22:23.

[1572] We will dig deeper into the concept of the afterlife in the next chapter. For now, it is enough to say that the first examples of Christian views of an afterlife come from Paul's letters and are reflected in this account in *Acts*. He seems to have aligned his learning as a Pharisee with his Christian convictions. See Browning Location 2916.

[1573] For example, Jesus's famous teaching that there were two spheres – the government and God – came out of hostile questions from Pharisees recorded in *Matthew* 22:15 and *Mark* 12: 13.

[1574] *Matthew* 12:14.

[1575] *John* 9:16.

[1576] *Matthew* 3:7.

[1577] *Matthew* 23:15. The Pharisee party numbered about six thousand in Jesus's time. See Jay Tolson and Linda Kulman *Newsweek* March 8, 2004.

[1578] *Luke* 7: 36-39, *Luke* 11: 37-54 and *Luke* 14: 1-23.

[1579] *Luke* 13:31: *"Just at that time some Pharisees approached, saying to Him, 'Go away, leave here, for Herod wants to kill You.'"* Note: Herod Antipas was a brutal ruler. It is an interesting coincidence that one of the early Christian martyrs was also called Antipas. In *Revelation* 2 the angel of Pergamum which was the capital of a Roman province was instructed: *"'I know where you dwell, where Satan's throne is; and you hold fast My name, and did not deny My faith even in the days of Antipas, My witness, My faithful one, who was killed among you, where Satan dwells.'"*

[1580] *Matthew* 23:2.

[1581] Maccoby, *Revolution in Judaea: Jesus and the Jewish Resistance* 108.

[1582] *John* 3: 1-21 Note: Josephus also mentioned Nicodemus. See Wilson, *Jesus A Life* 149.

[1583] *John* 7: 45-51. Interestingly, this is the same charge that was directed at Peter in the midst of his three denials according to *Mark* 14:70 and *Luke* 22:59.

[1584] *John* 19: 38-42.

[1585] This is a case in which some aspect of *Acts* is supported in Paul's letters: *Acts* 23:6; *Acts* 26:5 and *Philippians* 3:5. This latter verse is the first mention in world literature of the word "Pharisee." It is "a highly polemical passage. Paul boasts against his Jewish or Jewish-Christian opponents that he was *'according to the Law a Pharisee.'"* After that, *Mark* is the next document in history to mention Pharisees and it records the word twelve times. Neither author was neutral and both were writing to predominantly Gentile groups outside of Palestine. See Meier, *A Marginal Jew Rethinking the Historical Jesus Vlm III Companions and Competitors* 300.

[1586] *Acts* 22:3.

[1587] *Acts* 5:29-40.

[1588] *Acts* 23:6.

[1589] Akenson, *Saint Saul: A Skeleton Key to the Historical Jesus* 244. However, Josephus's claim to be a Pharisee is open to doubt. It may have only reflected his realization by the 90s of the Pharisees's survivability and surge. See

Meier, *A Marginal Jew Rethinking the Historical Jesus Vlm III Companions and Competitors* 300-02.

[1590] *Acts* 15:5.

[1591] *Acts* 5:37.

[1592] Maccoby, *Revolution in Judaea: Jesus and the Jewish Resistance* 40, 57, 62-3, 175.

[1593] For example, *Luke* 5:30 and 7:36-9.

[1594] For example, *Luke* 5:21.

[1595] *Mark* 12: 28-34; *Matthew* 22: 34-40; *Luke* 10:25-29.

[1596] Like Socrates (abt. 469 BC – 399 BC) Jesus asked more questions than he answered.

[1597] *Mark* 12:34.

[1598] *Matthew* 22:35.

[1599] *Luke*10: 29.

[1600] http://bible.org/seriespage/look-book-romans-11-17 (Accessed May 3, 2012).

[1601] Wilson, *Jesus A Life* 41.

[1602] If Paul according to *Romans* was also the apostle to the Jews, it is worth repeating that it was Peter who of the two was the first apostle to Gentiles. See *Acts* 2 (Pentecost) and 10:1–11:18 (Cornelius).

[1603] *Romans* 15:10: *"… from Jerusalem and round about as far as Illyricum I have fully preached the gospel of Christ."*

[1604] *Philippians* 3:5.

[1605] *Luke* 24:49, *Acts* 1:4. In each case, the disciples were to wait for the Holy Spirit.

[1606] *Acts* 28:14. Note: One theory holds that in his Gospel Luke located the sightings of the risen Jesus in Jerusalem to stress how the Christian message had moved from Galilee to Jerusalem and was to go to Rome. See Charlotte Allen, *The Human Christ The Search for the Historical Jesus* 254.

[1607] I draw much of this analysis from Ludemann, *The Earliest Christian Text I Thessalonians* Locations 178, 184ff, 209, 2864, 2918, 2929, 2978, 2998, 3109, 3138ff and I regret it if I have misstated Ludemann's point of view.

[1608] *Matthew* 26: 28 - Jesus at the Last Supper: *"For this is My blood of the* **covenant***, which is poured out for many for forgiveness of sins."* (Emphasis added).

Mark 14: 24 - Jesus at the Last Supper: *"And He said to them, 'This is My blood of the* **covenant***, which is poured out for many.'"* (Emphasis added).

Hebrews 8: 8-13: *"For finding fault with them, He says,*

'BEHOLD, DAYS ARE COMING, SAYS THE LORD WHEN I WILL EFFECT A **NEW COVENANT**
WITH THE HOUSE OF ISRAEL AND WITH THE HOUSE OF JUDAH;
NOT LIKE THE **COVENANT** WHICH I MADE WITH THEIR FATHERS
ON THE DAY WHEN I TOOK THEM BY THE HAND
TO LEAD THEM OUT OF THE LAND OF EGYPT;
FOR THEY DID NOT CONTINUE IN MY COVENANT,
AND I DID NOT CARE FOR THEM, SAYS THE LORD.
FOR THIS IS THE **COVENANT** THAT I WILL MAKE WITH THE HOUSE OF ISRAEL
AFTER THOSE DAYS, SAYS THE LORD:
I WILL PUT MY LAWS INTO THEIR MINDS,
AND I WILL WRITE THEM ON THEIR HEARTS.
AND I WILL BE THEIR GOD,
AND THEY SHALL BE MY PEOPLE.
AND THEY SHALL NOT TEACH EVERYONE HIS FELLOW CITIZEN,
AND EVERYONE HIS BROTHER, SAYING, "KNOW THE LORD,"
FOR ALL WILL KNOW ME,
FROM THE LEAST TO THE GREATEST OF THEM.
FOR I WILL BE MERCIFUL TO THEIR INIQUITIES,
AND I WILL REMEMBER THEIR SINS NO MORE.'

"When He said, 'A **new covenant***,' He has made the first obsolete. But whatever is becoming obsolete and growing old is ready to disappear."* (Emphases added).

Hebrews 10:15-17: *"And the Holy Spirit also testifies to us; for after saying,*

'THIS IS THE **COVENANT** THAT I WILL MAKE WITH THEM
AFTER THOSE DAYS, SAYS THE LORD:
I WILL PUT MY LAWS UPON THEIR HEART,
AND ON THEIR MIND I WILL WRITE THEM,'

He then says, 'AND THEIR SINS AND THEIR LAWLESS DEEDS I WILL REMEMBER NO MORE.'" (Emphasis added)

[1609] To be overly brief, Paul's relationship with his co-religionists, the Jews, at least as seen in the *New Testament*, could be summarized as follows:

- To the Christians he promised money. See *Galatians* 2:10 (*"They only asked us to remember the poor—the very thing I also was eager to do."*) and the discussion in Chapter 7.
- To the non-Christians he seemed to promise salvation without faith in Jesus. See *Romans* 11:26 (*"all Israel will be saved"*) and the discussion this Chapter.

[1610] To review: *"... then comes the end, when He hands over the kingdom to the God and Father, when He has abolished all rule and all authority and power. For He must reign until He has put all His enemies under His feet. The last enemy that will be abolished is death. 'For HE HAS PUT ALL THINGS IN SUBJECTION UNDER HIS FEET.' But when He says, 'All things are put in subjection,' it is evident that He is excepted who put all things in subjection to Him. When all things are subjected to Him, then the Son Himself also will be subjected to the One who subjected all things to Him, so that God may be all in all."*

[1611] *Acts* 25:19 - Festus to Agrippa.

[1612] Dennis Prager, *FrontPageMagazine.com* January 4, 2005.

[1613] A Christian departure from Jerusalem during the rebellion against Rome was a symbol of Jewish-Christian separation. See Charlotte Allen, *The Human Christ The Search for the Historical Jesus* 43.

[1614] Akenson, *Saint Saul: A Skeleton Key to the Historical Jesus* 100, 105, 121, 167, 228.

[1615] Maccoby, *The Mythmaker: Paul and the Invention of Christianity* cited by Akenson, *Saint Saul: A Skeleton Key to the Historical Jesus* 267-8.

[1616] Donald A. Hagner, "Paul in Modern Jewish Thought," in Donald A. Hagner and Murray J. Harris (eds.), *Pauline Studies: Essays presented to Professor FF Bruce on his 70th Birthday* (Exeter: Paternoster Press, 1980) 143.

[1617] Hengel and Schwemer xi-xiv, 1-5, 47, 133, 153ff, 173-174, 242, 291.

[1618] Sanders 14-15.

[1619] See Ludemann, *What Really Happened to Jesus A Historical Approach to the Resurrection* 14-15.

[1620] Johnson, *Jesus A Biography From a Believer* 217.

[1621] There is an interesting point to consider about this three year period. As seen in *Galatians* and possibly *II Corinthians* Paul was in occasional rivalry with the Twelve. Paul bolstered his role in at least two ways. First, although they had been selected by Jesus, he believed he had been selected by Jesus before he was even born. Second, although they had spent three years with Jesus, so had he. See *Galatians* 1:15–18. I owe this thought to Tabor, *Paul and Jesus How the Apostle Transformed Christianity* Location 1550ff and regret it if I have misstated Tabor's point of view.

[1622] As noted earlier, I work under the assumption that *I Peter* was not written by Peter. However its existence shows a certain regard for him in the early church.

[1623] This coheres with James DG Dunn's view: "The crucial impact of Paul's work was made during his mission in the Aegean, recounted in *Acts* 16-20. For one thing, it marked a decisive shift *westwards*." During this time Paul wrote most of his letters. "Paul's letters are the only Christian writings which can assuredly be dated to the first generation (thirty-five years) of Christianity. And it is these letters which ensured that Paul's legacy would continue to influence and indeed give Christianity so much of its definitive character.

"In other words, the eight or so years of Paul's Aegean mission stand alongside the three years of Jesus' own mission, the first two or three years of the Jerusalem church's existence and the initial expansion of the new sect led by the Hellenists." See James DG Dunn, *Jesus, Paul, and the Gospels* Location 2488.

[1624] Paul may have split with the Galatians in later years. The collection of money from the Galatians is mentioned in *I Corinthians* 16:1 but not later in *Romans* 15:26 or *II Corinthians* 8-9. Possibly, the collection was canceled due to a breakdown there:

- *I Corinthians* 16:1 – *"Now concerning the collection for the saints, as I directed the churches of **Galatia**, so do you also."* (Emphasis added).
- *Romans* 15:26 – "For **Macedonia** and **Achaia** have been pleased to make a contribution for the poor among the saints in Jerusalem." (Emphasis added).
- II Corinthians 8-9. See 8:1-2 - -*"Now, brethren, we wish to make known to you the grace of God which has been given in the churches of **Macedonia**, that in a great ordeal of affliction their abundance of joy and their deep poverty overflowed in the wealth of their liberality."* See 9:1 – *"For it is superfluous for me to write to you about this ministry to the saints; for I know your readiness, of which I boast about you to the **Macedonians**, namely, that **Achaia** has been prepared since last year, and your zeal has stirred up most of them."* (Emphasis added).

Galatia, Macedonia and Achaia were three different provinces in the Roman Empire. Galatia was in modern Turkey. Achaea was in modern Greece. Macedonia was north of Greece. See Browning Location 7248.

[1625] As noted earlier, there is a Gaius listed as a traveling companion of Paul. *Acts* 19:29 records a Gaius of Macedonia and *Acts* 20:4 records a Gaius from Derbe which is in modern Turkey. It is unclear whether this is the same person. Also, there is a Gaius listed as the recipient of *III John*.

[1626] Eusebius wrote that the authorities in Jerusalem turned on James the brother of Jesus because Paul got away from them by appealing to Rome: "But after Paul, in consequence of his appeal to Caesar, had been sent to Rome by Festus, the Jews, being frustrated in their hope of entrapping him by the snares which they had laid for him, turned against James, the brother of the Lord, to whom the episcopal seat at Jerusalem had been entrusted by the Apostles." See Eusebius Book II Chapter 23.

[1627] Eusebius wrote in the early 300s that Paul was beheaded. See Eusebius Book II Chapter 25. In 2006 archaeologists announced they had found an ancient sarcophagus that may well contain bones of the Apostle Paul. See Tabor, *Paul and Jesus How the Apostle Transformed Christianity* Location 140-155.

[1628] *Romans* 15: 24 and 28. Spain for Paul was an outpost. It fell to the Muslims in the 700s.

[1629] *Galatians* 5:14.

[1630] *Galatians* 6:2.

[1631] He had actually thought about this trip for years and had considered skipping it and just sending the aid through others. See *I Corinthians* 16: 1-4.

[1632] Paul Johnson, A History *of Christianity* 40. ●

[1633] Grant, *Saint Paul* 98-99. Of course, this brought certain problems. In Chapter 6 we saw how Paul conflicted with the Jewish-Christians in his lifetime. He or his writings probably also did with the emerging Church even as it became Pauline in theology. His "claim to apostleship direct from Christ and independent from the mother church of Christianity sets *an uncomfortable* precedent for similar claims in later years...." See James DG Dunn *Jesus, Paul, and the Gospels* Location 2980ff. In a way, Paul attempted to nullify later claimants to different versions of Christianity when he recounted in *I Corinthians* 15:8 that the risen Christ appeared to him "*last of all.*"

[1634] *Acts* 28:30-31.

[1635] See Crossan and Reed 7.

[1636] Akenson, *Saint Saul: A Skeleton Key to the Historical Jesus* 13. Note: David is mentioned in the *Old Testament* over nine hundred times and in the *New*

Testament fifty-five times. In the latter he is often listed as an ancestor of Jesus either in his genealogy or in a title "Son of David" which is in the very first verse of the first book of the *New Testament* and in other places.

In the *Old Testament* David's life is described in great detail in the *Books of I* and *II Samuel*. He was a shepherd and later a king. He was a poet, a warrior, a murderer and an adulterer. His failures as a father lead to rebellion in the government. Whether he wrote the *Psalms* or not, people have studied them to understand David's inner life and as noted he was described as a man after God's own heart - by the prophet Samuel in *I Samuel* 13:14 and by Paul according to the writer Luke in *Acts* 13:22. We know him at all phases in his life from the time he was a boy at home through the end of his life when he was old and weak. There were few if any miracles associated with his life and he had very human-like qualities. The first words of David that are quoted in the *Bible* are of him trying to learn if there might be some reward available if he can kill a giant soldier of the other side named Goliath who was taunting the Israelites. Here are David's words: *"What will be done for the man who kills this Philistine and takes away the reproach from Israel?"* (*I Samuel* 17:26). David does kill Goliath giving rise to an enduring metaphor. The scriptures report that Saul the first king of Israel loved David (*I Samuel* 16:21) although he later turned against him, that Saul's son Jonathon loved David (*I Samuel* 18:1) *and* that Saul's daughter Michal loved David (*I Samuel* 18:20) and even helped him, at risk to herself escape a death trap (*I Samuel* 19:11-17) although later she came to despise him (*II Samuel* 6:16-23 and *I Chronicles* 15:29). Did David exist as a real person? The evidence outside of the *Bible* is scant but there is a slight consensus that he reigned as king of Israel about one thousand years before Christ.

Two valuable recent books on David are: Robert Pinsky *The Life of David* (New York: Schocken Books a division of Random House, Inc. and Toronto: Random House of Canada Limited, Kindle Edition, 2005) and David Wolpe *David The Divided Heart* (New Haven and London: Yale University Press, Kindle Edition, 2014).

[1637] James DG Dunn *Jesus, Paul, and the Gospels* Locations 2892ff and 3151.

[1638] Wilson, *Paul: The Mind of the Apostle* 238-39.

[1639] Borg, *Jesus: Uncovering the Life, Teachings, and Relevance of a Religious Revolutionary* 30-1.

[1640] Akenson, *Surpassing Wonder: The Invention of the Bible and the Talmuds* 546-47.

[1641] Two of the three Romans who mentioned Christianity in the first hundred years of its existence, Pliny the Younger who wrote about Christians in 112 AD and Tacitus who wrote about them in 116 (referring to the persecution in 64) were friends. See Ehrman, *Jesus Interrupted: Revealing the Hidden Contradictions in the Bible (And Why We Don't Know Them)* 149. John Quincy Adams, while a young diplomat appointed by George Washington to the Hague, often diverted himself by making translations of classical literature. He referred to Tacitus as an "incomparable author." See Nagel, *John Quincy Adams: A Public Life, A Private Life* 98.

[1642] White, *From Jesus to Christianity* 94-99.

[1643] Ludemann, *What Really Happened to Jesus A Historical Approach to the Resurrection* 17.

Additional note: All four Gospels report that Jesus was crucified. But how he was prepared for burial and his actual wounds are inconsistently reported in the Gospels.

As to the preparation: *Mark* 15:46 records that Joseph of Arimathea had a linen cloth and wrapped Jesus's body in it. *Luke* 23:53 records the same. *Matthew* 27:59 records the same, adding that the cloth was clean. *John* 19:40 records that Joseph of Arimathea was joined by Nicodemus and that they placed the body in wrappings. Was the body of Jesus arranged for burial in a linen cloth (singular) or wrappings (plural)? It is hard to see how it could be both. Following the typology from Chapter 2, this difference may be Inconsistent and Irreconcilable. But is it Insignificant or Significant? I believe that it is Insignificant, but those favoring the Shroud of Turin might see the difference as Significant.

What is the Shroud of Turin? It is a linen cloth bearing the image of a man that some believe is the burial shroud of Jesus. The shroud is kept in a cathedral in Turin, Italy.

The Catholic Church has not endorsed the shroud but recent popes have commented on it:

- John Paul II called it "a mirror of the Gospel."
- Benedict XVI and Francis have both described it as "an icon."

The origin of the shroud is a matter of intense debate. Radiocarbon tests in 1988 concluded that the age of the cloth only goes back to the Middle Ages.

As to the wounds: *John* 19:34-37 records that Jesus's lifeless body was stabbed in the side by a Roman soldier while it was still hanging on the cross. John reports that this stabbing was in lieu of the normal Roman practice of breaking the legs of someone who was crucified which was to speed up the death. John tied the stabbing into *Old Testament* references so as to allude Jesus's roles:

- As a Passover lamb - "*Not a bone of Him shall be broken.*" This appears to be a reference to *Psalm* 34:20 and an allusion to Jesus being the Passover lamb as mentioned by John the Baptist in *John* 1:29 and Paul in *I Corinthians* 5:7. This allusion is also consistent with John's placement of the crucifixion on Passover rather than, as the Synoptics have it, on the day before Passover.
- As a Good Shepherd – "*They shall look on Him whom they pierced.*" This appears to be a reference to *Zechariah 12:10*. In *Zechariah* 12 we are told that God will defend his people. This may be an allusion to Jesus being a protector or, in the context of the *Gospel of John*, a Good Shepherd.

John 20:27 later records that the risen Jesus gave Thomas the opportunity to touch his side.

The Synoptics do not report the stabbing incident and Luke seems not even to acknowledge it as noted when the risen Jesus refers to his wounds in *Luke* 24:39 to his close followers: "*See My **hands** and My **feet**, that it is I Myself; touch Me and see...*" (Emphases added).

The differences between *John* and the Synoptics on this point may be Inconsistent but Reconcilable in that Jesus could have been wounded by nails in this hands and feet as well as by a stab to his side. I owe the thoughts on the burial shroud and the side wound to a work of fiction: Ian Caldwell, *The Fifth Gospel A Novel* (New York, London, Toronto, Sydney, New Delhi: Simon & Schuster, Kindle Edition, 2015). I regret it if I have misstated Caldwell's point of view.

[1644] Van Vorst 8,14,16. To quote Bart Ehrman: "Even though there are innumerable historical problems in the *New Testament*, they are not of the scope or character to call seriously into doubt the existence of Jesus. He certainly lived, and in my view he too was a kind of religious genius, even more than the later authors who wrote about him." See Ehrman, *Did Jesus Exist? The Historical Argument for Jesus of Nazareth* 37. Note: Both Bertram Russell (1872 – 1970) and Voltaire accepted the historicity of Jesus. See Van Vorst 8, 16.

[1645] *Matthew* 27: 15-22.

[1646] *Mark* 15: 6-14.

[1647] *Luke* 23: 18-23.

[1648] *John* 18:40.

[1649] *Mark* 15:6.

[1650] *Matthew* 27:15.

[1651] *Luke* 23: 16-25.

[1652] *John* 18:39.

[1653] "Scholars are almost unanimous in regarding the 'Passover privilege' as fictional." See Maccoby, *Revolution in Judaea: Jesus and the Jewish Resistance* 19.

[1654] *Matthew* 27:25.

[1655] Levine 95ff.

[1656] Spong 168-9.

[1657] Einhorn 136-42. As I noted in Chapter 5, I know of no other support for these views.

[1658] Collins and Price 35. Peter was reputed to have been buried on what is now Vatican Hill in Rome. In the 300s the emperor Constantine built a church which became St. Peter's Basilica over the cemetery. The workers filled in the tombs which had the effect of preserving them. The cemetery was discovered in the 1500s during the construction of a new St. Peter's Basilica and the workers left the tombs undisturbed. The cemetery was discovered again in 1939. At the deepest level a simple grave of an old man was found. In 1968 Pope Paul VI declared that the bones were St. Peter's. See Bunson 344-45. In 2013 Pope Francis displayed the bones publicly for the first time. See Nicole Winfield *The Associated Press NBCNews.com* November 24, 2013.

[1659] Finally, it should be noted that Hyam Maccoby speculates that Barabbas and Jesus were the same person. His evidence:

- There is no evidence or logic to the Passover Privilege.
- There is obvious dualism: Jesus stands for pacifism, Barabbas for violence.
- Barabbas means Son of God. His first name was Jesus.

His fallback position is that if they were not the same person, they must have been in league. See Maccoby *Revolution in Judaea: Jesus and the Jewish Resistance* 13-21 and 159-69.

[1660] *Mark* 15: 34, 44. This also is one of his most memorable statements. It is a raw human emotion and echoes that of his own disciples to him on the Sea of Galilee in a storm as quoted in *Mark* 4:38: *"Master, do you not care that we are perishing?" Matthew* 8:25 renders this: *"Save us, Lord; we are perishing." Luke* 8:24 reads: *"Master, Master, we are perishing."*

[1661] Stark, *Discovering God: The Origins of the Great Religions and the Evolution of Belief* 327.

[1662] For ease of writing and habit I will stick with a male pronoun.

[1663] James Madison (letter to Frederick Beasley, 20 November 1825) *PatriotPost.US* September 23, 2008.

[1664] Micklethwait and Wooldridge, *God is Back How The Global Revival of Faith is Changing the World* 94.

[1665] Borg and Wright, *The Meaning of Jesus Two Visions* (New York: HarperCollins Publishers, 1999 First HarperCollins Paperback Edition Published In 2000) 9.

[1666] McLennan 12.

[1667] McLennan 51.

[1668] Wright, *The Resurrection of the Son of God Christian Origins and the Question of God* Volume Three 5.

[1669] Starr, *California: A History* 158.

[1670] William Herbert Carruth (1859-1924) *Each In His Own Tongue* 1908.

[1671] *Justo L. Gonzales, A History of Christian Thought From the Protestant Reformation to the Twentieth Century* Volume III Revised Edition Location 1286.

[1672] Sagan, *The Varieties of Scientific Experience: A Personal View of the Search for God* Edited by Ann Druyan (New York: Penguin Press, 2006) x, xv. Here is a different feeling about the universe: Blaise Pascal (1623-1662) a mathematician and philosopher wrote: "Those infinite spaces frighten me." Pascal is famous for formulating the wager that people should believe in God because: If God exists you gain everything and if God doesn't exist you lose nothing. See Hitchcock 320.

[1673] Wills, *Head and Heart: American Christianities* 281.

[1674] Dennis Prager, *TownHall.com* August 19, 2008.

[1675] McCullough, *John Adams* 418. (Possibly Adams over-worried this issue. The World Values Survey two centuries later reported that only 14% of the French were atheists. See Stark, *The Triumph of Christianity How the Jesus Movement Became the World's Largest Religion* 374.

[1676] Winik 277.

[1677] Micklethwait and Wooldridge, *God is Back How The Global Revival of Faith is Changing the World* 60-61. We should recall that the Enlightenment was not only about political philosophy. It also had anti-religious elements to it. King Charles of Spain (who reigned 1759-88) made efforts to control the Church. Charles expelled the Jesuits from the Spanish empire in 1767 and influenced Pope Clement XIV to suppress the order six years later. The Jesuits didn't get approval from Rome to reconstitute themselves until 1813. That is why the Franciscans and Father Junipero Serra got the task of setting up missions in California. In isolated Paraguay after independence from Spain, a dictator, Dr. Jose Gaspar Rodrigues de Francia (1766 – 1840), a follower of the Enlightenment, fought the church. See Ondina E. Gonzales and Justo L. Gonzales 111ff, 137ff.

[1678] Paul Johnson, *The Quest For God: A Personal Pilgrimage* 6.

[1679] This verse records that Abraham's army pursued a military enemy *"as far as Hobah, which is north of **Damascus**."* (Emphasis added).

[1680] This is in the context of God promising Abraham a son. First, God promises his *"reward"* in *Genesis* 15:1. Abraham responds in *Genesis* 15:2: *"O Lord GOD, what will You give me, since I am childless, and the heir of my house is Eliezer of **Damascus**?"* (Emphasis added). In *Genesis* 15:4 and in the rest of the chapter God promises Abraham a son and descendants.

[1681] Georgi, *The Opponents of Paul in Second Corinthians*, 41ff, 52.

[1682] Tad Szulc, *National Geographic* December 2001.

[1683] http://en.wikipedia.org/wiki/Book_of_Abraham (Accessed May 3, 2012). Note: In the Mormon stronghold in Nauvoo in the 1840s, Joseph Smith's mother kept a collection of Egyptian mummies and scrolls which she charged a quarter for people to see. One relic was supposedly the leg of pharaoh's daughter who saved Moses as recounted in *Exodus* 2: 5-10. Joseph Smith claimed that one scroll was handwritten by Abraham and had the signatures of Moses and Aaron. See Beam Location 954ff.

[1684] Meacham, *American Gospel* 178. Note: John Adams was correct. Abraham indeed was a cross-cultural figure. Bruce Feiler has written: "Probably less than 1 percent of the stories told about Abraham appear in the *Bible*. The vast majority did not even come into circulation until hundreds, even thousands of years after he would have lived." See Feiler, Abraham *A Journey to the Heart of Three Faiths* (New York: Wm. Morrow *An Imprint of* HarperCollins*Publishers*, 2002) 27.

[1685] Paul cited Abraham more than he cited any person other than Christ. See David Van Biema *Time* September 30, 2002. Note: Paul valued Abraham because Abraham believed in God prior to circumcision. Plus, Paul wanted to describe Christianity in ways that would relate to Jewish history. See Feiler, Abraham *A Journey to the Heart of Three Faiths* 138ff.

[1686] Moreover, Paul often wrote on this theme:

- I *Thessalonians* 5:15 - "*...always seek after that which is good for one another and for all people.*"
- *Galatians* 6:10 – "*So then, while we have opportunity, let us do good to all people, and especially to those who are of the household of the faith.*"
- *Romans* 2:10 "*Be devoted to one another in brotherly love...*"

[1687] Note: This is all about good conduct without even any mention of loving God as in Jesus's commandment.

[1688] http://www.aomin.org/aoblog/index.php?itemid=1892 (Accessed May 3, 2012.) He also had doubt about *Revelation* saying, "There is no Christ in it." See Pagels, Revelations Visions, Prophecy and Politics in the Book of *Revelation* 3. Luther also thought that *Hebrews* and *Jude* had little worth. See Walker 349, 125. (Across the centuries, Martin Luther appears to have been someone from whom it was not difficult to coax an opinion. For example, he called parents who neglected the education of their children, "despicable hogs and venomous beasts." See. Micklethwait and Wooldridge, *God is Back How The Global Revival of Faith is Changing the World* 205.

[1689] Wilson, *Jesus A Life* 249.

[1690] Actually, it may have been forged in that someone other than James the actual brother of Jesus probably wrote it. See Ehrman, *US News & World Report Special Collectors Edition Mysteries of Faith* "Scripture's Imposters."

[1691] http://en.wikipedia.org/wiki/Antinomianism (Accessed May 3, 2012).

[1692] *James* 2:19.

[1693] The widows in these Pauline churches had high status. They were possibly identified with the Anna who greeted the baby Jesus in the Temple as recorded in *Luke* 2: 36-38. The gospel section reads that Anna was a widow, age 84. "*She never left the temple, **serving night and day with fastings and prayers**.*"

Nero James Pruitt

(verse 37). I *Timothy* 5:5 reads: *"Now she who is a widow indeed and who has been left alone, has fixed her hope on God and **continues in entreaties and prayers night and day**."* (Emphases added). See Browning Location 500.

[1694] CS Lewis, *Mere Christianity* (New York: Macmillan Publishing Company, a division of Macmillan, Inc., 1943, 1945, 1953) 129.

[1695] *Luke* 23:47.

[1696] *Acts* 2:22.

[1697] *Acts* 17:31.

[1698] Richard Bauckham makes a case that *Jude* is a Jewish-Christian text. See Bauckham, *Jude and the Relatives of Jesus in the Early Church* 178, 233.

[1699] *Documents of the Christian Church* second edition Selected and Edited by Henry Bettenson (London, Oxford and New York: Oxford University Press) First published, 1943. Second edition, 1963. First issued as an Oxford University Press paperback, 1967) 5.

[1700] Hitchcock 258.

[1701] Paul Johnson, *A History of Christianity* 274.

[1702] Manchester 184.

[1703] Hitchcock 245ff.

[1704] Walker 329ff. Or: "Erasmianism became a reform program with fluid boundaries, aimed at the simplification of the Christian life, made possible by a direct encounter with the Gospel as originally written." See Hitchcock 247.

[1705] Paul Johnson, *A History of Christianity* 275. See also MacCulloch 602. This of course is a reference to the *filioque* controversy.

[1706] Hitchcock 247.

[1707] *Justo L. Gonzales A History of Christian Thought From the Protestant Reformation to the Twentieth Century* Volume III Revised Edition 310, 318ff.

[1708] Paul Johnson, A History *of Christianity* 334ff.

[1709] David Gelernter, *Americanism: The Fourth Great Western Religion* (New York, London, Toronto, Sidney, Aukland: Doubleday, 2007) 32, 110-111.

[1710] Zev Chafets, *A Match Made in Heaven* (New York: HarperCollinsPublishers, 2007) 21.

[1711] Ahlstrom 6.

480

[1712] George C. Herring, *From Colony to Superpower: US Foreign Relations Since 1776* (Oxford: Oxford University Press, 2008) 4.

[1713] Feiler, *Time* October 12, 2009. Note: One of my ancestors was Moses Pruitt (1764 – abt. 1820) of Kentucky. He had a son, Abraham (1787 - 1856) also of Kentucky. From the review of some of Abraham's legal papers, it does not appear that he was literate.

[1714] Feiler, *America's Prophet Moses and the American Story* 134. (The Apostle Paul referred to this cloud In *I Corinthians* 10: 1-2: *"For I would not, brethren, have you ignorant, that our fathers were all under the cloud, and all passed through the sea; and were all baptized unto Moses in the cloud and in the sea;"*)

[1715] Campbell 328. Note: Irish playwright George Bernard Shaw (1856-1950) called Brigham Young "the American Moses." See Krakauer 196.

[1716] Waldman 159, 162. *PatriotPost.US* November 19, 2009. Washington was prone to say things that were very nonsectarian. For example: "May the father of all mercies scatter light, and not darkness, upon our paths, and make us in all our several vocations useful here, and in His own due time and way everlastingly happy." See *PatriotPost.US* April 30, 2008.

[1717] Paul Johnson, *The Quest for God: A Personal Pilgrimage* 39-40.

[1718] John Staffer, *Time* July 4, 2005.

[1719] Baptism:

- *Matthew* 3: 17 – *"This is My beloved Son, in whom I am well-pleased."*
- *Mark* 1:11 - *"You are My beloved Son, in You I am well-pleased."*
- *Luke* 3:22 – *"You are My beloved Son, in You I am well-pleased."*

Transfiguration:

- *Matthew* 17:5 - *"This is my dearly loved Son, who brings me great joy. Listen to him."*
- *Mark* 9:2 - *"This is my dearly loved Son. Listen to him."*
- *Luke* 9:35 – *"This is My Son, My Chosen One; listen to Him!"*

John 12

- *John* 12: 28 – After Jesus says, *"Father, glorify Your name,"* a voice from "heaven" responded: *"I have both glorified it, and will glorify it again."* The people present wondered if the voice was thunder or an angel (verse 29).

Note: In each of these three Transfiguration accounts, the disciples who were present were fearful. Additional note: In the account of the Transfiguration covered in *II Peter*, God is quoted in chapter 1 verse 17 more like the baptism statement: *"This is My beloved Son with whom I am well-pleased."*

¹⁷²⁰ Eric Reece, *Harpers* December 2005. (Benjamin Franklin edited the Apostles Creed to remove references to the miraculous. See Waldman 22).

¹⁷²¹ Gordon S. Wood, *Revolutionary Characters: What Made the Founders Different* (New York: The Penguin Press, 2006) 107.

¹⁷²² In this book I have stayed away from issues of the Trinity and am pretty close to Jefferson on this point, sort of a Unitarian. However, if pressed toward evangelical orthodoxy I would resonate with Robert Louis Wilken's view. He wrote that the fourth century was "a time of learned and sophisticated theological debate joined with low, dirty, partisan politics, of councils opposing or contradicting other councils, of disputes over the election of bishops, and of the exile of controversial bishops." Yet, he added that the councils of that era eventually "ensured that Christianity's distinctive understanding of God would become a permanent and enduring part of Christian tradition. Although Christians were unreservedly and unequivocally monotheistic and believed, along with Jews, and later with Muslims, that there is one God, they understood that God was not a 'solitary God,' as one church father put it. This affirmation, that God's inner life was triune, was a great impetus to Christian thinking and to spiritual life, for it affirmed that the deepest reality was communal."

¹⁷²³ Waldman 184,185 See footnote on p. 260. In another century, President Herbert Hoover echoed this sort of impatience with complex Christian doctrine. In 1933, by then out of office, he caustically remarked about columnist Walter Lippman that "Someday he will be buried with those who spent their lives in dialectics over the Nicene Creed." See Richard Norton Smith 171.

¹⁷²⁴ http://rotunda.upress.virginia.edu/founders/default.xqy?keys=FOEA-print-04-02-02-4012 Accessed December 23, 2014. Jefferson was paraphrasing the story of the less-famous Lazarus found in *Luke* 16: 19-31.

¹⁷²⁵ Russell Kirk, *The Conservative Mind: From Burke to Eliot*, Seventh Revised Edition (Washington DC: Regnery Publishing, Inc.: 1953, 1960, 1972, 1985, 2001 printing) 95.

¹⁷²⁶ Waldman 184,185. See footnote on p. 260. Pope Benedict XVI observed that "Justin concludes, since Christianity is the historical and personal manifestation of the *Logos* in his totality, it follows that 'whatever things

were rightly said among all men are the property of us Christians.'" See Pope Benedict XVI, *The Fathers* 20-21.

[1727] Waldman 260.

[1728] Mapp 62.

[1729] Brookhiser 208.

[1730] Micklethwait and Wooldridge, *God is Back How The Global Revival of Faith is Changing the World* 52, 53. See also Douthat 131. Note: President Jimmy Carter's experience was both similar and different to that of President Clinton. Carter was baptized in 1935. "I accepted Christ as savior and was baptized into the church at eleven. That was kind of a normal evolution for every young person in our church." After a 1966 loss in a run for governor, Carter was in a depression. His sister, a Pentecostal evangelist, met with him. As she later wrote: "I talked about my awareness of Christ and I shared with Jimmy how it was to come to a place of total commitment, the peace and joy and the power it brings." Jimmy later said that at that time: "I put my faith completely in God." And: "I recognized for the first time that I had lacked something very precious - a complete commitment to Christ, a presence of the Holy Spirit in my life in a more profound and personal way and since then I've had an inner peace and inner conviction and assurance that transformed my life for the better." And: "In 1967, I realized my own relationship with God was a very superficial one. I began to realize that my Christian life, which I had always professed to be preeminent, had really been a secondary interest to my life, and I formed a very close, personal intimate relationship with God through Jesus Christ."

See Balmer 11, 24ff.

[1731] Nagel 407. He followed his own father who had told him that he could not understand the eternal God hanging on a cross. Years later, Charles Francis Adams, John Adams's grandson, wrote that John Adams had rejected the Trinity, and Jesus's atonement for sins. See Mapp 62, 65.

[1732] From *Rights of Man* published in 1791. Quoted in Harvey J. Kaye, *Thomas Paine and the Promise of America* (New York: Hill and Wang: a Division of Farrar, Straus and Giroux, 2005) 75. Eugene V. Debs put a more negative twist on this sentiment during World War I: "I have no country to fight for. My country is the earth, and I am a citizen of the world." See Pietrusza *1920 The Year of the Six Presidents* 267.

[1733] Walter Isaacson, *Benjamin Franklin: An American Life* (New York, London, Toronto, Sydney: Simon & Schuster Paperbacks, 2003, 2004) 468-9.

[1734] Holzer 225.

[1735] This is a close paraphrase of *Matthew* 22: 37-39; *Mark* 12:30-31 and especially *Luke* 10:27.

[1736] Gelernter 33.

[1737] This inscription has its own history. In 1907, President Theodore Roosevelt said it was "eminently unwise to cheapen such a motto by use on coins..." Notwithstanding, in 1956 it was adopted as the national motto by Congress. In 1970 a Circuit Court found the phrase "of patriotic and ceremonial value" and not religious. The Supreme Court declined review. In 2003 Gallup found that 90% of adults approved of the phrase on currency. See Dru Sefton *Portland Oregonian* July 16, 2006. Along the way, in 1954, Congress added "under God" as used by Lincoln at Gettysburg to the Pledge of Allegiance. See Paul Johnson, *The Quest for God: A Personal Pilgrimage* 35.

[1738] Almost all of our modern presidents have relied heavily on prayer. In the middle of the Cuban Missile Crisis of 1962, President John F. Kennedy prayed at St. Matthew's Cathedral. President Lyndon Johnson repeatedly called for national days of prayer and reportedly prayed a dozen times a day. Jimmy Carter said: "There's no doubt that during my time as president, I prayed more intensely and more fervently for God's guidance than at any other time in my life. ... The problems were so complex that I sought counsel." *Bible*-toting Bill Clinton said, "I assure you that no president makes decisions like (an agreement with Haiti) without deep thought and prayer." See David Limbaugh, *OpinionJournal.com* September 16, 2008. The Reverend Jesse Jackson said this about President Clinton in 1998: "He knows even in a biblical sense the perils and treasures of leadership...He has a great sense of biblical journeys of leaders." See http://findarticles.com/p/articles/mi_m1355/is_n17_v93/ai_21237693 (Accessed May 3, 2012).

[1739] Wills, *Head and Heart: American Christianities* 441.

[1740] Meacham, *American Gospel* 153-4.

[1741] Beschloss 222. Truman also thought that the *Bible* promised the Jews a homeland. His favorite *Psalm* was *Psalm* 137: "*By the rivers of Babylon, there we sat down, yea, we wept, when we remembered Zion.*" See Beschloss 222.

[1742] Levine 92-3.

[1743] Joan Roughgarden, *Evolution and Christian Faith Reflections of An Evolutionary Biologist* (Washington DC, Covelo, London: Island Press, 2006) 54-55. See also Mark Lombard *Catholic Online* January 31, 2006 at http://www.catholic.org/national/national_story.php?id=18524 (Accessed November 21, 2012). See also Douthat 120.

[1744] Here is what he wrote in *Mere Christianity*: "I believe there is such a place as New York. I have not seen it myself. I could not prove by abstract reason that there must be such a place. I believe it because reliable people have told me so. The ordinary man believes in the Solar System, atoms, **evolution**, and the circulation of the blood on authority - because scientists say so." (Emphasis added). See CS Lewis, *Mere Christianity* 63.

[1745] Dinesh D'Souza, *What's So Great About Christianity* (Washington DC: Regnery Publishing Company An Eagle Publishing Company, 2007) 144-5.

[1746] McLennan 12.

[1747] Charles Darwin (1809-1882) in his *Origin of the Species* (1859) gave a great challenge to Christianity – although perhaps not deliberately. What were Darwin's experiences with the Christian religion? Here are some:

- Darwin and his wife were extremely close and she was a Christian. Before their marriage she asked him to read "our saviour's farewell discourse to his disciples which begin at the end of the 13th chapter of John. It is so full of love to them & devotion & every beautiful feeling. It is the part of the *New Testament* I love best."
- Darwin late-in-life said: "The plain language of the [biblical] text seems to show that the men who do not believe, & this would include my Father, Brother & almost all my best friends, will be everlastingly punished. And this is a damnable doctrine." At about the same time he said: "I gradually came to disbelieve in Christianity as a divine revelation." See Paul Johnson *Darwin Portrait of a Genius* (New York: Viking Published by the Penguin Group, Kindle Edition, 2012) 53, 141.

[1748] Micklethwait and Wooldridge, *God is Back How The Global Revival of Faith is Changing the World* 62, 96ff.

[1749] Charles Cerami, *Young Patriots* (Naperville, Illinois: Sourcebooks, Inc, 2005) 274.

[1750] Gelernter 77.

[1751] Micklethwait and Wooldridge, *The Right Nation* (New York: Penguin Press, 2004) 324 and Winston Churchill, *The Great Republic: A History of America* (London: Cassell and Co., 2002) drawn from Churchill's *History of the English-Speaking People* 31 Note: Cotton Mather called Rhode Island "the sewer of New England." See Micklethwait and Wooldridge, *God is Back How The Global Revival of Faith is Changing the World* 58.

[1752] Meacham, *American Gospel* 68-9.

[1753] Nathan Schachner, *The Founding Fathers* (New York: Putnam,1954) 123-4.

[1754] Kaye 74. Note: Some modern diversity consultants must think they are on the cutting edge in stressing that mere "tolerance" is not enough when they are just echoing American statesmen of two hundred years ago. See, for example: Ellie Y. Cross, Judith H. Katz, Frederick A. Miller and Edith W. Seashore, eds. *The Promise of Diversity* (New York: Irwin, 1994), Editor's Introduction.

[1755] The closest is this reference toward the end: "Done in Convention by the Unanimous Consent of the States present the Seventeenth Day of September in the Year of our Lord one thousand seven hundred and Eighty seven and of the Independence of the United States of America the Twelfth."

[1756] Micklethwait and Wooldridge, *God is Back How The Global Revival of Faith is Changing the World* 59-60. James Madison has also been credited with this quote. See Feiler, *America's Prophet Moses and the American Story* 94.

[1757] Waldman 133ff.

[1758] Meacham, *American Gospel* 245-6.

[1759] Herring 98. This was a very serious business. American vessels were plagued in the Mediterranean by Islamic pirates based in North Africa in the twenty or so years after independence. As envoys in France in the 1780s, Jefferson and Adams first dealt with American policy toward these Barbary pirates. They wrote the American Congress that they had asked the ambassador from Tripoli for justification for this piracy. "The ambassador answered us that it was founded on the Laws of the Prophet, that it was written in their *Koran*, that all nations who should not have acknowledged their authority were sinners, that it was their right and duty to make war upon them wherever they could be found, and to make slaves of all they could take as Prisoners." Jefferson wanted to send a naval force. Adams did not think the US was ready. "We ought to not fight them at all unless we determine to fight them forever." See Ellis, *American Sphinx The Character of Thomas Jefferson* (New York: Alfred A. Knopf, 1997) 75-76. This problem was initially addressed by bribes and eventfully by warfare. As noted, under Jefferson in the early 1800s US Marines attacked Tripoli to free American sailors.

[1760] The Dunkers were religious sect which had immigrated to America from Europe in the early 1700s. Their name came from their method of baptism by emersion.

[1761] Susan Dunn 149, 87, 88.

[1762] Nagel 160-1.

[1763] Johnson was later Vice President under Martin Van Buren. Johnson claimed to have killed the great Indian leader Tecumseh in the war of 1812. He was married common-law to a black woman.

[1764] Meacham, *American Lion: Andrew Jackson in the White House* 144-48, 344-45.

[1765] Meacham, *American Gospel* 134-35.

[1766] http://en.wikipedia.org/wiki/Articles_of_Faith_(Latter_Day_Saints) (Accessed May 13, 2012).

[1767] John Seigenthaler, *James K Polk* (New York: Times Books, Henry Holt and Company, *The American Presidents* Arthur M Schlesinger. Jr., General Editor,2003),12, 15.

[1768] Pietrusza, *1960 LBJ vs. JFK vs. Nixon: The Epic Campaign That Forged Three Presidencies* 265.

[1769] Meacham, *American Gospel* 246.

[1770] Susan Dunn 51ff. This echoed William Penn's comment one hundred years earlier that is quoted in Chapter 3 that: "liberty of conscience is everyman's natural right."

[1771] *Dennis v. United States*, 341 US 494 (1951) quoted in Jim Newton, *Justice For All: Earl Warren and the Nation He Made* (New York: Riverhead Books Published by the Penguin Group, 2006) 276.

[1772] Meacham, *American Gospel* 14.

[1773] Fundamentalists or at least evangelicals may be ready. Fifty-seven percent of evangelical Christians reported to Pew in 2008 that multiple religions can lead to salvation, although it is difficult to find an evangelical leader who would support this view. See http://religions.pewforum.org/reports# (Accessed May 3, 2012) and also Matthai Kuravilla *San Francisco Chronicle* June 24, 2008.

[1774] John R. Judis, *New Republic,* September 12, 1994.

[1775] Paul Johnson *A History of Christianity* 428.

¹⁷⁷⁶ CS Lewis, *Mere Christianity* 55-56. One of Lewis's similar formulations was as follows: Since Jesus claimed to be God or the Son of God or one with God, we are left with two choices. "Either he was a raving lunatic of an unusually abominable type or else He was, and is, precisely what He said. There is no middle way. If the records make the first hypothesis unacceptable, then you must submit to the second." To this, AN Wilson, one of his biographers responded: "Lewis's claim that 'the records' give us a stark choice about Christ – either he was a 'raving lunatic' or else 'He was, and is, precisely what He said' – is startling, to say the least. To what 'records' is he referring? Different books of the *New Testament* have different ways of describing the indescribable, that is, the nature of Christ, and the first three centuries of Christendom are a history of ceaseless dispute among the most learned doctors of the Church as to what this nature was, and how it was made manifest during the period of the Incarnation. This is not to deny the truth of the orthodox Christian belief. It is to point out that there is nowhere in existence a set of 'records' which could prove that Christ was either a lunatic or 'precisely what He said' He was."

More on CS Lewis: Lewis has been one of the great influences on evangelical Christianity during his life and in the half century since his death. (He died in 1963 on the same day as John F. Kennedy.) He was a professor at Oxford and friends with the writer JRR Tolkien. He was not a Christian when he first joined the faculty and in a conversation with Tolkien questioned Christianity: "What I could not see was how the life and death of Someone Else (whoever he was) 2000 years ago could help us here and now - except in so far as his *example* helped us." Lewis came to accept theism in 1929 and Christianity in 1931. He wrote years later that he was with a group on an outing to the zoo: "When we set out I did not believe that Jesus Christ is the Son of God, and when we reached the zoo I did."

At the time Lewis was 33, living with a woman named Jane Moore 58 who seems to have opposed his conversion according to Lewis's brother. Lewis had lived with Mrs. Moore since he was about 20 and Wilson has suggested and others believe that the relationship was sexual at least prior to Lewis's conversion. They continued to live in the same household until Mrs. Moore, suffering from dementia, went to a nursing home where, until her death in 1951, Lewis visited her daily. A few years later an American woman, Joy Davidman, who was separated from her husband and with whom Lewis had been corresponding came to England to visit him. The two were married in a civil ceremony in 1956 with the purported reason that Mrs. Davidman could legally stay in England. They later had a Christian marriage ceremony. Both Jane Moore in the post-World War I years and Joy Davidman in the

1950s were married women when Lewis began his relationships with them and this resulted in a certain amount of furtiveness in Lewis's behavior. This has surprised many of his evangelical followers in the United States. To them we would make these points:

- Certainly CS Lewis taught an orthodox sexual morality. As he wrote in *Mere Christianity* in 1943: "There is no getting away from it: the old Christian rule is, 'Either marriage with complete faithfulness to your partner, or else total abstinence.' Now this is so difficult and so contrary to our instincts, that obviously either Christianity is wrong or our sexual instinct, as it now is, has gone wrong. One or the other. Of course, being a Christian, I think it is the instinct that has gone wrong."
- We can admire him for his writings and teachings while not placing him on a pedestal. CS Lewis would certainly agree. To quote Lewis himself: "All reality is iconoclastic."

CS Lewis's works include *Mere Christianity, A Grief Observed, The Screwtape Letters, The Chronicles of Narnia,* a space trilogy and many more. Movies have been made about Lewis and his books. *Shadowlands* (1993) starred Anthony Hopkins as Lewis and Debra Winger as Joy Davidman. A film series based on the *Chronicles of Narnia* began in 2005.

See CS Lewis, *The Problem of Pain* (HarperCollins e-books, Kindle Edition, 1940, restored,1996) 13; AN Wilson *CS Lewis A Biography* (London and New York: WW Norton & Company, Inc., 1990) xvi, 58, 65-67, 117-18, 125-28, 164-5, 248-249, 257, 260; CS Lewis, *Mere Christianity* 89; CS Lewis A *Grief Observed* (NW Clerk, restored 1996 CS Lewis Pte. Ltd. Preface by Douglas H. Gresham copyright © 1994 by Douglas H. Gresham. HarperCollins e-books, 2009) 51

[1777] McLennan 63.

[1778] Cox 103.

[1779] MacCulloch 215.

[1780] Pagels, *Revelations Visions, Prophecy and Politics in the Book of Revelation* 137.

[1781] Arianism lost out, but it took centuries. Many of the barbarian tribes that took down the Western Roman Empire had come into Christianity through Arianism. The Goths had a bishop in Constantinople and a Gothic translation of the *Bible*. The Visigoths, Ostrogoths and the Lombards also converted to Arianism as did the Vandals. Military advances against the Germanic tribes by the Eastern Empire in the 500s dealt a blow to Arianism and finally, in a highly symbolic switch, in 589 the Visigoth king in Spain converted to Catholic Christianity from Arianism. See Victor Davis Hanson, *The Savior Generals How Five Great Commanders Saved Wars That Were Lost From Ancient Greece to Iraq* (New York, London, Sydney, New Delhi: Bloomsbury Press, Kindle Edition, 2013) Location 1182-1266ff, Hitchcock 103ff, Justo L. Gonzales, *A History of Christian Thought From Augustine to the Eve of the Reformation* Volume II Revised Edition Location 1004 and Ondina E. Gonzales and Justo L. Gonzales 21. MacCullough 221.

1782 Brownworth 83-90.

1783 Waldman 185. See also Wood 116. Unitarians are sometimes comically defined by a belief that there is at most one God. See George Will *Oregonian* December 3, 2007.

1784 Micklethwait and Wooldridge, *OpinionJournal.com* April 7, 2009.

1785 Potter 229.

1786 Arius's views got support in the seventeenth and eighteenth centuries. "(John) Locke's reasonable' Christianity was ... stripped of emotionalism, the personal relationship with Jesus, and the sinner's plea for mercy." This brand of Christianity became popular in Europe. Certain of these Christians called themselves Arians. The Arians were sometimes called Socinians after Lelio Sozzini sixteenth century Protestant who rejected the Trinity. See Charlotte Allen, *The Human Christ The Search for the Historical Jesus* 102. In the 1828 election presidential election in the US, John Quincy Adams was asked about his "ideas of the Trinity." He said that he was not a Trinitarian or a Unitarian. He said he "believed the nature of Jesus Christ was superhuman: but whether he was God, or only the first of created beings, was not clearly revealed to me in the Scriptures." See Robert V. Remini, *John Quincy Adams* (New York: Times Books, Henry Holt and Company, The American Presidents Arthur M Schlessinger. Jr., General Editor, 2002) 121.

1787 I owe this thought to Ehrman, *Jesus Interrupted: Revealing the Hidden Contradictions in the Bible (And Why We Don't Know Them)* 276 and regret it if I have misstated Ehrman's point of view.

1788 http://www.nytimes.com/2009/01/18/weekinreview/18lohr.html (Accessed May 3, 2012).

1789 Manchester 296.

1790 Schachner 64.

1791 Paul Johnson, *The Quest for God: A Personal Pilgrimage* 32.

[1792] Waldman 186.

[1793] http://www.beliefnet.com/resourcelib/docs/53/Letter_from_Thomas_Jefferson_to_John_Adams_1.html (Accessed May 3, 2012).

[1794] Wright, *The Resurrection of the Son of God Christian Origins and the Question of God* Volume Three 9-10, 209. I regret it if I have misstated Wright's point of view.

[1795] Jack Crabtree, Gutenberg College MacKenzie Study Center. *News and Views* May 2007 Vol. 24, No. 4. The distance between that sentiment and this one from a young John Adams in 1765 - "Let the pulpit resound with the doctrine and sentiments of religious liberty. Let us hear of the dignity of man's nature, and the noble rank he holds among the works of God" captures a lot about this book's message of the diversity within Christianity. See John Adams, *Dissertation on the Canon and Feudal Law,* 1765.

[1796] *I Corinthians* 15: 14-19.

[1797] Here are two: CS Lewis and NT Wright. CS Lewis discounts the purely visionary concept of the resurrection of Jesus Christ in a full chapter in *Miracles,* published in 1947. In that chapter he writes: "We have thought (whether we acknowledge it or not) that the body was not objective: that it was an appearance sent by God to assure the disciples of truths otherwise incommunicable. But what truths? If the truth is that after death there comes a negatively spiritual life, an eternity of mystical experience, what more misleading way of communicating it could possibly be found than the appearance of a human form which eats broiled fish?" See CS Lewis, *Miracles* Copyright 1947 in *The Complete CS Lewis Signature Classics* (New York: HarperOne *An imprint of* HarperCollins*Publishers* First Paperback Edition, *2007) 433.* NT Wright, near the end of a seven hundred page book published in 2003, describes first a visionary view of the resurrection and second an actual bodily resurrection (albeit with a new body) and then states: "I find this second option enormously more probable at the level of sheer history." See Wright, *The Resurrection of the Son of God Christian Origins and the Question of God* Volume Three 608-611. I regret it if I have misstated Lewis's or Wright's point of view.

[1798] White, *From Jesus to Christianity* 94- 99, 172.

[1799] *Acts* 1:15, describing a meeting prior to Pentecost, places about 120 people in a meeting. Pentecost, described in *Acts* 2, may have included more and, in fact, mentions that others joined the meeting in verses 5 and 6. Verse 41 states that about three thousand were baptized that day.

[1800] *Matthew* 28: 1-10; *Mark* 16: 1-8; *Luke* 24: 1-10 and 13-34; *John* 20: 1-18.

¹⁸⁰¹ By contrast, only eight people attested that they saw some golden plates from which Joseph Smith copied the *Book of Mormon* in the 1820s. Four of them were from a Whitmer family that was close to the Smiths. Mark Twain wrote of visiting the Mormons in *Roughing It* (1870-71) and noted about the *Book of Mormon's* authenticity that he "couldn't feel more satisfied and at rest if the entire Whitmer family had testified." Twain once noted that the phrase "and it came to pass" recurs about two thousand times in the *Book of Mormon*. See Ostling and Ostling 28. Note: In 1838 the entire Whitmer family was excommunicated by the Mormon Church after a leadership struggle.

¹⁸⁰² It must be noted that according to the *New Testament* there are two more resurrection appearances:

- *Acts* 7:56 – the Martyr Stephen as a the end of his speech at this trial said: *"Behold, I see the heavens opened up and the Son of Man standing at the right hand of God."*
- *Revelation* 1: 12-20 – As noted, the writer of *Revelation* was named John and was on the island of Patmos. He notes in *Revelation* 1:10 that he was *"in the Spirit"* and heard a *"loud voice"* and then: *"... I turned to see the voice that was speaking with me. And having turned I saw seven golden lampstands; and in the middle of the lampstands I saw one like a son of man, clothed in a robe reaching to the feet, and girded across His chest with a golden sash. His head and His hair were white like white wool, like snow; and His eyes were like a flame of fire. His feet were like burnished bronze, when it has been made to glow in a furnace, and His voice was like the sound of many waters. In His right hand He held seven stars, and out of His mouth came a sharp two-edged sword; and His face was like the sun shining in its strength. When I saw Him, I fell at His feet like a dead man. And He placed His right hand on me, saying, 'Do not be afraid; I am the first and the last, and the living One; and I was dead, and behold, I am alive forevermore, and I have the keys of death and of Hades. Therefore write the things which you have seen, and the things which are, and the things which will take place after these things. As for the mystery of the seven stars which you saw in My right hand, and the seven golden lampstands: the seven stars are the angels of the seven churches, and the seven lampstands are the seven churches.'"* (Revelation 1: 12-20).

Finally, there may have been two other individuals named in the *New Testament* who witnessed the resurrection. As noted, after the death of Judas, the remaining apostles selected a replacement and one of the qualifications for the job was that whoever was selected had to have been with the apostles and Jesus *"until the day he was taken up from us."* (Acts 1:22). Two men who met that criteria were Joseph of Barsabbas and Matthias whom they selected after prayer and the drawing of lots. It appears that these two also saw the risen Jesus although, of course, either or both of them may have been among the five hundred mentioned by Paul in *I Corinthians* 15.

[1803] *Acts* 10:41.

[1804] *Matthew* 28: 8-10. In 324 after Constantine secured his empire in the East he sent his mother Helena on a pilgrimage to the Holy Land. She built the Church of the Holy Sepulcher at the Empty Tomb after tearing down a temple of Venus which had been built by the Roman Hadrian supposedly to offend Christians in the 130s. In the early 1000s Tariqu al-Hakim the sixth Fatimid caliph in Egypt ordered the burning or confiscation of Christian churches. The Church of the Holy Sepulcher was then destroyed. Arab historian Yahya ibn Said of Antioch wrote that Hakim ordered his agents "to demolish the church (of the Holy Sepulcher) and to remove its symbols, and to get rid of all traces and remembrance of it." Said elaborated that they "seized all the furnishings that were there, and knocked the church down to its foundations, except for what was impossible to destroy...(and they) worked hard to destroy the tomb and to remove every trace of it,..." The next caliph allowed reconstruction of the Church of the Holy Sepulcher but the destruction of the cavern could not be fixed. See Brownworth 16 and Stark, *God's Battalions The Case for the Crusades* 79 and 90. Note: Protestant visitors in the 1800s discounted the possibility that the Church of the Holy Sepulcher could be the site of Jesus's tomb. However, this belief has received more support in recent times. See Charlotte Allen, *The Human Christ The Search for the Historical Jesus* 212-14. Further Note: Another view of Helena's pilgrimage is that it was undertaken because Helena was so disturbed by Constantine's murder of his wife and son for suspected plotting that she did the pilgrimage to Jerusalem to find the true cross, as a form of penance. See Hitchcock 57.

[1805] *Matthew 28: 16-19*

[1806] In sections that are very difficult, if not impossible, to reconcile with *Mark* and *Matthew*, Luke has Jesus giving his followers instructions not to leave Jerusalem. See *Luke* 24:49 and also *Acts* 1:3–4. This seems to foreclose appearances in Galilee. For Luke the ascension is important (*Luke* 24: 50-51 and *Acts* 1:6-10) because Luke couldn't have Jesus staying on earth eating and drinking as a human would because people would assume that like other people who had been raised from the dead he would eventually die as he grew older.

[1807] *John* does not have an ascension scene but does have Jesus saying earlier in *John* 6:62 that he was "**ascending** to where he was before." Additionally, as noted here he also has the risen Jesus telling Mary Magdalene in *John* 20:17:

"*Stop clinging to Me, for I have not yet **ascended** to the Father; but go to My brethren and say to them, 'I **ascend** to My Father and your Father, and My God and your God.'*" (Emphases added). *Matthew* and *Mark* do not have ascension stories. As noted, the author Luke covers it twice:

- *Luke 24:50-51 – "And He led them out as far as Bethany, and He lifted up His hands and blessed them. While He was blessing them, He parted from them and was carried up into heaven."*
- *Acts: 1:6-10 – "So when they had come together, they were asking Him, saying, 'Lord, is it at this time you are restoring the kingdom to Israel?' He said to them, 'It is not for you to know times or epochs which the Father has fixed by His own authority; but you will receive power when the Holy Spirit has come upon you; and you shall be My witnesses both in Jerusalem, and in all Judea and Samaria, and even to the remotest part of the earth.' And after He had said these things, He was lifted up while they were looking on, and a cloud received Him out of their sight. And as they were gazing intently into the sky while He was going, behold, two men in white clothing stood beside them."*

[1808] This may not be the negative that it is often portrayed to be. Possibly, the message to Doubting Thomas is that those who believe without an appearance are also blessed. I owe this thought to Borg and Crossan, *The Last Week: What the Gospels Really Teach About Jesus's Final Days in Jerusalem* 219 and regret it if I have misstated Borg's and Crossan's point of view.

[1809] Matthew's account is highly improbable. Would soldiers would have been party with the Jewish leaders in making up such a story that would show them to be derelict in their duty? Isn't it more likely that the early followers of Jesus were dealing with rumors that the resurrection had not occurred at all and thus confabulated a story that is unique to this Gospel?

[1810] *Matthew* 17: 1-9. See also *Mark* 9: 2-9 and *Luke* 9: 28-36. Note: As we have seen, the Jews of that time believed that Elijah had never died. According to Josephus, some believed the same of Moses. *Deuteronomy* 34: 1-8 holds that Moses died while in great health and noted in verse 6 that "no man knows his burial place to this day." See James DG Dunn *Did the First Christians Worship Jesus? The New Testament Evidence* 8.

[1811] *I Corinthians* 15:3: "*I delivered to you as of first importance what I also received....*" As noted, some of what Paul listed in this account of the resurrection of Jesus Christ got cut out of the growing narrative:

- The appearance of the risen Jesus to James the brother of Jesus.
- The appearance of the risen Jesus to the five hundred.

Also as noted, the only qualification to the latter is that the story of Pentecost in *Acts* 2 may be a reference to it.

It is also noteworthy that Paul left out of this account of the resurrection some events that later became quite significant such as the women finding the empty tomb or the actual ascension of Jesus into heaven as described by Luke in *Luke* and *Acts*.

As to the latter, however, two scriptural passages may cohere with what Luke wrote.

- Paul wrote to the Thessalonians about how they had begun *"to serve a living and true God, and to wait for **His Son from heaven**, whom He raised from the dead, that is Jesus,..."* (*I Thessalonians* 1:9-10. Emphasis added).
- To the Philippians, as noted earlier, Paul may be quoting a hymn about Christ which read that Christ had died on the cross after which **"God highly exalted Him**, and bestowed on Him the name which is above every name,..."* (*Philippians* 2: 9-10. Emphasis added). Each of these suggest, far more generally, Luke's claim of an ascension of Jesus Christ. See White, *Scripting Jesus The Gospels in Rewrite* Location 2695ff.

[1812] *Mark* 8:31-32; *Mark* 9:9; *Mark* 9:30-32 and *Mark* 10:32-34 - and, as noted, the angels tell the women that it has occurred.

[1813] *Mark* 16:6.

[1814] Wright, *The Resurrection of the Son of God Christian Origins and the Question of God* Volume Three 218.

[1815] *I Corinthians* 15:13 or 4:8.

[1816] *I Corinthians* 15:49.

[1817] *I Corinthians* 9:1.

[1818] *I Corinthians* 15:10.

[1819] *I Corinthians* 15:42, 50.

[1820] *I Corinthians* 15:44-46. Here is further explanation: In *I Corinthians* 15:45 Paul saw Jesus as a *"life-giving spirit."* In *II Corinthians* chapter 3 verses 17 and 18 he asserted *"Now the Lord is the **Spirit**, and where the **Spirit** of the Lord is, there is liberty. But we all, with unveiled face, beholding as in a mirror the glory of the Lord, are being transformed into the same image from glory to glory, just as from the Lord, the **Spirit**."* (Emphases added).

[1821] *I Corinthians* 15:20.

[1822] *I Corinthians* 15:36-38.

[1823] *II Corinthians* 3: 18 - 5:50.

[1824] *II Corinthians* 3:18.

[1825] *II Corinthians* 4:18.

[1826] I owe much of this thought to Sanders 45ff and regret it if I have misstated Sanders's point of view.

[1827] Paul and such Christian leaders as the Twelve, James the brother of Jesus and Peter were in consensus on this point. This bears repeating: As Paul wrote in *I Corinthians* 15:11 in discussing the resurrection: *"Whether then it was I or they, so we preach and so you believed."*

[1828] AN Wilson has said that the disciples on the road to Emmaus thought they had been with Jesus but instead had been with his brother James who may have resembled him. See Charlotte Allen, *The Human Christ The Search for the Historical Jesus* 310.

[1829] I owe these points to Borg and Crossan, *The Last Week: What the Gospels Really Teach About Jesus's Final Days in Jerusalem* 198, 200-1 201-202, and regret it if I have misstated Borg's and Crossan's point of view. Note: I have quoted four authors extensively in this book: Marcus Borg, John Dominic Crossan, Bart Ehrman and Elaine Pagels. I have also read negative criticisms of their works: Here is one example: "The cultural impact of figures like Pagels and Ehrman and Borg and Crossan has been almost entirely destabilizing. Rather than propagating an understanding of Jesus' identity that's more intellectually compelling than the orthodox portrait, all they've succeeded in doing is validating the idea that Jesus' identity is entirely up for grabs, and that one can be a follower of Christ without having to accept any constraints on what that 'following' might mean." See Douthat 178. I disagree.

[1830] Tabor, *Paul and Jesus How the Apostle Transformed Christianity* Location 1160ff. I regret it if I have misstated Tabor's point of view.

[1831] McLennan 80.

[1832] *I Corinthians* 1:18.

[1833] *Mark* 15:42-47.

[1834] *Matthew* 27:57.

[1835] *Luke* 23:50-51.

[1836] *John* 19:38-39.

[1837] I owe this thought to Ludemann, *What Really Happened to Jesus A Historical Approach to the Resurrection* 17ff and regret it if I have misstated Ludemann's point of view.

[1838] At least one scholar has cast some doubt on the claim that Jesus's body was cared for and buried by a person named Joseph of Arimathea who was a member of the Council or Sanhedrin. The oldest account of Jesus's death in *I Corinthians* 15 does not mention that he was buried by Joseph of Arimathea. Moreover, in the Synoptic accounts, the Sanhedrin – of which Joseph of Arimathea was a putative member - seems to have reached its conclusions unanimously. According to *Matthew* 26: 59 and Mark 14:55 the "*whole Council*" tried to get false testimony against Jesus. According to *Mark* 14:64 they "*all*" condemned Jesus. According to *Luke* 22:70 "*all*" of the Council interrogated Jesus. According to *Acts* 13:28-29 the Jewish leaders in Jerusalem who killed Jesus buried him. (Luke alone partially exonerates Joseph of Arimathea, writing that he "*had not consented*" to the Council's action (*Luke* 23:51). This line of reasoning holds that the role of Joseph of Arimathea was an idealized write-up of the aftermath of the crucifixion. See Ehrman, *How Jesus Became God The Exaltation of Jewish Preacher from Galilee* (New York: HarperCollins Publishers Inc., Kindle Edition, 2014) 151ff.

[1839] Besides the resurrection, there is one – and possibly two - direct teachings of Jesus that are evidence for an afterlife:

- *Matthew* 25:31 - 46: In this account, Jesus talks of a day of judgment with people divided into sheep and goats. The sheep are deemed righteous because of their caring for others. The goats are deemed unrighteous because of their apathy. Jesus concludes by distinguishing between them and saying that the goats "*will go away into eternal punishment, but the righteous into eternal life.*"
- *Luke* 16:19-25: In this account Jesus talks of the less famous Lazarus living in the afterlife in "Abraham's bosom" observed by a rich man who was living in torment.

[1840] *Acts* 4:2.

[1841] To quote Paul Johnson: "It has often struck me that the two most important questions about existence - is there a God and what happens after our death? - are not only unanswered but probably unanswerable." See Paul Johnson, *The Quest for God: A Personal Pilgrimage* 36.

¹⁸⁴² Mann 122. Or, as Stephen Hawking puts it: "I regard the brain as a computer which will stop working when its components fail. There is no heaven or afterlife for broken-down computers. That is a fairy story for people afraid of the dark." See *Time* May 30, 2011.

¹⁸⁴³ In *I Corinthians* 15: 29 Paul writes as part of his general argument that there is a life after death that *"If the dead will not be raised, what point is there in people being baptized for those who are dead? Why do it unless the dead will someday rise again?"* So, apparently, Paul's Corinthian followers practiced this ritual. No modern church does this with the exception of the Mormon Church which baptizes for the dead relatives of Mormons plus historical figures. There is controversy about this but there have apparently been instances of baptisms for dead relatives of famous non-Mormons. According to a researcher on the LDS FamilySearch data base: "Mormons have not only posthumously baptized President Barack Obama's mother into their faith, but may have performed the ritual for the President's African ancestors as well, including his father, grandfather and great grandfather..." See Matt Canham, *The Salt Lake City Tribune* July 22, 2009. Note: The doctrine of baptism for the dead emerged at a funeral oration in 1840 in Nauvoo. Joseph Smith cited *I Corinthians* 15:29. He introduced it as he observed in the audience a woman who had lost her young son to death before he was baptized. Records show that the audience was startled but also enthused. One person noted of Smith's sermon that it was a "very beautiful discourse."

The Mormons soon found other *New Testament* support for baptism for the dead: *I Peter* 3:18-20 and 4.6:

"For Christ also died for sins once for all, the just for the unjust, so that He might bring us to God, having been put to death in the flesh, but made alive in the spirit; in which also He went and made proclamation to the spirits now in prison, who once were disobedient, when the patience of God kept waiting in the days of Noah, during the construction of the ark, in which a few, that is, eight persons, were brought safely through the water........ For the gospel has for this purpose been preached even to those who are dead, that though they are judged in the flesh as men, they may live in the spirit according to the will of God."

Smith subsequently defended the practice of baptism for the dead in an editorial. He referenced the ancient theologian Chrysostom as reported by eighteenth century Protestant writer Charles Buck (1771–1815): "After any catechumen was dead, they hid a living man under the bed of the deceased; then coming to the dead man, they asked him whether he would receive baptism; and he making no answer, the other answered for him, and said that he would be baptized in his stead; and so they baptized the living for the dead." The editorial went on that "the church of course at that time was degenerate, and the particular form might be incorrect, but the thing is sufficiently plain in the scriptures." See Samuel M. Brown "Early Mormon Adoption Theology" *Journal of Mormon History* Summer 2011 Volume 37 No. 3 35-36.

When Smith was criticized for the doctrine he responded: "The doctrine of baptism for the dead is clearly shown in the *New Testament* and if the doctrine is not good then throw away the *New Testament*." The doctrine of baptism for the dead is seen by Mormons as one of optimism and works to embrace larger and larger groups of humans in the afterlife. See Ryan G. Tobler, "'Saviors On Mount Zion': Mormon Sacramentalism, Mortality, And the Baptism For The Dead" *Journal of Mormon History* Fall 2013, Volume 39, No. 4. 182-238.

[1844] *I Corinthians* 15: 29-32.

[1845] Ellis, *America's Creation: Triumphs and Tragedies at the Founding of the Republic* 14, 247.

[1846] Nagel 203-4. John Quincy Adams had an existential side. In 1824, he reflected at the graves of his ancestors in Quincy Massachusetts: "Pass another century and we shall all be moldering in the same dust or resolved into the same elements" and toward the end of life he said he was "one of the relics of the past." See Nagel 290 and 410.

[1847] Waldman 24. Who knows what the "hereafter" will be like? That is beyond the scope of this book except to note that whereas - if it exists - it is probably a wonderful place, it may not have always been. We learn in the *New Testament* that Jesus may have ejected evil from Heaven:

- *Luke* 10: 17-18 - "'*The seventy returned with joy, saying, 'Lord, even the demons are subject to us in Your name.' And He said to them, '**I was watching Satan fall from heaven like lightning**.'*"" (Emphasis added).

- *Revelation* 12:10-12 – "*Then I heard a loud voice in heaven, saying 'Now the salvation, and the power, and the kingdom of our God and the authority of His Christ have come, **for the accuser of our brethren has been thrown down,** he who accuses them before our God day and night. And they overcame him because of the blood of the Lamb and because of the word of their testimony, and they did not love their life even when faced with death. For this reason, rejoice, O heavens and you who dwell in them. Woe to the earth and the sea, because the devil has come down to you, having great wrath, knowing that he has only a short time.'*" (Emphasis added).

[1848] Note: She wrote these words in *Planned Parenthood v. Casey* (1992.)

[1849] Luther was referring to an account in the *Old Testament Book of Joshua*, chapter 10. In this story, Joshua, the Hebrew military commander who succeeded Moses, defeated an enemy army in the land of Canaan in a great slaughter, aided by God sending a hail storm against the enemy. Even more memorably, God prolonged the day at Joshua's request by making the Sun stand still so that the Hebrews could conclude the battle. As verse 14 states: "*There was no day like that before it or after it,...*"

[1850] This is a very close paraphrase of the second half of *Psalm* 93:1: "*Indeed, the world is firmly established, it will not be moved.*"

[1851] Manchester 89-90.

[1852] A Pawlowski CNN.com August 18, 2009; Sagan, *The Varieties of Scientific Experience: A Personal View of the Search for God* 155.

[1853] Seth Borenstein, Associated Press *San Francisco Chronicle October* 20, 2009 and CNN.com February 19, 2011. Note: The rate of discovery of new planets is amazing. To quote science writer Michael D. Lemonick: "For planet hunters business is booming. Astronomers estimate that our galaxy holds more than 100 billion planets and are now finding several each week. The pace of discovery is accelerating: in 2014 NASA's Kepler mission announced 715 new worlds in a single day." See Michael D. Lemonick, *Scientific American* "Secrets of the Universe Past Present and Future" Special Edition 2014 10.

[1854] In this I respectively dissent from the opinion of Pope Benedict XVI. He saw Arianism as promoting a view of "Christ, reduced to a creature 'halfway' between God and man, according to a recurring theme in history which we also see manifested today in various forms." I don't see Christ as a half-way creature. I see him as a human. See Pope Benedict XVI, *The Fathers* 62-63.

[1855] For more background see Justo L. Gonzales *A History of Christian Thought From the Beginnings to the Council of Chalcedon* Volume 1 Revised Edition 143ff.

[1856] *Acts* 10: 34-35.

[1857] Gibbs and Duffy 18-19. I have mentioned Billy Graham several times in this book and I want to balance any negative inferences with this quote from the intellectual and urbane Henry Kissinger who said of Graham in the late 1980s: "I went to see one of his crusades twenty years ago because I wanted to see what it was like, and I was very condescending about it. But at Madison Square Garden I was so moved that I thought I ought to meet him. I think he's a man of great substance, a man of great value." See Peter Schweizer and

Rochelle Schweizer, *The Bushes Portrait of a Dynasty* (New York, London, Toronto, Sydney, Auckland: Doubleday, 2004) 289-90.

[1858] Even today, most Americans believe that after death they will reunite with relatives and see God. See D'Souza *What's So Great About Christianity* 6 and Paul Bloom "Is God an Accident?" *Atlantic Monthly* December 2005.

[1859] Waldman 185.

[1860] Thomas Jefferson, letter to Thomas Jefferson Smith, 1825. See *PatriotPost. US* November 18, 2009.

[1861] Adrienne Koch, ed., *The American Enlightenment The Shaping of the American Experiment and a Free Society* (New York: George Braziller, 1965) 234.

[1862] There is evidence that some allied formally with Judaism as seen in *Acts* 6:1-6 which mentions a convert named Nicolas of Antioch who presumably later turned up in Jerusalem and converted to Christianity in time to become a proto-deacon.

[1863] Paul may have initially met many God-fearers in synagogues. *Acts* records that Paul often visited synagogues: 9:20 (Damascus); 13:5 (Salamis); 13:14 (Pisidian Antioch); 14:1 (Iconium); 17:1 (Thessalonica); 17:10 (Berea); 17:17 (Athens); 18:4 (Corinth); 18:19 (Ephesus); 19:8 (Ephesus again). (*Acts* 18:26 shows Apollos speaking out "boldly" in the synagogue in Ephesus.)

[1864] *Luke* 7: 3-5. This support from a God-fearer was not an isolated case. In 1976 an archaeological project in modern-day Turkey found an inscription from a third century synagogue in which a list of donors was preserved. Nearly half of the donors were listed separate from the Jews under the heading of "God-fearers." See MacCulloch 99.

[1865] Borg, *Evolution of the Word The New Testament in the Order the Books Were Written* 423ff.

[1866] *Acts* 8: 27-28.

[1867] Crossan and Reed 36ff.

[1868] *Acts* 17: 5-9 and possibly *Romans* 16:2.

[1869] *Acts* 18:7.

[1870] *Psalm* 90:12 – "*So teach us to number our days that we may get a heart of wisdom.*"

Printed in the United States
By Bookmasters